Voice, Text, Hypertext

Emerging Practices in Textual Studies

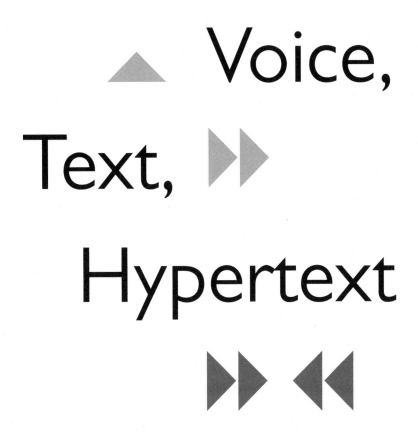

Voice, Text, Hypertext

EMERGING PRACTICES IN TEXTUAL STUDIES

Edited by

Raimonda Modiano, Leroy F. Searle, and Peter Shillingsburg

WALTER CHAPIN SIMPSON CENTER FOR THE HUMANITIES
in association with
THE UNIVERSITY OF WASHINGTON PRESS
Seattle and London

"Gerard Hopkins and the Shapes of His Sonnets" copyright © 2003 by Randall McLeod. This essay was produced by the author as camera-ready pages. The author's acknowledgments precede the notes to the essay.

Printed in the United States of America

Designed by Veronica Seyd

Library of Congress Cataloging-in-Publication Data

Voice, text, hypertext : emerging practices in textual studies / edited by Raimonda Modiano, Leroy F. Searle, and Peter Shillingsburg.
    p. cm.
    Includes index.
    ISBN 0-295-98305-1 (alk. paper)—ISBN 0-295-98306-X(pbk. : alk. paper)
    1. Discourse analysis. 2. Communication and culture.
I. Modiano, Raimonda. II. Searle, Leroy. III. Shillingsburg, Peter L.
P302.V59 2003
401'.41—dc21   2003001158

The paper used in this publication is acid-free and recycled from 10 per-cent post-consumer and aat least 50 percent pre-consumer waste. It meets the minimum requirements of American National Standard for Infor-mation Sciences–Permanence of Paper for Printed Library Materials, ANSI Z39.48–1984.

CONTENTS

PREFACE

This volume of essays concerning oral, material, and electronic texts offers a major contribution to scholarly debates in textual studies, a rapidly evolving field of ever-greater consequence in this age of technological revolution. It brings together eminent scholars from several countries (Australia, Belgium, Canada, the Czech Republic, England, France, and the U.S.) who confront the complexity of texts from diverse cultures (from ancient Near Eastern, Roman, and Indian to South Slavic and Czech), historical periods (from biblical and classical to medieval, Renaissance, and modern) and genres (from religious songs, oral epics, and sonnets to legal statutes, drama, fiction, and marginalia). While challenging prevailing editorial traditions through compelling illustrative examples, the essays take us on a rich historical journey that acquaints us with foundational systems of beliefs and textual practices in ancient and modern cultures. The stops on that journey include Israel in the third to sixth centuries C.E., where an oral Torah embodied in the figure of the Rabbinic sage gained authority equal to if not greater than that of its written counterpart (Martin S. Jaffee); ancient Near Eastern and Roman cultures, where sacred power was believed to reside not just in spoken and written words but also in the physical medium of their transmission, be it clay, papyrus, or lead curse-tablets (Scott B. Noegel, Phyllis Culham); ancient Greece, where odes to the Gods during Dionysian banquets were singular performative events that could neither be recorded nor duplicated, like the rule-bound literary genres to which they gave rise (Roger Chartier); the period from 1400 to 1700 in northwest India, where traveling singers continuously altered the songs and hagiographical narratives they collected for their repertoires (Winand M. Callewaert); eighteenth-century India, where the British vainly attempted to institute laws in accordance with Sanskrit texts they could not read and translations they could not understand (Ludo Rocher); nineteenth- and twentieth-century Serbia, where the recording, publication, and dissemination of oral epics was profoundly affected by the ideological and methodological predispositions of their editors (John Miles Foley); and twentieth-century Czechoslovakia, where a rich autonomous cultural life and underground literature flourished during the repressive Stalinist era but, ironically, suffered from critical neglect after the collapse of the Communist regime (Martin Machovec).

The geographical and historical range of these essays is matched by the diverse theoretical and practical issues they raise regarding the state and fate of texts as they move from oral performance or manuscript to inscription in codex or electronic form. The importance of understanding what happens to oral works in the process of textualization—of recovering the signature of orality in printed texts—is vividly illustrated in this volume (Chartier, Foley, Callewaert). That signature is also found where least expected: in annotated books, which make audible the conversation between reader and author (H. J. Jackson). The need to adjust editorial methods to the peculiarities of the material studied is exemplified both by the failure of a Lachmannian search for an original archetype that might account for oral variants in Bhakti literature of northwest India (Callewaert) and, conversely, by its appropriate use in the Italian editorial tradition, which focuses on medieval works with large numbers of surviving manuscripts (Conor Fahy). Also represented here is a critique of editorial practices that fail to take into account the bibliographic features of texts, or conceive of their materiality in an abstract way (Paul Eggert). That critique is rendered concrete by the radical exposure of how much of the "body language" of poems is lost through inattention to such spatial signifiers as indentation and leading (Randall McLeod), or through the placing of poetic fragments, written on portions of envelopes and resembling the existential condition of a flight of birds, within the restricted spatial dimensions of a book (Marta Werner).

The lure and shortcomings of electronic textuality are recurrent themes in this volume, which features an informed review of current technologies, each with built-in limitations for editorial ventures (Susan Hockey). Stern warnings about the dangers of overestimating the liberating and democratizing effects of the electronic revolution include the useful reminders that the shift from orality to literacy was far more consequential than the shift to electronic media has been, and that the invention of print was greeted by a past generation with the same sense of liberation from the tyranny of an older medium as expressed by this generation's "romanticists" of hypertexts and hypermedia (David Greetham). At the same time, candid assessments of the trials and errors that occur during the construction of complex electronic archives, for which neither individual nor a combination of available technologies suffice, lead not to discouragement but to the hope that the critical reflectiveness of traditional scholars will push technology forward as we attempt to imagine that which we don't know (Jerome McGann). Finally, the volume contains a forthright critique of the false motives supporting the pursuit of objective, scientific, complete, and definitive scholarly editions intended to render eternal service to an author's reputation, advancing instead a more modest but liberating view: that scholarly editions provide no more than editors' best interpretative thinking in handling given documentary evidence with as much clarity and accuracy as they can (Peter Shillingsburg). The volume also offers an examination of the textual condition in the context of contemporary critical theory, and against the historical background of modern literary study, where "scholarship" and "criticism" have been routinely opposed (Leroy F. Searle).

We have grouped the essays under various headings—"Textual Space," "Oral Text," "Material Text," "Subversive / Subverted Text," "Electronic Text," and "Textual Maintenance"—so that concerns shared by individual authors can become more readily apparent. Our placement of Jackson's essay after Chartier's, for example, is meant to highlight what might have otherwise been less apparent: namely, that both authors, in spite of the widely different literary material they discuss, challenge our contemporary assumption that texts imply a solitary reader with book in hand; instead, they direct our attention to clues in written texts that represent these texts as intended oral performances and social events—meant to be shared with an audience. Similarly, the grouping of Noegel's and Culham's essays with Eggert's, McLeod's, and Werner's is intended to demonstrate that notions of the materiality of texts were present in ancient cultures long before capturing the interest of contemporary textual scholars.

At the same time, our classification of the essays offered here does not exhaust the links that exist, across dividing boundaries, among the concerns of various authors. For example, the issue of how written works represent oral traditions is not dealt with exclusively by the authors included in the category of oral text but is also at the heart of Chartier's essay. Similarly, the subject of electronic editions is not treated just by Hockey and McGann; it comes up in several other essays (Greetham, Eggert, Shillingsburg, Jackson, Werner) and becomes a leitmotif in Noegel's attempt to show that ancient texts and cybermedia are more closely connected than we might have realized.

Taken together, the essays in this collection do two things admirably: they demonstrate the importance to any discipline of understanding the theoretical and practical problems involved in moving texts from their native times, places, and formats into a modern scholarly and, increasingly, electronic space; and they challenge the reader to formulate, by taking a close look at various past cultures, the "articles of faith" (Greetham) that will sustain textual studies—the oldest discipline dealing with the production, maintenance, preservation, and dissemination of texts—in the twenty-first century.

The exhilarating resurgence, in recent years, of textual studies as a field draws on a very long tradition and a hotly contested present. In the contemporary debates that form an important part of the background of these essays, the stakes are high because contemporary textual theories and methods have considerable consequences for our understanding of how texts are composed, altered, and interpreted. Practitioners in the field do not present a united front, nor do they pretend to have all the answers to vexing questions about the integrity, authority, historicity, and cultural contexts of texts. They do, however, show convincingly that variations in the form of texts cannot be separated from the meaning they convey, and that every reading is an act of textual appropriation. Likewise, there is broad consensus that heightened textual awareness should be the fundamental first stop in any discipline. When readers do not know the actual provenance of the text in hand, they provide, from their own imagination, fictional counterparts to "inform" the reading experience.

Textual study today does not match the old stereotype of a dry science of detecting and ordering the minutiae of text transmission, an activity somewhat akin to copyediting and proofreading, but done by people with doctoral degrees. The purpose of such mundane work, it was once thought, was to "establish" an identity between the work and the text to serve as the starting point for the more interesting and sophisticated tasks of interpreting and appreciating literature. These notions are now exploded and discarded, although of course they may persist. Textual critics today seldom claim that texts are "correct representations" of originating concepts, or of their times, or their agents of generation and change; they focus instead on the process of textual creation, transmission, and transformation, and their work encompasses "text" as composition, production, consumable commodity, performance, material, presentation, (re)presentation, and electronic apparition. What is at stake for readers and critics is a departure from the notion that the "established" text is a *fait accompli* and an invitation to actually understand the nature of the materials to be interpreted. Textual processes—in context, historicized, caught in acts of bias and manipulation by readers and editors exercising their own biases and manipulations—are presented by modern textual criticism as infinitely richer, more dicey, more dangerous, more slippery, and more satisfyingly useful than any "established text" or simple concept of materiality could ever be.

To laymen, written and printed texts offer a sense of security—witness the age-old question "Did you get that in writing?"— as if representational accuracy could provide comfort through the apparent stability of the written word. Textual scholars know, however, that the stability of written texts is belied by a variety of practical factors and theoretical concerns. On a practical level, written works as representations of oral traditions may introduce serious distortions or suffer from reduced credibility, just as many written works from ancient times may now be missing or have deteriorated through use, neglect, fire, or decay. Similarly, texts that were printed during the fifty years after the introduction of wood-pulp papers (that is, from the mid-1870s to about 1925) have suffered serious damage from chemical deterioration. More generally, written works of any period are problematic representations of historical meaning and intention and rarely indicate the state of revision they may represent, while reprinted materials can introduce and perpetuate errors. On a theoretical level, the idealized pursuit of "original" or supposedly authentic meanings of texts has been replaced by new desires to understand the processes of textual engagement, which inevitably involve social, political, and personal appropriations of texts. In a similar way, it is now common to note that the semiotic and semantic dimensions of language are inherently fluid, while the enabling contexts that had silently supported the text may undergo silent but spectacular changes that affect how texts are taken in new circumstances. The processes of textual transmission (copying, editing) are fraught with errors both innocent and sophisticated, while new formats seriously influence how readers interact with texts.

Responses to these changes in literary studies range from celebrations of interpretative freedom, at one extreme, to despair over the loss of certainty, at another. There was a time when the aim of textual study was to establish the best artistic text or the most authentic historical text as a universal standard that could form the foundation of all subsequent literary debate. That aim has been discredited for most scholars, both textual and literary, and new aims have emerged.

One branch of textual scholarship, *texte génétique*, associated with its most dedicated practitioners in France, traces the development of texts from inception through revision to abandonment (resisting the notion of any achieved perfection or finish), unworried by concerns for what the text ought to be, and glorying instead in the complexity, dexterity, and rich signification of actual textual evolution. For geneticists, the goal of understanding the processes of composition has superseded any desire for a standardized finished text.

Other scholars, pursuing the historical-critical *Editionwissenschaft* that is associated primarily with German textual studies, focus on the relations among variant versions of works, usually selecting some single extant version as a base text but insisting that the work is incomplete without its history of change (the work equals the text plus apparatus). Intentions are of no importance for such editors; instead, each historical, physical iteration of the text is a social / linguistic event, with its confluence of forces and contexts of signification, worthy of study as a separate entity.

Anglo-American textual studies is no longer dominated by a single school of thought. One cadre of editors, representing the dominant modes of the 1960s and 1970s, continues to produce clear reading texts representing the editors' understanding of what the authors probably intended, reporting the historical record primarily as superseded or questionable forms in an apparatus at the back. Other editors have tried to develop techniques that represent works as a textual flow or development, offering alternative texts on the text page itself. Still others focus on discrete but multiple textual manifestations for each work, without trying to establish a hierarchy or sense of superior texts. Among the newest types of textual work is that of electronic archivists, who attempt to combine the roles of collector of texts, textual guide, and archivist but who resist the editor's traditional role as arbiter of correctness.

Underlying all these new directions in textual studies is a new awareness of the complex communicative dynamics of written text. This awareness was influenced in part by the debates in literary theory that left formalism and structuralism in the dust of deconstruction and post-structural reconfigurations of authority. With the growing realization of the reader's role in determining the work, with the growing sense of the futility of objectivity, with the self-realization of the inevitable political power of interpretation (both in relation to the perceived author and with respect to other readers), with the growing understanding that interpretation had to deal primarily with the contingencies of the present and secondarily with the contingencies of an imagined past—with all these realizations taking root in literary theory and criticism, it became obvious to most textual scholars that the holy grail of definitive texts was a futile chase. It may come as a surprise to lay readers, however, that these changes began to take place in textual studies in the 1950s, although they did not reach a state of crisis until the mid-1980s. These changes were stoked by two emerging developments in textual criticism that have dominated discussions of textual criticism in the last ten years: first, serious exploration of modern works for which full histories of composition and production survive, and which rendered the pursuit of a single correct text far less interesting than tracing textual processes in social dynamics; and, second, exploration of increasing numbers of noncanonical or marginal texts, where gender and race bias in production processes forced a re-examination and clarification of textual goals.

Debates used to rage in textual studies over whether a work should represent an author's early or late intentions, and over whether the work should be studied as it appeared to its first public or in a form that the author intended but failed to achieve, either because lesser souls intervened or because the work did not reach completion. Such debates have given way entirely to new ones: about how to present the multiplicity and richness of variant texts, or how to represent agency in these processes, or how to construct electronic navigation aids to enable a sense of immediacy for users confronting a multiplicity of variant texts without losing their way, or how to minimize or eliminate the effects of editorial biases and misunderstandings. These debates usually raise questions about how to organize and represent complex textualities for literary critics who seldom demonstrate an inclination to think of works as textually problematic, however willing they may seem to think of texts as sites of interpretational contention and negotiation. It is curious that literary critics who have relished the indeterminacy of meaning seem unimpressed by the indeterminacy of texts. A willful ignorance holds textual complexity at bay.

None of these modern approaches to textuality strays far from concern about the role of the modern textual scholar in the representation or enactment of older texts for modern consumption. Literary theorists accustomed to "locating the subject," or to being conscious of the "situated self" and the "perceived other," will not find this concern to be strange. This debate, in its baldest form, centers on the question of an editor's critical interventions in textual representation. At one end of the editorial spectrum, where consciousness of the intruding subject is limited to a fearful potentiality rather than acknowledged as an inevitability, are those who promote a hands-off, objective accumulation of data. Such "editors" recommend the collection and reproduction of extant texts, with little or no editing. Fearing that offering too much guidance will make editors into advocates for one particular view or another, such scholars prefer a cautious approach to providing guidelines for understanding the accumulated texts. Also coming into vogue is a new philosophy that texts are best understood through what Randall McLeod has called "unediting," unveiling the obscuring effects caused by editorial misappropriation of original materials. At the other end of the spectrum, where the inevitability of the intruding subject is accepted, and where textual self-defense by well-informed readers is thought to be possible, are those who hold that an editor's duty is to make sense of the mountain of minute data involved in textual histories, in order to provide readers with the fruits of great labor and of wise though inevitably biased and limited judgment on the part of careful scholars who have exercised their critical faculties to separate what is relevant from insignificant details. Every approach to editorial and textual studies can be understood, in part, as an adjudication of these two poles: simple, accurate representation versus critical, interpretive added value.

The essays in this volume contribute significantly to the scholarly debates summarized here. They enter the debates at a point of momentous textual transformation—the Electronic Revolution—equal in magnitude to the Gutenberg Revolution. The essays arrange themselves in a narrative path that reflects simultaneously the development of textual technology in history and the development of sophistication in deployment of textual strategies. This collection provides overviews that indicate the philosophical and practical scope of the field and tentative maps of textual space. It explores the materials, lacunae, methods, and goals of oral texts. It confronts the implications of the instability, unexpectedness, and complexity of material texts. It raises questions about subversive and subverted texts; and it devotes considerable space to the problems and opportunities of electronic texts. By surveying ideologies, goals, methods, and strategies in textual studies in other languages and cultures, it shows how narrow, even parochial, has been the pursuit of textual awareness in America, and it offers a sardonic analysis of the editor's responsibility for the care and maintenance of texts in the face of temptations to think one's views are universally applicable or even desirable. The voices of written texts have rarely been so richly conceived and heard as in the essays contained in this volume.

We dedicate this volume to the students in the Textual Studies program at the University of Washington, those future textual scholars who will carry on the invaluable insights of the prestigious scholars gathered here.

Raimonda Modiano
Peter Shillingsburg

ACKNOWLEDGMENTS

This volume commemorates a major international conference ("Voice, Text, and Hypertext at the Millennium") held in October 1997 to inaugurate the University of Washington's program in textual studies. We would like first of all to express our sincerest thanks to the following units at the University of Washington, which contributed generously to the funding of the conference: the Walter Chapin Simpson Center for the Humanities; the College of Arts and Sciences; all departments in the Division of Humanities; the Graduate School; the Office of Research; the Department of History; the Comparative Religion and Jewish Studies programs; the History of Science Society; the Jackson School of International Studies; the Kenneth S. Allen Library Endowment Fund; the Center for West European Studies; the President's Fund; the Hilen Professorship; Russian, East European, and Central Asian Studies (REECAS); and the School of Medicine. We also obtained generous support from four neighboring universities, to which we owe special thanks: Pacific Lutheran University, Seattle Pacific University, Seattle University, and the University of Puget Sound. Numerous faculty members, students, and staff members provided inspiration, leadership, and countless hours of work in the planning and organization of the conference. Among them we would like to express particular thanks to Leroy Searle, former director of the Walter Chapin Simpson Center for the Humanities, and to the Simpson Center's staff members, especially Alex Aho, Marion Heard, and Lisa Spagnolo for handling a conference of tremendous administrative complexity; to librarians Sandy Kroupa and Helene Williams, and to Betty Bengston, former director of University Libraries; and to Keith Benson, George Bozarth, Michael Halleran, Jack Haney, Martin Jaffee, Fritz Levy, Tom Lockwood, Tilar Mazzeo, Paul Remley, Richard Salomon, Michael Shapiro, Míceál Vaughan, and Michael Williams. In the initial stages of recruiting for and planning the conference, we received invaluable help from David Greetham and a group of distinguished textual scholars from other institutions: George Bornstein, Anthony Edwards, Paul Eggert, T. H. Howard-Hill, Jerome McGann, Randall McLeod, Donald Reiman, and Jonathan Rose.

In the selection of essays for the volume, we were very fortunate to receive the expert advice of G. Thomas Tanselle and Kathryn Sutherland, for which we are extremely grateful. The help of assistants Lisa Spagnolo,

Alexander Schlutz, and Liz Browning was essential in preparing the manuscript for the University of Washington Press. We would also like to express our gratitude for the aid and support of Naomi Pascal and the extraordinary care and intellectual guidance of Xavier Callahan of the University of Washington Press, who lightened immeasurably our tasks as editors. Finally, it is hard to imagine what our labors or morale would have been without the generosity, enthusiasm, and dedication to this volume of our colleague Kathleen Woodward, director of the Walter Chapin Simpson Center for the Humanities.

The Editors

PART I

Textual Space

Emerging Questions
Text and Theory in Contemporary Criticism

LEROY F. SEARLE

As the essays in this volume make clear, the enterprise of textual scholarship and editing has certainly not been immune to the drama of contemporary theory in literature and the arts. For an earlier generation, the
vocation of editorial scholarship often seemed a haven (if not the very
citadel) of intellectual probity, in which one could practice a science—
mild and respectful, if sometimes dull—without being drawn into the
relatively unregulated life of literary criticism and theory, where, as I. A.
Richards remarked after a lifetime of experience with it, "an indecent
disregard of fact is still current form."[1] It has become increasingly clear,
however, that almost every issue that has made theory a matter of controversy, crisis, and polemical debate hinges on the representational status of texts. While texts are presumably instruments of communication,
they are also institutional facts and cultural interventions that may affect
one's sense of personal, religious, cultural, ethnic, or national identity,
just as they shape historical cultures in manifold ways. To put a complex point simply, the study of texts cannot be cordoned off from the
study of culture.

The essays collected here confirm this complexity, not in the mode of
ideological passion or advocacy, but as matters of inescapable though
problematic fact, whether the case in question is ancient or modern, oral
or printed or digital. Indeed, part of the importance of these essays collectively lies in their probity, even when they are sharpened or playful,
as investigations of textual complexities that reach far beyond the simple schema of a text as an author's privileged communication with the
public. More than that, they are the fruit of some two decades of intense
and often controversial work that has increased our collective textual
awareness, starting not from a primarily speculative posture but from
a profoundly critical commitment to the historicity and the concrete
materiality of texts.

In this sense, our understanding of the dimensions of textuality has
expanded, not merely as criticism and theory have contemplated the
death or decline of the intending author into an abstract "authorial
function,"[2] or by way of the indifferent habit of treating anything and

everything pertaining to culture as a "text" to be read, "theorized," and incorporated into the abstract rhetoric of a general cultural critique. For literary theorists, the better reason to attend carefully to the work of contemporary textual scholars is that they have neither simply followed the topoi and fashionable agendas of current theory nor treated textual complexity as just another source of paradox that follows the inexorable flow of power across the social field. The striking transformation of editorial traditions that appears to be in progress has arisen precisely from within those traditions, coming to conclusions that are remarkably similar to what one finds in contemporary literary theory, but differently derived. In this volume, accordingly, there is one strain of reflection that seeks to narrow if not collapse the difference between literary theory and textual scholarship, but another which draws more directly on those elements of editorial tradition that acknowledge texts as pivotal and highly specific historical transactions that we cannot afford to treat casually because they enable, just as they define and limit, the scope of collective social and cultural life.

What Wlad Godzich has treated elsewhere as the "culture of literacy" in its post-Hegelian, poststructuralist moment of crisis[3] is explored in these essays as an intricate mosaic of forces and influences, decisions and prohibitions, where any question pertaining to the authenticity of a text is transformed with sometimes startling swiftness into a far less tidy question of cultural authenticity. The essays here make vivid the reasons not to limit the idea of "literacy" to print, or of "text" to writing, as they show in case after case that what distinguishes a *text* from a casual utterance is not its formal medium so much as the weaving together of its elements, with careful and meticulous attention to *how* something is articulated, preserved, and transmitted. Whether we come at the question as writers or as readers, speakers, or listeners, we recognize texts to be intentional: they are *for* something (even if we are not sure what it is), just as they elicit our attention to the precise terms of their presentation. In the slogan of the architect Louis Sullivan (who borrowed it from Horatio Greenough), "Form follows function."[4] In cases where the intention of a text is overt, as in a manual for the repair of small engines or a textbook on medical physiology, the text itself ordinarily attracts little attention, because it appears to us subsumed in the subject it treats. But texts that seem to call attention to themselves foreground a common but intricate process, one that constitutes a subject in the very act of speaking or writing about it—and, in so doing, enormously complicates the problem of intentionality. This kind of textual self-reflexivity, whether in a philosophical essay, a religious recitation, a ritual pronouncement, or a literary work, demands that we attend to what *follows* from saying something in a particular way; and, more than that, it means that our projection of a future or possible pathway to what follows must depend not merely on our grasping the content, the message, but also on our apprehending that the method and the manner of the saying are evidence of an active power that the text invokes and incites.

Such problematic texts, however we may classify them, are the main subjects of the essays here, but a prevailing concern is to disclose a primary process of reasoning and thinking that textuality itself enables.[5] The examples, moreover, are various and frequently strange, from lead tablets, nailed down and not even meant to be read, to butterflylike pieces of an envelope, bearing poetic lines pinned to pages of a manuscript (see the essays in this volume by Phyllis Culham and Marta Werner). In this respect, the central theoretical issue with texts is not any presumed ontological priority of speech over writing, nor is it a contrary legislative authority of the book over the voice or even the indeterminacy of signification and meaning. It is instead a common logic of annunciation that defines and renders intelligible a common and collective cultural space. Texts capture our attention as sites that enable those transactions, both public and private, which are not merely linguistic expressions but give shape and body to culture itself.

This helps to explain why texts matter enough for us to fight over them, just as it goes some distance in clarifying why texts that seem to call attention to themselves, not as mere vehicles for information but as carefully and meticulously made things, seem fraught with intention and with the promise of meaning, all the more so as they may puzzle us. "Read me!" says the text; but when we do so, we have the uncanny sensation that the text is reading us. Textuality, in other words, is frequently a process of constitution and discovery, a specific mode of thinking that functions as one of the primary instruments of cultural legitimation. Texts allow us to see ourselves in thought, and to actively practice it, not in some splendid isolation but in and through others' words. In a precisely complementary way, meticulous textual attention allows us to understand cultures and practices that would otherwise be literally unimaginable to us.

It is striking in these essays, particularly to someone whose main arena of professional interest is literary criticism and theory, that though the field of textual studies has been equally seared by controversy, the familiar literary rhetoric of crisis is largely absent here, and the currently ubiquitous word *aporia*—Aristotle's term for getting stuck—doesn't appear at all. On the contrary, what we see is a trajectory of argument and inference that is theoretically vital precisely because it does not return upon its own puzzlements but keeps steadily in view the oddities and peculiarities of revealing textual examples, solidly anchored in specific documents and practices that provide a ground for evidence, no matter how weird or baffling the evidence itself may prove.

Considering the theoretical dimension of textual studies in this way is hardly the story of textual editors coming down out of the ivory tower and into the mosh pit of theory (showing, as David Greetham puts it in his essay, that they "can be as post-*anything* as the best of them"). It is, rather, that the editor's traditional task of establishing a text (as common legend avers Aristotle did with Homer so he could teach his most famous pupil, Alexander the Great) shows the editor first of all that there is nothing simple in the job, nothing obvious or cut-and-dried even in the reasons for doing it. Nevertheless, the editorial product, from Aristotle's time to the present day, is liable to be received by pupils and the public (and, of course, literary critics) as if the text in hand is just the way it ought to be—and against which liability we may encounter editorial and authorial antics, just to remind us that the texts do not materialize out of thin air, even if the idea of making them may seem to.

In what could provide an apt emblem for this problem, William Blake's "Introduction" to *Songs of Innocence* gives us a piper, caught up in his "songs of glee," descending quickly from his tune to an articulate song, to the written text, which in the act of being inscribed with his "rural pen" did not simply record his song but rather "stain'd the water clear." Nothing in textual studies belongs to the state of Edenic innocence, and textuality itself may be the very image of the Fall. But for Blake, as for contemporary textualists, it is no simple image of loss but of an ambivalent transformation. As the piper-turned-writer puts it, though his vision has vanished, he writes his songs "that every child may joy to hear."[6]

Now that contemporary critical theory is old enough to have a popular folk history, conveyed through textbooks, anthologies, and other simplified narratives of who caused what, I would suggest that the role of editorial scholarship may prove even more revealing because even in its fiercest controversies it has generally shied away from sudden or daring leaps of political rhetoric or the sweeping conceptual claims that are such a prominent feature of critical theory. Editors who come to their vocation from a longer explicit history are apt to understand in a quite distinctive mode that their work with texts plays a foundational but always problematic role in the development of intellectual institutions (a fact that, as a "theoretical" discovery, seems always to come as a shock) because they are immersed in the details of how it happens, not in the scandal that the glorious free-play of verbal intelligence should ever be confined in a definite form.

Ironically, the theoretical turn in textual studies since the 1980s is a direct outgrowth of success for the modern (that is, post-Renaissance) editorial project that first domesticated and then institutionalized the very idea of "standard" editions of major authors.[7] From the now hotly contested idea of a literary "canon" to the always hotly contested notion of a scriptural or religious "canon," the idea of establishing "standard" texts is inextricably bound up with establishing narratives of national, ethnic, or religious origin, negotiating privileges or rights that belong to the citizen, even to the point of defining what it means to be a person who belongs to some particular community, just as it is shaped by the particular values and commitments of the editors who do the work.

The turn to theory in criticism, by contrast, has been much more starkly associated with crisis, with seemingly impassable paradoxes, in part because textual editors since the early Renaissance *have* done their jobs so diligently. The Stephanus edition of Plato made it possible, for example, to actually *study* Plato instead of merely worshiping him, so as to see how slippery is his conception of forms, just as editions of Shakespeare or medieval romances both create and complicate the idea of (national) literary history. On a shorter scale, we could date the rise of contemporary theoretical criticism from the dramatic collapse of formalism and structuralism after 1965,[8] an event leading directly to radical forms of skepticism (by way of deconstruction) and to a rapidly escalating sense that perhaps the entire edifice of Western culture was erected on the sand of shifting signifiers, economic opportunism, and gross imperial ambitions. This pervasive mood of suspicion and crisis was accelerated, however, by democratic ambitions shaped by the same cultural history, which, since the end of World War II, have transformed higher education from a resource for the privileged few to a public project if not an entitlement for the many. Yet the very idea of public education as it emerged from Renaissance humanism was inescapably grounded in textuality, in the profound secular commitment to recover the authors (and thereby the authority) of the ancient world at a time of enormous turbulence and change. The culture of literacy, in this framework, takes shape as a culture of books, a culture of reading and writing, which is and always has been inflected at every turn by political and moral imperatives. As Richard Ohman and Evan Watkins have both pointed out with distinct but similar political intent,[9] taking an English class since the mid-1960s has become about as close to a cultural universal as anything could be: one could not pass through any level of schooling without it; and without some level of formal schooling, participation in the diverse goods of a modern society was severely constrained. On the international scene, for better or for worse, this trend appears to be continuing at an accelerating pace.

What has been less clear is that this drama of theoretical crisis has depended in part on what amounts to a studied indifference to the subtle revelations that textual scholarship can offer on topics of lively contemporary interest. For example, literary critics may move from this or that detail of the literary "canon" to a much broader discernment of social injustice, which appears everywhere as the imposition of oppressive and usually covert power by the privileged class. This makes a story that is at least easier to tell (and much easier to get upset about) than the richly particular studies of culture that take shape when one is trying to sort out precisely how British magistrates tried to accommodate Hindu law, or how Serbian folk poetry was actually recorded and disseminated, or how enormous bodies of religious songs may have been generated on the authority of long-since-inaccessible authors (see the essays in this volume by Ludo Rocher, John Miles Foley, and Winand Callewaert). But if one wants to pursue cultural studies, doing so from a textualist perspective has the considerable advantage of privileging the concrete, documentary details of the text as a basis for reasoning instead of trusting almost exclusively to the dialectical process of reasoning from what we already happen to believe and may fervently think we know.

No doubt this dialectical rhetoric of theoretical criticism and cultural studies has seemed hotter and more immediately relevant than the painstaking work of sorting out textual variants, or trying to make explicit the complex paradigms that come into play in the seemingly transparent activities of reading and writing. For example, the enterprise of foregrounding the historicity of reading, as explored in the work of Roger Chartier, like the examination of writing as an immediate response to what one reads, as in the revealing case of marginalia presented by Heather Jackson, discloses intimate dimensions in the life of culture that are remarkable not because they are indeterminate but because they are so surprisingly rich. To reiterate the importance of probity, what we see in these instances is a degree of accountability sufficient to risk the actual complexity of what is there, without evident prejudgment of what it might mean. We should make no mistake: the patience of these textual scholars is marking out a possible future for study in the humanities as they insist that we discipline our opinions and temper our judgments, keeping them much closer to concrete, specific evidence.

Perhaps nowhere is this imperative clearer than in the sober assessment, given in this volume by Jerome McGann and Susan Hockey, that we are far past the point of mere enthusiasm over hypertext and the Internet, now that we actually have some concrete experience of what happens to excited expectations when they come into hard contact with data structures, programming conventions, and a host of related choices we might not have even suspected we would have to make when we first embraced the idea of electronic or digital texts. As any casual surfer can see, moreover, what the World Wide Web routinely shows is less the radical democratization of textual production and dissemination than a kind of riotous global pursuit of the promises made by advertising and pornography, in the face of which the actual availability and use of electronic texts as educational and scholarly resources requires an increased degree of critical vigilance and forethought, not to break new ground so much as to preserve the vitality of intellectual and cultural links to the concrete history of textual production and reception.

Moreover, throughout this volume, the rather sharp and persistent reaction against earlier conceptions of textual scholarship seems itself a product of the same habit of probity, no matter how much it may appear to involve some transgression or violation of a sacred cultural trust. As Jerome McGann put it in 1982, the central problem lay in the "inadequacies in our basic views" of textual criticism, inadequacies that had become "unavoidable."[10] The very effort to arrive at a "definitive" text, or to isolate in any convincing way a putative "final intention" of an author, was itself the source of evidence that the objective was not only impossible but also wrongheaded by virtue of being vastly too simplistic. While this situation has an analogue in the collapse of formalism and structuralism precisely through the diligent pursuit of formalist and structuralist practices, the difference is that textual editors, working on historical materials, may be much less vulnerable to the a-historical misapprehension, currently abroad in criticism, that "theory" in literary study really only started in Baltimore in 1966.[11]

When critics take on the literary canon for its unfair exclusiveness, it is commonly with the sense of seeking out a mysterious and crafty enemy who is defending a prejudicial curriculum. But from a textualist point of view, what is at stake is first of all an encounter with the cumulative history of decisions to valorize certain texts over others (and certain editions of them over others), a history that it behooves us to understand in more specific detail.

The work assembled here marks a very significant collective advance in handling such questions or, at the very least, coming to terms with their intrinsic subtlety. Even as early as the 1950s, it was clear that the presumed opposition between literary criticism and textual scholarship was more a caricature than a description of work in the field. In 1963, for example, almost as a lull before the poststructuralist, postmodernist storm that was about to break in criticism, the Modern Language Association created a commission charged to update its 1952 report on the aims and methods of research in language and literature. The new report was to be an ostensibly conciliatory and synoptic pamphlet that treated linguistics, textual scholarship, literary history, and literary criticism as an integrated hierarchy of scholarly techniques and methods.[12] Northop Frye was commissioned to write the essay titled "Literary Criticism," where he treats earlier essays in the book as dealing with "the essential techniques to be learned by scholars in the humanities" but cautions those whose real interest is in criticism against becoming "*too* expert in them" because the difficulty of these techniques might persuade those interested in criticism that "if criticism is posterior to scholarship," to which "scholarly techniques are preliminary parts," then the enterprise of criticism must be something "requiring superhuman abilities."[13]

This intricate rhetorical display, coming right up to the edge of false modesty, accurately reflects a real problem of critical confidence; but, by treating the work of scholarship as "a ratio between accuracy and limitation of perspective," it simplifies, in a dangerous and invidious way, the difference it preserves. If scholarship depends, in other words, "on the kind of statement of fact that can be definitely verified or contradicted, the narrower in range it is likely to be."[14]

Fredson Bowers's "Textual Criticism" begins with a simplification that matches Frye's precisely. "Any critic or historian or linguist," Bowers begins, "would prefer to discuss a literary work on the basis of a sound text." But he proceeds in his very first paragraph to turn this seemingly obvious remark into the basis for an obviously polemical attack on F. O. Matthiessen (and, indirectly, on literary criticism itself), for finding deep speculative tension in the phrase "soiled fish of the sea" from Melville's *White-Jacket*.[15] Here is Bowers: "Unfortunately, credit for this metaphysical shock should properly go to the unknown compositor of the reprint consulted, whose memory or fingers slipped while trying to set 'coiled fish of the sea.'" In representing the case as "spectacular," however, Bowers inadvertently goes for his own bait, spectacularly overgeneralizing the example as "easily multiplied . . . when critics have relied in vain on corrupt editions for an accurate transmission of an author's words."[16] The case affords an almost perfect example of the elaborate but inconclusive debates that are precipitated when a surprising and anomalous detail throws scholars and critics back upon their most fundamental conceptions and opinions, debates that no amount of evidence, or of argument bearing only on the specific case in question, could possibly resolve. Either image, of "coiled fish" or "soiled fish," may be problematic, but the anomaly in this case lay not merely in whether it was Melville's genius or a compositor's inadvertence behind the phrase but also in the embedded matrix of ideas that scholars and critics had habitually relied on for deciding what would count as authoritative.

I mention this notorious example, not to carry on what has become an almost ritual practice of Bowers-bashing (or of trashing Frye) but to foreground the fact that Bowers's apparent immunity to doubt on the possibility of a "definitive" text, as an accurate reflection of the author's final intentions, has *exactly* the same roots as Frye's belief that the critic, broadening his scope to *"all* of the literature he knows," could understand the whole of literature as one gigantic anagogical object depicting the totality of an imagined human universe.[17] Both positions reflect the conviction that literature can be understood—or, more emphatically, that it could *only* be understood—as a collection of *objects* about which to reason. The irony is that the actual role of the author is thereby misleadingly simplified, as if he or she were the possessor of a superhuman competence to issue a text that fully expressed authorial intention, without lapse or remainder, or as if the text were the production of an unidentifiable spirit or zeitgeist in which the author is, in T. S. Eliot's unfortunate metaphor, only the catalyst in a chemical reaction.[18] Though Eliot's is just a variant of a much older figure in which the author is a conduit for communication from the gods (who, as Plato was perhaps not the first to suspect, must be crazy), neither version does anything to clarify the actual process by which specific words really are put in a specific order that is subject to change, whether by revision, excision, negotiated editorial intervention, or accident. In a precisely complementary way, the "text" is made into a fetish, a privileged site of power or influence, to be protected from tampering, revision, correction, or second thoughts.

In both cases, the theoretical slippage centers on mistaking the *integrity* of a text for its *authority.* When the text is objectified as the unique representation of the author's thought, its cultural authority is simply taken for granted—and made to depend on a fundamentally mystified conception of the artist as a "genius." Thus, when contemporary scholars and critics have turned to the putative "materiality" of the text, *not* as the image of authorial intention (since, in keeping with the contemporary commonplace, the author is either dead or distilled into an authorial function), but as the reflection of economic, political, or ideological forces in the social field, the mystification is of the same kind, only immeasurably worse, since it makes even the idea of intentionality impenetrable.

This distinction between integrity and authority is *not* transparent, however, because literary critics and textual scholars alike may simply assume, for example, that the integrity of the text ought to serve ipso facto as a guarantee of its authority, since it is extremely difficult to see how the text could be anything but an object—either materially, as a made thing, or ideally, as a "cognitive" object constituted by reading and interpreting. But this seemingly binary choice is illusory, wanting a third term to mediate between the seemingly incommensurable alternatives. The dilemma is that one is not, therefore, free to treat the concreteness and materiality of textual evidence as illusory, on the one hand, or, on the other, to presume, either through spurious appeals to common sense or through the invocation of ideologically saturated theoretical models, that the text is transparent with respect to significance or meaning. Neither will it suffice to take a relaxed, relativist attitude or improvise one's way through the problem with an eclectic gathering of cautions against essentialism, or commonplaces about material or epistemological contingency.

The idea of textual integrity reflects what is perhaps the deepest modern tradition in editing: the commitment to account precisely for the order of the words—not, in a manner of speaking, to cook one's books, or falsify the evidence, no matter how messy it might be. In this light, Bowers was correct in supposing that critics would rather have a "sound text," since perhaps the deepest modern tradition in criticism is a commitment to consider, by contemplative means, the cognitive "object" that is constituted in and through reading. But the very idea of "literature" as an essentially stable list of books, the "canon" of Western culture, is an historical and institutional accomplishment based squarely on the work of editors. Speculative contemplation of this fact does indeed make the admission unavoidable that any "edition," any version of a text, like any particular instance of interpretation, cannot be purified of the choices made and the interests served by the editor or interpreter. Yet what is at stake is not agreement between contemporary literary theory and textual scholarship in finding language indeterminate, or intention beyond our grasp; rather, it is agreement that the conception of *literature* as a collection of "objects" is fundamentally incoherent.

This is why the traditional assumption—that to guarantee the integrity of a text (these words in this order) is to settle the matter of authority—systematically produces controversy and ambiguity: words alone offer no transparent or untroubled pathway of access to meaning or to value. Just as the implicit face-off between Frye and Bowers is grounded in common presuppositions, current controversies between idealist and materialist conceptions of texts have a common ground in the metaphysical notion of the primacy of objects as, in some way, *given*.

Over the range of the essays collected here, one can discern, I think, an admittedly subdued sense of renewal, along with a sometimes excessive exuberance, in efforts to domesticate the idea that literary work (and literary *works*) depend above all on a process of exploration and discovery that may not be initially shaped by semiotic motives but by what Charles Sanders Peirce called "abduction," the leaps and lucky guesses that lead us to a hypothesis, or by the less docile experience of being carried away by a possibility, a relation, a coincidence that invites us irresistibly because it offers so rich a promise of meaning. Marta Werner's carefully incomplete and evocative reflections on marvelous fragments in the manuscripts of Emily Dickinson, or Randall McLeod's astonishing tour through the typographical exigencies lying behind the publication of Gerard Manley Hopkins's sonnets, are crucial reminders of the play and willfulness, the accident and contingency, that shape, condition, and liberate the imaginative. At a farther extreme, Martin Jaffee's demanding reflections on the spirituality of Torah as something embodied and woven as text into daily life and not only as something written on a scroll, or the studies by Scott Noegel and Phyllis Culham of cases in which the power of textual precision is conceived as divine verbal magic or as the execution of horrific curses—all this work reminds us that the human world is a world of words. But words in the studied text are almost never actually conceived as neutral signifiers but rather as living exponents of human power, whether we think of this power as secular or divine, aesthetic or political.

While it would be misleading to claim a unified theory in the sum of the essays in this book, it would be perhaps more misleading not to remark the consistency with which these authors are attempting to move forward, not by some declared rupture with the past but precisely by its renewal. In distinguishing between the integrity of a text and its authority, my point is that an insistence on the concrete details of how texts come to be, of exactly what words come in exactly what order, is perhaps the only way to avoid falling into a state of enthusiastic mystification or dangerously mistaken passion about the rightness of one's own opinions. In the effort to vouch for the integrity of a text, faith resides not in the belief that editorial accountability will deliver over to us an unproblematic and transparent object; on the contrary, it is more like the commitment that Peirce urged be inscribed "upon every wall of the city of philosophy: DO NOT BLOCK THE WAY OF INQUIRY."[19] In other words, integrity in textual matters lies in *access to the evidence,* such that someone who follows us can see precisely how we worked, what we considered, so as either to ratify the evidence or object and think it through again. Texts earn their authority not merely by their being integral, ostensibly faithful transmissions but also by our *assent to what they say,* to what they make possible, to what they mediate in specific and definite terms. Just as we would have serious reasons to distrust a study of human emotions if it were carried out in complete obliviousness to the point of actually *feeling* them, what comes into being when a text is studied is the result of the work of reasoning that does *not* set cognition and affect at odds. We ask these questions when particular texts actually count in our lives, and we have the actual experience of textual authority precisely and only as we assent to what follows from reading the text, by reasoning our way into the rich and expandable matrix of relations that integral, specific, and continent texts make intelligible to others as well as to ourselves.

This point is made all the more difficult because of the ease with which the repetition of incoherent ideas can come to seem theoretically advanced or intellectually courageous in following a line of inquiry no matter where it leads. Paul Eggert's very astute essay in this volume takes up the case of "materialist" editorial practices that literalize the idea of the death of the author, or the banishing of authorial intention, on the apparent warrant of the impossibility of deciding which of many variant texts (in this case, Shakespeare's plays) should be selected as authoritative. But, as Eggert points out, removing a vaguely idealist conception of authorial intention from consideration leaves the strict materialist in the awkward position of replacing that conception with an even more vague social, historical, or contextual intention, at the risk of confounding altogether the idea of a literary *work* as something not identical with the printed, material text in all its variants. A crude opposition between "materialist" and "idealist" conceptions does not become subtle just by repetition but rather, as Peirce might have argued, only shows the folly of ignoring the real power of ideas, on the one hand, or the equally real pressure and resistance of materiality, on the other.[20]

This issue is, I believe, central to the contemporary resurgence of interest in textual studies, as much as to the contemporary sense of malaise and uncertainty in literary criticism. On both sides of the aisle, furthermore, this relation between the text and the work has been the source of interminable controversies, not unlike Immanuel Kant's discovery of the Antinomies of Reason, where cogent but incompatible arguments can be made on both sides without the provision of anything that could decide between them. The collapse of formalism and structuralism, while tolerably (or intolerably) complete, has provided, in the general movement of deconstruction, a compelling rehearsal of the deficiency of the idea, ultimately Platonic, that the link between being and representation is simple and obvious. The appeal of the idea of authorial intention as having one and only one privileged expression, in the form of a definitive text, depends on the premise of common understanding that the only thing that could be represented is something that already exists. The negative or privative demonstrations that this is not the case, whether they examine meaning as a potentially infinite chain of signifiers or demonstrate that the material social context trumps the claims of individual intention, always stop short of providing an alternative explanation of how it is that we do in fact understand one another, that discourse ends not always in more discourse but in discrete intentional actions, or that individuals can in fact act effectively in opposition to the pressures of social and political history.

Deconstruction in all its forms is not only necessary but inevitable, precisely because the philosophical groundwork of our historical communities in the West is a philosophical formalism that tirelessly repeats the paradoxes of Plato's theory of Forms when we presume that the work must be identical with the text, or that the representation can be validated only in a one-to-one relation to the object it is presumed to represent. In this sense, it makes no enduring difference whether we take the position that a different text is therefore a different work or that different texts are but variants of one ideal work, because both positions derive from exactly the same insufficient philosophical assumptions about the relation between ontology and intelligibility.

Whether in critical or philosophical terms, getting beyond formalism is inordinately difficult because it requires of us that we discriminate, as Kant did in *The Critique of Judgment,* between common sense and common understanding *(sensus communis).* The former depends on the free play of our cognitive (and affective) faculties, whereas the latter is grounded in the historical contingencies of actual communities,[21] but what we ordinarily mean when we talk of "common sense" is just the sense of the community: the concepts and practices we have acquired, not because we have confirmed them by inquiry and reflection, testing them, as Keats put it, upon our nerves, but merely because they were already in common and communal circulation.

In the present case, the broad movement away from the idea of a single privileged representation as the "authoritative" text and toward the preservation of variants and revisions, including false starts and happy (or unhappy) accidents, is compelling because of what the evidence confirms over and over in actual cases: this is how imagination actually works, not by a perfect text springing Athena-like from the capacious forehead of an authorial Zeus. In this sense, preserving the integrity of a text already includes the idea of preserving the process by which it came into being. There is a stunning example in the manuscripts of Charles Sanders Peirce: a letter of application to the Smithsonian Institution for a grant to complete a very ambitious set of philosophical essays. Peirce trashes the requirement that he provide a letter of application of some fifteen or so pages, producing instead a brilliant document that, with serial revisions, runs to more than four hundred manuscript pages. But as he writes, the resulting letter (L 75) shows with stunning clarity how the pursuit, in words, of an idea or a possibility does not proceed down a single straight line of argument but circles back by fits and starts of sudden insight and self-correction.[22] Peirce frequently cautioned his readers (and perhaps himself) not to think that thoughts are in us, but rather to understand that we are in thought much as bodies are in motion or fish are in water.[23]

The problem is that the idea of the work, if the work is not to be identified with the material text, does not therefore dissipate into the circumambient gas of naive idealism, because the "work" of imaginative reasoning is not some kind of marble monument; it is our being led to think in a particular way, with exact verbal and formal guidance, so that we as readers must confirm what follows and what fits. This perspective is at least suggested in the insistence that we simultaneously take the word "work" as both a noun and a verb.

When we read Shakespeare's *Hamlet,* for example, the divergences between the folio and the quarto texts do not compel us to make a single, unambiguous choice, so long as we recognize that the "work" inevitably includes the reader's work of reasoning as he or she follows the text. In the case of the "bad" 1603 quarto, drastically shorter and evidently prepared for performance with a much smaller company, it is altogether clear that it does not *do* what the longer and later texts do.[24] In each case, we rely on the integrity of the text (whether it is the "bad" quarto, the "good" one, or the folio) as the *ground* of evidence: its integrity derives from the fact that it is stable.[25] The existence of other texts establishes a connection between a *relate* (one text) and a *correlate* (another text), both of which have their own integrity. But following one text— that is, reasoning with it—and then another (for as many variants as may be at hand) puts us in the unique position of being able to compare the correlates so as to recognize that the work *"Hamlet"* is what Peirce called an *interpretant* (in the language of his categories, a "third"): a mediating representation that is definite without being bounded, and, far from being merely a conventional or arbitrary signifier, is an aspect of reality (and a necessary constituent of meaning) wherein we can locate regularity and order that are not incompatible with variation.[26] As with any other general terms, from common nouns to laws of nature, our ability to recognize that all three texts are instances of *"Hamlet"* is no more surprising than our ability to recognize that Great Danes and Chihuahuas are both instances of *"Dog."* The materialist who would assert that *"Dog"* does not exist but only *dogs,* and the idealist who asserts the contrary, that the universal *"Dog"* is the *arché* and origin of all the many *dogs,* have both subscribed to the same self-contradictory story, which (driven by common understanding) assumes that "to be" can only mean to be a *thing.*

What makes a text authoritative depends on but is not guaranteed by its literal integrity, as these words in this order: rather, its authority is negotiated by our actually reasoning *with* the text. We choose one variant over another, not because we have fixated on some detail of its genesis but because of its function. Moreover, this is *not* an issue of interpretation. In exactly the same way as we can recognize different and distinct animals as all equally *dogs,* we can admit many interpretations of a literary work based on an integral text, without conflict, because the text is rich and deep enough to sustain them. In the case of *Hamlet,* the function of the work is to create that cultural space of thought and feeling wherein the relations represented in the text incorporate and implicate *us.*

In certain respects, I mean to suggest that current editorial practice, with its far more open and flexible view of how to handle variants by deferring the question of authority, assumes an intermediate position by default. Teaching editions, "critical" editions, scholarly editions, even "definitive" editions are still being produced, if for no better reason than that we have institutionalized the idea of textual authority through negotiations that culminate in the classroom. As teachers, we still demand books for classroom adoption that students can read with some confidence that the text will enable a specific community among its readers, no matter how widely dispersed.

Establishing a teaching text—or a performance script—is a complex historical negotiation that may be more or less extended or relatively brief, but it is not dissimilar to what happens to an author's manuscript upon submission to a publisher. The text—and the author—go through a generally harrowing process by which the author is as often as not chastened (or bullied) out of his or her crotchets by careful readers and watchful editors. From this point of view, the author's intention is to publish and disseminate the most satisfying, the best book he or she can manage—and it *never* happens in isolation. In this light, not the least of the damage done by editorial practices that have sanctified and mystified the notion of the author's intention is the substitution of an author's original draft manuscripts for published versions of works (as in the particularly vivid case of Faulkner's *Sartoris,* replaced by the "original" *Flags in the Dust,* which shows not only that Faulkner's editors had a hard time reading him but that the young Faulkner really needed editorial help). The decision to replace the earlier published novel with the "original," as if they were the same, ironically impoverishes scholarship and criticism in short-circuiting and falsifying the very process of negotiation by which texts actually do come into their cultural authority.

What is particularly exciting, however, is the broadening of such negotiations, with the intriguing possibilities of digital publication and dissemination so as to make available to students, scholars, and the general public the rich contingent record of working papers, multiple versions, and variants, examples of the work of the imagination as not simply mimetic or expressive but exploratory, dynamic, and self-correcting. In this context, once again, the intelligent cautions of Jerome McGann and Susan Hockey foreground the importance both of imagining what we do not know and of not forgetting what we do know. Texts on the Internet may be terrible replacements for printed books, just as they can be a superb means for preserving and disseminating them. But in the development of research archives on line, the electronic medium is perhaps even better suited to preserving variants, and even, with intelligent programming, to letting us see them and study them, not as objects to be valued as they are, but as the record of complex trajectories that do finally lead to works rich and coherent enough to sustain and affirm cultural continuity through times of dramatic change.

During the conference from which these essays derive, nothing was quite so vivid as the sense that the prospects for textual studies have never been so great. It is not because there are dramatic or revolutionary developments in the field that will transform us, either in the twinkling of an eye or, perhaps, even in another millennium. Instead, it was the sense that the value of meticulous work, by which the ordering of words occurs, emerges neither from the editor's will nor from the critic's obsession but rather from the continuous effort of authors and readers, editors and critics, to participate in a common work that has as its result a broadening horizon of intelligibility. There is nothing here that would warrant an extravagant gesture, like Kant's declaration in the *Critique of Pure Reason,* that he had brought about a "Copernican Revolution" in philosophy, when a more apposite claim might have been that his was really a Ptolemaic revolution, which put *us* at the center of the universe. But there is, in this collection of essays, enough to warrant renewed confidence in the cultural continuity that texts make possible, precisely through acceptance of the fact that they come into being not just by way of the insular author but in a deeply committed, inescapably difficult negotiation between author and editor, writer and reader, that shapes a text as a primary cultural product in which every formal detail counts.

It is, ultimately, a metaphysical transformation that will be required to domesticate the difficult idea that a representation is not a representation of a pre-existing entity, or that the integrity of a text—these words in this order—matters precisely because it is the condition for *doing* the work of textuality, a work of humane reasoning about relations that can be captured in words. Between the ancients and the first moderns there was a momentous millennium, which culminated, in the Renaissance, in the rebirth of texts as the confirmation that a culture, to be continuous, need be neither insular nor narrowly bound by time and space; and there has been another millennium between that accomplishment and our postmodern age, in which our anxiety appears to be that cultural continuity may have been ruptured beyond recovery.

That possibility, however, is defused and quieted, in modest but still remarkable ways, by a kind of exuberant patience, so generously in evidence in this volume. What is remarkable is the emergence here, as in other work, of a calmer, earned sense of a new reality wherein representation does not follow an already existent idea but rather produces things in the midst of exigencies that never were before. In this epoch, the work of textual studies is identical with the work of criticism in keeping our attention patiently fixed on what T. S. Eliot called the "intolerable wrestle / With words and meanings"[27] so that this time around we find it not only tolerable but bountifully liberating.

NOTES

Every effort has been made to ensure that references to the World Wide Web are correct and current, but some addresses may have changed or expired while this volume was in production. The reader is urged to use online search engines to locate current URLs.

1. I. A. Richards, "Grounds for Responsibility," in *Design for Escape: World Education through Modern Media* (New York: Harcourt, Brace, 1968), 39. The same motif has never been out of

play since, particularly among cultural conservatives alarmed by contemporary relativism and what they see as the unseemly circus of postmodern multiculturalism. Richards, however, was writing from the left, already anticipating such struggles over legitimacy precisely when one cannot claim probity for one's intellectual methods.

2. See Roland Barthes, "The Death of the Author," reprinted in Vincent Leitch et al., eds., *The Norton Anthology of Theory and Criticism* (New York: Norton, 2001), 1466–70; and Michel Foucault, "What Is an Author," reprinted in Hazard Adams and Leroy Searle, eds., *Critical Theory since 1965* (Tallahassee: Florida State University Press, 1986), 138–48.

3. Wlad Godzich, *The Culture of Literacy* (Cambridge, Mass.: Harvard University Press, 1998), especially "Introduction: Literacy and the Struggle for Theory," 1–35.

4. See Louis Sullivan, *Kindergarten Chats and Other Writings* (New York: Dover Publications, 1979); and Horatio Greenough, *Form and Function: Remarks on Art,* ed. Harold A. Small (Berkeley: University of California Press, 1947).

5. For a related discussion of literary texts as a form of reasoning, not identical with the kind of abstract calculation we usually associate with that term, but providing through imagination a ground for it, see Leroy F. Searle, "The Conscience of the King: Oedipus, Hamlet, and the Problem of Reading," *Comparative Literature* 49 (Fall 1997), 316–43.

6. William Blake, *Songs of Innocence and of Experience* (Princeton, N.J.: The Blake Trust, 1991).

7. I mention here only a brief sample of pivotal works, as other citations pervade this collection. See especially Jerome McGann, *A Critique of Modern Textual Criticism* (Charlottesville: University of Virginia Press, 1982); David Greetham, *Theories of the Text* (New York: Oxford University Press, 1999); George Bornstein and Ralph G. Williams, eds., *Palimpsest: Editorial Theory in the Humanities* (Ann Arbor: University of Michigan Press, 1993); and Philip Cohen, ed., *Devils and Angels: Textual Editing and Literary Theory* (Charlottesville: University of Virginia Press, 1991).

8. See my "Afterword: Criticism and the Claims of Reason" in Adams and Searle, eds., *Critical Theory since 1965*, 856–57.

9. See Evan Watkins, *Work-Time: English Departments and the Circulation of Cultural Value* (Stanford, Calif.: Stanford University Press, 1989), 20–21; 85–86. See also Richard Ohmann and Wallace Douglas, *English in America: A Radical View of the Profession* (New York: Oxford University Press, 1976).

10. McGann, *Critique,* 2.

11. The event referred to here is the celebrated conference at Johns Hopkins University that introduced the work of Jacques Derrida, and the practice of deconstruction, to an American audience. See Richard Macksey and Eugenio Donato, eds. *The Structuralist Controversy* (Baltimore: The Johns Hopkins University Press, 1972). See also note 8, above, and the introduction, by Hazard Adams, to Hazard and Searle, eds., *Critical Theory since 1965*.

12. James Thorpe, ed., *The Aims and Methods of Scholarship in Modern Languages and Literatures* (New York: Modern Language Association of America, 1963), viii. For the earlier version of this work, see James Thorpe, "The Aims, Methods, and Materials of Research in the Modern Languages and Literatures," *PMLA* LXVII (Oct. 1952), 3–37.

13. Northop Frye, "Literary Criticism," in James Thorpe, ed., *The Aims and Methods of Scholarship in Modern Languages and Literatures* (New York: Modern Language Association of America, 1963), 57.

14. Frye, "Literary Criticism," 63.

15. The case has long been a notorious common locus for pointing up both critical pretentiousness and editorial exaggeration. See, for instance, Frank Lentriccia's passing citation of the case (Lentriccia makes the common mistake of attributing the troublesome line to *Moby Dick*): "A legendary blooper was made by F. O. Matthiessen in his book *American Renaissance.* When he wrote about *Moby Dick*—a book almost as big as *Ulysses*—he put a lot of weight on the oxymoronic phrase 'soiled fish of the sea.' Actually, the manuscript shows that Melville was a lot less clever: It reads 'coiled fish of the sea'" (quoted from the "Ask the Expert" sec-

tion of Duke University's online alumni magazine, in a comment about the then forthcoming Kidd edition of James Joyce's *Ulysses*; see http://dukemagazine.duke.edu/alumni/dm13/quotes.html). For a fuller account of this celebrated imbroglio, see James Thorpe, "The Aesthetics of Textual Criticism," reprinted in *Principles of Textual Criticism* (San Marino, Calif.: Huntington Library, 1972). I am grateful to Peter Shillingsburg for additional background information on this episode.

16. Fredson Bowers, "Textual Criticism," in James Thorpe, ed., *The Aims and Methods of Scholarship in Modern Languages and Literatures* (New York: Modern Language Association of America, 1963), 23.

17. Frye, "Literary Criticism," 63.

18. T. S. Eliot, "Tradition and the Individual Talent (1919)" in *Selected Essays* (New York: Harcourt, Brace and World, 1960), 7.

19. Charles Sanders Peirce, *Reasoning and the Logic of Things,* ed. Kenneth Ketner (Cambridge, Mass.: Harvard University Press, 1992), 178.

20. I note here, by way of gratitude and acknowledgement, that Paul Eggert's original paper, presented at the conference, made some provocative preliminary use of Peirce's philosophy in developing his argument. What follows here, however, is independent. See especially in this context Charles Sanders Peirce, "The Rule of Mind," *Collected Papers of Charles Sanders Peirce,* vol. 6, ed. Charles Hartshorne and Paul Weiss (Cambridge, Mass.: Harvard University Press, 1931), ¶102 ff.

21. See particularly Immanuel Kant, *The Critique of Judgment,* trans. J. H. Bernard (New York: Hafner Press, 1951), 74–76.

22. One version of the text of L 75 is available at the Web site of Joseph Ransdell: http://members.door.net/arisbe/menu/library/bycsp/L75/L75.htm The manuscript of the letter is in the collection of the Houghton Library at Harvard University; a copy is in the files of the Center for the Study of Pragmaticism at Texas Tech University, Lubbock.

23. See, for example, Peirce, *Collected Papers,* vol. 2, ¶289nP1.

24. See Albert B. Weiner, *Hamlet: The First Quarto: 1603* (Great Neck, N.Y.: Barron's Educational Series, Inc., 1962).

25. I must add here that stability means no more than there being sufficient witnesses or documentary sources to confirm literally what the text includes or does not include. The work of explaining why certain things may be there and why others may not is precisely where editorial work is most consequential—and most risky.

26. For Peirce's primary account of his categories, see Charles Sanders Peirce, "On a New List of Categories," reprinted in *The Essential Peirce,* vol. 1: *Selected Philosophical Writings (1867–1893),* ed. Christian Kloesel and Nathan Houser (Bloomington: Indiana University Press, 1992). For a brief general introduction to Peirce, see Leroy Searle, "Charles Sanders Peirce," in Michael Groden and Martin Kreiswirth, eds., *The Johns Hopkins Guide to Literary Theory and Criticism* (Baltimore, Md.: The Johns Hopkins University Press, 1994).

27. T. S. Eliot, "East Coker," in *Four Quartets* (New York: Harcourt, Brace, & World, 1943), 13.

The Function of [Textual] Criticism at the Present Time

DAVID GREETHAM

As my disfigured title suggests, the presiding genius for the inaugura-
tion of the University of Washington's new textual studies program was
Matthew Arnold, that Arnold who, in most of his formal portraits, does
seem to embody Victorian angst, looking as if he has all the weight of
Western civilization on his shoulders (fig. 1), a responsibility that, some
might argue, is exactly what he wished. I am playing with Arnold, of
course, and with the enormously heavy cultural, political, and moral burden he placed on poetry and criticism;[1] but, like all games, this is serious play, with serious rules. By putting my textual variance from Arnold
in square editorial brackets, I am playing by the rules of our scholarly
editorial craft, or, as Fredson Bowers would have had it, "putting all my
cards on the table." To Arnold, the interpolation of "[Textual]" would
perhaps have been less of an ideological and procedural swerve than it
would be to a generation of literary critics at *our* "present time," here on
the edge of the millennium—a generation for whom *text* and *textuality*
are more frequently invoked as mystical qualities of network, web, and
matrix than as practical, evidentiary problems associated with the basely
material phenomena of papyrus, parchment, paper, or pixel.

As at the conference, in this volume I take it *as read* that Arnold,
ensconced within the high redoubts of positivist philology, would probably have felt more at home at the Seattle conference on bibliography, cod-
icology, paleography, textual editing, and so on, than would his latter-
day poststructuralist, postmodernist, postfeminist, postmarxist, post-
colonialist critical descendants. But it is an important battle (or, as I would
prefer to see it, crusade), not something taken as given, for I have frequently claimed that we textuists can be as post-*anything* as the best of
them—indeed, that we have often been *post* while they were still being
pre.[2] But my aim was not and is not to don the evangelical robes of the
proselytizer against any monstrous regiment of "nontextual" critics, but
rather to make use of our presiding Arnoldian genius as a guide to discussing the terms under which criticism, and specifically *textual* criticism, in the here-and-now of the late twentieth and early twenty-first
centuries, might deal with the moral charge given by Arnold, and how

Fig. 1. Matthew Arnold, from a photograph taken in 1886. Reproduced from Matthew A. Madden, *Matthew Arnold: A Study in the Aesthetic Temperament* (Bloomington: Indiana University Press, 1967).

it can successfully carry this mandate into the next thousand years of scholarly endeavor. I should assure the reader that, despite the forbiddingly serious nature of this theme, I hope to offer both *solas* and *sentence, game* as well as *ernst*, and I will begin this play by co-opting the figure of Arnold himself.

So there he is, immobile, sturdy, and *reliably* anxious, as solid as the positivist texts of his period. But here (fig. 2) is our familiar mischief-maker, Randall McLeod, *aka* McLeod M Cloud (or Clovd) or Leod, or McLod or the gender-bending Claudia Nimbus, at play in the fields of the text (not in the missionary position), the inventor of a portable collator ("in a handbag") that works by *preventing* the user from "reading" in order to "see."[3] What would Arnold have made of McLeod; or, more to my point, what will I make of the two of them? This: a digital morph, a "conflation" or "cross-fertilization" (both good, sound textual terms) of Arnold and McLeod (fig. 3).[4]

Fig. 2. Randall McLeod at his collator. Reproduced from *PMLA* 111:1 (January 1996), 39, and from Randall McLeod, "From 'Tranceformations in the Text of *Orlando Furioso*,'" in Dave Oliphant and Robin Bradford, eds., *New Directions in Textual Studies* (Austin: University of Texas Press/Harry Ransom Humanities Research Center, 1990), 61–85.

If this is play (and it is), it is *arduous* play (four hours to "write" a digital morph, which lasts a mere five seconds in presentation); and it is, again, very serious, with very clear rules of engagement. If we leave aside the merely technical for the moment, what does this morph accomplish, apart from showing that McLeod needs a better tailor and muttonchop whiskers? In print, the reader will have to imagine the live "morph movie" in which McLeod, upside down and back to front vis-à-vis Arnold, swerves pixel by pixel from one position on the start image of the storyboard to another on the end image (fig. 4), traversing through the center to come out on the other side (fig. 5), with pixels colliding with their counterparts, like subatomic particles in an accelerator (and subject to the same instability and quick decay), streaming from the opposite direction. Now, apart from suggesting that McLeod and his works are inherently decadent—in that they demonstrate the *decay* of our bibliographical perceptions[5]—what sort of moral or cultural emblem does such a traversal of matter illustrate? That question—the filtering of apparently fixed text through a new medium (digitization) and the likely

Fig. 3. Digital morph of Matthew Arnold and Randall McLeod.

results of this filtering, either in the collisions at the center or the decayed matter at the edges—underlies much of what I will address in this essay. The loss of presentational immediacy, however, is also serious, with its still different rules of engagement. In print, I must leave it with the reader only as a rather bare *phenomenon*. Make of it, as they say, *what you will*.

So, too, print alone cannot provide the direct experience of my second example, in another medium: a little jazz by Jelly Roll Morton, but with a textual conundrum. I asked the audience to listen to some music,

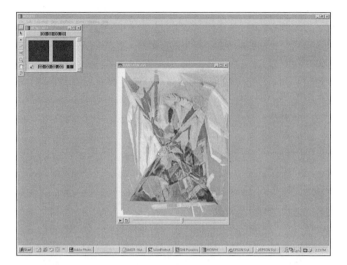

Fig. 4. Arnold-to-McLeod morph (transitional point).

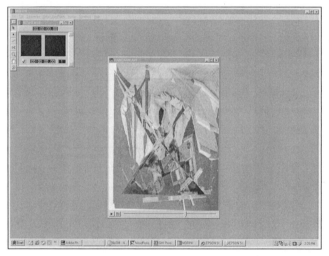

and then to consider *what* they had just heard—that is, to invoke a concept dearly beloved of Peter Shillingsburg:[6] What is the *agency* that is responsible for this music? Who "produced" it?[7]

Here's the problem. What the original audience heard sounded *much better* than it ought to have done;[8] it was an "ideal" text displayed through an "ideal" performance: not only "the text that never was" (that holy grail of the Anglo-American midcentury school of Greg-Bowers eclectic editing) but also a "performance that never was" (much as the *Oxford Shakespeare* produced by Stanley Wells and Gary Taylor has been cele-

Fig. 5. Arnold-to-McLeod morph (end point).

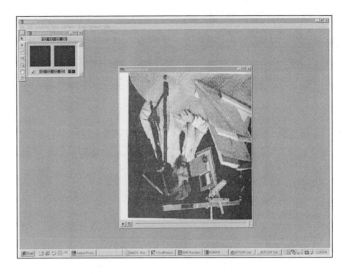

brated, or vilified—depending on the ideological persuasion of the critic—for attempting to shift editorial practice away from original authorial intention and toward ideal performance, in the process constructing acting texts that would be unrecognizable to the Burbages or any other member of the King's Men troupe). If we were reduced to representing what the original audience heard in the transmissional mode of conventional stemmatic rendering, it would probably look like figure 6.

And the problem with this mapping is that, like McLeod at his collator, reading his text upside down, the production stemma of Jelly Roll Morton is also upside down, in the sense that the expected hierarchical relations of such concepts as *authenticity, corruption,* and *descent* are inverted. Contrary to the orthodox wisdom of Lachmannian genealogy, where things only get worse in this worst of all possible corrupting worlds (as pristine authorial *ur*-texts are mangled and sullied by their progress through the competing agencies of scribe, compositor, publisher, and the author's well-meaning but inept spouse, sibling, or offspring), the *quality* of the text—what Aquinas might call its *quidditas,* or Joyce its *whatness*[9]—gets *better* as it encounters its own history of transmission, and particularly the technology in which that history is made manifest.

Here is the story. Jelly Roll Morton made a number of piano rolls in the 1920s, in addition to some acoustic recordings. The latter are, of course, woefully inadequate technically, for while one can just about dis-

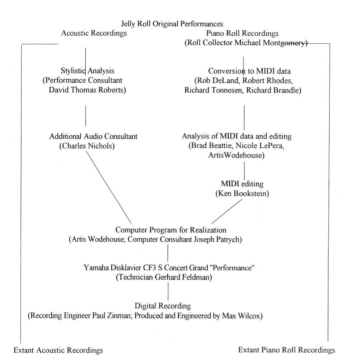

Fig. 6. Jelly Roll Morton realization (collaborative editorial project).

cern an actual Jelly Roll "performance" somewhere under the crackles, pops, and hisses of historicity, no amount of technical restoration, in the manner of, say, the notorious restoration of the Sistine Chapel frescoes,[10] will produce anything like what my original audience heard. So where did their musical experience come from? What was its agency? The story is of lost originals and editorial belatedness, of technological intervention in a text, and of the recuperation, through criticism, analysis, and judgment, of a new text not fit for the ages but very much a product of its own cultural moment. In other words, it is the story of what we, as textual critics in our various disciplines, have all been doing for many years, and the rationale for organizing another major, international conference on the subject. The technology of the piano roll is as unsatisfactory as that of the primitive acoustic recording, but for virtually the opposite reason. Where the acoustic recording is unrecoverably authentic, the piano roll is recoverably inauthentic in that the holes made in the roll are *permanent* (and perhaps analogous to the coded "instructions" in a digital recording), but they also (as did the first generation of CDs) offer only *approximations* or *normalizations* of actual sound. Jelly Roll Morton's style was famous for its Gregian "surface features," its "accidentals," if you like, and most of these could not be calibrated exactly on the crude but consistent mapping of the roll, where a note had to be firmly and unambiguously positioned in one and only one location.

So, rather like the California editors in what they did to Mark Twain's *Roughing It,* and rather like myself in what I have laid out for the editing of Hoccleve's *Regement of Princes,*[11] the editors of Jelly Roll decided to take the parallel but transmissionally unrelated evidence of both media (the acoustic recordings and the piano rolls) to produce an authenticity that *was* recoverable, and permanent. In the case of *Roughing It,* the Twain editors took the substantive text from the nonauthorial documents (newspaper articles, and so on) and then imported into these texts the accidentals practice observable in contemporary authorial documents of other works (primarily in other genres, correspondence, journals, and the like). In the case of Hoccleve, we took the substantive text from a scribal, nonauthorial copy of the *Regement* (there were no others) and then imported the accidentals usage recoverable from the holograph manuscripts of other works into this witness. The marriage of substance and accidence was forced upon the Twain editors by documentary circumstance; for the Hoccleve editors, it was a documentary opportunity: since Hoccleve was also a professional scribe as well as a poet (his hand produced the work of Chaucer, for example), we had holographs of virtually every Hoccleve poem, with the exception of the *Regement.* Why not try to produce the first-ever attempt at reconstructing the actual idiolect of a Middle English poet from separate documents that would otherwise not be susceptible to cross-fertilization? For the editors of Jelly Roll, the marriage was effected by an electronic shotgun: the Yamaha Disklavier CF3 concert grand. What Robert Hirst's team did for Twain and we did for Hoccleve, Artis Wodehouse, Brad Beattie, and Nicole LePera did for Jelly Roll Morton by analyzing the accidentals of the "authentic" acoustic recordings (some of them of the same *works,* though not the same *performances,* as those on the rolls) and then writing a computer program that could produce accidentals for the too-consistent and constraining rolls, which were then reconstructed and played *at,* or *on,* or *by,* or *with,* or *through* the Yamaha. My hesitation over the prepositions is, of course, a reflection of my problems with a Shillingsburg "agency" for the performance heard by the conference audience.

The piano keys, strictly speaking, *played themselves,*[12] and the only "digital" intervention was not the human finger but the binary switch. *Who* then—*what* then—produced the sounds that the audience experienced? And does this agency (or, more likely, do these agencies) support the idealism of Greg-Bowers, the socialization of Jerome McGann, the oral-

performance bias of John Foley, the cultural historicism of Jonathan Rose
and Elizabeth Eisenstein, the materiality of Randall McLeod and Marta
Werner, or the electronic intertextuality of George Landow, Peter
Robinson, or Susan Hockey (to mention only some of the distinguished
participants in the inaugural conference)?[13]

Well, as both original audience and present reader might expect,
given this rhetorical flourish, *all* of the aforementioned dispensations may
find some "sentence and solas" from my Jelly Roll *exemplum*. For example, when I told the story of the textual transmission to G. Thomas Tanselle
over lunch during the summer preceding the conference, he immediately
found that there was no real "conundrum" here at all. The combination
of the accidentals derived from one type of text with the substantives
from another, and then the refitting of them according to the technical
savvy of the latter-day editor, was, to him, a perfect example of eclectic
editing of the Greg-Bowers school. All that would be at issue was
whether the electronic "editors" had *successfully* interpreted authorial
intention at the level of both the substantives and the accidentals. And
I imagine that Tanselle, as one of our century's foremost analytical bibliographers, would also find the research into the technology of text production on the piano roll to have an inherent value, whether or not it led
to new "editions" of previously unrecoverable jazz classics. But then
Roger Chartier might see the Jelly Roll story as a further exemplification
of his work on the effect of medium on the cultural construction and social
cognition of texts, and Mary Keeler might find the computer intervention in and construction of textual form a nice parallel to her work on
Peirce, and Donald Reiman might find the variant states of the texts a
provocation for his principle of "versioning."[14] Without laboriously
spelling it all out, I think I can foresee some fruit in Jelly Roll for the social
textologists, the oralists, the genealogists, and most of the other dispensations represented at the conference and now in this volume.

And so, I could hear the audience thinking, what then? And what does
jazz have to do with that apostle of "high seriousness," Matthew Arnold,
evoked as our presiding genius? Has David Greetham just told another
of his "murie tales" at a stopping place on our textual pilgrimage? Is
the invitation for various rival dispensations to participate in the conundrum of Jelly Roll anything more than the by now obligatory obeisance
to interdisciplinarity and interstitial textuality? To make free with some
other *obiter dicta* of the Arnoldian genius, have we been given the opportunity to "see the object as in itself it really is"?[15] In considering the cultural fortunes of a jazz "classic," are we carrying out or flouting the critical
mandate of a "disinterested endeavour to learn and propagate the best

that is known and thought in the world"?[16] Can this piece of Jelly Roll
be regarded as a "touchstone" of poetic excellence by which all other
efforts in the same genre may be judged?[17] Or, as in Arnold's famous
invective against the English mind and the British constitution, have we
been guilty of "compromises, [a] love of facts, horror of theory" in supporting a "colossal machine for the manufacture of Philistines"?[18]

Leaving aside as unanswerable the question of whether the sternly
classical and antipopulist Arnold would have *liked* Jelly Roll (actually,
I think he would probably have hated him in the 1920s, when he was
merely popular, but greatly approved of him once he had achieved the
status of "classic"), I believe that the oppositions Arnold works with—
culture and anarchy, poetry and science, criticism and literature—do
have bearing on what has been done to Jelly Roll and may inform our
sense of what textual criticism has been, is now, and may be in the next
millennium, the ostensible occasion for the conference. And I specifically
chose a problematic case like Jelly Roll Morton to illustrate the Arnoldian
issue of the proper function of criticism and text in culture, in order to
point up another of Arnold's important intellectual, interdisciplinary
mandates: that the true "critic should try to possess one great literature
besides his own, and the more unlike it, the better."[19] That sentiment is,
after all, the rationale for any interdisciplinary gathering—the possession of the unlike and the recognition of dissimilitudes—and, for my
rhetorical purposes in an inaugural address, the status and condition of
Jelly Roll was so apparently *unlike* the status and condition of, say, the
Bible, William Shakespeare, Buddhist texts, Ezra Pound, W. B. Yeats,
Johannes Brahms, rabbinic texts, and the Czech underground[20] that it
could test Arnold's charge while undermining it by demonstrating that
the invitations posed by the unlike may enable us to see our own dispensations the more clearly.

So let us assume that Matthew Arnold would have approved of a
scholarly conference to practice what he called the necessary "disinterested love of a free play of the mind"[21] over the disparate textual objects
of our attention, and let us assume that his faith (even from the depths
of his cultural pessimism) in progress toward an "apparition of intellectual life"[22] might be sustained by the enormously varied scholarly
riches that were prepared for us at the conference. While I imagine that
most of us, even the most theoretically inclined, would distance ourselves from Arnold's claim that the "critic must keep out of the region
of immediate practice in the political, social, humanitarian sphere" and
that criticism "must maintain its independence of the practical spirit and
its aims"[23] (a credo that is hardly consistent with the eminently practi-

cal problems of scholarly editing and text encoding), it may be that some of us still yearn nostalgically for that positivist celebration of *disinterestedness* that marks Arnold's hope for the "universality of . . . ideas."[24] It is true that disinterestedness has taken some hard knocks of late (I have delivered some of them myself),[25] and that under the influence of cultural anthropologists like Clifford Geertz and James Clifford and postcolonial critics like Homi K. Bhabha,[26] the former claims for a textual definitiveness that would rise above the local circumstances of production and acculturation have been replaced by a recognition that there are national (even regional) and period *schools* of textuality, and that there is no unmoved still point from which an Arnoldian universalist textuality can be observed and created. Yes, the presence of, say, the *annales* school of socialized historical analysis in both *l'histoire du livre* and New Historicism (as opposed to the typical "great figure," author-centered historiography and textuality of Anglo-American criticism) accounts for the terms of "unlikeness" in the development of national discourses on text,[27] an unlikeness that was confronted by the participants in the conference. And, yes, as I have had to admit in my own case, the deeply personal can reinforce national prejudice in the construction of our textual identities and predilections[28] (as in Joseph Bédier's attempt, by ransacking the documentary *remaniements* of German soldiers captured or killed during the First World War, to demonstrate that the German language and German culture at large were barbarous and uncritical, to be resisted by French powers of critical analysis,[29] a claim that reinforced his rejection of Germanic Lachmannian stemmatics in favor of French "best text" theory). And, yes, as Ludo Rocher has demonstrated, there was often a deep cultural resistance in the Indian subcontinent to the "blasphemous" editing of Sanskrit texts according to the protocols of Germanic philology.[30] Yes, these national, ethnic, and personal prejudices do testify *against* Arnold's desire for, and faith in, the definitiveness and universality of *disinterestedness,* just as they do against the claim of timelessness made for the Platonized ideal-text editions produced under the auspices of Greg-Bowers copytext theory.

But one can easily see why the disinterested and the definitive might be a necessary rhetorical ploy in such time-*consuming* scholarly ventures as critical editing. No editor, having given a lifetime to the production of a definitive edition of *x*, wants to hear that his or her life's work is likely to be rendered passé with each shift of the critical wind; and no grant-conferring foundation or agency is likely to pour hundreds of thousands of dollars into a project that openly accepts its cultural contingency and the possibility that its very rationale, as well as its methodology, may be rooted in parochial and ephemeral principles. I recall that in a postdoctoral seminar I once directed, Stanley Fish claimed that the body of texts we call canonical literature needed a drastic critical swerve every decade or two in order to ensure these texts' *continuance* as canonical objects of study; thus his having practiced a form of reader-response criticism on, say, Milton, opened up Shakespeare et al. to similar resuscitation by other critics. The individual items in the canon might remain fairly stable in relation *to one another* but had to be continually reinvented in their relations with criticism.

Can textuists afford such continual refurbishing of their canon? While protean critics like J. Hillis Miller can constantly reinvent themselves, from phenomenology to structuralism to poststructuralism to postmodernism, it is the rare soul in *our* establishment who can match these swerves. Jerome McGann, as productive a fellow as one could wish, might declare (while still comparatively young and in good health) that, if he had his Byron edition to do all over again, he would do it differently.[31] But he can say this presumably because nobody expects that he *will* do Byron again according to his newer critical insights. Besides, he has been seduced by hypertext and D. G. Rossetti.[32] A postwar nutrition and the retaining of youthful energies long into even late middle age might mean that we now tend to outlive the editions of the authors we work on, rather than the other way around. As I look at the familiar features of my friend and colleague W. Speed Hill, who has just finished what *ought* to have been his life's work, the *Folger Library Edition of the Works of Richard Hooker*,[33] I can just about imagine that he might undertake an edition of, say, Bacon—but only just. I certainly do *not* expect him to reedit Hooker, because the ideological climate has changed since he began the edition thirty years ago.[34]

So it is easy to see why Arnold's invocation of permanence and definitiveness might still find a correspondent impulse in our textual breast, even if we know it is not really sustainable. But what of Arnold's other charges to criticism, perhaps most especially that it be a "criticism of life" and that (rather strangely) criticism must *precede* a "time of true creative activity,"[35] in a reversal of the usual sequence, and of the still widespread assumption that criticism (and particularly textual criticism) must act *upon* a previous body of literature? We do not need to suppose that Arnold was a closet deconstructor in presciently anticipating Geoffrey Hartman's claim that criticism is literature anyway (and needs only to study itself),[36] to be able to account for Arnold's apparent paradox. He was faced with the problem that, by his high standards of, well, "high moral seriousness," the poets of the previous Romantic period did not *know* enough and that therefore their apparent literary fertility was, as he said, "premature."[37] (Tell that to textually prolix Wordsworth, as energetic a text producer as one might wish for.) According to Arnold, there ought to have been a period of "concentration" (characterized by Burke's having "saturate[d] politics with thought")[38] *before* this Romantic epoch of "expansion."[39] Now, one could easily respond that, if any period of literary "expansion" had had a critical "concentration" to promote and provoke it, surely it was the Romantic period. What else were the prefaces to Wordsworth and Coleridge's *Lyrical Ballads* than a critical "concentration"? But, even if we set aside the problem that the prefaces were something of an afterthought, a reactive critique *after* the event,[40] Arnold's peculiar paradox may still hold. For by "criticism" he does indeed mean "criticism of life," and this is a heavy charge that few critics (or at least few English critics), before the Victorian investment in *earnestness,* could sustain.

As an avowed Aristotelian insisting that human action was the proper subject of poetry (and not, like Wordsworth, the *consciousness* of the poet), Arnold inherited his master's advocacy of poetry as superior to history (because of its "possessing higher truth and higher seriousness")—and he ran with it. If criticism was necessary *before* a "period of creative activity" (that is, if practice *required* theory to promote it), and if poetry was not only superior to history but was also necessary to the fulfillment of science and religion (indeed, was the only hope of a cultural crisis in which poetry must *replace* religion and philosophy), what a heavy responsibility this placed upon criticism. I occasionally feel that Arnold's worrying over such things as "culture" and "anarchy," and his having placed criticism in such a high moral profile, perhaps anticipated the New Critical charge for the critic, or, as Terry Eagleton has put it, citing Iain Wright, "the Decline of the West was felt to be averted by close reading."[41] To Arnold, this would not have been a joke, and to most textual critics, the Victorians included, it has not been a joke either.

Take the Alexandrian librarians on Homer, and take George Kane and E. Talbot Donaldson on *Piers Plowman.*[42] Both editorial projects place the closest reading of all at the center of their attempts to perfect a Homeric or Langlandian line; indeed, both share Arnold's peculiar faith in the power of the critical and textual "touchstone," the only "real estimate" for poetic truth, "the possession of the very highest poetical quality"[43] that will give us "the benefit of clearly feeling and of deeply enjoying the really excellent, the truly classic in poetry."[44] As usual, we can rely on the hardheaded Samuel Johnson to skewer such Arnoldian pretension: a century before, in his *Preface to Shakespeare,* Johnson had warned against such "touchstonery" with the barb "He that tries to recommend [Shakespeare] by select quotations, will succeed like the pedant in Hierocles, who, when he offered his house to sale, carried a brick in his pocket as a specimen."[45] Michael Suarez notes that this ignorance (or denial) of the "recall problem" in information science (that is, the need to construct an algorithm to calibrate the *proportion* of information retrieved from a textual corpus) would mean that a word search of *Fanny Hill* might paradoxically not only confirm Cleland's argument that the book was not obscene but also suggest that it was not even erotic![46] Taking on the supposed "polytheoricity" of Standard General Markup Language (SGML), Suarez quite properly notes that SGML proponents' faith in OHCO—that is, in text as an "ordered hierarchy of content objects"—and thus their faith in OHCO's neutrality and objectivity, is not naive as a faith in word searches but avoids the issue that the difference between "deep" and "shallow" encoding is a difference in critical theory and involves a slippage of OHCOs, just as the difference between "deep" editing of the Kane-Donaldson type[47] and the "shallow" editing enshrined in the tomes of the Early English Text Society is also critical and also produces OHCO slippage. With a larger version of Arnold's touchstones in our electronic pockets, there may be the temptation to think that we now *comprehend* the work. We do not.

Similarly, from these same Alexandrian librarians and their attempts to resuscitate a worthy and culturally "proper" Homer out of the corrupt oral and scribal transmission *remaniements*,[48] down to Petrarch and Boccaccio's disdain for the failures of the monastic guardians of classical culture,[49] down to Johnson's attempt to overcome the indecencies and improprieties inflicted on the body of Shakespeare's text by actors, prompters, scribes, and printers,[50] down to the claims of the Pennsylvania Dreiser and the Cambridge Lawrence to have rescued their authors from the damage of time and social constraint,[51] we have had an Arnoldian high moral seriousness as the raison d'être of textual criticism, usually couched in terms very similar to Arnold's repudiation of the "bourgeois" and the "Philistine." Textual criticism has been a criticism of life in that it has taken responsibility for righting the wrongs of history. A heavy load.

Are we still up to it? Or has the acknowledgment of contingency and *interestedness* over universality and *disinterestedness* made textual critics just as likely to trim their editorial sails and shift with the wind, as lesser mortals of the Fish and Miller variety have evidently done? Can we still endow poetry (and thus "[textual]" criticism) with an Arnoldian responsibility in the next millennium? For over two thousand years, textual criticism, as the oldest scholarly activity in Western culture, has had a major (though often unrecognized) role in the preservation and construction of that culture. Can it do so in the millennium we are about to see? If religion and philosophy had to be replaced by poetry and criticism toward the end of the nineteenth century, what are our articles of faith at the end of the twentieth and the beginning of the twenty-first?

I posed these questions in this form because I took it that our brief at that "millennial" conference and in this "millennial" volume was and is indeed, Januslike: to look back over the history of text and textuality and then to practice a little bibliographical "futurology." For some, including some of the participants at that gathering in Seattle, the bibliographical future is already written, and they are (inevitably) already critically ensconced in this future. To shake such securities (of, for example, the "demise of the book" and the "end of linearity"), one is tempted to mutter, deconstructively, that *everything* is *always* "already written," so why should the future of the book be any different? But we must acknowledge that there has been a messianic quality to bibliographical futurologists of late, in which the conventional textual trope of "overcoming the corrupt remaniements of the past" has *not* been balanced by the topos of "dwarves standing on the shoulders of giants." There has often been a moralistic hubris in declaring that the codex and all that it has wrought must be swept away if the malignancies of linearity and hierarchy are to be superseded in a brave new world of roseate intertextuality. While I like to think that I am no electronic Luddite (all of my current projects are based on and in electronic media, and I embedded some of my work in digital morphing in the original presentation of this essay), I confess to being uneasy about bibliographical millenarianism. Consider, for example, the themes of historical supersession and liberation technology that Paul Duguid records[52] in the apocalyptic textualism of a number of distinguished hypertextuists, from Stuart Brand, Richard Lanham, J. David Bolter, and others.[53] You know, of course, that "information wants to be free,"[54] that the "revolutionary" goal of hypertext is "freeing the writing from the frozen structure of the page" and "liberating the text,"[55] thereby removing a veil of distortion so that "what is unnatural in print becomes natural in the electronic medium";[56] you know that electronic text will "disempower . . . the force of linear print" and "blow wide open" the social limits imposed by the codex book, in the process democratizing the arts and allowing us to "create that genuine social self which America has discouraged from the beginning"[57] (I am not making this up!), and that liberation technology will free readers from the "tyrannical, univocal voice of the novel."[58] Many of us could add our favorite tropes of electronic millenarianism: I am particularly fond of "I have seen the future, and it is morphed"[59] and "We are all cyborgs."[60]

These messianic voices wallowing in the "pomo romance" of hypertext and hypermedia ironically often seem not only to have silently bought into the Enlightenment view—promoted by such conservative thinkers as Jürgen Habermas[61]—that modernity is a continual and irrepressible movement toward intellectual and cultural fulfillment; they also seem to have ignored the cautions expressed about electronic culture in that founding text of pomo, Lyotard's *The Postmodern Condition: A Report on Knowledge.*[62] As Charles Ess has demonstrated in a penetrating account of Habermas and electronic media,[63] Lyotard and the inheritors of the Frankfurt School are much less sanguine about the "liberation technology" and "communications rationality" of the "life on the screen," and, by contrast with the Panglossian optimism of Habermas, find that there is at least as much potential for control, constraint, and, well, hierarchy and linearity in pomo and electronic media as there is freedom and a democracy of reading. Indeed, some workers in the fields of the electronic text have gone even further than Lyotard: my fellow CUNY-ite Pati Cockram, in constructing a hypermedia archive of some of the Pound *Cantos,*[64] has persuasively argued that there is an ideological fitness as well as the obvious phenomenological one in representing Pound in hypermedia, for electronic coding can be an emblematically "fascistic" exercise of totalitarian control over an apparent freedom. And, while I hesitate to offer this speculation because I know it to be untrue of some of the pomo romanticists, I do feel that this romanticism of liberation technology has often conveniently repressed the confining, detailed, anally retentive *input* of electronic text, preferring instead to celebrate its superficial, phenomenological, fluid *output.* When, at the 1997 conference of the Society for Textual Scholarship, Jerome McGann found out that I was working on digital morphing, I will admit that the first attribute of the *construction* of digital morphs that came to my mind during our conversation was . . . "tedious." McGann nodded in agreement. As tedious as mapping out collation variants in fifteenth-century *anglicana formata* manuscripts? Quite. As tedious as cyclotron analysis of the inks of the forty-two-line Bible? Quite. As tedious as searching archives for an annotation of a seventeenth-century coterie poem? Quite. And, insofar as tedium has always been felt to be a necessary requirement for true scholarship, then, yes, digital morphing is as

Fig. 7. Digital morph of Michel Foucault and Power Ranger.

"scholarly" as anything else most of us may have done in our textual careers. For those who need raw empiricism, figure 7 is a morph I wrote, based on Sherry Turkle's MIT Web site on Foucault and the Power Rangers, again sadly *mis*represented in print.[65]

Yes, phenomenologically very fluid (at least in conference presentation): five seconds of feminist *écriture numérique*. But the storyboard opening and closing frames for even that very simple morph disclose another tale, a tale of constraint and hard construction. With, say, a comparatively modest 600 × 800–pixel frame (i.e., 480,000 possible choices for each pixel in every link in the storyboard), and with each replace-

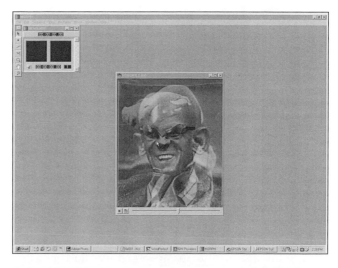

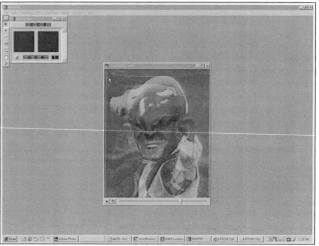

ment of each individual pixel having to be mapped through the 8 or 16 or 24 frames per second of the morph, and with each pixel deviation deriving from a conscious and specific constraining choice made by the morphist—well, you do the math. And that's only at the top level of constraint. Even after having selected the pixel displacements between the opening, closing, and intermediate frames (and multiple interstitial positions, in complex, multistage morphs), the morphist must then plot out such parameters as speed, compression, pixellation, and graphic radiation before "producing" the morph movie and modifying its direction, looping, and size. I have argued that this degree of individual mastering constraint in the morph input is as "masculinist," "totalitarian," and "hierarchical" as the output has been seen as "feminist," "fluid," and "nonlinear."[66]

Finally, the pomo romanticists and liberation technologists, in arguing for a supersession to end all supersessions, have proved themselves to be very poor (dare one say, ill-read?) cultural historians of bibliography. Those who argue that the codex is irremediably closed, fixed, and determined have clearly not encountered an Aristotle textbook from the thirteenth century (fig. 8), whose hospitable white spaces ("writing space," indeed, Mr. Bolter) are designed specifically to invite a *scriptible* intervention by what one should properly call, in the language of software contracts, the *end user* rather than the *reader*, except, of course, that there is no *end* in the constant recycling of texts in the moveable bibliographical feast we know as the medieval book, where, far from the univocal qualities the hypertextuists find in the codex, we are typically faced with the transient and shifting indeterminacies of the user-formulated *florilegium, collectanea,* and anthology manuscript.[67] The poet who used to be *myn auctor*, Thomas Hoccleve, was perhaps the first in English to attempt a bibliographical construction based on the concept of limited authoriality—a "collected works"—and he had (as I have already noted) the advantage of being a professional scribe as well as an author; but even he was powerless to stop the continual migration and intertextual hyperlinkings of his major work, the *Regement of Princes*. Whether or not one accepts the specific arguments of such bibliographical theorists and historians as Arnold Sanders (claiming that such devices as the book wheel and the chained book were already symptomatic of hypertextuality),[68] an electronic enthusiast ought surely to exercise some caution from the fact that the codex itself was celebrated in terms not unlike those now *attributed to hypertext*. As is well known, the codex, if not actually invented by Christians, quickly became associated with Christian writings, and particularly with Patristic sectarian polemics.[69] And why? Because it was felt to be, unlike the roll that preceded it, eminently nonlinear, nonhierarchical, and user-friendly. Just try conducting a debate based on the authority of multiple and variable Arnoldian textual "touchstones" within the medium of the roll as opposed to the codex (fig. 9): say, "*Vide* Ieronimus, *adversus Iovinianum, capitulum* at para 32, sect. 4, but *confer.* Augustinus *de Trinitate libri atque* xxix," and you'll very quickly see why the accessional freedom, the liberation of the text, that the codex seemed to provide was so welcome to sectarian feuding in the first few centuries of Christianity and could thereafter provide a similarly hospitable hypertextual linking for liter-

Fig. 8. "Works of Aristotle for the university student," Yale University, Cushing / Whitney Medical Library, manuscript 12.

ary critical commentary on the pagan classics and on the vernacular literatures.

Moreover, the work of such scholars as Harold Love[70] and Arthur Marotti[71] on the continuity (even the express bibliographical desirability) of "scribal publication"—long after the print revolution was supposed to have overcome text production in all but a few conservative bureaucratic areas (like law, civil administration, and social contracts, where immediacy and revision were valued over permanence)—must surely give some caution to all bibliographers who are tempted to see the apocalypse in every moveable type or pixel. Similarly, when

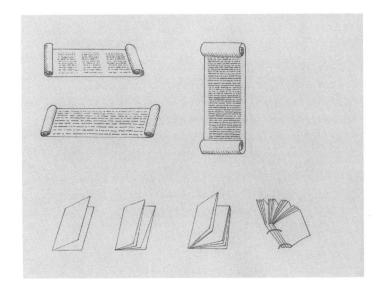

Fig. 9. Roll and codex.

D. F. McKenzie argues, from the evidence of the Short Title Catalogue, that anonymity was the preferred mode of attribution until the end of the seventeenth century (and not just for fear of censorship or punishment),[72] the Foucauldian thesis[73] of an epistemic disjunct in the construction of authoriality in this very period (or actually a little later in France) must be qualified by the bibliographical and cultural evidence for a decidedly ambivalent stance toward technological advances and the imposition of authority—what McKenzie refers to as the "anxiety of print."[74]

Obviously (or at least I hope it is obvious), I do not wish to suggest that the pomo romanticists of hypertexts are only that—romantics who prefer to ignore both bibliographical history and their own experience as the constructors of electronic texts, so seductive is the lure of the electronic medium. No, I do accept that *some* revision of our view of the "function of textual criticism at the present time" will have to be adopted and that it may result in a very un-Arnoldian perspective on canonicity, social responsibility, and textuality. But I do want to suggest that, to adopt McKenzie's terminology, the pomo romanticists do not have enough *anxiety*. The shift to electronic media is indeed a momentous one, perhaps even as momentous as the shift from roll to codex, though surely not as momentous as that from orality to literacy. But while accepting (even delighting in) some of the prodigies and marvels that electronic coding and production can achieve, I do think that the unthinking and promiscuous celebration of the democratic, liberational, imagined future of bibliography without an earnest, cautious, and scholarly awareness of its past will not only make some of the evangelical pronouncements I have recorded here look as embarrassingly foolish as most futurological prognostications turn out to be (what ever happened to quadraphonic sound and eight-track tape?); but, even more dangerously, these pronouncements may blind us both to the possible continuity of current bibliographical artifacts (dare one say it? THE BOOK) *and* to some of the dangers that any new medium may bring. I will close by illustrating these dangers, again as digital morphs.

In a presentation I made at Stanford at the invitation of Stephen Orgel, just before the Seattle conference,[75] I showed a morph that had occasioned some distress, leading to an injunction not to show it. The point, however, was to show the profound and sometimes disturbing homologies that can be discerned between the domain of texts and biological mappings, as suggested by earlier work I had done on the mapping of textual genealogy.[76] When applied to the accepted biological mappings of any modern family, with its distributions of unions and disunions, progeny and hyphenated parenting, all signs of domestic knowledge in our times, orthodox stemmatic theory, though based on biology, would have to acknowledge both *conjunctive* and *separative* elements in such morphs. That is, there is a blood, genetic relation between mother and child, and between half-siblings in different combinations (his, hers, ours, etc.— people in the same "family" between whom there are no genetic links). Our terms of kinship yield nothing in complexity to the cultural objects of Lévi-Strauss's structuralist reflections. But morphing knoweth not such laws, and the boundaries of identity, while still constrained by the morphist, may be stretched and disturbed. The responses of persons so represented, however, reveal other strata of affect: morphing a mother to her son may produce amusement or pleasure, but morphing one ex-spouse to another would produce an altogether different and vastly more dangerous emotion. When the morph becomes a phenomenological soup of identity-crossings, it is easy to understand why some among those subject to the crossing may not at all want to see it.[77] Should we then be surprised that identity-crossing in the domain of texts can provoke volatile emotions?

After that presentation at Stanford, when Stephen Orgel asked me to provide some morphs for an address he was giving at Cambridge on the indeterminacy of text, I made him the identity-bender shown in figure 10. In several ways, the recent movement of Chaucerian textual studies can be seen as a shift from the authority of the beautifully illuminated,

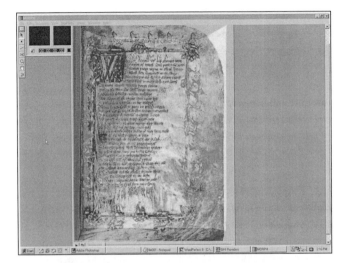

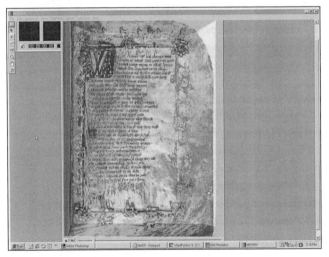

Fig. 10. Digital morph of Hengwrt to Ellesmere manuscript.

highly ornate, fully achieved presentation Ellesmere manuscript to the scruffy, work-in-progress, incomplete, and decidedly unachieved Hengwrt manuscript shown in the figure. I am sure you will immediately recognize in this shift the expected move from product to process, from teleology to fragment, that has marked the ideological shifts of recent textual study in many fields. But even leaving aside the question of whether the two manuscripts were in fact written by the same scribe at different periods of his professional career, we can digitally accomplish a frightening degree of both conflation and contamination with the click of a mouse (given, of course, that we have spent several days

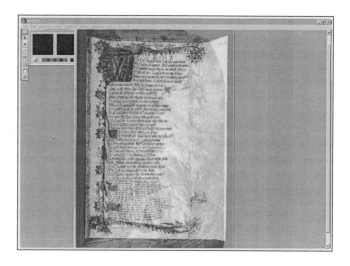

laboriously writing the morph; see fig. 10). I am told that when Orgel showed this contaminated monster, the strict and pure bibliographers did not exactly run fleeing from the room in the face of the textual Antichrist, but there was a feeling that something unholy had been made before their eyes.

Now, I delight in the unholy, the contaminated, and various other sorts of "free play" of a distinctly Derridean rather than Arnoldian sort. But I am conscious, *while I am playing,* of a nagging *anxiety* at what I have wrought, and of a moral uncertainty about the monstrous births that I have produced. It is not going to stop me doing it, any more than distressed responses would stop my mix-'n'-match genealogy. In fact, I could argue that my fascination with textual monstrosities and contaminations is just one more emblem of the postcolonial poetics of dispersal and alienation (of which digital morphing is a peculiarly powerful trope) that I have elsewhere characterized as the figure of textuality that has been the presiding figure for my own textual poetics.[78] As we turn the corner of what looks to be a momentous swerve in the history of text, I think we must look back to Arnold's "high moral seriousness"— and his charge that what we do as critics be a "criticism of life"—as well as forward to the new worlds braver than either Miranda or Aldous Huxley ever dreamed of. To Miranda, Ferdinand was an aberration, a morph, but a particularly seductive and exciting one. I confess to having been similarly seduced, as were many at the conference; but I would caution that we should at least be aware of the epistemological, cultural, and moral ramifications of this seduction, just as, in the midst of

George Landow's celebratory *Hyper-Text-Theory*, David Kolb recognizes that such basic intellectual and cognitive tools as the tripartite and sequential premises of the syllogism (or even good old QED) may become inoperative without "the unidirectional dependence demanded by argumentative structure."[79] And while I may intertextually intone, conflating *Star Wars* with the *Book of Common Prayer*, "May the Morph be with you," I am equally conscious of the burden in the ritual response: "And with you also."

NOTES

This essay was initially presented as the inaugural lecture in "Voice, Text, and Hypertext at the Millennium," a conference held at the University of Washington, Seattle, on October 29, 1997. While providing necessary documentation for the reader, I have preserved most of the functionally occasional (and celebratory) nature of the lecture, and in particular its references to the conference itself. The address was preceded by a very gracious introduction to my work, given by Randall McLeod, whose formidable bibliographical research has always been accompanied by, and often expressed in, a playful, deliberately unacademic style. Part of this serious playfulness has been his adoption of several variants on his authorial identity, including the transgendered "Claudia Nimbus" (via "cloud"); hence McLeod's appearance in my own essay as a foil to the high moral seriousness of Matthew Arnold, from whom, of course, the title of my address is co-opted. Parts of the original presentation and of this print version were made possible by grants from the Research Foundation of the City University of New York.

Every effort has been made to ensure that references to the World Wide Web are correct and current, but some addresses may have changed or expired while this volume was in production. The reader is urged to use online search engines to locate current URLs.

1. See, for example, such grandiose claims as "the future of poetry is immense, because in poetry, where it is worthy of its high destinies, our race, as time goes on, will find an ever surer stay" (in a passage where he finds that poetry has effectively displaced religion: "The strongest part of our religion today is its unconscious poetry"). This claim is found in Arnold's essay "The Study of Poetry," in R. H. Super, ed., *The Complete Prose Works of Matthew Arnold*, vol. 9: *English Literature and Irish Politics* (Ann Arbor: University of Michigan Press, 1973), 161. (All citations from Arnold in this essay are taken from the Super edition.) Note that Arnold is here quoting himself twice: from his general introduction to Thomas Humphry Ward, ed., *The English Poets* (London: Macmillan, 1880), for which the initial paragraph was taken from Arnold's preface ("On Poetry") to *The Hundred Greatest Men*; and from Super, ed., *Complete Prose Works*, vol. 6: *Dissent and Dogma* (1968), 189, where similar sentiments appear, as elsewhere in Arnold's oeuvre. In other words, the great cultural "burden" laid on poetry and criticism was central to Arnold's thesis and to much of his work. See also, for example (in Arnold, "The Study of Poetry"), "more and more mankind will discover that we have to turn to poetry to interpret life for us, to console us, to sustain us. . . . Without poetry, our science will appear incomplete; and most of what now passes for religion and philosophy will be replaced by poetry" (161–62); "the best poetry will be found to have a power of forming, sustaining, and delighting us, as nothing else can" (163); "the use of . . . criticism . . . is entirely in its enabling us to have a clearer sense and a deeper enjoyment of what is truly excellent" (165); and "it is by a large, free, sound representation of things, that poetry, this high criticism of life, has truth of substance" (174). Perhaps the most notorious example of Arnold's misplaced judgment in these lofty demands he made of poetry is his assertion that, while Chaucer does indeed possess "substance," he "lacks the high seriousness of the great classics" ("The Study of Poetry," 177). But what might to modern critics now appear an evaluative gaffe is a further indication of the earnest-

ness and sense of cultural responsibility that Arnold placed on poetry and criticism (a Victorian desideratum that is, of course, parodied in Oscar Wilde's play *The Importance of Being Earnest*). See also Matthew Arnold, "The Function of Criticism at the Present Time," in Super, ed., *Complete Prose Works*, vol. 3: *Lectures and Essays in Criticism* (1962). My play on Arnold's title is by no means the first co-option, as essays by T. S. Eliot ("The Function of Criticism") and F. W. Bateson ("The Function of Criticism at the Present Time") demonstrate. For an account of the influence of Arnold's essay and its thesis, see Super, ed., *Lectures and Essays in Criticism*, 476, where Super notes that Arnold's apparent rationale for his essay on the function of criticism—that his high claims for criticism in an earlier essay on Homer had been regarded as "excessive" (Arnold, "The Function of Criticism at the Present Time," 258)—was perhaps disingenuous, since, as Super says, "only one reviewer of the Homeric lectures seems to have quoted his sentence, and that with approbation" (474). Perhaps Arnold needed the idea rather than the fact of intellectual debate and opposition: he remarked to his mother, "I cannot do what I want without, now and then, a little explosion which fidgets people" (cited by Super, ed., *Lectures and Essays in Criticism*, 473). I readily admit to the same desire for an "explosion" and a discomforted audience in this Arnoldian tradition.

2. See, for example, David C. Greetham, "Contemporary Editorial Theory: From Modernism to Post-Modernism," in George Bornstein and Ralph G. Williams, eds., *Palimpsest: Editorial Theory in the Humanities* (Ann Arbor: University of Michigan Press, 1993), 9–28, and David C. Greetham, "[Textual] Criticism and Deconstruction," *Studies in Bibliography* 44 (1991), 1–30, both reprinted in David C. Greetham, *Textual Transgressions: Essays toward the Construction of a Biobibliography* (New York: Garland, 1998).

3. On the evidentiary function of McLeod's distinction between "reading" and "seeing," see the comments in David C. Greetham, "Textual Forensics," *PMLA* 111 (1996), 32–51, referring especially to Randall McLeod, "from Tranceformations in the Text of Orlando Furioso," in Dave Oliphant and Robin Bradford, eds., *New Directions in Textual Studies* (Austin: Harry Ransom Humanities Research Center / University of Texas Press, 1990), 60–85.

4. Note for the digitally impaired: a "morph" is a series of changing "frames" (to form a "morph movie") whereby one image is gradually transformed into another. This is accomplished by linking a specific pixel in one digitized image to another pixel in another and then, through various types and stages of electronic calibration, metamorphosing one image into another, with the understanding that the metamorphosis can be "arrested" at any intermediate stage. For a consideration of the textual implications of digital morphing, see David C. Greetham, "Is It Morphin Time?" in Kathryn Sutherland, ed., *Electronic Text* (Oxford: Clarendon Press, 1997), 199–226.

5. McLeod has frequently admonished twentieth-century bibliographers for their misreading of Renaissance bibliographical signification: "Renaissance books use different visual codes than ours. And not just neutrally different codes, but pointedly different, because we arrived at our codes by undoing theirs!" See McLeod, "from Tranceformations," 76.

6. The concept of agency is central to Shillingsburg's work, but see especially Peter Shillingsburg, "Individual and Collective Voices: Agency in Texts," in *Resisting Texts: Authority and Submission in Constructions of Meaning* (Ann Arbor: University of Michigan Press, 1997), 151–64.

7. For additional information on this "production," see Artis Wodehouse, Brad Beattie, and Nicole LePera, eds., *Jelly Roll Morton: The Piano Rolls* (New York: Nonesuch Records, 1997).

8. In the print medium, it is of course impossible to convey the point I was trying to make in the aural medium of the conference: simply printing a notated score would not demonstrate my argument about the "improper" technical quality of the sound reproduction. Readers will just have to take it on faith that the sound was indeed too good.

9. For a discussion of the function of *quidditas* in textual ontology, see David C. Greetham, *Theories of the Text* (Oxford: Clarendon Press, 1999), 47, 155, 161–62.

10. On the textual implications of the Sistine Chapel restorations, see Greetham, *Theories of the Text*, 54, 56; Kathleen Weil-Garris Brandt, "The Grime of the Centuries Is a Pigment of

the Imagination: Michelangelo's Sistine Ceiling," in Bornstein and Williams, eds., *Palimpsest;* Kathleen Weil-Garris Brandt, "Twenty-five Questions and Michelangelo's Sistine Ceiling," *Apollo,* Dec. 1987, 392–400; James Beck and Michael Daley, *Art Restoration: The Culture, The Business and the Scandal* (London: Murray, 1993); David Cast, "Finishing the Sistine," *Art Bulletin* 123 / 4 (1992), 669–84; and David Ekserdjian, "The Sistine Chapel and the Critics," *Apollo,* Dec. 1987, 401–4. See also Joseph Grigely, *Textualterity: Art, Theory, and Textual Criticism* (Ann Arbor: University of Michigan Press, 1997), especially 67, 68–69, 85–87.

11. Mark Twain, *Roughing It,* in Harriet Elinor Smith et al., eds., *Roughing It: The Works of Mark Twain* (Berkeley: University of California Press, 1993, 1996). See also David C. Greetham, "Normalisation of Accidentals in Middle English Texts: The Paradox of Thomas Hoccleve," *Studies in Bibliography* 38 (1985), 120–50, and David C. Greetham, "Challenges of Theory and Practice in the Editing of Hoccleve's *Regement of Princes*," in Derek Pearsall, ed., *Manuscripts and Texts: Editorial Problems in Later Middle English Literature* (Cambridge: Boydell and Brewer, 1987), 60–86, both reprinted in David C. Greetham, "Normalisation / Challenges in Editing Hoccleve," in *Textual Transgressions,* 123–97. The actual edition of the normalized text of Hoccleve was produced by Charles R. Blyth; see Thomas Hoccleve, *The Regiment of Princes,* ed. Charles R. Blyth (Kalamazoo: Western Michigan University Press for TEAMS Middle English Texts, 1999).

12. Since experiencing the refurbished Jelly Roll Morton piano rolls, I have come across two other authorial "conundrums" in the same medium. The first of these is a set of "compositions" created specifically for the piano roll over the past forty years by the American composer Conlon Nancarrow, who manually punches the holes in rolls to be played on a player piano and deliberately makes these compositions literally "unplayable" by human hands. Thus the texts of his music consist solely of the holes in the rolls, whereas in the case of Jelly Roll Morton the piano rolls attempt to replicate actual human performances. The piano keys in Nancarrow's music must "play themselves": there is no other "agency" possible or intended by the author; see Conlon Nancarrow, *Studies for Player Piano* (Wergo, 2000). The second conundrum is the gigantic *Überorgan* installation (330 feet long) created by Tim Hawkinson for the *Unnatural Science* exhibition at the Massachusetts Museum of Contemporary Art, in which a huge player console, "scored [by the artist] with dabs and dashes of black acrylic paint[,] winds over twelve photo-electric sensors arrayed like piano keys"; see Laura Steward Heon and John Ackerman, *Unnatural Science: An Exhibition,* exhibition catalog (North Adams, Mass.: Mass MoCA, 2000),75. In a further exemplification of the problems of authentic text and performance, Hawkinson's *Überorgan* is a pun on and a play with the interrelationships of music, human agency, and machine, for while the vast installation is technically a machine for producing otherwise "unplayable" music on a constructed musical instrument, it is also a simulacrum and representation of the human "organs": "Every internal organ has a particular tonal signature, a frequency with which it sympathetically resonates due to its specific shape and density. Every organism's body is, therefore, a concert hall filled with the orchestra of its organs. *Überorgan* poses (and answers) the question: what if there were a body so large that the sound of its organs could readily be heard?" (Heon and Ackerman, *Unnatural Science,* 75).

13. At the oral presentation, I was, of course, trying to be both expeditious and diplomatic in my selection of figures to represent these intellectual schools: I noted that those not mentioned in that particular performance of my text could mentally interpolate themselves as variants to those actually recorded, and that when I posted the talk on my Web site I would have a full hypertextual array of links to everybody on the conference program!

14. See, for example, the following works by Roger Chartier: *Cultural History: Between Practices and Representations,* trans. Lydia G. Cochrane (Ithaca, N.Y.: Cornell University Press, 1988); *The Cultural Uses of Print in Early Modern France,* trans. Lydia G. Cochrane (Princeton, N.J.: Princeton University Press, 1987); *The Culture of Print: Power and the Uses of Print in Early Modern Europe,* trans. Lydia G. Cochrane (Princeton, N.J.: Princeton University Press, 1987); "Meaningful Forms," trans. Patrick Curry. *Liber* 1 (1968), 8–9; *The Order of Books: Readers, Authors, and Libraries in Europe between the Fourteenth and Eighteenth Centuries,* trans. Lydia G. Cochrane (Stanford, Calif.: Stanford University Press, 1994); "Texts, Printing, Reading," in

THE FUNCTION OF [TEXTUAL] CRITICISM AT THE PRESENT TIME   49

Lynn Hunt, ed., *The New Cultural History* (Berkeley: University of California Press, 1989); and *Forms and Meanings: Texts, Performances, and Audiences from Codex to Computer*, New Cultural Studies series (Philadelphia: University of Pennsylvania Press, 1995). See also Mary Keeler, "Iconic Indeterminacy and Human Creativity in C. S. Peirce's Manuscripts," in George Bornstein and Theresa Tinkle, eds., *The Iconic Page in Manuscript, Print, and Digital Culture* (Ann Arbor: University of Michigan Press, 1998), 157–93; Mary Keeler and Christian Kloesel, "Communication, Semiotic Continuity, and the Margins of the Peircean Text," in David C. Greetham, ed., *The Margins of the Text* (Ann Arbor: University of Michigan Press, 1997), 269–322; and Donald H. Reiman, "'Versioning:' The Presentation of Multiple Texts," in *Romantic Texts and Contexts* (Columbia: University of Missouri Press, 1987).

15. "Of the literature of France and Germany, as of the intellect of Europe in general, the main effort, for now many years, has been a critical effort; the endeavour, in all branches of knowledge, theology, philosophy, history, art, science, to see the object as in itself it really is." See Arnold, "The Function of Criticism at the Present Time," 258. Note that, as in the opening citation, Arnold is again quoting himself, from his essay "On Translating Homer" (in Super, ed., *Lectures and Essays in Criticism*, 474). The textual ramifications of Arnold's much-quoted phrase are explored in David Greetham, "The Philosophical Discourse of [Textuality]," in Neil Fraistat and Elizabeth Loiseaux, eds., *Reimagining Textuality* (Madison: University of Wisconsin Press, 2002). In a similar play on the past / present, modern / postmodern, textual / hypertextual implications of Arnold's dictum, my colleague Gerhard Joseph examines the critical juxtapositions that Arnold's phrase poses for contemporary critics; see Gerhard Joseph, "Text versus Hypertext: Seeing Victorian Criticism as in Itself It Really Is," in Suzanne Anker, ed., *Knowing the Victorians* (Ithaca, N.Y.: Cornell University Press, forthcoming).

16. Arnold, "The Function of Criticism at the Present Time," 283.

17. "Indeed there can be no more useful help for discovering what belongs to the class of the truly excellent, and can therefore do us most good, than to have always in one's mind lines and expressions of the great masters, and to apply them as a touchstone to other poetry. . . . [s]hort passages, even single lines, will serve our turn quite sufficiently" (Arnold, "The Study of Poetry," 168). This Arnoldian concept of the "perfect" expression of the "master" poet is applied to textual analysis at various points in Greetham, *Theories of the Text*; see especially the chapter titled "Phenomenology and Reading of the Text" with reference to a disputed reading in Melville's *Typee*.

18. Arnold, "The Function of Criticism at the Present Time," 275.

19. Ibid., 284.

20. There were to be presentations on all these (and many other similarly disparate) topics during the conference proper.

21. Arnold, "The Function of Criticism at the Present Time," 268.

22. Ibid., 269.

23. Ibid., 275, 280.

24. Ibid., 265.

25. See, for example, the argument against a "pre-hermeneutic" disinterestedness in textual criticism in David Greetham, "The Resistance to Philology," in Greetham, ed., *The Margins of the Text*.

26. See, for example, Clifford Geertz, *The Interpretation of Cultures* (New York: Basic Books, 1973), especially "Blurred Genres: The Refiguration of Social Thought"; Clifford Geertz, *Local Knowledge: Further Essays in Interpretive Anthropology* (New York: Basic Books, 1983), especially "Thick Description: Toward an Interpretive Theory of Culture"; James Clifford, *The Predicament of Culture: Twentieth-Century Ethnography, Literature, and Art* (Cambridge, Mass.: Harvard University Press, 1988); James Clifford and George E. Marcus, eds., *Writing Culture: The Poetics and Politics of Ethnography* (Berkeley: University of California Press, 1986); Homi K. Bhabha, "Postcolonial Criticism," in Stephen Greenblatt and Giles Gunn, eds., *Redrawing the Boundaries: The Transformation of English and American Literary Studies* (New York: Modern Language Association of America, 1992); and Homi K. Bhabha, *The Location of Culture* (London: Rout-

ledge, 1996). For an account of how current anthropological and postcolonial theories have textual implications, see David Greetham, "Textual Imperialism and Post-Colonial Bibliography," in Greetham, *Textual Transgressions;* David Greetham, "Society and Culture," in Greetham, *Theories of the Text.*

27. For an account of the prejudice and function of national discourses of textuality, see Greetham, "Textual Imperialism and Post-Colonial Bibliography," and Greetham, "Society and Culture."

28. See the introduction ("Text as Transgression, Or How I Came to Live on the Margins") in Greetham, *Textual Transgressions,* an argument developing out of Reiman's call for a "personalist bibliography" in Donald H. Reiman, *Study of Modern Manuscripts: Public, Confidential, and Private* (Baltimore, Md.: The Johns Hopkins University Press, 1993) and from Miller's "personalist" feminist criticism in, for example, Nancy K. Miller, *Getting Personal: Feminist Occasions and Other Autobiographical Acts* (New York: Routledge, 1991).

29. On Bédier, see Alain Corbellari, "Joseph Bédier, Philologist and Writer," in R. Howard Bloch and Stephen G. Nichols, eds., *Medievalism and the Modernist Temper* (Baltimore, Md.: The Johns Hopkins University Press, 1996), especially 280–81.

30. Ludo Rocher, "Sanskrit Literature," in David C. Greetham, ed., *Scholarly Editing: A Guide to Research* (New York: Modern Language Association of America, 1995).

31. Jerome McGann, "What Is Critical Editing?" *Text* 5 (1991), 15–30.

32. See Jerome McGann, "The Complete Writings and Pictures of Dante Gabriel Rossetti: A Hypermedia Research Archive," *Text* 7 (1994), 95–105; Jerome McGann, "The Rationale of HyperText," *Text* 9 (1996), 11–32 (reprinted in Sutherland, ed., *Electronic Text*).

33. W. Speed Hill, ed., *The Folger Library Edition of the Works of Richard Hooker* (Cambridge, Mass.: Belknap Press of Harvard University Press, 1977); W. Speed Hill, Egil Grislis, John E. Booty, et al., eds., *Richard Hooker: Of the Laws of Ecclesiastical Polity: Index* (Binghamton, N.Y.: Medieval & Renaissance Texts & Studies, 1993).

34. For an account of the personal and institutional effects of this changing "intellectual climate" on such monumental editions as Hill et al., eds., *Richard Hooker,* see Greetham, *Textual Transgressions,* especially 24–28. See also the account by W. Speed Hill, "Editing Richard Hooker: A Retrospective," *Sewanee Theological Review* 2 (1993), 187–99 (special issue on Richard Hooker).

35. "Criticism first; a time of true creative activity, perhaps—which, as I have said, must inevitably be preceded amongst us by a time of criticism,—hereafter, when criticism has done its work" (Arnold, "The Function of Criticism at the Present Time," 269).

36. Geoffrey Hartman, "Literary Commentary as Literature," in *Criticism in the Wilderness: The Study of Literature Today* (New Haven, Conn.: Yale University Press, 1980).

37. "It has long seemed to me that the burst of creative energy in our literature, through the first quarter of this century, had about it in fact something premature. . . . And this prematureness comes from its having proceeded without having its proper data, without sufficient materials to work with. In other words, the English poetry of this first quarter of this century, with plenty of energy, plenty of creative force, did not know enough" (Arnold, "The Function of Criticism at the Present Time," 262).

38. Ibid., 266.

39. Ibid., 269.

40. See Paul M. Zall, *Literary Criticism of William Wordsworth* (Lincoln: University of Nebraska Press, 1966), x: "Wordsworth's initial strategy was to let the poems in the *Lyrical Ballads* of 1798 speak for themselves, with only a brief note that they differed from contemporary poetry by way of experiment. . . . For the edition of 1800, however, Wordsworth acceded to Coleridge's urgings for a prefatory essay explaining what he was trying to do and why." For a documentary account of the stages of composition of the *Lyrical Ballads,* see William Wordsworth, *Lyrical Ballads and Other Poems, 1797–1800,* ed. James Butler and Karen Green (Ithaca, N.Y.: Cornell University Press, 1993).

41. Terry Eagleton, "The Rise of English," in *Literary Theory: An Introduction* (Minneapolis: University of Minnesota Press, 1983), 34. Eagleton cites Iain Wright, "F. R. Leavis, the Scrutiny

Movement and the Crisis," in Jon Clarke et al., eds., *Culture and Crisis in Britain in the Thirties* (London: 1979),48.

42. For accounts of Alexandrianism, see the chapter on ontology in Greetham, *Theories of the Text.* For the controversy over the editing of *Piers Plowman* (especially the Kane-Donaldson edition), see David C. Greetham, "Reading In and Around Piers Plowman," in Philip Cohen, ed., *Text and Textuality: Textual Instability, Theory, and Interpretation* (New York: Garland, 1997), 25–57, and the references therein, together with Charlotte Brewer, *Editing Piers Plowman: The Evolution of the Text,* Cambridge Studies in Medieval Literature, no. 28. (Cambridge, England: Cambridge University Press, 1996).

43. Arnold, "The Study of Poetry," 170.

44. Ibid., 166.

45. Samuel Johnson, "Preface to Shakespeare" (originally published 1756), in Arthur Sherbo, ed., *The Yale Edition of the Works of Samuel Johnson,* vol. 7: *Johnson on Shakespeare* (New Haven, Conn.: Yale University Press, 1986),62.

46. Michael Suarez, "In Dreams Begins Responsibility: Novels, Promises, and the Electronic Edition," in Alexander Pettit, ed., *Textual Studies and the Common Reader: Essays on Editing Novels and Novelists* (Athens: University of Georgia Press, 2000), 160–79. See my fuller comments on Suarez's argument in "Now, Again, And 'Getting Beyond It All'" formerly at

http://www.intertextual.com

and soon to be at my next Web site. This was a respondent essay originally intended for Pettit, ed., *Textual Studies* but withdrawn when the contents of the volume changed.

47. On deep editing, see A. S. G. Edwards, "Middle English Literature," in Greetham, ed., *Scholarly Editing,* 184–203; Ralph Hanna III, *Pursuing History: Middle English Manuscripts and Their Texts* (Stanford, Calif.: Stanford University Press, 1996); and the textual introductions to the editions of the A and B texts in George Kane, ed., *Piers Plowman* (London: Athlone, 1960) and in George Kane and E. Talbot Donaldson, eds., *Piers Plowman* (London: Athlone, 1975).

48. For accounts of the Alexandrian editing of Homer, see, for example, George A. Kennedy, "Hellenistic Literary and Philosophical Scholarship: Alexandrian Philology," in George A. Kennedy, ed., *The Cambridge History of Literary Criticism,* vol. 1: *Classical Criticism* (Cambridge, England: Cambridge University Press, 1989); Rudolph Pfeiffer, *History of Classical Scholarship from the Beginnings to the End of The Hellenistic Age* (Oxford: Oxford University Press, 1968); and J. E. W. Sandys, *A History of Classical Scholarship* (Cambridge, England: Cambridge University Press, 1906–1908; reprinted in New York by Hafner, 1964).

49. For accounts of Renaissance attitudes toward medieval archives, see, for example, E. J. Kenney, *The Classical Text: Aspects of Editing in the Age of the Printed Book* (Berkeley: University of California Press, 1974).

50. Johnson's statement is a classic view of the "degeneracy" of Renaissance play texts, a persuasion that ultimately leads to Greg's famous and influential response to these supposed documentary conditions; see W. W. Greg, "The Rationale of Copy-Text," *Studies in Bibliography* 3 (1950–51), 19–36. Johnson claims, "It is not easy for invention to bring together so many causes concurring to vitiate a text. No other authour ever gave up his works to fortune and time with so little care: no books could be left in hands so likely to injure them, as plays frequently acted, yet continued in manuscript: no other transcribers were likely to be so little qualified for their task as those who copied for the stage, at a time when the lower ranks of the people were universally illiterate: no other editions were made from fragments so minutely broken, and so fortuitously reunited; and in no other age was the art of printing in such unskilful hands." See Samuel Johnson, "Proposals for Printing, by Subscription, the Dramatick Works of William Shakespeare," in Sherbo, ed., *Johnson on Shakespeare.*

51. For the debate over Dreiser, see the textual introductions to Theodore Dreiser, *Sister Carrie,* ed. James L. W. West III (Philadelphia: University of Pennsylvania Press, 1981) and to Theodore Dreiser, *Jennie Gerhardt,* ed. James L. W. West III (Philadelphia: University of Pennsylvania Press, 1992). See also the generally favorable review of West's edition by G. Thomas Tanselle in *Text* 8 (1995), 462–65, as well as the demurrals in Donald Pizer, "Self-Censorship

and Textual Editing," in Jerome J. McGann, ed., *Textual Criticism and Literary Interpretation* (Chicago: University of Chicago Press, 1985), 144–61, and, more generally, in Donald Pizer, "On the Editing of Modern American Texts," *Bulletin of the New York Public Library* 75 (1971), 147–53, 504–5. For Lawrence, see Charles L. Ross and Dennis Jackson, eds., *Editing D. H. Lawrence: New Versions of a Modern Author* (Ann Arbor: University of Michigan Press, 1995), especially the bibliography on editing Lawrence (239–49). See also the textual introductions to D. H. Lawrence, *Sons and Lovers,* ed. Helen Baron and Carl Baron (Cambridge, England: Cambridge University Press, 1992) and to D. H. Lawrence, *Women in Love,* ed. David Farmer, Lindeth Vasey, and John Worthen (Cambridge, England: Cambridge University Press, 1987).

52. Paul Duguid, "Material Matters: The Past and Futurology of the Book," in Geoffrey Nunberg, ed., *The Future of the Book* (Berkeley: University of California Press, 1996).

53. Some of the authors cited in this section were present in the original audience, so I made this part of the oral presentation an exercise in attribution, by deliberately not actually naming the enthusiasts or linking them with their more romantic flights of rhetoric, and thereby inviting the audience to do its own attributions. In this print version, I have to "come clean." As Duguid notes ("Material Matters," 92n27), the dictum "Information wants to be free" is widely attributed to Stuart Brand, *The Media Lab: Inventing the Future at M.I.T.* (New York: Viking Penguin, 1987), 202; to J. David Bolter, *Writing Space: The Computer, Hypertext, and the History of Writing* (Hillsdale, N.J.: Erlbaum, 1991), 21; and to T. Nelson, cited in E. Davis, "Techgnosis, Magic, Memory, and the Angels of Information," *South Atlantic Quarterly* 92:4 (1993), 613 (special issue titled *Flame Wars: The Discourse of Cyberspace*). It is perhaps quite appropriate that one of the most ubiquitous aphorisms of the pomo romanticists cannot be firmly traced to a specific documentary source but depends on hearsay and attribution: Bolter's "freeing the writing," and so on, in *Writing Space;* the "genuine social self" of Richard Lanham, *The Electronic Word: Democracy, Technology, and the Arts* (Chicago: University of Chicago Press, 1994), 21, 105, 219; the "univocal voice" of Thaïs Morgan, cited in George Landow, *Hypertext: The Convergence of Contemporary Critical Theory and Technology* (Baltimore, Md.: The Johns Hopkins University Press, 1992),10.

54. Brand, cited in Duguid, "Material Matters," 73.

55. Bolter, ibid.

56. Bolter, ibid., 75.

57. Lanham, *The Electronic Word.*

58. Landow, *Hypertext.*

59. Mark Dery, "Cyberculture," *South Atlantic Quarterly* 91:3 (1992), 501.

60. Donna Haraway, *Simians, Cyborgs, and Women: The Reinvention of Nature* (New York: Routledge, 1991),150: "By the late twentieth century, our time, a mythic time, we are all chimaeras, theorized and fabricated hybrids of machine and organism; in short, we are all cyborgs. The cyborg is our ontology; it gives us our politics. The cyborg is a condensed image of both imagination and material reality, the two joined centres structuring any possibility of historical transformation." For my comments on these pronouncements, see Greetham, "Is It Morphin Time?"

61. For an analysis of the significance of Habermas's "modernist" credo for textual theory, see Greetham, "The Philosophical Discourse of [Textuality]."

62. Jean-François Lyotard, *The Postmodern Condition: A Report on Knowledge,* trans. Geoff Bennington and Brian Massumi (Minneapolis: University of Minnesota Press, 1984).

63. Charles Ess, "The Political Computer: Hypertext, Democracy, and Habermas," in George Landow, ed., *Hyper / Text / Theory* (Baltimore, Md.: The Johns Hopkins University Press, 1994).

64. Pati Cockram, "A Hypermedia Archive of the Italian Cantos of Ezra Pound" (Ph.D. diss., City University of New York, 1999).

65. See Sherry Turkle's home page at
http://web.mit.edu/sturkle/www/PowerRanger.html.
See also Sherry Turkle, *Life on the Screen: Identity in the Age of the Internet* (New York: Simon

& Schuster, 1995), especially 258–59. For my discussion of this particular morph and Turkle's general thesis on identity, see Greetham, "Is It Morphin Time?"

66. For my arguments on the gendered significance of digital morphing, see Greetham, "Is It Morphin Time?"

67. See, for example, Stephen G. Nichols and Siegfried Wenzel, eds., *The Whole Book: Cultural Perspectives on the Medieval Miscellany* (Ann Arbor: University of Michigan Press, 1966) and the references therein. For an account of how bibliographical qualities of medieval and post-modern means of textual production militate against "modernist" views of authoriality, see David Greetham, "Romancing the Text, Medievalizing the Book," in Richard Utz and Thomas Shippey, eds., *Medievalisms: Essays Presented to Leslie Workman* (Amsterdam: Brepols, 1998).

68. Arnold Sanders, "Hypertext, Learning, and Memory: Some Implications from Manuscript Tradition," *Text* 8 (1995), 125–44.

69. See Colin H. Roberts and T. C. Skeat, *The Birth of the Codex* (Oxford: Clarendon Press, 1988).

70. Harold Love, "Scribal Texts and Literary Communities: The Rochester Circle and Osborn b. 105," *Studies in Bibliography* 42 (1989), 219–35; Harold Love, *Scribal Publication in Seventeenth-Century England* (Oxford: Clarendon Press, 1993).

71. Arthur Marotti, "Malleable and Fixed Texts: Manuscript and Printed Miscellanies and the Transmission of Lyric Poetry in the English Renaissance," and "Manuscript, Print, and the English Renaissance Lyric," in W. Speed Hill, ed., *New Ways of Looking at Old Texts: Papers of the Renaissance English Text Society, 1985–1991* (Binghamton, N.Y.: Renaissance English Text Society / Medieval and Renaissance Texts and Studies, 1993).

72. This case for anonymity was the burden of a presentation McKenzie made with the other coeditors of *The Cambridge History of the Book in Britain* at the 1983 conference of the Society for Textual Scholarship in New York. Some of the ramifications of this position for the cultural history of text are explored in Greetham, "Society and Culture," especially 416–17.

73. Michel Foucault, "What Is an Author?" in Paul Rabinow, ed., *The Foucault Reader* (New York: Pantheon, 1984).

74. D. F. McKenzie, "Speech–Manuscript–Print," in Oliphant and Bradford, eds., *New Directions in Textual Studies*, 86–109, especially 88.

75. David Greetham, "Digital Morphing and the Genetic Challenge," paper presented at "The Letter and the Spirit in Early Modern Literature," conference held at Stanford University, April 1997.

76. David Greetham, "Phylum–Tree–Rhizome," *Huntington Library Quarterly* 58 (1996), 96–126 (special issue titled *Reading from the Margins: Textual Studies, Chaucer, and Medieval Literature*).

77. Since the publication of Greetham, "Phylum–Tree–Rhizome," the analogous case I make from a "contaminated" rather than neat genetic phylogeny has been reinforced by evidence that "extensive horizontal transmission of genes occurred even after the emergence of the three [biological] kingdoms [bacteria, eukarya, and archaea], making the origin of life look more like a forkful of spaghetti than a tree"; see Nicholas Wade, "Life's Origins Get Murkier and Messier," *New York Times*, June 13, 2000, F2. This sort of "cross-fertilization" of collateral branches in biology makes the traditional "family tree" paradigm of textual descent much more difficult to sustain as a "scientific" model.

78. See especially Greetham, "Text as Transgression."

79. David Kolb, "Socrates in the Labyrinth," in Landow, *Hyper / Text / Theory*, 323–44.

The Text Between
the Voice and the Book

ROGER CHARTIER

This essay will examine the nexus of relations created during the sixteenth and seventeenth centuries between the forms of transmission of texts—or, to put it another way, the different modalities of their "performance"—and their possible reception by different audiences. Such an inquiry has a fundamental objective: to identify the modes of circulation and appropriation of works and genres whose original status, functions, and usages were not those implied both by printed inscription and by individual habits of silent reading.

I would like to show that the contemporary relationship to literary works and to genres cannot be considered either invariable or universal. Against the temptations of an "ethnocentrism of reading" it is necessary to recall how numerous are the ancient texts that in no way imply a solitary and silent reader in search of meaning, texts that, composed to be spoken or to be read out loud and shared before a listening audience, address a community of listeners and obey the laws proper to oral and communal transmission.

It is thus necessary to break with an uncritical posture, which assumes that all texts, all works, and all genres have been read, identified, and received according to the criteria that characterize our own relationship to the written word. It is a question, then, of historicizing the definitions and taxonomies of genres, the practices of reading, the forms of destination, and the figures of addresses as they have been bequeathed to us by the "literary institution." When we are confronted with works dating from the sixteenth and seventeenth centuries (and, a fortiori, from earlier periods, or from non-Western cultures), categories that we use without thinking ought to lose their assumed self-evidence and universality.

Let us consider, by way of illustration, a "tale"—a *cuento*, as its author, Borges, writes. It is a "fiction" entitled "El espejo y la máscara" ("The Mirror and the Mask"), published in the collection *El libro de arena (The Book of Sand).*[1] In it, Borges tells the story of a king and a bard. The High King of Ireland, after having defeated his Norwegian enemy, asks the poet Ollan to write an ode that will celebrate his triumph and establish his glory for all eternity: "Las proezas más claras pierden su lustre si no se las amoneda en palabras . . . Yo seré Eneas; tu serás mi Virgilio" ("The greatest deeds lose their luster if they are not coined in words . . . I will be Aeneas; you will be my Virgil"). Three times, at one-year intervals, the bard comes back before the king with the same poem, which is nevertheless different. Each time, the poetic writing, the aesthetic that governs it, the form of the text's publication, and the figure of its addressee prove to have been modified.

The bard composes his first ode according to the rules of his art, mobilizing all the knowledge that is his: a knowledge of words, images, verse, examples, genres, tradition. The poem is declaimed by its author "con lenta seguridad, sin una ojeada al manuscrito" ("slowly, confidently, without a glance at the manuscript") before the king, the court, the "School of Bards" and crowds of those who, "agolpados en las puertas, no descifraban una palabra" ("thronging the doorways, were unable to make out a single word").

This first panegyric is a "monument": it respects rules and conventions, summarizes all of Ireland's literature, and is set down in writing. Inscribed within the order of representation, it leads to belief in the exploits of the sovereign. Thus the decision is made that it should be preserved and disseminated: the king orders thirty scribes to copy it two times each. The bard is a good artisan who has faithfully reproduced the teachings of the ancients: "has atribuido a cada vocablo su genuina acepción y a cada nombre sustantivo el epíteto que le dieron los primeros poetas. No hay en toda la loa una sola imagen que no hayan los clásicos. . . . Has manejado con destreza la rima, la aliteración, la asonancia, las cantidades, los artificios de la docta retórica, la sabia alteración de los metros" ("You have given each word its true meaning, and each substantive the epithet given it by the poets of old. In your whole panegyric there is not a single image unknown to the classics. . . . You have skillfully handled rhyme, alliteration, assonance, quantities, the artifices of learned rhetoric, the wise variations of meters"). In recompense, the bard is given a mirror, the work of an artisan like himself, which, like the ode of praise, reflects what is already there.

The king, however, remains dissatisfied. The poem, although perfect, has remained lifeless. It has not produced any effects on body or soul: "Todo está bien y sin embargo nada ha pasado. En los pulsos no corre más a prisa la sangre. Las manos no han buscado los arcos. Nadie ha palidecido. Nadie profirió un grito de batalla, nadie opuso el pecho a los vikings" ("All is well and yet nothing has happened. In our veins the blood runs no faster. Our hands have not sought the bow. No one has turned pale. No one uttered a battle cry or set his breast against the Vikings"). The bard deserves a reward, but he must compose another work: "Dentro del término de un año aplaudiremos otra loa, poeta" ("Before a year is out, poet, we shall applaud another ode").

One year later, the poet is back before the king. His new poem is quite different from the preceding one. On the one hand, the new ode has broken all the rules, whether grammatical ("Un sustantivo singular podía regir un verbo plural. Las preposiciones eran ajenas a las normas comunes"; "A singular noun governed a plural verb. The prepositions were alien to common usage"), poetic ("La aspereza alternaba con la dulzura"; "Harshness alternated with sweetness"), or rhetorical ("Las metáforas eran arbitrarias o así lo parecían"; "Metaphors were arbitrary, or so they seemed"). The work in no way conforms to the conventions of literary art; it is no longer imitation but invention. On the other hand, this time the poet reads his work; he no longer recites it with the mastery that was his a year earlier. He reads with uneasiness, hesitation, uncertainty: "lo leyó con visible inseguridad, omitiendo ciertos pasajes, como si él mismo no los entendiera del todo o no quisiera profanarlos" ("He read it obviously hesitant, omitting certain passages, as if he did not completely understand them or did not wish to profane them"). This reading takes place before the king and the circle of men of letters, but the public has disappeared. This new text—strange, surprising—no longer belongs to the order of representation but, through invention, to that of illusion. It does not lead to belief in the exploits of the king; rather, it *is* these exploits, shown to the listening audience: "No era una descripción de la batalla, era la batalla" ("It was not a description of the battle, it *was* the battle"). The poem gives rise to the event itself, in its original force. Ekphrasis has been substituted for representation.

The poem captures and captivates its audience: "Suspende, maravilla y deslumbra" ("It astounds, it dazzles, it causes wonderment"). It exerts an effect on sensibility, an effect that the first ode in no way accomplished, despite its formal perfection. In order to characterize these effects, Borges goes back to the very vocabulary that belonged to Spanish Golden Age literature: *embelesar, maravillar, encantar.* At that time, fiction was thought of and described as a dangerous enchantment that annuls the gap between the world of the text and the world of the reader.[2] The poet's second ode is to be preserved, but it is destined not for the illiterate but only for the learned, and in small number: "Un cofre de marfil será la custodia del único ejemplar" ("An ivory casket will be the resting place of its single copy"). For his creation, which has the force of theatrical illusion, the poet receives an object of the theater, a golden mask, sign of the power of his invention. Yet the king wants a work still more sublime.

When the bard returns a year later, the ode that he brings with him is no longer written, and it consists of a single line. The bard and the king are alone. The bard utters the ode a first time, and then "el poeta y su Rey la paladearon, como si fuera una plegaria secreta o una blasfemia" ("the poet and his king savored it as if it were a secret prayer or a blasphemy"). Everything is turned upside down. The poem is inscribed within the order of the sacred, a prayer or a blasphemy, and it inhabits the poet like an inspired Word. The poet has not respected the rules, nor has he transgressed them. Like the Homeric bard or the lyric poet, he has been overwhelmed by inspired words not his own: "En el alba, me recordé diciendo unas palabras que al principio no comprendí. Esas palabras son un poema" ("In the dawn I woke up speaking words I did not at first understand. Those words were a poem"). Thus inhabited by a language other than his own, the poet has become other. "Casi era otro. Algo, que no era el tiempo, había surcado y transformado sus rasgos. Los ojos parecían mirar muy lejos o haber quedado ciegos." ("He was like another man. Something other than time had furrowed and transformed his features. His eyes seemed to stare into the distance or to be blind.")

The third ode, murmured, is an event, not a monument. It has not been written; it will not be repeated. It constitutes a unique experience, and there is no possible reading of it. Its mystery leads those who utter it, or hear it, to a forbidden contemplation. Says the poet, "Sentí que había cometido un pecado, quizá el que no perdona el Espíritu" ("I felt I had committed a sin, perhaps one the Holy Ghost does not forgive"). And the king replies, "El que ahora compartimos los dos. El de haber conocido la Belleza, que es un don vedado a los hombres. Ahora nos toca expiarlo" ("The one we two now share. The sin of having known Beauty, which is a gift forbidden to men. Now it behooves us to expiate it"). The king's third gift is thus an instrument of death: a dagger with which the poet commits suicide. The king's expiation takes another form, one appropriate for the "greater theater of the world," where roles are ephemeral and interchangeable: "es un mendigo que recorre los caminos de Irlanda, que fue su reino, y no ha repetido nunca el poema" ("he is a beggar wandering the length and breadth of Ireland—which was once his kingdom—and he has never repeated the poem").

Borges's fable takes us from monument to event, from inscription to performance. It designates, with the acuteness of a Cervantes, the different registers of opposition that organize written culture. These have to do with aesthetic norms (imitation, invention, inspiration), modes of the text's transmission (recitation, reading aloud, repetition to oneself), the nature of the addressee (the public at large, the learned, the prince or, finally, the poet himself), and the relationship between words and things (a relationship inscribed within the order of representation, of illusion, or of mystery). The "tale" of the mirror and the mask, of the poet and the king, thus provides points of reference that allow entry into analysis of the forms of texts' production, circulation, and appropriation, and that consider their variations across time, place, and community to be essential. The lesson does not account for the poetic fulguration of Borges's text, but it is perhaps faithful to what Borges wrote in a preface to *Macbeth:* "*Art happens* [El arte ocurre], declaró Whistler, pero la conciencia de que no acabaremos nunca de descifrar el misterio esético no se opone al examen de los hechos que lo hicieron posible" ("Art happens, declared Whistler, but the idea that we will never have done with deciphering the aesthetic mystery does not stand in the way of our examination of the facts which made it possible").[3]

The opposition I have suggested between the text as "monument" and the text as "event" was proposed by a historian of classical literature, Florence Dupont,[4] who underscores how insufficient the categories traditionally associated with the idea of literature are to an understanding of texts' production and circulation in antiquity. What are these fundamental notions that constitute the "literary institution"? First of all, there is the identification of the text with a writing that is fixed, stabilized, and manipulable because of its permanence. Then there is the idea that the work is produced for a reader—and a reader who reads in silence, alone and for himself, even if he happens to be in a public space. Finally, there is the characterization of reading as a quest for meaning, as a work of interpretation, a search for signification. The fundamental genres of Greek or Roman literature show that we must distance ourselves from these three assumptions in order to understand the reasons for these genres' production, the modalities of their performance, and the forms of their appropriation.

The ode, for example, should not be thought of as a "literary" genre but as a ritual speech act that takes place in a form of religious sociability essential to ancient Greece: the *symposión,* or banquet of Dionysiac drunkenness. The ode is a song addressed to the gods of the banquet, and above all to Dionysius, as well as a song inspired by the Muses, of which the singer is but the instrument. Far from being a product of individual creation, of poetic art, the banquet song manifests the overpowering of the speaker by sacred inspiration. The meaning of the text depends entirely on its ritual effectiveness. It cannot be separated from the circumstances in which the poetry is sung, since, by invoking the gods, it causes them to take part in the banquet. Irreducibly singular, the text can be neither written down nor repeated. It is a moment of surging forth: it is mystery, it is event.

It was in Greek antiquity itself that this poetic, ritual, singular Word was progressively transformed into "literature." During the festivals and competitions accompanying the cults of the city-states, or of the great panhellenic sanctuaries (such as Delphi and Epidaurus), the song inspired by the Muses became a genre that had its rules, and whose productions could be classified and judged.

This transformation of ritual event into poetic monument had considerable consequences. The most fundamental of these was the introduction of a gap between the circumstances of actual enunciation—namely, the poetic competition, which sought to crown literary excellence—and the fictional scene of enunciation in the poem itself, which reflected a vanished situation: that of the banquet where the ode had been sung for its ritual function. Primeval enunciation had become literary fiction. The banquet that it evoked was no longer a Dionysiac *symposión* but an imagined feast. A second effect of the transformation of ritual poetic word into literary monument was the need to assign it to an author. For that, mythical authors were needed, and each genre was associated with one author, considered to be its founder: Homer for the epic, Anacreon for lyric poetry, etc. The primordial author became the guarantor of the genre in which new creations could be inscribed. A third consequence was the possibility (or the necessity) of elaborating a poetics that stated the rules. The inspired Word that had overwhelmed the poet who conveyed it was now replaced by the idea of the work as creation and labor. That is why it was only with lyrical poetry, with Pindar or Baccylides, that the poem could first be compared to a woven textile, and poetic art to a craft. Nowhere in the *Iliad* or the *Odyssey* is the metaphor of verbal weaving, which was used to designate contests in eloquence, applied to the song of the poet, which in fact belongs not to him but to the Muses.[5]

When the production of the text is no longer attributed to the spontaneous irruption of the sacred Word, it comes to depend on correct application and imitation of the rules. That is why, according to Aristotle's *Poetics*, or at least according to Aristotle's commentators, a tragedy was to be judged, not on the basis of its theatrical performance, but through reading, which would gauge its conformity to the norms. The opposition between rules, on the one hand, and performance, on the other, as the fundamental criterion for the evaluation of plays, provided the foun-

dation for the polemical arguments mobilized during the literary
querelles of the seventeenth century—for example, those concerning
plays by Corneille[6] or by Lope de Vega.[7] In fact, this opposition set the
learned, who read plays in order to judge them on the basis of rules,
against those (starting with the authors themselves) who considered the
effects produced on an audience during a theatrical representation to
be of prime importance. In 1609, in his *Arte nuevo de hacer comedias en
este tiempo*, addressed to an academy of men of letters assembled in
Madrid by the Count of Saldaãna, Lope de Vega recalled that he was
the author of 483 *comedias* and added:

> Fuera de seis, las demás todas
> pecaron contra el arte gravemente.
> Sustento, en fin, lo que escribí, y conozco
> que, aunque fueran mejor de otra manera,
> no tuvieran el gusto que han tenido
> porque a veces lo que es contra lo justo
> por la misma razón deleita al gusto.

> Except for six, in fact all without exception
> have gravely sinned against the laws of the art.
> No matter, I uphold what I have written and I know
> that, if done otherwise, they would have been better,
> but they would not have enjoyed such favor,
> for sometimes that which runs counter to what is right,
> for that very reason is what pleases the most.

From these three features—the disjunction between the actual circumstances of enunciation and the fictive enunciation inscribed in the text;
the invention of founding authors; and the formulation of an *ars poetica*
stating what the rules ought to be—there follows another: the written
inscription of texts, which by the very fact of inscription constitutes a
scholarly canon, an object of apprenticeship, and a repertoire from which
to draw the citations, examples, and models necessary for composing
new texts. The trajectory of the Greek world thus takes us from a poetry
fundamentally linked to its performance, a poetry governed by the forms
of sociability and of the religious rituals in which it is sung, to a poetry
governed by the rules of the "literary institution." The end point of this
trajectory coincides with the constitution of the library and museum of
Alexandria, during the Hellenistic period. It was then that the fundamental categories that structure and constrain the order of modern lit-

erary discourse, as characterized by Foucault in two famous texts, "Qu'est-ce qu'un auteur?" and *L'ordre du discours*, were crystallized in the concept of the "work" (with its criteria of unity, coherence, and fixity), the category of the "author" (which assigns the literary work to a proper name), and, finally, "commentary" (identified with the work of interpretation, which brings meaning to light.)[8] The three fundamental disciplines of the "literary institution"—philology, literary history, and hermeneutics—were thus set in place at the end of a trajectory leading from "event" to "monument," and they found their formulation in the dream of a universal library.

This detour through antiquity suggests several fundamental lessons, which also apply to the beginnings of modernity. The first lesson defines the "literary institution" as consisting in the separation of texts from their ritual functions, and in their availability for pedagogy, citation, and commentary. The second lesson cautions against all forms of anachronism, that is, all forms of projecting as universal what are individual experiences localized in time and space—our own, for example. Readers in antiquity did not read an ode by Anacreon, a poem by Catullus, or the *Satyricon* as we read them, and from this fact stems the importance of a history of reading devoted to recording the historicity of the fundamental morphological differences that affect the construction of meaning.[9] The third lesson reveals a trajectory from inspired Word to controlled imitation, from the singularity of the speech act to its inscription in writing, from the ephemeral singularity of poetic performance to the repetitiveness of reading. These displacements, which characterize ancient literature, are not without parallels in modernity. Ollan, Borges's Irish poet, by making the same journey in reverse, attests to an enduring nostalgia for a lost orality, for the text as "performance."

Singling out the effects specific to the different modes of texts' inscription, transmission, and reception is a necessary condition for any historical understanding of literary works. We have only to follow the plan laid out by Pierre Bourdieu: "S'interroger sur les conditions de possibilité de la lecture, c'est s'interroger sur les conditions sociales de possibilité des situations dans lesquelles on lit . . . et aussi sur les conditions sociales de production des *lectores*. Une des illusions du *lector* est celle qui consiste à oublier ses propres conditions sociales de production, à universaliser inconsciemment les conditions de possibilité de sa lecture" ("Inquiring into the conditions of possibility of reading means inquiring into the social conditions which make possible the situations in which one reads . . . and inquiring also into the social conditions of production of *lectores*. One of the illusions of the *lector* [in the sense of the reader who comments and interprets—R.C.] is that which consists in forgetting one's own social conditions of production, and unconsciously universalizing the conditions of possibility of one's own reading").[10]

The fundamental aim of this remark consists in opposing the logic of practice, the "practical sense," to the logic of interpretation and commentary, which is a logic of the order of discourse. To impose a textual logic on practices is to submit them to categories foreign to them. On a smaller scale, this remark leads one to distinguish between the oral, communal, ritual performance of texts, which obeys its own laws, and a reading of the same texts as practiced by a reader who is in the position of a *lector* in search of meaning. Here we have a pertinent warning against any temptation to project our own relationship with ancient texts onto their readers or auditors in the past; this would be an error akin to the one that projects "into practices what is the function of practices for someone who studies them as something to be deciphered."[11]

Thus we face a difficult problem of method: how to reconstruct modalities proper to the *oral* dissemination and appropriation of ancient texts when for us these are by definition mute forms of orality. There are, it seems to me, three main strategies that allow us to confront this difficulty and grasp something of the specificity of oral performances by way of the written texts to which they are irreducible. The first strategy seeks to decipher in literary representations the practices of orality: recitation, song, reading aloud, etc. It is therefore a question of constituting the corpus of these forms of orality, which certain texts represent through the fiction of writing. This is the case with chapter 20 in Part I of *Don Quixote*, where Sancho tells his master a tale.[12] The description shows, with extraordinary acuity, the gap that separates Sancho's ways of telling a story from the expectations of a reader like Don Quixote. Sancho tells his story by multiplying repetitions, relative clauses, and broken clauses, constantly interrupting his story with references to the situation in which he finds himself with Don Quixote. Don Quixote, by contrast, expects a linear narrative without repetition or digressions. Cervantes thus shows the absolute gap between ways of speaking and ways of reading (or of listening to reading). Sancho tells his story the way stories *(consejas)* are told in his village. But Don Quixote becomes very impatient upon hearing this way of telling a story, so foreign to a reader, like himself, who is used to apprehending texts in written, stable, fixed form.[13]

Likewise, in chapter 5 of his *Propos rustiques et facétieux*, Noël Du Fail shows how a rich peasant, Robin Chevet, tells some old folk tales to his assembled household.[14] The features that Du Fail retains in order to characterize this recitation are the very ones that Cervantes uses to characterize the way in which Sancho tells his *consejas*—appeals to the audience, digressions, parenthetical remarks, repetitions, etc. This first path of inquiry is in no way to be understood as reducing the text to documentary status, but it does take account of the fact that literary representations of the practices of orality designate (while displacing them onto the register of fiction) the specific procedures that govern the oral transmission of texts.

The second mode of inquiry seeks to collect in the works themselves such practices as they have been defined by Paul Zumthor: "Par 'indice d'oralité,' j'entends tout ce qui, à l'intérieur d'un texte, nous renseigne sur l'intervention de la voix humaine dans sa *publication:* je veux dire dans la mutation par laquelle ce texte passa, une ou plusieurs fois, d'un état virtuel à l'actualité, et désormais exista dans l'attention et la mémoire d'un certain nombre d'individus" ("By 'indicator of orality,' I mean anything that, within the text, informs us about the intervention of the human voice in its *publication,* I mean in the mutations through which the text passed, once or many times, from a virtual state to its current form and henceforth existed in the mind and the memory of a certain number of individuals").[15] These indicators of orality, inscribed within the texts themselves, are not representations of oral practices but implicit or explicit devices that destine texts to addressees who will read them aloud or listen to them being read.

They may be indisputable, just as when a musical notation indicates that a text is to be sung, as in the case of broadside ballads or *romances.* They may be simply probable, as in the case of texts that are addressed to a double audience: those who will read, and those who will listen to the text being read to them. In all European languages, a couple of verb pairs mark this double reception: *to read* and *to hear, ver* and *oír* or *leer* and *escuchar, voir* and *écouter.* Prologues, notices to the reader, and chapter titles very frequently indicate this double nature of address and addressee, and this double circulation of the text.[16]

Other indicators, inscribed within the formal structure of a work, may equally suggest the oral destination of a text. A number of works—starting with the greatest, such as *Don Quixote* itself—are organized into short chapters perfectly adapted to the necessities of oral performance, which assumes a limited time of delivery so as not to tire the audience, and to account for the audience's inability to memorize an overly complex plot. Brief chapters, which are so many textual units, can be considered units of reading, closed in on themselves and separate. William Nelson has thus stressed how the rewriting of certain works (the *Amadigi* by Bernardo Tasso, or the *Arcadia* by Spencer) might be understood as the adjustment of the work to the constraints of reading aloud at a time when this practice was a major form of lettered sociability.[17] The division of the text into shorter units, the multiplication of autonomous episodes, and the simplification of the plot are all indicators of the adaptation of the work to a modality essential to its transmission. This is doubtless the case for a number of older verse or prose works, particularly collections of short stories in which a staged fictive enunciation (which imagines the presence of several storytellers within an enclosed space) possibly coincides with the real conditions of the work's circulation (through its being read out loud).

A third line of inquiry is more technical and more specific. It is devoted to transformations of punctuation, beginning with a hypothesized passage from oralized to grammatical punctuation—or, as William Nelson writes, a mutation that dates from the end of "the late seventeenth century" whereby "elocutionary punctuation indicative of pauses and pitches was . . . largely supplanted by syntactic punctuation." Verifying such a hypothesis poses a preliminary difficulty: to whom should the orthographic and graphic forms of ancient editions be attributed? According to various traditions of textual studies, the answer varies widely.

As far as analytical bibliography is concerned, graphic and orthographic choices are the doing of compositors. The compositors of ancient printing workshops did not all have the same way of spelling words or of indicating punctuation, hence the regular recurrence of the same forms in the different quires of a book, according to preferences of orthography or punctuation of the compositor who set the pages of the different printers' formes. This is precisely why "spelling analysis" and "compositor studies," which allow one to attribute the composition of such and such a sheet or forme to such and such a compositor, constitutes, with the analysis of damaged types and ornaments, one of the surest means of reconstructing the very process of making a book, through formes or *seriatim*.[18] From this perspective, on the basis of the study of printed works' materiality, punctuation, like graphic or orthographic variations, is considered to result not from the will of the authors who wrote the texts but from the habits of the compositors who set the printed pages.

From the perspective of the history of language, the essential role was played out elsewhere: in the preparation of the manuscript for composition, as practiced by the *corrector,* that is, the copy editor, who added capitals, accents, and punctuation marks and who thus standardized the spelling and established graphic conventions. Choices regarding punctuation, if still products of work connected with printing houses and the publishing process, are no longer assigned to compositors but to humanists: to the clerics, university graduates, schoolmasters, etc., that publishers and printers employed in order to ensure the greatest possible correctness of their editions. Paolo Trovato has reminded us how important it was for Italian publishers of the Cinquecento to insist on the "correctness" of their editions, a correctness praised in the books themselves with the phrase *"con ogni diligenza corretto."*[19] From this followed the decisive role of copy editors, whose interventions are spread out over several stages of the publishing process: preparation of the manuscript; stop-press corrections made during the printing process; proofreading; and the compilation of various forms of errata (corrections made in ink on individual printed copies, loose leaves that encouraged the reader to make corrections himself on his own copy, or pages added at the end of the book to list errata).

The role of copy editors and proofreaders in the graphic and orthographic fixation of the vernacular tongues was far more decisive than propositions for the reform of orthography that were advanced by writers who wanted to impose an "oral writing" entirely governed by pronunciation.[20] There was, for example, a wide gap between the moderation of the solutions chosen by French publishers and printers of the sixteenth century and the boldness of the reforms suggested by the authors of the Pléiade. Ronsard, for example, in his *Abrégé de l'Art poétique françois,* proposed doing away with "all superfluous orthography" (that is, all letters that were not pronounced); transforming words' written appearance to more closely resemble the way in which the words were spoken (for example, *roze, kalité, Franse, langaje,* etc., thus rendering *q* and soft *c* useless in French); and introducing letters in imitation of Spanish *ll* and *ãn* so as to facilitate correct pronunciation of *orgueilleux* or *Monseigneur.*[21] In the advice that he addresses to the reader as a preface to the first four books of the *Franciade,* Ronsard directly links punctuation marks and oral reading practices: "Je te supliray seulement d'une chose, Lecteur: de vouloir bien prononcer mes vers et accommoder ta voix à leur passion, et non comme quelques uns les lisent, plustost à la façon d'une missive, ou de quelques lettres Royaux, que d'un Poëme bien prononcé; et te suplie encore derechef, où tu verras cette marque ! vouloir un peu eslever ta voix pour donner grace à ce que tu liras" ("I will ask of you but one thing, Reader: to pronounce my verses carefully and to accommodate your voice to their passion, and not as some read them, more in the manner of a letter or some royal missive than of a well-read poem; and I also ask you once again that where you see this mark ! you raise your voice a little so as to give grace to what you are reading").[22]

If the practice of publishers and printers, far from these radical propositions, preserved some link with oralization, its innovations were limited to determining the length of pauses. Here, the fundamental text is that of the printer (and author) Etienne Dolet, entitled *La Ponctuation de la langue françoise*.[23] In 1540 he defined the new typographical conventions that were to distinguish, according to the length of the interruption or its position in the sentence, the *point à queue* (comma); the *comma* (semicolon), "which is placed in a suspended sentence and not always at the end point"; and the *point rond* (period), which "is always placed at the end of the sentence."

Language dictionaries from the end of the seventeenth century record not only the efficiency of the system proposed by Dolet (a system enriched only by the colon, which indicates a pause of halfway between that of the comma and that of the semicolon) but also the distance established between the reader's voice and punctuation, which, according to the terminology of Furetière's dictionary, has to be considered as demarcating logical rather than rhetorical divisions of discourse. In the examples that he proposes in the same dictionary, published in 1690, Furetière indicates that "ce Correcteur d'Imprimerie entend fort bien la ponctuation" ("this copy editor understands punctuation perfectly well") and that "l'exactitude de cet Auteur va jusques là qu'il prend soin des points et des virgules" ("this author is exact to the point of paying attention to periods and commas"). If the first example assigns punctuation to the technical skills proper to the copy editors and proofreaders employed by printers, the second implicitly reflects authors' common disinterest in punctuation.

Furetière points out, however, that there are authors who are attentive to the punctuation of their texts. Is it possible to find traces of this attention in printed editions of their works? Let us take the case of Molière. It would be very risky to attribute too directly to him the choices in punctuation to be found in the original editions of his plays, since, as has been shown for the 1660 edition of *Les Précieuses Ridicules,* punctuation varies from sheet to sheet, even from forme to forme, according to the preferences of the compositors.[24] Nevertheless, the different uses of punctuation that exist between the first editions of his plays, published shortly after their first Parisian productions, and the later editions allow one to reconstruct, if not the author's intention, at least the modalities of the implied destination of the printed text.

Molière's reticence concerning the printed publication of his plays is well known.[25] Before *Les Précieuses Ridicules,* Molière had never sent any of his plays to the printers, and he did so in this case only because he needed to get an advance on the publication of the text by Somaize and Ribou, made from a pirated copy and under cover of a license *(privilège)* obtained through deceit. There were financial reasons, since a play, once published, could be staged by any theatrical troupe; but there were also aesthetic reasons. For Molière, in fact, the theatrical effects of a play depended entirely on the *action,* that is, on performance. The address to the reader that opens the edition of *L'Amour Médecin,* produced at Versailles and then at the Theater of the Palais Royal in 1665, and published the following year, underscores the gap that exists between spectacle and reading: "Il n'est pas nécessaire de vous avertir qu'il y a beaucoup de choses qui dépendent de l'action: on sait bien que les comédies ne sont faites que pour être jouées; et je ne conseille de lire celle-ci qu'aux personnes qui ont des yeux pour découvrir dans la lecture tout le jeu du théâtre" ("There is no need to tell you that there are several things [in the play] that depend upon the action. It is generally known that comedies are written only to be acted; and I would have only those read this who have eyes to discover the acting in the reading of it").[26]

Punctuation is one of the possible devices (together with the image on the frontispiece and the stage directions) that allow something of the theater to be restored to the printed text and its reading. The punctuation in the first editions of Molière's plays, systematically compared to the punctuation adopted in later editions (not only in the nineteenth century but also as early as the eighteenth and late seventeenth centuries), clearly attests to its link with orality, either because it destines the printed text to being read aloud or recited or because it permits those readers who will read it in silence to reconstruct for themselves the actors' timing and pauses in the play. The passage from one form of punctuation to another has an effect on the very meaning of the works that is far from insignificant.[27] On the one hand, the original punctuation marks, always more numerous, portray the characters in different ways; thus the comma, present in the 1669 edition and later suppressed, after the first word ("Fat") in act I, scene 4, line 233 of *Tartuffe:* "Gros, et gras, le teint frais, et la bouche vermeille" ("Stout, and fat, with blooming cheeks and ruddy lips"); or the accumulation of commas and capitals that distinguish the Master of Philosophy's way of speaking from that of the Master of Dance in act II, scene 3 of *Le Bourgeois Gentilhomme.* On the other hand, the punctuation marks in the original editions give the reader the time needed to reconstitute or imagine the play of the actors. For example, in act II, scene 4, lines 586–94 of *Le Misanthrope* (the scene of the portraits), the 1667 edition contains six more commas than the modern editions, a fact that allows one to reconstruct how Célimène, or the actress playing the part, emphasized some words, introduced pauses, and elaborated on the mimicry. Finally, these original punctuation marks throw into relief words that are charged with particular meaning. The last two verses of *Tartuffe* do not contain any commas in the modern editions, but this is not the case in the edition of 1669: "Et par un doux hymen, couronner en Valère, / La flamme d'un Amànt généreux, & sincère" ("And, with my daughter's hand, reward Valère / For this, a love both generous and sincere"). The last word of the play is thus clearly designated as the antonym of a word that figures in the title, *Le Tartuffe, ou l'Imposteur*. These abundant punctuation marks, which point out certain pauses that are more numerous and, generally, longer than those retained in later editions, tell readers how they should read (or say) the lines of verse and emphasize a certain number of words, generally endowed with capital letters, which, along with the commas, have been suppressed in the later printed editions.

The inquiry that I have only sketched here raises several problems of a general nature. The first is that of dating the passage from rhetorical punctuation to grammatical punctuation. Is this passage organized around a single chronological trajectory, wherein the end of the seventeenth century would constitute a decisive moment? Does it obey different rhythms according to the genre? Or, following the hypothesis formulated by Philip Gaskell with regard to the "maske" of Milton's *Comus*,[28] should we not trace these variations back to the various destinations of the same text, contemporaneous with one another?

The second problem concerns the reasons and devices that convey attempts to restore the punctuation marks of oralization during the eighteenth century. From this point of view, the case of Benjamin Franklin would be exemplary. By imagining the various devices that would allow one to uphold the role of the public orator in the midst of a dispersed population, Franklin strove to reconcile the new definition of public and political space, which had the dimensions of a vast republic, with the traditional forcefulness of live speech, addressed to citizens assembled for deliberation.[29] On the one hand, authors of "public discourses" were invited, in their writings, to make use of the genres most directly linked to orality: proverbs, dialogues, and letters (which belong to the oratory genre). On the other hand, the apprenticeship of reading aloud, which points up the duration of pauses and voice pitches, was to have become a fundamental element of school curricula. Finally, a reform of typographical conventions was to have made the oralization of texts easier, thanks to an "expressive typography" that would play with italics, with capital letters added to certain words, or with new punctuation marks (for example, the introduction into English of the inverted exclamation point or the inverted question mark proper to Spanish, which, placed at the beginning of a sentence, would indicate from the outset how one was to pitch one's voice). By mobilizing these resources, with which he was quite familiar, since he had been a printer, Franklin aligned printed discourse as closely as possible with oratory performance and, by the same token, allowed different orators to reproduce an original discourse in identical fashion, and in different places. Thanks to reading out loud, and thanks to "expressive typography," the discourse of the "publick Orator" would be reproduced, in his very absence, as if he were "present." By contrast with Condorcet or Malesherbes, who were distrustful of the passions and emotions engendered by oratory rhetoric, Franklin thought it possible to overcome an apparently insoluble contradiction: around speeches, or on the basis of oral exchanges, how was one to organize a public space that would not necessarily be enclosed within the confines of the Greek city-state?

"If we offend, it is with our good will. / That you should think, we come not to offend, / But with good will. To show our simple skill, / That is the true beginning of our end."[30] In the prologue to the *Comedy of Pyramus and Thisbe,* Quince's faulty enunciation causes him to say the very opposite of what he wants to say, and what would have been suitable for him to say: "If we offend, it is with our good will / That you should think we come not to offend. / But with good will, to show our simple skill: / That is the true beginning of our end." Plays on faulty punctuation that reverses the very meaning of a text without changing a single word occurred more than once in Elizabethan literature. Let us just recall the unpunctuated "Eduardum occidere nolite timere bonum est" in Marlowe's *Edward the Second,* where the same phrase in the letter given by Mortimer to Lightborne can be understood, according to the position of the pause—after or before "timere"—as either ordering the murder of the king or as saving his life.[31] Such plays on punctuation indicate that the construction of a text's meaning depends on the forms that govern its inscription and its transmission. In opposition to every critical approach that considers the materiality of texts and the modalities of their performance to be without importance, the clumsy Quince reminds us that we need to identify the effects of the meanings produced by forms (whether those forms are manuscript-based, printed, oral, or electronic) in order to understand the various appropriations of texts, literary or not, in their full historicity.

NOTES

1. Jorge Luis Borges, "El espejo y la máscara," in *El Libro de arena* (Buenos Aires: Emecé Editores, 1975), trans. Norman Thomas di Giovanni, *The Book of Sand* (London: Penguin Books, 1979), 53–57.

2. B. W. Ife, *Reading and Fiction in Golden-Age Spain: A Platonist Critique and Some Picaresque Replies* (Cambridge: Cambridge University Press, 1985).

3. Jorge Luis Borges, "William Shakespeare: MacBeth," in *Prólogos con un prólogo de los prólogos* (Buenos Aires: Torres Aguero Editor, 1975), 142–47.

4. Florence Dupont, *L'Invention de la littérature: De l'ivresse grècque au livre latin* (Paris: La Découverte, 1994), trans. Janet Lloyd, *The Invention of Literature: From Greek Intoxication to the Latin Book* (Baltimore, Md.: Johns Hopkins University Press, 1999).

5. John Scheid and Jesper Svenbro, *Le métier de Zeus: mythe du tissage et du tissu dans le monde gréco-romain* (Paris: La Découverte, 1994), trans. Carol Volk, *The Craft of Zeus: Myths of Weaving and Fabric* (Cambridge, Mass.: Harvard University Press, 1996).

6. Hélène Merlin, *Public et littérature en France au XVIIè siècle* (Paris: Les Belles Lettres, 1994).

7. Lope de Vega, *Arte nuevo de hacer comedias en este tiempo* (originally published 1609), in Felipe Pedraza, ed., *Lope de Vega Esencial* (Madrid: Taurus, 1990), 124–34.

8. Michel Foucault, "Qu'est-ce qu'un auteur?" *Bulletin de la Société française de Philosophie* 64 (1969), 73–104, reprinted in Michel Foucault, *Dits et Ecrits, 1954–1988*, ed. Daniel Defert, François Ewald, and Jacques Lagrange, vol. 1: *Dits et Ecrits, 1954–1969* (Paris: Gallimard, 1994), 789–821, trans. *Language, Counter-Memory, Practices: Selected Essays and Interviews*, ed. Donald F. Bouchard (Ithaca, N.Y.: Cornell University Press, 1977), 113–38; Michel Foucault, *L'Ordre du discours* (Paris: Gallimard, 1970), trans. A. M. Sheridan Smith, *The Archaelogy of Knowledge* (New York: Pantheon, 1972), 215–37; Roger Chartier, *Culture écrite et société: l'ordre des livres, XIVe-XVIIIe siècle* (Paris: Albin Michel, 1997), trans. *The Order of Books: Readers, Authors, and Libraries in Europe between the Fourteenth and Eighteenth Centuries* (Stanford, Calif.: Stanford University Press, 1994); Roger Chartier, *Forms and Meanings: Texts, Performances, and Audiences from Codex to Computer* (Philadelphia: University of Pennsylvania Press, 1995).

9. Guglielmo Cavallo and Roger Chartier, eds., *Storia della lettura nel mondo occidentale* (Rome: Editori Laterza, 1995), trans. Lydia G. Cochrane, *A History of Reading in the West* (Oxford: Polity Press, 1999).

10. Pierre Bourdieu, "Lecture, lecteurs, lettrés, littérature," in *Choses dites* (Paris: Editions de Minuit, 1987), 132–43, trans. Matthew Adamson, *In Other Words: Essays Toward a Reflexive Sociology* (Stanford, Calif.: Stanford University Press, 1990), 94–105.

11. Ibid.

12. Miguel de Cervantes Saavedra, *Don Quijote de La Mancha* (originally published 1605), ed. Francisco Rico (Barcelona: Instituto Cervantes Crítica, 1998); see also Cervantes, *The Adventures of Don Quixote,* trans. J. M. Cohen, 2d ed. (London: Penguin, 1984).

13. Michel Moner, *Cervantes conteur: Ecrits et paroles* (Madrid: Bibliothèque de la Casa de Velázquez, 1989).

14. Noël Du Fail, *Propos rustiques et facétieux* (originally published 1548), in Pierre Jourda, ed., *Conteurs français du XVe siècle* (Paris: N.R.F. / Bibliothèque de la Pléiade, 1965).

15. Paul Zumthor, *La Lettre et la voix de la "littérature" médiévale* (Paris: Editions du Seuil, 1987).

16. Margit Frenk, "'Lectores y oídores'. La difusión oral de la literatura en el Siglo de Oro," presented at the meeting of the Asociación Internacional de Hispanistas, Venice, Aug. 25–30, 1980, and collected in Giuseppe Bellini, ed., *Actas del Séptimo Congreso de la Asociación Internacional de Hispanistas,* vol. 1 (Rome: Bulzoni Editore, 1981), 101–23.

17. William Nelson, "From 'Listen Lording' to 'Dear Reader,'" *University of Toronto Quarterly* 46:2 (1976 / 77), 110‑24.

18. D. F. McKenzie, "Compositor B's Role in the 'Merchant of Venice' Q2 (1619)," *Studies in Bibliography* 12 (1959), 75–89; Charlton Hinman, *The Printing and Proof-Reading of the First*

Folio of Shakespeare (Oxford: Clarendon Press, 1963); R. M. Flores, *The Composition of the First and Second Madrid Editions of Don Quixote, Part I* (London: Modern Humanities Research Association, 1975); Jeanne Veyrin-Forrer, "Fabriquer un livre au XVIè siècle," in Roger Chartier and Henri-Jean Martin, eds., *Histoire de l'édition française,* vol. 1: *Le Livre conquérant du Moyen Age au milieu du XVIIè siècle* (Paris: Fayard / Cercle de la Librairie, 1989), 336–69.

19. Paolo Trovato, *Con ogni diligenza corretto: La stampa e le revisioni editoriali dei testi letterari italiani, 1470–1570* (Bologna: Il Mulino, 1991).

20. Nina Catach, *L'Orthographe française à l'époque de la Renaissance: Auteurs, imprimeurs, ateliers d'imprimerie* (Geneva: Librairie Droz, 1968).

21. Pierre de Ronsard, *Abrégé de l'Art poétique françois* (originally published 1565), in Gustave Cohen, ed., *Oeuvres complètes,* vol. 2 (Paris: N.R.F. / Bibliothèque de la Pléiade, 1950), 995–1009.

22. Pierre de Ronsard, *Les Quatre premiers livres de la Franciade* (originally published 1572), ibid., 1009–13.

23. In Catach, *L'Orthographe française à l'époque de la Renaissance,* unpaginated.

24. Jeanne Veyrin-Forrer, "A la recherche des 'Précieuses,'" in *La lettre et le texte: Trente années de recherches sur l'histoire du livre* (Paris: Collection de l'Ecole Normale Supérieure de Jeunes Filles, 1987), 338–66.

25. Abby E. Zanger, "Paralyzing Performance: Sacrificing Theater on the Altar of Publication," *Stanford French Review,* Fall / Winter 1988, 169–85.

26. Molière, *L'Amour Médecin* (originally published 1666), in Georges Couton, ed., *Oeuvres complètes,* vol. 2 (Paris: N.R.F. / Bibliothèque de la Pléiade, 1971), 87–120.

27. Gaston H. Hall, "Ponctuation et dramaturgie chez Molière," in *La Bibliographie matérielle* (Paris: Editions du CNRS, 1983), 125–41.

28. Philip Gaskell, "Milton, *a Maske (Comus), 1634,*" in *From Writer to Reader: Studies in Editorial Method* (Winchester: St. Paul's Bibliographies, 1924), 28–61.

29. Jacob Melish, "'As Your Newspaper Was Reading': La culture de la voix, la sphère publique et la politique de l'alphabétisation: le monde de la construction de l'imprimé de Benjamin Franklin" (Paris: Ecole des Hautes Etudes en Sciences Sociales, mimeograph, 1992).

30. William Shakespeare, *A Midsummer Night's Dream* (originally published 1600), in Harold F. Brooks, ed., *The Arden Edition of the Works of William Shakespeare* (London: Routledge, 1979, 1993).

31. Christopher Marlowe, *Edward the Second* (originally published c. 1592), in J. B. Steane, ed., *The Complete Plays* (London: Penguin, 1969), 520.

Editing and Auditing Marginalia

H. J. JACKSON

Forty years ago, Princeton University Press undertook an edition of the collected works of Samuel Taylor Coleridge as part of its deluxe Bollingen Series, with funding from Paul Mellon and the Bollingen Foundation. To everyone's surprise, I think, the edition is now finished. Six of approximately thirty volumes were devoted to publishing the complete text of all the notes Coleridge is known to have written in other people's books, by which I mean books by authors other than himself, though it is also the case that he often wrote in books that belonged to other people. The edition of the marginalia was carefully designed and started by George Whalley of Queen's University in Canada, who completed the first two volumes; a year or so after his death, in 1983, I agreed to take it over. Volume 3 appeared under our joint names in 1992, volume 4 in 1999, volume 5 in 2000, and volume 6 with the cumulative index in 2001.

This seems a good moment to pause and reflect upon the special problems of editing marginalia, and to consider the value of this apparently trivial and ephemeral sort of writing. I chose the word "auditing" for the title of this essay because the word conveys the idea of assessment of worth, but also because it is close in sound to "editing" and has the root meaning of "listening to." A metaphor I like to use for the experience of coming upon handwritten notes in printed books, when you expect to be communing only with the author, is of a phone call in which suddenly another voice comes on the line, and you have to attend to it as well.

From a textual point of view, marginalia have equivocal status, if they have any status at all. They arise out of a prior, printed text; they could not exist without it; they do not make sense without it; they are naturally subordinate to it—some would say, parasitic upon it. *Editing* marginalia reverses the natural order by obliging us to put the cart before the horse and focus on the note rather than on the text. That is one reason for the incredulity that I encounter when I tell a layperson what it is I do. Another is the inherent absurdity of annotating annotations (which may themselves be notes upon notes): people find the regression confusing.

The problems associated distinctively with the publishing of marginalia are in the first instance practical problems having to do with presentation and format. How do you reproduce the effect of an annotated book? Is that indeed what you ought to be aiming at? There are not many precedents to go by. The printed glosses in early printed books imitated the handwritten glosses of manuscripts, being fitted in interlinearly, or in the margins, and in a smaller font, to distinguish them from the primary text and to show their derivative and subordinate status. *Handwritten* glosses—readers' notes—in the eighteenth century generally followed the same models, being written in ink with the intention of permanence, but keeping modestly to the margins and not overwhelming the text. Some twentieth-century scholarly editions of marginalia have attempted a facsimile format, printing the text full measure and the notes as little afterthoughts on the side, as, for example, in the 1938 edition of Boswell, with notes by Hester Thrale Piozzi.

But this technique would not do for Coleridge, whose notes sometimes go on for ten or twelve pages. Printing both text and notes in the same font might be easier on the printer and would have a pleasing neutrality about it, but it would make it difficult for the reader to distinguish the author's words from the annotator's. When Coleridge's notes began to appear in periodicals, in his lifetime, around 1820, they were at first published as independent, freestanding observations, but as soon as an extensive collection was planned, it became obvious that the notes could not always stand alone: the passage that had prompted the note would sometimes have to be printed as well. In *Literary Remains* and later Victorian editions, the original text is printed in small type, with the annotations printed full size. G. E. Bentley's edition of Blake's wonderfully abrasive notes takes the same approach.[1]

Publishers have also had to decide how much of the original text to include (just enough so that a reader could find it in another copy?) and in what order to present the notes (by subject? by date of composition?). The solution adopted by the Bollingen edition is to organize the marginalia alphabetically by the names of the authors annotated; to print all the notes from a book in book order, not chronological order; and to begin with about a paragraph of the text, printed in black, up to the point at which the marginal note begins, and then to present the note itself, printed in a reddish brown. The editor's notes are suitably subdued footnotes in a smaller font and double columns. This is an elegant if not perfect solution; on the face of it, the annotator and the annotated have different but equal standing, and the sequence on the page reproduces the order of composition.Here, in less elegant format, is a sample entry.

It starts by identifying the author and title, continues with the passage annotated and a translation of it, followed by Coleridge's note, and concludes with my explanatory footnotes.

Gotthilf Heinrich von Schubert *Ansichten von der Nachtseite der Naturwissenschaft* (Dresden 1808)

49 p 296

Die grössten Thiere der zweyten Reihe sind der Eisbär und der grosse bengalische Tieger, während sich die küorperliche Grösse in der ersten Reihe, nachdem schon früher die Geschlechter der Stiere und des Rosses, das Kameel und die Giraffen . . . aufgetreten, noch bis zu dem Elephanten, ja bis zu dem grössten bekannten Thier der Erde, (wenn wir den fabelhaften Kraken ausnehmen) zum Wallfisch erhebt.

[The largest animals of the second series are the polar bear and the great Bengali tiger, while physical size in the first series (after the earlier appearance of the bull and horse species, the camel and the giraffe . . .) reaches that of the elephant, and even that of the largest known animal on earth (if we exclude the legendary Kraken), the whale.]

Relata refero:[1] March, 1821. Lieutenant Matthews while off the Cape of G. H. on his return from the East Indies in Capt[n] Cochrane's Ship saw & the whole Ship's Crew saw with him, a Kraken with a vengeance![2] So he assured me on his word and honor: and authorized me to use his name, and to make enquiries of Capt[n] Cochrane. The vessel was going six knots an hour; & by his watch which he held in his hand the whole time they were ten minutes and a half in passing the enormous Lubber from Head to Tail, running close alongside it: and discharged a cannonade into it, at the moment of parting. Matthews (who is now the Lithographer at the Admiralty)[3] saw the Blood spout up, & Kraken surlily sunk down!—

1. "I report what has been said."
2. The kraken, a fabulous sea-monster believed to be the largest living creature, was said to be something like a jellyfish in shape: it rose to the surface of the ocean, producing the appearance of a cluster of islands; put out tentacles to gather in food; and, when satisfied—or disturbed—sank slowly out of sight. See W. Scott COPY C **3** for further references.
   The Navy List for 1821 includes three Captain Cochranes and three lieutenants named Matthews or Mathews, but the only record of a Matthews and a Cochrane working together dates from 1816–17, when Henry Bathurst H. Matthews (commissioned 13 Jun 1815, d 1827) served under Nathaniel Day Cochrane (commissioned 26 Mar 1806) aboard HMS Orontes in St Helena. Since C mentions the Cape of Good Hope, however, it seems unlikely that it was on the St Helena voyage that Matthews saw the kraken. The Orontes had previously been stationed at the Cape of Good Hope, and most probably Matthews's story refers to a period antedating his lieutenancy: cf John Marshall Royal Naval Biography Supplement pt 1 (1827) 123.
   3. The Navy Lists do not record any Lieutenant Matthews or Mathews employed at the Admiralty in or about 1821, though he might have been there in some minor office. What C can mean by "Lithographer" is also a puzzle: although the Admiralty had created the very important office of Hydrographer in 1795 there was no corresponding Lithographer, and the word in the sense of one who deals with stones, or geology, or landforms was already obsolete. Charts in C's day were usually engraved, although some experiments in lithography for maps and charts had been carried out in England since 1808, notably in the army: Michael Twyman *Lithography 1800–1850* (1970) 32–3.

This is a pretty typical note. Coleridge appears to have been reading along, accepting by and large what he found, until he was brought up short by Schubert's assumption that the kraken is purely imaginary. This provokes an objection. Perhaps the kraken is fabulous, but there is evidence to the contrary—and Coleridge cites what he has heard. From a biographical point of view, his reaction is not surprising: even if we know only *The Rime of the Ancient Mariner*, we know that Coleridge took an interest in travelers tales and kept an open mind about exotic and even supernatural phenomena. The note also adds a mite to our knowledge of his circle of acquaintance, for Lieutenant Matthews of the Admiralty does not appear to have been mentioned in any other biographical record. We gather, furthermore, by the context that Coleridge was not alone, and that the kraken was still a live issue in England, whatever its status in Germany: so we get a whiff of his and his contemporaries' uncertainty, subtly different from our own, about the world they inhabited.

It is a relatively straightforward note, not one that displays the sort of arcane learning that we sometimes find in Coleridge, and I am a little embarrassed by the amount of explanatory verbiage that I have added to it. Of course, it could have been worse. When you gloss material like this, you always have to weigh the estimated needs of your readership against its estimated patience. Samuel Johnson says that footnotes may be necessary, but that they are a necessary evil;[2] and Coleridge himself, trying to work with an up-to-date edition of the plays of Ben Jonson, has an irritable note[3]—not at all in his usual tone—saying, "What does this mean? Of course, a note being *needed*, there is none." I think I can see where further notes might have been useful to some readers. Should I have informed you about where Coleridge was and what he was doing in March 1821? Should I have identified the Cape of Good Hope, the East Indies, or the Admiralty? Should I have commented on the unusual word "Lubber" or drawn attention to the solecism of "six knots an hour"? Should I have given more of the interesting history of the kraken, demonstrating its endurance by reminding you of John Wyndham's popular science fiction story *The Kraken Wakes*,[4] or speculated about what it was that Matthews *did* see (perhaps a giant squid)? Guided by policy and precedent—not to mention the editor's personal limitations, which are sometimes glaringly evident—I decided that none of these was necessary, but that other basic requirements had to be met. In the process of trying to satisfy these basic requirements, however, I unearthed some new problems.

Coleridge's note is concrete and circumstantial, but when you scrutinize the details of it, it begins to look like a concrete sieve. He gives us a date, names, titles, exact measures ("ten minutes and a half [a *half*!] in passing the enormous Lubber from Head to Tail")—none of which is verifiable, and some of which are certainly wrong. Why did he pad out his note with such confident bluster as "now the Lithographer at the Admiralty" when it appears that no such office existed and, ipso facto, that Matthews didn't hold it? This note will be a treasure to the party that wishes to represent Coleridge as a pathological liar. I think myself that he was in the persuasive mode, and that he overdid it a bit, as we are all inclined to do. But then whom was he trying to persuade? Schubert? Schubert was never going to read this note. Himself? He was already prepared to suspend his disbelief and listen to witnesses. If this note had been written as a memorandum to himself, Coleridge would have needed only something like "Mem. Matthews" to bring it all back. Surely he must have been writing for the benefit of some future reader—someone who understood German (or he wouldn't be reading this book) and Latin (for Coleridge uses the phrase at the beginning without self-consciousness) but who would not know Lieutenant Matthews and would need to be told who he is, "the Lithographer at the Admiralty."

Coleridge began annotating books seriously when he was in his mid-thirties and friends asked him to do it. He would, as he said, "spoil" a book "to leave a Relic."[5] The volume of Schubert that contains the note about the kraken may have belonged to or been shared with Coleridge's close associate Joseph Henry Green, a successful London surgeon with whom Coleridge studied German philosophy, particularly the Nature-philosophy of Schelling and his followers. In this case, the annotations would constitute a study guide. Hence Coleridge, in his notes, repeatedly raises objections to Schubert's statements or proposes evidence counter to that adduced by him. At one point he says he is sick of the whole post-Kantian movement. Several of the notes in the volume imply a listener, and one of them contains a direct address: "Did you ever happen to hear Chinese Music?" Coleridge's own dating of notes like the kraken one proves that he read the book, or read *in* it, on at least four occasions in a five-year period. From this one title alone, then, we can find out quite a lot about Coleridge's knowledge of science, about his growing disenchantment with German philosophy of science, about his relationship with Green (if Green was in fact his imagined fellow student), and about his personality—not only the active fictional powers that generate Lithographers and the like, but also the engaging and eclectic curiosity that takes up, for instance, questions about the substance of comets and meteorites, the evidence for and against the kraken and the megatherium, and ways of getting fruit stains out of muslin. And in thus learning about him, we learn about his period, in what still seems to me the most reliable way—that is, through identification with one member of it.

When you examine Coleridge's notes carefully, as I have been obliged to do, you realize that many of them—*most*, I believe, and certainly the ones that we now consider the most engaging—were written for specific friends to read. For a long time I thought Coleridge was exceptional in thus making the writing of marginalia a social act, not a private one, but I was wrong. Having seen what Coleridge could do with a marginal note, I got curious about the conditions that produced those notes and enabled them to be treasured, published, and canonized as they have been. I began to read other people's marginalia, now more accessible than they used to be, thanks to online library catalogs. It should really come as no surprise to discover that when the absolute number of books in existence and the number likely to belong to any given individual were smaller than they are now, and when the recollection of manuscript culture was less remote, the prohibition against writing in books appears to have been weaker. Indeed, many kinds of notes were not only tolerated but encouraged.

In the century before Coleridge was an active annotator, people wrote mainly in their own books (not anonymously) to keep them up to date and to increase their usefulness. You could make a book—your own dictionary, for instance—go farther and last longer if you added stuff from other sources; it was also efficient to have your information all in one place instead of having to consult several volumes. So scholars collated their copies of classical works with other editions, and children put the translations of hard words directly into their textbooks. Lawyers kept records of new statutes, and of significant judgments that affected the law, by entering them in their copies of Coke upon Littleton and other handbooks. Amateur naturalists made notes in their field guides about the incidence of species of birds, butterflies, and plants in their own areas. Readers exercised their wits and displayed their knowingness, as they were meant to do, by filling in the blanks in satires and poems *à clef* with the proper names of the subjects, so that D——— of B———ck———m became "Duke of Buckingham." Those who were engaged in controversy carried their arguments over into the margins and endpapers of their opponents' works. The devout enriched their Bibles and prayer books with learned commentary and pious meditations. This sort of common use was continuous with earlier practice.

What happened that was new, I believe, in the eighteenth century was that readers began on a large scale to write *critical* notes in books, and to share them with others. My theory is that the replacement of marginal glosses with explanatory and critical footnotes, especially in editions of works in the vernacular, led readers to emulate the scholar-critics, not only to improve the work itself but also to show off their learning or acuteness. And to whom would they be showing off, if not either to an unknown future owner of the book or to a known contemporary? We do not know very much about the circulation of books in the period, though we can probably all think of instances of lending or exchange among literary figures—Thomas Percy begging for old books and manuscripts as he assembled the *Reliques of Ancient English Poetry*, for example. It is my impression that, for the most part, eighteenth-century owners saw themselves as the custodians, not the final resting place, of books and that there was a quite lively casual traffic in annotated books. In the Johnson circle, for example, we see Johnson sending back to Hill Boothby a book she had given him, that he had annotated on her behalf, and that he expected to get back from her again; Boswell acknowledging the help of a few readers, including at least one whose identity he did not know, who gave him their annotated copies of the *Life of Johnson* with suggestions for improvements in the second edition; and Hester Thrale Piozzi making up annotated Boswells as gifts for special friends.[6] These are circumstances that we have to take into account when we approach readers' notes in books.

For many areas in the new scholarly realm of textual studies—for example, reception history, reader response, and the history of reading practices—marginalia are potentially a gold mine. They bring us probably as close as we can get to a reader's immediate mental processes: turning to a notebook, or even to the endpapers of the book, involves just a little too much time for reflection, by comparison with a note written directly in the margin. But marginalia have to be treated with caution. First, there is probably no such thing as a perfectly spontaneous human utterance, let alone a critical reaction without an audience in prospect somewhere. Second, the special circumstances of the occasion of reading have to be factored in, as in the case of the practice of communicating marginalia in the late eighteenth century, or of Coleridge's writing for Joseph Henry Green. Third, and finally, we should realize that writing notes in books was and is an evolving practice governed by different conventions at different times. I am inclined to think that Coleridge's example acted as a stimulus to people in his orbit, and I am sure that the publication of his notes—particularly the large-scale operation of *Literary Remains*, the first volume of which appeared in 1836— changed the conditions of the art forever by making it for the first time conceivable that such notes *could* be published.[7] If ever there was a naive annotator, just irresistibly taken with the impulse to get down a note, the creature is gone the way of the dodo: we are all self-conscious now.

Samuel Johnson says that the general effect of notes is to "refriger-ate" the mind, meaning that you can be caught up in the text of a play or a romance or a lyric poem, but that explanatory notes put you off: they distract and eventually sicken you.[8] I don't know that this is true, even of explanatory notes (as opposed to critical or polemical ones), or even for the hypothetical "general reader." It seems to me that notes and text can generate momentum in tandem. In any case, Johnson's words are a serious warning to the would-be *editor* of marginalia. If we sup-pose that a reader has only so much attention to give and can spread it only so thin, and that the reader's attention is already divided between the text and the marginalia, then further layers of comment should be avoided, if possible, and otherwise kept to a minimum. This would be my advice in any case, for discursive notes tend to second-guess the use to which the material might be put, and we cannot be sure about that.

For the future, to those who might be interested in editing margina-lia, I would suggest that the most useful accompaniments to an edition would be a historically sensitive introduction, outlining the conditions in which the marginalia were written, and the briefest possible footnotes, performing only the most basic functions: translating foreign words; identifying people, places, and things that are not part of the standard equipment of conventionally educated readers nowadays; and identi-fying the sources of direct quotations. Apart from the translations, these notes would apply to the marginalia only, not to the original text. In the hypertext editions of the future (if hypertext ever becomes a medium in which it is economically viable to treat manuscripts), it might be desir-able to have images of all the annotated pages available so that the seri-ous student could see where a note falls on the page, whether the hand changes from one note to another, and whether the editor has made any errors in transcription. But for a reader who wants to reconstruct as closely as possible the annotator's experience of reading the book, and thereby to define the relationship between the text and the notes more precisely, it will be indispensable to have access to the whole work, not just to the annotated passages. Often a note that appears to be respond-ing to a particular passage is really addressing the cumulative effect of a narrative or an argument. (It's like a domestic quarrel: it wasn't really the way you squeezed the toothpaste that drove him mad.) For those purposes, students will at the very least have to be reading the whole text through, along with the edition of the notes. Ideally, they would have access to the actual annotated copy, which always shows features that the process of editing perforce has suppressed. But they would still be likely to need the supplement of the editor's explanatory notes; and so, since this is not an ideal world, a conscientious scholarly edition— with a complete text of the marginalia, ample selections from the source text, and footnotes that restore historical context—is the best instrument we have for making marginalia audible again.

NOTES

1. William Blake, *William Blake's Writings*, vol. 2, ed. G. E. Bentley Jr. (Oxford: Clarendon Press, 1978), 1349–1518.

2. Samuel Johnson, *Johnson on Shakespeare*, vol. 1, ed. Arthur Sherbo (New Haven, Conn.: Yale University Press, 1968), 111.

3. Samuel Taylor Coleridge, *Marginalia*, vol. 3, ed. George Whalley and H. J. Jackson (Princeton, N.J.: Princeton University Press, 1992), 181.

4. John Wyndham, *The Kraken Wakes* (London: M. Joseph, 1953).

5. Coleridge, *Marginalia*, vol. 1, ed. George Whalley (Princeton, N.J.: Princeton University Press, 1980), 372.

6. Samuel Johnson, *Letters*, vol. 1 (Hyde Edition), ed. Bruce Redford (Princeton, N.J.: Princeton University Press, 1992–94), 120; James Boswell, *The Principal Corrections and Additions to the First Edition of Mr. Boswell's Life of Johnson* (London: Dilly, 1793), 31; James Boswell, *Correspondence and Other Papers Relating to the 'Life of Johnson,'* ed. Marshall Waingrow (New York: McGraw-Hill, 1969), 327n10; James Boswell, *The Life of Samuel Johnson LL.D. with Marginal Comments and Markings from Two Copies Annotated by Hester Lynch Thrale Piozzi*, 3 vols., ed. E. G. Fletcher (London: Limited Editions Club, 1938).

7. Samuel Taylor Coleridge, *Literary Remains*, vols. 1–4, ed. H. N. Coleridge (London: Pickering, 1836–39).

8. Johnson, *Johnson on Shakespeare*, vol. 1, 111.

Spoken, Written, Incarnate
Ontologies of Textuality
in Classical Rabbinic Judaism

MARTIN S. JAFFEE

Students of culture are recovering these days from a recent addiction to global theories about "orality" and "literacy" as essential modes of cultural being. Whereas literary or ethnographic studies once assumed a nearly ontological gulf dividing cultures of the "spoken word" from those of "the book," those who have entered the discussion in the past decade or so regarding the Great Divide have become accustomed to working with more supple, sociologically grounded models for understanding the implications of oral and literate forms of cultural transmission.[1]

The hasty retreat from a misplaced ontologization of orality and literacy has, however, missed an important point: the academy's enthusiasm for positing a vast gulf between two hypostasized cultural forms was not entirely wrongheaded. The plausibility of the ontological dichotomization of orality and literacy among culture theorists is grounded, after all, in the empirical availability of cultures that posit precisely such a distinction. Scholars of orality and literacy merely missed what should have been obvious. Academic socialization, dependent as it is upon the transmission of tradition in sophisticated oral and written registers,[2] is itself a form of the very discursive dualism it hoped to cast in ontological terms. In this way, academic theory committed an elementary error—it uncritically replicated, in its own interpretive discourse, the data it sought to theorize, thus mistaking a contingent historical structure for a universal ontological one.

This essay attempts to save ontological thinking about orality and literacy while avoiding the error of what might be termed "misplaced ontologization." Its primary contribution is to insist that we study the ontologization of the written and spoken word as historically and culturally specific discourses without ethnocentrically projecting our results onto a global anthropological screen. The key is to root ontological reflection upon orality and literacy as deeply as possible in the social structures and communicative systems that sustain these dichotomies in the first place.

Accordingly, I explore here some ontological dimensions of the written and spoken word in early Rabbinic Judaism (from about the third to the sixth centuries C.E.).[3] At the center of my interest stands the common Rabbinic jurisprudential distinction between written revelation of law from Sinai (scripture) and orally transmitted legal tradition from sages (Rabbinic teaching).[4] This conception of the dual sources of Torah, I suggest, extended beyond a theory of how the two forms of knowledge were transmitted and taught. It was more than a theory of legal or theological sources. The distinction established as well a hierarchical distribution of ontological potency among the diverse textual embodiments of the tradition. Three principal types of such embodiments will concern us here: the written scroll of Mosaic Torah, the orally performed text of Rabbinic teaching, and the person of the Rabbinic sage. Each embodiment of Torah was distinguished from the others not only by the medium in which the text was transmitted and by the skills required for decoding its message but also by the fact that each textual medium enjoyed its own distinct place in a larger conception of Torah as the ontological foundation of the world.

The Puzzle of the Torah-Text in Rabbinic Culture

There is, in one respect, of course, no news in the announcement that Torah in Rabbinic culture sustained an ontological weight. The classical Rabbinic literature of late antiquity is familiar with the notion that Torah per se serves as a principal structure of cosmic order.[5] Like many Hellenistic intellectual systems within and beyond the borders of Judaism, the Rabbinic system rooted the being of the cosmos in an ultimately linguistic conception of mind.[6] My point, however, is that the Torah's ontological significance extended as well to the media in which texts of Torah were embodied and transmitted.

I can name, however, no passage that explicitly defines an ontological grid for classifying the diverse linguistic and nonlinguistic forms in which the Torah is conveyed as comprehensible human communication. While medieval Jewish Neoplatonic ontologies richly reflect such schemata,[7] I doubt that Rabbinic sages would have recognized in their own tradition anything corresponding to an "ontology of the written and spoken word."[8] Nevertheless, I believe that my discussion, while framed in terms foreign to Rabbinic discourse, sufficiently intersects it to enable a useful fusion of hermeneutical horizons.

Most of the evidence drawn upon here is well known to students of Rabbinic literature. The Palestinian and Babylonian Talmuds, in particular, are rich in materials—of a theological, historiographic, and legal character—that portray the Rabbinic literary heritage as an exclusively oral tradition, an "oral Torah" transmitted in a series of face-to-face encounters between Rabbinic sages and their disciples, beginning with Moses' instructions to his associates.[9] Yet, as students of Rabbinic literature increasingly recognize, written texts of Rabbinic teachings existed from a very early period.[10] It is also clear, however, that only in the Middle Ages did such written texts come to be regarded as authoritative versions of the orally delivered texts they represented.[11] Whereas medieval Talmudic commentators compared manuscript readings in order to establish a correct text, their predecessors in late antiquity consulted colleagues who had memorized the text.[12]

This is a puzzle. Early Rabbinic circles produced written versions of key elements of the oral-traditional curriculum, and the written versions themselves served as mnemonic cues aiding the memorization of texts for citation in learned oral exchanges. But these written versions bore no textual authority over oral citations in the way that a written copy of the canonical scriptures would have controlled oral variations of its text. An ontology of the written and spoken Rabbinic text must begin in reflection upon this situation. What is ultimately at stake in the privileging of the voice over the page in early Rabbinic pedagogy?[13]

In my view, inquiry into the Rabbinic ontology of oral and written linguistic texts is enriched by reflection upon the people who incorporated such texts into themselves and came to be viewed as their human embodiments. As I shall argue, the distribution of oral and written texts of Rabbinic tradition among overlapping ontological registers is sustained by a particular paideic system, namely, a system of discipleship to men believed to image in their own being the Torah that, ontologically speaking, sustains the world. That is to say, Rabbinic distinctions between the written and spoken media of Torah are intimately connected to the social dominance of the Rabbinic sage as a symbolic representation of Torah.

Discipleship in the Communities of Oral Torah

It is well beyond my scope to isolate here the various threads of Greco-Roman discipleship practice woven into Rabbinic patterns of discipleship in the third century c.e. and thereafter. It is sufficient to remind ourselves that, as the Second Temple period drew to a close, the Judaic landscape was dotted with a variety of ideologically diverse subcultures, which, for all that, bore strikingly similar social-structural characteristics.

In another place I have tried to grasp this common feature with the term "intentional communities."[14] Groups such as the Alexandrian Therapeutae, the Yakhad of Qumran, the Pharisees, and the primitive Jesus-communities all appear to have been conversionist associations formed to pursue a collective transformative discipline under the guidance of persuasive teachers. Among such teachers, the name *Torah* did not simply refer to the books they interpreted or to the substance of their teaching; more important, they seemed to exude Torah from their very persons, so that it took form in the contours of a human life. In such men, a principle of being had become tangible to the senses for interpretation and emulation. Around such embodiments of truth disciples gathered, eager to draw, by proximity and imitation, from the fountain of Torah that flowed, from its source in the suprasensible, eternal world of Heaven, into the sublunar world of becoming.

The fall of the Temple in 70 c.e., lamented bitterly in liturgically transmitted memory, proved for some of these communities an insurmountable obstacle. For others it was an opportunity. The delay in the Temple's restoration created an institutional vacuum in the economy of Judaic religious life that these communities quickly filled. The Jesus-communities, to mention one example, found here an opportunity to expand their communal life beyond the Jewish nation. Surely the distinctive disciple tradition that we know as Rabbinic Judaism, and that came to know itself as the tradition of oral Torah, emerged into self-consciousness in this period as well.[15] While its particular roots in the Second Temple milieu are probably beyond clear identification, the Torah of the Rabbinic sages was, by the beginning of the third century c.e., well on the path toward what it would ultimately become by the end of the tenth: the Torah of virtually all who regarded themselves as Israel.

Not every male Jew, of course, could or would actually apprentice himself to a Rabbinic sage and take up the life of a disciple. Yet the life of discipleship to the sage had become the primary milieu for generating the traditions of domestic custom, liturgy, and theological imagination that most Mediterranean and Middle Eastern Jews would by the seventh or eighth century regard as their own. These traditions, framed in texts of various kinds, would become the substance of transformative knowledge[16] held out to disciples for their personal appropriation. But at the center of that transformative life was the intense scrutiny of the words and deeds of the living sage himself. Let us now explore some of its characteristic contours as they appeared in the classical period of Rabbinic discipleship, beginning from the third century. This is the setting in which the distinctive ontological valuations of various media for the transmission of Torah will emerge.

The Texts of Oral Torah in Context

The third century marked a dramatic pedagogical revolution in the shaping of Rabbinic discipleship as a transformative project. At the heart of that revolution lay a vast, comprehensive legal text whose very name suggests its significance. The name is Mishnah. Philologically rooted in a stem that means "to repeat" (*šnh*), Mishnah often bears in the earliest Rabbinic literature the semantic sense of "tradition memorized through repetition" rather than denoting the title of a legal compilation. According to Rabbinic historical memory, the particular recension of memorized tradition called "the Mishnah of Rabbi" was compiled in the academy of the central political leader of early third-century Palestinian Jewry, Rabbi Judah the Patriarch. With Rabbi's Mishnah, a conspectus of tradition common to all sages and disciples replaced the diversity of traditions that had earlier been linked to the personal authority of specific first- and second-century teachers. By the middle of the third century it had begun to supplant all other textual formations of Rabbinic tradition as the primary curriculum for training Rabbinic disciples.

It remains unclear whether Rabbi Judah the Patriarch himself produced a written document of the entire Mishnah.[17] Most contemporary scholars of the Rabbinic literature acknowledge that the written texts of the Mishnah that survive in medieval manuscripts are not simple transcriptions of texts composed in purely oral circumstances. Rather, the Mishnah shows many signs that writing was used in its composition.[18] The point, however, is that, whatever the manner of its textual composition and preservation, the Mishnah was intended to be studied and analyzed in an exclusively oral interchange between master and disciple. By the late third century, the oral setting in which the Torah of the Mishnah was taught came to define its contents as well. The Mishnah was regarded as the primary repository of oral Torah, and many of its traditions were claimed to originate in Sinaitic revelation supplementary to the written Torah of scripture.[19]

The terms "written Torah" and "oral Torah," it must be stressed, did not at first describe the media in which texts were composed or preserved. Rather, they described the modes of their public performance as literature. Each mode was designated by a formal term denoting the character of the text's public declamation. The written Torah was "read" (*qr´*), in the sense that the text was sung aloud from a scroll in the course of its study and exposition. The oral Torah, by contrast, was "repeated" (*šnh*)—quoted from memory, without recourse to the mnemonic crutch of a written text.[20]

Both Torahs, then, existed in writing, and both were transmitted in an oral declamation that commonly included comment on and exposition of the text. What needs to be understood, then, is the significance of referring to texts of scripture as "written Torah" (despite the oral-performative setting of the written text's presentation) and to texts of the Mishnah as "oral Torah" (despite the fact that they had been committed to scrolls or other sorts of written surfaces). We can approach this puzzle by focusing more closely upon the entire question of the nature of textuality in early Rabbinic culture. As we shall shortly see, there is more to the concept of text in Rabbinic discipleship communities—and thus more to the concept of oral Torah—than first meets the eye.

The Text of the Written Torah

In a scribal culture rich in textual possessions, the scrolls of scripture—and particularly those on which were inscribed the Five Scrolls of Moses—were subject to the most stringent rules of production and use. Its copies were produced in scrupulous conformity to precisely defined norms that ensured a textual stability preserved in antiquity only for works regarded as cultural treasures.[21] These norms, themselves deemed part of the received tradition of oral Torah, governed the preparation of the textual surface and inks, the shaping of the letters, the orthography of the words, and the paragraphing of the text.[22]

The scroll of written Torah produced under such discipline, of course, communicated linguistically. Read in public ceremonies as a written message originally transcribed by Moses (or a prophetic descendant) at divine dictation, it transmitted the content of the covenantal revelation preserved for Israel's instruction, edification, and censure. The communicative power of the scroll of written Torah, however, was not confined to its merits as law, evocative narrative, or epic poetry—for the scroll was also a cultic object. Ceremonially conveyed in a procession during the liturgical rite of the synagogue, the scroll communicated metalinguistically, marking the tangible presence of God and serving as a relic of the reality of covenantal revelation.[23]

The written Torah's communicative life as symbolic icon will interest us later, in another context. For the present, we focus on its character as a verbal utterance, for it is precisely as utterance that we encounter one other aspect of its cultural presence as a text. While the written Torah was undoubtedly read aloud, studied, and interpreted as a document, it was also—especially for disciples of the sages—a text that was carried in the memory. The written Torah was *written*, and the proper way to recite it for liturgical purposes was to read out the written text; but it was deployed in the training of the disciple primarily in the form of proof texts and testimonia that adorned the citations of Rabbinic homiletical or legal teaching. And such testimonia had to be culled from memory, not from manuscripts.

We cannot read the surviving Rabbinic literature at all without encountering the sages' stunning ability to summon apparently obscure scriptural texts as rhetorical testimonia to various points of Rabbinic law and theology. This mastery of the scriptural text testifies to a comprehensive project of memorization that yielded a scripture known backwards and forwards, inside out and upside down. Stories of sages who could write scrolls of written Torah from memory may be apocryphal,[24] but the mind-stopping display of scriptural erudition obvious in nearly any Rabbinic exegetical discourse on scripture reminds us that the sages knew their scripture with a physical intimacy reminiscent of the Hebrew double entendre regarding the word "knowledge" (da'at). Scripture was first and foremost known through a possession as intimate as the taste in one's mouth, encountered textually as a presence lodged in memory, and brought to expression in the tongue's speech. In this crucial sense, the written Torah was an oral as much as a written text, a possession within the body as much as a material object in the world.[25] With this in mind, let us turn to some reflections on that other body of memorized text, the text of oral Torah.

The Text of the Oral Torah

The written Torah lived a crucial part of its life in the Rabbinic community in the medium of memory and speech. Yet, as pointed out earlier, its material presence in a scroll enabled it to serve, even unread, as an icon of the entire Judaic complex of cultural memory. In a mirrorlike reversal of this pattern, the oral Torah of the sages, no less a possession of memory, lived out a long shadow-life as a loosely arranged, textually polymorphous collection of written sources with no discernible iconic significance. Let me elaborate upon this, because it is precisely here that I wish to make my contribution to grasping the ontological dimension of textuality in Rabbinic culture.

The question of most interest concerns the meaning of the well-known rabbinic ambivalence toward the written text of oral Torah. The classic expression of that ambivalence is found in an exegetical tradition, transmitted in both the Palestinian and Babylonian Talmuds, that proscribes the study of oral Torah from written versions. I reproduce the crucial sections here from one of the Babylonian recensions.[26] In this version, in which sages of the middle to late third century dominate, the ques-

tion of writing is generated by a report that one sage, Rav Dimi, wanted
to send by letter the correct wording of a Mishnaic passage to his colleague, Rav Yosef. The ensuing discussion speaks to our interests:

> 1. Now, even if he had found someone to write the letter, could he
> have sent it? For surely, said R. Abba b. R. Hiyya b. Abba, said R. Yoha-
> nan: Those who write down legal traditions *(halakhot)* are like those
> who burn the Torah. And anyone who studies from them receives no
> reward.
>
> 2. R. Judah b. Nahmani, Resh Laqish's Announcer, expounded: One
> Scriptural clause says, "Write for yourself these things" (Exod. 34:27);
> while another says, "But these things are orally transmitted"[27] (Exod.
> 34:27)—this tells you that things transmitted in memory you may not
> recite from writing, and things transmitted in writing you may not recite
> from memory.
>
> 3. And a Tradent of the School of R. Ishmael reported an oral tradi-
> tion: "Write for yourself these things"—these things (i.e., Biblical texts)
> you may write, but you may not write legal traditions.

Despite the contentions of many scholars committed to an exclusively
oral model of the transmission of early Rabbinic tradition, such passages
as this hardly constitute compelling evidence that Rabbinic texts were
primarily unwritten.

Quite to the contrary, the passage's condemnation of the use of written copies of oral Torah is predicated on the fact that they were widely
disseminated—even through the mail. Other passages, in the Palestinian
Talmud in particular, know of Rabbinic teachings preserved in notebooks
and on walls.[28] A seventh-century synagogue in Israel's Bet Shean valley, moreover, has a section of the Palestinian Talmud reproduced in
mosaic tile on its floor.[29]

So, to resume my argument, it is not the proscription of written texts
of oral Torah that must be explained; rather, it is the ambivalence about
their existence.[30] For our passage reflects what is everywhere assumed
in nearly all Talmudic portrayals of sages and disciples in study: that
is, despite the existence of written versions, the Mishnah and other texts
of oral Torah were learned in the course of a face-to-face oral interchange
involving the memorization, recitation, comparison, and critical analysis of memorized texts.

How do we interpret the preservation of written versions of oral Torah
within a scholarly community refusing to make use of them in the for-

mal education of its disciples? This paradox of Rabbinic pedagogy opens a window onto the Rabbinic understanding of the relation between the written and spoken text of Torah. Behind that window, framed squarely in the center, stands the sage as the comprehensive embodiment of oral Torah, the model of the transformed individual. He, too, was a text. We well understand the Rabbinic ontology of the written and spoken word once we see how he was read.

The Master as Living Text

I will not speak here of disciples, such as Rav Kahana, who hid beneath the conjugal beds of their masters in order to observe the way of Torah in the erotic arts.[31] Such narratives of the master-disciple relationship have been mined for all they are worth by gender studies, and I have no interest in violating my neighbor's border.[32] Nor can I possibly condense here all the ways in which Rabbinic narratives about the acts and words of holy men assume that the rabbinic master and the Torah were, at some profound level, aspects of each other.[33] But I would like briefly to reflect on two typical stories about masters. Each in its own way offers us a powerful image of the sage's embodied act as a text that the disciple must learn to read and, ultimately, incorporate into himself.

There is, for example, a well-known story about the legendary first-century sage Hillel's unquenchable thirst for knowledge:

Our Masters repeated an oral tradition:

A pauper, a rich person, and a wicked person come to their judgment. They say to the pauper: Why didn't you devote yourself to Torah? If he replies: I was poor, and swamped by the need to find food—they say to him: And were you poorer than Hillel?[34]

For they said of Hillel the Elder that each day he would labor and earn a half-dinar. Half of it he would give to the registrar of the collegium, and half went to support himself and his dependents. One time he was unable to earn anything, and the registrar of the collegium denied him entry. So he climbed up and sat against the opening of the skylight in order to hear the words of the Living God from the mouths of Shemaiah and Avtalion.

Now that day was a Sabbath Eve in the dead of winter, and snow fell upon him from Heaven. When the Morning Star rose, said Shemaiah to Avtalion: Avtalion, my brother, on most days the house is bright, but today it is dark—is it cloudy out? They glanced and saw the shape of a man in the skylight. They climbed up and found him covered in three cubits of snow. They brought him down, bathed him, anointed him, and sat him next to the fireplace. They said: This Hillel—for him it's worth desecrating the Sabbath![35]

This narrative's directness as a moral tale about love of Torah masks some puzzles. What, for example, would possess a registrar to expel a poor disciple from the warm circle of Torah for the lack of a quarter-dinar? How is it that Shemaiah and Avtalion could be so oblivious to the plight of their disciple so as to notice it only because he was block-ing their light? I cannot solve these puzzles. But I do think I can help point to this story's obvious power within the sages' community of discipleship.

The key, I think, lies in the simultaneous centrality and absence of the teaching of Shemaiah and Avtalion. Hillel, after all, ascends to the roof of the collegium only to hear an echo of the words of the Living God proceeding from the mouths of Shemaiah and Avtalion. But notice that we never learn what he heard—or if, through the thick skylight, he heard anything at all. The story's point as a transmission of Torah, in fact, has nothing to do with what Shemaiah and Avtalion have to say; rather, it is about what Hillel did.

The story's meaning, in fact, emerges in the way our attention is deflected from the words of Torah uttered by the sages to the embodi-ment of Torah represented by the disciple. What sinks into the imagi-nation of disciples who ponder this story is a lesson formed by a graphic image: the hunched silhouette of Hillel's body, a black hulk against the pale, snow-filtered light of a winter morning. The words of the Living God may have proceeded from the mouths of Hillel's teach-ers, but their meaning is embodied in his own frozen form of devotion. This is what a disciple is, this is what must be emulated. More impor-tant than the oral Torah Hillel failed to hear is the oral Torah he became by his desire to learn. It is this trait of Hillel as disciple that makes him a powerful example of a sage, for the sage is nothing but the perfection of discipleship in the form of perfect obedience to Torah.

A more prosaically narrated and certainly more obscure incident pro-vides a second example of the sage as a text to be interpreted, over and beyond the words he can formulate as teachings. It concerns the pecu-liar spy-mission of the early fourth-century Babylonian sage Rav Yitzhak b. Rav Yehudah:

Once Ula made a visit to Pumbedita. Said Rav Yehudah to Rav Yit-zhak, his son: Go and bring him a basket of fruit for the Sabbath, and make sure to watch how he makes havdalah, the concluding Sabbath benediction.

Rav Yitzhak didn't go. He sent Abaye instead. When Abaye returned, Rav Yitzhak asked: What did he do? Abaye replied: When he held the cup he said "Blessed is the One who divides between the holy and the common," and nothing more.

Rav Yitzhak came before his father, who asked him: So, what did he do? He replied: Well, actually, I didn't go, but I sent Abaye. And he told me that he said "Blessed is the One who divides between the holy and the common."

His father replied to Rav Yitzhak: Mister's arrogant self-importance has denied Mister the merit of repeating the tradition directly from his mouth![36]

Let us reflect upon this for a moment. A great master, Ula, comes to town. At precisely that moment, a question regarding the proper wording of the benediction of havdalah has plagued the scholars. All know that the master can answer the question. But nobody asks him. Is the proper text of havdalah a kind of trade secret, generations after the first-century debates of the disciples of Shammai and Hillel? In any event, Rav Yehudah—himself an acknowledged master of tradition—designs a clever ploy as a way of getting the answer from Ula without asking it. He sends his son on a mission that conceals, within a gesture of homage, a hidden agenda. The son, above such nuisances, in turn deputizes a younger disciple, Abaye, who dutifully brings the fruit. It is Abaye—ultimately to become one of the great sages of Babylonia—who brings back the report of what he has observed, the all-important formula for havdalah as Ula has performed it.

This story, spare in its telling, is rich in the glimpse it offers of the sage as a living text. Ula could have reported in a second his formula for making havdalah. But the tradition he might have transmitted orally was of lesser authority, in Rav Yehudah's opinion, than actually being in the physical presence of the master as he realized the tradition in an act. The oral Torah was not fully present in discursive language at all. Its fullness was most richly available only as Ula embodied Torah in the actual holding of the cup and the recitation of the benediction.

This is precisely why Rav Yehudah sent his son on the mission, and it accounts as well for his anger upon learning of Rav Yitzhak's own failure personally to fulfill it. What Abaye gained was what Rav Yitzhak might never possess—the actual glimpse of Torah embodied in the form of Ula bent over his havdalah, the benediction on his lips. Of course, the story of Ula's havdalah could and would be transmitted as the verbal text of oral Torah—here it is, 1500 years later, in the Talmud—but this text is not the whole text, and it was not the whole text even on the day of its formulation for transmission as a tradition.

The whole text was there to be read only by those attending Ula. And future readings of that text would depend entirely upon the disciples' success in transmuting Ula's wordless text into the language of tradition. The oral Torah read from the text of Ula's actions was, ultimately, reduced to verbal texts. These texts, on the page, were inert as oral Torah but capable of revival in the form of voiced narrative, informing the minds and the actions of a chain of disciples and masters.

Conclusions

Let me now draw together and assess the significance of these various observations about discipleship as the matrix of Rabbinic understandings of the spoken and written text of Torah. Classical Rabbinic Judaism recognized as Torah only two classes of texts. One, the text of the written Torah, represented the physical relic of revelation, the written code by which the structuring principle of the cosmos was reconfigured in linguistic signs. Each letter enjoyed its own unique power of signification within the closed code of verbal revelation. Each, therefore, was preserved inviolate according to the best efforts of professional copyists.

The second type of text, the word and deed of the sage, represented the plenitude of revelation in its existential concreteness. Its units of meaning were not encoded in linguistic symbols but rather in the integration of thought, speech, and act that displayed the incorporation of Torah in a lived life. The scroll of scripture was Torah transformed into the code of written human language; the Rabbinic sage was Torah transformed into an embodied form of human being. Accordingly, even the text of the written Torah fulfilled the telos of its being only when its code was lifted by the sage's voice off the written scroll and incorporated into the oral Torah of his own life.

Between these two sorts of ontologically rich texts of Torah—the code of the written Torah, and its teleological unfolding in the oral Torah of the sage's thought, word, and deed—existed a range of texts suffering various forms of diminished or derivative being. There were, for example, texts utterly devoid of ontological potency insofar as they were precluded from consideration as texts of Torah. Greek "books of Homerus" or "external works" of pseudoscripture excluded from the Rabbinic canon would have fallen into such an ontologically empty domain. Such texts could never embody the ontological fullness of Torah, for they originated in the created order of derived being rather than in the creative order in which all being had its source.

But what of the other manuscripts imprinted with the mnemonic traces of the sage's words, disembodied from the personal presence of those who had received and transmitted them from the mouths of their masters? What of the texts of oral Torah written down? Unlike the scroll of written Torah, the written rendering of oral Torah was not a holy object. No professional scribe produced it; no legal norms governed its production or ensured its sanctity. In this it was like a secular book. But, unlike the secular book, it had a relationship to Torah.

This relationship explains the unique ontological sphere occupied by the manuscript of oral Torah. The conceptual content of oral Torah might be confined to such a text, but the ontological fullness of oral Torah was elsewhere. Written representations of oral Torah differed from all other writings primarily in terms of what they might, in the proper circumstances, become. Originating as Torah, in a transmission of oral teaching to Moses on Sinai, the written texts of oral Torah were inert traces of that revelation—of mnemotechnical value only. These mnemonic traces of revelation could be restored to life as Torah only in the mouths of sages and disciples. That is, the written script of Mishnah and other renderings of sages' traditions were unique among all writings in that they had once been Torah, were not now Torah, but could again become Torah.

The texts of written Torah were Torah even unread, by virtue of the coded revelation preserved on their parchment. Common texts could never be Torah no matter how they were read, for they were of purely human origin. But the texts within which the mnemonic traces of oral Torah were preserved could be restored to existence as Torah even though, in written form, they were common books. The vehicle of this transformation was the voiced performance of the disciple or sage, who could summon the texts of oral Torah from the internalized, immaterial scroll of memory.

Herein lies the substantive correctness of the Talmud Yerushalmi's assertion that oral traditions imparted to Moses are somehow "imbedded in the Mishnah."[37] The metaphor of embeddedness is important. The scribal copy of the Mishnah was not itself oral Torah, for no writing could contain oral Torah. Yet the copy retained the unique capacity to become oral Torah. It became so in a distinctive twofold performance—the memorized delivery of the text in public acts of learning, and, even more crucially, in the actual discipline of a life in conformity with the norms of the text.[38]

This last point is crucial, for delivery in speech was only a part of the transformation of texts into oral Torah. In truth, oral Torah was never merely a collection of words on or off a page. In the discipleship communities of the sages, oral Torah was a form of tradition that overcame anything written or spoken. Grounded in speech, it nevertheless absorbed all discourse into something even more concrete. This, as I have explained, was nothing less than the living presence of the master, whose very bodily motions were read as wordless texts disclosing the essence of Torah. The sage, then, the person of the living master, is our last crucial text of Torah. And the code he embodied could be read only by one devoted to his personal service.

In this sense, words—written on surfaces, or uttered in learned discourse and formal performances of tradition—formed only one element in the composition and comprehension of texts of oral Torah. The completion of texts, their genuine mobilization as a communication of Torah, was deferred beyond the linguistic word itself to the embodiment of the text in the form of a human act. Discipleship was the process that enabled one to read, as texts, the highly coded behaviors of sages and, in turn, to compose texts with one's own life that others might themselves learn to read.

NOTES

The present essay abridges and slightly revises Martin S. Jaffee, "A Rabbinic Ontology of the Written and Spoken Word: On Discipleship, Transformative Knowledge, and the Living Texts of Oral Torah," *Journal of the American Academy of Religion* 65:3 (1997), 525–49. Readers may wish to consult 529–32 of that article for a detailed discussion of the sociocultural model of religious discipleship that informs my study of Rabbinic sources. Portions of this essay in earlier forms were prepared for a variety of public presentations. The basic model of discipleship informing the original study was worked out in connection with the University of Washington's Comparative Religion Colloquium on Discipleship and the Transmission of Transformative Knowledge (February 1995). The implications of this model for reading the texts of b. Yoma 35b and b. Pesah. 104b were presented as the Ben Zion and Baruch Bokser Memorial Lecture at the Jewish Theological Seminary (March 1996). An attempt to draw out the implicit ontology of Rabbinic textuality was occasioned by papers presented to the University of Washington Jewish Studies Colloquium (May 1966) and to the American Academy of Religion Consultation on the Comparative Study of "Hinduisms" and "Judaisms" (November 1996). I am grateful to the many students and colleagues whose comments at these various occasions helped me to clarify my thinking. The final version of this essay has benefited from the criticism of two generous colleagues: Professors Marc Bregman of Hebrew Union College–Jewish Institute of Religion (Jerusalem) and Steven Fraade of Yale University. I also wish to thank a treasured colleague at the University of Washington, Professor Raimonda Modiano, for offering me the opportunity to submit my work to the remarkable collection of scholars gathered for the conference that engendered the papers in this volume.

1. See, for example, John Miles Foley, *Immanent Art: From Structure to Meaning in Traditional Oral Epic* (Bloomington: Indiana University Press, 1991); John Miles Foley, *The Singer of Tales*

in Performance (Bloomington: Indiana University Press, 1995); William Graham, *Beyond the Written Word: Oral Aspects of Scripture in the History of Religion* (Cambridge: Cambridge University Press, 1987); Mary Carruthers, *The Book of Memory: A Study of Memory in Medieval Culture* (Cambridge: Cambridge University Press, 1990). Influential representatives of the theoretical tendency to hypostasize or ontologize orality and literacy are Jack Goody and Ian Watt, "The Consequences of Literacy," in Jack Goody, ed., *Literacy in Traditional Societies* (Cambridge: Cambridge University Press, 1968), 27–68, a groundbreaking anthropological essay; the hermeneutical thought of Walter Ong, *Orality and Literacy: The Technologizing of the Word* (London: Routledge, 1982); and the historical study of Eric Havelock, *The Muse Learns to Write: On Orality and Literacy from Antiquity to the Present* (New Haven, Conn.: Yale University Press, 1986). Key figures in criticizing the ontological model and in proposing alternate ways of theorizing the orality-literacy spectrum include Ruth Finnegan, *Literacy and Orality: Studies in the Technology of Communication* (Oxford: Blackwell Publishers, 1988); John Halverson, "Goody and the Implosion of the Literacy Thesis," *Man* 27:2 (1992), 301–17; and, to an extent, Goody himself, in Jack Goody, *The Interface between the Written and the Oral* (Cambridge: Cambridge University Press, 1987).

   2. Edward Shils, *Tradition* (Chicago: University of Chicago Press, 1981), 100–28.

   3. Because of the preliminary character of this study, I have treated as a single "Rabbinic culture" what is in fact a highly complex family of cultures in Palestine and Mesopotamia. The most useful survey of classical Palestinian (in fact, Galilean) Rabbinism is Catherine Hezser, *The Social Structure of the Rabbinic Movement in Roman Palestine* (Tuebingen: Mohr Siebeck, 1997). For Mesopotamia, see Jacob Neusner, *There We Sat Down: Talmudic Judaism in the Making* (Hoboken, N.J.: KTAV Publishing House, 1978), and Isaiah M. Gafni, *The Jews of Babylonia in the Talmudic Era: A Social and Cultural History* (Jerusalem: Zalman Shazar Center for Jewish History, 1990), 177–204 (in Hebrew). An instructive attempt at a synoptic comparison of the two communities is found in Richard Kalmin, *The Sage in Jewish Society of Late Antiquity* (London: Routledge, 1999). In light of the historical complexity of Rabbinic culture, I claim for my "ontology" no more than a heuristic model that illumines basic aspects of Rabbinic thought as canonized in the Palestinian and Babylonian Talmuds and that might enable more refined studies in the literature. In so doing, I hope to avoid the acontextualism of Jose Faur, a pioneering theorist of the ontological dimensions of Rabbinic textuality; see Faur's *Golden Doves with Silver Dots: Semiotics and Textuality in Rabbinic Tradition* (Bloomington: Indiana University Press, 1986), 84–113.

   4. This is thematized in two complementary ways in classical Rabbinic thought. In jurisprudence, distinctions between laws derived from scripture *(de´oraita)* and laws instituted by Rabbinic scholars *(derabbanan)* identify the sources of the law and the consequent authority of specific rules. In addition, there is the distinction between written Torah *(torah shebikhtav)* and oral Torah *(torah shebe´al peh)*. This latter distinction has no jurisprudential force. It applies primarily to the textual forms for the transmission of authoritative teaching of all sorts—legal, homiletical, and historical. For further discussion, see Martin S. Jaffee, "How Much Orality in Oral Torah? New Perspectives on the Composition and Transmission of Early Rabbinic Literature," *Shofar* 10 (1992), 53–72, especially 58–61. On the specific role of the idea of oral Torah as an ideological component of classical Rabbinic culture, see Shmuel Safrai, "Oral Tora," in Shmuel Safrai, ed., *The Literature of the Sages,* first part, *Oral Tora, Halakha, Mishna, Tosefta, Talmud, External Tractates* (Assen / Maastricht and Philadelphia: Van Gorcum and Fortress Press, 1987), 5–120; Jacob Neusner, "Defining Rabbinic Literature and Its Principal Parts," in Jacob Neusner, ed., *Judaism in Late Antiquity,* part I, *The Literary and Archaeological Sources* (Leiden: E. J. Brill, 1995), 117–72; Martin S. Jaffee, *Torah in the Mouth: Writing and Oral Tradition in Palestinian Judaism, 200 BCE–400 CE* (Oxford: Oxford University Press, 2001), 84–99.

   5. The most frequently cited example is from the beginning of Bereshit Rabbah, a fifth-century commentary on the book of Genesis (Ber. Rab. 1:1). There the Torah is portrayed as a primordially existing structure, analogous to an architectural plan, that God consults to create the world.

6. See Gabriele Boccaccini, "The Pre-existence of the Torah: A Commonplace in Second-Temple Judaism, or a Later Rabbinic Development?," *Hennoch* 17 (1995), 229–49.

7. Gershom Scholem, *On the Kabbalah and Its Symbolism* (New York: Schocken Books, 1969), 32–86; Daniel Matt, "The Mystic and the Mizwot," in Arthur Green, ed., *Jewish Spirituality from the Bible through The Middle Ages* (New York: Crossroad, 1986), 367–404; Pinchas Giller, *The Enlightened Will Shine: Symbolization and Theurgy in the Later Strata of the Zohar* (Albany: State University of New York Press, 1993), 59–79; Barbara A. Holdrege, *Veda and Torah: Transcending the Textuality of Scripture* (Albany: State University of New York Press, 1996), 131–212; Elliot R. Wolfson, "Inscribed Speech / Spoken Inscription: Kabbalistic Cosmology and the Overcoming of the Oral-Written Dichotomy," presented at the annual meeting of the American Academy of Religion / Society of Biblical Literature, 1996.

8. Despite the arguments of Moshe Idel, *Kabbalah: New Perspectives* (New Haven, Conn.: Yale University Press, 1988), 17–34, I hesitate to posit an esoteric line of oral transmission linking the medieval formulations to early Rabbinic traditions of late antiquity that remain unattested in the surviving literature.

9. For example, b. Erub. 54b.

10. Guenther Stemberger, *Introduction to the Talmud and Midrash,* 2nd ed. (Edinburgh: T. & T. Clark, 1996), 31–37.

11. The entire question of the nature of Rabbinic compilations in late antiquity, particularly the degree to which manuscript versions were viewed as closed or canonical "works," is hotly disputed. For different perspectives, see Jacob Neusner, *Canon and Connection: Intertextuality in Judaism* (Lanham, Md.: University Press of America, 1987), 15–92; Jacob Neusner, "Defining Rabbinic Literature and Its Principal Parts"; Peter Schaefer, "Research into Rabbinic Literature: An Attempt to Define the Status Quaestionis," *Journal of Jewish Studies* 37 (1986), 139–52; Chaim Milikowsky, "The Status Quaestionis of Research in Rabbinic Literature," *Journal of Jewish Studies* 39 (1988), 201–11; Yaakov Elman, *Authority and Tradition: Toseftan Baraitot in Talmudic Babylonia* (Hoboken, N.J.: KTAV Publishing House, 1994), 1–46; Philip S. Alexander, "Textual Criticism and Rabbinic Literature: The Case of the Targum of the Song of Songs," *Bulletin of the John Rylands Library of Manchester* 75 (1993), 159–73; Martin S. Jaffee, "Oral Tradition and the Writings of Rabbinic Oral Torah," *Oral Tradition* 14 (1999), 3–32.

12. Saul Lieberman, *Hellenism in Jewish Palestine* (New York: Jewish Theological Seminary of America, 1950), 88–90.

13. In framing matters in this way, I acknowledge my debt to the important and ongoing work of Werner Kelber. See Werner Kelber, *The Oral and the Written Gospel: The Hermeneutics of Speaking and Writing in the Synoptic Tradition, Mark, Paul, and Q* (Philadelphia: Fortress Press, 1983); Werner Kelber, "Jesus and Tradition: Words in Time, Words in Space," in Joanna Dewey, ed., *Semeia 65: Orality and Textuality in Early Christian Literature* (Atlanta: Scholars Press, 1995), 139–68; Werner Kelber, "Modalities of Communication, Cognition, and Physiology of Perception: Orality, Rhetoric, and Scribality," in Dewey, ed., *Semeia 65: Orality and Textuality in Early Christian Literature,* 193–216.

14. See Martin S. Jaffee, *Early Judaism: Religious Worlds of the First Judaic Millennium* (Upper Saddle River, N.J.: Prentice Hall, 1997), 133–63. See also Steven Mason, "Philosophia as a Group-Designation in Graeco-Roman Society, Judaism, and Early Christianity" (1990; available at ftp://ftp.lehigh.edu/pub/listserv/ioudaios-l/Articles/smphilos). Such communities appear to have had much in common with various sorts of Greco-Roman "voluntary associations" characterized by restrictive membership rules, cultic activity, and table-fellowship. For an introduction to contemporary studies of this phenomenon and its connection to Judaism in late antiquity, see John S. Kloppenborg and Stephen G. Wilson, eds., *Voluntary Associations in the Graeco-Roman World* (London: Routledge, 1996).

15. Jacob Neusner, "The Formation of Rabbinic Judaism: Yavneh (Jamnia) from A.D. 70–100," in Wolfgang Haase, ed., *Aufstieg und Niedergang der Roemischen Welt,* part II, vol. 19.2 (Berlin and New York: Walter de Gruyter, 1979), 3–42; Shaye J. D. Cohen, "The Significance

of Yavneh: Pharisees, Rabbis, and the End of Jewish Sectarianism," *Hebrew Union College Annual* 55 (1984), 27–53.

16. See Jaffee, *Early Judaism*, 213–43, for my own understanding of this term in the context of early Judaism. Essentially, what I have in mind is knowledge derived from emulation of a sage's own example and teaching. Distinguished from the discursive knowledge gained from books, transformative knowledge works an ontological change in the knower. The transformation is commonly associated with an enhanced ability to participate in transmundane or transhistorical realities.

17. Stemberger, *Introduction to the Talmud and Midrash*, 133–40; Lieberman, *Hellenism in Jewish Palestine*, 83–99; Jacob Neusner, *Introduction to Rabbinic Literature* (New York: Doubleday, 1994), 21–25.

18. Martin S. Jaffee, "Writing and Rabbinic Oral Tradition: On Mishnaic Narrative, Lists, and Mnemonics," *Journal of Jewish Thought and Philosophy* 4 (1994), 123–46.

19. It is important to distinguish between oral tradition in Rabbinic Judaism and oral Torah. The former is a sociocultural form to which many forms of early Judaism may have contributed, and from which all drew. The latter is a distinctively Rabbinic ideological construction of the history and significance of oral learning, rooted in an ongoing tradition of jurisprudence and theology. I assume that Rabbinic oral tradition has preserved certain pre-Rabbinic Judaic traditions and that for this reason it can transmit very old material. Yet the ideological construction of oral Torah is probably a late-third-century development. See the discussions in Neusner, "The Formation of Rabbinic Judaism"; David Kraemer, "On the Reliability of Attributions in the Babylonian Talmud," *Hebrew Union College Annual* 60 (1989), 175–90; and Jaffee, *Torah in the Mouth*.

20. Birger Gerhardsson, *Memory and Manuscript: Oral Tradition and Written Transmission in Rabbinic Judaism and Early Christianity*, trans. Eric Sharpe (Lund and Copenhagen: Gleerup and Munksgaard, 1961), 28–29.

21. Lieberman, *Hellenism in Jewish Palestine*, 20–46; Wilfred Cantwell Smith, *What Is Scripture? A Comparative Approach* (Minneapolis: Fortress Press, 1993), 45–64.

22. Meir Bar-Ilan, "Scribes and Books in the Late Second Commonwealth and Rabbinic Periods," in Martin Jan Mulder, ed., *Mikra: Text, Translation, Reading, and Interpretation of the Hebrew Bible in Ancient Judaism and Early Christianity* (Assen / Maastricht and Philadelphia: Van Gorcum and Fortress Press, 1988), 21–38.

23. William Scott Green, "Romancing the Tome: Rabbinic Hermeneutics and the Theory of Literature," in Charles E. Winquist, ed., *Semeia 40: Text and Textuality* (Decatur, Ga.: Scholars Press, 1987), 147–68; Holdrege, *Veda and Torah*, 359–83.

24. For example, t. Meg. 2:5, y. Meg. 4:1, 74d, b. Meg. 18b.

25. See Paul Morris, "The Embodied Text: Covenant and Torah," *Religion* 20 (1990), 77–87. Cf. Carruthers, *The Book of Memory*, 189–220.

26. See b. Tem. 14b: cf b. Git. 60b; y. Pe'a 2:6, 17a and parallels.

27. Literally "in accordance with these words." The exegesis depends upon word play homologizing the biblical Hebrew *'al pi* ("in accordance with," literally "by the mouth of") to the Rabbinic phrase *'al peh* ("oral," "memorized").

28. See y. Ma'as. 2:4, 49d, y. Kil.1:1, 27a. See also Jaffee, *Torah in the Mouth*.

29. Jacob Sussman, "The Inscription in the Synagogue at Rehob," in Lee I. Levine, ed., *Ancient Synagogues Revealed* (Detroit: Wayne State University Press, 1982), 146–51.

30. Cf. Loveday C. A. Alexander, "The Living Voice: Scepticism Towards the Written Word in Early Christian and in Graeco-Roman Texts," in D. J. A. Clines, S. E. Fowl, and S. E. Porter, eds., *The Bible in Three Dimensions: Essays in Celebration of Forty Years of Biblical Studies in the University of Sheffield* (Sheffield: JSOT Press, 1990), 221–47.

31. For example, b. Ber. 62a.

32. See Daniel Boyarin, *Carnal Israel: Reading Sex in Talmudic Culture* (Berkeley: University of California Press, 1993); Michael Satlow, *Tasting the Dish: Rabbinic Rhetorics of Sexuality* (Atlanta: Scholars Press, 1995).

33. Neusner, *Introduction to Rabbinic Literature,* 566–68.

34. Elsewhere in classical Rabbinic literature, a strikingly similar formulation introduces a story regarding the Torah education of the great early-second-century c.e. sage Rabbi Aqiva. See Judah Goldin, *The Fathers According to Rabbi Nathan* (New Haven, Conn.: Yale University Press, 1983), 42, translating Avot d´Rabbi Natan, version A:6 / 15.

35. See b. Yoma 35b.

36. See b. Pesah. 104b.

37. See y. Pe´a 2:6, 17a; Jaffee, *Torah in the Mouth,* 125–56.

38. Steven Fraade, *From Tradition to Commentary: Torah and Its Interpretation in the Midrash Sifre to Deuteronomy* (Albany: State University of New York Press, 1991), 69–75.

Textualization as Mediation
The Case of Traditional Oral Epic

JOHN MILES FOLEY

The question of the textualization of oral epic addresses an important and complex area that has long received inadequate attention in research and scholarship. This "benign neglect" perhaps stems more from cultural predispositions about verbal art, technologies of communication, and our own deeply embedded dependence on texts than from any purposeful avoidance of the subject. Until relatively recently, investigators have tended to overlook just *how* an oral epic reached textual form, preferring to deal with it as a ready-made object that could be analyzed with available tools. Analysis and interpretation often began after the transcription was made, after the multidimensional performance was reduced to a form that scholarly culture found more manageable.[1] All of these assumptions mask an important part of the story.

In this essay I hope to tell at least one version of the tale that lies behind oral epics–become–books. Specifically, I am interested in the cultural matrices from which these works of art emerge, the roles of the informants and folklorists who contributed to the making of these works, the intersemiotic translation of performance to manuscript and print, and the myriad other issues that are submerged when we interpose our concepts of object and stasis between an oral epic and its bookbound reception.[2]

I propose to tell the tale of how South Slavic oral epic was textualized by the two major teams of investigators involved in its collection: first, the nineteenth-century Serbian scholar Vuk Karadžić and his network of amanuenses; and, second, the twentieth-century North American scholars Milman Parry and Albert Lord, with the important participation of their native assistant Nikola Vujnović, who was himself an epic singer.[3] In many ways, both groups were informed and limited by the historical periods in which they made their collections and by the theoretical predispositions that they brought to the enterprise of recording oral epic. Toward the end of the discussion, I will hazard a few comparative remarks that bear on two traditional epics surviving only in manuscript form—the Homeric poems and the Anglo-Saxon *Beowulf*—and whose textualization must therefore be reconstructed hypothetically.

Organizationally, I proceed by asking three basic questions: What gets recorded? What gets published? What gets received? In simplest terms, what gets recorded is a performance, but the nature of that performance necessarily varies from one instance to another, one subgenre to another, one investigator to another, and so forth. The Karadžić and Parry-Lord projects illustrate quite differently how various kinds of choices affect the outcome of the recording process. What gets published is usually a print transcription of a performance, with or without cues prompting the readership to appreciate other dimensions of the event, but not all transcriptions are created equal. The South Slavic case shows how unequal they can be, and how predispositions play a large part in what we might call "textual parallax." What gets received is essentially the reader's "take" on what he or she is offered in the published transcription. This part of the process cannot be detached from textualization because the very act of textualization always makes assumptions about the readership. Karadžić was creating a resource for a target audience, and so were Parry and Lord; the mere fact that these were manifestly different resources proves the importance of the projected audience's role in converting oral epic to a book.

Vuk Stefanović Karadžić

What Gets Recorded

Vuk Karadžić was, like all other collectors, a citizen of his time and place in history. A groundbreaking ethnographer and eminent lexicographer as well as what would be called a folklorist, he responded to the nineteenth-century European search for ethnic roots with benchmark accomplishments in many different fields. In addition to his massive Serbian dictionary,[4] which included words from the epic and nonepic oral traditions of Serbia that were found nowhere else in contemporary discourse, he published numerous volumes and essays on the customs and rituals of his people, and, not least, modified the Latin-based and Cyrillic alphabets to make them both entirely phonetic. But the accomplishment that was to have the longest-term importance for the widest cross-section of people (and this includes an international scholarly constituency as well as generations of schoolchildren) was his unparalleled collection of Serbian folk songs, *Srpske narodne pjesme.*[5]

Although he began publishing narratives from oral tradition as early as 1814, Karadžić's standard edition of Serbian folk songs in four volumes appeared between 1841 and 1862. Volumes 5 through 9 were posthumous publications, and four additional volumes, entirely unauthorized by Karadžić himself, were culled from his unpublished manuscript remains by Živomir Mladenović and Vladan Nedić and were issued in 1973–74.[6] These anthologies run the gamut from lyric to epic, and within epic from medieval to modern. For our purposes, the most significant part of the collection is volume 2 in the original standard series, in which, its editor specifies, "are the oldest heroic songs."[7]

For this as for other volumes, Karadžić employed two strategies for collection, both of which were informed by his personal history. For not only did he come from a family of traditional poets himself, but, having grown up in a village environment, he was aware of the realia of fieldwork: the morphology of performance, the need to deal with informants on an equal basis, and so forth. Early in his career he recorded most of the performances himself—by dictation, of course—and from many different poets. I say "poets" and not "singers" because in the Christian tradition of the early and middle nineteenth century many bards did not use the *gusle, tambura,* or other musical accompaniment, and apparently they recited rather than sang their poetry. As Karadžić grew older and his project expanded and matured, he more and more made use of a countrywide network of amanuenses who sent him transcriptions they had made, presumably but not absolutely dependably from oral performances. Even in this later period, however, he continued to deal personally with those poets he valued most highly, such as Old Man Milija and especially Tešan Podrugović, the highwayman *(hajduk)* who recited many of Karadžić's most memorable poems.

What got recorded, then, was an enormous, geographically diverse sample of what has come to be known in the native scholarship as the "classic Serbian literature" of its time. What is most significant, it was first and foremost a collection of *texts.* It had been written down by many different hands, and largely without the kind of context we modern investigators require. Because the focus was on unearthing a text that could be portrayed as an ethnic heritage, and also because this was, after all, the mid-nineteenth century, very little attention was paid to those process-oriented dimensions that distinguish an oral traditional performance from a literary text. In fact, one could fairly describe the act of collection as the initial step in translating an oral tradition into a text, with all of the linguistic and political complexities entailed in such a remaking.

One additional dimension of what got recorded should be emphasized. Karadžić's quarry was the Christian epic tradition of the Serbs, a type of narrative that many scholars of western European and Asian epics might choose to deny admission to the genre. The poems from this tradition are seldom more than three to four hundred decasyllabic lines in length, and, although they may constitute essentially the same story as a Moslem South Slavic epic of two thousand lines or more, still lack the elaborate descriptions of people, places, and events that we associate with the term and category "epic." Nevertheless, Serbian scholars have always treated these narratives as epic, and they do represent the most extensive and developed form within their ethnic orbit. We may add one further note in passing. While the portrayal of any work from oral tradition as a separate, freestanding item is inherently misleading in that it epitomizes the instance at the expense of the tradition, the case of the South Slavic Christian epics is especially problematic. Individual poems require a very substantial background to be merely intelligible, and the brief Christian narratives leave a great many gaps for the uninitiated reader. We would do better to think of Karadžić's poems as parts of a cycle—a strategy that, as we shall see, he adopted himself, if unconsciously or at least tacitly.

What Gets Published

From the many texts in his possession, both those he wrote down himself and those submitted via his network of collectors, Karadžić selected those that he thought would best represent the Serbian tradition. The first cut was made simply on the grounds of perceived quality. Karadžić included in his notes to the standard edition and elsewhere a realistic appraisal of his personal archive—a fair number of texts were confused or otherwise flawed, many were mediocre, and a relatively small group he considered up to the demands of his program—to reflect the precious ethnic heritage of Serbian poetry he had heard since he was a child. Let me add that this procedure of gross selection, based on qualitative evaluation, may have been prescriptive by our modern standards; nevertheless, it is also refreshing in another respect, namely, that Karadžić was willing to accept the fact that South Slavic oral poetry—like any other contemporary poetry, for example—was inevitably uneven. Some performance texts were poor, others average, and a few outstanding.

The second stage of selection was the much-discussed matter of Karadžić's editing, often compared, unfortunately, to the outright rewriting undertaken by the Grimms or some of the other nineteenth-century collectors and editors. Within his own period, in fact, Karadžić was criticized for his perceived "failure" to sufficiently edit the texts he published, to bring them into line—a reaction that serves as a good index of what the assumed editorial policy really was. Since that time, the tendency has usually been to overestimate the extent to which, probably under the influence of foreign exemplars, he interfered in the texts he wrote down or received.

Discovering the true story on this score is no easy task, since Karadžić followed the practice of destroying fair copies of texts as soon as they were sent to the publisher. The result is that the Archive of the Serbian Academy of Sciences holds very few manuscripts of the poems that appear in the second of his original, personally supervised volumes (the one containing "the oldest heroic songs"). The only survivors of his policy, then, are those poems that by chance occupied the other side of a text folio not selected for publication. I have personally examined these exceptional manuscripts in the academy archive and must report that I disagree with Mladenović and Duncan Wilson that Karadžić's editing was heavy, frequent, and noteworthy.[8] In fact, the editor interferes only seldom, and then very lightly and expertly. Specifically, he averages an added or substituted hemistich about every seventy-five lines, and a minor adjustment for dialect or incomplete syntax about every thirty to forty lines. These changes, along with orthographical corrections, address inconsistencies that may have stemmed from the process of recording via dictation: certainly the spelling and minor errors fall into that category, and many of the larger ones may as well. To impute absolute accuracy to the original transcription process would be naive even for a modern-day amanuensis; with a transcriber who may speak a different dialect, and who may know a different version of the poem being performed, the enterprise gains in complexity. (We shall see evidence of this in the case of Parry and Lord's assistant and transcriber, Nikola Vujnović.)

Two more aspects deserve mention in answering the question of what got published. One is the matter of the editor's handling of variant versions of the same poem. On this score, Karadžić's customary practice was to print only what he considered the finest version of a given tale, the one he judged the most finished poem. The sole exception to this rule was the occasional second, or even third, version of a particular narrative, labeled "Opet to isto" ("Again the same") and placed in sequence immediately after the initial text. It appears, although to my knowledge Karadžić never articulated it as a policy, that he included alternate versions only if they satisfied two conditions: they had to meet his general criteria for quality in their own right, and they had to offer his reader a significant variation of some sort (in overall story pattern or some smaller narrative action). These rare windows into the morphology of the Christian oral epic in nineteenth-century Serbia—rare because Karadžić was committed to the production of texts and a virtually literary heritage that would help his countrymen stand shoulder to shoulder with other European peoples—can be supplemented by perusal of his posthumous volumes, and especially by consultation of those many alternate versions he chose not to publish (as preserved in the Mladenović-Nedić edition of his manuscript legacy).[9]

Last on our list of what got published is Karadžić's actual configuration of his anthologies. In the second volume of his original standard collection he did not simply print the choicest available bits of the tradition, leaving each of them to make its own artistic case as a singular poetic creation. Rather, he provided an organic kind of structure to the overall presentation, organizing and sequencing according to groups and lineages of principal characters and interrelationships among semihistorical and highly mythologized events. Two examples of this textual strategy are the grouping of the stories surrounding the Battle of Kosovo in 1389 (the defining moment for Serbian heroism and identity vis-à-vis the Ottoman Empire), and the tales of the redoubtable Prince Marko (or Kraljević Marko), the mostly legendary figure who served the Turks as a forced mercenary and who took every opportunity to outwit his oppressors. In speaking of the narratives that collectively present Kosovo and Marko in volume 2, we would do better to recognize them as *cycles* of epics, with each (detached) poem incomplete in itself but contributing meaningfully to a highly resonant group.[10] By molding these individual poems into a cycle, Karadžić was in effect imitating the traditional process from which they derived, a process that never isolates but always contextualizes the singular in the plural, the one performance in the network of the epic tradition.[11] Although it was an artificial, facsimile enterprise, the creation of cycles in his anthology revealed Karadžić's own personal acquaintance with South Slavic epic as an ongoing presence and tradition that cannot be reduced to a sampler of individual items.

What Gets Received

In the interest of saving enough space to do some justice to Parry and Lord and the Moslem tradition, let me give short shrift here to the important question of what gets received. Elsewhere I have written of how traditional structures imply *traditional referentiality*, how composition implies and drives reception, how the "signs" of an oral epic open onto broad vistas of idiomatic meaning that, strictly speaking, are not a part of the literal performance or text. Using a homemade proverb—"Oral traditions work like languages, only more so"—I have tried to understand the depth and richness of the coding inherent in the special languages of oral tradition, especially but not exclusively in epic.[12]

Against that background it becomes very obvious that the history and methods involved in the textualization of oral epic are absolutely crucial to the process of reception. Editors of texts that derive from centuries of entrenched literary criticism explain that *any* act of edition is also necessarily an act of interpretation, that there is no such thing as "neutral" editing. How much truer is this for the oral or oral-derived epic performance, whose signals must undergo a profound semiotic translation even to appear in the "finished product" of the epic-as-book? Without further discussion, then, let us simply take note of the determinative role of the real and projected audience(s), or readership(s), for that product, as well as of the fact that making an experience into a text has a profound effect on what gets received.

Of course, in closer focus one can never separate traditional oral poetry from issues of identity and ideology, especially in the case of Serbia over the last two centuries. The reception of Karadžić's collections as the "classic Serbian literature" of its time arose from a combination of factors. First and most generally, in the nineteenth century many European nations embarked on a search for their ethnic roots by delving into their folklore and oral traditions; in this sense, Karadžić's collections and publications paralleled those of the Grimms in Germany, for example. Nor should we discount the longstanding identification that Serbs have felt with the epic hero Prince Marko, who in cleverly outwitting his Turkish oppressors has for hundreds of years served as a symbol of resistance and refusal to submit meekly to the Ottoman yoke. That function has been an important reason for the continuous popularity of songs about his exploits, whether as ongoing performances in the oral narrative tradition or as the collected, published, and received heritage of latter-day Serbs. Indeed, the close attachment between the songs and their many constituencies is mirrored even in the scholarly habit of referring to them unabashedly as *naše pesme* or *naša poezija* (our songs, our poetry).

More recently, this melding of oral tradition and ethnic nationalism has manifested itself in many fascinating and sometimes disturbing ways. Although modern citizens of Serbia seldom hear real-life performances these days, especially in urban areas, they have had repeated experience of Karadžić's poems from a young age throughout the school curriculum. Long before university courses in literature and folklore expose them to such material as a subject for higher-level study, elementary-school children are reading specially edited versions of *naše pesme*.[13] The songs are in their ears very early, and the fact that even the person in the street

has some familiarity with the tales collected by "our Vuk" has important implications. In addition to the fact that the media portrayed Tito's
death in May 1980 as the apotheosis of a folk-epic hero, complete with
verses and epithets drawn from the oral tradition, we may also point to
the cycle of traditional songs about Kosovo as an ongoing and dynamic
expression of Serbian proprietary interest in that region since before the
epochal battle fought (and gloriously lost) against the Turks in 1389.[14]
Over the last few years, the Milošević regime harnessed this nationalistic and ethnic sentiment—long incubated in the oral tradition and pro-
mulgated in print as a kind of cultural keepsake—to stoke the fires of
ethnic separatism and advance its political agenda.[15] One can safely
observe that Karadžić's tales, collected and originally published with a
certain kind of audience and purpose in mind, have experienced a series
of quite diverse receptions since their initial appearance in print about
150 years ago.

Milman Parry and Albert Lord

What Gets Recorded

The very first aspect that must be addressed herein is the question of
Parry's and Lord's core motivation in mounting their ambitious expedition to the former Yugoslavia for the purpose of collecting oral epic
from the South Slavs.[16] Why did they spend the better part of two years
in the hinterlands of Bosnia and Hercegovina, acoustically recording
more than seven hundred thousand decasyllabic lines on aluminum
disks—a "half-ton of epic," as Albert Lord characterized their yield on
more than one occasion? Why did they take the trouble to have a
Connecticut-based electronics firm design and produce a state-of-the-
art device that allowed inscription of those disks, and what was the impetus behind their hiring a native assistant to accompany them during
fieldwork, the same person who would later spend more than a year in
Cambridge, Massachusetts, writing out transcriptions of the audio
records?

We will be unfair to their methodology—both its numerous positive
aspects and its inevitable shortcomings—if we do not quote Parry's
own stipulation that "it was least of all for the material itself" that he
and Lord worked so arduously and creatively in the field.[17] Parry was
always primarily a classicist, and he was interested in one thing: a living analogy for the manuscript poems of Homer, a laboratory proof of
the phenomenon of composition-in-performance that he had posited
on the basis of the long-silent *Iliad* and *Odyssey* texts. If the formulaic
method he had so carefully demonstrated in Homer could also be

shown to be the root compositional strategy in the oral epics from then-Yugoslavia, then the circle, he felt, would be closed. Homer the ancient Greek *aoidos* would be mirrored in the South Slavic *guslar*.

This policy and priority had far-reaching consequences. Most centrally, it meant that Parry and Lord limited their sample of oral traditions to the single subgenre that most closely resembled the Homeric poems—namely, Moslem epic. In imposing this restriction, they were in one sense very wise in that only Moslem epic compares closely to the *Iliad* and *Odyssey* in length, elaborateness, and so forth. (An undesirable by-product of this focus emerged in later years as many investigators uncritically transferred the specifics of this single subgenre of oral tradition to create a universal model for all genres—but thereon hangs another tale.) Thus, what got recorded as part of their fieldwork project also determined what didn't get recorded: the shorter Christian epic anthologized by Karadžić was largely avoided; lyric or women's songs were collected but assigned a different status; and many other forms were never considered. This is certainly not to say that Parry and Lord should have conducted their fieldwork differently; on the contrary, they kept assiduously to a predetermined plan, and their archive is the richer for it. I observe merely that any decision about genres and subgenres to be examined or avoided has implications, immediate and long-term, for subsequent edition and scholarship.

To their great credit, Parry and Lord sought not texts but *performances,* and this was a significant step beyond what any other collectors had done in the former Yugoslavia. And, in an important departure from Karadžić, they of course did all of the fieldwork and recorded all of the performances themselves, with the invaluable cooperation of Nikola Vujnović. Whenever possible, they used their unique apparatus to encode the *guslar's* full-speed performance acoustically; these recordings were referred to as "sung" because the poet employed vocal and instrumental melodies as defining dimensions of performance. Songs that were voiced without melodic accompaniment, yet still recorded on the aluminum disks, were called "recited," while those taken down in the age-old way, by an amanuensis listening to a composing bard, were termed "oral-dictated." Lord came to the conclusion that this last category of performance, which he viewed as an opportunity for the singer to show his best because of the relaxed pace of the song, was the finest, and it was these he chose to compare most closely to the supposedly oral-dictated texts of Homer, as he saw it. In my work with the *guslari* from the region of Stolac,[18] I have not found the oral-dictated text such a dependable benchmark. Some of the singers adapted well to what is for all of them a new method of proceeding—speaking a line and waiting for the amanuensis to catch up—but most did not. This may be one place where the tyranny of a general rule runs roughshod over the specifics of individual talent, preference, and adaptability.

Because Parry and Lord were recording actual performances, they ensured that those who later examined them would be working with the "real thing." Another pioneering aspect of their investigation was Parry's insistence on multiple versions by the same singer, by different singers, in different regions, and so on. In this way he hoped to show dramatically how the principle of *multiformity,* or *variation within limits,* informed alternate performances. The South Slavic material illustrated beyond a doubt that at least the *junačke pjesme* ("heroic songs")—and by analogy, as Parry saw it, the Homeric poems as well—followed this pattern of rule-governed variation rather than memorization or wholesale reinvention. Although it is not widely known, they even conceived of a test, nicknamed the *proba* by Nikola Vujnović, to procure more examples of alternate versions. Via this ruse they told the singer, perhaps thirty to seventy lines into the song, that it would be necessary (for whatever avowed reason) to start over, thus generating two, three, or more successive versions of a song opening. The songs from the Stolac district are full of such alternate beginnings, and they are very instructive.

Having already mentioned Nikola Vujnović a few times, I should add a few words about his crucial role in determining what got recorded by Parry and Lord. As a *guslar* himself, Vujnović communicated easily and productively with the singers they encountered. The tenor of the conversations makes it clear that he was both an insider and an outsider and that he used both identities to good advantage. That is, he was able to bring to the table an insider's knowledge of both the tradition and its performance, and at the same time he could urge the research agenda of his academic employers, framing their inquiries in digestible terms. He was willing and able to cajole and flatter, but also to criticize and hold his singer-colleagues to a tough standard in their responses. As every field-worker knows, the answers one receives seldom match the questions posed, at least not literally, given discrepancies in cultural and cognitive categories. But Vujnović deftly and consistently uncovered much of great interest during the conversations, whether Parry and Lord actually intended the particular results or not, and he was their mainstay in discovering a context for the performances they were in the process of recording.

A brief example will illustrate the value of Vujnović's contribution beyond the more general functions of obtaining singers' repertoires and coaching them to perform certain songs. For one thing, inspired by Parry, he was especially tenacious about determining the *guslar*'s notion of a *reč u pjesmi* (a "word in a song"), a much misunderstood concept. Perhaps surprisingly, the singers were often able to distinguish between our contemporary, print-oriented sense of "word" as an entry in the dictionary, on the one hand (a definition that lacked any real meaning for them), and a traditional phrase or scene or story pattern, on the other. Thus, within the everyday conversational register, Vujnović and Salko Morić, an epic bard from Stolac, were able to agree that "Salko," the singer's name, was a word. And yet Morić also insisted that, when he was singing epic, the tripartite phrase *u pjanoj mehani* ("in a drinking tavern") was a single "word." In fact, he and his bardic colleagues often responded to Vujnović's request for "a word" by identifying a traditional unit of utterance—as large as an entire performance, and seldom smaller than a whole decasyllabic line. The difference is something that, for example, G. S. Kirk, author of *The Songs of Homer,* and general editor of the more recent *Iliad* commentary, was unable to see: a difference in two registers, two "ways of speaking."[19] And Vujnović, the person most immediately in charge of what got recorded, either acoustically or via dictation, was fluent in both tongues.

What Gets Published

From the "half-ton of epic" recorded in 1933–35 and, to a lesser extent, from later trips in the 1950s, it was left to Lord to decide what would get published. One strategy would have been to present an anthology of what he considered the best performances from all over the country, with a few alternate versions—essentially the Karadžić approach. But Parry and Lord had collected over a series of geographical areas and had become convinced that the basic organization of the epic tradition was regional.[20] For this reason, Lord chose to publish as the first two volumes of *Serbo-Croatian Heroic Songs* (hereafter *SCHS*),[21] a carefully selected group of performances from the Novi Pazar district, featuring five singers, with different songs by the same *guslar* and alternate performances of the same song by the same singer. In this fashion he hoped to sketch the tradition surrounding any given performance by placing it in its natural context. With this initial step taken, he and David Bynum then went on, in volumes 3–6, to sample the district of Bijelo Polje, with the master bard Avdo Medjedović and his performances rivaling the *Iliad* and *Odyssey* in length and elaborateness, and in volume 14 to the region of Bihać, where the presentational form of epic, here accompanied by the *tambura* rather than the *gusle,* differs in some interesting respects. For my part, I am working toward original-language and translation volumes of performances from the Stolac area, a part of central Hercegovina that especially favors the Return Song, the story of the *Odyssey*.[22]

Lord's strategy for textual representation also differed significantly from Karadžić's. Instead of interfering occasionally between bard and reader, he aimed at printing precisely what the singer said, "errors" and all, within existing editorial conventions. Only in this way, Lord reasoned, could Slavic specialists appreciate a living oral epic tradition without textual distortion; only in this way could comparative scholarship, and especially the classical scholar, find the South Slavic epic a useful analogy, a parallel that could help fill in the necessarily fragmentary picture of Homer as an oral poet.[23] Of course, the nonverbal aspects of the *guslar*'s epic performance were, as in Karadžić's *Srpske narodne pjesme*, silently deleted; the consideration of the role of vocal and instrumental melody, with rare exceptions like Béla Bartók and, most recently, Stephen Erdely, was to remain largely an unstudied dimension.[24] But Lord's insistence on an absolutely "literal" transcription, reflecting the actual performance as well as this kind of transcription could, was certainly a major step forward in the study of South Slavic epic both in itself and as an analogy for other traditions. What got published was now much closer to what got recorded and, in turn, what got performed.

I have already mentioned that the publication plan of *SCHS* called for proceeding region by region through the six major districts in which Parry and Lord collected, beginning with Novi Pazar and Bijelo Polje and continuing with Bihać in the initial volumes. Within each of these areas the internal strategy was to be the same: to present a selection of *guslari*, each with multiple instances of the same epic and, where possible, to include instances of the same epic sung by more than one singer. Like Karadžić, they sought to re-create a traditional context for the performances they were making available to a highly literate and very much "outside" world. Unlike Karadžić, however, they did so not by grouping song texts around historically and politically important figures or events but by attempting to simulate traditional multiformity, placing any one instance in its natural, resonant frame of reference.

The theory driving this plan for what got published was the *oral-formulaic theory*.[25] By presenting a digest of performances from a single area, with considerable overlap among singers and individual songs, Lord provided evidence for his tripartite scheme of compositional units: the formula (or traditional phrase), the theme (or typical scene), and the story pattern. And within its specified arena, the demonstration works very well. The South Slavic epic abounds with formulaic expressions based on the heroic decasyllable, including noun-epithet formulas as well as more loosely configured diction. Typical scenes are also very much in evidence: Arming the Hero, Assembly, Shouting in Prison, and Test of the Wife / Fiancée are only a few that appear in the Novi Pazar songs (the first two volumes of *SCHS*) and should also be quite familiar from the Homeric poems. And the large-scale dimension of story pattern informs all of the Parry-Lord songs in one way or another—the Wedding Song and Return Song are particularly prominent in their remarkable sample of Moslem epic.

The advantage in all three levels of structure is, of course, that the South Slavic epics actively and tangibly illustrate a traditional morphology that could in many cases only be hypothesized for the Homeric epics. Do you want to study the deployment of the noun-epithet formula *lički Mustajbeže* (Mustajbeg of the Lika) through an extensive sample of the phraseology? Then consider the literally hundreds of examples available in the work of numerous singers from one or more regions. Does the shape-shifting pattern of the Arming the Hero scene interest you? Then have a look at the dozens of heroes armed hundreds of times in related song texts. Are you embarked on the analysis of the *Odyssey* as a Return Song? Well, you have before you scores of Return Songs, with scores of different heroes in superficially different but generically linked situations, complete with wives and suitors and homecomings. Although the Parry Collection has not yet been used to full advantage, its unique comprehensiveness and depth allow for an unmatched perspective on one tradition of oral epic—both its characteristic structure and its characteristic art.

What Gets Received

Again, my comments in this third section will be brief, since relevant scholarship is available elsewhere.[26] One way to describe what gets received is to ask for whom the *SCHS* volumes were created. Unlike Karadžić, who was assembling a historical and political as well as a "literary" anthology for native speakers, many of whom already had considerable familiarity with the Christian epics, Parry and Lord strove to simulate an oral epic tradition almost exclusively for non-native speakers who had no experience of Moslem epic. With that in mind, we can appreciate how important the literal transcriptions in the original language are for Slavic specialists, as well as how significant the English translations are for comparatists. Both groups can profit from the regional constellation of performance texts in *SCHS*, with the resultant emphasis on the difference between an instance and a tradition of epic. And in the much understudied area of meaning and art, the Parry-Lord songs, both the published selections and, especially, the enormously larger archive of unpublished material, allow the serious evaluation of *traditional referentiality*, the ways in which the idiomatic implications of oral tradition inform each of its instances with a special force. This last aspect is the sense of the homemade proverb cited above: "Oral traditions work like languages, only more so."

Two Applications to Other Epic Traditions

Let me close with two brief examples of how the textualization of South Slavic oral epic can have a bearing on editorial and interpretive challenges in other, oral-derived epic traditions. The first example, having to do with Homeric epic, concerns a minor textual phenomenon with rather large implications for formulaic structure as a whole. The second, which has to do with a feature of the Anglo-Saxon epic *Beowulf*, concerns a fundamental and well-known property of that medieval work that the modern South Slavic analogy helps us to understand.

Textualization of Homer

One of Parry's earliest and most elegant insights was his explanation of metrical "flaws" in Homeric poetry as a function of formulaic combination and recombination. To take one general example, he argued that short-vowel hiatus—produced when one word ends with a short vowel and the next begins in the same way—resulted from the joining together of two pre-existent phrases in such a way that hiatus was created at the point of juncture. This phenomenon, Parry contended, stemmed from the fact that each phrase had an independent life of its own in the tradition. While in some cases a final or initial short vowel would be paired with a consonant, and no hiatus would occur, in other cases two vowels would be juxtaposed, and a metrical "flaw" would appear. Thus, according to Parry's diagnosis, the apparent necessity for a glottal stop between two short vowels very often marked a formulaic seam: one "part" ended there and another "part" began.

A look at the Parry-Lord versus the Karadžić song collections puts this phenomenon into a different—and, I think, clearer—perspective. Although Karadžić silently eliminated all traces of such sounds in his *Srpske narodne pjesme* texts, performed South Slavic epic makes generous use of hiatus bridges: consonants that, in performance, are inserted at points where hiatus would otherwise occur. These nonlexical phonemes smooth the aural pathway for a *guslar*, obviating the need for a glottal stop and allowing him to maintain vocalization (and sung melody) without interruption throughout the line—whatever combinations of phrases he might use. The singer Halil Bajgorić of the Stolac district, for example, has an impressive array of such continuant sounds: he can and does deploy [h], [j], [m], [n], and [w] to solve the inevitable phonetic problem generated by the exigencies of composition. These "extra" sounds are audible throughout the Parry-Lord acoustic records, of course, and as part of the policy of exact transcription they have also been maintained in the published textual record, though not at all consistently in the transcriptions made by Nikola Vujnović, himself a *guslar,* who perhaps did not "hear" them as part of the song or perhaps found it unnecessary or inappropriate to include what were strictly performance-based features in a textual record.

Indeed, the phenomenon of hiatus bridges makes one think carefully about the (transcribed) nu-moveable and (untranscribed) digamma in Homeric epic. Might these and other sounds also have participated in the ancient Greek poet's negotiation of short-vowel hiatus under analogous conditions? Might the interstices between Homer's formulas also have been smoothed—*in performance*—by such phonetic bridges rather than highlighted by the ragged breaks of (textually induced) hiatus per se? Audible analogies can point toward answers that reduction to a manuscript medium has silenced.

"Completeness" and Unity in Beowulf

Students and scholars alike have long been frustrated by what seems the incompleteness of the textual record of this unique Anglo-Saxon epic poem. So many moments, like the Fight at Finnsburh and the Heathobard episode, exist in parallel to but not within the main story. These events are mentioned only telegraphically, leaving present-day readers scurrying to the notes provided in Frederick Klaeber's standard edition or, better, to Adrien Bonjour's monograph on what he calls the digressions in *Beowulf,* written precisely to allay this difficulty.[27] And the difficulty is, of course, that we modern readers of the oral-derived epic text are not in on the tradition from which it springs. We simply do not know the background on which the poet depended for economical communication with the audience. While the poet could confidently cite a shorthand version of a given story, with the full expectation that the audience could expand it and make the connection to the main story, that strategy leaves the uninitiated outside the arena, struggling to make sense of what we perceive as partial exposition. This is a situation not confined to epics but common to most traditional works, to some degree: the very fact that the individual item emerges from a natural, idiomatic frame of reference makes interpretation more challenging for scholars of ballads, for instance, or of Native American tales, or even of the homelier genres from the former Yugoslavia, such as magical charms.[28]

The textualization of South Slavic epic illustrates the endemic importance of such a frame of reference, and of the varying need to simulate it for different readerships. Karadžić had much the easier task in that the audience he was addressing was likely to be broadly au courant with the background of *Srpske narodne pjesme,* particularly with the songs celebrating the Battle of Kosovo and Prince Marko. But Parry and Lord's *SCHS* project could not assume such a well-trained audience. Especially because we Western scholars are usually very narrowly trained, if at all, in the verbal art of eastern Europe, most of the information a *guslar* could take for granted within his tradition is simply not a part of his new audience's working knowledge. Not only does the new audience entirely lack fluency in the traditional way of speaking (as distinct from simple language competence), it is also wholly unfamiliar with what that idiom points toward. Who is Djerdjelez Alija? What does a Turkish hero's armor look like (especially the feathered headpiece)? What is the conventional role of women in Moslem epic? The *SCHS* audience is much in the same boat as the modern-day readership of *Beowulf,* needing extensive editorial apparatus and multiple songs and versions (or their equivalent) to gain even a glimpse of what Karadžić's readership already had available to them as a working interpretive "kit." In the present state of knowledge, we cannot ameliorate the situation beyond a certain point, since no real analogues to *Beowulf* have survived, but we can at least appreciate that the apparently "partial" nature of the text is not a paleographical or artistic blemish; rather, it demands another way of accessing background information. The "digressions" are symptomatic, not of a problematic text, but rather of the operation of traditional referentiality.

Conclusion

The textualization of South Slavic oral epic is a complex and fascinating area of inquiry, and I have had time to focus on only a limited number of issues here. Left aside were the myriad other collections and their common and idiosyncratic features. I especially regret not having the opportunity to treat the published anthology of Luka Marjanović,[29] whose two volumes of Moslem epic provide many analogues for the Parry-Lord songs, and, more generally, the published and unpublished holdings of Christian songs in the Zagreb archive. Then, too, there are the liminal cases of Bishop Njegoš and Andrija Kačić-Miošić,[30] poised on the cusp of oral tradition and texts, who seem to have been able to "textualize" their own personal epics, written in the special language of South Slavic oral epic by thoroughly literate, even scholarly, authors. This latter phenomenon leads us into the nature of the traditional register, its accessibility to composer and receiver, and related matters that I have no opportunity to discuss here.[31]

What we can say in closing is that South Slavic oral epics become books via a variety of routes, the two most prominent of which I have chosen for examination here. What emerges at the far end of the process as a volume on the library shelf must pass through many stages, from the initial decision about *what gets recorded* (effectively the root determinant of everything else) to the secondary decision of *what gets published* (not, as we have seen, an enterprise without choices) and on to *what gets received*. At every stage, theory and policy narrow the range of options, productively giving necessary definition and identity to whatever is collected, published, or read. It is this often unexamined process of manufacturing definition and identity that we must closely examine; in other words, rather than start our inquiry with the received text itself, we should begin by asking how this particular facsimile of an oral epic performance reached us in this particular form. South Slavic epic provides an opportunity to shed light on this process in an unambiguously oral tradition; perhaps it can also help to illuminate ancient Greek and medieval English texts that derive from oral epic traditions.

NOTES

Every effort has been made to ensure that references to the World Wide Web are correct and current, but some addresses may have changed or expired while this volume was in production. The reader is urged to use online search engines to locate current URLs.

1. On the history of textual editing of traditional oral works in general, see especially Elizabeth Fine, *The Folklore Text* (Bloomington: Indiana University Press, 1984). On the important approach through ethnopoetics, see especially Dell Hymes, *In Vain I Tried to Tell You: Essays in Native American Ethnopoetics* (Philadelphia: University of Pennsylvania Press, 1981). More recently, Lauri Honko has examined eleven different projects, from various parts of the world, in which oral epics were textualized and published; see Lauri Honko, *Textualising the Siri Epic*, Folklore Fellows Communications, vol. 264 (Helsinki: Suomalainen Tiedeakatemia, 1998). Honko and his colleagues have also provided a twelfth example via their own textualization of a South Indian oral epic; see Lauri Honko, ed. and trans., in collaboration with Chinnappa Gowda, Anneli Honko, and Viveka Rai, *The Siri Epic as Performed by Gopala Naika*, parts 1–2, Folklore Fellows Communications, vols. 265–66 (Helsinki: Suomalainen Tiedeakatemia, 1998). See further Lauri Honko, ed., *Textualization of Oral Epics* (Berlin: Mouton and De Gruyter, 2000), which contains essays by various scholars on the textualization of living oral epic traditions from around the world.

2. I regret not having the opportunity to take account in this essay of the potentially highly fruitful efforts now under way to provide electronic, hypertext editions of oral and oral-derived

epics; I think, for example, of ProVisual, *HyperKalevala* (Helsinki: Finnish Literature Society and Edita, 1996), or of the hypertext edition-translation of Halil Bajgorić's *Ženidba Bećirbega Mustajbegova (The Wedding of Mustajbey's Son Bećirbey)*, a Moslem South Slavic epic from the Milman Parry Collection, which I am currently completing. It may well be that electronic media, and particularly the Internet and multimedia computing, will make possible new levels of fidelity in the editing of traditional oral works.

3. Given present political conditions, I prefer to call the epics (and their singers and languages) by the general term "South Slavic," acknowledging, of course, that the material published by Karadžić was almost exclusively recorded in Serbia. Although "South Slavic" is employed by linguists to denote the language family that also includes Bulgarian, Slovenian, and Macedonian, it seems better to err on the side of inclusiveness rather than parochialism or segregation. Moreover, many of the songs, events, and characters instanced in one geographical and ethnic area can be found—albeit in localized form—in other geographical and ethnic areas.

4. Vuk Stefanović Karadžić, *Srpski rječnik* (originally published 1852) (Belgrade: Nolit, 1975).

5. Vuk Stefanović Karadžić, *Srpske narodne pjesme* (originally published 1841–62), vols. 1–4 (Belgrade: Nolit, 1975).

6. Živomir Mladenović and Vladan Nedić, eds., *Srpske narodne pesme*, vols. 1–4 (Belgrade: Srpska Akademija Nauka, 1973–74).

7. The editor's phrase is "su pjesme junačke najstarije."

8. See Živomir Mladenović, "Rukopisi narodnih pesama Vukove zbirke i njihovo izdavanje," in Živomir Mladenović and Vladan Nedić, eds., *Srpske narodne pesme*, vol. 1 (Belgrade: Srpska Akademija Nauka, 1973), esp. xxiv–lv. See also Duncan Wilson, *The Life and Times of Vuk Stefanović Karadžić, 1787–1864: Literacy, Literature, and National Independence in Serbia* (Oxford: Clarendon Press, 1970 / Ann Arbor: Michigan Slavic Publications, 1986), 317–18 of the 1970 edition; Wilson bases his opinion on comments by Thomas Percy, Bishop of Dromore.

9. Živomir Mladenović and Vladan Nedić, eds., *Srpske narodne pesme*.

10. For some translated samples of the Marko stories, see Milne Holton and Vasa D. Mihailovich, trans., *Songs of the Serbian People: From the Collections of Vuk Karadžić* (Pittsburgh: University of Pittsburgh Press, 1997), 159–214. On Marko as a figure both historical and legendary, see Tatyana Popović, *Prince Marko: The Hero of South Slavic Epics* (Syracuse, N.Y.: Syracuse University Press, 1988). For scholarship in English on the Karadžić poems, see Svetozar Koljević, *The Epic in the Making* (Oxford: Clarendon Press, 1980), and John Miles Foley, *Immanent Art: From Structure to Meaning in Traditional Oral Epic* (Bloomington: Indiana University Press, 1991), 96–134.

11. On the nature of cycles and their implied context, see John Miles Foley, "Epic Cycles and Epic Traditions," in John N. Kazazis and Antonios Rengakos, eds., *Euphrosyne: Studies in Ancient Epic and Its Legacy in Honor of Dimitris N. Maronitis* (Stuttgart: Franz Steiner Verlag, 1999), 99–108.

12. See further John Miles Foley, *Traditional Oral Epic: The Odyssey, Beowulf, and the Serbo-Croatian Return Song* (Berkeley: University of California Press, 1990); Foley, *Immanent Art;* John Miles Foley, *The Singer of Tales in Performance* (Bloomington: Indiana University Press, 1995); John Miles Foley, ed., *Teaching Oral Traditions* (New York: Modern Language Association, 1998); John Miles Foley, *Homer's Traditional Art* (University Park: Pennsylvania State University Press, 1999). On proverbs for understanding oral traditions, see John Miles Foley, *How to Read an Oral Poem* (Urbana: University of Illinois Press, 2002).

13. See, for example, Nada Milošević-Djordjević, ed., *Narodne epske pesme: Lektira za VII razred osnovne škole* (Folk epic songs: A reader for grade 7 of elementary school)(Belgrade: Nolit, 1978), which includes a selection of Marko tales.

14. I was living in Belgrade when Tito died, and was struck by the fact that the newspapers and electronic media portrayed him as a modern-day figure from legend, often quoting from the epic tradition (familiar to most of the intended audience, of course) to describe his heroic achievements as a warrior (a leader of the resistance against Nazi incursions during

World War II) and as a ruler (the president and leader of all of the ethnic minorities in the synthetic nation-state of Yugoslavia). On the poetic tradition surrounding the Battle of Kosovo, see especially the translated sample of Kosovo songs—the tip of a very large iceberg—in Holton and Mihailovich, trans., *Songs of the Serbian People*, 131–58.

15. Eye-opening in this regard is the regime's fostering of "neofolk" music to culturally leverage its position with the natural audiences for traditional forms: rural rather than urban, older rather than younger, and inward-looking and nationalistic rather than Western-leaning. On this phenomenon, see especially Eric D. Gordy, *The Culture of Power in Serbia: Nationalism and the Destruction of Alternatives* (University Park: Pennsylvania State University Press, 1999), 103–64. Let me add the observation that two of the neofolk lines he cites (130)—Mila braćo, došlo novo doba / Rodio se Milošević Sloba (Dear brothers, the new era has come / Sloba Milošević is born)—were composed within the traditional oral epic idiom: two ten-syllable lines "made" from formulaic phraseology common in the epic songs, and for that reason heavy with resonance and connotation.

16. For an account of Parry's and Lord's fieldwork and scholarship, see John Miles Foley, *The Theory of Oral Composition: History and Methodology* (Bloomington: Indiana University Press, 1988), 19–56.

17. For Parry's heretofore unpublished field notes, see Milman Parry, "Ćor Huso," *The Making of Homeric Verse: The Collected Papers of Milman Parry*, ed. Adam Parry (Oxford: Clarendon Press, 1971), especially 439.

18. Chiefly the singers Ibro Bašić, Mujo Kukuruzović, Salko Morić, and Halil Bajgorić. See further note 2 above, as well as Foley, *Traditional Oral Epic*, 42–50, and Foley, *Homer's Traditional Art*, chaps. 2–4. For a digest of South Slavic epics in the Parry Collection, see Matthew W. Kay, *The Index of the Milman Parry Collection: Heroic Songs, Conversations, and Stories* (New York: Garland, 1995).

19. See G. S. Kirk, *The Songs of Homer* (Cambridge: Cambridge University Press, 1960), and G. S. Kirk, ed., *The Iliad: A Commentary*, vols. 1–6 (Cambridge: Cambridge University Press, 1985–93). On "word" as a traditional unit of utterance, see especially Foley, *Homer's Traditional Art*, 66–88, and Foley, *How to Read an Oral Poem*.

20. In later work I have identified three levels of organization in South Slavic Moslem epic via the linguistic terminology of "idiolect," "dialect," and "language"; see Foley, *Traditional Oral Epic*, chaps. 5, 8.

21. Milman Parry, comp., and Albert B. Lord, ed. and trans., *Serbo-Croatian Heroic Songs / Srpskohrvatske junačke pjesme*, vols. 1–2 (Cambridge, Mass.: Harvard University Press / Belgrade: Serbian Academy of Sciences, 1953–54).

22. This comparison allows the establishment of a traditional morphology for the *Odyssey* and thus sheds light on crucial critical problems in Homer's poem, such as the order of narrative events (the celebrated sequence of "in medias res" turns out to be idiomatic), Penelope's heroism (she, not her husband, provides the narrative fulcrum), and the postreunion "ending" of the *Odyssey* (outside the story pattern, but traditional nonetheless); see further Foley, *Homer's Traditional Art*, 115–67.

23. On the philological dimensions of this comparison, see Foley, *Traditional Oral Epic*; John Miles Foley, "*Guslar* and *Aoidos*: Traditional Register in South Slavic and Homeric Epic," *Transactions of the American Philological Association* 126 (1996), 11–41.

24. See Béla Bartók, transcription of selections from *The Captivity of Djulić Ibrahim*, with notes, in Albert B. Lord, ed. and trans., *Serbocroatian Heroic Songs / Srpskohrvatske junačke pjesme*, vol. 1 (Cambridge, Mass.: Harvard University Press / Belgrade: Serbian Academy of Sciences, 1953); Stephen Erdely, *Music of South Slavic Heroic Epics from the Bihać Region of Bosnia* (New York: Garland, 1995).

25. For a history of the theory, see Foley, *The Theory of Oral Composition*; for a bibliography, see John Miles Foley, *Oral-Formulaic Theory and Research: An Introduction and Annotated Bibliography* (New York: Garland, 1985), with updates in the journal *Oral Tradition* and the entire bibliography available electronically at http://www.oraltraditiion.org.

26. See further Foley, *The Theory of Oral Composition;* Foley, *Traditional Oral Epic;* Foley, *Immanent Art;* Foley, *The Singer of Tales in Performance;* Foley, *Homer's Traditional Art.*

27. See Frederick Klaeber, ed., *Beowulf and the Fight at Finnsburg,* 3rd ed., with 1st and 2nd suppls. (Boston: D.C. Heath, 1950); Adrien Bonjour, *The Digressions in Beowulf* (Oxford: Blackwell, 1950). See also Theodore M. Andersson, "Sources and Analogues," and Robert E. Bjork, "Digressions and Episodes," in Robert E. Bjork and John D. Niles, eds., *A Beowulf Handbook* (Lincoln: University of Nebraska Press, 1997).

28. On these three examples, see, respectively, William Bernard McCarthy, *The Ballad Matrix: Personality, Milieu, and the Oral Tradition* (Bloomington: Indiana University Press, 1990); Larry Evers and Barre Toelken, eds., *Native American Oral Traditions: Collaboration and Interpretation* (Logan: Utah State University Press, 2001); and Foley, *The Singer of Tales in Performance,* 99–135.

29. Luka Marjanović, ed., *Hrvatske narodne pjesme,* vols. 3–4 (Zagreb: Matica Hrvatska, 1898).

30. See especially Albert B. Lord, "The Merging of Two Worlds: Oral and Written Poetry as Carriers of Ancient Values," in John Miles Foley, ed., *Oral Tradition in Literature: Interpretation in Context* (Columbia: University of Missouri Press, 1986), and Foley, *How to Read an Oral Poem.*

31. On the "rhetorical persistence of traditional forms," see Foley, *The Singer of Tales in Performance,* 60–98.

Bhakti Literature
An "Oral-Scribal" Archetype

WINAND M. CALLEWAERT

This essay deals with *bhakti* literature in northwest India between 1400 and 1700 A.D. This literature consists mainly of religious songs and hagiographical narratives. The songs were most often not written down by the original poets and were orally transmitted for a period varying from three centuries to fifty years before being written down. The first manuscripts now available are dated around 1600 A.D. I propose to describe a method that may enable the textual critic to go beyond the "written archetype" and approach the "oral archetype" of some of these texts.

It does no harm periodically to stir up academic or sectarian complacency and to remind ourselves that the *bhakti* texts we read and hear now may not even have been composed by the poets to whom they are attributed. For example, very few of the 100 songs of Kabir that Rabindranath Tagore translated into English are found in the critical editions of Kabir, and David Lorenzen even doubts that the most popular songs in the Kabirpanth of Banaras today were even composed by Kabir.[1] Moreover, during his recent fieldwork in Rajasthan, Bahadur Singh collected and recorded about 500 songs of Kabir sung by traveling singers, but hardly any of them are found in the existing critical editions. Mirabai is a similar case: if she died at the age of forty-three, in the sixteenth century, it is remarkable that at the end of the twentieth century there should be as many as 5,197 songs attributed to her.[2]

Singers changed texts to suit their musical purposes or to adjust to their audiences. Scribes may have changed texts because of laziness, or because they no longer understood the texts, or because they had sectarian or theological interests to defend (as when the values important to a guru who initiated a new trend were quickly overturned by different, often contrary, priorities).[3] More dangerous still is the notion that it may be worthwhile to look at the earliest manuscripts of the *Adi Granth* of the Sikhs and to consider whether there, too, scribal alterations reflect changing attitudes.

Changing attitudes reflected in a fresh text edition are of historical interest, but they also have a theological and devotional importance. Religious insights need constant rethinking if they are not to become obsolete. One way to rethink them is to go back to the earliest sources and to scratch from existing editions the layers of interpretation—and possibly also of manipulation—that the passage of time has seen added to the text. The textual critic's enterprise, therefore, has a social importance as well, especially in the living *bhakti* traditions.

Further, for the history of religions, fresh critical editions are needed that are not only based on new "ancient" material but also made with a new methodology. Otherwise, scholars and students will make studies of the influence of the Kabir of about 1500 A.D. on the Dadu sect of about 1600 A.D., using Kabir texts from 1700 A.D. Studies of this kind, often with titles like "A Comparative Study of . . . ," are abundantly available but do not necessarily reach correct conclusions. Finally, linguists and philologists, too, are often misled by wrong chronologies, which are based on editions that have relied on manuscripts from later periods.

In the different editions that I have prepared, I did not apply the same method to all the bhakti texts, although what I call the method of "oral-scribal archetypes" gave very good results for at least two texts. Even though so-called *bhakti* literature is in many ways uniform in its purposes and common elements, a single method could not be applied.

The "Scribal Archetype" Method:
The *Dadu Janma Lila*, or *Life Story of Dadu Dayal*

When Jan Gopal composed this hagiography, around 1620, he could not have imagined that, three and a half centuries later, his text would be edited "critically." The very idea of a critical edition probably never occurred to him: scribes were not supposed to make mistakes while copying; they certainly did not intentionally alter texts or add anything. But his *Life Story,* as now found in manuscripts, is a gold mine of sectarian interpolations and variants, illustrating the growing biases in the early group of Dadu's followers. Very soon in the history of the Dadu sect—one of the manuscripts with an enlarged text is dated 1654 A.D.—efforts were made to "explain" Dadu's Muslim origin and his association with the low caste of *dhuniyas,* or to emphasize his celibacy. I copied many old manuscripts of this text and found basically two versions, abbreviated as *E* (early) and *L* (later and expanded). I draw my examples in this essay from the critical edition of *The Hindi Biography of Dadu Dayal.*[4] Within thirty years after the composition of this biography, sectarian scribes had changed nuances and added stories in particular contexts, hoping thus to underline the divine status of Dadu. Not only has the critical edition brought out what is probably the most authentic version of the text, it has also highlighted the changing attitudes of scribes in the early period of scribal transmission.

The method for this edition may be called the traditional one: collecting the oldest manuscripts, collating texts, and looking for variants in order to discover a stemma that provides an inferential pathway to a scribal archetype, in the absence of an original text. On the basis of the study of variants, both minor changes and major interpolations, I reasoned that the shortest version, with the fewest encomiastic details, was most probably the more authentic one. In the English translation of the critical edition I included, with indentations, the interpolated lines of the expanded version. In the introduction to the edition I listed all the examples of intentional changes in the expanded version. This procedure gave a vivid picture of changing attitudes in the second generation after Dadu.

The Method of "Oral-Scribal Archetypes": The Songs of Namdev and Raidas

It was in the course of research on the songs of Namdev that I developed and tested my hypothesis about relationships among manuscripts representing singers' repertoires. With this hypothesis, much *bhakti* literature and its transmission during the oral and scribal periods can now be studied in a different light.

Namdev (ca. 1280–1350) was one of the most important *bhaktas* (poet-mystics) of Maharastra and is considered to be the earliest representative of the Bhakti movement in north Indian vernaculars. He stands at the origin of the movement in which, later on, great *bhaktas* like Kabir, Dadu, Nanak, and others developed as outstanding mystic reformers. Besides the numerous *abhangas*, or songs, in Marathi, there are many *pads* in "Hindi" bearing the name of Namdev and traditionally attributed to the Marathi Namdev. These *pads* have been very popular, as demonstrated by the abundance of seventeenth-century manuscripts containing them, *pads*and are still being sung today.

My study of Namdev, conducted in collaboration with Mukund Lath of Jaipur, has been exclusively based on manuscripts. The earliest available source is the Fatehpur manuscript of Jaipur (1582) and the *Adi Granth* (1604). The other manuscripts consulted are dated 1636, 1653, 1658, 1660, 1664, 1675, 1676, 1681, 1684, and 1698. For the *pads* of Namdev I started looking for manuscripts and copying them in 1973 and on each of my successive study tours. In these manuscripts we began to uncover a pattern in the repertoires of traveling singers.

In 1971 I came back from India, after six years of study, and had a clear picture of what my research would consist of: the copying of man-

uscripts and the preparation of critical editions of original texts and translations. I also saw that my work would necessarily include going to far-
away places in Rajasthan and to important institutions in the cities. On
the basis of the manuscripts found, I would reconstruct, I thought, the
archetypes of the *pads* I wanted to edit. Since scribes committed errors,
intentionally or unknowingly, these variant readings should enable me
to establish relationships among the manuscripts. On the basis of these
relationships, the stemma should allow me to reconstruct the "critical"
text: a classical, scholarly approach to manuscripts leading to the
Archetype! This was, after all, what I had been trained to do—but I did
not realize how little my training had prepared me for what the work
actually turned out to be.

Indian scholars have applied this method, with the same confidence,
to *bhakti* literature they have found in seventeenth-century manuscripts.
For example, as Professor Shukdev Singh of Benares, editor of the *Bijak*,
told me, "Kabir wrote down his own *pads,* and if we find a sufficient
number of manuscripts, we should be able to reconstruct what Kabir
wrote." Likewise, Parasnath Tivari has taken it for granted that we
should be able to reconstruct the original text of Kabir if we put together
all the little pieces that have survived in the manuscripts.[5]

I felt very comfortable with my project; it looked very simple and easy.
But that was wrong. The project became an exciting adventure, however, when we started to discover the singers in the manuscripts. Let
me illustrate this growing insight by giving a conjectural description of
the method of transmission of the songs of these early *bhakti* poets.

Traveling Singers

Let us imagine that we are traveling through northwest India in 1550
A.D., on sandy tracks or on bumpy roads after the rainy season. We spend
nights on temple floors and watch the audiences drawn by a family of
traveling singers who perform songs of *bhakti.* These singers, like the
Puranic bards, receive extended hospitality in accord with the quality
and the depth of their performances. They may not belong to a particular sect, and they sing what appeals most to local feelings. We are on
the way to Rajasthan after a visit to Benares, where a few years ago Raidas
died, and where the oldest members of the family of singers may have
heard a person called Kabir. This family of traveling musicians, a few
generations before, has perhaps been to Maharashtra and heard a poet
called Namdev. Therefore, the family's repertoire goes on expanding,
and some have started to feel the need to write down songs.

Such singers sang the songs most in demand, like the songs of

Namdev and Kabir, which they had learned from their fathers. The singers were artists, too, and, inspired by a particular environment, they added new songs, sometimes of their own creation, to the repertoire. Memory was their only way of recording, but as the repertoires grew bigger, some singers started to keep little (or big) notebooks as an aid to memory. The earliest manuscripts seem to have had these notebooks as their basis. The manuscripts of the seventeenth century that have been preserved are *copies* of these early notes, now lost: scholars of the twentieth century, in order to reconstruct and edit what the singers sang, have to rely on seventeenth-century manuscripts that are copies of the singers' scribbled notes. I must say "what the singers sang"; I cannot, of course, go so far as to say "what Namdev or Kabir or Raidas sang."

It is the ambition of a textual critic studying Shakespeare to bring out, by looking at the various versions available in manuscripts, the text "written" by the author. The textual critic of *bhakti* songs soon realizes that this is impossible in the case of a Namdev or a Kabir. Their songs were written down only long after they had died. If we want to reach the poets themselves, we have to walk on the path of the oral tradition. This oral tradition, unlike that of the Vedas, did not shun variety and creativity. Consequently, the oeuvre of Namdev and others has come to us in a multiplicity of forms, changing over both space and time. We should look for an analogy in the Puranas rather than in Shakespeare.

Rag *Clusters*

Fortunately, the manuscript tradition allows us to reach beyond the threshold of the first writing, and to go into the gray zone of oral transmission. How?

Indian musicians used to sing clusters of songs according to a particular mode, called a *rag*. It appears that first the singer sang a particular song in a particular *rag*, and then he grouped together the *pads* that were to be sung in the same *rag*. Consequently, a *rag* is like an identity card for the earliest period of oral transmission.

It was only later, when compilers took over, that *pads* were classified according to the main theme, but even in those collections the name of the *rag* was given with each song.

The same song could be sung to different *rags*; as a result, we find songs classified under different *rags* in different manuscripts. This variation in classification is not due to a scribe's intervention but stems from the oral period itself, when the songs were in the hands of the singers. Subsequently, the songs were transmitted under different *rags* and appeared as such also in the manuscripts. Therefore, by looking at the *rag* structure we are able to make a preliminary classification of the musical recensions.

When, for Namdev, Kabir, and Raidas, we compare the *rag* structure in the *Adi Granth* with that in the Rajasthani repertoires, we find considerable differences. The Panjabi singers handled a text that was not only morphologically but also musically very different from what their colleagues in Rajasthan had. I am tempted to propose that *pads* having the same *rag* in the *Adi Granth* and Rajasthani manuscripts are likely to have come from a very early common source. In fact, what we find in the seventeenth-century Rajasthani manuscripts is a variant musical version that may well be as old as the musical version from which the Panjabi singers drew their inspiration, if not older.

At what muddy or sandy crossroads did singing families go their own separate way, and at what point in the sixteenth century?

The First Composition and Transmission

In order to explain the variations in the texts of the songs in the manuscripts, it is useful to have an understanding of the process by which the songs of the Sants were transmitted. Clearly, the most direct transmission would have occurred if the Sant himself—let us say Kabir—taught one of his songs to one of his followers in a *guru sisya parampara*. In that guru-disciple tradition, the song was probably handed down in forms that did not vary much from the original. But even the original core text itself may not have been totally fixed, and so it is possible that disciples learning the same song from Kabir at different times during his life were not taught the same forms of the same core text. Transmission in guru-disciple relationship cannot have been the only form of oral transmission, however. Singers from outside the tradition may also have learned Kabir's songs by listening to Kabir or one of his disciples perform them.

While people in nonliterate societies have a considerable ability to learn and recall texts purely through hearing them, a version of a song learned through listening to it, even several times, may nevertheless not have been an exact copy of the original performance text. It is likely that the songs of Kabir, for example, would have been learned at third hand, by singers who had heard his songs being performed by other singers, who in turn had learned them by listening to Kabir or his disciples. Even those singers who had heard Kabir at first hand may have heard him at different times and perhaps remembered differently what he was singing. Because of this process of learning the songs at third hand during the period of oral transmission, there probably also would have been a conflation of core text and performance text. This possibility would suggest that the extant versions *in the manuscripts* probably represent texts created from an amalgam of what was once (commentorial) performance text and core text.[6]

The Pancavani

As an illustration of the exciting work involved in studying these manuscripts, I should like to briefly describe an important manuscript source of *bhakti* literature in Rajasthan. In seventeenth-century manuscripts in Rajasthan we frequently encounter a work called *Pancavani* ("The words of the five," "the five" being the great poets Dadu, Kabir, Namdev, Raidas, and Hardas). Three of these are also quoted in the *Adi Granth*. Many manuscripts that include the *Pancavani* are available, but nobody has bothered to compare them. Comparison is not an easy task, because each *Pancavani* is about 1.6 megabytes of text—roughly the equivalent of 330,000 words. Parasnath Tivari used one *Pancavani* manuscript for his edition of the Rajasthani recension of Kabir's songs. He considered the compiled *Pancavani* as one manuscript tradition in which, around 1600 A.D., the songs of the five great gurus were written down. They were written down from memory and neatly classified according to *rag* in the way a singer would remember them.

Looking at the consistent order—Dadu, Kabir, Namdev, Raidas, Hardas—in all the *Pancavani* manuscripts, we may be tempted to imagine that the numerous *Pancavani* manuscripts we have today all go back to a single archetype compiled by one of the learned disciples of Dadu. It may seem to us that this archetypal exemplar served as the basis for all later copies, the earliest now extant being dated 1636 A.D. But then came my discovery. Looking at different manuscripts, I noticed that the internal classifications of the *rag* clusters, and of the songs within these *rag* clusters, were not identical. What I faced was the amazing fact of several compilers independently writing down, from memory, the *Vanis* of the five gurus. Thus, by looking at the *Pancavani* manuscripts, we were able to go beyond the imagined scribal archetype and into the time of oral transmission. In a way, we were able to reconstruct an "oral archetype," supposedly much closer to the original version.

Because of a plainly direct link with different musical traditions, we find in the manuscripts variants that were introduced during the oral / singing tradition, along with those produced by scribes. A detailed comparison of these musical variants[7] in the Rajasthani manuscripts and in the *Adi Granth* suggests the hypothesis that the singers walking on the Rajasthani roads around 1550 and singing the songs of

Namdev (or of Kabir, and so on) drew their repertoires from a common source. But this source is different from the source that gave us the *Adi Granth* repertoires.

Language as a Clue?

Traditionally, language has been considered a reliable clue to the authentic version of a text. Many textual critics have used language to define the genuineness of a text, a line, or a song. They have also used it as a norm for modifying a text. In the cases of Namdev, Kabir, Raidas, and many others, however, the linguistic test was often contradicted by the musical *(rag)* pattern in which the songs had been arranged. For example, the songs of Namdev, which were found under the same *rag* in all our manuscripts and presumably belonged to an old layer of the oral tradition, were linguistically quite a mixed bag: we had some songs in almost pure Gujarati, others in a kind of Marathi-Rajasthani, and still others in Braj. Which Namdev were we talking about, and what language did he use?

When we constructed a tentative stemma on the basis of the similar order in which the songs had been arranged under the heading of a *rag*, our efforts were continually contradicted by dissimilarities in the arrangement of the oral and scribal variants. The result was a totally blurred and confused pattern, if a stemmatic pattern appeared at all. A computer count of variants showed that there was not even any relationship between two manuscripts of the same musical recension, nor was there consistency even within a single manuscript. These findings suggest very nebulous interactions among singing traditions. If we seek to establish "original texts" for these songs on the basis of stemmatic clues, we deceive ourselves, for the simple reason that an authoritative text perhaps never existed. The original composer himself may even have changed the song as the years went by.

Once Namdev had composed his songs, they very soon became the property of singers who handled them according to their own inspiration, musical genius, and particular dialects. Singers may well have combined several of the versions that they had heard. We may also assume that it was mostly the capable singers—those who were more poetic and creative—who prevailed, and we notice the consequences of that creativity in the stemmatic chaos before us.

What, then, were we looking for in these *bhakti* songs? We were looking for a text that is found in many musical traditions. We tried to isolate an old Rajasthani core, without suggesting that the songs of this core were in any way close to the poet. And, most important, each song separately was considered an independent recension, sometimes with a better reading in one manuscript than in another manuscript.

Kabir: Impossible to Reach?

Nearly 600 years after Kabir was born in Banaras (perhaps around 1400), and after at least 80 years of scholarship, do we have any certainty that the songs attributed to Kabir, and published in critical and uncritical editions and translations, are actually by Kabir? My research suggests that this conclusion is very doubtful. Between Kabir and our computer age lie 150 years of oral transmission—which has never stopped—and nearly 400 years of scribal transmission. We have no oral recordings of Kabir scolding his audiences, and I take it for granted that he did not write down his compositions. What we have are manuscripts in which his popular repertoire was written down, first by traveling singers and, later, by devoted scribes, in a more respectful and professional way. But what of Kabir do we have in those repertoires?

Among scholars there is no consensus on the authenticity of any of the songs attributed to Kabir. With due respect to the oral traditions that survive to the present day, my approach to the problem of authenticity starts with a search for the earliest manuscripts. Even if, in the case of Kabir, that approach may not give us complete certainty about which songs are authentic and which definitely are not, at least it can question the claims made in the current editions. All we can say with any certainty, I argue, is that the versions of Kabir's songs found in seventeenth-century manuscripts are the versions that were commonly used and sung by singers at that time. Moreover, the songs that occur in most repertoires, and in different regions, are more likely to have been composed by Kabir. Three kinds of collections of Kabir's songs have been preserved in northern India: the "eastern" or *Bijak* tradition, the "western" or Rajasthani tradition, and the *Adi Granth* or Panjabi tradition.

The singers traveling the Rajasthani roads around 1550 A.D. probably drew their repertoires from a common source. But this source was different from the source that gave us the repertoires preserved in the *Adi Granth*. When we compare the *rag* structure of the songs of Kabir in the *Adi Granth* with the *rag* structure of the songs in the Rajasthani repertoires, we find considerable differences. The Panjabi singers handled a text of Kabir that was musically and morphologically very different from what their colleagues in Rajasthan had.[8] Most songs of Kabir that I looked at in three Rajasthani manuscripts were classified in them under the same *rag*, and I am tempted to propose that songs having the same *rag* in the Rajasthani manuscripts *and* in the *Adi Granth* are likely to have come from a very early common source. Can that "early common source" be Kabir himself?

Kabir's songs, like Namdev's, are also very likely to have become the property of singers who handled them in diverse ways. As already mentioned, singers may well have combined several of the versions they had heard and then passed new textual combinations on to their students.

To conclude, writing about Kabir's theology, literary qualities, or unique language is a quick way to produce an outdated article—which is to say, an inconclusive and problematic argument. With the manuscript material now at hand, we can no longer rely on the existing editions. Charlotte Vaudeville very wisely reduced the number of *sakhis* that she quoted in her 1993 translation, by comparison with the 1974 edition,[9] but I suggest that we have to be even more severe. A fresh critical edition of the oeuvre of Kabir should be prepared, using all the ancient manuscripts and applying the hypothesis about the oral variants in the manuscripts. With that hypothesis we can go back further in time in the western or Rajasthani recension than Tivari managed to do.

NOTES

1. See David N. Lorenzen, *Praises to a Formless God: Nirguni Texts from North India* (Albany: State University of New York Press, 1996), 205.

2. See Winand M. Callewaert, "The 'Earliest' Song of Mira (1503–1546)," *Annali, Istituto Universitario Orientale* 50:4 (1990), 363–78.

3. A clear example involves the life story of Dadu and a critical edition that exposed such changing attitudes, apparently creating displeasure within the Dadu sect; see Winand M. Callewaert, ed. and trans., *The Hindi Biography of Dadu Dayal* (Delhi: Motilal Banarsidass, 1988).

4. Ibid.

5. See Parasnath Tivari, *Kabir-granthavali* (Allahabad, 1961).

6. For examples of commentorial additions to a core text, see Winand M. Callewaert and Peter Friedlander, *The Life and Works of Raidas* (Delhi: Manohar Book Publications, 1992), 69ff.

7. For an analysis of differences in *rag*, inversion of stanzas or of lines (or of singing units within a line), addition of "fillers," and so on, see Winand M. Callewaert and Mukund Lath, *The Hindi Padavali of Namdev: A Critical Edition of Namdev's Hindi Songs* (Leuven: Orientalia Lovaniensia Analecta / Delhi: Motilal Banarsidass, 1989), 63ff.

8. For his critical edition of the songs of Kabir, Parasnath Tivari finally selected 200 songs. Of these, 121 are also found in the *Adi Granth,* and of these 121 common songs, only 55 are classified under the same *rag* as in the Rajasthani manuscripts. Out of the 35 songs under *rag gaudi* in the Rajasthani tradition, 31 have the same *rag gaudi* in the *Adi Granth;* under *rag asavari,* 8 out of 23; under *rag ramkali,* 3 out of 6; under *rag bhairu,* 8 out of 11; and under *rag vasant,* 4 out of 5. For the other *rags,* the versions have no songs in common. See Tivari, *Kabir-granthavali.*

9. See Ch. Vaudeville, *Kabir* (Oxford: Clarendon Press, 1974); Charlotte Vaudeville, *A Weaver Named Kabir* (Delhi: Oxford University Press, 1993).

PART III

Material Text

Text, Script, and Media
New Observations on Scribal Activity
in the Ancient Near East

SCOTT B. NOEGEL

Living in an age of microchips and monitors, one might think that the ancient eras that saw the heyday of the stylus share nothing in common with our baud-rate generation. Yet, as Edward Mendelson wrote in a report on Web sites created by Benedictine monks,

> the relations between modern Web sites and medieval scriptoria, or writing rooms, is even closer than these monks may have guessed. The technology that connects millions of pages on the World Wide Web derives ultimately from techniques invented by the scribes and scholars who copied out the Bible more than a thousand years ago.[1]

Mendelson's report focused primarily on the similarity of biblical cross-referencing systems to Web links, but it also offered new ways of looking at the role of media within the matrix of ancient scribal culture:

> The marginal references to the Bible and the hyperlinks of the World Wide Web may be the only two systems ever invented that give concrete expression to the idea that everything in the world hangs together—that every event, every fact, every datum is connected to every other. Where the two systems differ drastically is in what their connections mean.[2]

Mendelson's remark illustrates how cybermedia have forced us to rethink both modern and ancient text-related issues and suggests that these two types of issues may not be altogether dissimilar or, at least, unworthy of comparison. Indeed, I would suggest that our modern experiences as technophiles offer new insights into issues of text and context in scribal systems antedating even the Middle Ages.

In this essay, I would like to take a step in this direction by examining scribal activities in ancient Egypt, Mesopotamia, and ancient Israel from the standpoint of the following cyberinduced issues: the cultural context of, and attitudes toward, script and various textual media; the formative role of a script and the physical medium in shaping the cultural conception of language; the cultural significance of the compositional structure of various written media; and the cognitive function of images as text. My remarks will be exploratory and will remain cursory but will, I hope, suggest new avenues for research.

I begin with the general ancient Near Eastern cultural context of script and the textual medium, a context that cannot be understood without acknowledgment of the ancient widespread belief in the inherent power of words, both human and divine.[3] As Georges Contenau has written,

> Since to know and pronounce the name of an object instantly endowed it with reality, and created power over it, and since the degree of knowledge and consequently of power was strengthened by the tone of voice in which the name was uttered, writing, which was a permanent record of the name, naturally contributed to this power, as did both drawing and sculpture, since both were a means of asserting knowledge of the object and consequently of exercising over it the power that knowledge gave.[4]

The belief in the written and spoken power of words derives, ultimately, not from a courtly social matrix, where a king's word was law, but rather from religious associations attached to the very invention of writing. In the earliest texts from ancient Sumer (ca. 3300 B.C.E.), we find a pictographic cuneiform (or "wedge-writing") system employed to record the daily activities of religious authorities who were concerned foremost with the number of sacrificial animals and foodstuffs brought to the temple. The pictographic script gradually would become syllabically oriented over the next five hundred years, but would forever retain its connection to the images that the original signs represented. By 2500 B.C.E. this system had become rich in what we would call "literary" allusive sophistication and was employed by a variety of different language groups.[5] Throughout the more than three-thousand-year history of Mesopotamia, both writing and reciting constituted sacred acts, and the highly protected technological privilege of a select few who were not just scholars but also magicians, physicians, and priests. Thus in second-millennium documents we hear that writing is the "cosmic bond of all things"[6] and the secret of scribes and gods. In fact, the Mesopotamian gods also kept ledgers, or "tablets of life," on which they inscribed the destinies of individuals.[7] Moreover, the Mesopotamian creation myth Enuma Elish, which was recited during a ritual enactment of the myth on the fourth day of the new year festival, begins with an act of speaking that brings all things into existence.

Writing appeared in Egypt around 3000 B.C.E., in the form of the hieroglyphic script, a writing system that worked on phonetic, syllabic, and logographic levels. Though genetically unrelated to the Mesopotamian system, hieroglyphic Egyptian similarly expanded, over time, its repertoire of signs while retaining and multiplying their visual associations. The pictographic nature of the script permitted scribes to write in multiple directions: right to left, left to right, even top to bottom, and sometimes alternately left to right and then right to left, in "boustrophedon" (literally, "as the ox plows") fashion. Also, as in the Mesopotamian system, hieroglyphs were the tools of an elite priesthood expert in medicine and magic. The scribes guarded and boasted of their technological secrets, with a zeal that rivals even Microsoft.[8] Writing was, to use the Egyptian expression, "the words of the gods" *(mdw-nṯr)*, and the scribal art was to the Egyptians an occupation without equal.[9] The ibis-headed god Thoth is credited with the invention of writing and is said to be "excellent of magic" and "Lord of hieroglyphs." He appears writing the hieroglyphic feather sign representing the word *Ma'at*, which stands for the cosmic force of equilibrium by which kings keep their thrones and justice prevails. The link between writing and *Ma'at* suggests that Egyptian scribes viewed the scribal art as integral to maintaining this cosmic equilibrium.[10]

The spoken word was equally potent in Egypt. Execration and prophetic texts abound and bespeak a belief in the efficacy of spoken words. The oracular use of speech is evident in the term for the Egyptian temple's innermost sanctum or, literally, "the Mouth of the House" *(r3–pr)*.[11] The written and the spoken word similarly play prominent roles in the Egyptian description of creation.[12]

The Hebrew Bible displays a belief in the power of words similar to the belief evidenced in Egyptian and Mesopotamian records. This is not surprising, since Israel became a cultural conduit and receptacle for Egyptian and Mesopotamian influences, and since in Canaan (which eventually would become the land of Israel) writing first appeared in cuneiform script.[13] Even as the Israelites rejected parts of the cosmopolitan culture they inherited, the belief in the power of words prevailed. Thus, while the biblical legal code states that the Israelites rejected all forms of magical praxis and divination, the very presence of laws prohibiting such practices, and references to speech and words found elsewhere in the Bible, imply a belief in the power of words on a par with

Mesopotamian and Egyptian dogmata.[14] Also, God's creation in Genesis takes place by fiat, and the Israelite holy of holies is called a *debîr*, a word derived from the Hebrew root for "speaking."[15] A belief in the power of words explains why the prophets often speak in the past tense about events they predict for the future. Once spoken, an event is as good as realized.[16] The written word apparently was no less important, for as the God of Israel informs Moses in Exodus 32:33, "Whoever has sinned respecting me, him will I blot out from my text *[sepher]*." Job, too, cries out, "Oh that my words were written! Oh that my words were inscribed in a text *[sepher]*" (Job 19:23).

Despite their obvious differences, Mesopotamian, Egyptian, and Israelite cultures had in common a conception of words as vehicles of power, of creation by fiat, and of the oracular use of written and spoken words. This observation greatly affects how we understand the written words that these cultures have left us. What we label "literary" or "rhetorical" was to them a deployment of power—of divine and, in many cases, magical import—as demonstrated by the ubiquitous appearance of wordplay in these texts.[17] Since words are deemed loci of power, puns and paronomasia must have more power because they magnify meaning through association.[18] In the Mesopotamian and Egyptian scripts, wordplay often takes place purely on a visual level, suggesting that the visual dimension of the sign, like the spoken word, conveys power.[19] Drawing on technojargon, we might say that written puns provide multiple links. Other devices, such as chiasm, acrostics,[20] and parallelism, might not be mere embellishments but rather manifestations of divinity and vehicles by which scribes harnessed the power of words.

The power of images extended beyond the script to iconography and the plastic arts. In Egypt, for example, sculptures also read as hieroglyphic signs, and drawings functioned as tools of magic.[21] This is why Egyptian pharaohs wore sandals with soles that depicted the ritual annihilation of their enemies. By placing their foes beneath their feet, they could magically trample them daily. Since art was language in Egypt, drawings and sculptures also carried verbal dimensions.[22] The name, being essentially a word, was also a locus of power that could be handled in written form only by experts familiar with the dangers of this power. This is why pharaohs possessed one secret name, and why cartouches were essentially hieroglyphs bound by the magical power of a knotted rope. We also see the belief in a tie between one's name and one's existence in usurping pharaohs' blotting of their predecessors out of existence by chiseling their names from inscriptions.

The belief in the power of words, despite its importance, is seldom incorporated into studies on ancient writing and literacy, yet even a scribal error, an accidental slip of the stylus, could have devastating consequences. An accurate memory is everything, copying is sacred, and knowledge of the associative subtleties embedded in a text is tantamount to secret knowledge of the divine.[23] The richer the allusive language, the more portents embedded in the text—or, in cyberlanguage, the more links embedded in a text, the more influential it is.

Our experiences with cybermedia, especially because we are biased users of particular platforms, also urge us to explore the various physical media to which ancient scribes committed their words and their cultural attitudes. For the Mesopotamians, the medium of choice was clay. Most of the writings that have survived, ranging from administrative and divinatory texts to poems and paeans, are in clay. There are a few documents in other materials, such as stone, but stone was not native to Mesopotamia (or to Egypt, for that matter), and so such materials were reserved for monumental inscriptions.

While clay as a writing medium might appear a mundane topic, documented religious beliefs about clay allow us to appreciate more fully the Mesopotamian scribes' approach to their material. It is of import, for example, that the Mesopotamians saw clay as the medium with which the gods mixed blood to form the first living mortal. The placental afterbirth also was called "clay," and the expression "baked brick" was an idiomatic term for "newborn," similar to the vulgar English idiom "bun in the oven," equating the womb with a heat source.[24] Clay is also the material that the Mesopotamians used to build their homes. Thus it is the material of creation, both for gods and for humans. When a scribe impressed a stylus into moist clay, he was, in a sense, participating in creation. He was giving form to language.

Several other examples can be mentioned that reveal the intimate connections among architecture, creation, and language in Mesopotamian culture. Ea, the god of magic, is said to have "built" his words,[25] and the gods did not "create" humans but rather "built" them (as we find also in the book of Genesis 2:22, in connection with Eve). We also find in Mesopotamia the use of clay cones inscribed with prayers and temple dedications. These cones were driven into temple walls and sometimes buried in the cornerstones of buildings, much like modern time-capsules. They were rarely intended for human eyes, and, once set into temple walls, would become the words that magically held the temple together and gave it longevity.[26] If the medium is the message, then in ancient Mesopotamia the message was constructive; it was creation, a message reminiscent of modern technophrases like "build a cyber-portfolio" and "create a Web site."

In Egypt, clay is the medium of builders, but papyrus is the preferred medium of scribes. Here, too, we find a religious attachment to the written medium, both in the script and in the Egyptian mythologies.[27] Thus the hieroglyphic sign representing a papyrus clump denotes concepts like "flourish," "joy," and "life" and appears as an apotropaic symbol on magical amulets. Several deities, such as the life-giving Nile god Hapi, appear with the papyrus hieroglyph, a fact that illustrates the connection of papyrus to divinity and creation. In Egyptian belief, papyrus pillars also held up the sky, and papyriform columns architecturally supported Egyptian temples, suggesting the forces of creation. As in Mesopotamia, the architectural connection to the creative aspect of writing obtains at the linguistic level as well. In Egyptian, the term "house" can mean a stanza of poetry, and "bricks" and "walls" can refer to stichs and lines.[28] With computer terminology in mind, I note that at an inscription at Edfu an unrolled papyrus scroll is referred to as "magic spread out," thus characterizing scrolling and unscrolling as acts of magical praxis.[29] In fact, the word "magic" (ḥk3) appears with the determinative for a scroll. Writing on papyrus, therefore, was to those who employed the materials of magic and creation much as employing clay was to the Mesopotamian scribe.

Such observations are suggestive as a backdrop when we examine scribal activity in the Hebrew Bible. The Hebrew word for writing surface, *sepher*, is used for a wide variety of media that include stone, clay, papyrus, parchment, and potsherds, and the verbs used for writing occur with equal variety.[30] Moreover, the words "scroll" and "tablet" often appear side by side, and both appear as media for containing sacred words. Yet the Israelites, unlike their superpower neighbors, evidently did not attach special religious significance to their written media (whether scroll, parchment, or tablet), even though the Hebrew Bible portrays words as loci of power and the creation of the first mortal from clay.[31] It is the writing alone that is sacred, and the medium becomes sacred by default. It is as if the conception of the text transcended the written page. Even if we look to Jewish tradition as contained in the later Talmudic tractate *Sepher Torah*, we find that the parchment used for the Torah scroll must come from ritually clean animals, but this attaches no religious significance to the animal from which the parchment was taken.[32]

The intimate connection between physical media and religious beliefs as reflected in these media also compels us to look anew at the composition of ancient Near Eastern texts. For example, the number of tablets and verses comprising a particular ritual text may be not so much a function of space considerations as a consequence of cultural conceptions of certain numbers. For example, the Mesopotamian creation account was neatly composed on seven tablets, and seven was a well-known sacred number in Mesopotamia.[33] I am reminded of the rabbinic observation that the first line in the biblical creation of Genesis begins with seven words, the number seven playing a prominent structural role in that composition. The Mesopotamian Epic of Gilgamesh was redacted into twelve tablets that possibly correspond to the sexigesimal system of the Mesopotamians.[34] It is of note that the scribe who redacted the epic came from a family of exorcists steeped in the magical sciences.[35] I could cite other ancient Near Eastern texts, both biblical and extrabiblical, that illustrate such numerically allusive compositional structures.[36]

In line with this observation is the use of numbers to represent words and names, a practice that appeared first in Mesopotamia and, later, in the rabbinic interpretive strategy known as Gematria. In Mesopotamia this practice was not literary whimsy; it was how divine secrets were derived from texts.[37] Many gods' names also can be read as numbers; thus the number thirty may be read as Sin the moon god; Ishtar, as fifteen; Enlil, as fifty; and so on.[38] The connection of deities to numbers is widespread and perhaps helps us to understand the numerical significance of later non-Mesopotamian divinities, such as the God of Israel, who, we are told in Deuteronomy 6:4, is One.[39] It also may explain the preoccupation that later Jewish scribes, such as the Masoretes, had in the ninth century c.e. with counting all the words and verses in the Bible. In fact, the tradition of counting letters and words must be far more ancient than the Masoretes, for it is embedded in the very word *sopher*, "scribe"— literally "one who counts," or who "gives an account" as we might say.[40]

Finally, our inquiry into ancient cyberesque conceptions of media naturally leads us to an examination of images as text. Throughout the Near East we find a fascinating conceptual correspondence between pictures and writing, surpassing even the power of a Nike symbol. In Egypt, the word *tɔt* means not only "written words" or "letters" but also an "artistic image," "form," or "sign."[41] To Egyptians, the sculpted image of a god was both an image and a living word. Thus the New Kingdom book of the dead depicts the weighing of the pharaoh's heart against the feather of truth *(Ma'at)* but would never show Pharaoh's heart tipping the scales. Had the scribe illustrated this, Pharaoh would not have entered into the afterlife, since the images enscripted Pharaoh's future.

Within the broader cultural conception of word as image and its association with creation, the Israelites appear somewhat anomalous, since the Bible's ten commandments specifically prohibit the creation of graven images but demand the transmission of divine knowledge by way of the written and spoken words. Moreover, although the Hebrew word for an alphabetic letter (*'ôt*) also means "sign, portent," the Bible nowhere connects the two semantic ranges or attaches religious import to particular letters outside the tetragrammaton, or sacred name of God, Yahweh. I believe that this puzzle can be solved, at least in part, with acknowledgment of the generative role that the sacred script (and, in the case of the Israelites, a consonantal script) played in ancient Near Eastern religions. Although the Hebrew script evolved from pictographic signs,[42] and the Old Canaanite script that preceded it had adopted the directional flexibility of hieroglyphic Egyptian, by the time of the Israelites it had lost its pictographic associations, and its direction had become fixed. Thus its associative dimension was limited to such sound devices as paronomasia; and, by contrast with the Egyptian and Mesopotamian conceptions of writing as an act of creation, the book of Genesis reports creation as solely an oral work, even though later Jewish tradition recalls the role of the alphabet in the creative process.[43] I cannot help wondering if the nonpictographic script played a partial role in shaping the ancient Israelite conception of creation.

Since I have written at length about ancient scribes, it is only appropriate that I conclude by quoting one of them. The citation comes to us from the stylus of a nameless Egyptian master of script, and although it was written at a time and in a place wholly foreign to us, it reminds our tech-savvy world that the utility of technology depends upon the quality of its use, and that its quality provides for its own legacy. Here are the words of the sage:

> As for the erudite scribes from the time of those who lived after the gods, they could prophesy what was to come, their names have become eternal, [and though] they are no more, they finished their lives, and all their relatives have been forgotten. They did not make for themselves pyramids of metal, with coffins of iron. They were not able to leave heirs in children, pronouncing their names, but they made heirs of themselves in the writings and in [the scrolls of wisdom] which they composed.[44]

NOTES

1. Edward Mendelson, "Monastery of Christ in the Desert, New Mexico," *New York Times Book Review*, June 2, 1996.

2. Ibid.

3. Sheldon W. Greaves, "The Power of the Word in the Ancient Near East" (Ph.D. diss., University of California, Berkeley, 1996); J. N. Lawson, "Mesopotamian Precursors to the Stoic Concept of Logos," in R. M. Whiting, ed., *Mythology and Mythologies: Methodological Approaches to Intercultural Influences,* Melammu Symposia II (Helsinki: Neo-Assyrian Text Corpus Project, 2001), 68–91.

4. Georges Contenau, *Everyday Life in Babylon and Assyria* (London: Edward Arnold, 1955), 164.

5. For the development of writing and its relationship to "magic," see Jean Bottéro, *Mesopotamia: Writing, Reasoning, and the Gods* (Chicago: University of Chicago Press, 1992); Jean Bottéro, "Symptômes, signes, écritures en Mésopotamie ancienne," in J. P. Vernat et al., eds., *Divination et Rationalité* (Paris: Éditions du Seuil, 1974), 70–197.

6. A. W. Sjöberg, "In Praise of the Scribal Art," *Journal of Cuneiform Studies* 24 (1972), 126–31.

7. Shalom M. Paul, "Heavenly Tablets and the Book of Life," *Journal of the Ancient Near Eastern Society of Columbia University* 5 (1973), 345–53.

8. See, e.g., the famous Egyptian texts known as "The Satire on the Trades" and "In Praise of Learned Scribes," translated in James B. Pritchard, *Ancient Near Eastern Texts Relating to the Old Testament* (Princeton, N.J.: Princeton University Press, 1950).

9. For the connections among writing, speech, and "magic," see Robert Kriech Ritner, *The Mechanics of Ancient Egyptian Magical Practice,* Studies in Ancient Oriental Civilization, no. 54 (Chicago: Oriental Institute of the University of Chicago, 1993). The importance of writing also can be seen in the word *rḫ,* "knowledge," which contains the papyrus scroll determinative.

10. On the possible origin of the deity Thoth, see Carleton T. Hodge, "Thoth and Oral Tradition," in Mary Ritchie Key and Henry M. Hoenigswald, eds., *General and Amerindian Ethnolinguistics: In Remembrance of Stanley Newman* (Berling: Mouton de Gruyter, 1989), 407–16; for more about Thoth, see also Ritner, *Mechanics of Ancient Egyptian Magical Practice,* 35. On *Ma'at,* see Jan Assmann, *Ma'at: Gerechtikeit und Unsterblichkeit im alten Ägypten* (Munich: Verlag C. H. Beck, 1990) and, more recently, Emily Teeter, *The Presentation of Maat: Ritual and Legitimacy in Ancient Egypt,* Studies in Oriental Civilization, no. 57 (Chicago: Oriental Institute of the University of Chicago, 1997).

11. Adolf Erman and Hermann Grapow, *Ägyptisches Handwörterbuch* (Hildesheim: Georg Olms Verlag, 1995), 92.

12. Cf. the role of the scribal god Thoth in the Memphite Theology.

13. A. Leo Oppenheim, *Ancient Mesopotamia: Portrait of a Dead Civilization* (Chicago: University of Chicago Press, 1977), 236.

14. See, e.g., I. Rabinowitz, *A Witness Forever: Ancient Israel's Perception of Literature and the Resultant Hebrew Bible* (Bethesda, Md.: CDL Press, 1993).

15. Contra Francis Brown et al., eds., *A Hebrew and English Lexicon of the Old Testament* (Oxford: Clarendon Press, 1951), who propose an Arabic cognate *dabara* "back, behind." See also the ancient Greek and Latin translations that treat the word as if connected to the common Hebrew verb *dābar,* "speak."

16. E.g., Ezekiel 29:13. Compare Psalm 85, which begins by telling us that God has restored the captivity of Jacob and forgiven the iniquity of his people and then concludes with a prayer for the enactment of these very events.

17. For an accessible treatment of the subject of wordplay, see Scott B. Noegel, ed., *Puns and Pundits: Word Play in the Hebrew Bible and Ancient Near Eastern Literature* (Bethesda, Md.: CDL Press, 2000).

18. Similarly, see Scott B. Noegel, "Atbash in Jeremiah and Its Literary Significance: Part 1," *Jewish Bible Quarterly* 24:2 (1996), 82–89; Scott B. Noegel, "Atbash in Jeremiah and Its Literary Significance: Part 2," *Jewish Bible Quarterly* 24:3 (1996), 160–66; Scott B. Noegel "Atbash in Jeremiah and Its Literary Significance: Part 3," *Jewish Bible Quarterly* 24:4 (1996), 247–50.

19. See, e.g., Carleton T. Hodge, "Ritual and Writing: An Inquiry into the Origin of Egyptian Script," in M. Dale Kinkade et al., eds., *Linguistics and Anthropology: In Honor of C. F. Voegelin*

(Lisse, The Netherlands: Peter de Ridder Press, 1975), 331–50; Scott B. Noegel, "Wordplay in the Tale of the Poor Man of Nippur," *Acta Sumerologica* 18 (1996), 169–86.

20. See, e.g., W. M. Soll, "Babylonian and Biblical Acrostics," *Biblica* 69 (1988), 305–32; H. M. Stewart, "A Crossword Hymn to Mut," *Journal of Egyptian Archaeology* 57 (1971), 87–104.

21. Ritner, *Mechanics of Ancient Egyptian Magical Practice*, 111–43.

22. See M. Etienne Droiton, "Une figuration cryptographique sur une stèle du Moyen Empire," *Revue d'Égyptologie* 1 (1933), 203–29. See also Scott B. Noegel, "Moses and Magic: Notes on the Book of Exodus," *Journal of the Ancient Near Eastern Society* 24 (1997), 45–59. Mesopotamian iconography conveying textual information also is known. See, e.g., I. L. Finkel and J. E. Reade, "Assyrian Hieroglyphs," *Zeitschrift für assyriologie* 86 (1996), 244–68; J. A. Scurlock, "Assyrian Hieroglyphs Enhanced," *Nouvelles Assyriologiques Brèves et Utilitaires* (1997), 85–86.

23. Alasdair Livingstone, *Mystical and Mythological Explanatory Works of Assyrian and Babylonian Scholars* (Oxford: Clarendon Press, 1986).

24. See the important brief note in Anne Draffkorn Kilmer, "The Brick of Birth," *Journal of Near Eastern Studies* 46 (1987), 211–13.

25. See, e.g., the remark about Ea, god of magic, in Enuma Elish XI: 175–76 *mannuma ša lā ᵈEa amatu ibann[u]* (lit.) "Who other than Ea can build word / ideas?"

26. Oppenheim, *Ancient Mesopotamia*, 234–35.

27. Papyrus was associated with the Deltan cosmology of the god Ptah, who created all life from a primeval papyrus thicket. Some Egyptian myths did involve clay, such as the myth of Khnum, a ram-headed god responsible for making humankind on a potter's wheel. Nevertheless, it is Ptah and papyrus that concern us here.

28. Cf. the Talmud Bavli Meg 16b, Talmud Yerushalmi Meg 3:8 (74b), Sot 12:9, which refer to Moses' Song at the Sea in Exodus 15 as composed of alternating stichs of "one-half brick over a whole brick, and a whole brick over a half-brick."

29. Cf. Isaiah 34:4, "All the host of heaven shall dwindle away, and the heavens shall be rolled up like a scroll *[sepher]*."

30. E.g., *kārat*, "cut"; *hāqaq*, "engrave"; and *kātab*, "inscribe." The latter covers not only writing with ink but also inscribing; see, e.g., Exodus 31:18 and Isaiah 44:5.

31. Note also the semantic range of the Hebrew word *bayit*, which means "house" as well as "dynasty, family."

32. This does not rule out, of course, the possibility that the animals from which parchment was made possessed a sacred significance in the period before the Israelites began to use the material.

33. For the use of seven in ancient Near Eastern literature, see W. R. Dawson, "The Number 'Seven' in Egyptian Texts," *Aegyptus* 8 (1927), 27–107; S. E. Loewenstamm, "The Seven-Day-Unit in Ugaritic Epic Literature," in S. E. Loewenstamm, ed., *Comparative Studies in the Bible and Ancient Near Eastern Literatures, AOAT* [Alter Orient und Altes Testament] 204 (Neukirchen-Vluyn: Neukirchener Verlag 1980), 192–209; Scott B. Noegel, "The Significance of the Seventh Plague," *Biblica* 76 (995), 532–39.

34. See, e.g., Wolfgang Heimpel, "The Sun at Night and the Doors of Heaven in Babylonian Texts," *Journal of Cuneiform Studies* 38 (1986), 127–51.

35. See W. G. Lambert, "A Catalogue of Texts and Authors," *Journal of Cuneiform Studies* 16 (1962), 59–77. P. A. Beaulieu, however, convincingly suggested to the American Oriental Society (March 20, 1996) that this author belongs to a family of *kalû*, "lamentation priests." The difference in profession matters little here, since both occupations required a knowledge of "magic."

36. See, e.g., the praise of Enlil, which contains fifty lines, fifty being the number of Enlil's name. This was pointed out to me by Professor Anne Kilmer of the University of California–Berkeley, who also informs me that she has collected a great deal of information on this topic and is preparing it for publication under the title "Weaving Textual Patterns: Symmetry in Akkadian Poetic Texts"; see, provisionally, Anne Draffkorn Kilmer, "Fugal Features of Atra-

Hasis: The Birth Theme," in M. E. Vogelzang and H. L. J. Vanstiphout, eds., *Mesopotamian Poetic Language: Sumerian and Akkadian,* Cuneiform Monographs, no. 6 (Groningen: Styx Publications, 1996), 127–39. We might add to this the so-called acrostics, which are found in the Bible and in Egyptian and Mesopotamian literature (see n. 20 above). For the use of numbers in biblical and rabbinic compositions see Robert Gordis, *Poets, Prophets, and Sages: Essays in Biblical Interpretation* (Bloomington: Indiana University Press, 1971), 95–103.

37. Livingstone, *Mystical and Mythological Explanatory Works;* Laurie E. Pearce, "The Number-Syllabary Texts," *Journal of the American Oriental Society* 116 (1996), 453–74.

38. See, e.g., Jean Bottéro, "Les noms de Marduk, l'écriture et la 'logique' en Mésopotamie ancienne," in Maria de Jong Ellis, ed., *Essays on the Ancient Near East in Memory of Jacob Joel Finkelstein,* Memoirs of the Connecticut Academy of Arts and Sciences, no. 19 (Hamden, Conn.: Hamden Books, 1977), 5–28.

39. I cautiously add here Gemini and the Trinity. The relationship between numbers and gods was first espied by K. Jaritz, "Geheimschriftsysteme im alten Orient," *Adeva Mitteilungen* 8 (1966), 11–15, and was applied to the biblical material by Cyrus H. Gordon, "His Name is 'One'," *Journal of Near Eastern Studies* 29 (1970), 198–99.

40. It is of interest to note Z. ben Hayyim's observation that the word *masorah* is related to the tradition of scribal counting; see Z. ben Hayyim, *"mswrh wmswrt,"* Leshonenu 21 (1957), 283–92.

41. Note that $t\rho t$ is written with the determinatives $w\underline{d}3t$, "magical eye of Horus," and the papyrus scroll.

42. The discovery in October 1999 at Wadi el-Ḥol, Egypt, of an early alphabetic script related to the inscriptional hieratic of early Middle Kingdom Egypt may shed light on this issue. Several of the letterforms discovered there relate closely to those in the so-called proto-Sinaitic script, found several centuries later in the Sinai.

43. See, e.g., the explanation of the raised letter *he-* in $b^h br'm$ as "with the *he* . . . he created them [the heavens and the earth]" (Midrash Rabbah 1:10).

44. I have based this rendering, with some modification, on the translation of John A. Wilson in Pritchard, *Ancient Near Eastern Texts Relating to the Old Testament,* 431.

Magical Texts and Popular Literacy
Vulgarizations, Iterations, or Appropriations?

PHYLLIS CULHAM

Epigraphers study texts engraved on stone, bronze, or other durable surfaces. Most ancient epigraphy to date has had as its first goal "publishing" the text painstakingly read on the durable surface and then trying to see behind it to an *ur*-text. Work on public documents has often attempted to understand if not recover the "original" governmental pronouncement that is assumed to lie behind the epigraphical monument. Scholarship on private texts, such as those on tombstones, has been more open to investigation of authorial identity and intent, although it, too, has been interested in recovery of a professionally generated *ur*-text in the form of handbooks or other models. In short, epigraphical editing falls under Gary Taylor's claim that "editing seeks to establish texts that are proximate to a source of value."[1] This essay, too, goes partway on that traditional hunt for the *ur*-text, but I would also like to redirect attention toward the entirety of the text-bearing object.

I believe that considering the physical nature and manufacture of the text-bearing object will enable epigraphers to address their usual textual concerns as well as raise other profitable questions. Did divergences from an ancient *ur*-text always amount to deficiencies? Could they have been creative appropriations of the power to make a text? Did users of handbooks or models attempt pure replication, or did they view these aids as platforms from which they could generate new products for consumers? How much of the power of a text lay in its resemblance to an *ur*-text, and how much in the handling of the object that bore the text? Epigraphers often study generators of texts, both the governmental elite and economically successful purchasers of gravestones, and sometimes even ask questions about envisioned readers. Yet the actual makers of the physical texts that survive are considered only as potential sources of "error" in textual transmission from elite source or model to consumer. This essay attempts to ask what could happen at that "scribal" or mediating level between authoritative text and consumer.

Recent work on the topic of literacy in antiquity supplies a more general social perspective from which we can approach these issues. William V. Harris's deeply comparative approach went a long way toward eliminating the concept of a stark literate / illiterate dichotomy and toward recognition of several types of literacy.[2] Harris tended to minimize literacy in the ancient world as a whole and in the Roman republic with which this essay is concerned. More recently, Mireille Corbier has tackled the preconception (which my colleagues tell me is epidemic among modern historians) that literacy is always associated with socially elite status and even defines it or confers it in some cases. Corbier notes that "scribal literacy" was hardly a socially elite phenomenon in Rome, where the senatorial class spoke and senators' slaves wrote.[3] Surely Greek scribes or secretaries cannot have given themselves many airs, and freeborn, if poor, Romans would not have been inclined to defer to them socially. Hopkins suggests that Roman life would inevitably have led to encounters not with literary but with governmental-style, record-keeping literacy, which in turn would have inculcated concepts of cataloging and bringing order to masses of data.[4] This recent scholarship supplies the social and cultural context in which we can view one selected set of curse tablets, not simply as texts but as a collective object.

We will focus on five lead curse-tablets with the average dimensions of 32 cm. by 12 cm. They were folded or rolled, and then a nail 12.7 cm. in length was driven through them. Their texts were originally "published" in 1912.[5] The text-bearing object no longer exists; it was inevitably destroyed in the process of detaching and unrolling the lead tablets to recover the texts. Each tablet was damaged in proportion to how close it had been to the head of the nail. When the tablets were unrolled, much of their substance crumbled into illegible or unplaceable fragments.[6] Although all the tablets bear versions of the same curse, the argument that follows depends mainly on the text cursing Plotius, since that tablet was farthest from the head of the nail. Here is Fox's reconstructed text of the Plotius curse, followed by my translation, for the reader's benefit. For consistency with other citations, however, Fox's translation will be cited henceforward as *P*.[7]

Bona pulchra Proserpina, [P]lut[o]nis uxsor,
seiue me Saluiam deicere oportet,
eripias salutem, c[orpus, co]lorem, uires, uirtutes
Ploti. Tradas [Plutoni] uiro tuo. Ni possit cogitati
sueis hoc uita[re. Tradas] illunc\onibus

Febri quartan[a]e, t[ertian]ae, cottidia[n]ae,
quas [cum illo l]uct[ent, deluctent; illunc]
eu[in]cant [uincant], usq[ue dum animam
eiu]s eripia[nt. Quare ha]nc uictimam
tibi trad[o, Prose]rpi[na, seiu]e me,
Proserpin[a, sei]ue m[e Ach]eruosiam dicere
oportet. M[e mittas a]recessitum canem
tricepitem, qui [Ploti] cor eripiat. Polliciar
illi te datururn t[r]es uictimas—\us
palma[s, ca]rica[s], por[c]um nigrum—
hoc sei p[erfe]cerit [ante mensem]
M[artium. Haec, P]r[oserpina Saluia, tibi dabo]
cum compote fe[cer]is. Do tibi cap[ut]
Ploti Auon[iae. Pr]oserpina S[aluia],
do tibi fron[tem Plo]ti. Proserpina Saluia,
do [ti]b[i] su[percilia] Ploti. Proserpin[a]
Saluia, do [tibi palpebra]s Plo[ti].
Proserpina Sa[luia, do tibi pupillas]
Ploti. Proser[pina Saluia, do tibi nare]s,
labra, or[iculas, nasu]m, lin[g]uam,
dentes P[loti], ni dicere possit
Plotius quid [sibi dole]at: collum, umeros,
bracchia, d[i]git[os, ni po]ssit aliquit
se adiurare: [pe]c[tus, io]cinera, cor,
pulmones, n[i possit] senti(re) quit
sibi doleat: [intes]tina, uenter, um[b]licu[s]
latera, [n]i p[oss]it dormire: scapulas,
ni poss[it] s[a]nus dormire: uiscum
sacrum, nei possit urinam facere:
natis, anum, [fem]ina, genua,
[crura], tibias, pe[des, talos, plantas,
digito]s, ungis, ni po[ssit s]tare [sua
ui]rt[u]te. Seiue [plu]s, seiue paruum
scrip[tum fuerit], quomodo quicqu[id]
legitim[e scripsit], mandauit, seic
ego Ploti ti[bi tr]ado, mando,
ut tradas, [mandes me]nse Februari[o
e]cillunc. Ma[le perdat, mal]e exset,
[mal]e disperd[at. Mandes, tra]das, ni possit
[ampliu]s ullum [mensem aspic]ere,
[uidere, contempla]re.[8]

Good and beautiful Proserpina, wife of Pluto,

unless it would be fitting for me to call you Salvia

Snatch away Plotius' health, body, complexion, strength, and
abilities.

Hand him over to your husband. Let him be unable to avoid this
by use of schemes.

Hand him over to the fourth-day, the third-day, the everyday
fevers.

Let them wrestle and tussle with him.

Let them conquer and overwhelm him and snatch away his life.

Thus I consign him as a sacrifice to you, Proserpina,

unless it would be fitting for me to call you Acheruosia.

Send me the three-headed dog so that he can rip out Plotius'
heart.

Promise [your husband] that you will give him three sacrifices:

dates, figs, and a black pig.

if he completes this before the month of March.

These will I give you, Proserpina, when you have done for me as
I've prayed.

I give you the head of Plotius, slave of Avonia.

I give you the forehead of Plotius, Proserpina Salvia.

I give you the eyebrows of Plotius, Proserpina Salvia.

I give you the eyelids of Plotius, Proserpina Salvia.

I give you the pupils of Plotius, Proserpina Salvia.

I give you the nostrils, lips, ears, nose, tongue and teeth of Plotius

so that he may be unable to speak about what afflicts him;

his neck, shoulders, arms, and fingers so that he may be unable
to help himself in any way;

his chest, liver, heart, lungs, so that he will not even know what
afflicts him;

his intestines, belly, navel, and sides so that he may be unable
to sleep;

his shoulder-blades so that he may be unable to sleep soundly;

his sacred part so that he may be unable to pass urine;

his buttocks, anus, thighs, knees, legs, shins, feet, ankles, soles,
toes, and nails

so that he may be unable to stand by his own strength.

Should there be a great written curse, or even a small one,

in any manner whatsoever under the rules of magic

in which he has drafted something and entrusted it to writing

so I similarly hand him over to you and consign him,

so that you may hand him over and consign him in the month
   of February.
Let him perish horribly. Let him die horribly. Let him be utterly
   wiped out horribly.
Hand him over, consign him so that he may not
look forward to, see, or anticipate any other month.

Little is known about the physical context in which the tablets were
recovered, since an anonymous donor gave them to The Johns Hopkins
University at the beginning of the twentieth century, with the cryptic
information that he believed they were from Rome.

These texts represent an opportunity extremely rare in the study of
antiquity. Public documents are infrequently preserved in multiple
copies, and private ones are almost never duplicated. Even so, the
uncommon cases in which there are multiple epigraphic copies are usually those in which there is an effort to recover an *ur*-text, not to study
the process by which the physical text-bearing object was actually generated or to consider how these texts problematize such concepts as
"author," "original," "error," and even "editor." Nor have magical texts,
as opposed to funerary texts or business accounts, featured in any scholarship I can find on popular reading and writing in antiquity. We can
begin by following McGann's advice to "make a careful distinction
between the linguistic and the bibliographical features of texts"[9]—in this
case, between the written content and the object created by five lead
tablets and a nail. If we consider magical text and object together we
can look for answers to our initial questions—in this particular case, asking where meaning and power lie: in the repetition of magical words?
in the construction of a perfect edition, namely, the text-bearing magical object? in the hands of the writer? in the actions of the object's user?
in the arcane knowledge possessed by the author of the now invisible
ur-text? Can the roles of "author," "reader," and "editor" be carefully
sorted out?

At first glance, the object-with-nail seems to come from a primitive
world of sympathetic magic. Some scholars, discussing similar tablets,
have suggested that the act of piercing the tablets was meant to injure
the cursee sympathetically.[10] That hypothesis is not possible in this case,
since the tablets embody the curser, if they may be said to embody anyone. They use assertive first-person language, even the emphatic first-
person pronoun *ego,* not normally expressed in Latin (see *P* line 41, as
well as the aggressive series of the first-person-singular verb *do* in *P* lines

18–24). Surely Gager is right to suggest that we think of the nail as expressing a more abstract metaphor, yet one based on daily life.[11] The curser wished to finalize the deal with the deity, "nailing it down," as it were, and to make sure that his words bore real weight. Nails were certainly associated with relief as well as with pain in the Roman world, as attested by Livy's belief that the very early Roman republic had a custom of driving nails to prevent plague.[12] The idea of finality is implicit in Etruscan depictions of Fate (Roman Fortuna) with nails as well as in the driving of nails to count off years at one shrine to Fortuna.[13]

There are curse tablets in which the lead does stand in part for the victim.[14] Those examples do not have the feature of first-person speech in words attributed to the curser. The first person of these tablets is not the author of the model, nor even the writer of these particular tablets, but the user of the object, the person who might have rolled the tablets and, I believe, driven the nail and deposited the tablets at some sacral site, thereby becoming, if not an author, a compositor of the physical text and its message.

As already noted, we do not know how this object was placed, but in general such tablets were deposited at temple sites and graves. This was surely an attempt to communicate with deities rather than an attempt to consign to perdition, sympathetically, an object representing the victim. Chthonic deities were believed to associate themselves with tombs. Tomlin, who worked on British curse-tablets, believed that lead was considered particularly appropriate for dark and weighty matters,[15] and one can see how someone wishing to communicate something to the infernal deities would pick a substance known for sinking. Certainly, the use of lead in curse tablets persisted even after more convenient materials like papyrus were available, and a majority of surviving texts written on lead are curses.[16] The potential for harm, therefore, lay in the text-bearing object, not in the words of the text per se, a point to which we will return later. The physical medium was part of the message, as was the site of the text. Involvement of the curser in construction and deposition would easily have justified the first-person language of the texts, even if the curser was not the writer. These circumstances offer a strong contrast with the earlier culture of the Near East, as discussed in Scott Noegel's essay in this volume. Although there is a similar respect for medium, the written word per se is not magic until it is appropriately objectified. Nor, as we will see, does it have to be passed on exactly as received.

We can now examine the Plotius text, how it was generated, and whether it was generated by the curser. We have already noted the first-person verbs and the pronoun *ego,* but another example illustrates the formal and formulaic nature of many of the expressions in the text, namely, Fox's translation of *P* lines 1–2: "Good and beautiful Proserpina, wife of Pluto, / whom perhaps it is fitting for me to call Salvia." This is not daily language and may reflect the use of a compendium of curses or magic. Another section of the text offers us chantable language: lines 18–24, with the repetitions of "do tibi" ("I give you"). Lines 6–8 give us a heaping of fevers and of verbs paired after one pronoun, which may suggest formulaic expression from a handbook, but, admittedly, it may also suggest a memorable, even chantable, folk spell. The repeated *do* was also chantable. If we had only one tablet, this catalog might appear to be the hallmark of originally oral, popular composition, in which case these texts might have been considered attempts to preserve and reinforce an oral performance of spells by one or more people. Nevertheless, all the anatomical items that occur in those separate sentences appear in the same order in all the tablets, a hint that their striking if boring consistency results from the use of a written model. Fox suggested, on the basis of the resemblance between these first-century B.C. curse tablets and other curse tablets from second-century A.D. Latium, that handbooks were circulating locally near Rome. Those tablets resembled these in their excruciatingly detailed cataloging of the body parts to be afflicted, as well as in their tendency to curse the victim downward, from head to foot, although their catalogs were different from and less systematic than the catalog with which we are concerned.[17]

A better indication of the use of a handbook is the striking reference, in *P* lines 38–42, to writing; Fox's translation reads as follows: "In what manner he [Plotius] has according to the laws of magic composed any curses [i.e., against me] and entrusted it to writing, in like manner I consign him to thee." The Latin syntax may not be clear, but the sentiment is unmistakable. There are obvious Greek parallels for both the legalistic construction and the sentiment, which suggests in turn that we are dealing with a model that harks back to the handbooks circulating in the eastern Mediterranean.[18] The Romans associated magical books with foreign cults, and so they would not have been put off by a little foreign flavor in their perhaps incompletely translated models.[19] The slightly exotic formulation might even have been considered a guarantor of authenticity, and therefore of potency. Certainly this fussily formulaic balancing of the curse account echoes neither a popular chant nor a passionate, unchanneled outpouring of resentment.

A final piece of evidence that we are dealing with a text closely derived from a handbook has heretofore been overlooked. *P* lines 33–34 hand the victim's *viscum sacrum* over to the goddess so that the victim will not be able to urinate. The grammatically incorrect *viscum*, which should be *viscus* as a third-declension neuter, must be the male organ, often the explicit target of Greek curses.[20] One might be able to take it as a misspelling of *vesica*, "bladder," if not for the neuter adjective *sacrum*. Admittedly, the term *viscus* does often refer to the uterus, but the ancients understood as well as we do that in women the reproductive system and the urinary tract do not share a channel. It makes no sense to call down upon a uterus the curse of an inability to urinate. If one wanted to curse a woman's *viscus*, one would presumably curse her with sterility, and there are parallels for such curses.[21]

The leading recent scholars on curse tablets argue that even the educated elite feared curses because they believed them to work, having seen what they believed to be the results of curses in the many unpleasant events of premodern life.[22] If it is true that curse tablets were feared because they appeared to produce results that could be commonly observed, we would expect to find that all curses leveled at a victim sought medically plausible results. For example, one would curse a victim with the prospect of producing oozing skin sores, not with the prospect of his skin turning purple and sprouting mushrooms. Women, premodern or not, are highly, highly unlikely ever to experience difficulty in urinating for any significant time; all the vicissitudes of life made and make the opposite, incontinence, much more likely.[23]

Men, by contrast, face prostatitis from both age and sexually transmitted diseases (STDs). STDs may also produce ulceration in the urethra; the scarred tissue then contracts. Repeated intubation, including self-intubation with reeds, could be expected to exacerbate the scarring until the victim experienced an impassible stricture. The consequences for the premodern victim were generally unpleasant and humiliating, extremely painful, and a prolonged route to death. Now, that is a worthwhile curse![24]

These medical observations are of great significance for the tablets with which we are concerned, because poor Plotius and the male victim whose name does not survive (just a male pronoun remains) are a minority of victims. One would presumably not curse the male organs of the three female victims unless one were copying a pattern, and (this may be significant later) unless one were a little vague on the significance of the Latin term one encountered, or with which one translated one's Greek model. It is a mistake one might be more likely to make if one were a professional writer of curses, not the personally involved, aggrieved curser who knew the victims all too well. Nevertheless, a person fearfully inexperienced at magic might have made the mistake in the course of following a model slavishly. It is not asking too much for a curse to be anatomically correct.[25] In short, a single model from a handbook must lie behind the tablets we are discussing, and its use of the phrase *viscum sacrum* shows the actual writer of these tablets failing to adapt the curse completely to three of the five victims. In performing the currently admired editorial function of conserving the standardized text, he failed at accomplishing the ends of the curser, even if he was the curser, and he may even have subverted (inadvertently) the "true purpose" of the "author."

The foregoing material has led us to conclude that the "author" of the original model curse, the writer of the tablets, and the curser might well not have been the same person. It is not clear (and this essay will not be able to resolve the question) whether the "author" or the writer is also the translator from a Greek model. We have already seen that the writer is not fully in control of the model; nevertheless, he is confidently making texts which will become a new, unique object. No one has doubted Fox's original conclusion that one writer did all five tablets: the handwriting is easily within the range of variation we can expect from ourselves when we grow tired of writing, change position for comfort, or attempt to adjust our writing to fit the space; that seems to me to argue for some facility and comfort with the process, since the writer is not trying painstakingly to produce a "best" handwriting. Nor has anyone argued with Fox's initial observation that the handwriting on the tablets resembles other cursive scripts on walls, wax tablets, and papyrus of the first century B.C.[26] There are spots where the writer is unable to complete a word and must append it below, on the next line (e.g., *P* lines 4 and 14). That feature might be taken as evidence of marginal literacy, as displayed in the inability to read ahead and estimate correctly, if not for the appropriate syllabic division in those lines, and if not for another example at line 29 of the Maxima Vesonia text, as well as the visible cramming at the ends of lines—a clear indication of the writer's reading ahead and being aware of the medium.[27] The Avonia and Maxima Vesonia tablets (see n. 7) both continue the text for a few lines on the back. In each case, the tablet was turned in midsentence, without a break in syntax and without the introduction of confusion, facts that speak for some sophistication in copying. They also illustrate that the writer believed he had the ability to create a new text-bearing object—a new edition, if you will—and did not have to preserve the appearance and configuration of an arcane archetype.

As the catalogs of body parts show, the three legible tablets do differ from one another in a number of ways; the question is what those differences tell us about how the texts were generated. These catalogs occur in the accusative, since the curser is handing the items over to Proserpina. I will not discuss all the "vulgar" spellings here, although some of them may reflect popular pronunciation. The catalogs certainly illustrate the confusion over gender and declension in Latin that reigns throughout the tablets, although I will concentrate on three more particular examples, which may offer additional pointers to the identity of writer and curser.[28]

P lines 18–26 specify that the person to be cursed is Plotius, the slave of Avonia, although that information is not given until about halfway through the tablet, at line 19. None of the other cursees are so identified. Clearly, the writer has exercised an editorial function and clarified a text where he believed clarification was necessary; the question is why. The writer might have been the curser, who so hated Plotius that he only belatedly realized that a goddess with a broader perspective might not know which of the hundreds of Plotii in Rome had been consigned to her. Or he might have been a dispassionate professional writer of curses who unthinkingly followed his usual practice of inserting a name into the matrix of the curse, until he belatedly realized that Rome was full of Plotii and that he had better specify which of them was meant.

There are also revealing variations in the catalogs. The Avonia tablet clearly offers the properly organized, efficient text of one catalog: *intestina, venter, umblicus, scapulas latera ni possit dormire.* Clearly, the Plotius text initially omitted *scapulas* in lines 31–33. When the author realized he had omitted a term, he had to repeat a whole clause, *ni possit dormire,* in order to keep the syntax complete while getting the term back in. In other words, he recognized while still writing that he had made a mistake, and he generated sound new text to cover it and yet keep the catalog complete. Finally, there are reversals of order in the last catalog, at *P* lines 35–37. The Avonia text reverses *femina anum,* and the Vesonia text reverses *tibias crura.*

What these three examples show us is that the writer is concerned with fulfilling the intent of the curser (however he may fail on occasion) and with cursing everything the model permits him to curse. In contrast to what we see in the Near Eastern material, he is not aiming at the perfect verbal repetition of a charm or spell. He does not have to throw out a "defective" tablet; it suffices that the meaning is clear. The efficacy must have lain in the proper handling of the new object and in communicating the meaning to the god, not in the flawless incantation of a formula. The variation in the catalogs seems to point to an inscriber who did not copy painfully and slowly with awe, but to one who looked at the model and copied a few to several words at a time, with confidence in his ability to function as an editor in glancing back over the model and catching and adding omitted items. The magic did not lie in the matrix of words but in the constructed object bearing them.

We can move closer to this question of the identity of the writer and the curser. It intersects with both the Graecisms and the "vulgarisms." First, the Greek flavor: Proserpina is herself Greek, and she is attested as Salvia only here. That must refer to the *Soteira* epithet applied in Greek to the same deity. The only parallels for evoking Cerberus in a curse come from Attica. The texts that concern us here are unique in offering dates to Proserpina and Cerberus, but dates were used in magic in Babylonia and Assyria. These examples of Greek and eastern Mediterranean influence could all have been transmitted by handbook.[29]

The inconsistent genitives in the Avonia and Vesonia tablets are different. In many cases, the tablets use normal Latin first-declension genitives in -*ae*, but the Avonia tablet definitely has *Avoniaes* in at least four lines. The Vesonia tablet has *Vesoniaes* only once. Greek genitives turn up in other curse tablets, and the Greek *eta sigma* probably lies behind this -*es* ending.[30] Since the names inserted in the matrix of the curses were not in the handbook, we may suspect that the writers of these and similar Greek-flavored curses were people who originally spoke Greek or were comfortable in a bilingual setting—just the sort of setting in which eastern Mediterranean handbooks were kept and perhaps translated.

That brings us to the second significant aspect of the language, namely, its colloquialism and old-fashioned qualities, e.g., *illunc, luctent, liguam, uxsor, seive, seic, deicere,* and *ungis* and *navis* as accusatives. The pleonastic piling up of colorful verbs, which we noted earlier, is typical of the enthusiasm of popular speech.[31] What are we to make of texts that contain both colorful speech, like that of rascals in Plautus, and expressions from arcane books from the eastern Mediterranean? Here we must recall the cultural context with which we began. These texts clearly support the arguments of scholars like Corbier, who has pointed out that literacy was not an altogether elite phenomenon in the Roman world, and Hopkins, who has argued that even those who were unable or disinclined to read literary texts for pleasure still acquired, by observation, the habits of systemization and cataloging.[32]

Surely both Corbier and Hopkins are describing the milieu in which our tablets originated: a society in which those who encountered inscriptions, whether or not they read them, had a sense of the respect and attention one could get if one had the right medium. One thinks of Ramsey MacMullen's phrase "epigraphic culture."[33] One historian of Latin has recently denied that there was a Roman *culture cabalistique*; she quotes the aphorism *verba volant, scripta manent,* claiming that there was an argument at the end of the Roman republic about whether writing ought to hold out a standard at which speech could aim or whether it ought to represent speech.[34] The writer of the texts we have been examining made the second assumption: that writing ought to represent speech. He was not imitating Near Eastern models, which attempt to compile power by repeating catalogs of sacred names, or to mystify by using nonsense words. He was constructing a text that would serve as a secure mechanism for carrying words across distance and time, all the way to the gods, and the speech he heard every day supplied words good enough for the task. He intended to convey his meaning to his selected deity, not to compel her merely by the precise repetition of an incantation.

But was this writer / editor the curser? Probably the use of the hand-book tips the scales in favor of the professional consultant at magic. The use of such materials was socially frowned upon and even dangerous to the practitioner. Roman law of the later imperial period condemned the practitioner of curses to crucifixion or to facing animals in the arena, and the mere owner of a manual was, according to social class, deported to an island or beheaded. Surely few people other than serious practitioners would have kept such suspicious materials around just on the chance that they might have to curse a neighbor! The holder of the hand-book was a sort of gatekeeper to useful texts, and a powerful figure in his ability to multiply the number of these texts, yet he was also in the power of his neighbors.[35]

Gager, however, and others have argued that curse tablets worked because they were public in some sense. They presumably worked upon the victim through suggestion, as well as, if Gager is right, through publicizing accusations against the cursee and through demonstrations, by way of ill-effects, of how the gods despised him. Certainly curse tablets were frequent in the Roman world, in spite of their illegality.[36] There were certainly shrines where some were posted, although those were surely viewed as one more type of prayer to a locally respected deity.

People who kept suspicious books may have been viewed as fearless and dangerous people in their neighborhoods. A curser may have dropped oblique hints meant to evoke fear in the victim, but surely the harsh penalties, and the usual practice of deposit at fearful sites in the middle of the night, kept the actual creation of objects such as those examined here a secret between the writer and the curser. Such commissions were probably proposed and accepted only among people already known to each other, or among those brought together by trusted friends. They presumably lived in geographical proximity. Some cursers may have been sufficiently literate to read over the tablets they had ordered, and the service may have consisted largely of the use of the model. The first-person subjects of the texts examined here were presumably justified by the importance of creating the magical object with the nail and depositing it properly—both acts presumably performed by the curser. Cursers may have concluded that their curses worked simply because of the higher rates of disorders that might affect people even in the prime of life. Some of the items Gager cites seem to point to the converse, namely, that people who suddenly became ill assumed that they had been cursed. Failure to produce illness may have been ascribed to some flaw in deposition.[37]

Whoever commissioned the tablets we have been discussing was confident in his use of literacy and in the text that was generated, even if he could not fully practice literacy. He had defined a problem closely and had determined to deal with it thoroughly, to the extent of commissioning five tablets. The writer did not fear that a mystically constituted text of magic words had power beyond his ability to manipulate it and its letters. He did not need to duplicate an *ur*-text exactly. He could rely on his own judgment as the actual maker of texts. He, not the remote author of the *ur*-text, guided the consumer in the handling of the text-bearing object. That physical process was as important in achieving efficacy as was the text itself. The maker of the text, whether originally a speaker of Greek or of Latin, was comfortably cosmopolitan in his dealings with the other culture.[38] He saw writing as an instrument for his use. It rendered the speech he used daily permanent and weighty. There is nothing in these texts that reflects the far-reaching power of a literate elite of the kind Goody has envisioned, guarding its arcane knowledge and skills closely.[39] To the contrary, the instrument of writing enabled the wielder of the tablets, literate or not, to communicate even with the gods, to assert what he wanted, and to use a weapon against neighbors or competitors he feared. We cannot isolate neat categories labeled "author," "editor," and "reader," since the texts that emerged from this process were collaboratively generated by the maker of the text from the expressed wishes of a consumer who might never have read the text-bearing object.

This close observation of one object and its texts in historical context has shown how much we can learn about the generation and transmission of texts with their "vastly complex indeterminacies" if we remember that "every part of the production process is meaning constitutive."[40] In the world of ancient popular culture, at least, texts may claim power even without attempting exact iteration or claiming a place in a hierarchy of accuracy. The tablets examined in this essay may have been replete with "errors" or even "vulgarisms," but the editor who produced them had confidence in his abilities.

NOTES

1. Gary Taylor, "The Renaissance and the End of Editing," in G. Bornstein and R. G. Williams, eds., *Palimpsest: Editorial Theory in the Humanities* (Ann Arbor: University of Michigan Press, 1993), 130.

2. William V. Harris, *Ancient Literacy* (Cambridge, Mass: Harvard University Press, 1989).

3. Mireille Corbier, "L'Ecriture en quête de lecteurs," in J. Humphrey, ed., *Literacy in the Roman World* (Ann Arbor: University of Michigan Press, 1991), 105.

4. Keith Hopkins, "Conquest by Book," in J. Humphrey, ed., *Literacy in the Roman World* (Ann Arbor: University of Michigan Press, 1991), 139.

5. William Sherwood Fox, *The Johns Hopkins Tabellae Defixionum* (Baltimore: The Johns Hopkins University Press, 1912).

6. Parts of the tablets still adhered to the nail, but some tablets were reduced to a "promiscuous heap of brittle chips of lead" ranging in size from one-fourth of a square cm. to forty square cm.; see Fox, *Tabellae Defixionum*. Fox, even to learn that he was dealing with the remnants of five separate tablets, had to work painstakingly from slight variations in the color and thickness of fragments. He finally identified 210 legible pieces that could be placed in tablets, but he was unable to make use of about 300 tiny crumbs. Efforts to separate additional pieces from the nail by using sulphuric acid had to be abandoned, since the chips that were detached were illegible and had been rendered crumbly. The legibility of many fragments was additionally compromised by chemical changes inflicted on the surfaces of the tablets by undetermined environmental conditions.

7. The two closest to the head of the nail (those tablets cursing Aquillia and an unknown) are so badly damaged as to be useless for the discussion that follows. The argument in this essay examines only the bottom three tablets, those that target Plotius, Avonia, and Maxima Vesonia, in that order, counting upward. Since all the tablets used the same model, substituting only the name of the victim and introducing other changes to be discussed in the text, each aids greatly in restoring the others' texts. I will cite lines from the Plotius tablet unless a comparison of two tablets is needed for the point being made. I will indicate restorations only when there is some question that affects the argument.

8. Fox's *editio princeps;* text supplemented from the other tablets.

9. Jerome McGann, *The Textual Condition* (Princeton, N.J.: Princeton University Press, 1991), 66.

10. See, for example, R. S. O. Tomlin, *Tabellae Sulis* (Oxford: Oxford University Committee for Archaeology, 1988), 84. Piercing and otherwise acting upon figures of victims had a long history in the ancient Near East and the Mediterranean; see Erica Reiner, "Magic Figurines, Amulets, and Talismans," in A. E. Farkas, P. O. Harper, and E. B. Harrison, eds., *Monsters and Demons in the Ancient and Medieval Worlds* (Mainz: Phillip von Zabem, 1987), 74–88, and Christopher A. Faraone, "Binding and Burying the Forces of Evil," *Classical Antiquity* 10 (1991), 165–79. But even the use of figurines was not always meant to harm the object. Some love charms using figures were meant to bind the target to the lover; see John Gager, *Curse Tablets and Binding Spells from the Ancient World* (Oxford: Oxford University Press, 1992), 15, 78ff, and Fritz Graf, *Magic in the Ancient World* (Cambridge, Mass.: Harvard University Press, 1997), 138ff. It is even less likely that the piercing of tablets was meant to injure the victim sympathetically, as maintained by E. Kagarow, *Griechische Fluchtafeln* (Leopoli: Societas Philologa Polonorum, 1929), 8.

11. Gager, *Curse Tablets,* 18.

12. Livy 7.3.5.

13. On the significance of nails among the Etruscans, at shrines to Fortuna, and in Horace, see Otto Wilhelm von Vacano, *The Etruscans in the Ancient World* (Bloomington: Indiana University Press, 1960), 12–13. My colleague Samuel Nelson has called my attention to African nail fetishes, and I was fortunately able to see two of these at the Seattle Art Museum while attending the conference that produced this volume. Those nail fetishes seem to share the concept of completion, as well as that of making a binding deal. The idea is that two disputants or simply negotiators reach an accord, often with mediation, and drive a nail into the village's nail-bearing figure as confirmation that the discord is at an end, and / or that the bargain is irrevocable. Other uses of nails are possible; my colleague David Appleby has pointed out to me the medieval ceremony of *transpunctio,* in which a defective document is ritually cancelled by being pierced with a nail, as in the case of a parchment document discussed by Janet L. Nelson, *The Frankish World* (London: Hambledon, 1966), 65.

14. Gager, *Curse Tablets,* gives the examples of no. 20, where the victim is to be buried as the lead tablet is buried; no. 21, where the curser hopes his rivals' passions will cool as their names are cooling on the cold lead in the ground; and no. 66, where the curser asks that his victims' tongues become lead if they speak ill of him. In his commentary on no. 66, Gager does not argue that the text is always or even usually to be identified with the victim. See also Graf, *Magic in the Ancient World,* 133. Graf is altogether more skeptical about the significance of medium and deposition, since he believes in a generally Mediterranean-wide adherence to papyrus models. He notes aptly that lead was a cheap writing medium, common enough, and need not have been selected for a specific magical trait; nevertheless, the medium could have *suggested* inevitable physical effects, such as sinking.

15. Tomlin, *Tabellae Sulis,* 82.

16. On the popularity of leaving little messages to the gods at sacral sites, see Mary Beard, "The Written Word in Roman Religion," in J. Humphrey, ed., *Literacy in the Roman World* (Ann Arbor: University of Michigan Press, 1991), 38, and Richard Cavendish, *The Powers of Evil* (New York: Putnam, 1975), 122. On the persistence of lead, see Christopher A. Faraone, "The Agonistic Context of Early Greek Binding Spells," in C. Faraone and D. Obbink, eds., *Magika Hiera* (Oxford: Oxford University Press, 1991), 8.

17. See Augustus Audollent, *Defixionum Tabellae* (Paris: Fontemoing, 1904), no. 190, lines 5–13: *mem(b)ra* (limbs); *colorem* (complexion); *figura(m)* (shape); *caput* (head); *capillos* (hair); *umbra(m)* (spirit or shade); *cerebru(m)* (brain); *fru(n)te(m)* (forehead); *supercilia* (eyebrows); *os* (mouth); *nasu(m)* (nose); *me(n)tu(m)* (chin); *buccas* (cheeks); *labra* (lips); *verbu(m)* (speech); *vultu(m)* (face); *col(l)u(m)* (neck); *iecur* (liver); *(h)umeros* (shoulders); *cor* (heart); *pulmones* (lungs); *i(n)testinas* (gut); *ve(n)tre(m)* (belly); *bracchia* (forearms); *digitos* (fingers); *manus* (hand); *u(m)b(i)licu(m)* (navel); *vesica(m)* (bladder); *femina* (thighs); *genua* (knees); *crura* (shins); *talos* (ankles); *planta(s)* (soles); *digitos* (presumably toes this time). Letters in parentheses were supplied by the editor to "correct" the text. Clearly, the items in this list did not all come

from the same handbook, if indeed they came from one. The list resembles the catalog with which we are concerned, in its failure to decline in standard fashion and in its syncopation of *umbilicum* through the removal of a syllable with a short vowel. It engages in a confusing repetition (of *digitos*) unparalleled in the catalog that concerns us. It mixes tangible anatomy with such intangibles as the soul and the faculty of speech. Perhaps this writer was working from memory.

18. Faraone, "Agonistic Context," 19. Professor Brent Vine, commenting on the presentation of an earlier version of this paper at the International Epigraphical Congress in Rome, September 1997, said that the same syntax could be found in Oscan material and that an Oscan model was as likely as a Greek one to lie behind this sentence. (His belief in the priority of Oscan also extended to other grammatical features of the text, which will be discussed later.) But Professor Vine's hypothesis seems unlikely, given the fact that the Greek material has an earlier origin, and that it is more frequently found and more widely distributed; and Professor Vine was willing to agree that a Greek model might lie behind both this Latin material and the Oscan material. Nor have other scholars whom I consulted supported the idea of any significant Oscan cultural influence on Roman legalism; rather, they support the reverse proposition, especially with respect to periods as late as the first century B.C.

19. See Eugene Tavenner, *Studies in Magic from Latin Literature* (New York: Columbia University Press, 1966), where Livy 26.1.6–12, among others, is cited.

20. *Viscus* ordinarily refers to the abdominal organs (cf. modern the English "viscera" and the *viscera interania* of Audollent, *Defixionum Tabellae,* nr. 250; as Fox notes, the word is more common in the plural). The tablets with which we are concerned are the only examples known to me that use the term to refer to the urethra or any other part of the urinary tract. They are also apparently unique in pairing *viscus* with *sacrum*. In the OLD and other lexica, *viscera* is thought sometimes to mean "testicles," but the cited reference to Pliny, *Natural History* 20.142, is quite ambiguous and may even refer to the general abdomen; in Petronius 119, lines 120–21, *viscera* certainly refers to the male genitals but need not refer to the testicles in particular. The *viscum sacrum* in our text could easily refer to the male genitals in general or to the penis in particular. Fox (*Tabellae Defixionum,* 44) cites as parallels *tylos* and *psola,* which are more explicit and are certainly not applicable to both sexes.

21. For *viscus* as "uterus," see Ovid, *Fasti* 1.624, or Seneca, *Nat.* 3.25.11. The Greek *kysthos* of one parallel (see Fox, *Tabellae Defixionum,* 44) echoes the *cunus* of another in that both seem to be generally descriptive of the female genital region and are certainly not parallels for any concern with a specifically urinary function, let alone attributions of a urinary function to the uterus. The one example Fox adduces of a specifically urinary curse uses the specific *visica,* presumably *vesica,* "bladder." One might suspect *viscum* here of being a corruption of *vesica* if not for the effort to make the word unambiguously if incorrectly an obviously neuter form, an effort emphasized by its pairing with *sacrum*.

22. Tomlin, *Tabellae Sulis,* 101; Gager, *Curse Tablets,* 23.

23. Interview with Janice Bird, M.D., a gynecologist, Annapolis, Maryland, April 24, 1997. See also J. Walton, P. Beeson, and R. P. Scott, *Oxford Companion to Medicine,* vol. 2 (Oxford: Oxford University Press, 1986), 1414. These authors easily demonstrate.that common injuries from childbirth and common effects of infections in the urethra and bladder result in incontinence, exactly the opposite of impeded urination. Although it is possible that a completely prolapsed uterus might temporarily impede the ability to urinate, the overfull bladder would eventually spill over, producing the typical incontinence. Any kidney stone so large and in such a position as to block urine completely would produce excruciating pain in the side and / or back for a painfully lengthy time before moving into the genital region; again, one who intended to produce that result would curse the kidney itself rather than anything in the genital region (as some curses do.)

24. Today, one-third of men over sixty experience benign hypertrophy of the prostate to the extent that its enlargement produces discomfort by making urination difficult. Prostatitis from infections is relatively common even among men between the ages of twenty and twenty-

five and sometimes produces enlargement. Sexually transmitted diseases may produce scarring in the male urethra as a result of ulceration. The scarred tissue then contracts. Although
women also commonly experience infection of the urethra through STDs, such strictures are
apparently not a problem, according to Janice Bird (see n. 23, above). Gout, too, may produce the inflammation of urethritis, and gout is largely a disorder of males, although there is
some disagreement about what percentage of gout victims are women. In any case, when women
get gout, they get it later in life, and it does not produce urinary-tract problems at the same
rate. See Walton, Beeson, and Scott, *Oxford Companion to Medicine*, vol. 1, 252, and vol. 2,
1410ff; Gordon MacPherson, *Black's Medical Dictionary*, 3rd ed. (London: A. & C. Black, 1992),
609.

25. See Gager, *Curse Tablets*, no. 80, a tablet engraved on both sides: side A curses a male,
and side B a female; the similar curses include items common to both genders yet are gender-
specific in other ways.

26. Fox, *Tabellae Defixionum*, 51.

27. I have not offered any standard letter count per cm., since the cursive script's shape
varies, apparently according to the writer's position. Nevertheless, the cramming is obvious
even in facsimile.

28. E.g., the Avonia text preserves *liguam* as a vulgar spelling and / or pronunciation of
linguam; the Vesonia text syncopates *oriculas* as *oriclas,* wrongly inflects *labra,* and leaves the
final -*m* off *linguam.* The Plotius text has "Ploti" for "Plotum" at line 41. All the texts synco-
pate *umbilicus* as *umblicus* and treat it and *venter* as neuters. Fox (*Tabellae Defixionum,* 49)
suggests that the writer forgot that the catalog of nouns would be in the accusative, since
he wrongly thought they were neuters rather than masculine nouns and hence could be
nominative.

29. Gager, *Curse Tablets,* 240; Fox, *Tabellae Defixionum,* 39.

30. Professor Brent Vine, in his comments at the 1997 International Epigraphical Congress
in Rome (see n. 18 above), also identified these genitives with the Oscan -*as* genitive but did
not follow up by explaining why the -*aes* ending that actually occurs on the tablets does not
more closely resemble the addition of a Greek -*es* (*eta sigma*) ending to an unmodified Latin
name.

31. L. R. Palmer, *The Latin Language* (London: Faber & Faber, 1954), 74, 257.

32. Corbier, "L'Ecriture in quête de lecteurs"; Hopkins, "Conquest by Book."

33. Ramsay MacMullen, "The Epigraphic Habit in the Roman Empire," *American Journal of
Philology* 103 (1982), 233.

34. F. Desbourdes, *Idées Romaines sur l'écriture* (Lille: Presses Universitaires de Lille, 1990),
79–80, 140.

35. As in Paulus, *Sententiae* 5.23.15–18. See also J. H. W. G. Liebeschuetz, *Continuity and
Change in Roman Religion* (Oxford: Oxford University Press, 1979), 127–38. A modern par-
allel illustrates the social possibilites of having a reputation yet avoiding official notice; see
Vassos Argyrou, "Under a Spell: The Strategic Use of Magic in Greek Cypriot Society,"
American Ethnologist 20 (1993), 260–61, in which an elderly Cypriot claims to have learned
his prayers (magical spells) from "a very old book" allegedly written by King Solomon. Although
Argyrou reports that Greeks from all over the world visit the informant, the Cypriot is reluc-
tant to talk to someone he believes to be a journalist because he doesn't want problems
with "the priests." Although he eventually agrees to the interview, he is not forthcoming and
keeps stressing his devotion to Christianity. Argyrou notes that this attitude is typical of his
Cypriot informants in its assumption that anyone can perform magic if he gets access to the
instructions.

36. Gager, *Curse Tablets,* 22–24.

37. Ibid.

38. Anne-Marie Tupet, "Rites Magiques dans l'Antiquité Romaine," *Aufstieg und Niedergang
der Römischen Welt* 2:16.3 (1986), 2591–92.

39. Jack Goody, *Literacy in Traditional Societies* (Cambridge: Cambridge University Press, 1968).

40. Ralph G. Williams, "I Shall Be Spoken: Textual Boundaries, Authors, and Intent," in G. Bornstein and R. G. Williams, eds., *Palimpsest: Editorial Theory in the Humanities* (Ann Arbor: University of Michigan Press, 1993), 66; McGann, *The Textual Condition*, 33.

The Way of All Text
The Materialist Shakespeare

PAUL EGGERT

I

This essay is a commentary on a recent proposal for understanding afresh Shakespeare's works and how they functioned in their time, by focusing resolutely on their material dimension. The meanings to which those physical features testify have in the past been ignored, it is argued, by the traditional methods and assumptions of Shakespeare editing. I have some significant caveats to offer to such an account: they are drawn from my experience of editing some works of the nineteenth and twentieth centuries. But I am quite prepared to believe that there is a sense in which the materialist case holds, and not just for Shakespeare. Hugh Amory commented recently that editing effaces much bibliographical evidence simply by deeming it irrelevant: because Fredson Bowers saw the aim of editing as being to "strip away . . . the veil of print"[1] from authors whose manuscripts were not extant, he effectively "shrank . . . bibliography"[2] in the minds of its practitioners by excluding from the editor's purview those features that literary holographs lack but that printed texts contain: typefaces and variations in typefaces, page design, publishers' information, ornaments, binding, illustrations, running heads, and so on. Thus editors have traditionally concerned themselves with establishing the text of the work, and with documenting its rejected forms, in the belief that the text, taken as a sequence of letterforms and punctuation, could be isolated from its physical presentations.

I first felt the effects of this shrinking in my initial foray into critical editing, in the mid-1980s. I was editing D. H. Lawrence and Mollie Skinner's *The Boy in the Bush,* using Lawrence's autograph manuscript as my copy-text. (This manuscript is his very extensive reworking of Skinner's lost, original version.) I realized that the Cambridge Lawrence Works series had found only a limited and rough-and-ready way of dealing with the variations in presentation of text between manuscript and print versions. This seemed odd to me in an edition that routinely reported in a single, comprehensive apparatus all variations in the collated states, whether of wording or punctuation. What was the difference, I wondered, between, say, routinely recording whenever one print presented a chapter title in capitals as against the manuscript's mixture of upper and lowercase (variant in accidentals), but not recording that another print used a drop capital instead of an ordinary capital to commence the first paragraph? A very fine line was being drawn: it depended on an unspoken acceptance of Bowers's remarkably convenient position.

I aired my concern and came up with a workable if not ideal solution: like most complete works editions, the Cambridge Lawrence was having to evolve as it went along. Because I was bound, on copy-text principles, to preserve Lawrence's styling in manuscript as far as possible, I had first of all to recognize when a typist or typesetter had done something that in any way changed the communicative capacity of its features. This led me to isolate those elements that no reader could expect would go unchanged as a manuscript text of a novel entered print (line and page endings, the provision of headers, page design, choice of typeface, etc.) and then to describe, as silent categories not reported individually in the apparatus, those things about which a reader might be unsure (such as the various house stylings of chapter titles and numbers, or of the openings of first paragraphs of chapters, and the differing indentations and type sizes in the presentation of songs, correspondence, and biblical quotations). As I drew up these descriptions for my note on the text, I was aware of what I was excluding; but then I reflected that it was Lawrence's text I was supposed to be editing. Nevertheless, any critical edition allows itself to be read against the grain, via its recording of textual variations.[3] Thus the textual apparatus should preferably be as generously inclusive as the reading text is rigorously exclusive. Some years of working on this particular project meant I had been, as it were, semiotically cohabiting with the novel's various typists, typesetters, and in-house editors: their work had communicated added meanings to me, probably because of the microscopy of attention I brought to it.

As a result of that experience and others, I do *not* think, for instance, that an indented quotation means the same thing (in the sense of having the same meaningful effect) when, upon entering the realm of print, its size is reduced from that of the surrounding text. The staggered layout across the page of the three lines of a complimentary close to a personal letter written in the manuscript *does* have a meaning (one sees it when, reflecting the different mood of the character, Lawrence presents— whether consciously or unconsciously—the next one in the manuscript differently). That meaning can and will be changed upon its graphic translation into typescript and print. Thus I insisted that the typesetter break the press's standard layout rules in order to reflect, as best print could do it, the layouts in the manuscript; and I did manage to report photographically, in the apparatus, the variant forms of the character Mad Jack Grant's drawing of a skull and crossbones.[4]

It was with some personal interest, then, that I read an article published in 1993.[5] In it, Margreta de Grazia and Peter Stallybrass pursue a broader kind of bibliographic approach, which does not see text as essential and physical features as dispensable.[6] They are interested in the paper and typography. They also point out that plays in Shakespeare's quartos and Folio show diversity of titles and names of the same character, and that the quartos and most of the Folio fail to provide lists of dramatis personae (with the differentiation between characters and the unity of character that such lists would come to imply when finally provided at the beginning of each play in Rowe's edition of 1709). And they remind us of the variability of orthography, with the lexical fields that variant spellings can invoke, but that are silenced by regularization and emendation.

The postulation in the 1970s and 1980s of a "revising Shakespeare"— whose revising hand could be detected in the early editions—was the first stage of the new response to textual and paratextual variability.[7] Thus we have seen, for instance, multitexted *Lear*s and *Hamlet*s.[8] But this shift, as de Grazia and Stallybrass point out, only broadened the sustaining category of authorship while leaving it essentially in place. This has been, they argue, a catastrophe for the study of Shakespearean texts. They trace its source to the eighteenth century, when, in deference to a newly felt concern for modernization and regularization, the tradition of eighteenth-century Shakespearean editing gradually removed the potentially rich variability in presentation of the early printings. This reflected the new view of Shakespeare as the Bard, who had access to the eternal truths of human nature: his plays came to be regarded as expressive of his genius, and their textual authority was located in its hidden presence. Because textual confusion was incompatible with it, there would be very many attempts to draw eclectically on the Folio, the quartos, and the existing editorial tradition in order to fix an ideal text, called Shakespeare's, for each play. An illusion of transparency was thus produced between the text and its source of textual authority, by eighteenth-century and later reading and editorial practices.

In other words, according to de Grazia and Stallybrass, we have been living with a Shakespeare of our own creation. As they are aware, this argument begs some fundamental questions about the nature of the literary work, and it assumes and extends some existing questions about authorship. But, as I will show, this is not to say that the questions have been answered: indeed, the rest of this essay is a critique of the materialist position that de Grazia and Stallybrass espouse.

II

Although editing is less heroic than art conservation in that it does not run the risk of irreparably changing or destroying the physical object, it shares with conservation the need for its working methods to be justified in relation to an argued conception of the work in question. Diminishing the importance of the link of authorship to the literary or artistic work usually involves linking the work instead either to its historical audiences or to the material practices of the period of its first production. These arguments, if they are to prevail, demand fundamental shifts in our normal conceptions of the work. Broadening the purview of bibliography, however, puts considerable strain on traditional bibliographic terms. G. Thomas Tanselle's proposals to redefine some of these terms are a relevant response,[9] but they seem to me to misconceive the new intellectual pressures. In an attempt, apparently, to retain some continuity of present-day editorial thought with that of the heyday of copy-text editing, Tanselle has proposed that whatever source of textual authority (whether authorial or not) an editor may decide upon as the basis of the editing practice, a distinction needs to be made between the achieved text of an extant document and the intended but unachieved text of the work.

Tanselle eschews the term "ideal text"; but whether one uses the term "intended text" or "ideal text," the effect is the same if one assumes that the work, from the point of view of one's editorial orientation, *has* a single text. A Neoplatonic idealism sustains the assumption: this transhistorical ideal holds separately for each of the possible grounds of a work's textual authority. Thus Tanselle lowers the philosophical heat by acknowledging nonauthorial grounds for textual authority; but the gas of idealism that is burning is the same as before, only now there are a number of pots upon the stove. The idealism, of course, is the very thing that the Shakespearean materialists, the sociological editors and theorists who have been influenced by Jerome McGann and D. F. McKenzie, and those working in the German documentary tradition have been rejecting.[10]

Encouragingly, de Grazia and Stallybrass recognize that acceptance of the materialist approach to Shakespeare involves "a need to reconceptualize the fundamental category of a *work* by Shakespeare";[11] unfortunately, however, they do not provide that reconceptualization. As part of their demonstration of the significant textual multiplicity they find in the Folio and quartos, they have to resort to such terms as "single texts," as opposed to different "versions" of the "same play."[12] But they enclose the latter terms self-consciously within quotation marks, as if they are not going to indulge in the kind of stemmatic relationship and text-critical terminology that allow a work's identity to be plotted. In a very 1990s way, they wish to celebrate and liberate textual difference, not confine it within editorial categories. I am not sure that a work by Shakespeare *is* a fundamental category: it might better be thought of historically, as de Grazia and Stallybrass themselves show; but the concept of the work is fundamental, at least in the pragmatic sense.

Michel Foucault once promised that he would deconstruct the concept of the work, just as he did the concept of authorship in his famous 1969 essay.[13] As far as I know, he failed to do so; but his concept of discourse subsequently did it for him, by dissolving the work into a site of unstable discursive inscriptions. De Grazia and Stallybrass take poststructuralist thinking, including Foucauldian thinking, for granted, but they bring bibliography to bear on it and find, as a result, that a rich lode of historical practices—to do with papermaking, typography, conceptions of character, etc.—may be revealed by close scrutiny of the Folio and quartos. They attempt to graft bibliographic evidence onto ideas of discursive practice. This is to the good, but the poststructural context also traps them into a binary, for, on the one hand, they seek to discredit the "solitary genius immanent in the text" as an "impoverished, ghostly thing" in order, on the other, to privilege "the complex social practices that shaped, and still shape, the absorbent surface of the Shakespearean text."[14] The binary was perhaps necessary for the authors to draw attention to their argument, but it has more than a touch of iconoclasm about it, and although it appears to offer a brave new clarity, it begs questions of its own.

De Grazia and Stallybrass comment, for instance, on the variable spellings in the early printings:

> Whether Holinshed or Shakespeare or a given scribe or compositor of either author's work determined a given form is less significant than the capacity of a word in the language's preregulative or generative phase to take multiple forms. This is precisely what baffles the project of retrieving the correct word, for it is a semantic field and not a single word that needs to be retrieved.[15]

But retrieved for what end, we are entitled to ask. The answer is an abstraction: for multiplicity's sake, for the sake of exemplifying the complex discursive and material practices—the "diversity of labors" that de Grazia and Stallybrass designate as the new materialist "object of analysis," now to replace the figure of the immanent Author formerly believed to be legible beneath the Shakespearean text.[16] Unfortunately, this new emphasis on the material "surface" leaves the reader out of the equation almost as much as did the Authorial paradigm that it explicitly sets out to replace.

Given de Grazia and Stallybrass's warning that the editorially constructed Shakespearean work can no longer be considered self-identical, the newly attuned reader is likely to be looking for a cause of the rich ambiguity of the original text's orthography at this or that point. Such a reader might wish to imagine the text as a form of communication. In that case it *would* matter whether the editor could judge if the spelling were Shakespeare's: the reader might want to appreciate his way of tracking across the then-available linguistic field. If, however, the reader wished to imagine the text as something bearing passive witness to social, linguistic, stage, or print-shop conditions contemporary with Shakespeare—to look *at* rather than *through* the pages of the early printings, as de Grazia and Stallybrass advise us to do[17]—then the editor would have much the same problem as before, given that the same ink traces on paper remain the primary evidence. Only now the reader needs to be sure that the ambiguity is *not* Shakespeare's, not author-intentional. To do that, the editor has to judge who *was* responsible. To abrogate this responsibility would be to ignore human agency as a form of explanation in favor of a social-discursive paradigm. It would be to trade one abstraction (authorship, which, whatever its illusions, has at least spawned finely differentiating analytical methods) for another abstraction ("materiality," as de Grazia and Stallybrass call it, which so far has not).

Graham Holderness, Bryan Loughrey, and Andrew Murphy, in their response to de Grazia and Stallybrass's article, contest the definition of materialism. While accepting the major contention that "the text [should be] stripped of its mystery and spurious autonomy," they object to de Grazia and Stallybrass's redefining of the text as only "an element in a material process of production and circulation" when it should be read also "as eloquent . . . of its own self-dispersal within the continuum of that process."[18] They see de Grazia and Stallybrass's position as a misreading of Marx: "The object forming the commodity does not in Marx simply disappear into an undifferentiated process of production."[19] They argue that a printed "text's specific identity" comes from its "exchange-value" being "more manifestly marked than its use-value"; in this, it differentiates itself from the manuscript or the prompt book or the script of a particular performance, whose use-value is in each case identical with its exchange-value, used up either in the physical performance or, in the case of a manuscript, turned into scrap paper.[20] We are told that "we have (erroneously) been accustomed, by the theory and practice of modern editing, to identify [these] as analogous elements within a larger whole"[21]—by which I presume they mean "the work" (which de Grazia and Stallybrass have already told us needs to be redefined), except that the respondents do not use the word.

Dispensing with the notion of the work is easier said than done, although it is certainly a brave idea if not altogether consistent with the fact that the respondents cite various works in their footnotes, including works written by themselves. (I have elsewhere discussed the way in which the library catalog as a positivist mechanism cannot do without authorship;[22] the librarian's concept of the work is equally fundamental.) But some revolutions happen more slowly than others, so it is probably fairer simply to observe that it is not clear how the Marxist notions of value secure the "text's specific identity." The respondents insist on the text's functioning as a commodity and therefore on its use to people, or for a purpose. They thereby incorporate into their terminology the purchaser of the book or theater ticket, but that is not quite the same thing as incorporating a readership (which de Grazia and Stallybrass have begun to do, if only by virtue of the new reading practice they are advocating). In other words, "value" seems to confer the status of object on the text at the expense of its living effects on its readers. Furthermore, reliance on differentials in use-value and exchange-value might well separate prompt book from foul papers from printed book, but differentials do not obviously separate the prompt books or sets of foul papers or printings of two different works (as traditionally defined).

In addition, a tendency on the part of Holderness, Loughrey, and Murphy to run together what I will refer to below as the textual and documentary dimensions of works (e.g., they refer to "the text that was printed, sold and preserved")[23] means that little allowance can be made for the categorical difference between unique objects (autographs) and printed texts as exact or variant copies of the state of a work (allographs). The respondents see both categories as "various discrete and to some degree incommensurable textualizations produced by historical contingency" that have been "coloniz[ed] by the modern edition" and that "pass under such generic titles as '*King Lear*' or '*Hamlet.*'"[24] No theory of the literary work can get very far without taking account of the autographic–allographic distinction: in this circumstance, "textualization" is little more than gestural.

The need to keep the "text" separate from the notion of the printed book or, more generally, from the notion of the document can be seen here: in reaction against the belief that the ideal text of the work is secured by the authorial presence, the Marxist materialists transfer all the phenomenological weight onto the idea of the text as physical commodity—in other words, onto the documentary dimension. My argument elsewhere has been that, adapting Theodor Adorno's phrase, the two dimensions are incapable of disconnection: that they negatively constitute one another and that this constitution requires human agency at every step, from composition to reception.[25] To stress one dimension at the expense of the other is, I believe, inevitably to produce a flawed and partial account.[26]

III

Having in many ways discredited the illusion (as they see it) of the work's "uncontaminated origin" in Shakespeare-as-Author, de Grazia and Stallybrass do not in fact start again from scratch. Rather, their substitution of performance or materiality seems to keep them in a state of sharp reaction to authorship. Perhaps this goes with the patch. Shakespeare studies sometimes strike the outsider (such as I am) as a privileged but enclosed workshop with a disproportionately high number of very intelligent but resource-challenged inmates. Lacking the documentary— and, to a lesser extent, the contextual and biographical—riches that later periods have in abundance, some Shakespeareans seem to enjoy nothing so much as taking a blowtorch to their inherited organizing tropes and then rejecting, with indignation, the resulting scars.[27] This impression is perhaps unfair, but it is true that the materialists mock the "purely imaginary and idealized status" of foul papers.[28] Yet if they had nourished their editorial thinking in, say, the literature of the nineteenth and twentieth centuries, where autograph manuscripts are plentiful and not at all imaginary, different conclusions might have emerged.

De Grazia and Stallybrass's argument, like that of Holderness, Loughrey, and Murphy, is being hindered, I believe, by a conflation of basic terms. I would have thought that proposals about a materialist Shakespeare ought consistently to distinguish the physical dimension from the mental—that is, the prints and the hypothesized foul papers and prompt books from (hypothesized historical) producers' and readers' engagement with them in raising textual meaning. Edward Pechter's objection to de Grazia and Stallybrass's essay is that "they demonstrate merely that Shakespeare's texts *may* be studied as an aspect of the history of printing."[29] But his term "texts" (which repeats theirs) confusingly incorporates mentalized meanings (whether of today's readers or of Shakespeare's contemporaries), when what Pechter actually means is "books" or "printings," for he immediately nominates printing history as the appropriate discipline for de Grazia and Stallybrass's interest—an interest that he then seeks to reduce in importance by differentiating it from literary criticism.[30]

It is not surprising that literary critics sometimes get bibliographic terminology wrong. Strangely, however, the materialists are equally at fault. Peter Stallybrass, in his reply to Pechter, says that "writers do not necessarily *control* the pointing of literary texts—or, to put it more strongly, do not control the literary object itself."[31] This formulation seems either to swallow up the manuscript or the printing as a physical object within the notion of text or, conversely, to reify the literary text as an object, thus doing away with its documentary foundation altogether. Again, de Grazia and Stallybrass, in their joint article, say that "the Shakespearean text is thus like any Renaissance book, a provisional state in the circulation of matter."[32] What is "provisional" here? the physical document? the mentalized text? both? Running the two together allows the term "text" to float free and allows the indefinite deferral of explanations involving personal agency (in the acts of writing, copying, revising, typesetting, and printing, which enabled and embodied the circulation).[33]

This is a poststructuralist reflex at work, and one wonders what has happened to materialism at this point: notions of text as fluid, decentered, unoriginated, in discursive circulation, have been around for so long that one scarcely notices any more the bibliographic black hole into which the thinking has slipped. Holderness, Loughrey, and Murphy refer tellingly to the "striking penetration of bibliographical preoccupations into theoretical and critical debate."[34] But if materialism is to have a future, then its practitioners will have to keep a closer eye on the implications of the documentary dimension for their understanding of the textual, and particularly for the questions of personal agency that the documentary dimension so imperatively raises.

Materialist arguments usefully underline editing's bibliographic selectivity and the danger of failing to see past the reading practices of one's own period, especially the likelihood of falling under the spell of an authorial creature of our own culture's (inherited) imagining. Even when authorship is stripped of its aura (as de Grazia and Stallybrass powerfully urge, like Walter Benjamin before them),[35] the need remains

for explanations, not so much of textual origination as of textual acti-
vation: why the linguistic text as written, or as printed, took such and
such a shape, and no other. Personal agency as an explanatory mode
will not go away; it is powerful and familiar, even if it can and does create ideological illusions when it is puffed up into the unitary self
believed to lie behind the text or the artwork: the real Shakespeare, say,
or the true Leonardo.[36] When removed from the cultural pressure-cooker,
however, personal agency offers less abstract explanations than materialist invocations of "a productive and reproductive network" are ever
likely to do.[37]

IV

If the notion of Authorship is a historical distortion gradually created
by the marketplace in the era of the printing press, then the concept of
the Work would also seem to be in trouble, since its ontology is conventionally secured by authorship. The free-floating term "text," as a
metonym for a work or a book, was until fairly recent times a booksellers'
and students' convenience (as in the term "textbook"); it was given a
new and looser currency by the poststructuralist movement. Discourses
came to be seen as inscribing both texts and people, who could then be
imagined as the provisional sites of discursive traces, rather than as
unified or stable entities. The poststructuralist carriage of de Grazia and
Stallybrass's argument will, I think, finally force them to abandon the
term "work." It is not clear how they will then show that the Folio and
the two quarto *Hamlets* have any relation to one another—something
they currently assume, by dint of tradition. Bibliography can restore the
concept of the work, through its interest in the physical traces of textual
activity (the text-in-deposition, as it were), traces that reflect postulated
intentions to mean this rather than that (the text-in-communication) on
the part of the people responsible for those physical traces. The work
as a (lowercase) concept can make sense as a regulative principle: a container within which to distinguish and interpret the activity of personal
agency on the part of those who can be identified as having taken part
in the creation and production of meanings, and as having left their documentary traces.

Any two copies of a single printing are usually physically variant in
minute and sometimes in larger ways, even in nineteenth- and twentieth-
century printings; and optical collation of different impressions often
reveals minor corrections, or the making good of damage to plates. A
new edition can introduce thousands of variations in styling and wording, and it usually involves changes in typeface, page design, and bind-

ing. So well is bibliography able to describe and analyze variation, both within and between editions, that the concept of the work seems to arise naturally from these empirical methods. That it does not arise harmlessly is the burden of the materialist case. Nevertheless, to make the editorial decision that a particular work can tolerate a certain amount of variation before its variant texts and presentations constitute a different work is to engage in an interpretative act: the "work" emerges as a principle allowing the editor and the reader to regulate that variation. The decision also has to do with the physical capacity of the edition to contain and document this variation, and with the willingness of the publisher to risk the resulting financial outlay. The editor normally feels a duty to make this interpretation with some regard to the aim that the author (or other textual authority) had in mind: whether, for example, there was commercial pressure to get a novel ready for the Christmas market, or the need to revise a script for an upcoming performance of a play at a new venue with a changed cast of actors, or the need to write an occasional poem. The editor's use of the regulative principle will usually respect the original commercial pressures under which the work took shape. There are, of course, notable exceptions; such editions are usually controversial.[38]

How is the reader to engage profitably with the thousands of newly recovered details that editions reveal? Take away personal agency and intention, and "the work" is in danger of becoming too bloated to have any meaning, or, apparatus-free, it will retain only its popular meaning in the marketplace of "book" or "title" or "text," where the documentary and textual dimensions blur harmlessly but unenlighteningly in whatever experience the reader has. But if the reader wishes to examine that experience and starts asking the harder questions about textual identity and authority, then the problem of definition arises.

Will the situation differ in the electronic medium? To the extent that we move to a hypertextual environment where the reader is empowered to move about at will, textual authority will probably be said to be transferred to the reader, and the concept of the work may conceivably be seen as a superseded historical blip, yoked to the period of the printed book. Kathryn Sutherland has already referred to the work as a "manifestly relegated term."[39] Nevertheless, the transfer of authority to the reader is partly illusory, given the facilitating hand of the programmer who chooses the links and paths that can be followed, and also given the (continuing) linear nature of text, whatever bite-size chunks it is cut up into. In addition, readerly authority has always been a familiar experience, as when, empowered by printing technology, we turn from reading text to textual apparatus to explanatory notes. Jerome McGann once dubbed it "radial reading."[40]

It is not clear to me that the editor-archivist's interpretative duty in relation to agency and intention will necessarily be lessened in the electronic medium. Indeed, that medium's capaciousness, if taken advantage of, will only increase the load upon the reader. The need for archives that do not so much *contain* as *argue* will surely emerge. I have speculated elsewhere[41] about a possible application to D. H. Lawrence's writings: an agent-centered archive intended to trace the interweaving filaments of Lawrence's writing in its multiple forms in any one period, rather than respecting (as do the Cambridge Lawrence volumes) the commercial, Work-oriented pressures that in nearly every case brought the dynamics of his thinking and writing to a temporary full stop in the act of publication. In such an environment, the boundaries between works would become more relaxed, and some of the pressure would be taken off the decision of what, in any particular case, constitutes the work. If such an approach proved feasible, it would amount to an alternative principle of organization.

But this is crystal-ball gazing; for now, I see no way around the concept of the work. The act of reading remains an act of (always provisional) completion of the work via the available reading practices: as I see it, the reader participates in the textual dimension and, in doing so, asks questions, prompted by those practices, about the meaning of the letterforms and the other physical features that he or she encounters.[42] De Grazia and Stallybrass are advocating a new reading practice, which is a healthy sign; but they show little interest in how reading or the reader needs to be incorporated into the definition of the work. They obviously have more to do here of a philosophical nature.

Unless the letterforms and features are imagined as having come into physical being in a miraculous way, questions arise about the agencies and intentions involved in their genesis and transmission. Bibliography shows us how complex the answering of those questions can be. To recognize only the bibliographic multiplicity—to gaze *at* the pages, as the materialists enjoin us to do—seems to have no editorial outcome of a kind that might assist readers in answering their questions. The materialist pursuit offers a newly sensitized way of looking at the early printings, and for this it is valuable; but it explicitly denies readers an agented focus by which they might raise this attentiveness into evidence so as better to understand why they react as they do to what they read.

Comprehensiveness needs to be attended by explanation and interpretation, if it is not, like Tennyson's undersea monster the Kraken, to come to the surface only to die. The sharpening tool, I believe, remains what it has been: personal agency, even if, in the form of the Author, it has proved lately to be the Exxon *Valdez* of the editorial coastline. If any editorial policy emerges from the materialist case, it will—even if it takes a capacious electronic form—have to compromise on the aim of comprehensiveness if only because it will be unable to represent fully its own reception. And, to the extent that it ignores personal agency as an explanatory paradigm for dealing with variation, it will, I predict, have dumped upon us another big cleanup job. Semiotic flow is one thing, but we continue to need boundaries to make sense of it. For editors, this is the way of all text.

NOTES

1. Fredson Bowers, *Textual and Literary Criticism* (Cambridge: Cambridge University Press, 1966), 18, 81. This statement is repeated with slight variation in Fredson Bowers, "Textual Criticism," in Oscar James Campbell and Edward G. Quinn, eds., *A Shakespeare Encyclopaedia* (London: Methuen, 1966), 869.

2. Hugh Amory (review of G. Thomas Tanselle, *The Life and Work of Fredson Bowers*), *TEXT* 9 (1996), 469.

3. See Paul Eggert, "Reading a Critical Edition with the Grain and Against: The Cambridge D. H. Lawrence," in Charles L. Ross and Dennis Jackson, eds., *Editing D. H. Lawrence: New Versions of a Modern Author* (Ann Arbor: University of Michigan Press, 1995), 27–40. Cf. the distinction made between linguistic text and "bibliographic coding" in Jerome J. McGann, *The Textual Condition* (Princeton, N.J.: Princeton University Press, 1991), passim.

4. See D. H. Lawrence, *The Boy in the Bush*, ed. Paul Eggert (Cambridge: Cambridge University Press, 1990), 489. For an account of the meaning-bearing importance of quotation styling and paragraphing in Coleridge's manuscripts and prints, cf. J. C. Mays, "Reflections on Having Edited Coleridge's Poems," in Robert Brinkley and Keith Hanley, eds., *Romantic Revisions* (Cambridge: Cambridge University Press, 1992), 139.

5. Margreta de Grazia and Peter Stallybrass, "The Materiality of the Shakespearean Text," *Shakespeare Quarterly* 44 (1993), 255–83.

6. For her earlier work along similar lines, see Margreta de Grazia, "The Essential Author and the Material Book," *Textual Practice* 2 (1988), 69–86, and Margreta de Grazia, *Shakespeare Verbatim: The Reproduction of Authenticity and the 1790 Apparatus* (Oxford: Clarendon Press, 1991). I commented on de Grazia's "The Essential Author" in Paul Eggert, "Textual Product or Textual Process: Procedures and Assumptions of Scholarly Editing," in Philip Cohen, ed., *Devils and Angels: Textual Editing and Literary Theory* (Charlottesville: University Press of Virginia, 1991), 67–69.

7. See Stanley Wells and Gary Taylor, with John Jowett and William Montgomery, *William Shakespeare: A Textual Companion* (Oxford: Clarendon Press, 1987). The ground had been broken in Gary Taylor and Michael Warren, eds., *The Division of the Kingdoms: Shakespeare's Two Versions of King Lear* (Oxford: Clarendon Press, 1983). For an overview, see Grace Ioppolo, *Revising Shakespeare* (Cambridge. Mass.: Harvard University Press, 1991).

8. William Shakespeare, *The Complete King Lear 1608–1623*, ed. Michael Warren (Berkeley: University of California Press, 1989); William Shakespeare, *The Three-Text Hamlet: Parallel Texts of the First and Second Quartos and First Folio*, ed. Paul Bertram and Bernice W. Kliman (New York: AMS Press, 1991).

9. See, e.g., G. Thomas Tanselle, "The Varieties of Scholarly Editing," in David C. Greetham,

ed., *Scholarly Editing* (New York: Modern Language Association, 1995), 26; G. Thomas Tanselle, "Textual Instability and Editorial Idealism," *Studies in Bibliography* 49 (1996), 43–44n76.

10. See McGann, *The Textual Condition;* D. F. McKenzie, *Bibliography and the Sociology of Texts: The Panizzi Lectures, 1985* (London: British Library, 1986); Paul Eggert, "The Shadow across the Text: New Bearings on German Editing," *TEXT* 11 (1998), 317–30. For a fuller response to Tanselle's argument, see Paul Eggert, "The Work Unravelled," *TEXT* 11 (1998), 41–60.

11. See de Grazia and Stallybrass, "The Materiality of the Shakespearean Text," 255.

12. Ibid., 268.

13. See Michel Foucault, "What Is an Author," trans. Josué V. Harari, in Paul Rabinow, ed., *The Foucault Reader* (London: Penguin, 1986).

14. See de Grazia and Stallybrass, "The Materiality of the Shakespearean Text," 283.

15. Ibid., 266.

16. Ibid., 280.

17. Ibid., 257.

18. Graham Holderness, Bryan Loughrey, and Andrew Murphy, "'What's the Matter?' Shakespeare and Textual Theory," *Textual Practice* 9 (1995), 104.

19. Ibid.

20. Ibid., 104–5.

21. Ibid., 105.

22. See Paul Eggert, "Social Discourse or Authorial Agency? Bridging the Gap between Editing and Theory," in Paul Eggert and Margaret Sankey, eds., *The Editorial Gaze* (New York: Garland, 1998), 97–116.

23. Holderness, Loughrey, and Murphy, "'What's the Matter?,'" 104–5.

24. Ibid., 117.

25. For a case about defining the work by using some aspects of Adorno's philosophy, see Eggert, "The Work Unravelled."

26. Thus I would rather entertain a Marxist aesthetic that, while rejecting the potential fetishism of the "work" as a commodity, as well as the authorial aura that sustains it, would unravel the work into the textual labor of its producers and readers, the physical expression of which labor would be seen as the work's documentary traces (manuscript, prompt book, prints, etc.).

27. Thus, for instance, Holderness, Loughrey, and Murphy, in "'What's the Matter?,'" want to link Bowers's phrase "to strip the veil of print from a text" not with a Neoplatonic idealizing but with Salome's dance. They conclude, "In the absence of the authentic body or manuscript, the manipulation of such discarded coverings as the printed texts . . . remains a source of sexual or editorial pleasures" (97). However, I believe that Bowers was implicitly comparing (justly or not) editing to art conservation, which typically removes a painting's top layers of varnish, since they are far more liable to have discolored and darkened than is the paint underneath. Holderness and his colleagues' attempt to disunify the authorial presence behind the phrase by probing the vulnerable metaphor seems willful to me, even perverse—its own kind of violation. There is a lot of this kind of maneuvering in their essay; see, for example, 98–99.

28. See de Grazia and Stallybrass, "The Materiality of the Shakespearean Text," 276–77.

29. Edward Pechter, "'Making Love to our Employment; Or, The Immateriality of Arguments about the Materiality of the Shakespearean Text," *Textual Practice* 11 (1997), 54.

30. With suitable qualification, the term "texts" might have done unambiguous service, but only by acknowledging the physical, documentary basis from which those texts were raised; see n. 33 below.

31. Peter Stallybrass, "Love among the Ruins: Response to Pechter," *Textual Practice* 11 (1997), 74.

32. See de Grazia and Stallybrass, "The Materiality of the Shakespearean Text," 280.

33. At this point in their argument, de Grazia and Stallybrass are in fact about to discuss the life cycle of paper in Elizabethan and Jacobean England. They mention the "diversity of labors"

(ibid., 280) that the "circulation of matter" must have involved. This seems promising as a way of reducing the abstraction "materiality" to knowable confines; but the underlying philosophical point that they will have to face—if they do indeed mean to "reconceptualize the fundamental category of a *work* by Shakespeare" (ibid., 255)—is the relationship between literary document and physical object (paper and ink). Normally we think there is no gap. But if, as I argue elsewhere (see Eggert, "The Work Unravelled"), document and text are negatively constitutive of one another, then there *is* an inherent gap between document and physical object: the object as paper and ink becomes a document (gets into the documentary dimension) only in the act of reading (the textual dimension).

34. Holderness, Loughrey, and Murphy, "'What's the Matter?,'" 94.

35. "The presence of the original is the prerequisite to the concept of authenticity," now superseded in an age of mechanical duplication: see Walter Benjamin, "The Work of Art in the Age of Mechanical Reproduction," *Illuminations,* ed. Hannah Arendt, trans. Harry Zohn (London: Fontana, 1992), 214.

36. For an account of the most recent conservation of Leonardo's *The Last Supper,* see Paul Eggert, "Where Are We Now with Authorship and the Work?," *Yearbook of English Studies* 29 (1999), 89–102. The method adopted has been to strip off the overpainting of all previous restorations in order to reveal the work as it left Leonardo's hand—even though only fragments remain. See also the discussion of the conservation of Michelangelo's Sistine Chapel in Paul Eggert, "Editing Paintings / Conserving Literature: The Nature of the 'Work,'" *Studies in Bibliography* 47 (1994), 65–78.

37. See de Grazia and Stallybrass, "The Materiality of the Shakespearean Text," 276.

38. Two examples are Theodore Dreiser, *Sister Carrie,* ed. James L. W. West III (Philadelphia: University of Pennsylvania Press, 1981), and D. H. Lawrence, *Sons and Lovers,* ed. Helen Baron and Carl Baron (Cambridge: Cambridge University Press, 1992). Both editions restored versions of the novels that had been altered substantially by people other than their authors (but with the authors' general agreement), to ensure commercial publication.

39. Kathryn Sutherland, "Looking and Knowing: Textual Encounters of a Postponed Kind," in Warren Chernaik, Marilyn Deegan, and Andrew Gibson, eds., *Beyond the Book: Theory, Culture, and the Politics of Cyberspace* (Oxford: Office for Humanities Communication, 1996), 16.

40. Jerome J. McGann, "Theory of Texts," (review of D. F. McKenzie, *Bibliography and the Sociology of Texts*), *London Review of Books,* Feb. 18, 1988, 21.

41. Eggert, "Where Are We Now with Authorship and the Work?"

42. For a proposal of a definition of bibliography as including the study of readership, see Paul Eggert, "Document and Text: The 'Life' of the Literary Work and the Capacities of Editing," *TEXT* 7 (1994), 10.

Gerard Hopkins and the Shapes of His Sonnets

RANDALL McLEOD

For Tom Vogler, on his retirement from the classroom, 2001

Thirty-five uncritical years ago, I bought my once-perfect-bound but now-disintegrating 16mo Penguin paperback: "*POEMS AND PROSE OF GERARD MANLEY HOPKINS* SELECTED WITH AN INTRODUCTION AND NOTES BY W. H. GARDNER" — as its title page declares.[1] On the following recto, Gardner dedicates his edition to another of his clan, one who will figure as prominently in this essay as Hopkins himself: "TO THE MEMORY OF ROBERT BRIDGES . . . FRIEND AND ADVISOR OF GERARD MANLEY HOPKINS, PRESERVER AND FIRST EDITOR OF HIS POEMS." On the back of the title page, facing this editorial salute, lies an unattributed note, which I didn't think to read until well after deciding to write this essay. Varying densities of ink between its paragraphs and also asymmetries of its layout suggest a paste-up of various historical layers. One of them states, "This selection first published in 1953 | Reprinted 1954, 1958, 1960, 1961, 1962, 1963, 1964." More darkly inked is the identification of the printer: "Cox & Wyman Ltd., London, Fakenham, and Reading" — far away from "BALTIMORE . MARYLAND", named at the base of the title page in this the seventh reprinting, 1964. Was it Gardner's *selection* that Cox & Wyman reprinted, I wonder, or was it the actual *setting* of Monotype Bembo identified in a note as the fount of the first edition?

Copies of the first printing and reprinting answer some of my questions: the printer was Unwin Brothers, Woking and London; and the covers say "*Two Shillings and sixpence*", whereas my cover says "$1.25".[2] As the typeface and column width of all three editions are identical and as their page layouts generally match, mechanical collation of them is possible: my seventh reprinting was neither from type standing from the first printings nor from photographic images of them. Later Penguin "reprintings" represent at least one *resetting* of the earlier Penguin texts. And, as we shall see, there are unacknowledged revisions to the reset text from one printing to another. When I bought my copy, I knew nothing of this complex evolution, or that it called into question the identity of Hopkins' text.

13

THE WINDHOVER:

To Christ our Lord

I CAUGHT this morning morning's minion, king-
   dom of daylight's dauphin, dapple-dawn-drawn Falcon, in his
     riding
Of the rolling level underneath him steady air, and striding
High there, how he rung upon the rein of a wimpling wing
In his ecstasy! then off, off forth on swing,
   As a skate's heel sweeps smooth on a bow-bend: the hurl and
     gliding
Rebuffed the big wind. My heart in hiding
Stirred for a bird, – the achieve of, the mastery of the thing!

Brute beauty and valour and act, oh, air, pride, plume here
   Buckle! AND the fire that breaks from thee then, a billion
Times told lovelier, more dangerous, O my chevalier!

   No wonder of it: shéer plód makes plough down sillion
Shine, and blue-bleak embers, ah my dear,
   Fall, gall themselves, and gash gold-vermilion.

14

PIED BEAUTY

GLORY be to God for dappled things –
   For skies of couple-colour as a brinded cow;
     For rose-moles all in stipple upon trout that swim;
Fresh-firecoal chestnut-falls; finches' wings;
     Landscape plotted and pieced – fold, fallow, and plough;
     And áll trádes, their gear and tackle and trim.

All things counter, original, spare, strange;
   Whatever is fickle, freckled (who knows how?)
     With swift, slow; sweet, sour; adazzle, dim;
He fathers-forth whose beauty is past change:
         Praise him.

15

HURRAHING IN HARVEST

UMMER ends now; now, barbarous in beauty, the stooks arise
  Around; up above, what wind-walks! what lovely behaviour
  Of silk-sack clouds! has wilder, wilful-wavier
eal-drift moulded ever and melted across skies?

walk, I lift up, I lift up heart, eyes,
  Down all that glory in the heavens to glean our Saviour;
  And, éyes, heárt, what looks, what lips yet gave you a
apturous love's greeting of realer, of rounder replies?

nd the azurous hung hills are his world-wielding shoulder
  Majestic – as a stallion stalwart, very-violet-sweet! –
hese things, these things were here and but the beholder
  Wanting; which two when they once meet,
he heart réars wíngs bold and bolder
  And hurls for him, O half hurls earth for him off under his feet.

16

THE CAGED SKYLARK

s a dare-gale skylark scanted in a dull cage
  Man's mounting spirit in his bone-house, mean house, dwells –
That bird beyond the remembering his free fells;
  nis in drudgery, day-labouring-out life's age.

By whatever arbitrary channels my 1964 version of the text of Hopkins' poetry descended from his to my unwitting hands, the Penguin "reprint" has been Hopkins for me—comfortable fragments all these years. (Tom says his copy is now just the same—fragments.) Here is where many of my generation began reading Hopkins in earnest, and here is where I will start to dig myself out of complacency. In this essay, I want to unedit my way back to 1953, to the first of Gardner's Penguin versions, and beyond, to his Oxford editions, and eventually to the earliest witnesses of Hopkins' sonnets—in order to reveal the shape-shifting of Gardner's editions (but of any editor's, really).[3] Specifically, I want to demonstrate that the gestures—the shapes—of Hopkins' sonnets are often ones that others have given them. This essay, then, is about the body language—the appropriated body language of Hopkins' sonnets. By scrutinizing especially the rather homely graphic features of (horizontal) indentation of verses and (vertical) extra leading[4] of lines (to invoke only two dimensions of typographical layout), we can witness a startling variety of sonnet shapes in this edition. Focusing on such merely physical aspects of poetry on the page, we will nevertheless home in on issues at the very core of Hopkins' poetry—rhythm and rhyme. The reader is alerted, before we begin, to expect many more material facts than are conventional or convenient in literary criticism, and these observed from unfamiliar angles. To prepare for this protracted demonstration of sonnet morphology, you might just lay in a ruler (a centering ruler would be good) and even a protractor.

Look at the poems in the previous opening—I mean really look. Reproduced there are my Penguin pages 30–31. They offer two fourteen-line sonnets: on the verso lies "THE WINDHOVER : | *To Christ our Lord*" (numbered 13); and on the recto lies "HURRAHING IN HAR VEST" (numbered 15). (You *do* see that space?) These sonnets exhibit the same pattern of indentation for corresponding verses. By what convention shall we contrast their depths? We could differentiate lines either as *flush left* or as *tabbed*—a distance of 3mm (or of ⅛″, as the British layout artist or typesetter may have conceived the matter). But I prefer to speak of them algebraically, as *both* tabbed—to two different depths: 0mm and 3mm. I deem this phrasing more useful, since the first tab in this edition proves to be a parameter, not a constant zero throughout. (Contrasting the first tabs of these two sonnets with that (or those) of "Pied Beauty", between them, will make clear the fluidity of the first tab.)

Now, Hopkins did not comment on spatial formatting in his sonnets, but he addressed the indentations of the opening stanzas of "The Wreck of the Deutschland", the ambitious poem this priest began in December 1875, after a decade-long silence since he had joined the Society of Jesus. And so I have chosen to angle into the indentations of his sonnets through those of the two stanza structures of "The Wreck", which he wrote before the bulk of the sonnets. (I will not take up leading until I return to the sonnets.) This digression will serve to begin laying before readers disquieting features of the editorial history of Hopkins' text.

Though Hopkins' "hand was out at first", as he wrote to R. W. Dixon on October 5–10, 1878, almost three years after he composed "The Wreck", the poet-priest eventually had "realized on paper" "the echo of a new rhythm", one that had long been "haunting [his] ear".[5]

111 Mount Street, Grosvenor Square, W. Oct. 5, 1878

Very Reverend and Dear Sir . . .

You ask, do I write verse myself. What I had written I burnt before I became a Jesuit and resolved to write no more, as not belonging to my profession, unless it were by the wish of my superiors; . . . But when in the winter of '75 the Deutschland was wrecked . . . I was affected by the account and happening to say so to my rector he said that he wished someone would write a poem on the subject. On this hint I set to work and, though my hand was out at first, produced one. I had long had haunting my ear the echo of a new rhythm which now I realized on paper. . . . However I had to mark the stresses in blue chalk, and this and my rhymes carried on from one line into another and certain chimes suggested by the Welsh poetry I had been reading (what they call *cynghanedd*) and a great many more oddnesses could not but dismay an editor's eye, so that when I offered it to our magazine the *Month*, though at first they accepted it, after a time they withdrew and dared not print it. After writing this I held myself free to compose, but cannot find it in my conscience to spend time upon it; so I have done little and shall do less. . . .

Believe me, dear Sir, very sincerely yours

Gerard Hopkins.

Oct. 10.

Let us look at the visual structure of Gerard Hopkins' rhythmic "echo . . . on paper" as filtered through Robert Bridges.

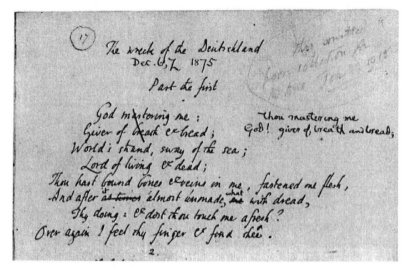

Here is the start of this poem on p. 15 of Ms B, the latter of the extant manuscripts, both in the hand of Hopkins' "advisor and friend", as Gardner curiously styled Robert Bridges, his editorial predecessor. (The autograph in which Hopkins had to mark the stresses in blue chalk is now lost.) Using Ms A (which he had written out from Hopkins' manuscript), Bridges copied the poem again into Ms B; and on December 14, 1883 he passed it to the poet (who, more or less scrupulously, had not kept copies of his own work, and who was therefore dependent on Bridges' transcription), whereupon Hopkins revised it, and sent it, three months later, to Coventry Patmore. As you can see, Hopkins deleted Bridges' transcription of the first two lines and penned them anew, revised, to the right, with the indentations intact. His more striking changes were to diction and punctuation, and consequently to rhythm. But do note for future reference the subtleties of penmanship, which hint at differences of the two men's graphic habits: Hopkins wrote out Bridges' "&" as "and"; and he did not retain his friend's characteristic space before the semicolon, at the end of v. 2.

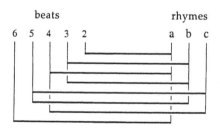

Bridges' transcription of the poet's lost Note to the reader of this poem, supposedly composed for the abortive publication in *The Month*, will be my next jumping-off point. Now, this Note is not actually in my copy—or in any prior Penguin. I learned of it only recently from Norman MacKenzie's *The Poetical Works*, 1990, which is the first edition to place it in the body of the book—as a preface to this poem. Not until Gardner's collaboration with MacKenzie on the next Oxford edition, 1967, did the Note become public at all—and then only in the endnotes (pp. 255–56). In other words, in the editorial tradition, it has taken this preface a century to come home.[6]

Note—Be pleased, reader, since the rhythm in wh:
the following poem is written is new, strongly to mark the
beats of the measure, according to the number belonging to
each of the eight lines of the stanza, as the indentation
guides the eye, namely two & three and four and three &
five & five & four & six; not disguising the rhythm &
rhyme, as some readers do, who treat poetry as if it were prose
fantastically written to rule (which they mistakenly think the
perfection of reading) . . . .

I quote this first quarter of Hopkins' Note, surviving only in Bridges' transcription[7] (where its abundant ampersands surely originated), in order to allow the poet to introduce the topic of rhyme. Except for one additional extract on this subject, below (p. 195), the Note deals with rhythm, with Hopkins' pioneering "sprung rhythm", as he named it in another part of the letter to Dixon just quoted. At the bottom of the page opposite is a model of the eight verses of the stanza, for immediate contrast of its rhythms and rhymes.

Let me discuss rhythm first, as does Hopkins. The jagged left side of my model reports five tabs over the eight verse lines of the stanza as Hopkins' hand realized it on paper (and as Bridges must faithfully have copied it). I have aligned with the beginning of each verse the number of beats the poet asks the reader to mark. (The risers here actually correspond to Bridges' ruled guidelines, still visible on some pages.[8]) Indeed, the differences of the tabs do guide the reader's eye *toward* (if not precisely *to*) the rhythm of his verses: there is an inverse correlation of the progressing tabulations of verse lines across the page with their diminishing numbers of beats. A more intuitive way to state the matter is to say that this order of tabbing

tends to accommodate longer verses, and so minimizes problems associated with wrapping—not only of a new tab for the latter part of a
verse (which, even if it is right,[9] distracts from Hopkins' symbolic indentations), but also of disproportionate internal spacing of the former part
of the verse in printed versions. (In the Penguin settings, this former
part typically extends flush right, and is therefore prone to awkward
compression or expansion—as if it were a justified setting of prose.)[10]

Now, Hopkins' Note did not inform the reader that the initial line has
two beats in only the first ten of the thirty-five stanzas. Nor did it need to:
from the eleventh stanza on, the poet's retabbing of the first verse leftward,
so as to align its start with that of the second verse, conveys the message
silently; and it guides the reader's eye toward a three-stress rendering
of both of these lines through all of PART THE SECOND.[11] To this extent,
the body language of the poem speaks relatively unambiguously—if
editors would only "dare" to follow copy: for, in the second edition, 1930,
Charles Williams silently undid this feature of indentation in stanzas
11–35. I see a more pervasive problem in Ian Lancashire's 2002 internet
edition, *Representative Poetry*, where indentation appears throughout as
a function of rhyme, not rhythm; and so this change of rhythm goes
unmarked in his edition.[12] At the foot of the facing page, I have placed a
model of his commonsense misrepresentation of the copytext, Ms B. (To
contrast it with the previous model, simply lift the present leaf.)

But even in ideal spatial formatting, there are problems for the
reader who is pleased to mark the beats. Consider the following
representations of the first three lines of the poem—with their alleged
two, three, and four beats, respectively.

    God mástering me ;
    Giver of breath & bread ;
   Wórld's stránd, swáy of the séa ;

    God mástering me ;   Thou mastering me
    Giver of breath & bread ;   God! giver of breath and bread;
   World's strand , sway of the sea ;

Represented first is Bridges' Ms A transcription of the lost manuscript.
Below left is his copying of Ms A in Ms B; and Hopkins' revision of its first
two lines is to the side. (These two last versions appear together in the
photograph from Ms B on p. 182.) Writing home, Hopkins voiced doubt
that readers would be able to scan his new verses unless he actually
marked the stresses. Just how literally he meant this can be gauged from

stresses in Ms A, where Bridges blue-pencilled in a score of them in this first stanza alone. (Four stresses, for example, are marked in v. 3.) But in the photograph of Ms B, only a lone example of them survives—in "theé", v. 8. This accent is heavily inked; and it is in Bridges' hand. In v. 6, more accents appear, this time in Hopkins' purple pencil—"álmost únmade". These three stresses in Ms B are all that remain of the original score of them in Ms A (which supposedly were copied from the lost holograph).

St Beuno's. June 26 '76

My dearest Mother, . . .

You ask about my poem on the Deutschland. You forget that we have a magazine of our own, the *Month*. I have asked Fr. Coleridge the editor, who is besides my oldest friend in the Society,[13] to take it, but I had to tell him that I felt sure he wd. personally dislike it very much, only that he was to consider not his tastes but those of the *Month*'s readers. He replied that there was in America a new sort of poetry which did not rhyme or scan or construe; if mine rhymed and scanned and construed and did not make nonsense or bad morality he did not see why it shd. not do. So I sent it. . . .

June 28—I have heard from him this morning. The poem was too late for July but will appear in the August number. He wants me however to do away with the accents which mark the scanning. I would gladly have done without them if I had thought my readers would scan right unaided but I am afraid they will not, and if the lines are not rightly scanned they are ruined. Still I am afraid I must humour an editor, but some lines at all events will have to be marked. . . .

You must never say that the poem is mine.

With best love to all I am your loving son

Gerard M. Hopkins S. J. . . .

"You must never say that the poem is mine."[14] Was the author's identity to be kept secret?—or was Hopkins not the author? (The first version is actually signed with a bardic name: "Brân Maenefa"—which means Crow or Raven of Maenefa.[15])

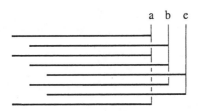

In some verses, v. 3 in Ms A, for example, marked stresses are scarcely necessary: there are only four obvious places for the requisite four beats. But where guidance is required, as it is in both versions of vv. 1–2, the poet provided none. Problems surface immediately. In his revision of the first v. 1, which was originally end-stopped, Hopkins replaced the initial word, "God", with "Thou", and moved the holy name to the end of the phrase, where it now enjambs into the second verse. *God!*—how, with the same three beats, is one ever to scan this augmented second verse? Only with difficulty, it seems, by removing the beat from "giver", which it must have borne in the earlier version, to give it to "God", the "giver". But as "giver" now alliterates with "God", does it not beg for even more stress in the revision than it had formerly? How is a reader ever to divine Brân Maenefa's intentions in this central aspect of Hopkins' poetic?

The first two (posthumous) appearances of this stanza in print were edited by Robert Bridges: in *The Spirit of Man*, an octavo anthology published by Longmans, Green and Co. in 1916; and in the first edition of Hopkins' *Poems*, also an octavo, published by Humphrey Milford in 1918. (Oxford University Press printed both titles.)[16]

GOD mastering me ;
Giver of breath and bread ;
World's strand, sway of the sea ;
Lord of living and dead ;
Thou hast bound bones and veins in me, fasten'd me flesh,
And after at times almost unmade me with dread,
Thy doing ; and dost Thou touch me afresh ?
Over again I feel thy finger and find Thee . . .

I

Thou mastering me
God ! giver of breath and bread ;
World's strand, sway of the sea ;
Lord of living and dead ;
Thou hast bound bones and veins in me, fastened me flesh,
And after it almost unmade, what with dread,
Thy doing : and dost thou touch me afresh ?
Over again I feel thy finger and find thee.

The earlier derives from Ms A, but eliminates all the poet's studied indentations and idiosyncratic accentuation. The later, however, does respect Hopkins' tabs and verbal revisions to Ms B; and at least the editor's textual notes for this edition report some of his accents (though none for this first stanza in either manuscript). Obviously, neither of Hopkins' first editors, Fr. Coleridge or Dr. Bridges, welcomed visual indications of rhythm. Nor (as we shall see) do most of the editors who follow.[17]

The title page of the first Oxford edition, in 1930, the year of Bridges' death, respectfully states: "*Edited with notes by ROBERT BRIDGES*". Then comes "SECOND EDITION *With an Appendix of Additional Poems, and a critical Introduction by CHARLES WILLIAMS.*" Although it is a resetting, this edition strove to appear typographically identical with the first in their common parts (and so it too can be mechanically collated).[18] It supplemented Bridges' work, but sought not to disturb it; and so the second edition represents no real advance in communicating Hopkins' markings of his beats. (As the twig was bent, so grew the tree.) And, as I said earlier, in its tabbing of the first line of every stanza of "The Wreck" to a single depth, it represents less than an advance. I suppose that the editor of the second edition did not know Hopkins' unpublished Note or understand the change of beats in v. 1, and he may simply have deemed he was repairing Bridges' inconsistency. Is it not fair to say that this second edition represents editing building on editing, not directly on evidence? (Is it not the beginning of apostolic succession?)

Gardner's title page for the next Oxford edition, 1948, takes a slightly more ambitious stand; but, as we might expect from his dedication in the Penguin edition to "Bridges the advisor", to whom "no adequate tribute can be paid"[19], Gardner was not about to tamper with tradition.[20] His title page declares, in now familiar but still strange words, that this is "*The First Edition with Preface and Notes by ROBERT BRIDGES*" and then adds "*Edited with additional Poems, Notes, and a Biographical Introduction by W. H. GARDNER*". It too sounds like an edition based not directly on Hopkins' work, but rather like an edition of an edition of it, which the title page curiously names the "*Third Edition*"! — without otherwise glancing at the unnamed second editor (the superseded apostle?).[21] (And, to add to the confusion, on turning the title page, we learn that this third is also the *first* American edition.)

Because his Oxford text is derivative, I won't need to quote Gardner's rendition of the first stanza of "The Wreck" from the body of this edition, even though it is a new setting of type. One note (from p. 221) does deserve to be quoted in full, however. There, off stage, as it were, Gardner selectively quoted his predecessor, subtly establishing his independence by rewriting the bulk of Bridges' notes. Here, for the first time, an editor of Hopkins comments in detail on the rhythm of "The Wreck" — and so the editorial tradition begins its slow break from Bridges.

(Before we start, please note for future reference Gardner's now out-of-date convention: even when he centres a quotation of Hopkins' verse in his editorial commentary, he encloses it in quotation marks.)

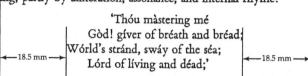

Stanza 1. Here, as throughout the poem, the meaning is 'fetched out'
by the stressing; and the stressing is indicated partly by the meaning, partly by alliteration, assonance, and internal rhyme:

> 'Thóu màstering mé
> Gòd! gíver of bréath and bréad;
> Wórld's stránd, swáy of the séa;
> Lórd of líving and déad;'

←—18.5 mm—→   ←—18.5 mm—→

In Part the First the distribution of the stresses in the eight-line
stanza is 2–3–4–3–5–5–4–6; in Part the Second the first line has
three stresses, as the alignment of A and B (printed in the 1st Edition and now restored) clearly shows.—l. 5: 'Thou hast bóund
bónes and véins in me . . .'.—l. 8, *finger*, cf. st. 31, l. 6.

The string of numbers below the quoted verses ("2–3–4–3–5–5–4–6")
suggests strongly that Gardner, unlike Williams, knew Hopkins' Note
on rhythm. But, as he did not divulge its existence, it is the editor, not
the author, who appears as the authority on "stressing" (l. 2), which is
the term Gardner substitutes for Hopkins' "beats". Gardner holds up alliteration, assonance, and internal rhyme as indicators of stressing, which
are all, of course, qualities one accesses only through *reading* the verses,
as opposed merely to *looking* at them. Here, in the notes, the quotation of
Hopkins' verse is loaded with accents, whereas, in deference to editors
Coleridge and Bridges and to the typographical conventions of English
poetry, the verses in the body of the edition appear without them: only in
the notes may this part of the poet's art dismay the eye.

Now, the four accents in the third line must derive from the lost
autograph, copied thence into Ms A by Bridges; but the other ten accents
in this quotation originate with Gardner himself, including the two grave
accents (a mark Hopkins did not employ to mark rhythm[22]). There is
nothing gravely wrong, of course, with an editor's offering his own acute
scansion in a note, for readers of Hopkins do need much help with his
rhythms, and are grateful for it. But doesn't the editor need to say when
and where the scansion is already the poet's? *No* beats by Hopkins need
defence—even if they should be wrong-headed, or even if the poet may
have himself wavered from one draft to another, as in the following
differences between Ms A and Ms B—

almóst unmáde   álmost únmade

(neither of which follows the stresses of colloquial English)—for they
are simply evidence. But *all* explanatory stresses by an editor, no matter

how correct they may be, do need explanation, because they constitute his own interpretation. As you can see, I am insisting that interpretation *always* be distinguished from evidence. Editing not so identified is not critical editing. (And what editing is critical?)[23]

Gardner's stresses may be satisfying, even pleasing, but are they supported by his rules? If the concept of alliteration that he has singled out justifies the two acute accents he reads in "bréath and bréad", why does it not also justify two where he reads only one in "Gòd! gíver"?—or, if it justifies only one, why that of the second word, and not of the first? (Does it have to do with assonance, present in "breath" and "bread" but not in "God" and "giver"?) When the editor's rules are not self-evident, is it not better to go with the author's unstated rules (or even lack of them) and his inconsistent written accents, rather than to confound his practice with the editor's?

Having eliminated the author, this editor runs in a hermeneutic circle of his own making: "the meaning is 'fetched out' by the stressing", he says, "and the stressing is indicated . . . by the meaning". Of course, it is absurd to think that Hopkins was against reading or against literary interpretation. He wrote to Bridges that all his verse was "as living art should be . . . and that its performance is not reading with the eye but loud, leisurely, poetical (not rhetorical) recitation, with long rests, long dwells on the rhyme and other marked syllables".[24] But, as Hopkins' Note has it (to which the reader of Gardner's edition has no access), it is rather the immediate appearance of his poetry on paper that "indicates": the poet's focus here is on the visual communication of his rhythms. And what of the poet's written accents (which even his Note did not note)—at times blue, always odd? Even before reading an accented word, one knows where "strongly to mark the beats of the measure". And in Hopkins' injunction not to disguise rhyme, the poet implies a role for the mere termination of each verse, as well as for its subtly differentiated beginning. All—all such body language is prior to reading, and is part of the mere *look* of poetry. *Denk nicht, sondern schau!*[25] Wittgenstein's admonition to behold rather than intellectualize seems made for the editor of the manuscripts of "The Wreck of the Deutschland".

There was further slippage when Gardner adapted his note titled "Rhythm" from the Oxford edition for the Penguin. I quote it atop the next page, along with two lines before it, to establish the column width. We are in a tabbed subsection, and so the apparent column width (tab 2 to tab 9) is only 80mm, not the full 85mm shown in the span of 1–9. ("1", by the way, is the tab for the page number, but it is not visible in this extract.)

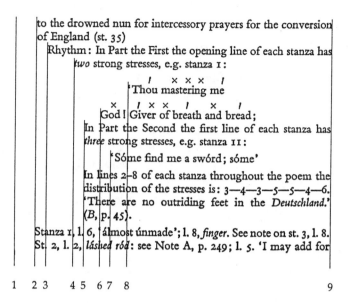

to the drowned nun for intercessory prayers for the conversion
of England (st. 35)
   Rhythm: In Part the First the opening line of each stanza has
two strong stresses, e.g. stanza I:

       /   x x x   /
      'Thou mastering me

      x   / x x   /   x   /
    God I Giver of breath and bread;
In Part the Second the first line of each stanza has
three strong stresses, e.g. stanza II:

      'Sóme find me a swórd; sóme'

In lines 2–8 of each stanza throughout the poem the
distribution of the stresses is: 3—4—3—5—5—4—6.
'There are no outriding feet in the *Deutschland*.'
(*B*, p. 45).
Stanza I, l. 6, 'álmost únmade'; l. 8, *finger*. See note on st. 3, l. 8.
St. 2, l. 2, *láshed ród*: see Note A, p. 249; l. 5. 'I may add for

1   2 3   4 5   6 7   8   9

What a deformed note! The paragraph on rhythm may begin (l. 3) with indentation appropriate for a line of prose (to tab 3), but its continuation at an even more inward tab (4), where a quoted verse might go, rather than where prose should (to the tabbed-in left margin, 2), is not. There follows a line of accents, all but centered, for a line of verse below it, beginning with the editor's quotation mark (which I asked you to look out for). After extra leading, another accented verse follows (tabbed to 6), all but centred against the first. (These verse tabs may seem appropriately to guide the eye; but not quite at *this* distance from each other—7mm, not the 6mm of the body of the book.) What may initially appear to be a third, unaccented, verse follows, tabbed to a new depth (5), a little short of where we might expect the third verse to begin. But, really, this line is prose, as its being right-justified argues (and as its content proves).

The setting of the 1954 edition helps identify the error: extra leading that should follow the second verse, to separate it from the prose (and which was present there in *1954*), has been set instead above the second row of accents. The third "verse" line is tabbed confusingly to the third depth in as many prose lines (5), and this tab endures to the end of the paragraph, instead of reverting to the previous (incorrect) margin for prose (4), as it did in *1954*, and would again, I see, in the reset *1985* Penguin Classic edition (p. 222)—or instead of going where it really belongs (to 2). Consonant with this confusion of verse and prose is the fact that the editorial quotation mark that precedes the first verse never closes. Nor did it in the settings of *1953* or *1954*. In *1985*, the scansion is finally identified as editorial. Thus, some care eventually was taken to improve the note; but the closing quotation mark needed after v. 2 is still absent in *1985*, and the following prose line, still wrongly tabbed, continues to pose as verse.

Now, the purpose of Gardner's note is to detail Hopkins' changes of rhythm and tabbing in the first line of the stanza. But when he ultimately adduced an example of the three-beat first line from PART THE SECOND to contrast with the two-beat first line of PART THE FIRST, Gardner did not tab it to the depth (8 or 6) of either of the verse lines already quoted (it should have gone to 6), but rather to 7—where it is centred in the "Rhythm" section (2–9). Here it sits pretty; but it fails to guide the reader's eye to the editor's own point, let alone Hopkins'.

And do note the new height and slope of the acute accents in v. 3, which Penguin quotes with modest extra leading above and below it. These accents are *in* the line of verse, not set above it, as in the first two. (The problems accents pose to English typesetters!) Now, Gardner had not reported these accents in the body of his edition: they have come in the back door. Nor does he now divulge their source. (Bridges had blue-pencilled them into Ms A, but had not repeated them in Ms B.)

Made only worse in a decade of reprintings, all this spatial and typographic incoherence is apt: it is the *very* kind of error that an editor will make who claims that Hopkins' stresses are "indicated" by non-visual means. In Gardner's marking up the lines with acute accents and x's, which replace and supplement acute and grave accents in his earlier edition (all without any of Hopkins' own colourful calculus, his "blue chalk"), the editor counteracts the instructions of the poet's Note. (Hopkins had written to his mother on his fears of having to humour an editor, and to Dixon about how his oddnesses could not but dismay an editor's eye; his difficulties seem to inhere in editing itself, and are not peculiar to the poet's unsuccessful struggle with his "oldest friend", the editor of *The Month*.)

More important, Gardner misquotes the third verse, beginning with one quotation mark, when he also needed another, to indicate that the verse adduced already had one, for it is reported speech: Death is the "me" of this line from PART THE SECOND ("'Sóme find me a swórd; sóme'"), whereas the "me" of the first line of the poem ("Thou mastering me") is the persona. Like the inconsistent tabbing, the misquoted quotation marks inscribe the awkward interface of editing with the materiality of the poem: the misquotation confounds the editor's voice with the poet's—and with that of Death.

In Part the First the distribution of the stresses in the stanza is, as G. M. H. says, 2–3–4–3–5–5–4–6; but in Part the Second the first line has *three* stresses, as the alignment in both A and B clearly shows. In L. I, p. 45, the poet warns R. B. not to look for '*hangers or outrides*': 'There are no outriding feet in the *Deutschland.*'

St. 1: Here, as throughout the poem, the meaning is 'fetched out' by the stressing; and the stressing is indicated partly by normal word-accent and syllabic strength, partly by contextual suggestion, and partly by allitera- tion and assonance. In A, all the stresses are marked in ll. 3, 5, and 8 (see below); in B, only two stresses are marked, the 2nd and 3rd ('álmost únmade') in l. 6, which is a recast of A:

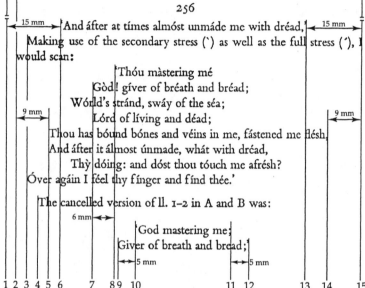

256

← 15 mm → 'And áfter at tímes almóst unmáde me with dréad,' ← 15 mm →

Making use of the secondary stress (`) as well as the full stress ('), I would scan:

Thóu màstering mé
Gòd! gíver of bréath and bréad;
Wórld's stránd, swáy of the séa;
Lórd of líving and déad;
Thou has bóund bónes and véins in me, fástened me flésh,
And áfter it álmost únmade, whát with dréad,
Thỳ dóing: and dóst thou tóuch me afrésh?
Óver agáin I féel thy fínger and fínd thée.'

The cancelled version of ll. 1–2 in A and B was:

6 mm ← →

'God mastering me;
Giver of breath and bread;'

← → 5 mm   ← → 5 mm

1 2 3 4 5 6   7   8 9 10   11 12   13 14   15

The problems did not vanish in Gardner and MacKenzie's collabo- ration in the next Oxford edition, 1967. Intelligently, at the top of this extract from pp. 256–57, the note on the changing format of the first line of the "Wreck" stanza in PART THE SECOND is now *outside* the note to the first stanza. But why doesn't the subsequent note on "fetching out" in the first line of discussion of Stanza 1 also now go outside, since it pertains to interpretation of the meaning of the whole poem?

What remains of the note to Stanza 1 has also been revised. Clues to stressing the edited poem are changed: "normal word-accent and syl- labic strength" and "contextual suggestion" are in; "internal rhyme" is out. But again, there is utter silence on what the poet himself pleads, that we mark the beats as indentation guides the eye. In the next sentence, the editors deal with the poet's written accents; responsibly, stresses derived from Hopkins' annotations are at last ascribed to him in detail, manuscript by manuscript. (But do realize that the poet's accents still make no appearance on centre stage—in the *body* of the volume.) From the statement and the example the editors offer, one has difficulty reconstructing where Hopkins' own accents fell. It's the same old defect: the model mixes the poet's accents with the editors'—or with the *editor's*, rather: for, although one expects the plural "we" at the end of l. 2 on p. 257, "I" is abruptly identified as the author of the scansion. (Which of the two editors is now in charge?) Problematic in the previous edition, accents are problematic in this one too: there seems to be a mixture of styles or founts. Note the contrasting slopes of the acute accents in the following phrase, blown up for clarity. (You *did* bring your protractor?)

I féel thy fínger

Despite the faster rise of the accent over "e" (by about 15°), "é" is situated quite normally under the kerned curl of the "f". Despite the less raked, and therefore more accommodating, accent on the "i", however, a pigeonhole appears between it and the preceding "f". In Penguin, "f" and "i" usually form a ligature, the crossbar of the "f" joining the "i" at its upper serif, and the curl of the "f" absorbing the dot of the "i"; but here it is the accent that absorbs the dot. The stand-alone "i" after "f" is thus doubly awkward. In English settings, accented letters in proportionally spaced founts are obviously a challenge. (A poet in manuscript, Hopkins never had to face this problem, as his poor editors must.)

But a greater spatial oddity lies in the tabbing again, where no typographical obstacle exists. It is hard to say what is the basis of positioning of the whole stanza in this edition. It may be that one of its middle lines (v. 5) is tastefully centred between tabs 2 and 15 (at 9mm from each), or it may be that its farthest left projection (v. 8) was arbitrarily tabbed to 3 (also used for beginning a prose paragraph) and the rest of the tabs ranged as a consequence of that decision. In any event, the revision of vv. 1–2, quoted at the bottom of this extract, are all but centred in the whole column, between tabs 1 and 15, and so they fail to align with the first two lines of the stanza above, which—and this is the editors' whole point—they revise. These two revised lines are ever so slightly right of centre in the column; but they are exactly centred relative to each other, as my 5mm measurements show. However, as the distance between tabs in the stanza above is 6mm, not 5, local typographical aesthetics seems to have over-ridden the systematic tabulations that are to guide the eye.

The problem extends to the prose line before the two final verses. I don't see why it should be the start of a paragraph, but if it must be, it needs to indent only to 3 (the tab for the start of the preceding paragraph), not to 4. (It seems to have been indented from the tab for the leftmost verse line, immediately above, as if verse established the margin for prose!) It looks like an undefined thing—a "paragraph within a paragraph". In this edition, the quotation marks are all in place, but, by virtue of the confused tabulation, the visual separations of poet from editor and of poetry from prose are still problematical. The lack of extra leading between the two topmost lines of p. 257 (the first one verse, the second prose) also tends to collapse genres.

I indicated that Hopkins' Note appeared late in the editorial tradition. But to open the "POEMS (1876–1889)" section in the Penguin, which begins with "The Wreck", Gardner does indeed have a note by Hopkins—and one on rhythm! This same note had appeared here in Bridges' and Williams' editions too, though Bridges had originally planned it *after* the poems. One has to read the fine print to learn they all knew that this "AUTHOR'S PREFACE" was written around 1883, close to Bridges' drafting of Ms B—many years, therefore, *after* Brân Maenefa wrote "The Wreck". On this latter occasion, it was not associated with that poem in particular—certainly not by Bridges when he copied Hopkins' poems into Ms B, for it appears on five leaves that Hopkins attached to or inserted in this manuscript after Bridges had sent it to him. Eventually, Bridges removed this note when the manuscript came back to him from Patmore, and we do not know its original location. If Hopkins had actually placed it at the front of Ms B (where it presently stands), it would have been very far indeed from the poem that the editorial tradition now uses it to introduce.

Hopkins' note reads like a general response to Bridges' transcription of his poetry or to its presentation to Patmore, rather than one particularly about "The Wreck of the Deutschland". In any case, the designation "AUTHOR'S PREFACE" is certainly a misnomer, for the original document is untitled. It is, rather, the "EDITOR'S PREFA-tory *placement* of Hopkins' note. If his *post*script was *pre* anything in Ms B, its position alone would have guided Patmore's eye to see it so. Certainly in his editorial structuring of Ms B, Bridges had postponed "The Wreck". When, later, following chronology in his ordering of Hopkins' poems in his 1918 edition, Bridges positioned "The Wreck" toward the front of the volume, he spoke of it as being "like a great dragon folded in the gate to forbid all entrance": "The editor advises the reader to circumvent the dragon and attack him later in the rear", or even to start with Stanza 16. Bridges' advice from the notes at the back of the book short-circuits his own chronological order in the body. But my point is that the order is already wilfully non-chronological by virtue of the specific placement and contrived titling of this "AUTHOR'S PREFACE".

I will return to this "preface" later in this essay, when editorial shaping comes into focus again. But now back to my model on p. 182. As we know, the profile of its left side mimics that of Hopkins' stanza and telegraphs its *rhythm*. But, on the right side, I have arbitrarily drawn out the representation of each line of verse to various lengths in order to encode the structure of *rhyme* in this stanza (and in all the stanzas of the poem)—*ababcbca*. As you can see at a glance, and have already seen in the contrasting Lancashire model, p. 185, there is no correlation to speak of between the rhymes of the poem and Hopkins' tabs of its verse lines. One concludes that the tabs of the "Wreck of the Deutschland" stanza guide the eye to register rhythm alone—not rhyme.

In its only other reference to rhyme, Hopkins' Note speaks of

> letting the scansion run on from one line into the next,
> without break to the end of the stanza : since the dividing
> of the lines is more to fix the places of the necessary rhymes
> than for any pause in the measure . . .

Here, the poet does allow that rhyme is "necessary"; but his main point is about rhythm—the running on of the scansion without break.[26] Of course, if running on had been his only goal, Hopkins might have written out the verses as if they were prose (but he had already knocked prose in this context), or by *not* varying the depths of tabulation, which now appear as jagged breaks ("fantastically written to rule", one wants to say). And so, we may detect a conflict—a tolerable one, but a conflict nevertheless—this time between the poet's stated aim, to let the scansion run on (to let the rhythmic *sound* run on), and his actual *visual* breaking of flow by these busy tabulations.

But what of the busy tabs of our two sonnets, "The Windhover" and "Hurrahing in Harvest"? Try reading them as a key to metre. Well, you won't get far, for they seem to have five-beat lines throughout. The visual coding of these sonnets, unlike that of the "Wreck" stanza, uses indentation to telegraph only end-of-verse *rhymes*—not rhythm at all.

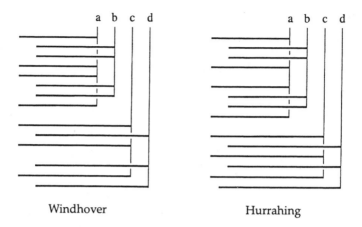

Windhover   Hurrahing

Don't these models confirm that notion? It is not by accident that the first eight horizontal lines in each are of one single length, and all the last six are of another. These correspondences indicate that rhyme and indentation in octave and sestet are tightly linked in Hopkins' sonnets.

But, if a function of these indentations is to telegraph rhyme, we have a problem. Consider the "Windhover" structure as it appears on p. 30 in the Penguin: there are four rhymes per sonnet, but only two tabs—two tabs, that is, if you ignore a third depth—do you?—the tab for the wrapped latter halves of vv. 2 and 6. Well, it is hard to ignore them, especially as the symbolic tabs, which guide our eyes, tend to generate these non-symbolic wraps (which *bewilder* our eyes) by limiting the space available after the indentation for printing a verse intact on a single line.

But even if we do ignore wraps in "The Windhover", its four dis-criminations of rhyme will be seen to map onto only two tabs. Imagine mapping north, south, east, and west onto only half of those dimensions—south and east, say. Some subtlety is *bound* to be lost. (Where, for example, would you locate Seattle?) This telegraphing of rhyme, if that is the function of the tab, is systematic, but it is also ambiguous, for the tabbing is a reductive reflection of the rhymes.

As we become sophisticated at reading body language, I suppose we learn that at the major strophic threshold in either sonnet, between octave and sestet, the symbolism of the tabbing needs to be understood as cleared (of the *a* and *b* rhymes) and begun again at the same depths (for the *c* and *d* rhymes). This resetting comes as the reader passes over the first extra leading in "The Windhover". But the next extra leading, between its tercets, does not occasion a change of association of rhymes with tabs. Similarly, in "Hurrahing in Harvest", extra leading between quatrains does not mark such a change. Thus, like indentation, extra leading sends an equivocal message about rhyme.

But extra leading has a more reliable function than to indicate change of rhymes. Although these two sonnets agree in the structure of indentations and rhyme, their extra leading is different. In the former, as we saw, extra leading isolates octave and tercets; in the latter, it isolates quatrains and sestet. Such leading silently but vividly parses the poems in strophes and sub-strophes. In body language, therefore, the leading in this opening of the Penguin edition offers the eye two distinct strophic structures, even though these two poems have the same structure of rhymes and symbolic indentations.

Now, while reading Hopkins' sonnets, it is a pleasure also to take in their communicative postures. (This feat comes with practice.) And it is instructive, when more than one sonnet is visible in an opening, also to contrast their body languages, for they almost always carry themselves differently. Certainly, the sheer variety of visual styling is a striking feature of Hopkins' poetry in this, as in most editions. (But you won't see it in the Pterodactyl Press *Sonnets* (San Francisco, 1980). There, the dominant structure of tabs (shown on the left) is reversed for just the six "sonnets of desolation" (on the right). In this inauthentic editorial tabbing, a mere two shapes fit all, whatever the rhyme scheme.)

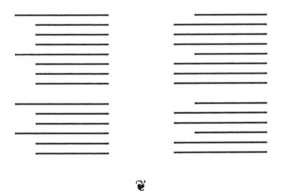

At the bottom of the recto of the Penguin opening under consideration since the start of this essay, there begins a new poem, "THE CAGED SKYLARK" (numbered 16). At a glance, a poem can often reveal itself as a sonnet solely by its shape. But the coming of the end of the page after merely the fourth verse makes us unsure whether this quatrain is the start of a sonnet at all, and, if it is, which, if either, of the two previous shapes might pertain. If we turn the leaf (Let me just cut and then paste to bridge this recto with the verso*h no*—how could (Excuse me for just a moment, please*Now* look what you've made me

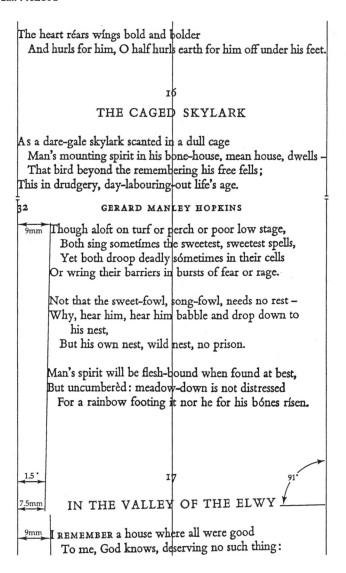

The heart réars wíngs bold and bolder
And hurls for him, O half hurls earth for him off under his feet.

16

THE CAGED SKYLARK

As a dare-gale skylark scanted in a dull cage
  Man's mounting spirit in his bone-house, mean house, dwells –
  That bird beyond the remembering his free fells;
This in drudgery, day-labouring-out life's age.

32   GERARD MANLEY HOPKINS

9mm Though aloft on turf or perch or poor low stage,
  Both sing sometimes the sweetest, sweetest spells,
  Yet both droop deadly sómetimes in their cells
Or wring their barriers in bursts of fear or rage.

Not that the sweet-fowl, song-fowl, needs no rest –
Why, hear him, hear him babble and drop down to
    his nest,
  But his own nest, wild nest, no prison.

Man's spirit will be flesh-bound when found at best,
But uncumberèd: meadow-down is not distressed
  For a rainbow footing it nor he for his bónes rísen.

1.5ʺ   17   91°

7.5mm   IN THE VALLEY OF THE ELWY

9mm I REMEMBER a house where all were good
  To me, God knows, deserving no such thing:

—yesyes it *does* look like a sonnet, one that ends in leaded tercets, just as
"The Windhover" did.

I found myself hesitating in the last sentence, because, although I had
asked you to monitor the SUBTLETIES OF SYMBOLIC INDENTATION, the
left margin of my cut-and-paste job appeared unexpectedly—well, it
appeared rather jagged. (I'm sorry. I had hoped to seem more in control
of my essay.) I see now that, when I joined the two images, I had a choice
of what to align vertically—either the zero tabs on both pages, or what
is centred on them (such as the titles and the running headline). I chose

centering, never thinking my choice was partial. But *look* at the result. The horizontal dimension of layout—the tabbing—was redefined over the page break! Hopkins was not the author of these asymmetries. Nor, I suppose, was Gardner? (There must have been unacknowledged hands at work in this Penguin text.) But I see that either arbitrary option for aligning my paste-up would have exhumed the *cadavre exquise* of Penguin's *mise en pages* for a poem, like this one, that extends over a page break. The principle of this layout appears to be that the left margin of a block of verses on a given page (*i.e,* its first tab) is a function of line lengths in that block alone.[27] And the vertical is also redefined: the different amounts of leading apparent above and below each poem number, "16" and "17", also point to local spatial accommodations of verse on a page. (But who ever notices such a change from one opening to another?)

So—both horizontal and vertical dimensions were at play when the verse was shoehorned into the Penguin page layout. The poem in space proves to be more slippery than we bargained for.

Let us see whether we can find a rationale for the horizontal reorganization. At the very top of the illustration, the last two verses before "The Caged Skylark" fill the column width, 85mm.[28] And, a little lower, taken together, the flush-left first verse of "The Caged Skylark" and its flush-right second verse fill the column width. When we track the poem overleaf, onto p. 32, we find that the remaining lines of "The Caged Skylark" are all shorter than the longest on p. 31; in the interest of symmetry again, perhaps, a new tab for the margin comes into effect, 9mm or so in from the left edge of the column (as established by the position of the page number, "32"). Again, by chance, the first and second verses after the page break establish the maximum width of the first quatrain there (which is less than the full width of the column this time), and this width (ending all but 9mm from the right margin) may have served as the standard for centering— even though each of the following tercets has a greater width. It seems, therefore, that, in both parts of this poem that ventures across a page break, the Penguin edition centres merely *proximate* lines of verse against the centred titles or running heads in their vicinity.[29]

Whatever hazy definition of "proximate" may apply here, a basic principle seems clear enough: the first tab of each block of a poem divided by a page-break is a function of the line lengths merely of that block. Such a rationale of layout is thus local and bibliographical, not global, not literary. In other words, Penguin layout focused on the appearance of individual pages (or openings perhaps), not on the whole of a poem that runs over a page break. By centering the start of the text block on p. 32, the layout avoided lopsidedness (to the left), which would have resulted if the tabs for the first part of the poem had persisted from p. 31. (Some may see no problem with an aesthetic rationale that shifts margins from page to page within a poem. But it is a close cousin of the confused tabbing we witnessed in Gardner's note on the two different stanzas of "The Wreck".)

One needs to proceed carefully in such formulations, for on close reading—you *do* believe in close reading?—space may not behave as systematically as one expects. The first line of the first tercet on p. 32 actually bows up slightly at the right end. (I'm on the level. Can you not see this deviation now that I point it out?) And the last line of the second tercet bows down, doesn't it? (Where's your ruler?) Furthermore, the left margin of all the verses of this poem that fall on p. 32, though straight, is not quite vertical. Doesn't it tilt clockwise a degree and a half? And I suppose you can now detect with the naked eye a one-degree tilt in the same direction in "The Windhover", on p. 31 of the Penguin. Or did you see it all along? (Who *needs* a protractor?) In the poem lower down on p. 32, the title and verses of "IN THE VALLEY OF THE ELWY" are straight and parallel, as would have been apparent if I had photo-quoted more than just the first two verses of the poem. (But why take up space representing normal things?) As a block, however, the poem tilts counter-clockwise a degree. Yes? The spatial disorder of this page is quite apparent when we bring together, without realignment, some of its remote lines—a Random Anthology of the two curvaceous verses already mentioned, one from each tercet of the upper poem, and the straight but tilted title below it. (Gravol, anyone?)

> Not that the sweet-fowl, song-fowl, needs no rest –
> For a rainbow footing it nor he for his bónes rísen.
> IN THE VALLEY OF THE ELWY

Whatever ideal format the editor and production staff (the unacknow-ledged legislators of this anamorphic literary world) may have wished to impose on the text of this page, close reading reveals it as materially chaotic. Surely, we are not dealing with the direct printing of a setting of a page of Monotype Bembo; rather, it seems, these were lines on paper, possibly stripped in during one revision or another somewhere in the seven reprintings over a decade—somewhere in the seven descending spirals in the mist of the journey of this our. Yes, the cockeyed layout of the Penguin page hints at prior states and reveals its text as patchwork.[30]

Back to the bigger picture now—and to a summary. We began our thinking about the tabs of a sonnet as a function of its rhymes; but the establishment of a different left margin (the first tab) for each block of verses of a poem like "The Caged Skylark" that falls across a page break is a function of local symmetry on each page. Here, then, is further ambiguity in the spatial manifestation of Hopkins' poetry: it responds to bibliographic accidents, not merely to poetic substantives. Our . monitoring the retabbings in a poem charts somewhat the awkward fit of poetry in the discontinuous structure of the codex. (We began by monitoring merely horizontal and vertical; but now we are reading in a third dimension as well.)

The discontinuous structure of the codex. I also hesitated as I cut and pasted the text shown on p. 198, because I was ceasing to be guided by that abstraction, the "*fourteen*-line sonnet". Both THE INCREMENTAL PAGE NUMBER and THE AUTHOR'S NAME distractingly bisect the octave—or was it two separate quatrains to begin with? If it was, why not compute an extra line for the "invisible lead" at the page break? (We *can* read such space now.) Isn't this sonnet thus *fifteen* lines? Or *sixteen*, if you count the extra leading after the intrusive headline? Or *seventeen*, if you count the extra leading after the title? Or *eighteen*, if you count extra leading after the number of the poem? And two more, for leads above and below the first tercet? And more for the big space after the latter tercet?

Of course, every book is discontinuous from one page, leaf, or quire to the next; and the bibliographic links at such points, like pagination, or catchwords (now very rare) or signatures (still occasionally found— witness this very edition)

THE STARLIGHT NIGHT

LOOK at the stars! look, look up at the skies!
    O look at all the fire-folk sitting in the air!
    The bright boroughs, the circle-citadels there!
Down in dim woods the diamond delves! the elves'-eyes!
The grey lawns cold where gold, where quickgold lies!
    Wind-beat whitebeam! airy abeles set on a flare!
    Flake-doves sent floating forth at a farmyard scare!
Ah well! it is all a purchase, all is a prize.

C

and headlines—all can jostle the book's literary contents, not only its actual letters, but also its semantic spaces.

What should one read when one reads? What should one ignore? In particular: *Has the octave of "The Caged Skylark" opened out of its own nature or been forced open by bibliographic accident?* Though we cannot readily answer such a question in this, the typical state of literary consumption—that is, with both our eyes on a copy of a single edition (now in one of its openings, now abruptly in another)—at least we can observe a new pattern of indentation in the sestet of this poem, a pattern that seems, again, to be responsive to rhyme. And so, to return to our original topic—remember?—we do, indeed, have a new shape of sonnet. Three sonnets thus far—and three different sonnet shapes.

In considering the layout of these Penguin pages, I have opened a can of worms. Before I restore the lid, let one more wriggle out—to show how contradictory the layout of this edition can be. (It's definitely for the birds, Tom.) What the "AUTHOR'S PREFACE" called a "Curtal-Sonnet", the eleven-line poem "PIED BEAUTY" (numbered 14), begins on p. 30 and ends atop p. 31. Opposite, I have spliced the two halves of this poem (along with verses of the adjacent poems, to establish the margins). As you see, the second block is not centred on p. 31, nor does it align with the flush-left margin of the sonnet below, "HURRAHING IN HAR VEST" (or with that of "THE CAGED SKYLARK", lower still). When we consider the poem spliced together across the page break, we may wonder why its parts stand horizontally just where they do. Neither the separated nor joined parts are centred. In the upper part, the beginning of the first verse does not align with the beginnings of the flush-left verses of the sonnet above it. Nor can the notion of symmetry of this whole first block explain its location, for v. 5 of "Pied Beauty" ends about 1mm from the right margin, whereas no line starts closer than 6mm to the left margin (established by the placement of the page number). If we consider only lines "proximate" to the title, however, we may detect a rationale for the layout, for the left edge of v. 1 and the right edge of v. 3 (which mark the bounds of a "curtal-quatrain") are both 6mm from the adjacent margins. Along with the title, they form a centred mass on *that* page.

But for whatever reason the poem sits where it does (if there is a reason), note that in this poem, the margin of the verses on the first page *is* conserved on the second.[31] This conservation across the gut-

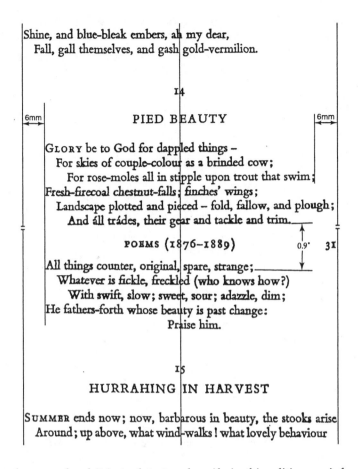

Shine, and blue-bleak embers, ah my dear,
 Fall, gall themselves, and gash gold-vermilion.

14

6mm   PIED BEAUTY   6mm

GLORY be to God for dappled things –
 For skies of couple-colour as a brinded cow;
  For rose-moles all in stipple upon trout that swim;
Fresh-firecoal chestnut-falls; finches' wings;
  Landscape plotted and pieced – fold, fallow, and plough;
  And áll trádes, their gear and tackle and trim.

POEMS (1876–1889)   0.9"   31

All things counter, original, spare, strange;
 Whatever is fickle, freckled (who knows how?)
  With swift, slow; sweet, sour; adazzle, dim;
He fathers-forth whose beauty is past change:
   Praise him.

15

HURRAHING IN HARVEST

SUMMER ends now; now, barbarous in beauty, the stooks arise
 Around; up above, what wind-walks! what lovely behaviour

ter—however hard it is to detect and verify in this edition—reinforces graphically the unity of the separated stanzas. The rationale of the layout of the two parts of this poem (unlike that of "The Caged Skylark") implies a global, not a local unity. Worldly wise, many of us have already learned in life to read between the lines of a sonnet; but who has ever thought to read between its pages? Here on the outer forme of Sheet C, where pp. 30 and 31 stood head to head when they emerged from the press, but now, after folding and cutting, stand side by side, disconjugate—*here*, in these disregarded places, is where subtle (and vulnerable) aspects of a poem's unity may be hiding.

The eccentricity of the lower block (on p. 31) against the centred running headline above it gives the end of this poem a rather pied look. So does the tilting of the same block—by almost a degree. Are you *looking* at poetry yet? (Anybody can just *read* poetry.) Lastly, the closing

"Praise him." is also eccentric, as comparisons with the centred "15" below it or the running head a half dozen lines above it make evident. Given all this seeming lack of control, one wonders whether the conservation of the tabbing over the page break is merely accidental.

Here is the splice across the page break in the *first* Penguin edition, 1953. Protractor handy?

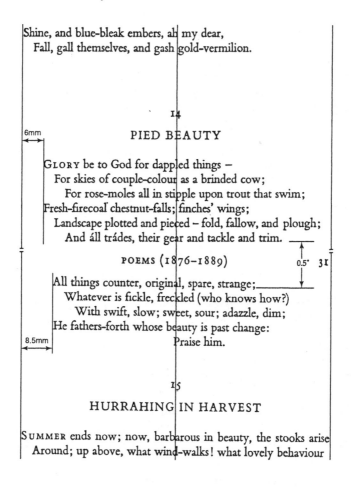

Shine, and blue-bleak embers, ah my dear,
    Fall, gall themselves, and gash gold-vermilion.

14

6mm

PIED BEAUTY

GLORY be to God for dappled things –
    For skies of couple-colour as a brinded cow;
        For rose-moles all in stipple upon trout that swim;
Fresh-firecoal chestnut-falls; finches' wings;
    Landscape plotted and pieced – fold, fallow, and plough;
    And áll trádes, their gear and tackle and trim.

POEMS (1876–1889)   0.5"   31

All things counter, original, spare, strange;
    Whatever is fickle, freckled (who knows how?)
        With swift, slow; sweet, sour; adazzle, dim;
He fathers-forth whose beauty is past change:
                    Praise him.

8.5mm

15

HURRAHING IN HARVEST

SUMMER ends now; now, barbarous in beauty, the stooks arise
    Around; up above, what wind-walks! what lovely behaviour

Perhaps this layout sought to tab the start of the last line, "Praise him.", to the centre? It is actually *off*-centre, of course, as my drawn-in axis makes clear—but by less than a millimetre. If the layout was eye-balled, rather than precisely measured, the present position may have looked close enough. (Certainly, the tilt argues for an imprecise means of placement— a manual, not a mechanical means.)

In the 1985 resetting as well, the two blocks have different first tabs.

Shine, and blue-bleak embers, ah my dear,
  Fall, gall themselves, and gash gold-vermilion.

14

PIED BEAUTY

GLORY be to God for dappled things –
  For skies of couple-colour as a brinded cow;
    For rose-moles in all stipple upon trout that swim;
Fresh-firecoal chestnut-falls; finches' wings;
  Landscape plotted and pieced – fold, fallow, and plough;
  And áll trádes, their gear and tackle and trim.

POEMS (1876–1889)   31

All things counter, original, spare, strange;
  Whatever is fickle, freckled (who knows how?)
    With swift, slow; sweet, sour; adazzle, dim;
He fathers-forth whose beauty is past change:
            Praise him.

15

HURRAHING IN HARVEST

SUMMER ends now; now, barbarous in beauty, the stooks rise
  Around; up above, what wind-walks! what lovely behaviour

The first tab of the poem aligns again with that of "The Windhover", as in 1953. But the start of its second stanza (or is this one solid poem arbitrarily split by the page break?) is even farther right. Thus, the identical tabbing of the first lines of each stanza of "Pied Beauty" in my 1964 Penguin is lost in the 1985 edition—but the last line *is* now precisely centred.

(I will leave tectonics for the moment, but, towards the end of the essay, I'll return to this question of the drift of "Praise him.")

Useful for comparison to the positioning of the greatly indented last line of this curtal sonnet are the four greatly indented lines of the twenty-four-line, multiply caudate sonnet "That Nature is a Heraclitean Fire". As the model overleaf shows, the interweaving of the rhymes blurs the boundaries of the tails (as does the occasional enjambment). The long lines are tabbed to the same (zero) depth—and it seems that they all have six beats, three on each side of a caesura.

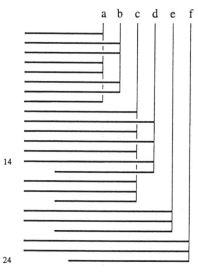

Heraclitean Fire

Our problem comes into focus with the four tails, all greatly indented, the first three to 24mm, the fourth to 27mm. As they express four different rhymes and as each rhymes only among the unindented lines that precede it, the tabbing cannot be for rhyme. And so we need to ask whether it is for rhythm. As the first three tails can readily be scanned with three beats each, the ultimate question concerns the scansion of the uniquely indented final tail, or "burden" line, as I hear it called.[32] Here is the setting of the poem in my 1964 Penguin, from v. 14 to the end, v. 24.

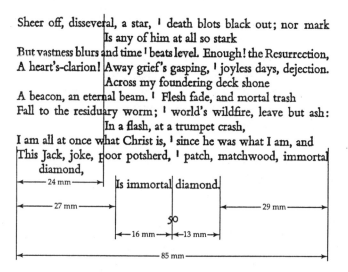

My excerpt includes the centred "50" from the following poem to show that the last verse of "Heraclitean Fire" is not quite centred, and also to make more plausible the notion that it may sit where it does merely to differentiate its tab from that for the three preceding short lines. Does this positioning mean that the last line does not have three stresses, like the other, less indented, short lines? This question is hard to answer, as Hopkins did not mark any beats in the last line—or in the end of the penultimate line, which uses two of the same words. Now, through Gardner's 1948 Oxford edition the last line was not extra-indented. Such indentation first appeared in his Penguin, and it appears again in his co-edition with MacKenzie, and again in MacKenzie's own solo edition, both from Oxford. None of these editions comments on the extra indentation or the scansion of this last line— nor does Catherine Phillips' 1998 Oxford World Classics paperback edition, which offers an unprecedented *three* tabs among the four short lines.

veral, a star,
|Is any of
rs and time |
n! Away grie
|Across
ernal beam.
uary worm;
|In a flas
what Chris
poor pots

|Is imm

There is only one surviving manuscript of this poem. Hopkins created a single deep indentation for the first three half lines, but also (and this is key) he atypically used the same depth to begin the wrapped portions of nearby verses. I will represent this tab by a vertical line in the following transcription of the end of the manuscript. The long penultimate verse wraps as you see here, quite to the right of the former tab. And the final, one-word, verse, "Diamond.", which follows immediately, is very close to the depth of this new wrap—perhaps an "agreement by attraction", as grammarians say.

Thís Jack, jóke, poor pótsherd, | patch, matchwood, is immor-
                        tal diamond,
                        Diamond.

It is far-fetched to think that there could be any symbolism in the subtly fluctuating indentation of the wrapped lines: in handwriting, we do not expect such precise alignments as we do in print. And it is not as if the wrapping of the penultimate line took place at the caesura, say. But the question remains whether the similarly deep indentation of the last verse is symbolic. Does it telegraph a changed number of beats? Or is it merely a mechanically consistent aligning of this short verse with the *local* example of the wrap, which just *happens* to be more deeply indented than before?

The problem is intractable, especially since the revised last verse, "Is immortal diamond.", which is potentially of three stresses, was originally merely "Diamond.", which, though it is itself trisyllablic, sounds awkward as verse with anything more than a beat or two. In revising the two last verses (spread over three lines),

> Thís Jack, jóke, poor pótsherd, │ patch, matchwood, is immor-
> tal diamond,
> Diamond.
> Is immortal diamodnd.

should Hopkins also have realigned the last line well to the left?

A note at the bottom of the page says that this sonnet is "provisional only". That is why editing will never answer such a question, and is consigned to being provisional itself. That Gardner, MacKenzie and Phillips have no notes about their novel indentations suggests they are not aware of the symbolic evocation of their spatial formatting or of the ambiguity of the manuscript. It seems that their later editions are merely recycling this (likely unconscious) aspect of Gardner's editing —or unsupervised waywardness of the typesetter.

Lost? Once one starts squinting at space before verses, between strophes and poems, or between the pages of a printed book, whether over the fore-edge of the leaf or across the gutter, and also between layers of revision in a provisional manuscript source—why, it is possible to wander forlorn in all directions. So, having, I hope, somewhat stretched our sense of literary space (with sonnets of eleven lines or sonnets of twenty four), let me set all this pied beauty aside for the moment, and return to the original focus—indentation and line spacing within the standard fourteen-line sonnet.

We may be able expeditiously to answer our deferred question (whether the octave of "The Caged Skylark" ought to split into quatrains) by looking to Gardner's source—though it has taken me (an average reader, a slacker on a modest budget) three and a half decades to wake up to the critical problem and to move toward the source—with a visit to my local library, and eventually to the Bodleian, where Hopkins' manuscripts are on deposit. As we know, Gardner's Penguin edition derives from his own 1948 Oxford University Press edition. There, the poem is laid out on a single page: the answer is that this Penguin page break does indeed correspond to the extra leading in the Oxford edition. "The Caged Skylark" would have constituted a third sonnet shape for its extra leading alone. (This question proves easy to answer, don't you think?)

But not so fast: this solution to the problem of "The Caged Skylark" throws in doubt the structure of "Hurrahing in Harvest", just before it (which had seemed secure in Gardner's Penguin), for, in Gardner's 1948 Oxford edition,[33] the page breaks between the second quatrain and the sestet—where mere leading had appeared in the Penguin. *O Lord*—the same editor, but different texts—because different tectonics.

38

Hurrahing in Harvest

SUMMER ends now; now, barbarous in beauty, the stooks arise
　　Around; up above, what wind-walks! what lovely
　　　　behaviour
Of silk-sack clouds! has wilder, wilful-wavier
Meal-drift moulded ever and melted across skies?

I walk, I lift up, I lift up heart, eyes,
　　Down all that glory in the heavens to glean our Saviour;
　　And, éyes, heárt, what looks, what lips yet gave you a
Rapturous love's greeting of realer, of rounder replies?

～ 74 ～

And the azurous hung hills are his world-wielding shoulder
　　Majestic—as a stallion stalwart, very-violet-sweet!—
These things, these things were here and but the beholder
　　Wanting; which two when they once meet,
The heart rears wings bold and bolder
　　And hurls for him, O half hurls earth for him off under

Is it possible that, at this source, a reader who would not "stand upon page endings" would regard this sonnet essentially as a quatrain followed by a ten-verse unit (one *accidentally* divided into four-verse and six-verse blocks)? You might think such a question silly, because a ten-line unit would blur the essential structural division of THE SONNET between octave and sestet? Yes?

50

Justus quidem tu es, Domine, si disputem tecum : verum-
tamen justa loquar ad te : Quare via impiorum prospera-
tur ? &c.

THOU art indeed just, Lord, if I contend
With thee ; but, sir, so what I plead is just.
Why do sinners' ways prosper ? and why must
Disappointment all I endeavour end ?

POEMS '89   69

Wert thou my enemy, O thou my friend,
How wouldst thou worse, I wonder, than thou dost
Defeat, thwart me ? Oh, the sots and thralls of lust
Do in spare hours more thrive than I that spend,
Sir, life upon thy cause.   See, banks and brakes
Now, leavèd how thick ! lacèd they are again
With fretty chervil, look, and fresh wind shakes
Them ; birds build—but not I build ; no, but strain,
Time's eunuch, and not breed one work that wakes.
Mine, O thou lord of life, send my roots rain.

No, not in Hopkins. Compare "THOU art indeed just, Lord", photo-
quoted here across a page break (pp. 68–69) in Charles Williams' second
edition, 1930. (I'm inching back to origins along a library shelf!) Again,
of course, the page break after v. 4 in this edition means that we do not
know for certain whether there should *ideally* be any extra leading in this
sonnet. But that uncertainty need not delay our present enquiry, for the
only indentation, in v. 5 of this sonnet (the first line after the page break),
is sufficient in itself to sculpt—do allow me this indulgence—to *sculpt*
a terminal ten-verse block. This unique indentation helps obscure the
passage from octave and sestet, which is prominent in all the previous
sonnet models. (Certainly, the poet's construction of this ten-verse block
does not look accidental, for Hopkins runs his syntax from the eighth
verse into the ninth, never opening the expected gap between octave and
sestet.)

Whether "Hurrahing in Harvest" or "Thou art indeed just, Lord"
are sonnets in which there should ideally be extra leading after the first
quatrain is something we might hope to establish by going back from this
second edition to the first, to Bridges' editi—*oh oh*, I see the sonnet breaks
there in just the same place (across pp. 69–70)—well, go back beyond

that, then, to Hopkins' own manuscribble, squinting to see if any line-spacing there, in the source of all sources, corresponds to the page breaks of the printed editions. But how much time do we have? Would all the seventy years God gave Adam to sweat in be enough? And, of course, manuscript may not itself prove to be the Promised Land. Cannot a handwritten poem be interrupted by a page break as readily as a printed one? We will soon see such in "The Windhover" (pp. 233-34)—where confusion about the symbolism of the tabs potentially attends the turning of the leaf it is written on? Isn't the Muse mediated (and ready to nod) at *every* stage? And can't there be more than one manuscript? And how many of them are in only the author's hand? In how many is authorship mixed, as we already saw at the start of "The Wreck" in Ms B?

In this short time, we have ventured far into uncertainty. But at least in "Thou art indeed just, Lord", we have certainly ventured upon a new sonnet shape! In the three previous shapes, indentation telegraphed rhyme. But the lone indentation in v. 5 marks—well, what does it mark? A strophe? A verse paragraph? A division of argument? On the level of body language, it doesn't really matter what it marks: there is a conspicuously different shape and that shape guides the eye to one end or another, be it rhythm or rhyme or something else altogether. In fact, every sonnet we have observed thus far uniquely guides (uniquely *teases*) the eye. Four sonnets: four shapes. We *see* there are four sonnet shapes, even before we read a word.

The next opening displays pp. 46–47 in my Penguin. I don't suppose I need me to point out that, though the verses of "AT THE WEDDING MARCH" (numbered 29) are level, the margin established by the first tab tilts a degree clockwise, forming at the top, left side, and bottom of the poem, three sides of a "parallelogram"? Easier to see, certainly, is that "THE CANDLE INDOORS" (numbered 27) offers yet another unique sonnet shape, one with no indentation at all, and extra leading before the sestet. Below it, "THE HANDSOME HEART : | *at a Gracious Answer*" (numbered 28) has extra leading between quatrains and between tercets. This too is a new utterance in the body language of the sonnet, isn't it?— an ambiguous one, by virtue of the page break, for it is unclear whether we should also read extra leading between octave and sestet. Similarly, a break at the bottom of the next page, p. 47, divides the first quatrain of "FELIX RANDAL" from the rest of the—*Is* it a sonnet?—overleaf.

27

THE CANDLE INDOORS

SOME candle clear burns somewhere I come by.
I muse at how its being puts blissful back
With yellowy moisture mild night's blear-all black,
Or to-fro tender trambeams truckle at the eye.
By that window what task what fingers ply,
I plod wondering, a-wanting, just for lack
Of answer the eagerer a-wanting Jessy or Jack
There/ God to aggrándise, God to glorify. –

Come you indoors, come home; your fading fire
Mend first and vital candle in close heart's vault:
You there are master, do your own desire;
What hinders? Are you beam-blind, yet to a fault
In a neighbour deft-handed? are you that liar
And, cast by conscience out, spendsavour salt?

28

THE HANDSOME HEART:

at a Gracious Answer

'BUT tell me, child, your choice; what shall I buy
You?' – 'Father, what you buy me I like best.'
With the sweetest air that said, still plied and pressed,
He swung to his first poised purport of reply.

What the heart is! which, like carriers let fly –
Doff darkness, homing nature knows the rest –
To its own fine function, wild and self-instressed,
Falls light as ten years long taught how to and why.

Mannerly-hearted! more than handsome face –
Beauty's bearing or muse of mounting vein,
All, in this case, bathed in high hallowing grace . . .

Of heaven what boon to buy you, boy, or gain
Not granted! – Only . . . O on that path you pace
Run all your race, O brace sterner that strain!

29

AT THE WEDDING MARCH

GOD with honour hang your head,
Groom, and grace you, bride, your bed
With lissome scions, sweet scions,
Out of hallowed bodies bred.

Each be other's comfort kind:
Déep, déeper than divined,
Divine charity, dear charity,
Fast you ever, fast bind.

Then let the march tread our ears:
I to him turn with tears
Who to wedlock, his wonder wedlock,
Déals triumph and immortal years.

30

FELIX RANDAL

ᴱᴸIX RANDAL the farrier, O is he dead then? my duty all ended,
Who have watched his mould of man, big-boned and hardy-
    handsome
ining, pining, till time when reason rambled in it and some
atal four disorders, fleshed there, all contended?

48   GERARD MANLEY HOPKINS

Sickness broke him. Impatient, he cursed at first, but mended
Being anointed and all; though a heavenlier heart began some
Months earlier, since I had our sweet reprieve and ransom
Tendered to him. Ah well, God rest him all road ever he
    offended!

This seeing the sick endears them to us, us too it endears.
My tongue had taught thee comfort, touch had quenched thy
    tears,
Thy tears that touched my heart, child, Felix, poor Felix Randal;

How far from then forethought of, all thy more boisterous
    years,
When thou at the random grim forge, powerful amidst peers,
Didst fettle for the great grey drayhorse his bright and battering
    sandal!

Yes, each of these two Penguin page breaks (pp. 46–47 and 47–48) corresponds with extra leading in the source. And so, as close readers — as
close *collators* of different editions — we might convince ourselves that,
despite appearances, the two sonnets, "The Handsome Heart" and
the wrap-bedeviled "Felix Randal", have the same structure of leads
and indentation.[34] Let's not read so narrowly, though, Fellow Close
Readers, that we fail to notice that the top two lines of "Felix Randal"
on p. 48 are, infelicitously, more darkly inked, less "etched", than the
lines following, or that after them there appears to be extra leading,
or that the centres of the top two lines (and the author's name above)
bulge up ever so slightly over the bottom half, OK?[35]

GERARD BULGER HOPKINS

Surely, then, it can't be extra leading that causes such irregular spacing.
Again, we must be witnessing the behaviour of flexible paste-up paper,
not of rigid metal monotype. (Mechanical collation suggests that the two
bowed verses at the top of the page could possibly have derived from the
setting of the earlier edition, but the rest must have been reset.) I see that
the text remains out of line in a later reprint, 1967; but by 1985, at least,
it was reset, as you can see atop the next page. There is no extra leading
here, but the wrapped last line of this excerpt (8.2) is now flush left. The
end of the second quatrain therefore begins as verse (begins with a capital
on "Tendered") but ends as prose (as the gross internal spacing of 8.1 and
the lower-case beginning of "offended" in 8.2 suggest).[36]

48   GERARD MANLEY HOPKINS

> Sickness broke him. Impatient, he cursed at first, but mended
> Being anointed and all; though a heavenlier heart began some
> Months earlier, since I had our sweet reprieve and ransom
> Tendered to him. Ah well, God rest him all road ever he

8.2   offended!

But at last, in "Felix Randal", we do have a repetition of sonnet shape in my Penguin reprint. We have it, that is, if we search across the gutter or over the leaf, and down the long road to where we can read this edition against its immediate source—and then leap in the faith that no earlier sources will undo us. And we also have it if we overlook the subtle irregular inking and overlook the irregular spacing between lines, and the bowing of the lines themselves, and the shifting of tabs in future editions, and overlook the mixing of different settings of type and of layers of paste-up, and of the metamorphosis of verse into prose, and—and so conclude that the same shape is actually *not* the same shape. (As indeed it is not.)

Thus far, we have encountered seven sonnets with six (or seven) unique shapes. Throughout my Penguin, I can count thirty-one fourteen-line sonnets in all, and discriminate over a dozen and a half different sonnet shapes among them. (Among other things, the page breaks make me approximate here.) In the following section of the essay (pp. 215–22), I have constructed schematic models for these myriad shapes, laid them out analytically, and discussed their varieties. Now, at last, we can begin a systematic, a scholarly—a really *scientific*—discussion of the varieties of these aspects of Hopkins' body language.

But in the section after that (pp. 222–28), I have somewhat *de*-constructed them, and so I invite you to become *less* systematic—and why not, since everything seems fluid in Hopkins' text? (So, please don't get too attached to these models.) The present thread picks up again at the bottom of p. 228. *You* choose where to go next.

Constructing the Models

Overleaf, begins the display of my models. Of course, they include the two shown above, for "The Windhover" and "Hurrahing in Harvest", now as Models 17 and 18. Each model is arbitrarily numbered, sequentially, in the box at the upper left. Together they serve to map

Group 1: Models 1–6

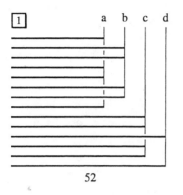

52

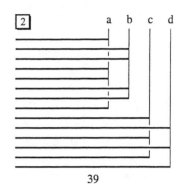

39

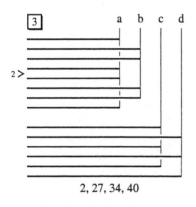

2, 27, 34, 40

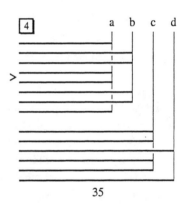

35

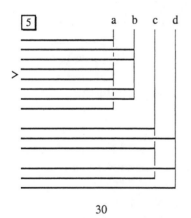

30

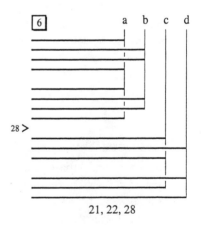

21, 22, 28

Hopkins' sonnets as they appear in the Penguin edition, in terms of their various indentations, extra leadings, and rhymes. As before, I have not reproduced line lengths proportionally; nor have I indicated which lines wrap. I have also evened out the shifting tab settings in sonnets that cross from one page to another. But I do show where there are page breaks, as I will explain in a moment (on p. 219).

My encoding of the rhymes is straightforward. One may quickly deduce from this display that each fourteen-line sonnet has only four rhymes—two in the octave, two in the sestet. The structure of rhyme looks constant in the octave (*abbaabba*), but seems to vary in the sestet (between *ccdccd* and *cdcdcd*). There are thus only two structures of rhyme for all of Hopkins' fourteen-line sonnets. Extra leading and indentation, however, greatly enrich the texture of this structural simplicity, as the range of all twenty models will demonstrate.

For ease of description, I have arbitrarily arranged the models in three Groups (Models 1–6, 7–14, and 15–20), rather than in the sequence of their appearance. A table provided below (p. 281) correlates the numbers and titles in the Penguin with my Model numbers.

It turns out that only four pairs of sequential sonnets in the Penguin edition have the same shape (12–13, 21–22, 41–42, and 44–45), and only one of these four pairs (21–22) lies wholly within the same opening and also does not divide across the gutter, so that a reader can actually perceive the unambiguous repetition of shape at a glance. Generally speaking, therefore, for a reader of Gardner's Penguin edition, a dominant impression, opening after opening, is of the ubiquity of sonnets and of their shifting shapes.

Group I (Models 1–6): The obvious common feature of the six models in the first group is that all verses of each sonnet have the same tab. Models 1 and 2, which have no extra leading, present the poems as solid blocks, and so it is not immediately obvious that they are traditional sonnets—for who can tell at a glance the precise differences of blocks of thirteen, fourteen or fifteen lines?

As noted, Hopkins' fourteen-line sonnets use Italianate rhyme structure in the octave: *abbaabba*. The structural difference between these first two models, therefore, lies merely in the rhymes of the sestet, *ccdccd* or *cdcdcd*, and not in any shaping of the left margin or in any extra leading. My marking of this subtlest of differences here at the outset in two models such as these may seem trifling. But hold on.

Group 2: Models 7–14

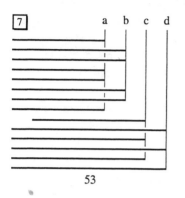

53

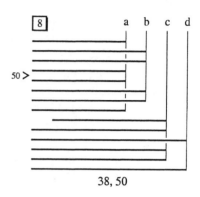

38, 50

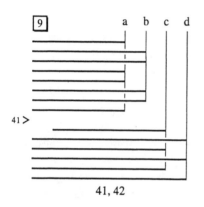

41, 42

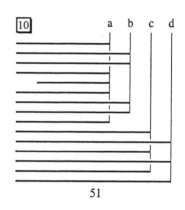

51

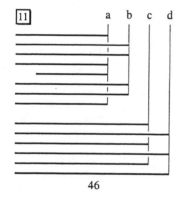

46

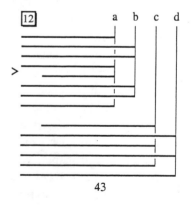

43

Group 2 continues atop p. 221

Models 3 and 4 contrast with the first two in their use of extra leading after v. 8. The graphics of this first group now telegraphs a distinctive sonnet shape: octave and sestet. As we have already seen, page breaks make one unsure about the structural division of a sonnet by leading. The wedges on the left of Models 3 and 4 identify areas of uncertainty for just those sonnets of the Penguin edition that are specified by number—the sonnet numbered 2 in the case of Model 3 and (by default) numbered 35 in the case of Model 4. Take Model 3, with its "2" in the wedge. The shape as drawn (with its solid octave) is accurate for Sonnets 27, 34, and 40; but, in Sonnet 2, the page break after v. 4 means we cannot know from this edition alone whether the octave should continue across this bibliographic divide or should break there. So as not to multiply models without clear evidence, I have, where possible, arbitrarily grouped such equivocal examples with verifiable actualizations of the models. In Model 4, the same problem arises. But this time there is no other example to associate it with; and so my simpler design (with no extra leading in the octave) is, again, arbitrary. (Model 18, however, does provide an unequivocal example of quatrains with extra leading between them but with a solid sestet; and so Model 4 would be defensible with extra leading after v. 4.) Only reference to an earlier source than the Penguin might resolve this kind of uncertainty.

In Model 6, there is definitely extra leading between the quatrains; but Model 5 equivocates at this point. In both these models, the sestet splits into tercets. The second tercet in each model inverts the rhyme scheme of the first—*cdc* then *dcd*. Now, merely listening to the sonnets being read, we may *hear* these sestets as three *cd* rhymes in a row; but *visually* they do break into two parts, and the inversion of the rhymes in the second half is slowly brought to our awareness when, having looked at the sonnet and been guided visually, we begin to sound it out. In other words, one has to read through sonnets like these to discover the effect of diversity in the same unindented visual structure. But in Group 3—to look ahead to Model 17, for "The Windhover"—this same inverted structure of rhymes in the extra-leaded tercets is there telegraphed through indentations; and thus, by contrast, the viewer of "The Windhover" intuits the rhyme structure *before* reading the sonnet or at least before *finishing* it. Models 5 and 6 therefore offer an interesting tension between graphic parallelism and phonetic inversion, but such tension is not present in Model 17.

To sum up: evidently, this first group of models offers us a variety of sonnet shapes: a full-poem block, which may not immediately appear as a sonnet, and a variety of shapes that do so: octave-sestet, octave-tercet-tercet, and quatrain-quatrain-tercet-tercet.

Group 3: Models 15–20

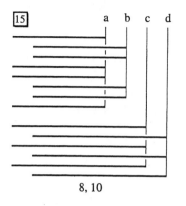

8, 10

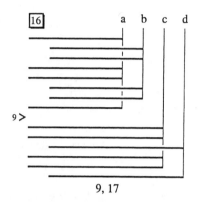

9, 17

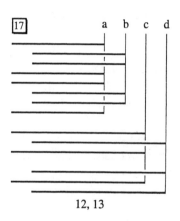

12, 13

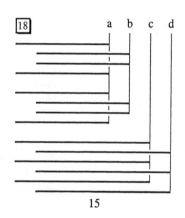

15

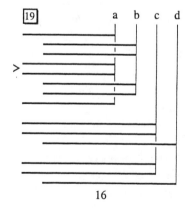

16

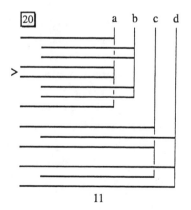

11

Group 2 continues from p. 218 (and concludes)

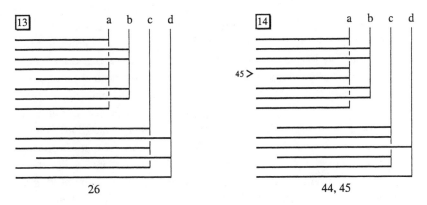

Group 2 (Models 7–14): Each Group-2 model shows one, two, or three indented verses. In Models 7–9, just the first line of the sestet is indented; consequently, these models clearly display themselves as sonnets. (In Model 9, extra leading of this verse compounds the effect.) Model 10 (for "Thou art indeed just, Lord", now on a single page) has indentation of only the first line of the second quatrain; consequently, the poem may not as readily register visually as a sonnet. In Model 11, the same indentation is supplemented by extra leading before the sestet—and thus the silhouette of a sonnet is more obvious, as it is also in Models 12–14, not only by virtue of these same features, but also by indentation at the start of the sestet at least. In Models 13 and 14, these effects combine with additional indentation within the sestet and now highlight by various means all the strophic divisions of an Italianate sonnet—octave, sestet, quatrains, and tercets. As in Models 5 and 6, the sestet of Model 13 displays itself as parallel tercets; but, again, when we read to the end, we find the scheme of rhymes inverted. In this group, too, Hopkins set at odds the structures of sight and sound. But Model 14, which has indentation and leading identical to those features in Model 13, is not inverted.

Group 3 (Models 15–20): In the models of Group 3, indentation (of six or seven verses) does not mark strophes. Rather, it largely telegraphs rhyme. Strophes are now signaled exclusively by extra leading. In this group, each poem is quite recognizable as a sonnet, as they all have extra leading between octave and sestet, and some also at the midpoint of each—but not necessarily in both simultaneously. (My qualification stems from the fact that, though Models 19 (for "The Caged Skylark") and 20 could be graphed as having extra leading at all the major strophic divisions (between quatrains, between octave and sestet, and between tercets), the occurrence of a page break after the first quatrain in each of them means that this most vivid of sonnet shapes is never actualized for these two models in my Penguin (though it is in Hopkins' manuscripts).

On p. 219, I first commented on the structure of indentations in the sestet of Model 17; let me now continue. In this model, the second tercet inverts the indentations of the previous tercet, whereas that of Model 20 repeats them. But look at the structure of rhyme in the final tercet of these two contrasted models. It is the same! In Model 20, (for "The Lantern Out of Doors"), therefore, the indentation of the sestet proves an unreliable guide to its rhyme. The eye and the ear are in tension again. Even if we allow indentation to be a function of rhyme, it is not a straightforward function of rhyme. It may sometimes be inverted. And therefore such indentation is not merely a slavish and mechanical function. On occasion, it can be seen as artful, paradoxical, ironic, playful, teasing. These are terms we easily associate with the diction of Hopkins' poetry, of course, but not so readily with its physical structure—and that is why it is a novel thrill to use them now.

So much for detailed scrutiny of the models. They bear out the conclusion you may have come to already: Hopkins was precocious, not only in diction but also in graphic styling. Should we be surprised? He was a very accomplished draftsman as well as a poet.[37] Among his other gifts, Gerard Hopkins was a spatial thinker.

If you want to move immediately to Hopkins' manuscripts, you can turn now to p. 229. But before *I* get there, I'll need to take some of the starch out of these models.

Deconstructing the Models

Let us come at these constructions from a different direction. Indentation and extra leading should not generate much debate. Is there any doubt about what constitutes symbolic indentation? Is it not readily distinguished from the obligatory extra-indentation of wrapped lines to show continuity? Nor is there doubt about symbolic leading, except where its presence cannot be detected at page breaks. But rhyme—well, rhyme is quite another matter. Eye rhymes, archaic rhymes, and dialect rhymes defy the ear, and do offer a challenge to these models.

In an early letter to his mother, Hopkins reported on a rhyme that had stirred his father's protests: "Pool" and "renewal". The poet's defence: "it must be looked at partly as a freak, partly as a necessity."[38] This particular freak survives only in the poet's letter, but he was not to be stopped. Who is more daring in rhyme than Gerard Hopkins? In "Hurrahing in Harvest", look at these four rhymes behaviour   wilful-wavier   Saviour   gave you a

which equivocate di- and trisyllable. Unlike the other three rhymes, the last, with no letter r, reveals Hopkins' southern English speech, with its silent final r in the first three rhymes and concomitant gliding of the preceding vowel. But what is astounding in any English accent is the location of the rhyme: now contained in one word, now spread across three (where there could scarcely be a "pause in the measure").

Even more startling are these rhymes in "Spelt from Sibyl's Leaves" (numbered 39 in Penguin):[39]

stupendous   overbend us   end, as- | [tray]   end us

Here, the third example shows the two syllables of the rhyme interrupted by a comma: "end, as-". Also strange is that, though the rhyme comes, as we expect, at the *end* of the line, the latter syllable of the rhyme is the *first* syllable of a word that enjambs into the next line.[40] Although an oscilloscope and a phonetician in a white coat may force us to accept that a single rhyme binds these four words or phrases or fragments together, so much about them registers as dissimilar in the contexts of metre, syntax, syllable, punctuation, and word that they are scarcely to be conceived as rhyming. One might *reason* by the second reading (or the tenth) that since such combinations as these must rhyme, this must be a sonnet, and the self-assured model adduced, Model 2, must, in theory, be apt. But, to our *feelings*, Hopkins' sonnet structure is coy—provocatively so; and (God be praised) it strives against norms.

These models are not advanced, therefore, as if they were beyond debate. My caution here is not merely scholarly. It pertains, rather, to Hopkins' ambition and to our sheer excitement and bafflement on reading his poetry. He risks abolishing all rules, while harvesting rules where they were never deemed to grow, until he sowed the ground. The models are, therefore, something that may germinate in our darkness as we read, and struggle, and read again. But one's doubts about a model are not to embarrass us: for the struggle for the poem *is* the poem. The proffered models could not nail down these elusive sonnets even if we wished them to. At best, each model functions like an asymptote, approaching but never tangent to the arc of its sonnet.

The previous two examples of rhyme are hard to locate. But in "The Windhover" the location of rhymes is too obvious: the first eight lines all end in "ing". One might conceive, therefore, that the model for this octave should be radically simplified—not as I showed it, in Model 17 (where indentation telegraphs rhyme), but as in 17A.

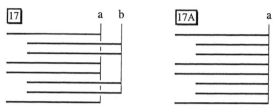

Indeed, one editor, Ian Lancashire, sees it as just that: "**Rhyme:** aaaaaaaaabcbcbc." With the reduction of all the octave rhymes to *a*, the tabulations of his *Representative Poetry* version, which are the same as in my Penguin edition, now seem absurd. They no longer telegraph the architecture of the rhymes (just as pilasters, be they ever so graceful, say nothing of what supports the ceiling). But a *close* look—I mean a closer *listen*—does reveal a subtle but regular differentiation of rhyme—"-ing(-)" *vs* "-ding". And this differentiation is indeed one that matches the indentations of these lines. (Were they pillars after all, then?) Here are the rhymes. See if you don't agree with me.

king- | [dom]

        riding

        striding

wing

swing

        gliding

        hiding

thing

Well, if you did agree, you're in trouble. For the first two *b* rhymes are more extensive than merely "-ding": they rhyme "riding" and "(-)riding". So, if you were discerning enough to separate "-ing(-)" from "-ding" (as I set you up to do), why not also separate "-ing(-)" from "-ding" and from "(-)riding"? But this challenge is itself challenged in the second quatrain, because, for "gliding" and "hiding", "-iding" is the *b* rhyme, not "(-)riding". On closer scrutiny, this "-iding" proves ultimately to be the common denominator of all four *b* rhymes. As the indentation supports this recondite notion of structure, my model survives. (Hurrah!) But who would deny that the poet might have been playing off traditional structure (advertised in the tabs, and made to *appear* solid, as in my projection of Model 17) against a more complex notion of structure, barely audible in the subtle variety of *b* rhymes?—*and* their cousins, the *a* rhymes? As we have already seen structural antics in this poet's "Thou art indeed just, Lord", our surprise should not surprise us.

We are not done yet, for there is as much difficulty really in determining the *a* rhyme as the *b*. As one goes from the end of the first quatrain to the start of the second, the rhyme words of these adjacent lines are obvious enough, despite the enjambment which obscures them: "wing" and "swing". One can be forgiven, therefore, for thinking in passing that the basis of the rhyme is "(-)wing", especially since the preceding *a* rhyme in this class, "-ing-", is wickedly hidden in the middle of "king-Idom". But by the end of the second quatrain, with its rhyme on "thing", the *a* rhyme certainly has to be, we calculate, retrospectively — retro*audially*, rather — less than "(-)wing", has to be "-ing(-)". Again, with great good fortune, Model 17 survives — but, again, only in tension with tempting variations of itself. It survives not only in tension with Model 17A, which collapses the *b* rhyme into *a*, but also with Model 17B,

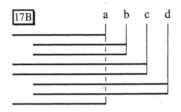

which multiplies *a* and *b* (in lines with opposed indentations) respectively into *c* and *d* (in lines also with opposed indentations):

a: -ing(-)   *b*: (-)riding   *c*: (-)wing   *d*: -iding

Aptly, *a* and *c* show one indentation, *b* and *d* another — "aptly", for the *c* rhyme more or less includes the *a*, and the *b* includes the *d*.

This last modeling certainly challenges our sense of octave structure. By habit, we are so apt to divide an octave into two quatrains that we can miss experiencing this example as three couplets sandwiched within — within a fourth couplet, as it were. It seemed that all my original models offer only four rhymes per sonnet, two per octave, two per sestet; but this transgressive sonnet flirts with three rhymes — and with six. Model 17 needs dialectical buttressing from 17A and 17B to make it begin to map onto our ambiguous reaction on first reading "The Windhover" — and to map onto Hopkins' sheer danger and dazzle.

If we focus on regional accents, there is yet another way to challenge this model. The first rhyme word in the earlier drafts of this poem (see Ms B, below, p. 264.) was simply "king". Only in revision did the rhyme shift from the end of this word to the middle of another, "king-I dom". Only then did it shift subtly from "-ing" to "-ing(-)".

In that earlier version, the point I am about to make does not apply, but it does apply in the revision (for which I made the model). In the speech of Liverpool, where Hopkins was living three years after he first drafted "The Windhover", you will hear the voiced velar stop [g] explode at the end of "king": not [kɪŋ], as I pronounce it (in my Ontario accent), without a final stop or plosive, but [kɪŋg], as the Beatles pronounce it, with a final stop and plosive, [g] — and, in fact, in Liverpool, one hears this stop and plosive at the end of all the other (end-of-word) rhymes in the octave. However, in this northern English accent, just as in my own, you won't hear the [g] when "-ing-" occurs in the *middle* of a word, as it does in the "king-|dom" of Hopkins' revision — the sound of which is [kɪŋdəm] (not [kɪŋgdəm]). In any English accent I know of, when two voiced stops or plosives occur next to each other medially, only the first really stops and only the second really explodes. (Contrast the Polish surname "Bogdan", (the equivalent of "Theodore")[41] — which has a single medial stop, [g], directly followed by a single medial plosive, [d] — with the same name arbitrarily extended by a vowel between these two consonants: "Bogọdan". With this new vowel in place, [g] is now also a plosive (and [d] is now also a stop).) In Liverpool, Hopkins' brilliant revision of the first rhyme word means that my Model 17 no longer pertains for the first line — or pertains there only as an eye rhyme.

Conversely, the following rhymes in the octave of Hopkins' "No worst, there is none" (numbered 42) may seem to work *only* in Liverpool, where all four of them might be deemed to end in [ɪŋg]

wring   comforting   sing   ling- | [ering]

— whereas, in my own accent, [ɪŋ] is the basis of the rhyme, and I voice the verse-ending plosive [g], so prominent in Liverpool, only in the first "g" of "lingering". But, to be more subtle still, this [g] is actually articulated (in both accents) at the start of the *next* syllable. Formerly, in "as-|tray", we saw a rhyme *ending* before the last syllable of a word enjambed. In Scouse, however, the rhyme straddles the enjambment. Hopkins' word division forces speakers with either accent to pronounce the "ering" that opens v. 8 with an initial [g]: as [lɪŋ | gərɪŋ] — or, in Liverpool, as [lɪŋ | gərɪŋg] — with a final [g].

Our sense of the structure of a sestet can also be challenged by close linguistic scrutiny. In this, my last deconstruction, it will be grammar that touches on rhyme. Consider "The Starlight Night" (numbered

9), which is reproduced below, p. 276. I will set out the rhyme words here in two columns, as a function of indentation in the Penguin. The two tabs in the sestet prepare us for two rhymes. Obviously (to start somewhere), the indented "sallows" and "hallows" lines do rhyme, on "-allows". We can represent the end of this rhyme as [oz]. The rhyme of the remaining four words ("vows", "bows", "house" and "spouse") to speak only of the vowel quality of "vows" and "bows", is on the diphthong [-au-], not [-o-]; and so, it seems clear enough that we must now be into the other rhyme in the sestet. But whether "vows", "boughs", "house" and "spouse" *all* rhyme among themselves (as Model 16 proposes) is the troubling question. Of "vows" and "boughs" there is little doubt; they rhyme on [-auːz], and the vowel, a diphthong, is long ([ː]). But "house" and "spouse" will rhyme with them exactly only if they are verbs. Should they be nouns, their terminal sound is [-aus], a shorter vowel and an unvoiced consonant.[42] Are they nouns or verbs, then? When we encounter the first of these two rhyme words of the latter tercet, "house" and "spouse", the context is so unusual that it will not spell out the grammar for most readers

vows
boughs
      sallows
house
spouse
      hallows

> These are indeed the barn ; withindoors <u>house</u>
> The shocks.

—and hence will not reveal how we are to sound the final consonant of "house", whether to rhyme it with "vows" and "boughs" on [z], or on [s] instead. Only belatedly, when we come to the word "the" before its potential rhyme-mate, "spouse", in the continuation of the partial line I just quoted,

> The shocks. This piece-bright paling shuts the <u>spouse</u>
>   Christ home . . . .

will many readers retroactively decide that "house" is a noun—and thus deem it ends with [s]: hence, [haus], *not* [hauːz]. As in our uncertainty about the octave of Model 17, we can regard the entire sestet of this sonnet as a cluster of slant rhymes, *c*, as shown in 16A,

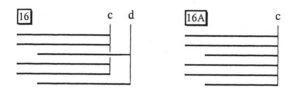

not of two rhymes, *c* and *d*, as my Model 16 has it. But the argument just advanced can as easily grant the sestet three rhymes: [-oz], [-aʊs], and [-aʊːz]—as in Model 16B: an initial couplet, standing on its own, and with its own (zero) indentation, followed by two more pairs, with contrasting indentations, one pair (with zero indentation) sandwiched within the other (indented).

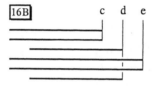

To maintain my Model 16 for this sonnet, therefore, I must also hold that [-aʊs] and [-aʊːz] are slant rhymes (despite their different final consonants and different vowel lengths), and therefore that all four words ("vows", "bows", "house", and "spouse") rhyme on *c*. But, finally, I must also forbid [-os] (in "hallows" and "sallows") to slant into their association (despite the same final consonant and the same (short) vowel length as one of the *c* rhymes, and also despite the shared "-ows" spelling), and therefore hold that "sallows" and "hallows" must evince a *d* rhyme—which is all a very very convenient and self-serving and overly subtle argument—even if it *is* true. (Well, it's *plausible* enough.)

My Model 16 alone obviously does not tell the whole story, any more than Model 17 alone tells the whole story. No, these models are frequently couched in doubt, and that is an essential part of their heuristic value. We cannot have *analysis* of Hopkins' poetry without doubt—because we cannot have his *poetry* without doubt.

If you find the whole matter hard to get straight, you are in excellent
company. As he drafted and revised his sonnets, the poet himself had
difficulty shaping and maintaining their body language.

Hopkins led off with a sense of genre; only in revision did this poem
become titled "God's Grandeur".

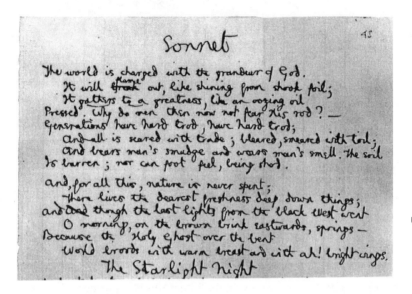

When this sonnet was printed, it conformed to Model 15. But of the
four surviving drafts, the one shown here initially veered away from
that model, for the pattern of indentation of the first three verses of
the sestet repeated the pattern of the first three verses of the octave.
But eventually "And", the first word of the indented third verse of the
sestet, v. 11, was deleted and rewritten (full-size, please note) in the
unindented position: "And" → "And". The poet's correction was not
to diction, but merely to spatial location: evidently, this line required
indentation to match that of the lines it rhymed with.[43] For the poet,
configuration was part of God's grandeur.

The same observations apply to the (full-sized) revision of "Is" at the
start of v. 8 in another manuscript of this same poem (shown overleaf):
"Is" → "Is".

But contrast the configuration of two other revisions, one at the start of v. 3 ("It" → "Goes") and one at the start of v. 9 ("Yet" → "And, "). The handwriting of these two revisions is small, and they appear above not beside the deletions (the second one situated in what hitherto had been the line spacing between octave and sestet). Had these substitutions been written out to the left of the start of each verse, they could have been full-sized. But in that location they would have confounded the codes of indentations, which Hopkins evidently strove to maintain.

For future reference, note two curious features of this manuscript. First, there are notations of rhythm: "∞" above "with" and "grandeur" (v. 1), "nature" (v. 9), and "over" (v. 13). (One supposes it is the vowel in each underlined cluster that is the object of the annotation, but it spreads imprecisely over consonants too.) Second, there is wrapping of the last word of two long verses (6 and 14) to the middle of the following line. Evidently, Hopkins had a strong sense of the vertical axis of the body of his verse on a page. (We will see more of it below.) Such centred wrapping certainly avoids equivocation with his more modest symbolic indentations at the starts of verses.

Atop the next page, in another version of this sonnet, now titled "God's Grandeur", on a part of the leaf severed by Robert Bridges (not shown here), v. 6 began without indentation; but Hopkins

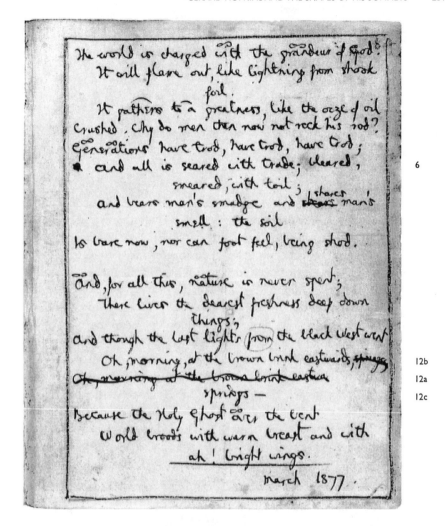

caught the misplacement after one letter, blotted it out, and began again, in the indented position, well to the right.

Verse 12 tells a different story. It seems to have begun (12a) after the (now filled-in) line spacing that divided the tercets. The sestet had not been divided here in earlier drafts; nor had this twelfth verse previously begun flush left: it looks as if Hopkins was changing from Model 15 to 20. But, after this twelfth verse was all but completely written out (almost to the end of "eastward"), the poet seems to have reacted to the lack of indentation or to the presence of line spacing above it or to both. Having struck out as much of the verse as he had written, Hopkins began it again verbatim, but indented now, in the line above (12b), hitherto blank (thus bringing this version back to Model 15). Having all but completed the verse in this new location, he seems to have deleted its last word, "springs", and written it again (12c), centred, with a dash after it now, under the deleted version of the verse (12a). All this trouble—and, again, it seems to be concerned merely with the posture of the sonnet, not its diction.

The metrical symbol "∞" now also appears in "Generation" (v. 5) and in "And" (v. 9) (a second stage of revision for this word). Also, ties or slurs occur over "gathers" and "to a" (v. 3).

The earlier version of "The Windhover", opposite, also has false starts (in vv. 1, 4, 7, and 11). But I will focus on the consequences of the small page size for writing out a sonnet with long verses. In the lower right corner, "[T. O." tells us to "Turn Over" the leaf. On the verso, we find the concluding tercet. Its lines' running the length of the page there obviates the need for wrapping any of them, whereas six of the eleven verses written horizontal on the recto do wrap. But because the two parts of the sonnet cannot be seen at the same time (though the last tercet is visible as show-through on the recto), the code of the indentations across the page break is easy to get wrong (I'm not saying it *is* wrong), and, once wrong, is hard to detect. (Recall the similar difficulty in detecting a shift in the margin in a printed poem when it crosses a page break.) Hopkins did not revise his indentations on the verso of this copy; but in a later one, where the sonnet fits on a single page, he line-spaced the last tercet, and he did reverse the indentations of each of its lines, relative to how they appear here. (This revision gives point to remarks above (pp. 219 and 221–22, relative to Models 5, 6, 13, 17 and 20) concerning parallel or inverted schemes of indentation in the tercets, and to supporting or contradictory relationships between the structures of indentation and rhyme.)

In "The Lantern Out of Doors" (Model 20), inversion was surely intentional. Hopkins began v. 12 tabbed, as he had the former *d*-rhyme verse. But then he struck out "Chris" and began again with no tab, as for a *c*-rhyme verse: "Christ minds . . ."; and so he continued, inverting tabs to the end of the poem. For MacKenzie, v. 12 was "begun correctly . . . but put wrong". (But who's to say *this* wrong wasn't just right?)[44]

Having arrived at such holographs as these, we may think we have attained the source, The Author in His Cell, where all the questions of line spacing and indentation we have been preoccupied with should find their authoritative (but contestable) answers. Well—read on.

The Windhover

caught this morning morning's minion, king   1a

Of daylight's dauphin, dapple-dawn-drawn Fal-   1b

con — — he was riding [striding

Rolling, level underneath him steady air, and

Hung so and rung the rein of a wimpled wing   4a, 4c

in an ecstacy; then off, — forth on swing,   4b

As a skate's heel, sweeps smooth on a bow-

—bend: the hurl and gliding

Rebuffed the big: wind. My heart in hiding   7a

stirred for a bird — for the mastery of the thing!   7b

te beauty and valour and act, O air, pride, plume,

                here   [a billion

buckle! And the fire that breaks from thee then,   11a

Times told lovelier, more dangerous, O my   11b

                chevalier!   = [T. O.

the wonder of it: stress; plod makes plough down sillion
'Shine, and blue-bleak embers, ah my dear,
Fall, gall themselves, and gash: gold-vermilion.

St. Beuno's. May 30 1877

I see no other writ-
ten . . . as . . . written . . . prize

Poems

of

Gerard Manley Hopkins

now firſt publiſhed

Edited with notes

by

ROBERT BRIDGES

Poet Laureate

LONDON

HUMPHREY MILFORD

Long after Hopkins' death in 1889, Robert Bridges, who had been collecting his friend's drafts for the last decade of the poet's life, mostly as they were mailed to him, edited and published his poems in 1918 in an edition of 750 copies, with a dedication to Hopkins' mother, rendered in Latin by A. E. Housman.[45]

Dare one speak the truth? Hopkins was not to be trusted with his own work. We have already heard him tell Dixon that he burnt his poems on becoming a Jesuit. Perhaps his diary entry on the "slaughter of the innocents" is a reference to this conflagration.[46] And, when he returned to poetry, like Keats, he mailed drafts to friend or family, often keeping no decent copies for himself—or any copies.[47] And was not Bridges also suspect? When his own letters came back to him after Hopkins' death, Bridges burned them. (Reluctantly, one assents to Dr. Bridges' right to privacy.) Though he generally saved most of the letters Hopkins had addressed to him (so bequeathing to posterity almost half a conversation), Bridges also edited some of them by fire.[48]

Robert Bridges

This world is unto God a work of art
Of which the unaccomplished heavenly plan
Lives in his masterpiece and grows with man
Unto perfection and success in part.
The ultimate creation stayed to start
From the last creature for whom all began:
Who child in what he is and what he can
Hath yet Gods judgement and desire at heart.

    Knowledge denied him/ and his little skill
Cumbered by laws he never can annul/
Baffled by qualities adverse and ill/
With feeble hands/ few years and senses dull/
His art is natures nature/ and love still
Makes his abode with the most beautiful.

One's sense of Bridges' graphic designs on his friend's remains begins on this title page, with the swash *P* in the title and *M* in "*Manley*", the three examples of swash and kerned *R* in the editor's name, and the kerned *k* in "*Hopkins*". Even more striking are the old ligatures in "*firſt publiſhed*" (not actually tied in my Palatino fount). Long-s disappeared from English books in the early nineteenth century, but traces of it remained in writing (where it had started), as in Bridges' own hand (see below, p. 250, vv. 2 and 7) and in some of his publications in print.

In the 1840s, Whittingham and Pickering revived long-s in Caslon Old Face for the title pages of their reprints of seventeenth-century authors. This styling had an antiquarian aura. Pickering's 1844 edition of Herbert's *Temple* reintroduced long-s in the body as well—and here its aura is scholarly. (This trend culminated in Grierson's 1912 edition of Donne.) Notably, the use of long-s in Thackeray's 1852 first edition of *The History of Henry Esmond, Esquire* by Smith, Elder, and Company artistically evoked the period of the novel's setting, a century and a half earlier.[49] And I see a long-s on Dante Gabriel Rossetti's woodblock title page for his sister Christina's *Goblin Market*, 1862. But these revivals in mid-nineteenth-century typography (or woodblock, in the case of Rossetti) were sporadic. By the end of the Great War, when Hopkins' *Poems* appeared, the long-s of its title page was scarcely apt: for a poet ahead of his time, such typography looked backwards.

Unlike Hopkins, Bridges was his own contemporary. Should we be surprised, then, that in 1889 Bridges brought out one of the anonymous editions of his own book of sonnets, *The Growth of Love*, from the Daniel Press at Worcester College, Oxford, in an astonishing black-letter type, the recently discovered seventeenth-century Fell types, with long-s, its attendant ligatures, Caxtonian commas, and even ragged-r (though this letter was not set according to convention)?[50] (*Growth* xᴠj is shown opposite.) Hopkins teased Bridges about aiming for oblivion by descending into "Daniel's den"; and the remark stung him.[51]

I cannot recall an original edition of sonnets that appeared in black letter since Thomas Watson's *Hekatompathia, or Passionate Centurie of Loue*, 1582, three centuries earlier, shortly before Sidney's *Astrophel and Stella*, 1591, decisively stamped a roman face on the English sonnet.[52] Bridges' antique typeface thus evokes the world of the English sonnet that began in 1557, with Tottel's black-letter miscellany, *Songes and Sonettes* (where Wyatt and Surrey's sonnets first appeared in print) and seems to have ended a mere two generations later. In English poetry, and in sonnets in particular, black letter may well have looked rustic ever since Spenser's *Shepheardes Calender* (1579).

Now, Hopkins was intensely aware of the medieval, as his study of Welsh poetry and of alliterative verse suggests; and Bridges even characterized his Catholicism as "medievalizing".[53] But the poet certainly did not programmatically cultivate the antique. One would not guess from his English verse that Hopkins was a teacher of ancient Greek. "I look on archaism as a blight," he had written to Patmore on August 16, 1883, while commenting on Dixon's *Mano: A Poetical History: of the Time of the Close of the Tenth Century*. In the same letter he spoke against the "trick" of "writing in italics". (I suppose he meant *setting* italic in or instead of roman.) Given these pronouncements, one wonders how the poet would have taken to the italic title page of his *Poems*, 1918, and to its long-s,[54] for to Patmore Hopkins voiced dislike of the long-s (and, by implication, the long-i) that he had seen in "a Puseyite spiritual book",[55] where, in his ridicule, "Conſider (ij) O my ſoul" would be mentally heard by contemporary readers as "*Confider idge o my fowl.*" (Unlike Bridges' calligraphy, Hopkins' inelegant scrawl had no long-s.)

Robert Bridges' framing of the contents of his 1918 edition is no less self-consciously "*brockered*" — this is the editor's very word (and also his italics) — than the typeface of his title page. As his own unsigned poem on the last page of the preliminaries introducing his friend's poetry lovingly puts it, Bridges' hands gathered Gerard's coy legacy, and bid him "*display*" his "*plumage of far wonder and heavenward flight*" to the "*chaffinch flock*" (vv. 13–14).[56] One supposes that this flock is of lesser "plumes".

Our generation already is overpast,
And thy lov'd legacy, Gerard, hath lain
Coy in my home; as once thy heart was fain
Of shelter, when God's terror held thee fast
In life's wild wood at Beauty and Sorrow aghast;
Thy sainted sense trammel'd in ghostly pain,
Thy rare ill-broker'd talent in disdain:
Yet love of Christ will win man's love at last.

Hell wars without; but, dear, the while my hands
Gather'd thy book, I heard, this wintry day,
Thy spirit thank me, in his young delight
Stepping again upon the yellow sands.
Go forth: amidst our chaffinch flock display
Thy plumage of far wonder and heavenward flight!

Chilswell, Jan. 1918.

On p. 70, before the "Unfinished Poems & Fragments" of this edition, the last plumage the editor has the poet display is "*To R. B.*"—a sonnet to Robert Bridges himself. (Hopkins had enclosed it in the last letter he sent to his friend, two months before he died.[57] This conciliatory letter survives, but Bridges burnt the two "bitter" ones before it.)

51

To R. B.

THE fine delight that fathers thought ; the strong
Spur, live and lancing like the blowpipe flame,
Breathes once and, quenchèd faster than it came,
Leaves yet the mind a mother of immortal song.
Nine months she then, nay years, nine years she long
Within her wears, bears, cares and moulds the same :
The widow of an insight lost she lives, with aim
Now known and hand at work now never wrong.
   Sweet fire the sire of muse, my soul needs this ;
I want the one rapture of an inspiration.
O then if in my lagging lines you miss
The roll, the rise, the carol, the creation,
My winter world, that scarcely breathes that bliss
Now, yields you, with some sighs, our explanation.

Thus, the "*gatherer*" framed the 1918 edition as a dialogue of two poet friends, at the start of which (three decades after the friend's death) Bridges invoked Hopkins to "*Go forth*"; and the poet was set up to reply to the editor at the end of the edition. So it is that, in his frame, Bridges' edition reversed the historical order of their voices. Seeing the first printed edition of Hopkins' poetry from the perspective of this editorial contrivance, I want—I *need* now to be able to separate authorial and editorial strains. How much Hopkins is really Hopkins? How much Hopkins is Bridges?

Overleaf are the models for these two sonnets, Bridges' call to the left, Hopkins' "answer" to the right. Neither shape indents lines to telegraph rhyme, but they do both mark off the sestet by indentation, and thus at a glance readily identify themselves as sonnets. The lone indentation in Hopkins' sonnet registers as a strophic marker. The indentation of v. 13 of Bridges' might appear to do the same. But as it proves Italianate rather than Shakespearean, the last two lines are not

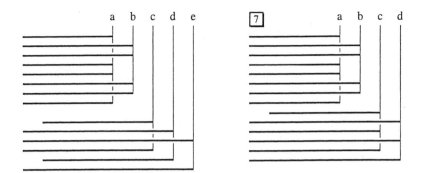

really a structural feature—are not a rhyming couplet. Perhaps, since analysis shows that all of Bridges' indentations in this sonnet occur after, and only after, all his full stops, the indentations might be deemed a function of sentences. In any case, it looks as if Robert Bridges could match Hopkins as a shaper of sonnets—as an examination of his own sonnets will show.

The anonymous first edition of Bridges' *The Growth of Love, A Poem in Twenty-four Sonnets* appeared in roman type from Edward Bumpus, in 1876. Essentially, all its sonnets conform to one model.[58]

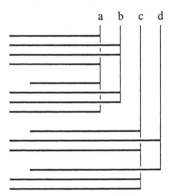

From the Daniel Press, a roman-type version followed in 1889 (in only 22 copies); it now had 79 sonnets, all conforming to Model 7 (the same structure, curiously, as Hopkins' "answer"); and it was reissued in black letter in the same year. A final version, in roman again, and now under the author's name, appeared from Smith, Elder, & Company in 1898, with merely 69 sonnets, and the body language was different yet again. There were also departures from the invariant rhyme scheme of the first two editions. Thus, there are now a total of four Shapes (A–D), all with the same structure of leading. Each shape offers several patterns of rhyme, however—two for each of A–C, and four for D.

I thus now offer a total of ten models for four shapes of indentation in this third and final *Growth,* 1898. The various models show Bridges always indenting for strophes, rather than (or more than) for rhyme. Yes—yes, it looks as if Robert Bridges, like Gerard Hopkins, was a prodigious shaper of sonnets.

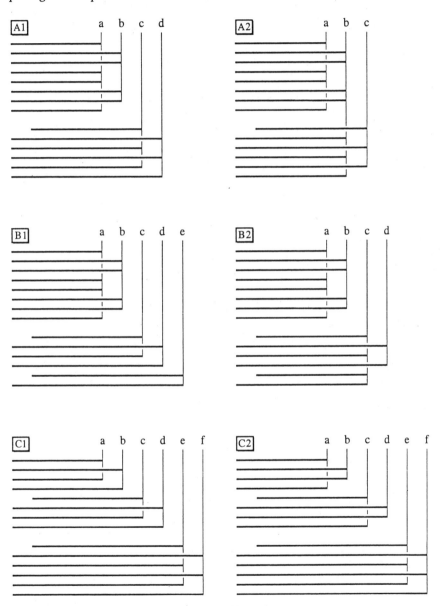

(Well, dear reader, that's because Robert Bridges *was* Gerard Hopkins.)

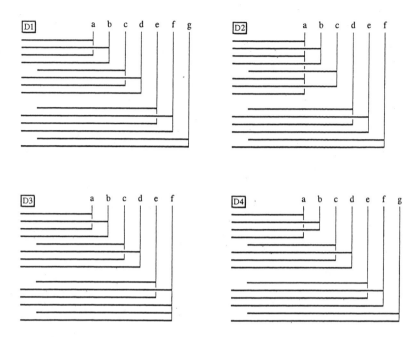

Underlying—*belying*—R. B's editing of *"To R. B."* is Hopkins' fair copy (opposite), very different in structure from Bridges' representation of it in *1918*.[59] Here, no indentation or extra leading marks the strophes; rather, multilevel braces yoke each quatrain and tercet, but also octave and sestet.[60] Ignoring these late innovations (Hopkins' gift to Bridges the poet), Bridges the editor reworked the sonnet graphically, merely tabbing v. 9; he thus forged a shape that somewhat resembled that of his own inaugural sonnet in *Poems* (Bridges the editor's gift to Hopkins). The same bracing occurs in Hopkins' manuscript for "Thou art indeed just, Lord". The "sculpting" of its final ten-line block (which I made so much of on p. 210) was not Hopkins' art at all![61]

AN editor of posthumous work is bounden to give some account of the authority for his text . . . .

So begins the editor's "PREFACE TO NOTES", p. 94, a *preface* at the *back* of the first edition of *Poems*. He then details the four notebooks, A, B, D, and H, that constitute his documentary authority. I shall omit descriptions of D and H, and will speak more of B later in the essay.

Gerard M. Hopkins.

To R. B.

The fine delight that fathers thought; the strong
Spur, live / and lancing like the blowpipe flame,
Breathes once and, quenchèd faster than it came,
Leaves yet the mind a mother of immortal song.
Nine months she then, nay years, nine years she
                    long
within her wears, bears, cares and combs the same:
The widow of an insight lost she lives, with aim
Now known and hand at work now never wrong.
Sweet fire the sire of muse, my soul needs this;
I want the one rapture of an inspiration;
O then if in my lagging lines you miss
The roll, the rise, the carol, the creation,
My winter world, that scarcely breathes that bliss
Now, yields you, with some sighs, our explanation.
                            april 22 1889

> A is my own collection, a MS. book made up of autographs—by
> which word I denote poems in the author's handwriting—pasted
> into it as they were received from him, and also of contemporary
> copies of other poems. These autographs and copies date from '67
> to '89, the year of his death. Additions made by copying after that
> date are not reckoned or used.

This manuscript represents an early collaboration between Bridges
and Hopkins. On receipt, Bridges pasted Hopkins' mailings to him
into his notebook (where they were mixed, in some undefined way,
with his own copies of Hopkins' work). He neglects to mention that he
also cut these manuscripts into pieces and rearranged them to fit the
small format of his album. Bridges finished his layout with red ruling
around the edges of these pasted-in cuttings, and sometimes also
across them. In general, manuscript ruling serves to guide a scribe; but
here, as it *follows* writing, it is purely decorative (as it is in those often-
encountered printed books of the sixteenth and seventeenth centuries,
in which the red ruling followed printing and preceded binding). The
critical point is that Hopkins' autographs do not descend physically
intact through Bridges' Procrustean and cosmetic reformatting.

Some of Bridges' alterations are strikingly apparent in the
photograph of "The Windhover" (on p. 233). To fit Hopkins' leaf into
his notebook, Bridges trimmed off the title, and then pasted it back so
as to overlap a deleted version of the first verse. He excised the bottom
margin, but pasted a snippet of it, with Hopkins' instruction to turn
the leaf ("[T. O."), close to the last verse. Thus did Bridges shepherd a
humble note, one outside the poem; but he obliterated an early draft of
one of its verses—and, of course, he sacrificed the overall integrity of
the document.

The next topic in Bridges' "PREFACE TO NOTES" is Hopkins'
"peculiar scheme of prosody" (95). Here, he quickly turns to the poet's
"very elaborate system of marks, all indicating the speech-movement".
This topic takes him from symbols of Hopkins' own invention to
conventional punctuation and finally to indentation—where I will pick
up the thread. Of his editorial response to all these, Bridges first speaks
of Hopkins' unique symbols (pp. 95–96):

> . . . the intention of the rhythm, in places where it might seem
> doubtful, has been indicated by accents printed over the
> determining syllables : in the later poems these accents correspond
> generally with the author's own marks; in the earlier poems they do
> not, but are trustworthy translations.

In justification of his "trustworthy translations", the editor first quotes from Hopkins' letters and then shifts to punctuation in this edition:

> ' This is my difficulty, what marks to use and when to use them : they are so much needed and yet so objectionable. About punctuation my mind is clear : I can give a rule for everything I write myself, and even for other people, though they might not agree with me perhaps.' In this last matter the autographs are rigidly respected, the rare intentional aberration being scrupulously noted.

And Bridges continues respectful:[62]

> And so I have respected his indentation of the verse ;   but in the sonnets, while my indentation corresponds, as a rule, with some autograph, I have felt free to consider conveniences, following, however, his growing practice to eschew it altogether.

Having bowed "rigidly" and "scrupulously" to authority, Bridges throws it over for the indentation of sonnets—but just of sonnets (Hopkins' major genre). And Bridges neglects to say anything about extra leading or multilevel bracketing, also powerful forms of spatial organization. The scrupulous editor is free, "free to consider conveniences". Although, "as a rule", Bridges reports that he follows the authority of some manuscript, he also claims to follow what he detects as Hopkins' "growing practice, to eschew" indentation altogether, by which he alleges Hopkins' *diminishing* practice of indentation. Are there not, conveniently, two masters here, or more? Surely all an editor need do is "follow some manuscript". Authority, in such a vision of editing, reposes in documentary evidence. Should the author's manuscripts as a whole progressively eschew indentation, so be it: let the editor choose an early manuscript for copy and accept the indentation that comes with it; or let him choose a late manuscript, and accept its alleged lack of indentation. (One need not follow both an actual manuscript and the perceived tendency of other manuscripts.) But our argument need not be subtle here. If this editor was stripping away indentation from early Hopkins in the name of late Hopkins, how is it that there are more than a dozen different structures of indentation among the Models—including Model 7—for "*To R. B.*", which we know from the only manuscript of that poem, just shown, has no indentation at all? Recall that this is the poem Bridges contrived as the answer to his own unsigned inaugural poem. Well, he contrived its body language too.

Didn't I say earlier that Hopkins used twenty different shapes for thirty-one fourteen-line sonnets? But, indeed, it was *Robert Bridges* who used twenty different shapes for these sonnets. You see, Gentle Reader, the editor followed conveniences. But not to worry—*just* in the sonnet (or so he assures us), the rare intentional aberration being scrupulously noted. In other words, dammit, we have come this far in the essay, constructed all these dumb models for Hopkins' sonnets (even *de*constructed them), and now—now it is not clear whether we have been mapping *Hopkins* at all.

Let's explore editorial conveniences. Three years before his edition of Hopkins' *Poems*, Bridges, poet laureate since 1913, produced *The Spirit of Man*, a patriotic anthology, dedicated to the King. Emery Walker's calligraphic title page is a feast of ampersands and swash italics—and ligatures: in long-s ("*permißion*", l. 5), round-s ("*Majesty*", l. 6), and "Th" ("**The**, l. 9). These italic effects align with the Italian *cinquecento* through a quotation from "Michelangelo's Fresco of the Creation of Adam in the Sistine Chapel" (Y3r). The Spirit of Man is indeed the emphasis here, for God is edited down merely to His right forearm.

Part of the war effort, this anthology gathered old and new prose and verse in English and French. (The French were allies.) Among the English poems were a few by Yeats. (Some Irish were also allies?)

THE LAKE ISLE OF INNISFREE

I WILL arise and go now, and go to Innisfree,
    And a small cabin build there, of clay and wattles
        made ;
Nine bean rows will I have there, a hive for the
        honey bee,
    And live alone in the bee-loud glade.

I WILL arise and go now, and go to Innisfree,
And a small cabin build there, of clay and wattles made ;
Nine bean-rows will I have there, a hive for the honey-bee,
    And live alone in the bee-loud glade.

The
Spirit of Man
An Anthology in English & French
from the Philosophers & Poets
made by the Poet Laureate in
1915
& dedicated by gracious permiſsion
to His Majeſty
The King

Longmans Green & Co, London
New York, Bombay, Calcutta & Madras
1916

On p. 246 are the setting of both the 1895 Unwin edition of Yeats' *Poems*,[63] Bridges' source, and his rendition of it. The *Spirit of Man* version is untitled, as are all the editor's selections—and so that variant is not surprising. Both versions of v. 2 end in a semicolon, but Bridges' punctuation is poorly printed, and looks like a colon. Real variants do occur in the spellings of "bean rows" ("bean-rows") and "honey bee" ("honey-bee"). The most important variants for our purposes, however, are the indentations of vv. 2 and 4 in Yeats' *Poems*, but only of v. 4 in *The Spirit of Man*. The poet's' metre is irregular, but the last line of every stanza is conspicuously shorter than the first three. This is the only line that Bridges indents, thus calling attention to its length. But the stanza rhymes *abab*, and that scheme is what Yeats' indentation guides the reader's eye to. In his note to this, the first of his eight quotations from Yeats (no. 26), Bridges says,

> I owe special thanks to my friend Mr. Yeats for his sympathy in this book, and for allowing me to use his beautiful poems so freely.

Thus does Bridges edit spatially another poet than Hopkins, and in another genre than the sonnet. Whoever the author, whatever the genre, it must have been convenient for Bridges as a rule to have been bounden scrupulously to follow conveniences freely.

But stoutly resisted were the changes he proposed to Rabindra Nath Tagore, who had been named Nobel Laureate for Literature in 1913, the very year Bridges had become Poet Laureate. Eventually, Bridges enlisted Yeats' assistance in changing the Bengali poet's mind. Now, Tagore had earlier accepted revisions from Yeats to the English prose translation of *Gitanjali* (*Song Offerings*); and it was Yeats who had written the introduction to that publication. Relenting under his collaborator's solicitations, Tagore allowed Bridges his way.[64]

> I have to thank him and his English publisher for allowing me to quote from this book, and in the particular instance of this very beautiful poem, for the author's friendliness in permitting me to shift a few words for the sake of what I considered more effective rhythm or grammar.

Atop the next page is an excerpt from Tagore's *Gitanjali* 67; Bridges' rendition (# 38) follows. The anthologist's "more effective rhythm and grammar" do not comprehend his shiftiness in indentation, or his re-punctuation (of comma and period to exclamation), or his typographic changes ("thou beautiful" → "Thou Beautiful"), or of number ("colours"

O thou beautiful, there in the nest it
is thy love that encloses the soul with
colours and sounds and odours.

O Thou Beautiful ! how in the nest thy love embraceth
the soul with sweet sounds and colour and fragrant
odours !

→ "colour"). Tagore's "thou" dictated forms like "didst"; but he avoided the archaic third-person singular, as did not the editor laureate
("that encloses" → "embraceth").[65] Indeed, Bridges changed *diction*
("there" → "how"), and he invented it too ("sweet" and "fragrant").[66]

Six Hopkins poems appear in *The Spirit of Man*. Three are sonnets:
"The Candle Indoors", "In the Valley of the Elwy", and "The Handsome
Heart". The last of them is unproblematic; it conforms to Model 6 in
both Ms A and Ms B, and in both the 1916 and 1918 publications. But
the other two are problematic indeed. The only manuscript of "In the
Valley of the Elwy" that Bridges knew conforms to Model 16, and that
is its structure in *1918*. But in *The Spirit of Man*, he shaped it according
to Model 8 (# 358). (Hopkins' draft for his sister, which Bridges did not
know, had no indentation and it line-spaced after each quatrain and
between tercets, looking like the left side of Model 6, therefore—though
the structure of rhymes in the tercet is different.) More complicated
still is "The Candle Indoors" (# 269). On p. 251 are *The Spirit of Man*
and *1918* versions. Their verbal differences are authorial variants, for
here, at least, Bridges was rigid and scrupulous and unaberrant with
diction.[67] The shape of Bridges' *1918* version conforms to Model 3, but
that of the *Spirit of Man* is unprecedented. (I will call it Model 21, for
ease of reference.) It combines the indentations of Models 7 and 10; and
so it resembles Model 12, but without its extra leading.

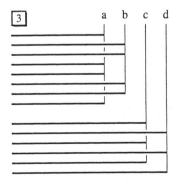 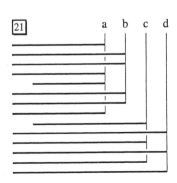

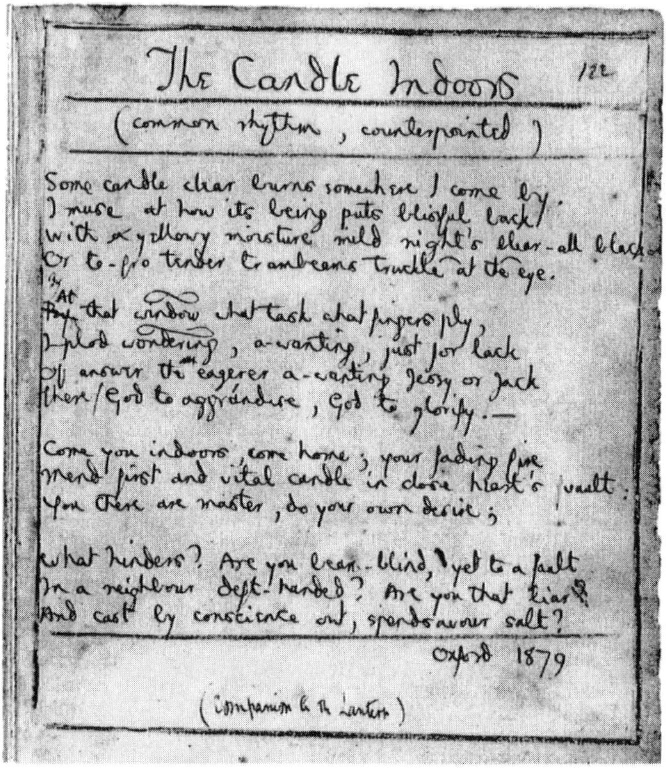

The Candle Indoors 122

(common rhythm, counterpointed)

Some candle clear burns somewhere I come by.
I muse at how its being puts blissful back
With yellowy moisture mild night's blear-all black,
Or to-fro tender trambeams truckle at the eye.

By At that window what task what fingers ply,
I plod wondering, a-wanting, just for lack
Of answer the eagerer a-wanting Jessy or Jack
There/God to aggrándise, God to glorify.—

Come you indoors, come home; your fading fire
Mend first and vital candle in close heart's vault:
You there are master, do your own desire;

What hinders? Are you beam-blind, yet to a fault
In a neighbour deft-handed? Are you that liar?
And cast by conscience out, spendsavour salt?

Oxford 1879

(Companion to the Lantern)

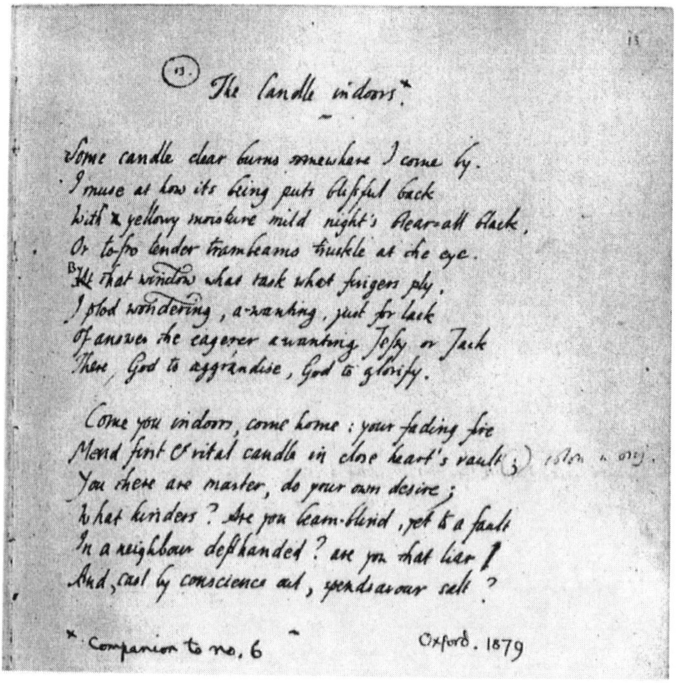

13

(13) The Candle indoors.*

Some candle clear burns somewhere I come by.
2 I muse at how its being puts blissful back
With yellowy moisture mild night's blear-all black,
Or to-fro tender trambeams truckle at the eye.
By that window what task what fingers ply,
I plod wondering, a-wanting, just for lack
7 Of answer the eagerer a-wanting Jessy or Jack
There, God to aggrándise, God to glorify.

Come you indoors, come home: your fading fire
Mend first & vital candle in close heart's vault;
You there are master, do your own desire;
What hinders? Are you beam-blind, yet to a fault
In a neighbour deft-handed? are you that liar
And, cast by conscience out, spendsavour salt?

* Companion to no. 6 — Oxford. 1879

SOME candle clear burns somewhere I come by.
I muse at how its being puts blissful back
With a yellowy moisture mild night's blear-all black ;
Or to-fro tender trambeams truckle at the eye.
    At that window what task what fingers ply,
I plod wondering, a-wanting, just for lack
Of answer the eagerer awanting Jessy or Jack
There, God to aggrandise, God to glorify.—
    Come you indoors, come home ; your fading fire
Mend first and vital candle in close heart's vault :
You there are master, do your own desire ;
What hinders ?   Are you beam-blind, yet to a fault
In a neighbour deft-handed ?   Are you that liar ?
And cast by conscience out, spendsavour salt ?

26

The Candle Indoors

SOME candle clear burns somewhere I come by.
I muse at how its being puts blissful back
With yellowy moisture mild night's blear-all black,
Or to-fro tender trambeams truckle at the eye.
By that window what task what fingers ply,
I plod wondering, a-wanting, just for lack
Of answer the eagerer a-wanting Jessy or Jack
There   God to aggrándise, God to glorify.—

Come you indoors, come home ; your fading fire
Mend first and vital candle in close heart's vault :
You there are master, do your own desire ;
What hinders ?   Are you beam-blind, yet to a fault
In a neighbour deft-handed ?   Are you that liar
And cast by conscience out, spendsavour salt ?

And what of the author's two manuscripts that Bridges consulted? Only Ms A is shown opposite, above, but both conform to Model 6. They have no indentations, and their line spacings isolate the quatrains and tercets. Neither is a convenient source for Bridges' shapes.

Opposite, below, is Ms B, with Bridges' long-s in *"blifsful"* and *"Jefsy"* (vv. 2, 7). Without commenting on his friend's reformatting of Ms B, Hopkins changed diction in vv. 3 and 5, added counterpoint signs in vv. 5 and 6, and accented "aggrándize", v. 8, in purple pencil. Punctuation was altered in v. 10 and was added to in vv. 10, 13 and 14.[68] But did Hopkins' silence thereby authorize Bridges' change of format?

At the bottom of Ms A, Bridges echoed Hopkins' note in Ms B. In his 1918 edition, Bridges accepted the poet's changes of diction, but he almost totally followed his own changed outline and even his internal spacing after "There", v. 8, a substitute for the poet's slash. Thus, in *1918* the editor edited his own editing.

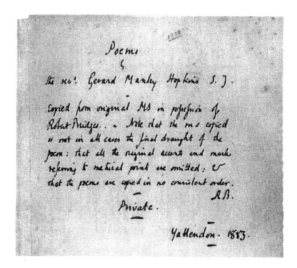

The world has long known that to get to Hopkins one had to go through Bridges. We may have understood from this fact merely our debt of gratitude—for without Bridges the preserver there would now *be* no Hopkins. But the evidence has revealed that when we go through Bridges, hoping to arrive at the poet, Hopkins is not all there—nor are we finally alone in his presence. We can now look to understand the word "shape" in my title in very precise terms—as *alienated* shape. We can read Bridges' hand in Ms B and in his subsequent publications as a record of his editorial manipulation of Hopkins' poetry.

Only by glimpsing such details of Ms B did I think to regard it as the primary scene of editing, therefore displacing Bridges' 1918 edition. Of course, in our print culture, we are accustomed to think of a mass-produced letterpress book as what constitutes an edition. But smack in the middle of my blind spot lies B, an edition in manuscript—on an intimate scale, a single copy: it had an author, an editor, and a reader.

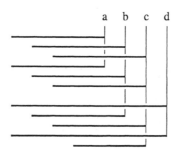

Let me now tell again the familiar story of Ms B, but from an unfamiliar perspective. This manuscript was compiled in 1883, six years before the author's death and thirty-five years before Bridges' brought out his edition of Hopkins' *Poems*, in 1918, which everyone speaks of as the first edition, but which, if you'll indulge me, is only the first among the *posthumous* editions (all print editions being posthumous). In 1883, the first edition, in manuscript, was a collaboration between Bridges and the still-living Hopkins. Like so much of Hopkins' life, it was not ideal. It was an edition of compromises, and it had a very limited circulation. It was, as it were, ill-brockered. There was only one outside reader, Coventry Patmore—and his reaction was not favorable.[69]

Now, Hopkins had met Patmore in the summer of 1883, when the latter had visited the Jesuit College at Stonyhurst to hand out prizes on Speech Day. The priest impressed the recent convert to Catholicism by talking knowledgeably of poetry and of his friend. Did Mr. Patmore not know him?—Robert Bridges, the poet?—all the while Hopkins never once mentioning his own writing. But, having introduced Patmore to Bridges, the modest priest was in a position to be helped in turn by his old friend. Did Mr. Patmore know that Father Gerard wrote verse too? asked Bridges. No? Well, would he not like to see a sample of his work? And Patmore agreed. Bridges wrote out Ms B for him, copying and reshaping poems from Ms A. As his cover annotation implies, Bridges extracted Hopkins' poems without regard either to their order of composition or to something almost the same, their sequence in A. Most obviously, as we know, he postponed the daunting early work, "The Wreck of the Deutschland", conveniently placing it after examples of Hopkins' more accessible genre, the sonnet. Like any edition, this one was guided by a sense of audience. Ms B attempted to persuade and ingratiate. As its calligraphy attests, it strove to be beautiful.

Bridges began his introduction of the old friend to the new with a transcription of the winning curtal sonnet "Pied Beauty".[70] If you turn to the next opening, you will see it cut in three, curtailed to fit the constraints of the album of Bridges' Ms A. We are now poised for a more complex view of the shape of this poem than was developed earlier in the essay. Opposite is my model for its body language, as Hopkins set the poem to paper.[71] It has four rhymes, and an unprecedented four tabs.

Pied Beauty

(Curtal-sonnet : sprung rhythm) with

× when the last syllable (a
single stressed syllable
of the pair-verse (as supplied
by stress) as strengthens the
"supplies) this × etc.
...

· Glory be to God for dappled things —
For skies of couple-colour as a brinded cow;
For rose-moles all in stipple upon trout that swim;
Fresh-firecoal chestnut-falls; finches' wings;
Landscape plotted and pieced — fold, fallow, and
            plough;
    And all trades, their gear and tackle and
            trim.

· All things counter, original, spare, strange;
    Whatever is fickle, freckled (who knows how?)
    With swift, slow; sweet, sour; adazzle, dim;
He fathers-forth whose beauty is past change:
            Praise him.

St Beuno's, Tremeirchion. Summer 1877.

This poem is idiosyncratic from its first written mark. Astoundingly, the opening utterance breaks not mere silence, but organized silence, since it begins with a so-called "great colon". You may already have noticed great colons in the manuscript of "The Windhover" (above, pp. 233–34), where they occur over half a dozen times. Note especially "sheer" in v. 12; there, a regular colon before it contrasts with a great one after. (Occasionally in "Pied Beauty" too, the great colon is preceded by punctuation proper: a semicolon in v. 4, and commas in vv. 7 and 9.) This contrast of great and small colons clearly shows that they are not to be confused: the small colon is a function of sentence structure; the great colon, a function of prosody.

Through the first of the two blocks of verses, there are three indentations for three rhymes—*abc*. Progressive indentations can trouble the fit of long verses: v. 5 typically turns down for the (centred) last word and punctuation of the verse; but the end of v. 6 (preceded by "[") turns up, into the right end of this same mostly blank line—thus keeping clear the symbolic line spacing between stanzas.

Now, in a fourteen-line sonnet, one does not always know whether the symbolic value of a specific indentation to telegraph a particular rhyme will hold across extra leading. It never does between Hopkins' octaves and his sestets; it always does between his quatrains. And usually it does between his tercets (as in Model 19); but sometimes, it does not (as in Model 20). So, in crossing the line spacing in "Pied Beauty", we seem to have passed, as it were, from "octave" to "sestet"; and we might well expect, therefore, that when we start off the second stanza at the zero tab, there will be a new rhyme, *d*—not *a* (the former rhyme for that tab). And we are right. But, to our surprise, the second verse of the "sestet" shares not only the indentation of the second verse in the "octave", but also its very rhyme, *b*. It thus contradicts the conventional notion that the symbolic tabs are reset. (It is as if, having moved out, we find ourselves still at home.) Similarly, as we read on into the next two verses, the first of them matches the indentation and rhyme (*c*) of the corresponding line of the "octave", but the fourth one (*d*) does not. Again, we are reminded of similarity with but also difference from the patterning of the "octave". (We have not seen quite such a trick before, though the sestets of Models 5, 6, 13, and 20 also set the eye and ear at odds.)

Let us focus now on the last verse of the poem, a mere two mono-syllables. This verse indents to an unprecedented depth for a *c* rhyme, far beyond even the axis of the page, on which Hopkins usually positions the wrapped portion of a verse (as he does for v. 5 in this very draft). The last verse sits in the "Amen position", as Peter Stallybrass, recalling his days as a choirboy, explained it to me on seeing a photograph of the manuscript; and Anne Coldiron echoed this notion, when I described the layout to her. Such an evocation from the position and the content of the verse may very well be what Hopkins aimed at. But, startlingly, this indentation also makes for graphic alignment of the great colon in this last verse with the one in the previous verse. I say "startlingly", for, until I saw this, I thought of prosody only as temporal. But here Hopkins coordinates his prosodic marker spatially. As his indentations guide the eye, so do these aligned colons.

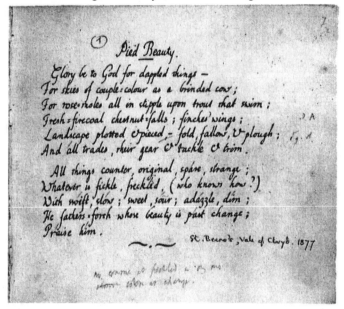

Bridges' rendition of this, the first poem in Ms B, is beautiful;[72] but it unpies Hopkins' art. For his two stanzas and three tabs, Bridges offers two verse paragraphs, each with a lone opening indentation. In such a diminished graphic structure, the eye cannot anticipate or over-see any pattern of rhyme or (and here's the fun of it) be faked out by its mixed signals. Consequently, when we eventually under-hear the *four* rhymes, which we are not able to predict, they will not surprise us by having unexpectedly played off against the indentations—or by the way two of the rhymes (*a* and *d*) double up at one depth, but one of them (*c*) spreads over two depths. In Bridges' simplified scheme, the flush-left last line simply has nowhere else to go. It sits left merely because it is short, rather than juts right because it says *Amen* or is configured prosodically with a rhythmic marker in the line above. Centred above the first verse is Bridges' dash; below the poem, he has his last say, graphically—another centred, symmetrical flourish, reminiscent of the one he placed after Hopkins' poem to him (see p. 239 above). But some of us came for Hopkins the eccentric.

In *1918*, Bridges was truer to the poet's scheme of indentation:

13

Pied Beauty

GLORY be to God for dappled things—
  For skies of couple-colour as a brinded cow ;
    For rose-moles all in stipple upon trout that swim ;
Fresh-firecoal chestnut-falls ; finches' wings ;
  Landscape plotted and pieced—fold, fallow, and
    plough ;
  And áll trádes, their gear and tackle and trim.

All things counter, original, spare, strange ;
  Whatever is fickle, freckled (who knows how ?)
    With swift, slow ; sweet, sour ; adazzle, dim ;
He fathers-forth whose beauty is past change :
      Praise him.

—but his positioning of the last line is still off. Now, it—it what?— extends to the axis of the page? (the right side of the "13", actually)—or is it perhaps centred relative to the previous line? The spirit of Bridges' symmetrical flourishes in Ms B may live on, even though these marks did not themselves survive into *1918*.

And there is a meandering history that follows Bridges' printed edition. In Charles Williams' second edition, 1930, the line inched right to centre, as the "14" below it allows one to deduce.

He fathers-forth whose beauty is past change :
    Praise him.

14

In Gardner's third edition, 1948, shown atop the next page, "Praise him." crept farther right—and right out of symmetry, though the end of this last line almost aligns with the end of the title (not shown here). In addition, the last line happens to be symmetrically disposed relative to the (indented) longest line of the poem (also not shown here).

> He fathers-forth whose beauty is past change:
> Praise him.

38

In my 1964 Penguin, this last line appears slightly more right.

> He fathers-forth whose beauty is past change:
> Praise him.

15

But Penguin wasn't always there. Recall the setting of the first Penguin edition of "Pied Beauty", 1953, above, p. 204 (where the tabs were reset for the second half of the poem, which fell on another page).[73]

> He fathers-forth whose beauty is past change:
> Praise him.

15

In this retabbing, 2.5mm farther in, the start of this last line comes further right, all but to the centre of the page. The Penguin layout artist's positioning of this latter half of the poem is not quite as far right as usual (as the slightly left positioning of the page number and the slightly off-centre running head show). If this block had been exactly centred, the page number would have gone flush right, and "Praise him." would have begun on the very axis of the page. (For all I know, trying to achieve such centring may have been the goal of retabbing the left margin after the page break?)

At least by the ninth Penguin reprinting, 1967, I see, "Praise him." went slightly left, to symmetry again in the page formatting.[74]

> He fathers-forth whose beauty is past change:
> Praise him.

15

In Gardner and MacKenzie's 1967 Oxford edition, "Praise him." ventured very far right, to a position close to that in Ms A. Here the "p" of "past" and the "P" of "Praise" almost exactly align.

> He fathers-forth whose beauty is past change:
> Praise him.

Outside the Oxford tradition, in Walford Davies' 1979 Dent and Sons edition—where I hope God is watching—it ventures *very* far right, seemingly well in the orbit of the small colon of the line before.

> He fathers-forth whose beauty is past change:
>   Praise him.

In Catherine Phillips' 1986 Oxford Authors edition, is the last line a split hair right of where we saw it in the previous Oxford edition?

> He fathers-forth whose beauty is pást change:°
>   Práise hím.

—then ever so slightly right in MacKenzie's 1990 Oxford edition?

> He fathers-forth whose beauty is pást chánge:
>   Práise hím.

But (again outside the Oxford tradition) in Paul Hunter's 2002 *Norton Introduction to Poetry*, the line shoots farther left than ever among the indented versions. But on what authority?

> He fathers-forth whose beauty is past change;
>   Praise him.

And by what authority does Hunter erase the gap between the two stanzas? And what is the authority for the same deletion in Ian Lancashire's 2002 *Representative Poetry*? And is he the only editor to shunt "Praise him" so *very* far left that its tab aligns it precisely with the other *c*-rhyme lines?[75]

But I do hope poor Hopkins is *not* watching all this to-ing and fro-ing. The poet's final line runs loose in the history of editing because it is unanchored by his "much needed and yet so objectionable" marker, his great colon. The great colon has vanished from all of these modern representations of "Pied Beauty" (and the representations of every other poem in which it is found), just as it has vanished from—surely *because* it has vanished from—Bridges' Ms B, which step-fathered-forth the printed tradition. But was it not by this idiosyncratic sign that Gerard Hopkins here aligned his written words, and thus configured his poetry spatially as a function of rhythm?

Why has no modern editor followed Hopkins' Ms A in its great colon, even those who are willing to restore odd accents, as Phillips and MacKenzie are? Not only must justice be done, must it not also be *seen* to be done? It is not enough that recent Oxford editions should finally (for the moment) have driven the last line of "Pied Beauty" more or less homeward. Why not also show the author's very means to *rivet* it in place?—*objectionable*, yes, *inconsistent*, indeed *offensive* (as Hopkins apologized for his markings to Bridges)—but *necessary*, as he also claimed, poetic. As a reader, I want to *see* Gerard Hopkins' great colon. I want Father Gerard's body language.

For me, it is not enough to be offered just the poet's acute accents, which some editors allow, and some even invent. Yes, even these accents are problematic. In Phillips' edition, you can see three of them at the ends of the last two lines of Mss A and B. But MacKenzie's 1990 edition adds a fourth, on "chánge". Wherever did it come from? The answer is that, unlike Phillips, who simply ignored the great colon (How can one ignore a great colon?), MacKenzie converted it to an acute accent on the following vowel. But such a substitution leaves no way of representing the difference of an isolated acute-accented syllable from one immediately preceded by a great colon. Look at MacKenzie's handling of "⁚ slów" in v. 9 and of "⁚ hím" in v. 11 (the latter being one of the very lines under consideration). They appear merely as "slów" and "hím". In other words, his translation of great colons into nearby acute accents cannot register the redundancy of the stresses. For what gain does he sacrifice the author's graphic key to the precise indentation of the last line? In this editor's hands, Hopkins' poetry becomes less dangerous—and oh more cavalier.

But when we do have access to Hopkins' great colons, what poetry will we not *see*? Hand in hand, my eyes move from v. 11 to the rest of the page. (The world is all before them.) I now apprehend another great colon in about the same place in the first verse of Stanza 2. And so I realize that three of the verses of "Pied Beauty" (vv. 7, 10, 11) align on this mark—and two of them, vv. 7 and 10, even rhyme. I also note that vv. 6 and 9 roughly align great colons, and they too rhyme. And the first verses of each stanza also align on their colons. Hopkins' quirky visual cues are everywhere—What *do* they mean?—everywhere, that is, except in *all* the editions, including the first, Bridges' Ms B.

Alas, must there not be a great variety of sonnet shapes in Hopkins' own hand out *there* somewhere, *somewhere*? But my con- and decon- structed models (pretty as they are) don't pie enough to be accurate guides to them. These comely models will have to stand as my flawed

𝔐onument to 𝔯obert 𝔅ridges
1844 – 1930
𝔓oet 𝔏aureate

and to all subsequent editors—if not quite to the poet they re-present.

•
•

> Dearest Bridges, . . . I had not meant Mr. Patmore to know I wrote
> poetry, but since it has come naturally and unavoidably about there
> is no more to be said and you may therefore send me your book and
> I will point it and make a few corrections. You were right to leave
> out the marks: they were not consistent for one thing and are always
> offensive. Still there must be some. Either I must invent a notation
> applied throughout as in music or else I must only mark where the
> reader is likely to mistake, and for the present this is what I shall
> do . . . .   [October 24, 1883][76]

Having drafted his edition without Hopkins' metrical marks, Bridges
sent it on to Hopkins for him to consider and then to pass on to
Patmore. Notice the hint of alienation from the project implied by
Hopkins' reference (not the only one) to "your book", when referring
to the transcription of his own verses. The first of his tasks that the poet
referred to was to point this manuscript: "there must be some" points,
even though they are "always offensive". When Hopkins said that it
was "right" for Bridges to "leave out the marks", he had not conceded
they were unnecessary. Rather, he anticipated that he himself would
reintroduce some marks, perhaps rendering consistent his various
practices over the years.

Having received it, Hopkins read Ms B closely from mid-December
1893 to early March 1894, by the end of which busy time he had
relocated to Dublin. He eventually increased the volume of verse in
Ms B by a third. He also inserted or appended (we don't know which)
five leaves, with six pages of prose, beginning "The poems in this
book . . .". This note was devoted to rhythm, and it seems to have
been written to supplement or compensate for Bridges' presentation
of Hopkins to Patmore. As we know it from its introductory role in
modern editions, it is in its own right something of "a great dragon
folded in the gate". This note can be read not only as an indication of
the fundamental importance of prosody for this poet, especially in addressing another poet, like Patmore, but also as a reaction to Bridges'

having transcribed the poems in Ms A without the poet's stresses and without his headnotes on the rhythm of each poem—such as we have seen above the verses in drafts of "The Windhover" (pp. 233–34) and "The Candle Indoors" (p. 250), and even cut away from the title in "Pied Beauty" (p. 254).[77]

Here and there in Bridges' transcriptions, Hopkins altered diction and added punctuation and accents, revising in every sonnet—but always leaving their newly contrived shapes, Bridges' shapes, alone, as we have already seen in detail, p. 250, in "The Candle Indoors". Bridges could have rendered the shape of that sonnet conservatively as Model 6. But in 1918, he configured it as Model 3, which corresponds to his own reworking of Hopkins in Ms B, but which does not correspond to either of the author's own drafts.

Let us explore in detail Hopkins' revisions of marks and diction in Bridges' transcription of "The Windhover" into Ms B. (See the reproduction in the next opening.) Hopkins' own drafts are represented by Models 17 and 20. (Recall that, in the Ms-A version shown on pp. 233–34, he reversed indentations when he wrote the latter tercet overleaf, perhaps in error, perhaps not.) By contrast, in Ms B, Bridges' format is Shape 2 (which matches the left-hand side of Model 9). (See p. 269 for "Shapes", which will now complement my models.)

As I said, Hopkins did not revise Bridges' shaping of this sonnet in Ms B, and so my discussion of his considerable revision will have to focus on other details—for example, the wedge-shaped accent (or *sforzando*) in v. 10 of Hopkins' autograph, Ms A.

[a billion
Buckle ! Ánd the fire that breaks from thee then,

Who but Hopkins would ever have thought to place stress here, on a mere coordinate conjunction,[78] *and* in the aftermath of an exclamation, one, moreover that follows an enjambed foot—**and** in a line that seems otherwise to have its full complement of stresses? (The effect of the start of the line is like the tight rhythm of a spondee—but with a full stop pushing it apart from within.)[79] When Bridges wrote out Ms B, he generally edited out such metrical markings

Buckle ! & the fire that breaks from thee then, a billion

—thereby forcing the poet's hand when he subsequently revised the manuscript en route to Patmore. (Note that, in this specific restyling,

Bridges also replaced the poet's Germanic "Ånd"—until its last word, this alliterative line is all Germanic—with "&", which is a stylized rendering of Latin *et* (as Palatino makes graphically clear).[80] Bridges' Latin styling is not inconsistent with his elegant italic.)

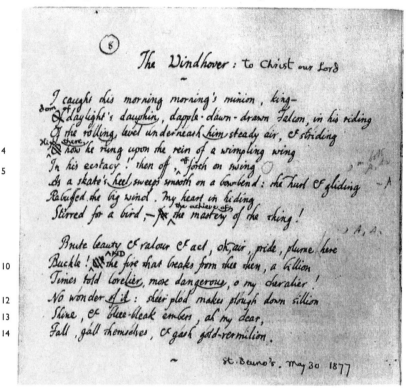

There are two editorial issues to discuss here, metrical stress and graphic rendering of the diction. In vv. 3, 6, 9, 10, 13, and 14, Bridges typically employed ampersand to replace each of the six examples of Hopkins' *un*accented, entirely lowercase "and" in this poem. But, in the stressed conjunction from v. 10 of "The Windhover", the poet's use or the editor's non-use of a capital initial is surely significant. In the manuscripts of this poem in Hopkins' hand, the initial capital in "Ånd" and the exclamation mark before it are each capable of signaling a sentence break; and together they do so decisively—never mind that what follows eventually proves to be no sentence at all (as it lacks a verb). By contrast, Bridges' "&" seems to make the word for which it stands, and also the remainder of the line, merely a continuation of the sentence that began in the previous line and reached one of its therefore *internal* climaxes with the exclamation mark just after the enjambed "Buckle". (For Bridges, a sentence is a sentence.) Certainly, as the editor's "&" cannot register the presence or absence of capitals, it falls short even of Hopkins' prosaic "And", let alone his excessively poetic "Ånd".

Now, Hopkins reacted to only this one of Bridges' seven substituted ampersands in "The Windhover", and to only this and one other of his eight omissions of the *sforzando* (in vv. 1, 5, 8, 9, 10, 12, and 14). The poet decisively deleted Bridges' ampersand with *three* strokes (not the mere one or two he used in his three other deletions in this poem) and, in the narrow track between this line and the one above it, he restored his original diction—atypically printing, not writing, it out, ånd with all three of its letters in caps. Responsive to Hopkins' last inscription, Bridges ultimately presented the line like this in *1918*, indented.

Buckle ! AND the fire that breaks from thee then, a billion

The editor's *small* caps appear in all the Oxford editions, and in many other editions from other presses (where occasionally they appear full size).[81] This small-cap setting of the usually unprepossessing conjunction is now a compelling landmark in our graphic experience of this strange poem. It symbolizes an unresolvable problem in Hopkins' prosody. Did the poet specifically intend small caps—which occur only here in all of Bridges' editorial rendering of Hopkins' verse?—or was it that the modest space the transcribing editor had left between lines of verse curtailed the size of the revising poet's characters—which are tiny not only here but also in all four of his other interlinear alterations (which are, however, rendered at normal size by all editors)? Certainly, we can note, where Hopkins added to the generously line-spaced title, he did indeed write his characters larger. The question, then, is this: Is Hopkins' unprecedented use of capitals (whatever their size) purely in his own voice—*hand*, rather—or are they not provoked by the editor's having substituted his "&" for the poet's "And" with its stressed initial capital?—as if Hopkins were responding to the substitute ampersand: "Dammit—can't you SEE the word is stressed?"[82] In the typographic rendering of this second word of v. 10 of "The Windhover" in printed texts from *1918* on, is it really possible for us to isolate the poet's "pure self-expression" from his reaction to editorial simplification, restyling, and tight spacing in Ms B?

Hopkins' diction may be clear enough in this instance, but his beats and stresses are as problematic as ever. They bear the mark of their assertion against eyes and ears closed to them. The presence of caps after the first letter of "AND" puts in doubt whether this conjunction should still be read merely as the start of a sentence, and not the reading Bridges' ampersand created (or also that reading)—the continuation of a sentence. As usual, the text is the struggle for the text. This particular text is a sign of the unresolved contest between poet and editor for the eye of the reader—initially Patmore, now all of us.

Hopkins had similar struggles with the editor elsewhere in this poem, and in two of these cases, diction does become problematic.[83] He did not accept Bridges' removal of any of his seven ties but restored them—and even added two more. But, though he acquiesced in the editorial deletion of all seven of his great colons, Hopkins twice wrote out verbal substitutions for them, and one of these also has punctuation. As he never defined the great colon, his substitutions for it may point us toward its intended prosodic effects.[84]

	Ms A (Hopkins)	Ms B¹ (Bridges)	Ms B² (Hopkins)
12	sheer **:** plod	*sheer plod*	*shéer plód*
12–13	sillion I **:** Shine	*sillion I Shine*	*síllion I Shine*
14	gash **:** gŏld-vermilion	*gash gold-vermilion*	*gásh góld-vermílion*
4	**:** O	*O*	High there, ⌄🜨
5	off , **:** forth	*off , forth*	*off , ⌄ᵒᶠᶠ forth*

Some of Hopkins' changes of stress or of diction may, of course, simply be ones he had meditated for years without influence from Bridges, but which he had not yet written down. These may be among the few "corrections" he wrote Bridges he would make. One such may be the brilliant change in v. 1 of "king I Of" to "king- I dom of", which relocates the rhyme from the end of "king" to the middle of the reworking of it as "king- I dom". (This change occurs in a verse that Bridges had *not* altered). But some of Hopkins' changes laid out in the chart may have been unpremeditated reactions specifically to his friend's revised presentation. Certainly, his new accenting of existing words (in vv. 12–14) and, more strikingly, his substituted or added monosyllables (in vv. 4–5) seem to fill in metrical gaps occasioned by Bridges' removal of great colons.

The new diction evident in the last two examples will strike most readers as happy changes, for we have known this beautiful poem only as it is presently worded — which is as it has been *changed*. Countenancing this new diction (now that we know some of the history of the text), we must be prepared to recognize it as scar tissue — as proud flesh.

Considering conveniences as he copied, Robert Bridges created the first six sonnet shapes shown on p. 269. (Column *d* in the Table on p. 281 records the Shape of a given sonnet in Ms B.) In Shapes 1–6, I map only extra leading and indentation, not also rhyme, as I did in my styling of the models. Some of these structures of indentation and line spacing are already familiar. Shape 1 resembles Models 3 and 4; Shape 2, Model 9; Shape 6, Models 5 and 6. The left sides of Shapes 3, 4, and 5, however, are not ones we have seen before. In Bridges' layout of Ms B, there is one sonnet per page, and so, at the most, two sonnets per opening. Of the eight openings that he gave over to fourteen-line sonnets in this manuscript, only two of them offer the same shape of sonnet. Even with a modest number of different shapes at his disposal, Bridges may thus be said to have cultivated structural variety. But, of course, Hopkins' own shaping in Ms A, Bridges' source, was also conspicuously various. (And it had the not inconsiderable virtue of being authentic.)

Hopkins gave up altering two sonnets in Bridges' redaction and cancelled them and a third. In the numbering of Ms B, they are Sonnets 4 and 7, and 14: "The Starlight Night" and "Walking by the Sea", and "The Handsome Heart". He wrote them anew in the first blank pages following where Bridges' copying had ended, changing the name of the second of them to "The Sea and the Skylark". In revision, Hopkins did not repeat any of Bridges' reconfigurations. Rather, he reworked the different shapes of these sonnets — Shapes 5 and 4 and 1 (which shapes they had assumed for the first time in Bridges' transcription), as Shape 7, one that Hopkins had never used before.

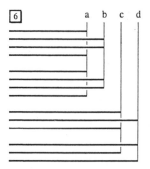

In *1918*, Bridges rendered "The Handsome Heart" as Model 6, a shape he derived from Ms A. But in Ms B he had offered Shape 1, which the poet cancelled and *twice* rewrote as Shape 7. Given his own space, Hopkins could have reverted to his earlier structure, but he continued to evolve. (Here it rather looks as if he was responding to—even surpassing—Bridges' tendency to indent the first lines of selected strophes.)

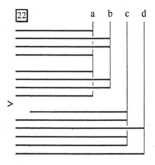

In *1918*, Bridges configured "Ribblesdale", as you see in Model 22 (as I will call it for convenience), which is not a shape of any of Hopkins' three other drafts of this poem, which could all have been rendered by either Model 1 or Shape 6, but which Hopkins rendered as Shape 7 when he entered it in Ms B.

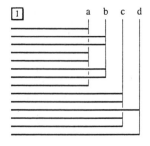

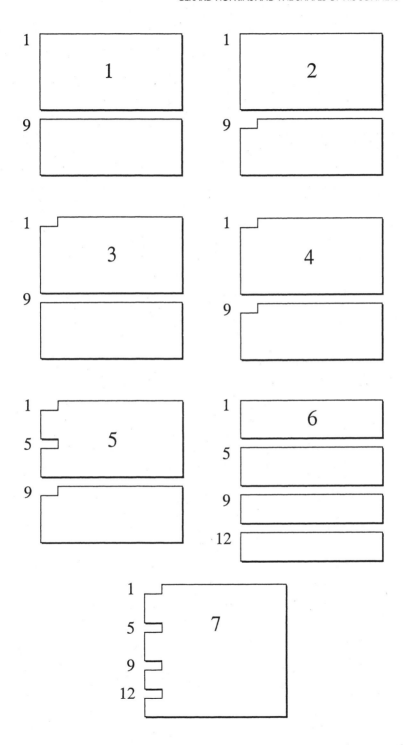

Nor is Model 22 the shape of any of Hopkins' drafts. This published configuration reflects the shape-shifting editor, but not our shape-shifting poet.

In the past, Hopkins often telegraphed rhyme when he indented. In this unprecedented use of Shape 7, he actually indented like Bridges, marking strophically, therefore, and not as a function of rhyme. Whether Hopkins was here bending with the editor to edit, he did resist Bridges' line spacing, eliminating it in all three of his revised Shapes in Ms B. Hopkins thus seems to have been partly Bridges' accomplice in adapting and altering of his own work; but he also partly resisted Bridges. When the editor claimed to respect, among other things, the later Hopkins' eschewing of indentation, he could not have been thinking of the later use of Shape 7 (against Bridges' Shapes 4 and 5). And with regard to Bridges' Ms B versions of sonnets which Hopkins did not delete and reconfigure, how are we to know but that in *1918* Bridges was merely honouring a projection of his very own editorial styling onto an acquiescent Hopkins? How can we tell the poet from the editor? How can we isolate the interactive shares of their collaboration, especially when in Ms B Hopkins sometimes, as MacKenzie has noted, imitated Bridges' hand?[85]

It is only a few days since I sent the MS book to Mr. Patmore . . . he acknowledged it this morning.   [March 7, 1884][86]

Mr. Patmore did not on the whole like my poems, was unconverted to them.   [April 16, 1884]

Coventry Patmore has kept your MS book a long time, as though it were to give himself the opportunity of repentance for not admiring all the poems, and indeed appears to look on his condition as one of guilt and near to reprobation — which is very odd of him. And I believe it will be of no avail and that like Esau and Antiochus he will not get the grace and is in a fair way to die in his sins.   [July 18, 1884]

After his cool response to Hopkins' work, Patmore returned Ms B to Bridges in person in July 1884, from whom Hopkins begged it as a boon, a godsend.

Dearest Bridges,—I am extremely glad to hear from both of you that you and Mr. Patmore were so well pleased with one another.

You did not, I hope, let him hear my remark about the MS book.

That book could be the greatest boon to me, if you are so good as to offer it—a godsend and might lead to my doing more.

[August 3, 1884]

Dearest Bridges,—I must let you have a line to acknowledge, with many thanks, the receipt of the MS book and two or three very kind letters.

I had an interesting letter from Mr. Patmore all in praise of you. . . . It always seems to me that poetry is unprofessional, but that is what I have said to myself, not others to me. No doubt if I kept producing I should have to ask myself what I meant to do with it all; but I have long been at a standstill, and so the things lie. It would be less tedious talking than writing: now at all events I must stop. [August 21, 1884]

From then till his death, Hopkins promised Bridges that he would copy his new work into Ms B, promised that their collaborative effort (this first edition, as I have called it) would grow. "The" book and "your" book eventually was even spoken of as "my book".

My Dear Bridges,— . . .

I hope soon to enter a batch of sonnets in my book and when I do that I can send you copies. They are thin gleanings of a long weary while, but singly good.   [November 2, 1887]

My Dear Bridges,— . . .

At Monasterevan I tried to get some outstanding and accumulated sonnets ready for hanging on the line, that is in my book of MS, the one you wrote most of, and so for sending to you. All however are not ready yet, but they will soon be. . . . It is now years that I have had no inspiration of longer jet than makes a sonnet, except only in that fortnight in Wales: it is what, far more than direct want of time, I find most against poetry and production in the life I lead. Unhappily I cannot produce anything at all, not only the luxuries like poetry, but the duties almost of my position, its natural outcome—like scientific works. . . . All impulse fails me: I can give myself no sufficient reason for going on. Nothing comes: I am a eunuch—but it is for the kingdom of heaven's sake.   [January 12, 1888]

The project was for the new work to be inscribed in Ms B, and only then for it to be returned to his friend, "who wrote most of" it—a revised first edition. But, half a decade later, whether it was *the* MS book, or *your* MS book, or *my* book, *the one you wrote most of*—the manuscript was dead. Promise after promise had gone unfulfilled; Hopkins had hung on the line only four new poems and extended one and written a new version of another. In June, 1889, half a decade after he had received the manuscript, the poet eunuch was dead too.

We are not dealing here with writer's block *per se*, for Hopkins did continue writing his last, best, desolate sonnets, which "came like in-spirations unbidden and against my will", as he wrote to Bridges.[87] But there seems to have been a block to transcribing these painful masterpieces of new work into the old unsuccessful edition, though he had assured Bridges he would do so. Of course, like the rest of us, Hopkins both struggled to write and struggled against writing. But in addition, he seems to have both assented to (even been inspired by), but also resisted Bridges' editorial format. It is this potential for conflict in the collaboration of this manuscript, more than its poor success with its first audience, that indelibly marks Ms B for me and makes it crucial to bring it into focus: this manuscript combines inextricably the scene of writing and the scene of editing.

Why had this first edition, this modeling of Hopkins' poetry, remained vague to me for so long, when I thought I knew the individual drafts of poems well from MacKenzie's archive of facsimile photos, which does, after all, include every text in Ms B?[88] Well, B does not appear as a coherent entity in MacKenzie's project, for it is not a documentary facsimile. The photographs of it appear in varying magnifications and croppings interspersed with the contents of other manuscripts. Now page edges show; now they do not. Pages are presented without regard for their original verso or recto positions, or for the contents of whole openings. As an example of reformatting, consider how MacKenzie displays "Pied Beauty" in Ms A. As we saw, Bridges had cut in three the leaf it was written on, and laid it out on facing pages with its lines vertical. But MacKenzie presents this opening of Ms A as a single page, with lines horizontal and the blank middle of the album's verso removed, along with its gutter. Precisely where Bridges the editor had cut and pasted, MacKenzie the editor has also cut and pasted—essentially *un*editing Bridges' work. He has thus gone a long way to restoring an earlier appearance of Hopkins' document. But he has taken us far away from what Michael Warren calls the "existential text", which embodies Bridges' problematic collaboration.

The facsimile editor has certainly chosen exciting and instructive juxtapositions of the evidence for comparisons of drafts within the limits of a codex format. The editorial sequence of the facsimile generally matches that of MacKenzie's other monumental project, his 1990 *Poetical Works*, which aims to order items by date of first draft. A chronology of origins of individual poems is thus very clear; but the chronologies of compilation, copying, and revision are not. Had they been so, they should have made Ms B vivid, allowing me to grasp it as an edition with its own strata, a project in which the poet and his friend, with many compromises, faced the daunting (indeed impossible) task of making Hopkins visible and acceptable to an age constitutionally unable to see him or accept him. (I suppose that only the eventual publication of a facsimile of Ms B will compensate for this blind spot in Hopkins studies.)

There is another reason that Ms B became visible to me late. This explanation also has to do with rearrangement. Recall that in *1918*, Bridges took the note on rhythm, which had joined Ms B at the eleventh hour, titled it for the first time, and placed it opposite and immediately after his own introductory (but late) poem, "OUR *generation is already overpast*". (In an earlier plan, by contrast, Bridges had suggested to Daniel, "a long note by G. H. on his own poems" was to come *after* them.)[89]

When the first words of Hopkins' Preface in Bridges' 1918 edition read "THE poems in this book . . .", one is hard put not to understand "this book" as the one in hand, rather than Ms B. Indeed, I still remember my incredulity when I first read these words. As I vaguely knew that Hopkins had resisted publication and that he had died long before his work appeared in print, I (wrongly) took the reference to "this book" to imply that Bridges himself was the author of the "AUTHOR'S PREFACE"—just as I (rightly) had guessed he was the author of the first unsigned poem in this book of Hopkins' verse. Of course, my interpretation was shortsighted, as I would have known if I had taken care to read the fine print of Bridges' brief note to this phrase at the bottom of the page. ([1] That is, the MS. described in Editor's preface as B. This preface does not apply to the early poems.) But the editor's preface, "PREFACE TO NOTES", is actually, as we know, at the *back* of his edition, remote from the reader's view at this point. Taking the book from the front cover, we will come to the editor's defence of his disposition of the author's text very late in the day, if at all, and will have learned by then that the order of Hopkins' poems in *1918* is basically chronological. That

Hopkins' late prose immediately follows the editor's even later poem at the front of the book represents further non-chronological shaping of Bridges' edition. This time, through the placement of the Preface, the author is made retrospectively to authorize his *Poems*.

My confusion of editor and author was naive, but this is a naiveté which few readers can avoid as they enter the 1918 edition for the first time. The confusion is intuitively apt: the literary friendship of Bridges and Hopkins did not itself transcend such confusion—as Bridges' editing or the work of later editors also did not.

After the "AUTHOR'S PREFACE" in *1918* come the three "EARLY POEMS" that the footnote tells us the preceding Preface does not apply to. Then follows the bulk of Hopkins' poetry in a section entitled "POEMS 1876–1889". Now, Hopkins had sent Ms B to Patmore in 1884. So, the note to the author's Preface should have raised the question of whether the Preface did not apply to these latest poems, from mid-1884 to 1889, as well. But it does not. This lapse further indicates Bridges' non-chronological use of Hopkins' note: it states the author's mature philosophy at the outset, as if it were a thing before or outside Hopkins' oeuvre, instead of engaged in it at a particular moment, and, as I have made out, was possibly provoked by Bridges' editing out the poet's accents and his remarks on rhythm in the very document, Ms B, to which Hopkins attached or appended it.

Now, Bridges' detailed editorial notes at the back of *1918* do stipulate one by one which late poems are present in Ms B. But very few people will ever seek out this scattered information, or, having done so, be able to organize it without the manuscript to hand. And though this totality can be gleaned, its actual sequence cannot be discovered.

Bridges' extraction and repositioning is not merely metaphorical. When Patmore returned Ms B and Hopkins' note to Bridges, he physically removed the note and placed it in Ms A. What Bridges then forwarded to Hopkins had thus once more stripped out the artist's prosody—last time the accents, this time the theory. I suppose Hopkins was left with no copy of his note in the last five years of his life. (Had he possessed one, might he not have revised it, just as he continued to revise the poems in Ms B?) Bridges' behaviour with this note contrasts with his behaviour concerning Hopkins' new poems at the back of Ms B, which he merely copied out for himself rather than removing them before returning Ms B to Hopkins. (His different attitude to the inserted note and the inscribed poems can scarcely be explained by his respect for the physical integrity of the album that formed the basis of his manuscript, of which the note was not an intrinsic part, as respect of physical integrity was not Bridges' strong suit, as his cutting up the autographs to fit the album of Ms A shows.)

After Hopkins' death, Ms B returned to Bridges, who eventually placed the note in it.[90] His locating this text at the start of *1918* as "AUTHOR'S PREFACE" continued the history of its unrootedness. Bridges defended the placement of "The Wreck" as "logically as well as chronologically in the front of his [Hopkins'] book".[91] But it was *not* the first written of the poems Bridges included, a fact that challenges what the editor meant by "chronologically". Essentially, Bridges projected the book backwards from the poet's achievement, not forward from his origins.

And this backwards projection persists. Hopkins' prose note for Ms B is also prefatory in Vol. 2 of MacKenzie's otherwise chronologically arranged facsimile of the poetry manuscripts. In his 1990 edition, it lies elsewhere, before the Note to "The Wreck" — still out of chronological sequence. This editor generally exorcized his predecessor; but here Bridges' ghost lingers. Equally problematic is MacKenzie's naming of this "famous long Preface on rhythm".[92] In *The Later Poetic Manuscripts*, he styles it "Metrical preface to MS. B" (vi), "Metrical Preface to Hopkins's Mature Verse" (23), "Metrical Preface to Hopkins's Mature Poems" (23), or "Metrical Preface to B" (24). "[*Author's Preface on Rhythm*]" (362) is the title from his *Poetical Works*; and he quotes (p. 23) Bridges' index to Ms A, where it is called "A preface to his poems MS."

To what extent does the growth of this latest branch of editing straighten the twig bent in *1918*? I shall conclude with a look at the shape of "The Starlight Night". I illustrate it overleaf by cutting and pasting from MacKenzie's 1990 edition. (Here we go again.) His editing marks an exciting advance over Bridges' because, more than others, he conserves many of Hopkins' odd markings (though not, as we saw, the great colons). Note, for example, the poet's ties in vv. 2 and 6 of this sonnet. But this fidelity to copy introduces a typographic oddity: as the usual leading is too tight to accomodate these ties, extra leading now holds the last three lines of each quatrain off from the first.

112   The Starlight Night

Look at the stars! look, look up at the skies!
    O look at all the fire-folk sitting in the air!
    The bright bóroughs, the circle-citadels there!
Down in dim woods the diamond delves! the elves'-eyes!

140   *Poem 112*

The grey lawns cold where gold, where quickgold lies!   5
    Wind-beat whitebeam! airy abeles set on a flare!
    Flake-doves sent floating forth at a farmyard scare!—
Ah well! it is all a purchase, all is a prize.

Buy then! bid then!—What?—Prayer, pátience, alms, vows.
Look, look: a May-mess, like on orchard boughs!   10
    Look! March-bloom, like on mealed-with-yellow sallows!
These are indeed the barn; withindoors house
The shocks. This piece-bright paling shuts the spouse
    Christ home, Christ and his mother and all his hallows.

And there is the familiar problem of shifting tabs across the page break and the question whether the break should correspond to leading between the quatrains. But this question can be answered, without recourse to an earlier edition, through an expedition into a daunting two-and-a-half-page note at the back of the book (for the editor has anticipated our question, though few readers will begin the journey toward the revelation, and fewer still will abide the outcome). Opposite, I quote the first quarter of the note, just to the bottom of p. 363. First, under "*MSS.*" come descriptions of seven sigla in five documents: F, H^1, A^1, A^2, H^2, B^1 and B^2, all by Hopkins, except B^1, by Bridges. (Images of their structures are displayed on p. 279.) Hopkins began to annotate Bridges' transcription of the poem in B^1 but then deleted it altogether and eventually rewrote it at the back of Ms B—as B^2. It is this his final version, the seventh manuscript listed, that is "Taken as *Text*" for the Oxford edition. But, as Bridges was free to consider conveniences, so is MacKenzie, whose note on this manuscript continues: "but layout follows MSS 1–4." The very last section of this excerpt is "*Layout.*" — and we can look to it for more details. The three-line note opens with the sigla of these first four manuscripts ("F, H^1, A^1, A^2"), and a reference to which lines they indent in common ("indent ll. 2, 3, 6,7, 11, 14").

112 The Starlight Night

MSS. **1.** F—autograph fair copy, with No. 111, sent to his mother 3 Mar. 1877 (L. iii. 144–5, with facsimile).

    2. (H¹) H. i. 30ʳ—autograph fair copy, with musical marks, and later revisions of ll. 4, 13 at ft.

    3. (A¹) A, pp. 79–80—autograph fair copy, sent to RB (3–8 Apr. 1877, marked 'II,' because accompanied by No. 111—see L. i. 38, 40), and mounted in album A. Note adds 'To be read, both of them, slowly, strongly marking the rhythms and fetching out the syllables.' No counterpoint signs.

    4. (A²) A, p. 92—later autograph fair copy, with rev. l. 13 from ft. of H¹, dated March 1877. '(Standard rhythm opened and counterpointed)'; 'opened' is nowhere defined, but seems different from 'sprung leadings' (the omission of the first slack in an iambic line) in Nos. 113, 117: see Introd. pp. xxviii–ix. This or MS A² of No. 111, was prob. sent to RB 8 Aug. '77. (L. i. 42); otherwise it was given to him in London that summer. Mounted in album A. Publ. by RB in Miles, *Poets and Poetry of the Century*, viii (1893), 167.

    5. (H²) H. i. 31ʳ, 30ᵛ—autograph fair copy, corrected in ll. 13, 14, and with later drafts of ll. 3–5 made on the verso of H¹ (= H² ft.). Counterpoint signs match those of 1879 on (music turns over two syllables); layout pre-1884.

    6. (B¹) B. 8ᵛ—transcript of A² by RB (1883), inscribed in album B; rev. by GMH, who also added metrical marks. Finally he crossed it through and wrote 'See later'.

    7. (B²) B. 27ᵛ—final autograph fair copy, inscribed in album B (1883–4) before GMH sent it on to Patmore. Taken as *Text*, but layout follows MSS 1–4. Transcript in album A (p. 78) by RB made Aug. 1884 (no authority).

Counterpoint signs. F, A¹ *none*   H¹, A² 3 boroughs   9 patience   H², B¹, B²
music turns, some reversed 3 boroughs   9 patience   H² *ft. only* 4 The diamond
wells quick through dimwoods   5 The grey lawns coldjaunting, there golddew
lies;   H² 14 home, Christ's mother, and all Hallows, Christ's Hallows!

Slurs. F, H¹, A¹ below the line; A², H², B¹, B² above words

Layout. F, H¹, A¹, A² indent ll. 2, 3, 6,7, 11, 14, line space after 8 only. H² no indenting, but line spaces after 4, 8, 11. B¹ RB's transcript, of no authority. B² indents ll. 1, 5, 9, 12; no line spaces.

And finally comes what we seek: "line space after 8 only". The answer is that the page break which interrupts the poem in this edition should *not* be understood to interrupt the octave of this sonnet, as extra leading would in a setting on a single page. For MacKenzie, the relevant model, therefore, is Model 16, as it was for Bridges. Are you clear on all this? The editor understands no line spacing at his page break, but only one after v. 8. But why?—that's not the shape of the poet's last revision, as you can see in "B²" (in the next opening), and which the *Layout* note confirms, when it states that "B² indents ll. 1, 5, 9, 12" and that there are "no line spaces". Do you undertand that the editor derives shape from the earliest drafts, which *do* have line spacing in v. 8, but diction from the latest draft, which does *not*? Does that make sense?

    Curiously, of the indentations and line spacing of B¹ (Bridges' transcript of A²), we learn nothing. "It is of no authority", says MacKenzie. But why of no authority?—we may ask. I understand well why Bridges' *later* transcript of B² into Ms A lacks authority, as MacKenzie claims (in his discussion of Ms 7). But if authority is muddied in the collaboration of Ms B, don't we need to know all we can about B¹ too, not just about B²? After all, the superscripts designate merely earlier and later states of the same contested first edition, in which B² is conditioned by B¹.

Now, two of the copies written by Hopkins (A¹ and A²) were what Bridges saw; and B¹ is what he *did* with what he saw. B¹ is what Hopkins saw—himself reflected in his friend—and B² is what *he* did with what he saw. Doesn't the resemblance of B¹ to the shape of Hopkins' novel replacement of it, B², speak to Bridges' likely having influenced his friend's graphic styling? And if Bridges' shadow lies across the poet's last revision, how can it lack authority?

MacKenzie's editorial practice is not neutral. It follows his decision to sunder form and content, and to seek out and fuse different historical embodiments of each. His consequent declaration that B¹ lacks authority deflects our scrutiny of his judgment, by depriving us of some of the evidence of the text—some of the *final* evidence—which inheres generally in Ms B, and is not to be limited to Hopkins' own specific hand in it—for the textual evidence is of collaboration, a collaboration that Hopkins' revision may not have transcended.

Like *1918*, MacKenzie's edition of this poem takes shape from the *earliest* manuscripts on odd scraps of paper that Hopkins had to hand; but the diction of these editions stems from Hopkins' *latest* go at the poem, on a page in Bridges' manuscript edition, where the two poets were interacting with each other, as the unprecedented body language of Hopkins' reformatting of his sonnet suggests. In offering mature diction in the young body, or a mature note as a preface, these editors school us with an anachronistic ideal work. As with this poem, so potentially with the whole corpus, which took no final shape, but exists in a myriad of transitional forms interrupted by death.

What disorients me about the image of "The Starlight Night" from this latest Oxford edition is that it shuffles off the inextricable confusion of Hopkins' poetic creation in his relationship to Bridges, in their relationships to Patmore—all difficult relations of difficult men—and erects instead an editorial convenience, a synthesis of earliest and latest versions. To the notes, MacKenzie has subordinated the actual struggles of poetry—its details, details, details. In seeking a release from such struggles in the body of the edition, in proffering the reader

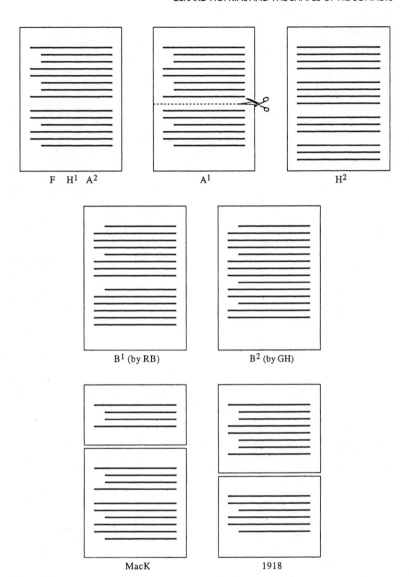

F   H¹ A²   A¹   H²

B¹ (by RB)   B² (by GH)

MacK   1918

a single fix for the multiple versions of this sonnet, editing vitiates the poet's struggle for the text, vitiates the reader's struggle for the text—which struggle *is* the text, which is the struggle for poetry, which *is* poetry. *God* is in the details.

~~Chris~~
Christ minds

NOTES

1. My thanks first and foremost to Lord Bridges for permission to study and to reproduce manuscripts by Robert Bridges and Gerard Hopkins, now on deposit at the Bodleian Library. For facsimiles of them, see Norman H. MacKenzie's invaluable *The Later Poetic Manuscripts of Gerard Manley Hopkins* (New York & London: Garland Publishing, 1991). (As the images in this essay are often not to size, check there for original measurements. His scale, is on p. [vii].) Thanks also to librarian Colin Harris and his colleagues for facilitating access to the manuscripts and for help with photography. Thanks as well to Oxford University Press for permission to reprint copyright material from editorial commentaries by Gardner (pp. 188, 190, and 192) and by MacKenzie (p. 277) and also his text of "The Starlight Night" (p. 276).

I am grateful to Michelle Faubert, University of Toronto, and Chris Jones, St. Andrews University, for reading early drafts of this essay, and to Linda Gough, a former student of Hopkins at Erindale College, University of Toronto, whose discerning term-essay on Hopkins and Bridges, along with Jean-Georges Ritz's *Robert Bridges and Gerard Hopkins, 1863–1889: A Literary Friendship* (London, New York and Toronto: Oxford University Press, 1960), led me to see the relationship of these two poets with more balance. Thanks also for careful proofreading of an earlier version to Xavier Callahan. (The mistakes are mine.)

Thanks for computer help to Pamela Harris, Rishi Arora, Stefan Neuffer, and Brandon Besharah; to him and Alison Dias for artwork; to her and Steve Jaunzems for photography. With their generous help, I was able to prepare this essay as camera-ready copy.

I am grateful for fellowships while I was engaged in this project—from the Social Sciences and Humanities Research Council of Canada and the Mellon Foundation (for tenure at the Folger Shakespeare Library).

Tom Dunne, *Gerard Manley Hopkins, A Comprehensive Bibliography* (Oxford: Oxford University Press, 1976), xix, quotes Maurice Charney's assessment that much criticism of Hopkins' poetry developed as a defence of him against Bridges. The present essay may seem to fit this mould. But my own understanding of my work is that I am mindful of the integrity of textual evidence and wary of editing and of its simplifications, appropriations, and displacements: I defend Hopkins' text against Bridges' editing, more than Hopkins against Bridges. As I hold textual evidence to be graphic before it is verbal, photography is a more efficient means of quotation than the keyboard. Ultimately, therefore, my defence is of *opsis* against a domineering *logos* (to use the terms in which Tony Hammond described my project to me).

2. For the first, 1953, Penguin printing, I examined copies in the Fisher Library, University of Toronto (end H665 A105 1953a) and Campion College Library, University of Regina (PR 4803 H44 A17 1953); for *1954*, copies at Trinity College, University of Toronto (PR 4803 .H44 A17 1953 [sic]) and Library of Congress (PR 4803 H44 A6 1954). Thanks to Jacqueline Roy for advising me about the readings of the Campion College Library copy.

3. In the academy, one often uses a text ready to hand, without much concern for its accuracy. According to Norman H. MacKenzie, ed., *The Poetical Works of Gerard Manley Hopkins* (Oxford: Oxford University Press, 1990), 424, I. A. Richards used the comfortable fragments of Robert Bridges' *The Spirit of Man* version of Hopkins' "*Spring and Fall. To a young child*" (Poem 9) as an anonymous test poem in his *Practical Criticism* (Kegan Paul, Trench, Trubner & Co.: London, 1930, 2nd impression of 1929 ed., "with a few alterations"), Poem VI. The body of Bridges' anthology offers no titles, dedications or attributions (they are found in the Index), but it does print what looks like centered headlines in italics, the contents of which change page by page. The one for this page, "*Sorrow's Springs*", is a quotation from Hopkins' poem, above which is one by Rimbaud in French. According to the first page of Bridges' "Preface", the page-headings", as he calls them, which are "sufficient guide" to the "various moods of mind", "allowed free play" in the "sequence

[Notes continue on page 282]

TABLE

Gardner's numbers for the sonnets in the Penguin edition appear in Column *a*, and the titles (or first lines) follow in *b*. My Model numbers are given in Column *c*. (In the body of the essay, on pp. 216, 218, 220 and 221, the numbers that appear below each model are from Column *a*; the numbers in the boxes at the upper left are from Column *c*.)

Column *d* relates to a matter discussed on p. 267 and displayed on p. 269, the six different Shapes that Bridges used to represent the fifteen of Hopkins' sonnets that he transcribed into Ms B; Shape 7 represents Hopkins' reworking of three of these transcriptions.

a	b	c	d
2	"Let me be to Thee as the circling bird"	3	
8	God's Grandeur	15	5
9	The Starlight Night	16	5 → 7
10	Spring	15	4
11	The Lantern out of Doors	20	5
12	The Sea and the Skylark	17	4 → 7
13	The Windhover	17	2
15	Hurrahing in Harvest	18	5
16	The Caged Skylark	19	4
17	In the Valley of the Elwy	16	2
21	Duns Scotus's Oxford	6	2
22	Henry Purcell	6	3
26	Andromeda	13	6
27	The Candle Indoors	3	2
28	The Handsome Heart	6	1 → 7
30	Felix Randal	5	3
34	"As kingfishers catch fire"	3	
35	Ribblesdale	4	
38	"To what serves Mortal Beauty?"	8	
39	Spelt from Sibyl's Leaves	2	
40	(The Soldier)	3	
41	(Carrion Comfort)	9	
42	"No worst, there is none."	9	
43	"To seem the stranger lies my lot"	12	
44	"I wake and feel the fell of dark"	14	
45	"Patience, hard thing!"	14	
46	"My own heart let me more have pity on"	11	
50	St. Alphonsus Rodriguez	8	
51	"Thou art indeed just, Lord"	10	
52	"The shepherd's brow"	1	
53	To R. B.	7	

of context", where "there is no logical argument". Bridges removed all twenty-four of Hopkins' accents, and he edited away vv. 3 and 4, representing them merely by two bold dots after the question mark at the end of v. 2—which dots Richards in turn boldly edited away. (Without these parts of the poem, Richards' Cambridge students and his and Bridges' readers lacked essential keys to interpret Hopkins' poetry.)

But Richards also derived his text from *Poems*, 1918—although there is no visible trace of this source in the final product: for Richards claims to have "omitted" the accent on "will", v. 9, which had thus far appeared nowhere but in *1918*, where it was one of thirteen accents. (Richards' credits, by the way, mention only Humphrey Mosley, the printer of *1918*.) Of this accent on "will", Richards states, "This mark I omitted, partly to see what would happen, partly to avoid a likely temptation to irrelevant discussions" (p. 83)—as if rhythm and stress could ever be irrelevant in Hopkins. Now, the word "will" is underlined in Ms A, but bears an accent in Ms B, presumably an addition by Hopkins to Bridges' transcription, which eschewed accents and underlining. In the earlier Mss A and D, Hopkins provided accents four to a verse—in vv. 1 3, 5, 11, 13 and 14. Bridges' 1918 edition offers only twelve of these (and also accents "will", in v. 9).

In *1918*, the accent on "áre" in v. 1 is almost invisible. This fact must explain why the 1930 edition omits it (and also why F. R. Leavis omits it in *Gerard Manley Hopkins: Reflections After Fifty Years* (Second Annual Hopkins Lecture), Hopkins Society (London, 1971), 8). The illegibility or lack of the accent in v. 1 is very influential in these representations: it prevents or slows the reader's understanding of the metre, for the first verse was the only one in which Bridges had given all four accents. (Leavis also omits the subtitle and the accent on "is", v. 14; and in his extract of v. 3, he drops the accent on "like".) Thus, no line of this poem appeared in print with an unambiguous four beats until Gardner's third edition, 1948—over half a century since the poem was first printed.

It is instructive to see Bridges' note (U5r) for his editing of the French poem: "8. Arthur Rimbaud. *Chanson de la plus haute Tour*. From ' Les Illuminations ', 1872–3. He gives a later version of this poem in ' Une Saison en Enfer ', whence I take the form of the refrain at end of quotation." In this poem too there are several uses of double bold dots, signaling omissions. Thus, both the poems on this page are severely compromised.

4. "Leading" rhymes with "bedding", not with "bleeding". A technical term from letterpress printing, it refers to thin strips (originally) of lead, which are less than type height (so as not to print ink). Leads separate lines of characters. (In manuscripts, the corresponding effect is called "line spacing".) A strip of lead that *is* type-height, and therefore able to print a line, is called a "rule".

Further to my distinction of *logos* and *opsis* in n. 1: W. H. Gardner's "Sonnet Morphology", 71–108, in vol. 1 of his two-volume *Gerard Manley Hopkins (1844–1889): A Study of Poetic Idiosyncrasy in Relation to Poetic Tradition* (New Haven: Yale University Press, 1948), is a learned example of the *logos* approach. As Gardner nowhere includes physical space, shape, or form in his concept of morphology, it is not surprising that he neglects tabbing in his quotations from "God's Grandeur" (p. 78) and from "The Windhover" (p. 78)—and again, from other of its verses (pp. 98 and 99), in both of which v. 2 is misrepresented: first, too little indented, then too much. (In the latter, the "dom" of "king- | dom" indents as if it were a wrap, instead of the beginning of a verse.) Gardner thereby fell into a predictable misunderstanding, for this is an error we are all likely to make on first reading—and it may even be a trap that the wily poet created for us when he revised the sonnet. (I see that Edith Anne Robertson also mis-tabs v. 2 in *Translations into the Scots tongue of poems by Gerard Manley Hopkins* (Aberdeen: Aberdeen University Press, 1968), 22.) Quoting the poetry as a critic, Gardner introduces various indentations in lines of "*That Nature is a Herclitean* [sic] *Fire*", though Gardner the editor tabs these lines alike in his Penguin edition. The critic's defence of the codas of this poem is that they "are not mere excrescences : they are organic members of a well-proportioned poetic body" (108). To the *logos*, it seems, the well-proportioned body is an abstraction that need not map onto material.

5. Letter III, in Claude Colleer Abbott, ed., *The Correspondence of Gerard Manley Hopkins and Richard Watson Dixon* (London, New York, and Toronto: Oxford University Press, 2nd rev. imp., 1955), 12–16. In Letter XXII (Aug. 7, 1868) to Bridges, in Claude Colleer Abbott, ed., *The Letters of Gerard Manley Hopkins to Robert Bridges* (London, New York, and Toronto: Oxford University Press, 2nd rev. imp., 1955), Hopkins stated that he could not send the promised "*Summa*", "for it is burnt with my other verses . . . I kept however corrected copies of some things which you have and will send them that what you have got you may have in its last edition.", 24. (Hopkins' use of "edition" applied to a manuscript supports my use of the term, on p. 252, to describe Ms B.)

6. As a guide to this poem from 1876, Gardner and MacKenzie, editors of the fourth edition (London, New York, and Toronto: Oxford University Press, 1967), refer the reader to the "AUTHOR'S PREFACE", which, like Bridges, they place just before "*The Wreck*", though, also like Bridges, they assert that this document "must have been written in 1883 or not much later", 253. This modern edition thus continues to project features of Bridges' edition, including Housman's dedication to the poet's mother and Bridges' dedicatory poem. By his 1990 edition, MacKenzie, now the sole editor, had concluded that this document, composed for the occasion, had accompanied Ms B, when Hopkins sent it on to Patmore in March 1883, but when it returned to Bridges, he placed it in Ms A, before sending Ms B on to Hopkins again. It was later mounted in the front of Ms B, where it sits now, perhaps where Hopkins originally had placed it, perhaps not. Strangely, MacKenzie retained the "Authors Preface" in this anachronistic position before "The Wreck". The "Preface" and then the undated "Note", which now precede the poem, together figure in MacKenzie's headline, "Author's Prefaces on Rhythm", but not in his index. It seems that the two prose pieces and "The Wreck" reverse chronological order.

7. MacKenzie, *Later Poetic Manuscripts*, 30–31 (showing pp. 24–25 in Ms A).

8. For example, see MacKenzie, *Later Poetic Manuscripts*, 42, 62, and especially 65 (for Ms A, 31 and 41, and Ms B, 20v). (He reports Bridges usually erased these guidelines, 42.)

9. In my 1964 Penguin, wraps occur in vv. 3, 5, 6, and 8 of the "Wreck" stanza (as functions of standard 16mo type size and column width). Indentations for wrapped portions breed confusion, not only because they create non-symbolic tabs among those that Hopkins had made symbolic, but also because they sometimes are inappropriately tabbed to symbolic depths. For 23.3.2 (by which I mean the second of two lines of v. 3 in st. 23), the tab is typically 9mm more than that for 23.3.1. This new depth creates an unprecedented tab; hence, it may be thought not to compromise Hopkins' system, though it does offer confusingly to expand it. The depth of 14.5.2, however, is 12.5mm more than that for 14.5.1. As this depth is 0.5mm more than the symbolic tab for verses 14.1, 2 & 4, a ruler may be required to show it *just* misses the symbolic depth;

She drove in the dark to leeward,
She struck – not a reef or a rock
But the combs of a smother of sand : night drew her
Dead to the Kentish Knock ;
And she beat the bank down with her bows and the ride of
her keel ;
The breakers rolled on her beam with ruinous shock ;
And canvas and compass, the whorl and the wheel
Idle for ever to waft her or wind her with, these she endured.

14.5.2

For 17.5.2, the depth is, inconsistently, 6mm more than that for 17.5.1 and certainly aligns exactly with the tab for vv. 17.3 & 7; and so, in this position, it does confound Hopkins' spatial symbolism. Similarly, the tab for 25.6.2 is 12mm more than that for 25.6.1, and this distractingly brings the start of 25.6.2 exactly to the tab for vv. 25.1, 2 & 4. Obviously, Penguin has no formula for indentation of the wraps. Measuring 6mm,

9mm, 12mm, and 12.5mm more than the indentation of the first half of the lines in question, they have no consistent extra depth.

(Indentation errors in *1918* occur at 8.7, which aligns with 8.2 & 4 instead of 8.3; and at 17.4, which aligns with 17.3, instead of with 17.1 & 2.)

10. For examples, see vv. 8 and 12 of "Felix Randal" in my Penguin edition, p. 48 (on pp. 213–14 of this essay), where the justified portions of each verse before the wrap show greater spacing between words. Contrast the exaggerated spaces of the former of these settings, "Tendered to", in the justified 8.1, with the normal spacing of "fleshed there" in v. 4, which is not justified. The latter setting is shown upside down and mirror image, and both of them appear in triple magnification, in order to facilitate contrast, along their baselines, of the spaced letters "-d t-", present in both settings. The spacing between these letters in the justified portion of v. 8 is about 167% of normal.

Tendered to
ɥǝꜱlɟǝd ʇɥǝɹǝ

In distended spacing like this, the rendering of printed verse feels subjected to the material conditions of printed prose. The problem goes back to limits that Hopkins the poet strove against—limits to the length of the English verse line. In publishing practice, these limits are mirrored in conventional page width and point size. (See nn. 33 and 36).

11. In the manuscripts, the transition from the two-beat to the three-beat version of the first line is oddly marked. The first letter in each of the first lines of sts. 11 and 12 (where the new rhythm comes into effect) stands at the old indentation; but a flourish, or ornament, or lead-in stroke precedes each of them, effectively realigning the start of each first verse leftward with that of the second verse. Does the flourish before the first line of st. 12 serve merely to correct the misalignment of words or is it (also) symbolic? Supporting the latter notion is the reduplication in Ms B of the flourish from the start of this verse at the top of 17r as part of the catchword on 16v. Since the catchword there stands alone in the bottom right corner of the page, it cannot be expected to communicate anything about placement in the body, and therefore it tends to read as symbolic.

12. http://eir.library.utoronto.ca/rpo/. The edition is "1996–2000" and the "recent editing" is dated "2:2002/3/14".

13. Bernard Bergonzi, *Gerard Manley Hopkins* (New York: MacMillan, 1977), 53. Henry Coleridge was a convert from Anglicanism. He was a friend of John Henry Newman's, both of whom attended the Holy Week retreat at the Birmingham Oratory, where Hopkins was in the last stage of his conversion.

14. Letter LXXV (June 26, 1876), Claude Colleer Abbott, ed., *Further Letters of Gerard Manley Hopkins, Including his Correspondence with Coventry Patmore* (London, New York, and Toronto: Oxford University Press, 2nd rev. ed., 1956), 138–39.

15. MacKenzie, ed., *Poetical Works*, 1990, 353, n. 7.

16. Photographs from *1918* are from a copy in the Thomas Fisher Rare Book Library, University of Toronto (end H665 A15 1918): "with holograph drafts of poems by Frank Preuett (1893–1962); also with his autograph". (It is Preuett's scrawl across the top of the title page, shown on p. 235 of this essay.) In this copy, point holes on the bottom edges of D3, E3, F4, G3, G4, H4 (possibly), and I3 argue that the printer's sheet was double what one would assume from the volume's being gathered as octavo. If each printer's sheet that entered the press contained sixteen leaves, both inner and outer formes of each octavo quire could have been imposed in a single chase, which could have printed both sides of the sheet, by the work-and-turn method. (This was the method used to print Matthew Arnold's *The Strayed Reveller*, 1849, as two different orders of offsetting, one found in half

the copies, the other in the other half, bear out.) In such a format, the print-run of each sheet would have been only half the number of volumes produced. Thus, for the 750 copies, only 375 exemplars of each sheet would need to have been printed.

I am grateful to Richard Landon, Director of the Fisher Library, for permission to reproduce images from this copy, and to Curator, Linda Joy, for assisting with photography.

17. The difficulty even for editors sympathetic to Hopkins' graphic oddities sounds out in Catherine Phillips' 1986 Oxford Authors edition of the poems, *Gerard Manley Hopkins* (Oxford and New York: Oxford University Press, 1986), xli: "Cost and editorial opinion at Oxford University Press have restricted metrical marks in the text to simple stresses". (This restriction was gone, however, when MacKenzie brought out his 1990 Oxford edition, and he went to great lengths to record and display Hopkins' idiosyncratic markings; but even then the poet's great colon still was not reproduced.)

18. "It seemed better (and it was in accordance with Dr. Bridges's own wish) to give these additional poems in an Appendix rather than to rearrange the original book. . . . the present volume is a reprint of the book which Dr. Bridges made, with an Appendix of sixteen other poems. . . . Dr. Bridges had given general approval, and the text was with the Printer when his death took place. This edition therefore becomes a memory not only of Gerard Hopkins but also of the poet, his friend, to whom all readers of either owe so great a devotion" (from the introduction to the second edition, 1930, ix–x).

19. "Bridges the advisor" derives from Gardner's Penguin dedication (see p. 177, above). The reference to "no adequate tribute" comes from Gardner and MacKenzie's 1967 edition, v.

20. In the introduction to Gardner and MacKenzie's 4th ed., 1967, xiv–xv, Gardner states: "Twenty years ago, when the present writer was invited to prepare a considerably enlarged Third Edition (1948), he gladly acceded to the publisher's request that the new collection should be firmly based on the historic First Edition and on the augmented text of 1930. . . . For the much needed Third Edition I accepted, with a few emendations, the text of the poems and fragments of the poet's maturity (1876–89) as these works had been edited and printed by Bridges; and as the text of the already collected additional early poems I adopted, with one or two corrections, the versions which seemed to have been competently transcribed from the MSS. by Bridges or Williams. I regret now that I did not look more closely to find those errors of transcription which have since been detected."

A cancel-slip tipped in between Acknowledgements and Contents pages in the 1967 Penguin reprint allows us to read between the lines of Gardner's previous statement: "This new reprint incorporates, as did (prematurely) the 1966 reprint, some thirty improved readings which are among the many established mainly by my fellow editor, Professor N. H. MacKenzie, for the new Fourth Edition of *Poems of Gerard Manley Hopkins* (O. U. P. 1967). In acknowledging this debt I must warn readers that whenever new emendations in this Penguin reprint coincide with readings in the Oxford Fourth Edition, the text of the Fourth Edition is the *earlier*— the authoritative source." (quoted from the copy in Victoria College, University of Toronto: PR 803 H44A6 1967). See n. 23

21. Gardner and MacKenzie do refer to him, positively, in the introduction to the fourth edition: "This [the second edition] was augmented by an Appendix containing sixteen more pieces (most of them early poems) and was graced by an appreciative Introduction from the pen of the new editor, Charles Williams, who had chosen the additional texts after consultation with Bridges.", xiv. "Charles Williams . . . boldly enlarged the Hopkins's [sic] canon and introduced a firmer note of editorial appreciation." , v.

22. He did use the grave accent, however, to show that a normally silent letter should be pronounced, as in "quenchèd" ("To R. B.", v. 3, which poem is reproduced on p. 239 of this essay).

23. In the fourth edition, 1967, xvi, Gardner gives credit to MacKenzie's role in separating editor from poet (*i.e.*, separating "Bridges" (and Gardner!) from "Hopkins"): "I wish to pay tribute to my coadjutor's work in restoring many true readings, and in

making good sense of certain passages, mainly in the early poems, which through faulty transcription had formerly been obscure. He convinced me of the desirability of printing, whenever possible, the latest of two or more variants, and the expediency, at this stage, of differentiating in the Notes between the scansions indicated in the poet's MSS. and those proffered by the editor as guides to the poet's probable rhythmical intentions." See n. 20.

24.   Letter CXLIII (Dec. 11, 1886), Abbott, ed., *Letters ... to Robert Bridges*, 245–48, 246. Abbott presumes "*Poems*, 32" (*i.e.*, "Spelt from Sibyl's Leaves") was the poem Hopkins meant to enclose in the letter. "I mean to enclose my long sonnet, the longest, I still say, ever made; longest by its own proper length, namely by the length of its lines; for anything can be made long by eking, by tacking, by trains, tails, and flounces.... This sonnet shd. be almost sung: it is most carefully timed in *tempo rubato*.", 246.

25.   Remark 66, *Philosophical Investigations*. The German text, with a revised English translation, G. E. M. Anscombe, trans. (Cambridge, Mass.: Blackwell, 2001), 27. My thanks to Jeff Dolven for this reference.

26.   Further on this matter, see Hopkins' afterthought, 3v, in his so-called "Preface" to Ms B. (MacKenzie, *Later Poetic Manuscripts*, p. 26): "Remark also that it is natural in Sprung Rhythm for the lines to be *rove over*, that is for the scanning of each line immediately to take up that of the one before, so that if the first has one or more syllables at its end the other must have so many the less at its beginning; and in fact the scanning runs on without break from the beginning, say, of a stanza to the end and all the stanza is one long strain, though written in lines asunder." See also n. 39.

27.   That is why I said (at the base of p. 180) that the first tab in a poem is a parameter, not a fixed constant.

28.   This distance can most easily be measured in the prose sections of the book.

29.   For a good example of centering by proximate lines, consider p. 46 in my 1964 Penguin, shown opposite. My guidelines and measurements demonstrate that the last line of the upper poem and the first line of the lower one are centred. Just above and below these proximate, centered lines of verse are other lines that extend beyond my right vertical guideline; evidently these extravagant lines are far enough away from the proximate lines not to disrupt their balancing act (though in each poem the extravagant line is merely *two* away from the closer proximate line).

15

The Gaged Skylark

As a dare-gale skylark scanted in a dull cage

2   Man's mounting spirit in his bone-house, mean house, dwells—

That bird beyond the remembering his free fells ;

This in drudgery, day-labouring-out life's age.

Though aloft on turf or perch or poor low stage,

6   Both sing sometímes the sweetest, sweetest spells,

Yet both droop deadly sómetimes in their cells

Or wring their barriers in bursts of fear or rage.

Not that the sweet-fowl, song-fowl, needs no rest—

10   Why, hear him, hear him babble and drop down to his nest,

But his own nest, wild nest, no prison.

Man's spirit will be flesh-bound when found at best,

But uncumbered : meadow-down is not distressed

14   For a rainbow footing it nor he for his bónes rísen.

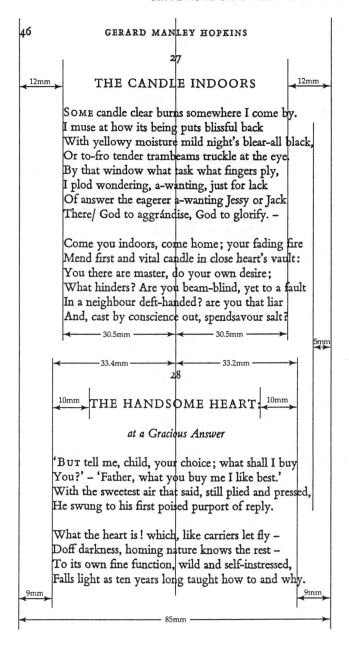

46   GERARD MANLEY HOPKINS

27

|←12mm→| THE CANDLE INDOORS |←12mm→|

SOME candle clear burns somewhere I come by.
I muse at how its being puts blissful back
With yellowy moisture mild night's blear-all black,
Or to-fro tender trambeams truckle at the eye.
By that window what task what fingers ply,
I plod wondering, a-wanting, just for lack
Of answer the eagerer a-wanting Jessy or Jack
There/ God to aggrándise, God to glorify. –

Come you indoors, come home; your fading fire
Mend first and vital candle in close heart's vault:
You there are master, do your own desire;
What hinders? Are you beam-blind, yet to a fault
In a neighbour deft-handed? are you that liar
And, cast by conscience out, spendsavour salt?

|←———— 30.5mm ————→|←———— 30.5mm ————→|

|←5mm→|

|←———— 33.4mm ————→|←———— 33.2mm ————→|

28

|←10mm→|THE HANDSOME HEART:|←10mm→|

at a Gracious Answer

'BUT tell me, child, your choice; what shall I buy
You?' – 'Father, what you buy me I like best.'
With the sweetest air that said, still plied and pressed,
He swung to his first poised purport of reply.

What the heart is! which, like carriers let fly –
Doff darkness, homing nature knows the rest –
To its own fine function, wild and self-instressed,
Falls light as ten years long taught how to and why.

|←9mm→| |←9mm→|

|←———————————————— 85mm ————————————————→|

30. In the second edition, 1930, the first (zero) tab of "The Caged Skylark" (shown opposite) is flush left. Verse 2, the longest, wraps, and vv. 6 and 14 are unnecessarily stretched to the right margin, while v. 10 (which will soon be our focus), is compressed against it, and so avoids wrapping.

In the first Penguin edition, 1953, the poem is divided by the page break (just as it is in the 1964 edition, reproduced above, on p. 198). The first and fourth lines of the first quatrain start flush left, and, there being a wide enough text block in this edition, v.2, the longest, does not wrap this time, despite its indentation. If this width of text block persisted overleaf, no wrapping would be needed there either. But overleaf the left margin of the sonnet is now tabbed in some 9mm, as is v. 1 of the sonnet below, "In the Valley of the Elwy", a poem of relatively short lines. As a result of this repositioning of the left margin within the sonnet, the second largest verse of "The Caged Skylark", v. 10, now wraps. The wrapped phrase "his nest," is 10mm long. But even taking into account the space that would have been needed before it, it could have fit on the previous line, with tightening of the spaces between words—or just the word "his" could have been accommodated without respacing throughout the consolidated 10.1. In *1964* the wrapping is multiply conditioned, as I will now explain.

As you can see above, on p. 198, there is disproportionate extra leading between "The Caged Skylark" and "In the Valley of the Elwy". In this layout, the top and bottom lines of this page align with the corresponding lines of the facing recto (not shown here), where "The Loss of the Eurydice" begins. Had "In the Valley of the Elwy" followed "The Caged Skylark" with more typical extra leading (such as is shown above "The Caged Skylark"), the awkward space would have appeared instead at the bottom of that page—where it could not, by the way, have been satisfactorily filled by bringing over several lines from the recto; for there would have been room on the verso to receive only the title of "The Loss of the Eurydice" and not also one of its four-line stanzas—and a stand-alone title would have been too ugly for words. Given these facts, the layout artist can be supposed to have welcomed the wrapping of v. 10 in "The Caged Skylark", as it helped diminish the awkward space between the two sonnets, and to stretch out this verso so as to align it with the top and bottom of the recto. Thus, the arbitrary new tabbing of the second half of "The Caged Skylark" and the wrapping of its v. 10 seem to be coordinate aesthetic functions, which help to balance layout in the verso-recto spread.

Now, there is something very odd about the wrapping of v. 10 in terms of what I said in n. 10. There, I spoke of the custom of fully justifying the first line of a wrapped verse, and of the consequent Procrustean spacing to be found throughout it. But look carefully. 10.1 in the *1964* Penguin "Caged Skylark" happens *not* to be justified against the right margin of the page and its internal spacing is unexceptional. However, in this later edition, the right end of 10.1 does align with the right end of the longest line in the sonnet below (not shown here)—about 6mm from the right margin of the text block. It seems that once it was centred left to right on the page, the compact shape of "In the Valley of the Elwy" must have dictated tabs and margins to the verses above it! The later sonnet may thus be said to have caged "The Caged Skylark".

In the 1953 printing, where this wrapping of 10.1 originated, v. 10 shows a similar but significantly different layout. 10.1 is the longest line on the second page of "The Caged Skylark". Verse 10 of "In the Valley of the Elwy", below it, is the longest line on the page, a mere 0.5mm longer than 10.1 in "the Caged Skylark". It may be that this small discrepancy points to revision in "The Caged Skylark" (and the subsequent argument suggests this notion is plausible). In any case, these variant lengths establish an *approximate* position of the internal right margin, against which 10.1 of "The Caged Skylark" seems to be justified. In the resetting of the 1964 Penguin, the line breaks at "to", the same word as in *1953* (in merely verbal imitation of copy, one supposes), but no longer under the influence of the absolute right margin, for in the 1964 setting, 10.1 is no longer the longest line on the page (as is clear in the illustration above, p. 198). A comparative reading of the dimensions of v. 10 in *1953* and *1964* thus reveals the greater arbitrariness of the location of the break in the later printing.

Our reading of the 1964 printing is where I want to bring these points home. I have suggested that, having become aware of the discrepant horizontal positioning of the two blocks of "The Caged Skylark" over the page break, we can intuit a disunity in

The Hiſtorie of King Lear.

Gloſt. Hartie thankes, the bonnet and beniz of heauen to
ſaue thee. *Enter Steward.*

Stew. A proclamed prize, moſt happy, that eyles head of thine
was framed fleſh to rayſe my fortunes, thou moſt vnhappy traytor, briefly thy ſelfe remember, the ſword is out that muſt de-
ſtroy thee.

Gloſt. Now let thy friendly hand put ſtrength enough to't.

Stew. VVherefore bould peſant durſt thou ſupport a publiſht
traytor, hence leaſt the infection of his fortune take like hold on
thee, let goe his arme ?

Edg. Chill not let goe ſir without cagion.

Stew. Let goe ſlaue, or thou dieſt.

Edg. Good Gentleman goe your gate, let poore voke paſſe,
and chud haue beene ſwaggar'd out of my life, it would not haue
beene ſo long by a fortnight, nay come not neare the old man,
keepe out, cheuore ye, or ile trie whether your coſter or my bat-
tero be the harder, ile be plaine with you.

Stew. Out dunghill, *they fight.*

Edg. Chill pick your teeth ſir, come, no matter for your foyns.

Stew. Slaue thou haſt ſlaine me, villaine take my purſe,
If euer thou wilt thriue, burie my bodie,
And giue the letters which thou find'ſt about me
To *Edmund* Earle of *Gloſter*, ſeeke him out vpon
The *Britiſh* partie, ô vntimely death ! death. *He dies.*

Edg. I know thee well, a ſeruiceable villaine,
As dutious to the vices of thy miſtres, as badnes would

Gloſt. What is he dead ? *(deſire.*

Edg. Sit you down father, reſt you lets ſee his pockets
Theſe letters that he ſpeakes of may be my friends,
Hee's dead, I am only ſorrow he had no other deathſmā
Let vs ſee, leaue gentle waxe, and manners blame vs not
To know our enemies minds wee'd rip their hearts,
Their papers is more lawfull.

Let your reciprocall vowes bee remembred, you haue many
opportunities to cut him off, if your will want not, time and place
will be fruitfully offered, there is nothing done, If he returne the
conquerour, then am I the priſoner, and his bed my gayle, from
the lothed warmth whereof deliuer me, and ſupply the place for
K your

the projection of the poem. But, if turning the leaf is too disorienting for such a critical realization to take place, a similar message appears anyway in the remainder of the poem on the second page: as we discern the "premature" break in 10.1, we are, in fact, reading intertextually. This break is not dictated by the Muse of the poem—is not, for example, a caesura, is not part of an enjambment. Rather it is a response to the spatial formatting of the poem that follows it on the page (a long-line poem is trying to look as trim as it companion) and to the over-abundant leading between poems on that page (the sonnets are trying to stand tall). It is also a response to the inflexible layout of the next page, and to the legacy of various solutions to the problem in previous Penguin "reprintings".

Examples of internal right-justification are not hard to come by. They are, for example, very common in the first quarto of Shakespeare's *King Lear*, 1608 (STC 22292), where we are dealing with letterpress, not monotype, and not with paper paste-ups or film. Take, for example, K1r, a page that mixes verse and prose. None of the verse lines in the lower half of the page comes close to spanning the full text block, as the prose lines do; but nevertheless one of the verses, that ending "would | (desire.", wraps (see the upper arrow), even though the width of the text block of this page could easily have accommodated the wrapped word at the end of the previous line, to make up a complete verse. Note that the tightly packed line of verse identified by the lower arrow comes to a stop at the same internal limit, in the word "deathsmā" (i.e, "death's-man"), which must have been tilde-contracted to fit the reduced measure. For the verse lines in this part of the page, a restricted length in the composing stick must have saved the compositor laborious justifying of the ends of each verse line with numerous spacing types. I suppose that a few pieces of furniture expeditiously filled in the right end of this group of short lines when the compositor moved them from his stick to the galley, where they joined the longer lines, for the top of the page, and were eventually followed by equally longer lines, for the base.

31. It may seem that there is a rule here: that poems continuing overleaf (from recto to verso) can get away with juggling their left margins, whereas poems that continue across the gutter (from verso to recto), like "Pied Beauty", are on show the whole time and cannot pull any fast ones. But there are examples to contradict this notion: "The Lantern Out of Doors" (pp. 28–29) continues across the gutter but has different zero tabs on each side of it.

32. Stephan Welliser, *"That Nature Is a Heraclitean Fire and of the Comfort of the Resurrection": A Case-Study in G. M. Hopkins' Poetry* (The Cooper Monographs), (A. Francke Verlag: Bern, 1977), 7. (A paste-on cancel on the title page corrects "Hopkin's" to "Hopkins'".) I also see the term "burden-line" in Gardner's "Sonnet Morphology", 107.

33. The page widths for Ms-A versions of "The Caged Skylark" and "Hurrahing in Harvest" are so narrow that, respectively, eight and six verses of each sonnet wrap. The body language of its symbolic indentation is thus quite obscured by the high ratio of letter size to page width.

Perhaps to accommodate his long lines without wrapping, Hopkins often wrote his poems so that the rules of the paper run perpendicular to the verses (*i.e.*, with the leaf in "landscape" position). In MacKenzie's *Later Poetic Manuscripts*, such rules can be made out on pp. 93 (see p. 229 of this essay, where I hope they will reproduce), 126, 190, 200, 272–73, 279, 283, 310–11, 316, 330, 339, 342, 344–46, and 348–49. (There may be other examples in the manuscripts that are not apparent in facsimile because of the high-contrast photography.)

Hopkins' writing across the rules is an apt symbol for the irregularity of his poetry and of his disregard for the prepared "portrait" model of communication. His practice offers a strong contrast to Bridges' red-ruling of the separate fragments into which he cut Hopkins' manuscripts in order to fit them into his album. See n. 60.

34. One is rather tempted to say the same "lack of indentation", but as I am speaking algebraically, zero indentation still counts. (There are, in effect, three different "grounds zero" on this Penguin page alone.)

35. The first Penguin edition omitted the comma after "Impatient", in v. 5, the first line of verse on the page. I presume that when the line was reset to include the comma, v. 6 was also reset.

36. In *1985*, the same wrong wrapping applies to "years" in the second tercet, but not to "tears" in the first, which remains as it was. On the previous page, the wrapping is also not changed. In this revised state, therefore, two of the five wrapped portions of verses are flush left. (Justified 12.1 offers another good example of disproportionate spacing.)

37. For examples of his drawings, see R. K. R. Thornton, ed., *All My Eyes See: The Visual World of Gerard Manley Hopkins* (Sunderland, England: Ceolfrith Press/Sunderland Arts Centre, 1975).

38. Letter LXXVII (Sept. 23, 1876) in Abbot, ed., *Further Letters*, 141–42, 141.

39. In his "Author's Preface", 101, Robert Bridges (who was the editor, of course, not the author) first drew attention to rhythms "rove over" from the end of one line to the start of the next (as discussed in n. 26). The concept impinges on rhyme, as to these—in "The Wreck": *leeward : drew her | D[ead] : endured* (st. 14); *rest of them! : unconfessed of them— : breast of the | M[aiden]* (st. 31); *Providence : of it, and | S[tartle]* (st. 31); *door | D[rowned] : reward : Lord* (st. 35). Here are some others. In "To what serves Mortal Beauty": *danc- | [ing] : glance : countenance : chance ; form : warm : storm : swarm | [-èd]*. In "The Loss of the Eurydice": *all un- | [warned] : fallen*. In "To seem the stranger": *dear : near | hear : wear | [-y]*. In "My own heart let me have more pity on" [so it reads in *1918*]: *awhile : smile | ['s] : mile*. In *Poems*, 1918, Bridges stated the general principle: "His intention in such places is that the verse should be recited as running on without pause, and the rhyme occurring in

their midst should be like a phonetic accident, merely satisfying the prescribed form." Here Bridges is certainly in accord with the passage I quoted from Hopkins' Note on p. 195 of this essay. But to Patmore, Bridges confided: "He has . . . an absolutely wrong notion of rhyme. He does not consider that it makes necessary any pause in the rhythm." (quoted from p. 118 of Catherine Phillips, *Robert Bridges: A Biography* (Oxford and New York: Oxford University Press), 1992). Bridges also found some of Hopkins' rhymes "hideous" purely on a phonetic basis, as this one in "The Bugler's First Communion"—*boon he on : Communion*. "When he indulges in freaks, his childishness is incredible." (*Poems*, 1918, 99).

40. Following Hopkins' later manuscripts, MacKenzie, *Poetical Works*, 1990, offers a further twist to the word "as- | tray": "as- | Tray". Formerly, Hopkins had written "a- | Stray". As the word means "off the street" (from L. *strata* via OFr. *estraier*), the poet's earlier usage was etymological, as one might expect from a professor of Classics. Hopkins' revision, however, forsakes etymology for the "logic" of his rhyme. (The lower-case "t" in "tray" originated with Bridges, who wrote an incredulous "Sic!" beside Hopkins' capital "T" in Ms A.)

41. Thanks, Ron Bogdan, Folger Shakespeare Library.

42. It would be interesting to know to what extent matching vowel length was sought out in rhymes before and after the Great Vowel Shift. After the Shift, vowel length ceased to be phonemic in English, and therefore speakers of Modern English are generally not aware of it. (Contrast the vowel lengths in the shorter "bit" and the longer "bid".)

43. Of course, there is a slim chance that Hopkins wrote "And" twice in a row, left to right, at the start of the line, before he caught the mistake (one of dittography, not of placement). But both the tight distance between the two settings of "And" and the slightly farther-left placement of the unindented one than the start of any unindented line before it in the poem argue that the deleted "And" was the first to be written. Furthermore, the fact that the next unindented line, v. 12, begins as far left as the protuberant "And" in v. 11 implies that the deletion of one "And" and the addition of the other occurred before v. 12 was begun.

44. *Later Poetic Manuscripts*, 104. In his 1990 edition, *Poetical Works*, published the previous year, MacKenzie makes no reference to this alleged nod, and he follows the inverted scheme. This editor holds for a rationale of indentation; but Hopkins may simply have "irrationalized"—or, in the spirit of "Pied Beauty", gone "counter". It is interesting that MacKenzie celebrates Hopkins' metrical oddity, but not that of his spatial formatting.

45. This dedication appeared again at the front of the second edition. In the third and the fourth, it was placed well into the volume and identified as the dedication to the first edition. It does not appear thereafter. In Gardner's Penguin editions, the dedication is to Bridges. In MacKenzie's 1990 edition, it is to members of his own family.

46. Michael Krotowski's deflating phrase is "Burning of the Duplicates". See n. 5.

47. Hopkins' letter to Bridges (Letter LIII, Feb. 15, 1879) in Abbott, ed., *Letters . . . to Bridges*, 65–67: "When I say that I do not mean to publish I speak the truth. I have taken and mean to take no step to do so beyond the attempt I made to print my two wrecks in the *Month*. . . . All therefore that I think of doing is to keep my verses together in one place—at present I have not even correct copies—, that, if anyone shd. like, they might be published after my death. . . . I cannot in conscience spend time on poetry, neither have I the inducements and inspirations that make others compose. Feeling, love in particular, is the great moving power and spring of verse and the only person that I am in love with seldom, especially now, stirs my heart sensibly and when he does I cannot always 'make capital' of it, it would be a sacrilege to do so. Then again I have of myself made verse so laborious.", 66.

48. Letter 106 (Aug. 10, 1889) from Bridges to Dixon (in Donald E. Stanford, ed., *The Selected Letters of Robert Bridges: with the Correspondence of Robert Bridges and Lionel Muirhead* (London and Toronto: Associated University Presses; Newark: University of Delaware Press, 1983), vol. 1, 188–89): "The last letter he wrote to me I have, but very

strangely it happened that the only two letters of his which I ever destroyed were the two which he wrote me preceding that . . . it was very like a sort of quarrel. He said in his last letter that he had been joking, and he added a sonnet (very sad) in 'explanation' but it did not read like joking, and the letters were rather bitter, so that I put them in the fire—of course I wish now that I had not done so.", 188. He also destroyed a half sheet, "the verse on which seemed of no account.", (MacKenzie, *Later Poetic Manuscripts*, 369).

There was destruction of correspondence by the Jesuits too. Father Wheeler, who dealt with Hopkins' effects, wrote to Bridges (Oct. 27, 1889): "Letters which I recognized by your writing or initials I set apart to forward. Many others I destroyed" (Abbott, ed., *Letters . . . to Robert Bridges*, vi).

49. These notes on long-s are partly drawn from the Textual Introduction to F. Harden's edition of Thackeray's *Henry Esmond* (New York: Garland, 1989), 407–08.

50. Despite the historical typographical consciousness implied by the presence of long-s in the Palatino fount in the body of this essay, the ragged-r (which looks like "2") is not available in black letter. Traditionally, it follows letters like w, h, y, b, d, o, and p, which, in this style have rounded right sides. Witness their shapes in CloisterBlack (also used on p. 262 of this essay): ꝡ, ꜧ, ꝑ, ꝏ, ꝺ, ꝋ and ꝓ—where the shapes of ꝡ and ꝺ are markedly different on their right sides than their roman counterparts. A traditional use of the ragged-r is seen in Daniel's setting of "wo_r_k" (v. 1); but the setting of the common-r in "wo_r_ld" earlier in the line is not traditional. There seems to be no rhyme or rhythm to Daniel's settings of common-r and ragged-r. (The fount of these notes, by the way, is Gill.)

All the sonnets in Bridges' 1889 publication conform to Hopkins' Model 9.

51. The *impresa* for the Daniel press was Daniel in the lion's den, with the motto, "MISIT ANGELVM SVVM"—"He sent his Angel". See the bibliography of the Daniel Press by Falconer Madan in *The Daniel Press: Memorials of C. H. O. Daniel, with a Bibliography of the Press, 1845–1919* (Oxford: Printed on the Daniel Press in the Bodleian Library, 1921). In 1899, Daniel printed in black-letter excerpts from Bridges' *The Yattendon Hymnal*. Bridges' *Shorter Poems*, issued in five parts in 1893–94 was, according to Madan, "the most considerable publication of the Daniel Press", 113. It was "a volume to be desired, the black letter giving", he claimed, "just the check to hasty reading which thoughtful and elaborate poems need.", III.

Bridges had other productions from this press in the Fell pica, which eventually became popular with Oxford University Press. (For more on Bridges' and Daniel's pioneering typography, see Catherine Phillips, *Robert Bridges, A Biography* (New York: Oxford University Press, 1992), 181.)

Daniel's use of long-s can be seen in plates VI, (1876), VII–VIII (1881), XII (1890), and XIII–XIV (1895) of *The Daniel Press.* (Pl. XV shows the third of Daniel's hand presses.)

52. In Watson's work, italics quotes Italian sonnets and translates them into Latin. His headnotes are in roman.

53. Bridges applied this term to Dolben, his cousin, who was also a convert to Catholicism. (He was another whose poetry Bridges edited, in 1911.)

54. Underlining of reported speech appears in Bridges' hand in st. 11 of "The Wreck" in Ms A; a pronoun "we", v. 5, is also underlined, evidently for stress; it is also accented. MacKenzie holds that this underlining likely derives from Hopkins' lost autograph. Bridges did not copy the underlining of Ms A into Ms B. Bridges generally did not favour shifts of fount (italics in print being the equivalent of underling in manuscript). (See MacKenzie, *Later Poetic Manuscripts*, 42n).

Soon after Hopkins' death, Bridges planned a volume of his verse from the Daniel Press, and he even went so far as to "suggest italics for memoir and early poems, and common type for POEMS" (Letter 109 (Oct. 11, 1889) in Stanford, *Selected Letters of . . . Bridges*, 1.190–91). Bridges' wife, Monica Waterhouse, is said to have influenced her husband's hand. Her *A New Handwriting for Teachers* appeared in 1898, and advocated the use of italic script (Phillips, *Robert Bridges*, 180).

55. Letter CLXIV (Aug. 16, 1883) in Abbott, ed., *Further Letters*, 295–96, 296.

56. A knowledge of the bibliographic structure of this edition informs a literary understanding of it. The editor's Contents page appears as the last recto of the half-sheet of preliminaries. As the Contents lists only Hopkins' works, there is no mention of Bridges' sonnet, which nevertheless appears on the next verso, the last page of preliminaries—within the survey of the Contents (we may suppose), but before the first title to which it refers, "Author's Preface ... p. 1", on the first recto of the new sheet, B, which faces Bridges' sonnet across the gutter. Technically, Bridges' sonnet may be thought to keep to its own side of the fence, but it effectively insinuates itself into the *"Go[ing] forth"* of *"gathered"* Hopkins, which, as Bridges styles it, his sonnet provokes, with the gratitude of the poet's spirit in Hopkins' closing sonnet.

Conventionally, Sheet B, with the beginning of Hopkins' text, would have been printed first, and the preliminaries printed last, or at least later. Thus, Hopkins' "To R. B." would likely have been printed before Bridges' invocation. Reading the book, we reverse that order.

The common, italic, typeface Bridges planned for both his memoir and Hopkins' early poems in the abortive Daniel Press volume (see n. 54) suggests a comparable elision of editor and poet.

57. Letter CLXXI (Apr. 29, 1889), the last from Hopkins to Bridges, Abbott, ed., *Letters ... to Robert Bridges*, 303–06: "I believe I enclose a new sonnet. But we greatly differ in feeling about copying one's verses out: I find it repulsive, and let them lie months and years in rough copy untransferred to my book. Still I hope to send you my accumulation. This one is addressed to you.", 304. (This sonnet was originally numbered "52" in Penguin, and then "53", at least by *1963*—not "51", as in *1918*. It is thus graphed by Model 7.)

58. Each first verse starts with a large capital, which extends into the line below. Thus, the second line of each sonnet in this edition is spaced off the left margin by the capital. I do not show this indentation in the model for the following reasons. The extra long first verse of Sonnet 22 happens to wrap onto a second line (where it is indented). In the setting of this sonnet alone, the second verse begins without indentation in l. 3, which is beyond the downward reach of the large cap of v. 1. And so, I take this unusual flush-left position of v. 2 as authorization to disregard the indentation of the second verses in all other sonnets, as being merely a mechanical function of the large cap at the start of the preceding verse, and not a symbolic placement.

59. The model for this sonnet (Model 7) was first used in *Robert Bridges and Contemporary Poets*, 1893 (vol. 8 of Alfred H. Miles, *The Poets and the Poetry of the Century*), 170. (Bridges edited this section of Miles' work.) He reused the model in *1918*.

60. To judge by the present line lengths, if Hopkins had not written in landscape format, he would have had to wrap a total of nine verses. See n. 33.

I see that a third poem, "Tom's Garland", the last Hopkins inscribed into Ms B after it returned to him in 1884, is similarly braced. This twenty-verse sonnet has two terminal tails, each with a brace. But, significantly, there is no additional brace uniting the two of them, as we might have expected from the manuscript of "Thou art indeed just, Lord". (In other words, braces do not always appear in layered combinations.) These three poems are dated September, 1887 ("Tom's Garland"); March 17, 1889 ("Thou are indeed just, Lord"); and April 22, 1889 ("To. R. B."). Hopkins usually repeated the date of original composition in later drafts, and so these annotations are unreliable for dating his initial use of braces. But bracing certainly seems to have been his last experimentation with the physical shaping of his sonnets. MacKenzie (*1990*) is the first editor to display the braces.

61. I *do* wish I had known all this before I made my damned models—or before I brought you this far into the essay. Sorry. Won't happen again.

62. The text varies in the second edition, 1930: "And so have I ...".

63. Reproduced by permission of A. P. Watt Ltd. on behalf of Michael B. Yeats.

64. Robert Bridges, ed., *The Spirit of Man* (London, New York, Bombay, Calcutta &

Madras: Longmans Green & Co: , 1916), Poem 38 and n.

65.   In "Robert Bridges and the First Edition of Gerard Manley Hopkins's *Poems*" (in Eugene Hollahan, ed., *Gerard Manley Hopkins and Critical Discourse* (New York: AMS Press, c. 1993), 297, Catherine Phillips defends Bridges against the charge (from Hopkins among others) of deliberate antiquing. His verb endings in "–eth", she suggests, were rather a cultivation of "sibilance, to which we are now practically deaf"—though I think "thibilanthe" would be more apt. As this example transforms not only Tagore's sound, but also his diction and grammar, I read it primarily as a cultivation of editorial arrogance.

66.   A full account of Yeats' quick acquiescence and Tagore's prolonged resistance is documented in their correspondence with Bridges and in his with them—which, in this case, he did not burn. See Richard J. Finneran, ed., *The Correspondence of Robert Bridges and William Butler Yeats* (Toronto: MacMillan, 1977), esp. 25 and 40–43. He also cites Mary M. Lago, ed., *Imperfect Encounter: Letters of William Rothenstein and Rabindranath Tagore, 1911–1941* (Cambridge, Mass.: Harvard University Press, 1972), esp. 177–202. (*Gitanjali* is dedicated to Rothenstein.) Here Bridges uses a more frank term in his annotation to his correspondence: "verbal alterations" (179).

67.   Bridges did follow Model 6, however, when he edited the poem for vol. 8 of Miles' *The Poets and the Poetry of the Century*, 1893, 168.

68.   He deleted "a" in v. 3, changed "At" to "by" in v. 5, and deleted the question mark at the end of v. 13. He added the accent in "aggrándize" (v. 8), "~" over the vowels in "window" and "wandering" in vv. 5 and 6, and also noted the place and date, in the lower right. He left "are" in v. 13, where his own two drafts both show "Are". ("Are", with an initial capital, is in both Bridges' published versions.) In v. 8, the exaggerated space between "There" and "God" is sometimes empty, and sometimes it contains a slash or a comma.

69.   Letter CLXXVI D (Mar. 20, 1884) in Abbot, ed., *Further Letters*, 2nd ed., 352–54: "My dear Mr. Hopkins,—I have read your poems—most of them several times—and find my first impression confirmed with each reading. It seems to me that the thought and feeling of these poems, if expressed without any obscuring novelty of mode, are such as often to require the whole attention to apprehend and digest them; and are therefore of a kind to appeal only to the few. But to the already sufficiently arduous character of such poetry you seem to me to have added the difficulty of following *several* entirely novel and simultaneous experiments in versification and construction, together with an altogether unprecedented system of alliteration and compound words;—any one of which novelties would be startling and productive of distraction from the poetic matter to be expressed." To Bridges he wrote that Hopkins' "poetry has the effect of veins of pure gold imbedded in masses of unpracticable quartz. . . . His genius is, however, unmistakable, and is lovely and unique in its effects whenever he approximates to the ordinary rules of composition" (May 2, 1884).

70.   Hopkins wrote two curtal sonnets, the other titled "Peace" (which has different spatial formatting), and he provided an arithmetic account of them at the end of his notes on metre associated with Ms B: "Curtal-Sonnets . . . are constructed in proportions resembling those of the sonnet proper, namely 6 + 4 instead of 8 + 6, with however a halfline tailpiece (so that the equation is rather $12/2 + 9/2 = 21/2 = 10 \frac{1}{2}$)." (In *1918*, "12/2" appears mistakenly as "12/8".)

Curiously, the first two editions print "halfline" as a single word, but without the fl ligature used elsewhere in these texts. Gardner's Oxford and Penguin editions used the ligature. When Gardner edited with MacKenzie, the ligature was dropped, but "halfline" still appears as a single word. Phillips' Oxford Classics edition, 1998, offers "half line"—two words.

71.   Note that this model does not attempt to capture the great indentation of the last line, a subject to be taken up shortly.

72.   In "Bridges and the First Edition of . . . Hopkins's *Poems*", 298, Catherine Phillips holds that "Bridges' beautiful transcriptions of Hopkins's poems showed Hopkins in a

practical way that Bridges valued his work." Certainly, Bridges' creation of Ms B is a sign of such value; but its "beauty" is problematic, as its aesthetic is frequently at odds with Hopkins'. Beauty is not neutral.

73. The column width of this edition is 1mm less, and so the length of each full line of type is shorter. The line height, however, remains the same. Thus, superimposing the images of these two Penguin editions would show that the stanzas occupy the same height on the page, though not the same width. The extra leading between poems is variable: above "14" (not shown here) it is different in the two editions, but it is equal above "15".

74.   One might think that "revisions" in a reprinting must mean "corrections", and so Gardner may have deemed them (if ever he read proofs of "reprintings", the resetting of which he had not been informed of, or where he had not requested specific changes). But later settings can be erroneous, as when, in the start of the third line of this very poem , "Rose moles all in stipple", which was correct in the 1967 "reprint", changed to "For rose-moles in all stipple" at least by the 1988 reprint. (The error was still in the class text my students used a decade later.)

75.   Lancashire, "RP edition: RPO 1996–2000". "Recent editing: 2:2002/3/14". (See n. 12 for the web address.) The copy text is Ms B. This editor also records "Rhyme: abcabcdbede", an unprecedented precipitation of e rhymes out of c. But this wrong analysis is contradicted by his four-tab indentation scheme, which aligns e and c verses. Unlike Hopkins, who tabs the verses with a and d rhymes alike, the editor rationalizes and gives d a separate tab: Lancashire's "Práise hím." aligns with his other verses with c and e rhymes, but Hopkins gave this line a unique tab, thereby conspicuously escaping any previous rationale of his graphic styling. Although poet and editor both use four tabs in the second strophe, they agree on the tabbing of only two of its five lines. Models for Bridges' and Lancashire's shapes can be contrasted with that for Hopkins' own in Ms A, shown above on p. 252.

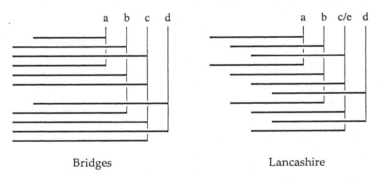

a   b   c   d   a   b c/e d

Bridges   Lancashire

76. Letter CX, Abbot, Letters ... to Robert Bridges, 186–89, 189.

77. MacKenzie offers another possible reason for Hopkins' inclusion of this note (one anticipating the audience rather than reacting to the editor, as I suggested): "Hopkins's autograph preface on Rhythm (ff. 1–5) may have been written specifically for Coventry Patmore's benefit, because of the latter's interest in metrical law, and have been inserted in album B before it was posted to Patmore in 1884" (Later Poetic Manuscripts, 361). ("Inserted" is used loosely here, I think, as we don't know where these extra pages were placed relative to Ms B when Hopkins sent them to Patmore.)

78. Concordances of Hopkins' verse do not show accents. Nor do they gloss a common word like "and" (except when it occurs in hyphenated compounds). But, in Ms B, I do see the conjunction stressed in "The Lantern Out of Doors", v. 14: "Their ránsom, théir rescue, & first, fást, last friend." (The only other manuscript of this poem, Ms A, has none of these accents.) Obviously, Hopkins could add a stress to one of Bridges' ampersands.

The dynamics here are especially interesting, as the three syllables of "rescue⁀,&" are to be uttered as two, and the second stressed. (The tercet containing this verse is the one which Hopkins began indented, as if for Model 15, but then revised as Model 20. See pp. 222 and 232.)

79. Without the stress on the conjunction, the metrics of this line is clear to Hopkins scholars. But with it, the line seems to have too many beats. See Edward A. Stephenson, *What Sprung Rhythm Really Is* (Alma, Ontario: The International Hopkins Association, Monograph 4, 1987), 71–72, where he builds on an idea of Gardner's, that the *sforzando* is indeed allowed stress—but not so as to count in the metrical scheme! Paradoxically, in a stuffed line, one ending in "billion", the parsimonious critic strives to rein in the metre to a mere six beats. But isn't the point to go extravagant? (See Gardner, "Sonnet Morphology", 94, n. 3(a), where both ">" and "AND" are regarded, paradoxically, as "*Heavy stress* (non-metrical)".)

Hopkins himself encouraged paradoxical thinking about another of his metrical oddities, the "outriding foot", which is, "by a sort of contradiction, a recognized extra-metrical effect; it is and it is not part of the metre; not part of it, not being counted, but part of it by producing a calculated effect which tells in the general success" (quoted from my 1964 Penguin edition, 228–29).

80. Throughout Ms B, Bridges frequently substituted ampersand for "and". But he kept "And" (with an initial capital) for the beginning of a verse, the opening of a parenthesis, and once, at least, for the beginning of a sentence in mid verse. He also kept "and" for the last word in a verse. Here are examples of the structures in which Bridges wrote out "And" rather than his usual ampersand. Bridges' transcription of "God's Grandeur" has four verses that begin with "And", each following punctuation (a period or semicolon) at the end of the previous line. In "The Candle Indoors", by contrast, his "And" beginning a line of verse falls in the middle of a sentence. In st. 31 of "The Wreck of the Deutschland" "and" (in lower case) appears in mid sentence at the end of a verse (v. 7)—where it falls in the middle of a rhyme (*Providence : of it, and* | S[*tartle*]). "The Leaden Echo and The Golden Echo", v. 45, has "and" following an opening parenthesis. Verse 2 of "The Lantern Out of Doors" offers the clearest structural parallel to v. 10 of "The Windhover". This time, Bridges used "And" rather than "&" in mid line at the beginning of a sentence. (The line below it, by the way, offers "&" in the middle of a sentence and verse. There are three other ampersands, and the last, in v. 14, is stressed.)

81. In the note to p. 123, however, MacKenzie's facsimile sets the word in large caps, a typographical style that may have been forced on him because of fount restrictions in the apparatus.

82. I suppose Hopkins could have more simply emended by placing a wedge over Bridges' ampersand, as he placed an acute accent over Bridges' ampersand in "The Lantern out of Doors" (see n. 78). But such an unprecedented mark would presumably have referred to the entire logo and not just to a letter (the vowel) in the English word that the ampersand stood for. (Of course, "AND" all in caps also stresses the whole word.) In his representation of the stresses in this poem in "Sonnet Morphology", 99, Gardner draws ">" from Ms A, but places it over the *second* letter of "AND", a consonant.

83. Bridges' copy for Ms B was the later Ms-A version ("Another version"), not the one shown above, on pp. 233–34. (It can be seen in MacKenzie, *Later Poetic Manuscripts*, 122.) The beginning of v. 4, ": Hung so and rung" in the final reading of Ms A¹, became ": O how he rung" in Ms A².

84. In Letter XXXV (Aug. 8, 1877) in Abbot, ed., *Letters . . . to Robert Bridges*, 42–43, Hopkins offered revisions to "The Caged Skylark" with two "great colons" (as he termed them himself). (One of them occurs, startlingly, after the first syllable of a word: "un:cumberèd".) He also pointed out to Bridges that he had not yet thought of this symbol when he wrote "The Wreck of the Deutschland", in 1875. I see the great colon for

the first time in "The Lantern Out of Doors", 1877. But, as I already noted (n. 60), Hopkins dated revisions with the date of original composition.

See MacKenzie, *Poetical Works*, lxi, for an ingenious argument for dating "The Lantern" between 24 February and 25 July on the basis of line-spacing and indentations. (MacKenzie subsequently thought Hopkins had corrupted the indentation in his immediate revision in Ms A. (See n. 44)

Editors are inconsistent in their regard for and analysis of the great colon. In his "Sonnet Morphology", 101, Gardner quotes the Ms A version of "Henry Purcell" as an example of Hopkins' successful attempt to "grapple" with "the equal division of the alexandrine". But his transcription omits much necessary evidence. He reflects only one of the three line spacings of the manuscript, that after the octave, and neglects those between the quatrains and tercets (as does Ms B); and, of the eight great colons, he offers merely the first three, rendering only the first two of them bold. As he omits all great colons from his editions, it is not surprising that this attempt to represent them in a critical argument is clumsy, even though they are key to it. (I see, however, that by the fourth impression, 1966, all the great colons were in place in this poem, although the third is still not bold.)

According to Edward Stephenson, *What Sprung Rhythm Really Is*, 42, "A great colon within the line usually means that metrical stresses fall on the syllables before and after it. At the beginning of a line, it indicates that the following syllable is stressed." (Gardner, however, had defined it as a "*Normal* stress (Metrical)... before the stressed syllable", 94, n.) In any event, these alleged rules do not explain at least three of the five colons in the chart on p. 266 of this essay: those in vv. 12–13, 14, or 5. (And what are we to do with v. 13 of "Hurrahing in Harvest": "The heart : rears : wings : bold<er> and bolder"? MacKenzie (*1990*) offers "The héart réars wíngs bóld and bolder", which evades the issue of Hopkins' *redundant* stress on "rears" and "wings", which both have great colons before and aft.)

Alas—or hurrah—Hopkins' metrical indications do not form a stable and consistent system.

85. MacKenzie, *Poetical Works*, xxxix, "In other places where he wished to revise, with misplaced aesthetic zeal he imitated Bridges' graceful italic script so closely that no knowledge of their respective hands is sufficient to determine who made the change."

86. The next seven excerpts from Hopkins' letters come from Abbott, *Letters ... to Robert Bridges,* Letter CXI, 189–91, 190; CXIII, 191–92; CXV, 193–94, 194; CXVI, 194–95; CXVII, 195–97; CLIV, 263–64, 264; CLVII, 268–72, 270.

87. Letter CXXX (Sept 1, 1885), 220-23, in Abbott, *Letters ... to Robert Bridges*, 221.

88. MacKenzie, *Later Poetic Manuscripts*, 361–63, does, however, offer a very helpful "Contents of Ms. B", which gives a detailed mapping of the manuscript and correlates its pages with plates in the facsimiles and the numbering of his 1990 Oxford edition. But he does not report the numbering of the poems in this very manuscript! MacKenzie also identifies the major historical layers of the manuscript, so that one can understand what parts of it Patmore would have seen and which came later. My delay in visualizing Ms B entire stems from my plunging into the photo-facsimiles of the body of MacKenzie's book, and coming late to his apparatus at the back of it. I could have read more wisely, but I suppose my *modus operandy* is not atypical. Anyway, though I now know how to reconstruct Ms B out of the facsimile images, I still cannot see it whole, as a facsimile of that text alone would allow me to do.

89. See n. 54.

90. MacKenzie, *Later Poetic Manuscripts*, 361.

91. *Poems*, 1918, p. 106.

92. MacKenzie, *Poetical Works*, xxxix

The Flights of A 821
Dearchivizing the Proceedings of a Birdsong

MARTA WERNER

For Randall McLeod (Random Cloud)

flight: *(flait),* sb.[1] 1.a. *The action or manner of flying or moving through the air with or as with wings. . . . e. Of birds or insects: a migration or issuing forth in bodies. . . .* 2.a. *Swift movement in general; esp. of a projectile, etc. through the air. . . .* 3. fig. *a. A mounting or soaring out of the regular course or beyond ordinary bounds; an excursion or sally (of the imagination, wit, intellect, ambition, etc.). . . .* †4. *A state of flutter or agitation; a trembling, fright. . . .* 6.a. *The distance which a bird can or does fly. . . .* 6.b. *The distance to which a missile may be shot. . . .* 8. *A collection or flock of beings or things flying in or passing through the air together. . . .* 9. *The young birds that take wing at one time, e.g., the* March Flight *or the* May flight. . . . 10. *A flight-arrow. . . .* **flight,** sb. [2]. 1.a. *The action of fleeing. . . . as from danger . . . an absconding. . . .* **flight,** sb. 3. Obs. a. *A flake of snow.* b. *A violent storm (of snow). . . .* **flight,** v. †2. intr. *To fluctuate, change. . . .* [3]. † a. *To migrate, flit, fleet* (obs.). . . . *to fly in flights. . . .* 4. trans. *To set flying. . . .*

—*Oxford English Dictionary*

I. Signs & Wonders

Among Dickinson's late papers is a manuscript—one text, several texts?—especially marked by the signs of flight. The manuscript, here identified by its catalog number, A 821, constitutes a kind of exit text. It may have been composed in a few minutes, or even seconds, in the early spring of 1885, since one line of the text reappears, slightly altered, in three fair-copy drafts of a letter from Dickinson to Helen Hunt Jackson, composed in March of that year but apparently never completed or mailed. In Thomas H. Johnson and Theodora Ward's *The Letters of Emily Dickinson,* this text is annexed to these drafts as a footnote. Its provenance, however, and the date of its composition, remain unconfirmed. I found it first by accident, in the Amherst College Library, when it fell (rose?) out of an acid-free envelope, out of the space of claustration. If I had not held it lightly in my own hands, I would never have suspected the manner in which it was assembled. Although its brevity and immediacy place it outside the reach of conventional classificatory gestures, it bears a striking affinity to the genre David Porter names "small, rickety infinitudes."[1] Look at it now, flying on the page, vying with light (fig. 1).

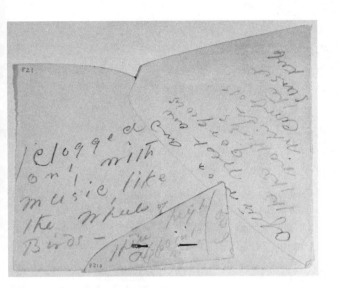

Figure 1.   A 821 / A 821a. Last decade. Lines penciled on two fragments of envelope held together with a straight pin.

Far away, so close!—Wim Wenders

II. Taxonomy of Paper Wings

A 821 is a "sudden" collage made of two, possibly three, sections of envelope.[2] The principles of its construction are economical, even austere. The larger section of the collage is the inside of the back of an envelope, the address face of which has been torn or cut away. One vertical crease bisects the document, turning the halved envelope into a diptych resembling the hinged leaves of the codex book Dickinson had long since abandoned and the wings of the bird the manuscript is becoming. Initially, the leaves / wings appear to have been folded, perhaps even pinned, closed; at rest, the manuscript is not yet transformed into a fully living figure. Another section of text, perhaps the last, is composed on an unfolded triangular corner of the envelope's severed seal; it has been designated by the cataloger "A 821a."[3] A single straight pin, still in place in June 1997, imps[4] the collage elements together while also spreading open the larger envelope fragment to reveal a blurred message about an imminent transition, or about the desire of writing to intervene between the visible and the invisible. The unfolding of the manuscript creates a strange visual rhyming of wings.

On the right wing, the lines "Afternoon and / the West and / the gorgeous / nothings / which / compose / the / sunset / keep" slant upward into the west.

Figure 2.   A 821 / A 821a, rotations.

On the left wing, the lines "Clogged / only with / Music, like / the Wheels of / Birds -" slant diagonally upward into the east.

On the smaller, pinned wing, writing rushes beyond the tear / terminus where the seen meets the unseen in "their high / Appointment."

Are we day or are we night?—Peter Greenaway

The singing of birds marks—some believe causes—both the break and the close of day.[5] If we read from left to right across the contours of the open wings, A 821 / A 821a appears to record the moment when day falls into night. Yet the grammar—*syntax*—of wings is the grammar of discontinuity. The slight variations in the handwriting on opposing wings suggest that the texts they carry were composed on different occasions; moreover, on each wing, writing, inscribed by Velocity, rushes in opposite directions. To access the text(s), and to answer the question of where we have arrived, we must enter into a volitional relationship with the fragment, turning it point by point, like a compass, or a pinwheel—like the *wheels of thought*. 360 degrees. As we rotate the text, disorienting and orienting it at once, day and night, each a whir of words, almost converge in the missing body spaces just beyond the light seams showing the bifurcation in the envelope, then fly apart in a synesthesia of sight and sound (see fig. 2).[6]

How do you know but ev'ry Bird that cuts the airy way,
Is an immense world of delight clos'd by your senses five?
                                                    —William Blake

Joy and Gravitation have their own ways - —Emily Dickinson

III. Gravity Fields

The three fair-copy drafts of Dickinson's last letter to Helen Hunt Jackson, composed across parts of eleven leaves of fine Irish linen stationery, shifting between prose and verse, respond to Jackson's letter of February 3 containing news of her prolonged suffering from a broken leg:

Santa Monica / Cal. / By the Sea. / Feb. 3. 1885

My dear Miss Dickinson,

Thank you heartily for the fan. It is pathetic, in its small-ness - poor souls - how did they come to think of making such tiny ones. - I shall wear it sometimes, like a leaf on my breast. -

Your letter found me in Los Angeles, where I have been for two months & a little more. - Sunning myself, and trying to get on my feet. - I had hoped by this time to be able to go without crutches, and venture to New York, for the remainder of the winter - but I am disappointed. So far as the broken leg is concerned, I could walk with a cane now: but the whole leg having been badly strained by doing double duty so long, is obstinate about getting to work again, is very lame and sore, & I am afraid badly given out - so that it will take months for it to recover. - I dislike this exceedingly; - but dare not grumble, lest a worse thing befall me: & if I did grumble, I should deserve it, - for I am absolutely well - drive the whole of every afternoon in an open carriage on roads where larks sing & flowers are in bloom: I can do everything I ever could - except walk! - and if I never walk again it will still remain true that I have had more than a half centurys excellent trotting out of my legs - so even then, I suppose I ought not be rebellious. - Few people get as much out of one pair of legs as I have! -

This Santa Monica is a lovely little Seaside hamlet, - only eighteen miles from Los Angeles, - one of the most beautiful Seaside places I ever saw: green to the *tip* edge of the cliffs, flowers blooming and choruses of birds, all winter. - There can be nothing in this world nearer perfection than this South California climate for winter. - Cool enough to make a fire necessary, night & morning: but warm enough to keep flowers going, all the time, in the open air, - grass & barley are many inches high - some of the "volunteer" crops already in head. - As I write - (in bed, before breakfast,) I am looking straight off towards Japan - over a silver sea - my foreground is a strip of high grass, and mallows, with a row of Eucalyptus trees sixty or seventy feet high: - and there is a positive cackle of linnets.

Searching here, for Indian relics, especially the mortars or bowls hollowed out of stone, with the solid stone pestles they used to pound their acorns in, I have found two Mexican women called *Ramona,* from whom I have bought the Indian mortars. -

I hope you are well - and at work - I wish I knew by now what your portfolios, by this time, hold.

Yours ever truly
Helen Jackson.[7]

Dear friend -

To reproach my own Foot in behalf of your's, is involuntary, and finding myself, no solace in "whom he loveth he chasteneth" your valor astounds me - It was only a small Wasp, said the French Physician, repairing the sting, but the strength to perish is sometimes withheld - though who but you could tell a Foot.

Take all away
from me, but leave
me Ecstasy
And I am richer
then, than all
my Fellow men -
Is it becoming
me to dwell so
wealthily,
When at my very
Door are those
possessing more,
In abject Poverty?

That you compass [glance at] "Japan" before you breakfast, not in the least surprises me, clogged [thronged] only with Music, like the Wheels [Decks] of Birds -

Thank you for hoping I am well - Who could be ill in March, that month of proclamations? Sleigh Bells and Jays contend in my Matinee,

and the North surrenders, instead of the South, a reverse of Bugles -
   Pity me, however, I have finished Ramona -
   Would that like Shakespeare, it were just published! Knew I how to
pray, to intercede for your Foot were intuitive - but I am but a Pagan -

   Of God we ask
   one favor,
   that we may
   be forgiven -
   For what, he is
   presumed to know -
   The Crime, from
   us, is hidden -
   Immured the whole
   of Life
   Within a magic
   Prison
   We reprimand the
   Happiness
   That too com-
   petes with Heaven -

May I once more know, and that you are saved?

Your Dickinson -[8]

   The epistolary relation is grounded in and exposed to time.[9] Before
Dickinson could complete and mail a finished copy of the letter, before
she could finish her last sentence, the newspapers announced Jackson's
death. Her carefully drafted response to Jackson's morning letter of
February 3 reaches its destination only belatedly, in the subjective night
of its intended recipient.[10]
   How can we ever verify the degree of match between what is transmitted and what is received?
   Cut to A 821 (fig. 3): "Clogged only with Music, like the Wheels of
Birds -"
   A 821 may be a poem-breaking-out-of-prose, a time-shifted bird
flown out of the constellations of March, a letter's vanishing point, a
translation of speed or spirit into a kind of handwriting, a dart that
returns immediately to the sender. What it conveys is not a "message"
but the sensation of *seeing*, for the last time.[11]
   In the visual linguistics of both an earlier mystical imagery and an

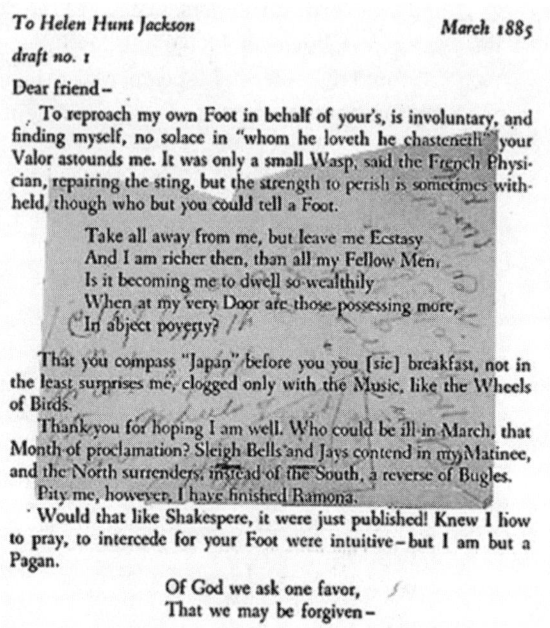

Figure 3. A 821 / A 821a, rising out of the letter drafts. Reprinted from Thomas H. Johnson and Theodora Ward, eds., *The Letters of Emily Dickinson*, 3 vols. (Cambridge, Mass.: Belknap Press of Harvard University Press, 1958), letter 976.

To Helen Hunt Jackson   *March 1885*

draft no. 1

Dear friend –

   To reproach my own Foot in behalf of your's, is involuntary, and finding myself, no solace in "whom he loveth he chasteneth" your Valor astounds me. It was only a small Wasp, said the French Physician, repairing the sting, but the strength to perish is sometimes withheld, though who but you could tell a Foot.

> Take all away from me, but leave me Ecstasy
> And I am richer then, than all my Fellow Men,
> Is it becoming me to dwell so wealthily
> When at my very Door are those possessing more,
> In abject poverty?

   That you compass "Japan" before you you [sic] breakfast, not in the least surprises me, clogged only with the Music, like the Wheels of Birds.

   Thank you for hoping I am well. Who could be ill in March, that Month of proclamation? Sleigh Bells and Jays contend in my Matinee, and the North surrenders, instead of the South, a reverse of Bugles. Pity me, however, I have finished Ramona.

   Would that like Shakespere, it were just published! Knew I how to pray, to intercede for your Foot were intuitive – but I am but a Pagan.

> Of God we ask one favor,
> That we may be forgiven –

Edenic physics, wings / wheels are signifiers for immateriality, for bodies that are not subject to the laws of gravity, and which can communicate between time and eternity.[12] By composing A 821 / A 821a on the reverse of an empty, unaddressed envelope, no longer the container for a message, but the message itself, Dickinson creates a template for a flight that is also a trope for her late, contrapuntal communications, in which "arrival" is another word for "departure," and where reaching a final destination involves a radical displacement—the loss of all topoi. Unlike the letter, a narrative of illness and death, boundlessly gravid, the undated because dateless fragment is a site of radical temporality. Bird of paradox and paradise, A 821's defection from the linear narrative of the letter signals the annihilation of continuity, the instantaneous translation from one condition into another. A 821 flies to the outermost edges of Dickinson's production, then out of this world.

   In August (perhaps) of 1885, on postal wrappers, Dickinson composed the following ex-static postscript to Hunt Jackson: "Dear friend, can you walk were the last words that I wrote to her - Dear friend I can fly - her immortal soaring reply -."[13]

And if there's no gravity, who needs hours?—Peter Greenaway

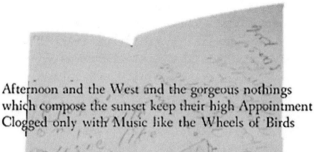

Figure 4. A 821 / A 821a, superimposed over the printed text of the fragment.

Afternoon and the West and the gorgeous nothings which compose the sunset keep their high Appointment Clogged only with Music like the Wheels of Birds

IV. Imprints

When A 821 was published as a footnote following the letter drafts addressed to Hunt Jackson,[14] it was denied its autonomy (autonomies), and the motion of its wings was arrested: subsumed under the metrics of the letter and reset in immovable type—pinned into a single temporality and spatiality—the iconic implications of the manuscript vanish; the conjunction of writing and sensuous representation manifested by the fragment-becoming-bird fails to take place. Lines broken according to the conventions of typesetting "prose" break the wings of the text, transgress the light internal junctions, the imbrications and tracery, as well as the outer edges of the envelope fragments, that mark the limits of a thought or the junctures between (flights of) thoughts. In the printed text, moreover, the music of the invisible bird is no longer audible. The syntactical discontinuities created by the folding and unfolding, the conjoining and breaking away, of A 821 / A 821a's word-wings are resolved via an editorial reordering of the text fragments into a smooth grammatical flight. The gravity of the "sentence" checks the flight of the image (fig. 4): "Afternoon and the West and the gorgeous nothings which compose the sunset keep their high Appointment Clogged only with Music like the Wheels of Birds."[15]

A vision has become legible.

V. Flight Paths

If you saw a bullet / hit a Bird - —Emily Dickinson, A 828

Figure 5. A 821 / A 821a, some possible trajectories of flight, bird's-eye view. Pinholes have been highlighted.

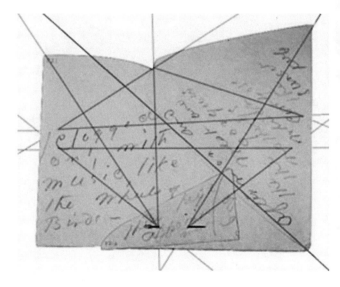

> . . . *and with new pinions refresh*
> *Her wearied wings, which so restored did flye*
> —Henry Vaughan

A bird's lost powers of flight may be restored by imping the feathers of another to it. Pinned to the body of A 821, the small arrow-wing called A 821a appears to mend (i.e., complete) the text on the right wing and also to name the fragment's destination, "their high / Appointment." Yet this wing, hardly more than a feather, did not always determine the arc of A 821's flight. On the body of A 821 four additional sets of pin-pricks, two along the outer edges of the left wing and two along the outer edges of the right wing, are signs of at least four previous trajectories or changes in course. Perhaps A 821, like A 821a, was once imped to other, more expansive wings out of which it has fallen or from which it is still ascending. The wings of a *letter,* perhaps. Alternatively, several small fragments like A 821a may have been appended to the extremities of A 821 to help pilot earlier, apprenticeship flights of brief duration, flights that missed their marks or found them suddenly. Like birds that migrate only so long as the "drive" is present, the durations of the fragments' previous flights, the timings and directions of their collisions and releases, and the relations among them remain mysterious, most completely unrecoverable. Pinned, unpinned, repinned, the fragments' flights shatter the deep, one-point perspective of the letter, reveal the extraordinarily complex and conflicted intentions of the writer (fig. 5).

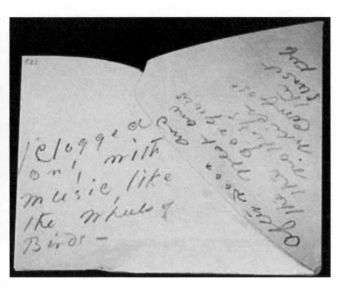

Figure 6.   A 821, sans pinned slip.

The pin complicates the play among past, present, and future, keeps the texts / birds flying in a splintered mode of time, in the "terrifying tense" of pure transition.[16] For here, the expectations of closure or *parousia*— "their high / Appointment"—may be endlessly postponed, or reversed, with the drop of a pin (fig. 6).

The caesuras and sudden discontinuities initially perceived in the opening of A 821 / A 821a's wings are intensified in the linking and breaking away of lap- or lost wings. To say the least, the common meter of the hymn found in Dickinson's early, bound poems has not survived this latest flight. On the contrary, in the (un)pinned texts of the 1870s and 1880s one hears an acceleration followed by snapping or short-circuiting of lyrical wires. In the late texts it is not often the unification (i.e., "completion") but the juxtaposition of texts that pinning brings about. In place of melody and measure come suddenness and syncope:[17] "meter with neither more nor less, but an impossible measure";[18] " + No Bird - but rode in Ether -."[19]

VI. A Flight of Fragments: Toward a Bibliography of Departures

W. H. Hudson says that birds feel something akin to pain (and fear) just before migration and that nothing alleviates this feeling except flight (the rapid motion of wings).

—Lorine Niedecker

Figure 7. "She died - this was the way she died -." Reprinted from Ralph W. Franklin, ed., *The Manuscript Books of Emily Dickinson*, vol. I (Cambridge, Mass.: Belknap Press of Harvard University Press, 1981), fascicle 7, c. 1859.

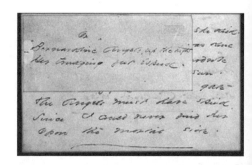

A certain set of operations repeated again and again, like the rapid motions of wings, may signify that a further migration is about to take place . . .

A few early harbingers of later flights appear scattered throughout Dickinson's fascicles (the bound packets of her poems) and the sets (gatherings of loose sheets perhaps prepared for binding). The first pinned fragment appears in fascicle 7, composed in 1859. It carries an alternate reading, one of the first variants to occur in the fascicles, for the fifth and sixth lines of the poem beginning "She died - this was the way she died -." It is inscribed on the verso of a small slip of notepaper but inserted as a recto (fig. 7).

Two more pinned texts appear in the fascicles bound in 1862, one in fascicle 16, the other in fascicle 19. In both instances the pinned slips— here small, but whole leaves of notepaper—carry the final, overflow lines of the poems to which they are fastened. Here, pinning appears to be a kind of binding, *double-binding:* a slip carrying the variant or final lines of a poem is pinned over a poem that is itself stab-bound into a fascicle (figs. 8, 9).

Yet the pinned slips carrying variants, endings, and variant endings also announce a crisis at and of the limits of the text. In the unbound leaves of the sets, themselves vulnerable to scattering, the association of pinned slips with the bodies of poems is more tenuous. In the final instance of pinning in the sets, the pin is deployed as an extreme mark of punctuation, a dash doubled and made material: it writes the poem apart (fig. 10).

If pinning was initially used as an alternative method of binding, a way of associating variants and overflow lines with poems, it immediately declared its difference from binding. Unlike binding, which is premeditated, permanent, and serial, pinning is instantaneous, temporary, random. In the 1870s and 1880s, as the "data" to be explained by poetry became more and more extreme, Dickinson's compositional practices

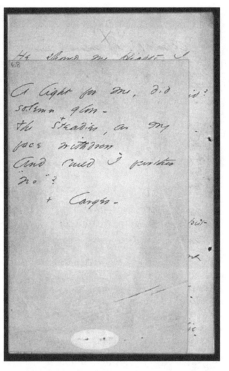

Figure 8. "He showed me Hights | I never saw -." Reprinted from Ralph W. Franklin, ed., *The Manuscript Books of Emily Dickinson*, vol. I (Cambridge, Mass.: Belknap Press of Harvard University Press, 1981), fascicle 16, c. 1862.

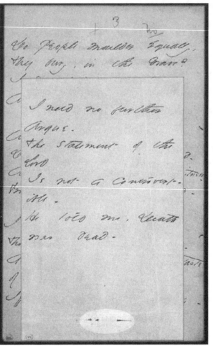

Figure 9. "Do People moulder Equally." Reprinted from Ralph W. Franklin, ed., *The Manuscript Books of Emily Dickinson*, vol. I (Cambridge, Mass.: Belknap Press of Harvard University Press, 1981), fascicle 19, c. 1862.

Figure 10. "Of the Heart that | goes in, and closes the | Door." Reprinted from Ralph W. Franklin, ed., *The Manuscript Books of Emily Dickinson*, vol. 2 (Cambridge, Mass.: Belknap Press of Harvard University Press, 1981), set 6c, c. 1866.

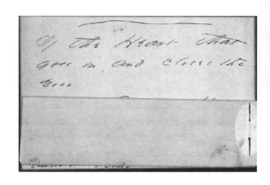

registered that extremity. Fragments, fractions of poems cut into smaller and smaller units of time / paper, are part of the countdown to the end of a century. Fragments pinned and unpinned are at once evidence of Dickinson's furthest expression of her aesthetics of "choosing not choosing" and evidence of her willingness to lose / loose the idea of the final version, the text one could be finished writing.

Winds blow through the textual histories of these wings.

> *The swallow is already far away. I am sure it was a flock of swallows,*
> *one swallow doesn't make a spring. . . .*
> —Michel Serres

VII. Narratives of Wings, Pinned and Unpinned

The nature of Dickinson's connection to the pinned, often fragmentary texts she left behind in her last, most precipitous flight remains mysterious. Here, I offer five possible visual narratives of pinning / unpinning—narratives of closure, of openness, of autonomy and intertextuality, of collision and syncope, and of lost pins / lost provenances— before offering a final variant flight of A 821, A822. Readers should add narratives as they like.

Narratives of Closure

At times, two or more fragments, pinned together, carry a complete poem draft. In the cases below (figs. 11–15), even the loss of the pin would not necessarily result in the permanent dissociation of text fragments; rather, each text fragment contains a clue linking it with the other(s), and making possible the reassociation of even widely scattered fragments.

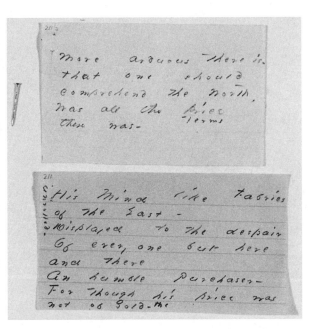

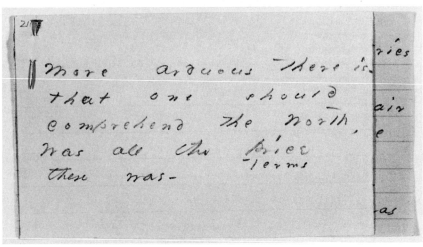

Figure 11. A 211a/A 211, c. 1878. Pencil. "His Mind like Fabrics / of the East -," poem-draft with variants, composed on two fragments of stationery (A 211: cream, blue-ruled stationery, 70 x 127 mm.; A 211a: white, gray-ruled stationery, 70 x 144 mm.), pinned together. Though it carries the poem-draft's closing lines, A 211a was pinned over A 211.

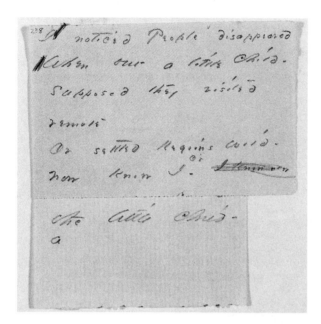

Figure 12. A 238 / A 238a, c. 1869. Pencil. "I noticed People disappeared," poem-draft with variants, composed on two fragments of stationery (A 238: laid, off-white stationery, 66 x 113 mm.; A 238a: laid, off-white stationery, 109 x 84 mm.), pinned together. A 238 is pinned over A 238a.

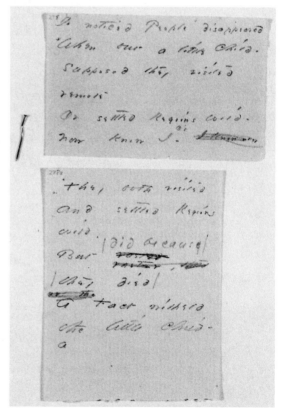

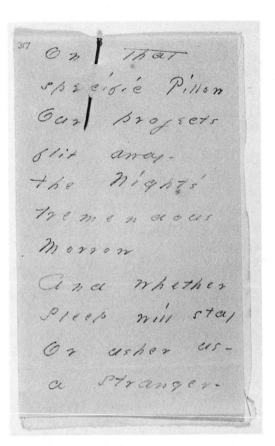

Figure 13.   A 317/A 317a, c. 1881. Pencil. "On that / specific Pillow," poem-draft with variants, composed on two fragments of stationery (A 317: cream stationery, 125 x 76 mm.; A 317a: slit envelope, 129 x 77 mm.), pinned together. A 317 is pinned over A 317a.

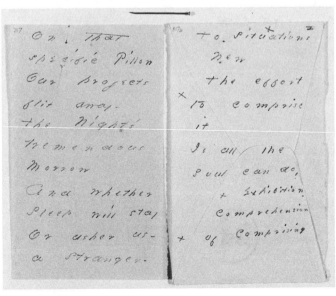

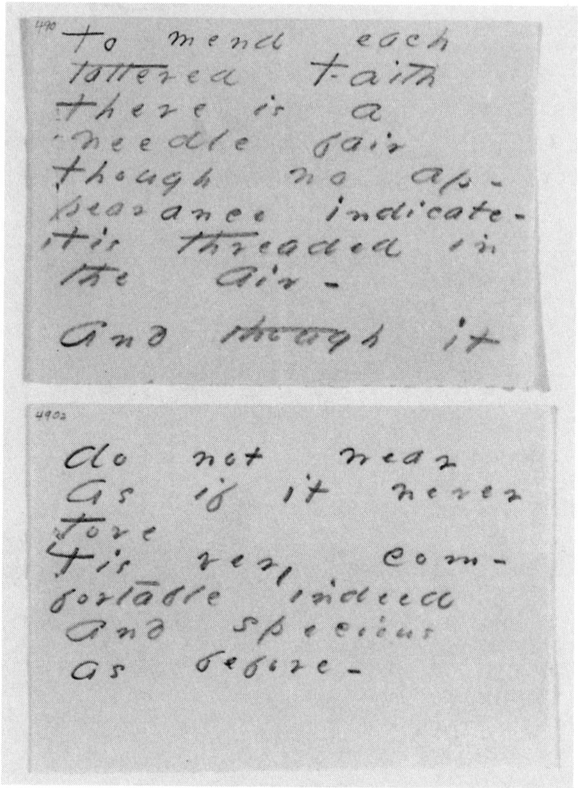

490

To mend each
tattered Faith
there is a
needle fair
though no ap-
pearance indicate -
'tis threaded in
the Air -

And ~~though~~ it

490a

do not wear
As if it never
tore
'Tis very com-
fortable indeed
And spacious
as before -

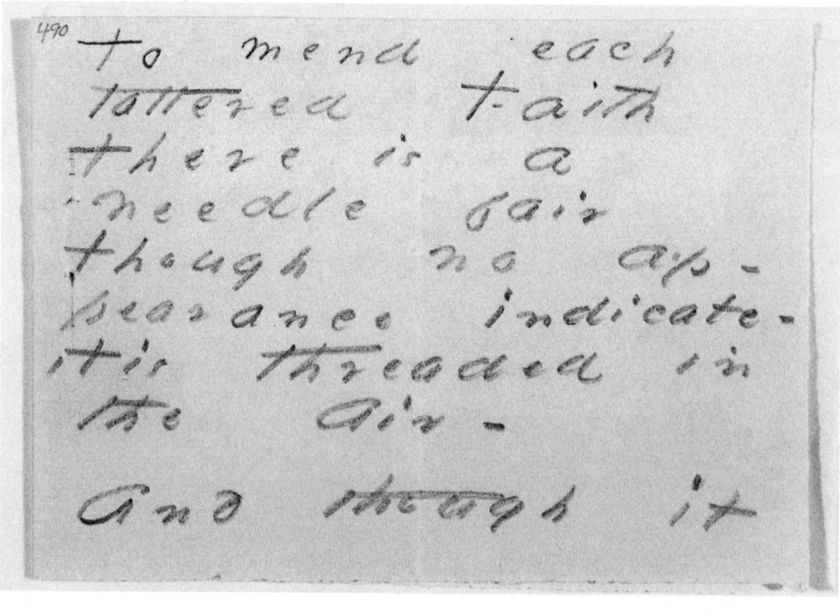

490

To mend each
tattered Faith
there is a
needle fair
though no ap-
pearance indicate -
'tis threaded in
the Air -

And ~~though~~ it

Figure 14.A A 490 / A 490a, c. 1878. Pencil. "To mend each / tattered Faith," poem-draft composed on two fragments of PARIS stationery (A 490: 68 x 97 mm.; A 490a: 68 x 101 mm.), pinned together. A 490 is pinned over A 490a.

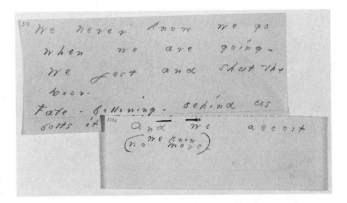

Figure 15. A 513/A 513a, c. 1881. Pencil. "We never know we go," poem-draft with variants, composed on two fragments of stationery (A 513: wove, white, blue-ruled, 139 x 59 mm.; A 513a: off-white, faint-ruled paper, 34 x 114 mm.), pinned together. A 513a is pinned to the bottom edge of A 513.

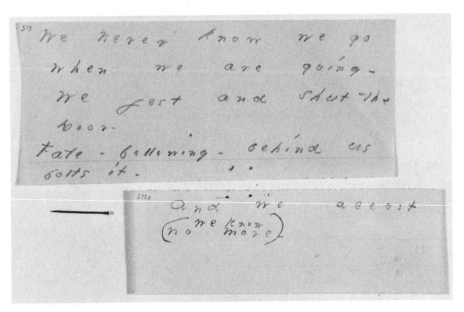

Figure 16. A 462/A 462a, c. 1873. Pencil. "There is no Frigate / like a Book," poem-draft with variants, composed on two fragments of stationery (A 462: white, blue-ruled stationery, 65 × 100 mm.; A 462a: wove, white stationery water-marked A PIRIE & SONS 1871, 41 × 137 mm.), probably pinned together at one time. Three sets of pinholes are visible on A 462; three pin-holes are visible on A 462a. The pins are missing.

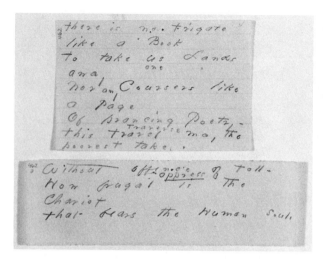

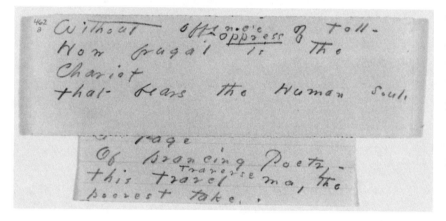

Narratives of Openness

At times, pinned documents are marked by more than one set of pin-holes (figs. 16–18; see also fig. 21), evidence of multiple (conflicting?) sets of intentions, many of which remain unrecoverable. Here pinholes marking departures may also function as points of entry. At risk in the unpinning of texts is not simply the loss of an end, but the conversion of ends and beginnings in the texts' successive encounters with the unforeseen.

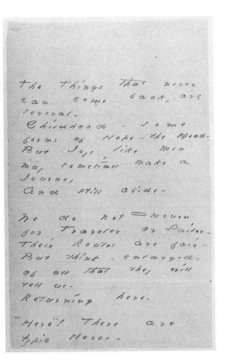

Figure 17. A 445 / A 445b, A 445a, c. 1881. Pencil. "The things that never can / come back, are several," poem-draft with variants, composed on two fragments of cream, blue-ruled stationery, embossed CONGRESS (A 445: leaf, 202 x 129 mm.; A 445a: 120 x 100 mm.), and pinned together. A 445a is pinned to the verso of A 445. Two sets of pinholes are visible on A 445; two pinholes are visible on A 445a.

Figure 18. A 366, A 366a / A 366b, c. 1876. Pencil. "Summer - we all have / seen," poem-draft with variant lines / passages, composed on two fragments of stationery (A 366: leaf, quadrille stationery, 185 x 124 mm.; A 366b: quadrille stationery, 126 x 120 mm.), once pinned together. A 366b appears to have been folded and pinned in half, then pinned to A 366. Four sets of pinholes are visible on A 366; three sets of pinholes are visible on A 366b. The pins have been lost.

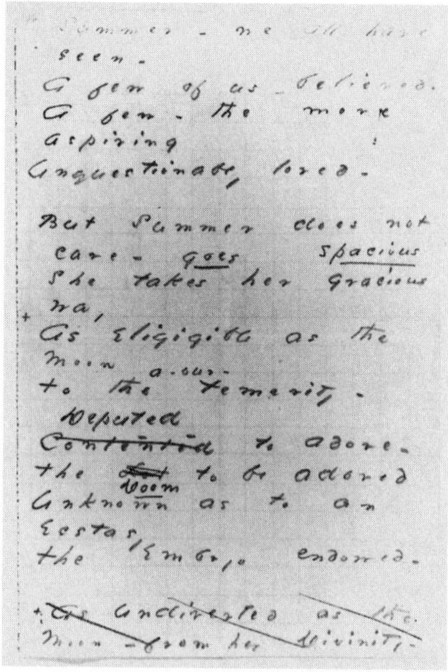
Summer - we all have
seen -
A few of us - believed -
A few - the more
aspiring
Unquestionably loved -
But Summer does not
care - goes spacious
She takes her gracious
way,
+ As Eligible as the
moon
to the temerity -
Deputed
Contented to adore -
the Doom to be adored
Unknown as to an
Ecstasy
the Embryo endowed -
+ As Undiverted as the
Moon - from her divinity -

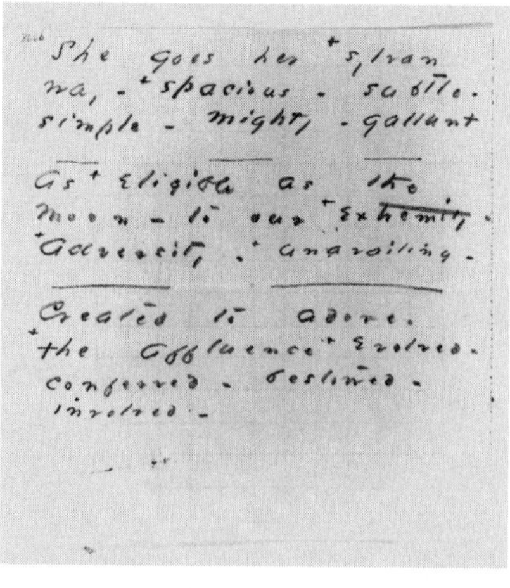
She goes her + way, -
+spacious - subtle -
simple - mighty - gallant
As + Eligible as the
Moon - to our +Extremity -
+Adversity, + unavailing -
Created to adore -
+the Affluence + Evolved -
conferred - bestowed -
involved -

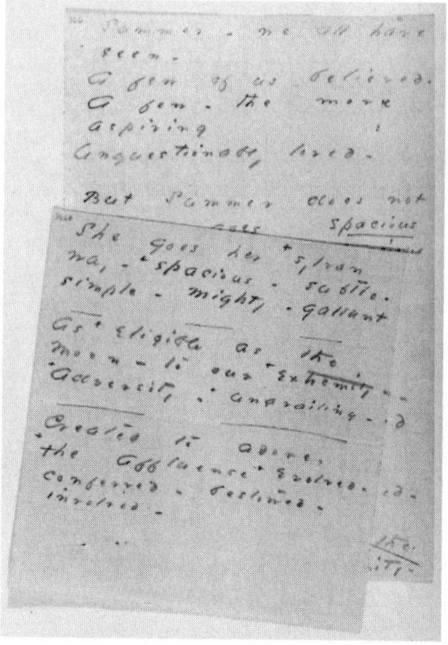

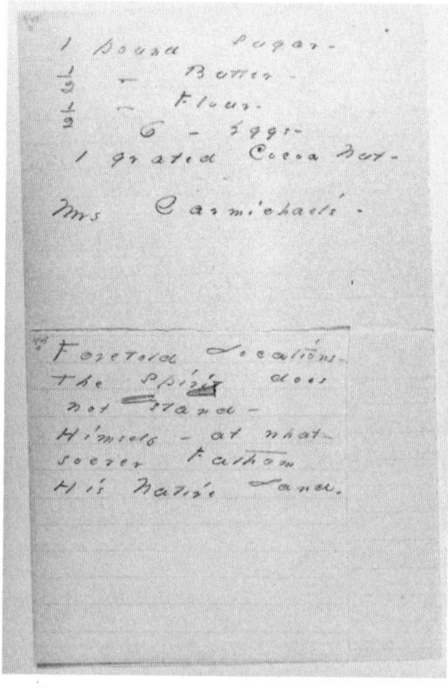
1 pound Sugar -
1/2 - Butter -
1/2 - Flour -
6 - Eggs -
1 grated Cocoa Nut -
Mrs Carmichael's -
Forever'd Locations -
The Spirit does
not stand -
Himself - at whatsoever Fathom
His Native Land.

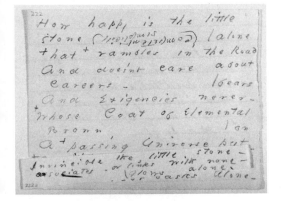

Figure 19. A 222, A 222b / A 222a, c. 1881 or 1882. Pencil. "How happy is the little stone," poem-draft with variants, composed on two fragments of stationery (A 222: white, blue-ruled stationery; A 222a: WESTON'S, 16 x 125 mm.), pinned together. A 222a, which carries a variant for the opening lines, is pinned over the opening lines of A 222. The pin passes directly through the word "associates."

Narratives of Autonomy and Intertextuality (Poems and Their Variants)

At times, the pinned slip carries a variant that, unpinned, could sue for autonomy from the poem "proper," for new status as a brief but electric lyric (figs. 19–22). These unpinned slips perhaps realize the desire for autonomy implicit in the variant lines penciled at the far limits of the poems in the fascicles like glosses or codas, extending the poems' limits but still held fast within their gravitational fields.

At still other times, the texts carried by two separate fragments may be lines or stanzas of a single poem, lines of two autonomous poems—or both (figs. 23, 24). The fragments and the texts they carry often appear symmetrical; they may be easily, cleanly, bisected.

Figure 20.   A 334, A 334a / A 334b, c. 1872 or
1873. Pencil. "Power is a familiar / growth -,"
poem-draft with variants, composed on two fragments of stationery (A 334: white, blue-ruled stationery, embossed CONN. VALLEY, 101 x 126 mm.;
A 334b: wove, white stationery, 22 x 126 mm.),
pinned together. A 334a, which carries a variant
for the final line of the poem, is pinned over the
first line of A 334. The handwriting on A 334b
differs from the handwriting on A 334 / A 334a,
suggesting that the variant line was composed at a
later time.

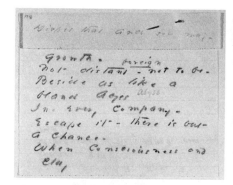

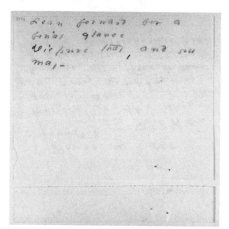

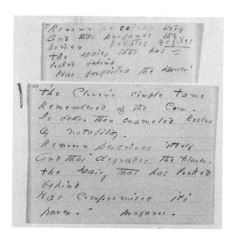

Figure 21.   A 388 / A 388a, c. 1872. Pencil. "The
Clover's simple Fame," poem-draft with variants,
composed on two fragments of stationery (A 388:
white, blue-ruled stationery, 104 x 138 mm.; A 388a:
white stationery, watermarked A PIRIE & SONS 1862,
44 x 113 mm.), pinned together. A 388a is pinned
over A 388; it covers the first stanza of A 388. Two
sets of pinholes are visible on A 388.

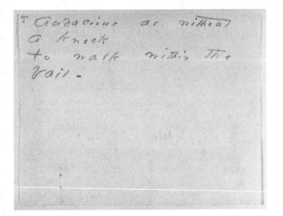

Figure 22.   A 404, A 404a / A 405, c. 1875 or 1876. Pencil. "The last of Summer / is a Time," poem-draft with variants, composed on two fragments of stationery (A 404: quadrille stationery, 119 x 91 mm.; A 405, wove, white stationery, 18 x 127 mm.), pinned together. A 405 is pinned over the opening three lines of A 404.

Figure 23. A 401 / A 401a, c. 1874. Pencil. "The Infinite a / sudden Guest," poem-draft composed on two fragments of stationery (A 401: wove, white stationery, watermarked A PIRIE & SONS, 33 x 110 mm.; A 401a: quadrille stationery, 25 x 118 mm.), pinned together. A 401 is pinned over A 401a.

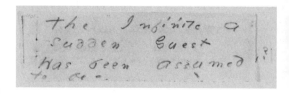

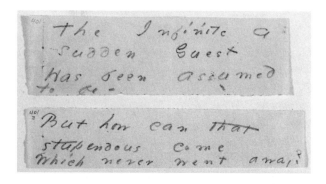

Figure 24. A 478 / A 478a, c. 1884. Pencil. "Though the / great Waters / sleep -," poem-draft composed on two fragments of WESTON's LINEN RECORD (A 478: 80 x 126 mm.; A 478a: 95 x 126 mm.), pinned together. A 478 is pinned over A 478a.

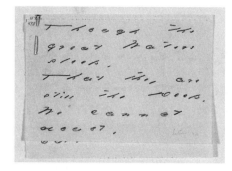

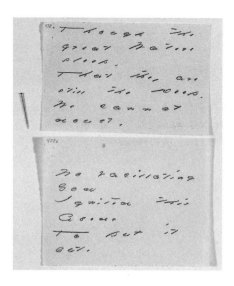

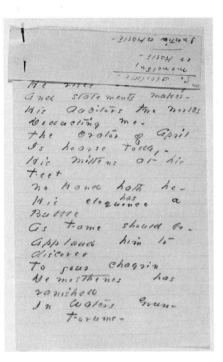

Figure 25. A 210 / A 210a, c. 1875 or 1876 / undated. Pencil. Two texts composed, respectively, on a leaf of white, blue-ruled stationery (202 × 125 mm.) and on a scrap of heavy white stationery (32 × 126 mm.), and pinned together. A 210 carries a poem-draft, with variants, beginning "His Mansion in the / Pool"; A 210a carries the last lines of "The mind lives on the heart," "so absolute / monotony / or Haste - / Inertia or Haste," as well as trials for the last word of "Not any more to be lacked." The relationship between the pinned texts is unclear: they are inscribed in different hands, perhaps at different times, and the lines inscribed on A 210a seem unrelated to the text inscribed on A 210. A 210a has been pinned, upside down, over the first three lines of the poem-draft.

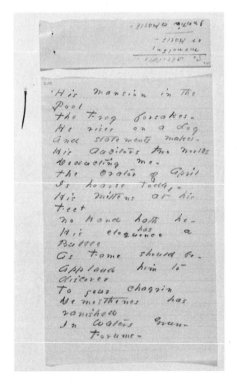

Narratives of Collision or Syncope

At times, texts bearing no relation to one another are "suddenly" associated by pinning (figs. 25, 26). If the texts were unpinned, the association between them would be permanently broken, revealing a gap between the wings.

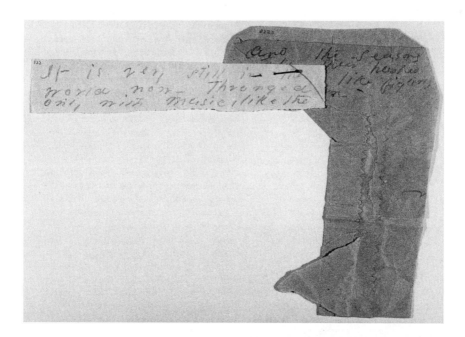

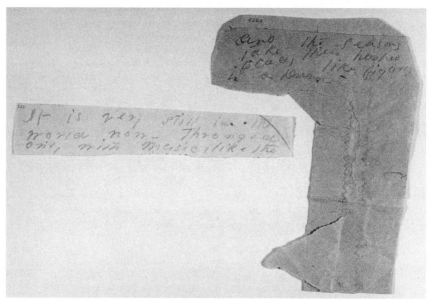

Figure 26.   A 822, A 822v / A 822a, c. 1885. Pencil. "It is very still in the / world now -," lines, extrageneric, composed on two fragments of paper (A 822: off-white wrapping paper, 30 x 167 mm.; A 822a: brown paper bag, 161 x 106 mm.), pinned together. A 822 is pinned to A 822a and covers part of the text carried by that document.

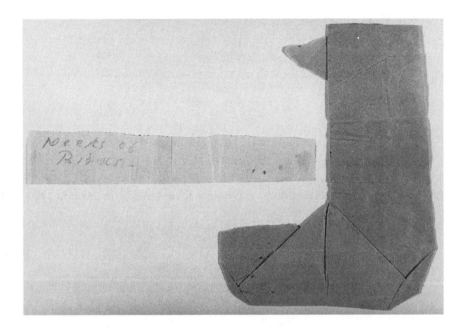

Narratives of Lost Pins / Lost Provenances

At times, multiple pinholes are visible on the documents, suggesting past associations, now lost (fig. 27).

Figure 27. A 287, c. 1884. Pencil. Fragment, composed on a slip (21 x 126 mm.) of wove, white stationery. Two pinholes are visible on the document, suggesting that A 287 was once associated with another text, now lost. The slip A 287 may have been attached to another copy of the message draft A 637, in which a variant of the line "Most Arrows" appears (though there are no corresponding pinholes).

VIII. Scatters: Writing Outside

High up, a mile high, perhaps two miles high, hundreds . . . of pale grey
birds flew south, like pages of flickering paper let loose from a small book
caught up in a wind. . . .

—Peter Greenaway

In order to determine whether or not certain kinds of birds possess homing instincts, a person known as a "liberator" throws several up into the
air, then turns and turns again, each time releasing more birds in different directions. The birds are then watched out of sight, and the points
at which they disappear from view are recorded. When a significant number of vanishing points has been noted, a scatter diagram is drawn up
for study. At times, for reasons that are not yet fully understood, large
numbers of birds returning to the original release point lose their way
and drift widely across the migration axis. These drifts, sometimes called
"radical scatters," both solicit and resist definitive interpretation.[20]

Freed from the forty bound fascicles, the accumulated libraries of her
poetic production, and whirling confusedly around the absent center of
the "book," Dickinson's (un)pinned fragments resemble the distant and
disoriented migrants that do not come fully into focus and that no longer
constitute a clearly delimitable constellation. At times, one or two or even
several appear to be in closest touch with one another; at other times,
texts / wings separated and dispersed by "paragraphs of wind"[21] seem
remote from each other, unassimilated and unassimilable to the larger
figure, whose moving edges and outlines also drift and blur. Moreover,
even if chance were to discover the breakaway fragments, carefully
inventorying and appending them to their "original" bodies, it would
still be impossible to establish the order of pinnings and unpinnings, or
the distances (seconds, minutes, hours, days, years) between them.
Fragments are "small, rickety infinitudes";[22] they try their chances.
Dearchivized, they fly to the lyric's scattered ends: the "proceedings of
a birdsong," the vibration of poetry freed from all devices.[23]

The late (un)pinned fragments are "escapes": texts with no place in
an official record—the official record of an "edition" or, more important,
the narrative (plot) of literary history / linear chronology. Intended by
Dickinson to be temporary and occasional in a way different from what
we suspected, they reveal the liaison between poetics and teleologies as
essentially specious. Belonging to an economy of indeterminacy in
which "discretion, stability and autonomy" are no longer givens but only
"effects of certain relations," they call for an alternative aesthetics, for

what Ira Livingston has recently called a "chaology of knowledge," perhaps, in which chaos is seen as "a logic at work in the epistemological
processes."[24] Instead of classifying them according to conventional bibliographical and generic codes, we need to find ways of not naming them
as they flash by; instead of binding them in chronological order into a
book, we need to discover ways of launching them into circulation again
and again, ways of expressing the unpredictably varied, stunningly beautiful reorderings of the texts-birds as they cross the sky / page / screen
of our reading. Ideally, the editor—and, no less so, the reader—of these
writings would assume the role of the liberator, throwing the (un)pinned
fragments high up into the ether, following them until they were out of
sight, noting their vanishing points, and, whenever possible, the modalities of their different returns.[25]

It has been a long winter.

NOTES

This essay was originally written in response to Randall McLeod's "FIATfLUX," a reading of
George Herbert's "Easter-Wings" given at the twenty-fourth annual Conference on Editorial
Problems, University of Toronto, Nov. 4–5, 1988. McLeod's work on Herbert was later published in Randall M. Leod [pseud.], ed., *Crisis in Editing: Texts of the English Renaissance* (New
York: AMS Press, 1993). I am deeply indebted to McLeod's work and friendship. His careful
reading of an early draft of this essay and his contributions in criticism give him the status of
collaborator.

Thanks are also due to the curator and the staff of the Amherst College Library, Special
Collections, for their assistance with my research and for their many kindnesses. John Lancaster,
curator, permitted me to view all of the manuscripts included in this essay. Daria D'Arienzo,
head archivist, provided critical information about the conservation of the documents. Donna
Skibel, archives associate, assisted me in locating materials on bird migrations between 1860
and 1886.

I wish also to thank my research assistant, Patrick Bryant, a doctoral candidate at Georgia
State University, for his contributions in criticism and his help with the many technological aspects
of this project.

The quotation "Far away, so close!" is the title, translated from German, of Wim Wenders's
1993 film *In Weiter Ferne, so nah!* The film begins, significantly, with a passage from Matthew
6:22 ("The light of the body is the eye").

The quotations attributed to Peter Greenaway are from his book *Flying Out of This World*
(Chicago: University of Chicago Press, 1994), 31, 114, 149.

The quotation attributed to William Blake is from *The Marriage of Heaven and Hell* (Oxford:
Oxford University Press, 1975).

The first of the display quotations attributed to Emily Dickinson is from Thomas H. Johnson
and Theodora Ward, eds., *The Letters of Emily Dickinson,* 3 vols. (Cambridge, Mass.: Belknap
Press of Harvard University Press, 1958). The second is from manuscript 828 in the Emily
Dickinson Collection, Amherst College Library; from this point on, the letter "A" followed by
the catalog number will designate a manuscript from that collection.

The quotation attributed to Henry Vaughan is from "Isaac's Marriage," in Leonard Cyril
Martin, ed., *The Works of Henry Vaughan,* vol. 2, 2nd ed. (Oxford: Oxford University Press,
1957), 48–49.

The quotation attributed to Lorine Niedecker is from a letter dated Jan. 30, 1968, in Lisa Pater Faranda, ed., *"Between Your House and Mine": The Letters of Lorine Niedecker to Cid Corman, 1960 to 1970* (Durham, N.C.: Duke University Press, 1986), 149.

The quotation attributed to Michel Serres is from *Genesis,* trans. Geneviève James and James Nielson (Ann Arbor: University of Michigan Press, 1995), 58.

Finally, with respect to part VI of this essay, "A Flight of Fragments: Toward a Bibliography of Departures," it should be noted that the word "flight" could be a term used for the classification of certain kinds of textual materials, especially those materials unsusceptible to collection, as in "a flight of fragments." A complete inventory of the pinned documents among Dickinson's papers has not been—perhaps cannot be—done. This bibliography is illustrative, not exhaustive. Unless otherwise noted, the images of the manuscripts of Emily Dickinson are reproduced courtesy of the Special Collections and Archives, Amherst College Library.

1. David Porter, "Assembling a Poet and Her Poems: Convergent Limit-Works of Joseph Cornell and Emily Dickinson," *Word & Image* 10:3 (1994), 199.

2. Although I have not done a complete inventory of texts composed by Dickinson on envelopes, a large number of such texts exists, many of which have clear iconic value. Two are especially relevant to this essay: A 109, beginning "A Pang is more / conspicuous in Spring / In contrast with the [those] / things that sing, / Not Birds entirely - but / Minds" (1881) and H 323, beginning "The / Bird her / punctual / Music brings" (1883).

3. I have assumed that Dickinson is the first author of the pinnings and unpinnings. The often jarring associations of text fragments suggest an aesthetics at odds with the editorial aesthetics of order. Since her death and the scattering of her papers, however, it is certain that the manuscripts have been pinned and unpinned by others—editors, catalogers, etc.

4. To graft or engraft; in falconry, according to the *Oxford English Dictionary,* "to imp" means to graft feathers into a bird's wing so as to remedy losses or deficiencies and thus restore or improve the bird's powers of flight. I am indebted to the discussion of imping in Randall McLeod, "FIATfLUX," especially as that work appears in McLeod, ed., *Crisis in Editing,* 129–35.

5. See Leonard Lutwack, *Birds in Literature* (Gainesville: University Press of Florida, 1994).

6. For a compelling reading of the connection between writing and seeing, see Françoise Lucbert, "The Pen and the Eye: The Politics of the Gazing Body," in Stephen Melville and Bill Readings, eds., *Vision and Textuality* (Durham, N.C.: Duke University Press, 1995), 251–55.

7. Johnson and Ward, *The Letters of Emily Dickinson,* letter 876a.

8. Ibid., letter 876, redaction of A 817, A 819.

9. The connection between the idea of destination and the idea of death is noted by Jacques Derrida, *La carte postale* (Paris: Aubier-Flammarion, 1980), 39.

10. On August 6, 1885, the *Springfield Republican* noted, "Mrs. Jackson is reported at the point of death in San Francisco, where she has been steadily declining for the past four months." She died six days later, on August 12. In a letter to Thomas Wentworth Higginson, apparently composed on the day the *Springfield Republican* ran the story, Dickinson wrote, "I was unspeakably shocked to see this in the Morning Paper - She wrote me in Spring that she could not walk, but not that she would die - I was sure you would know. Please say it is not so. What a Hazard a Letter is! When I think of the Hearts it has scuttled and sunk, I almost fear to lift my Hand to so much as a Superscription." Shortly afterward, she wrote to Hunt Jackson's widower: "She said in a Note of a few months since, 'I am absolutely well.' I next knew of her death." The letter to William Jackson confirms the March-to-August suspension of correspondence between Dickinson and Hunt Jackson. For the complete texts of the letters to Higginson and Jackson, see Johnson and Ward, *The Letters of Emily Dickinson,* letters 1007 and 1009, respectively.

11. Cf. John Berger, *The Sense of Sight* (New York: Vintage, 1985), 147: "People talk of freshness of vision, of the intensity of seeing for the first time, but the intensity of seeing for the last time is, I believe, greater." Dickinson's late writing, particularly her fragments, mark the edge of perception itself. This marking accounts, perhaps, for our perception of the fragments themselves as both infinitely distant and infinitely close.

12. See, for example, the extended exploration of flight iconography and iconology in Clive

Hart, *Images of Flight* (Berkeley: University of California Press, 1988). See also Marina Warner, *The Inner Eye: Art Beyond the Visible* (London: National Touring Exhibitions, 1996).

13. A 857.

14. See Johnson and Ward, eds., *The Letters of Emily Dickinson*.

15. Ibid., letter 976n.

16. I have appropriated the phrase "terrifying tense" from Leslie Scalapino's "Objects in the Terrifying Tense / Longing from Taking Place," in Juliana Spahr, Mark Wallace, Kristin Prevallet, and Pam Rehm, eds., *A Poetics of Criticism* (Buffalo, N.Y.: Leave Books, 1994), 37.

17. See Catherine Clément, *Syncope: The Philosophy of Rapture,* trans. Sally O'Driscoll and Deirdre M. Mahoney (Minneapolis: University of Minnesota Press, 1994).

18. Michel Pierssens, "Detachment," *New York Literary Forum* 8–9 (1981), 166.

19. A 828.

20. For a discussion of "random scatters," see G. V. T. Matthews, *Bird Navigation* (Cambridge: Cambridge University Press, 1968), 42, 86, 107, 108, 114, 134, 140. See also Donald R. Griffin, *Bird Migration* (Garden City, N.J.: The Natural History Press, 1964), 160–62.

21. Thomas H. Johnson, ed., *The Poems of Emily Dickinson,* 3 vols. (Cambridge, Mass.: Belknap Press of Harvard University Press, 1955), poem 1175; R. W. Franklin, ed., *The Poems of Emily Dickinson: Variorum Edition,* 3 vols. (Cambridge, Mass.: Belknap Press of Harvard University Press, 1998), poem 1247.

22. Porter, "Assembling a Poet and Her Poems," 199.

23. "The proceedings of a birdsong" is a reference to Wilhelm Raabe, *Die Akten des Vogelsangs,* cited in Anselm Haverkamp, *Leaves of Mourning: Hölderlin's Late Work, with an Essay on Keats and Melancholy,* trans. Vernon Chadwick (Albany: State University of New York Press, 1996), 5.

24. Ira Livingston, *Arrow of Chaos: Romanticism and Postmodernity* (Minneapolis: University of Minnesota Press, 1997), vi, 16.

25. I have compiled an electronic archive of Dickinson's late fragments: http://www.press.umich.edu/webhome/werner/siteform.pdf.

The archive is divided into two groups, never mutually exclusive: trace fragments, which appear, sometimes altered, in other Dickinson texts; and autonomous fragments, which are not linked to other texts but were nevertheless saved by Dickinson. The goal is to illuminate the play of autonomy and intertextuality in Dickinson's writing by allowing users to see how various fragments appear in, or near, more than one document. The electronic archive will allow scholars to work with Dickinson's texts in unedited form and draw on them in a nonlinear manner consistent with the approach I advocated in Marta L. Werner, ed., *Emily Dickinson's Open Folios: Scenes of Reading, Surfaces of Writing* (Ann Arbor: University of Michigan Press, 1995), but was not able to implement, bound as I was by the codex format.

PART IV

Subversive / Subverted Text

Reinterpreting Text
When Revealed Sanskrit Texts
Become Modern Law Books

LUDO ROCHER

In 1772, the British East India Company appointed a new governor of Bengal, Warren Hastings, "one of the most remarkable figures in India's history."[1] Hastings did not wait long to promote the adoption of a juridical plan that was to become one of his major legacies on the Indian subcontinent.[2] According to the plan, "in all religious suits regarding inheritance, marriage, caste and all other religious usages and institutions, the laws of the Koran with respect to the Mohamedans and those of the Shaster with respect to the Gentoos shall invariably be adhered to."[3] In other words, in 1772 the British authorities in Calcutta decided that Indian Hindus and Indian Muslims should not be ruled by British laws, which they would not be able to understand, but by their own laws, which they had cherished for many centuries.[4] In this essay, I will not deal with the Indian Muslims, who, according to the plan, were to be governed by the laws of the Koran. I will restrict myself to the Hindus, who were to be ruled by the laws of "the Shaster."

The term "Shaster," used in the judicial plan of 1772, corresponds to the Sanskrit term *śāstra*, which is the collective name for the voluminous body of Sanskrit texts (the *śāstras* and their commentaries) dealing with the Hindu *dharma*. The term *dharma* has no appropriate English equivalent; it refers to the aggregate of all the rules by which a Hindu must live, including rules that we would label rules of law. Modern scholarship has established that the several *dharmaśāstras* were composed somewhere between 500 B.C. and 500 A.D., but in the Hindu tradition these texts were attributed to ancient *rishis*, that is, "sages" or "seers." They are part of the Vedas, the sacred, revealed texts of Hinduism. Being sacred, the *śāstras* are superhuman and timeless; they proclaim eternal truths, and they should not be interfered with by human beings.[5] One of the adjectives used to describe *dharma* is *sanātana*, "eternal."[6]

From the end of the eighteenth century onward, and throughout the colonial period, the courts of law in India, as well as the highest court of appeal, the Judicial Committee of the Privy Council in London, have indeed, to the best of their abilities, based their judgments in cases involving Hindus on the *śāstras*. The goal of this essay is to show how and why, despite the best intentions to remain faithful to the law of the *śāstras*, the British could not avoid departing from the original intent and meaning of the sacred texts when it came to applying them in the courts of law. As Thomas Babington Macaulay later said, "the decision was far-sighted policy—not a matter of course."[7]

Background

It is important to note that, right from the start, the British found themselves at a triple disadvantage.

The first disadvantage was that the *śāstra* texts were composed in Sanskrit, and no Englishman entrusted with the administration of justice among Hindus had any knowledge whatever of that language.[8] After trying other solutions, which proved unsuccessful,[9] this disadvantage was remedied: some courageous Englishmen decided that there was only one way to administer the law of the *śāstras* properly—namely, to study Sanskrit themselves. A very few of them did, and in 1794 Sir William Jones, a judge in the Calcutta Supreme Court, produced an English translation of the most famous of the *śāstras*, a text attributed to Manu, the mythical ancestor of all Hindus.[10] The text became known as *The Laws of Manu*. Other translations—of commentaries first, of basic texts other than Manu's only later[11]—were to follow, but the shared disadvantage of not having access to the original Sanskrit texts continued to haunt the courts in India and in London. As late as 1899 the Privy Council lamented, "In examining this question their Lordships are again at a great disadvantage in not knowing Sanskrit."[12]

The second disadvantage was that the British not only did not know the language of the *śāstra* but also had no idea of the extent of the texts they were supposed to administer in the courts of law. It was possible, and legal, for the advocate of a party to a lawsuit to present the judge with a shastric text that neither the advocate of the opposing party nor the judge had ever heard of.

The third disadvantage was that even the translations proved to be of relatively little help. The rules contained in the *śāstras* often were as foreign and unintelligible to the early translators—and, a fortiori, to those who had to use the translations—as British law would have been to the Hindus. The *śāstra* was the product of a complex and different civilization with which even the most devoted British enthusiasts at that time were only vaguely familiar.[13] To quote the Privy Council once again, "It is quite impossible for us to feel any confidence in our opinion, . . . when that opinion is founded upon authorities to which we have access only through translations, and when the doctrines themselves, and the reasons by which they are supported, or impugned, are drawn from the religious tradition, ancient sages, and more modern habits of the Hindus, with which we cannot be familiar."[14]

It is against the background of this triple anomaly—the courts' not having access to and not knowing the extent of the laws they were supposed to administer, and their being ignorant of the historical context in which the *śāstra* had originated—that we must analyze and try to understand the changes that the law of the *śāstra* underwent in Anglo-India.

Changes from Within Traditional Hindu Law

Law Versus Religion

The British soon realized that the laws contained in the *śāstra* rarely corresponded to their idea of what "law" was supposed to be. Hindu legal texts, they felt, were inextricably mixed with what they called "religion."[15] Faced with this situation, the courts decided that it was their duty to administer law, but not religion, with which they were supposed not to interfere. For example, the text of the *śāstra* explicitly declares the adoption of a single son invalid; indeed, if one adopts a single son, one removes him from his natural family, in which he is the prime person who can perform the necessary ritual at the time of his father's death. The British gradually came to the conclusion that performing the *śrāddha* ritual at the time of one's father's death belonged to the sphere of religion and was therefore irrelevant with respect to the validity of the "legal" act of adoption. In a landmark decision, the Privy Council wrote, "The British rulers of India have in few things been more careful than in avoiding interference with the religious tenets of the Indian peoples. They provide for the peace and stability of families by imposing limits on attempts to disturb the possession of property and the personal legal status of individuals. With the religious side of such matters they do not pretend to interfere. But the position is altered if the validity of temporal arrangements on which temporal courts are asked to decide is to be made subordinate to inquiries into religious beliefs."[16] As a result, from 1899 onward treatises on Hindu law have ordained unequivocally that "an only son may be given and taken in adoption."[17] In cases such as this one, the British introduced a nonexistent dichotomy in the text of the *śāstra*, between what they considered to be law and what they considered to be religion. They dutifully applied the legal aspects of the *śāstra* but did not interfere with (that is, they disregarded) the religious aspects of the texts.

Human Commentaries Outweigh Revealed Śāstras

Not only was the text of the *śāstra* difficult to understand, often it either was ambiguous, and therefore susceptible of different interpretations, or failed to provide answers to legal questions that the judge had to deal with. In these circumstances, the British learned not only that the Sanskrit commentaries on the original *śāstras* were more comprehensive, in that they took into consideration the entire *śāstra* literature, but also that each individual commentator had worked out his own coherent system for interpreting the often incoherent and contradictory *śāstras*. Hence the British turned for help to the commentaries (as indicated earlier, although not a single ancient *śāstra* had been translated in the period that immediately followed the appearance of Jones's *The Laws of Manu*,[18] the commentaries were being translated, in ever-increasing numbers).

Since the commentaries had originated in different parts of India, the British assumed that they represented the way in which the text of the *śāstra* had been interpreted and applied in various parts of India. They introduced the concept of regional schools of Hindu law, thus admitting that the same *śāstra* text could mean different things in different parts of the subcontinent.[19] "The duty . . . of an European judge who is under the obligation to administer Hindoo law, is not so much to enquire whether a disputed doctrine is fairly deducible from the earliest authorities, as to ascertain whether it has been received by the particular School which governs the District with which he has to deal."[20] What that meant was a convenient but totally untraditional reversal of authorities; the meaning of the text of the ancient, revealed, and unalterable *śāstra* was now made subordinate to the differing interpretations of human commentators: "It is clear that in the event of a conflict between the ancient text writers and the commentators, the opinion of the latter must be accepted."[21] To be sure, the *śāstras* continued to be quoted in every legal decision, but the judges no longer were under the obligation to inquire what the original *śāstra* texts meant. They could be satisfied with the sometimes forced interpretations the commentators gave the *śāstras,* to make them fit into an overall system. In other words, the courts of law distanced themselves from the texts of the *śāstras* themselves, relying on them only indirectly, via the medium of interpretations provided by commentators.

Custom Outweighs Written Texts

The British distanced themselves even further from the text of the *śāstra* by cleverly using a means that the *śāstra* itself provided them with: the *śāstras* indeed do say that, in addition to their own rules, rather unspecified customs of clans, castes, villages, guilds, etc., are valid sources of *dharma* "as long as they are not contrary to the Vedas." The British were only too happy to comply, and soon it became a principle of Anglo-Hindu law that "under the Hindu system of law, clear proof of usage will outweigh the written text of the law."[22] Once again, this did not mean that the *śāstra* texts were easily discarded. They remained at the center of every debate, but their authority was now weighed in the balance against the authority of unwritten custom. The burden of proof that a custom was fully established, and that it ought therefore to overrule the text of the *śāstra,* invariably lay with the party who made such a claim; and yet, once the court had accepted that a custom was "valid," it did outweigh the text of the *śāstra.*[23]

Changes from Outside Traditional Hindu Law

The jurisprudential debates in the Anglo-Indian courts of law, and in the Privy Council, debates that centered on the text of the *śāstra* but relied on it in ever more different ways, were preserved in an endless series of law reports. These reports make fascinating reading; many of them are the work of eminent jurists, and some of them run to hundreds of pages. Nevertheless, the law reports were the work of Englishmen—and of an increasing number of British-trained Indian lawyers, who acted exactly as their teachers did[24]—with the result that purely British principles gradually began to infiltrate legal decisions, and purely British principles began to determine the role of the *śāstra* in these decisions.

Precedent

One such principle, borrowed from common law jurisprudence, is that of precedent. In Hindu law, too, it became common practice that if earlier cases had been decided on the basis of a certain interpretation of the *śāstra,* then it was appropriate to apply the same interpretation to the case at hand. Even when the advocate for one of the parties or a member of a Full Bench happened to know Sanskrit and demonstrated in court that the interpretation given to a text of the *śāstra* in earlier decisions had been wrong, a protracted discussion on the correct meaning of the *śāstra* text could be cut short by the Latin maxims of *stare decisis* and *communis error facit ius.*[25] In this connection, we can note that the maxim of *communis error facit ius* has also led to a development of a different nature: succession and inheritance in the *śāstras* are intestate, and there are no rules dealing with wills, and yet wills were occasionally recognized in Indian courts of law. When the validity of a will was challenged in 1867, the Privy Council ruled as follows: "It is too late to contend that, because the ancient Hindu treatises make no mention of Wills, a Hindu cannot make a testamentary disposition of his property. Decided cases, too numerous to be questioned, have determined that the testamentary power exists."[26] The undisputed novelty of wills in Hindu law notwithstanding, Indian jurists were prepared to claim them as integral parts of the *śāstra*.[27]

Factum Valet

A number of British legal principles that were introduced into the law of the *śāstra* had a long history in British law, and their refinement in British jurisprudence resulted from circumstances inherent in British society. A case in point is the maxim of *factum valet*, or, stated more completely, *quod fieri non debuit factum valet*, "if something that ought not to be done has been done anyway, it becomes law." There is a substantial body of jurisprudence on *factum valet* in Britain, but applying or even adapting that jurisprudence to Indian situations and to Sanskrit *śāstra* texts was bound to lead to some rather hybrid decisions.[28]

Justice, Equity, and Good Conscience

There were also rules in the *śāstra* that, to the British, were incompatible with their principle of "justice, equity and good conscience."[29] For instance, all *śāstras* agree that inheriting the property of a deceased person involves not only receiving his or her assets but also paying his or her debts, even when the debts exceed the assets, or when there are no assets whatever. A text attributed to the sage Bṛhaspati states, in the most general terms, "The father's debt must be paid first of all, and, after that, a man's own debt."[30] The British called this duty on the part of the heir "the pious obligation." They were prepared to accept the principle of the pious obligation as long as the debts did not exceed the assets, but an heir's being forced to pay debts larger than the assets violated their sense of justice, equity, and good conscience: debts were to be paid to the extent of the assets only.

In the case of the pious obligation, the British only narrowed the application of the *śāstra* texts, but the application of justice, equity, and good conscience went farther than that. The *śāstras* provide detailed rules on who can inherit and who cannot. Those who cannot inherit are those who are physically or mentally incapable of performing the necessary rites for the deceased (*śrāddha*). Inheriting property and performing the rites for the dead are indissolubly linked in the Hindu *śāstra*.[31] For instance, according to *The Laws of Manu*, the following are excluded from inheriting property: "No share is given to a man who is impotent or fallen, or blind or deaf from birth, or a madman, an idiot, or a mute, or devoid of virile strength."[32] All these are individuals who, for different reasons, are either unable or considered unqualified to perform the rituals for their deceased ancestors.[33]

At one point, two sisters of a murderer claimed the inheritance of their brother's victim. Their lawyers argued that the murderer, according to the *śāstra*, was his victim's heir, that he did not fall within the category of individuals who cannot inherit, and that, therefore, the inheritance belonged to them. Right from the beginning, the question was not so much whether the murderer himself could inherit but rather whether, for the sake of inheritance, he was to be considered existent or nonexistent. The case went from a lower court (which ruled in favor of the sisters), via an appeal to the Bombay High Court (which ruled in favor of their cousin), to the Privy Council in London.[34] Their Lordships discussed the case at great length, once more examining the *śāstra* texts on individuals who were entitled to inherit and on those who were not, but they concluded:

> Before this Board it has been contended that the matter is governed by Hindu law, and that the Hindu law makes no provision disqualifying a murderer from succeeding to the estate of his victim, and therefore it must be taken that according to this law, he can succeed.
>
> Their Lordships do not take this view.... The alternative is between the Hindu law being as above stated or being for the purpose non existent, and in that case the High Court have rightly decided that the principle of equity, justice and good conscience excludes the murderer.[35]

Legislative Acts

The principle of justice, equity, and good conscience presents one example of situations in which the British actually made some texts of the *śāstra* obsolete. This tendency also surfaced in a number of acts that the British imposed on Hindus during the last century of colonial rule. The earliest two, the Caste Disabilities Removal Act (1850) and the Hindu Widows' Remarriage Act (1856), clearly demonstrate the direction in which British interference with the *śāstra* was progressing: taking measures for the protection of the lower castes,[36] against restrictions imposed on women,[37] etc.

Epilogue

The *śāstra* suffered a far greater setback after Indian independence. In 1955–56, the Indian Parliament in Delhi enacted four laws that together overruled much of the *śāstra* and its development under British rule.[38] Section 4 of the Hindu Marriage Act unequivocally expresses the purpose of the new legislation:

> Save as otherwise expressly provided in this Act,—
>
> (a) any text, rule of interpretation of Hindu law or any custom or usage as part of that law in force immediately before the commencement of this Act shall cease to have effect with regard to any matter for which provision is made in this Act;
>
> (b) any other law in force immediately before the commencement of this Act shall cease to have effect in so far as it is inconsistent with any of the provisions contained in this Act.[39]

The Hindu Marriage Act[40] provoked a book whose subtitle, *Epitaph for the Rishis*, seemed to suggest that the law of the *śāstra* had come to an end.[41] It had, to a large extent, and yet S. V. Gupte, commenting on section 4 of the Hindu Marriage Act, points out that, notwithstanding its title ("Over-riding effect of the Act"), the section "also means that after the coming into operation of this Act any other law which was in force immediately before the commencement of this Act would continue to be in force provided it has not been repealed by this Act and to the extent to which its provisions are not inconsistent with this Act."[42] Even though, as far as marriage is concerned, "such matters are indeed few,"[43] there are broader areas of Hindu family law that remain beyond the purview of the four acts of 1955–56. These aspects continue to be governed by "the Shaster" as I have described it in this essay. Even today the law courts in India decide cases related to the pious obligation, and other cases, according to the law of the *śāstra* as it existed prior to independence.[44]

The laws of Manu and those of the other ancient sages, the *rishis*, may have been interpreted differently in the course of several centuries, and they may have been largely abrogated in more recent times, but they are still on the minds of the legal profession in India. The post-1956 editions of the classical treatises on Hindu law continue and will continue to devote lengthy introductions to the *śāstra* as long as "the enactments which have so far found place on the statute-book leave an undetermined residue."[45]

NOTES

The following abbreviations are used in legal citations included in the notes to this essay:

Bom.: Indian Law Reports, Bombay

F.B.: Full Bench

I.A.: Indian Appeals

M.I.A.: Moore's Indian Appeals

P.C.: Privy Council

1. See Robert E. Frykenberg, "Warren Hastings," in Ainslee T. Embree, ed., *Encyclopedia of Asian History*, vol. 2 (New York: Scribners, 1988), 38.

2. Hastings did so against strong opposition; see Alexander Dow, *Enquiry into the State of Bengal* (London: 1772), 11, 14: "To leave the natives to their own laws would be to consign them to anarchy and confusion. . . . It is therefore absolutely necessary for the peace and prosperity of the country that the laws of England in so far as they do not oppose prejudice and usages which cannot be relinquished by the natives should prevail. The measure, besides its equity, is calculated to preserve that influence which conquerors must possess to retain their power."

3. The plan was drawn up by the Committee of Circuit, of which Hastings was president, and was adopted by the president and council at Fort William on August 21, 1772. On April 11, 1780, the paragraph quoted here became law as section 27 of the Administration of Justice Regulation. Note that it exclusively bears on family law and thereby excludes procedure, criminal law, etc., even though these, too, were integral parts of "the Shaster." They were replaced by the Penal Code (1860), the Indian Evidence Act (1872), the Code of Criminal Procedure (1898), and the Code of Civil Procedure (1908).

4. See Sir William Jones's letter to Hastings's successor, Cornwallis, dated March 9, 1788, in Garland Cannon, ed., *The Letters of Sir William Jones* (Cambridge: Cambridge University Press, 1970), 794: "Nothing indeed could be more obviously just, than to determine private contests according to those laws, which the parties themselves had ever considered as the rules of their conduct and engagements in civil life; nor could anything be wiser than, by a legislative act, to assure the Hindu and Muselman subjects of Great Britain, that the private laws, which they severally hold sacred, and a violation of which they would have thought the most grievous oppression, should not be superseded by a new system, of which they could have no knowledge, and which they must have considered as imposed on them by a spirit of rigour and intolerance."

5. The question of whether the *dharmaśāstras* actually contained the laws by which Hindus lived in ancient India is still debated; see Ludo Rocher, "Law Books in an Oral Culture: The Indian *Dharmaśāstras*," *Proceedings of the American Philosophical Society* 137 (1993), 254–67.

6. See Dinshah Fardunji Mulla, *Principles of Hindu Law*, 10th ed., ed. Sunderlal T. Desai (Bombay: N. M. Tripathi, 1970), 3: "It was an article of belief with the ancient Hindu that his law was Revelation, immutable and eternal."

7. Cited in George Claus Rankin, *Background to Indian Law* (Cambridge: Cambridge University Press, 1946), 4.

8. The situation was different in the case of Indian Muslims. Several Englishmen at the time knew Persian, and some also knew Arabic.

9. One such solution, adopted in 1772 and abandoned in 1864, was to appoint Indian pandits as "law officers." These pandits consulted the *śāstras*, formulated decisions on the basis of the texts, and handed their decisions over to a British judge to pronounce his verdict. On the growing dissatisfaction with the system, see Jones's letter to Cornwallis in Cannon, ed., *The Letters of Sir William Jones*, 795.

10. William Jones, *Institutes of Hindu Law; Or, the Ordinances of Menu, According to the Gloss of Culluca, Comprising the Indian System of Duties Religious and Civil Verbally Translated from the Original Sanscrit* (printed in Calcutta, 1794, by the order of the government).

11. The reason why commentaries were preferred over the ancient texts will become clear later in this essay.

12. *Sri Balusu* v. *Sri Balusu* (1899) 26 I.A. 113, 146 (P.C.).

13. See the testimony, after his return from India, of George C. Rankin, chief justice of Bengal, in the preface to Rankin, *Background to Indian Law:* "I have been impressed at times with the peculiarity of the fate of very learned and able friends of mine who, as the reward of exceptional knowledge and skill in the business matters of England and Scotland, are suddenly required to turn a large part of their attention to Indian appeals. What at first do they think of them or make of them? What is their approach? . . . Not many people in this country have any settled notion of what we are doing in India administering law to Indians, nor have any means of readily acquiring a well-founded notion of how we come to be doing so or of the principles we apply. Certain I am that when I went to India in 1918 to engage upon the task, I had the smallest amount of information and no real explanation of many facts of historical importance."

14. *Rungama* v. *Atchama* (1846) 4 M.I.A. 1, 97–98 (P.C.).

15. See Ludo Rocher, "Hindu Law and Religion: Where to Draw the Line?" in Malik Ram Felicitation Committee, ed., *Malik Ram Felicitation Volume* (Delhi: Malik Ram Felicitation Committee, 1972), 167–94.

16. *Sri Balusu* v. *Sri Balusu.*

17. Mulla, *Principles of Hindu Law,* 502.

18. Yājñavalkya's *dharmaśāstra* was translated more than half a century later (by A. F. Stenzler, in 1849, into German). Most translations still used today were published in F. Max Müller, ed., *The Sacred Books of the East,* vols. 2 (*Āpastamba and Gautama,* trans. G. Bühler, 1879), 7 (*Viṣṇu,* trans. J. Jolly, 1880), 14 (*Vasiṣṭha and Baudhāyana,* trans G. Bühler, 1882), 25 (*Manu,* trans. Bühler, 1886), and 33 (*Nārada and Bṛhaspati,* trans. J. Jolly, 1889). More recent publications include Richard W. Larivière, trans., *Nārada* (Philadelphia: Department of South Asia Regional Studies, University of Pennsylvania, 1989), Wendy Doniger and Brian K. Smith, trans., *The Laws of Manu* (New York: Penguin, 1991), and Patrick Olivelle, trans., *The Dharmasūtras: The Law Codes of Āpastamba, Gautama, Baudhāyana, and Vasiṣṭha* (Oxford: Oxford University Press, 1999).

19. On the origin of the schools of Hindu law, see Ludo Rocher, "Schools of Hindu Law," in J. Ensink and P. Gaeffke, eds., *India Maior: Congratulatory Volume Presented to J. Gonda* (Leiden: Brill, 1972), 167–76. The most drastic and far-reaching division within Hindu law pertains to the law of succession and inheritance. The British selected two twelfth-century commentaries as the principal sources on inheritance law: Jimūtavāhana's *Dāyabhāga* and Vijñāneśvara's *Mitākṣarā,* for Bengal and for the rest of India, respectively. According to the *Mitākṣarā,* every male born into a joint family acquires by birth an undefined but real right of ownership in the family property—a concept that severely restricts the power of the head of the family. The *Dāyabhāga,* working from the same body of *śāstra* texts, concludes that the right of ownership originates only after the disappearance, by death or otherwise, of the previous owner of the property. As a result, in Bengal the head of the joint family was given nearly unlimited rights to dispose of family property as he pleased. Both commentaries were translated in a single volume; see Henry Thomas Colebrooke, *Two Treatises on the Hindu Law of Inheritance* (Calcutta: Hindoostani Press, 1810).

20. *Collector of Madura* v. *Moottoo Ramalinga* (1868) 12 M.I.A. 397, 436.

21. *Atmaram* v. *Bajirao* (1935) 62 I.A. 139, 143 (P.C.).

22. *Collector of Madura* v. *Moottoo Ramalinga,* 397, 436.

23. See Pandurang Vaman Kane, *Hindu Customs and Modern Law* (Bombay: University of Bombay, 1950).

24. They acted as their teachers did, that is, to the extent that Indian jurists were prepared to justify innovations introduced by the British as inherent parts of traditional Hindu law; see Ludo Rocher, "Indian Response to Anglo-Hindu Law," *Journal of the American Oriental Society* 92 (1972), 419–24.

25. See *Apaji Narhar* v. *Ramchandra* (1891) 16 Bom. 29 (F.B.), in which one judge demonstrated that Colebrooke's translation of a passage from the *Mitākṣarā* was in error. He was overruled by the majority of the Full Bench.

26. *Beer Pertab* v. *Rajender Pertab* (1867) 12 M.I.A. 1, 37–38. Wills among Hindus, including wills written in Indian languages, were officially sanctioned by the Hindu Wills Act (1870). Hindu wills created a complex body of jurisprudence; see Arthur Phillips and Ernest John Trevelyan, *The Law of Hindu Wills*, 2nd ed. (London: Thacker Spink, 1914).

27. See n. 23 above. For arguments that wills were not unknown in classical India, see Pandurang Vaman Kane, *History of Dharmaśāstra*, vol. 3 (Poona: Bhandarkar Oriental Research Institute, 1946), 816–17. Typically, Kane invokes a *śāstra* that "makes a very near approach to the modern conception of a will."

28. See J. Duncan M. Derrett, *"Factum valet:* The Adventures of a Maxim," *International and Comparative Law Quarterly* 7 (1958), 280–302. On the claim that the maxim was referred to in Jimūtavāhana's *Dāyabhāga*, see Ludo Rocher, "Jimūtavāhana's *Dāyabhāga* and the Maxim *factum valet*," *Adyar Library Bulletin* 59 (1995), 83–96.

29. See J. Duncan M. Derrett, "Justice, Equity and Good Conscience," in J. Norman D. Anderson, ed., *Changing Law in Developing Countries* (London: Allen & Unwin, 1963), 114–53.

30. For this and other *śāstra* texts to the same effect, see Ludo Rocher, "Hindu Law of Succession: From the Śāstras to Modern Law," *Revue du Sud-est asiatique* (1967), 20.

31. See Ludo Rocher, "Inheritance and Śrāddha: The Principle of Spiritual Benefit," in A. W. Van den Hoek et al., eds., *Ritual, State and History in South Asia: Essays in Honour of J. C. Heesterman* (Leiden: Brill, 1992), 637–49.

32. Doniger and Smith, trans., *The Laws of Manu*, 220.

33. The scholarly literature on *śrāddha* is vast. For a detailed study, see Pandurang Vaman Kane, *History of Dharmaśāstra*, vol. 4., 2nd ed. (1st ed. 1953) (Poona: Bhandarkar Oriental Research Institute, 1974), 334–551. See also, more recently, Marcelle Saindon, *Le Pitṛkalpa du Harivaṃśa* (Sainte-Foy, Quebec: Presses de l'Université Laval, 1998), 45–71.

34. See Ludo Rocher, "Can a Murderer Inherit His Victim's Estate? British Responses to Troublesome Questions in Hindu Law," *Journal of the American Oriental Society* 107 (1987), 1–10.

35. *Kenshava* v. *Girimalappa Channappa* (1924) 51 I.A. 368, 372–73 (P.C.). To prevent a murderer or his relatives from using the text of the *śāstra* again to claim the inheritance of the victim, the Hindu Succession Act (1956), even though it abrogates all Hindu law as it existed before the commencement of the act, explicitly disqualifies from inheritance, in section 25, "a person who commits murder or abets the commission of murder."

36. According to the *śāstra*, any person who became an outcaste lost his right to inherit. The Caste Disabilities Removal Act contains only one article: "So much of any law or usage now in force within the territories subject to the Government of the East India Company as inflicts on any person forfeiture of rights of property, or may be held in any way to impair or affect any right of inheritance by reason of his or her renouncing, or having been excluded from the communion of any religion, or having been deprived of caste, shall cease to be enforced as law in the Courts of the East India Company, and in the Courts established by Royal Charter within the said territories."

37. According to the *śāstra*, a Hindu widow, even a very young widow whose marriage had not been consummated, was not allowed to remarry; marriage being a lifelong commitment, divorce was prohibited. The Hindu Widows' Remarriage Act is subtitled "An Act to remove all legal obstacles to the marriage of Hindu widows." Article 1 reads: "No marriage contracted between Hindus shall be invalid, and the issue of no such marriage shall be illegitimate by reason of the woman having been previously married or betrothed to another person who was dead at the time of such marriage, any custom and any interpretation of Hindu law to the contrary notwithstanding."

38. These four laws were the Hindu Marriage Act (1955), the Hindu Succession Act (1956), the Hindu Minority and Guardianship Act (1956), and the Hindu Adoptions and Maintenance Act (1956).

39. The same formula is repeated, in nearly identical terms, in the three acts of 1956.

40. Or, rather, the Hindu Marriage Act (1955) as amended by the Marriage Law (Amendment) Act (1976).

41. J. Duncan M. Derrett, *The Death of a Marriage Law: Epitaph for the Rishis* (Delhi: Vikas, 1978).

42. Shankar Vinayak Gupte, *Hindu Law of Marriage* (Bombay: N. M. Tripathi, 1961), 102.

43. Mulla, *Principles of Hindu Law,* 612.

44. Ibid., 323: "The pious obligation of sons, grandsons, great-grandsons to pay the ancestor's debts to the extent of their interest in the joint family property is not abrogated by the Hindu Succession Act, 1956."

45. Ibid., 69.

Czech Underground Literature, 1969–1989
A Challenge to Textual Studies

MARTIN MACHOVEC

The notions of an underground culture and an underground literature entered unofficial Czech culture at the beginning of the 1970s. It was only after 1989, however, that prominent Czech literary historians, critics, and book reviewers invoked these notions to speak of a certain branch of Czech literature—or, perhaps more properly speaking, to speak of a few twigs on that branch, works whose publication had been infrequent if not wholly suppressed in Czechoslovakia between 1948 and 1989. Clearly, the term "underground" was imported to Czechoslovakia toward the late 1960s and early 1970s from the United States, and it came to have a particularly close connection, as we will see, with the movement generally associated with the Plastic People of the Universe, a Czechoslovakian rock group. Some Czech artists of the early 1970s, by identifying with the notion of the underground, not only acknowledged the influence of the American underground scene but also came to recognize and discover some of their own ancestors, whose art and way of life provided both inspiration and an autochthonic, endogenous cultural background.

First, however, it should be stressed that the notion of the underground in the Czech cultural setting involves more than a literary trend or orientation, and more than artistic activity. Rather, the notion of the underground can be understood in connection with a particular worldview (weltanschauung) or attitude toward life. As such, the "underground" is a notion that carries significant social, political, and psychological weight, and texts of the Czech underground must be interpreted in light of this fact. For scholars and editors in the area of textual studies, these are circumstances bristling with problems and difficulties, since the very conditions for the production and dissemination of "texts" are intimately bound up with the political and psychological reality of a profoundly disrupted cultural life.

The history of the Czech underground begins with the arrival and ends with the collapse of the totalitarian, Stalinist (and, later, neo-

Stalinist) regime. The Czech underground sought to preserve authentic cultural values, undistorted by totalitarian demagogy and ideology, through an insistence on the continuity of a creative process unconstrained by any kind of censorship or taboo. In this sense, the Czech underground (or *podzemí*) was from its inception remarkably similar to the medieval Jewish ghetto, where enough room was preserved for inner freedom despite isolation from the world outside. Thus the Czech cultural underground was always a question of politics, since its very existence amounted to indirect indictment of an inhuman political system.

The Czechoslovak Surrealist Group, with its revolutionary, provocative proclamations and its artistic ferment in prewar Czechoslovakia, aroused keen interest in several poets who were young at the beginning of the 1950s. They were lauded for their outlook on the world and their attitude toward life. Twenty years later, they won recognition as virtual founders of the underground movement that will be discussed in this essay. The first of these crucial writers was the poet and philosopher Zbyněk Fišer (1930–), who in 1948 adopted the pseudonym Egon Bondy. Then came the poet Ivo Vodseďálek (1931–); Jana Krejcarová (1928–1981), daughter of Milena Jesenská, herself famous as Kafka's "friend"; Vladimír Boudník (1924–1968), who later won fame as a graphic artist; and the now world-renowned Czech writer Bohumil Hrabal (1914–1997), more than ten years older than most of the writers just named. Despite Hrabal's relative visibility, not to mention his success in getting some of his works officially published (if in considerably censored and distorted form)—a success enhanced when the original versions of these works were published in Czechoslovakia after 1989—the key role in forming and articulating the Czech underground (or "protounderground") was played by Bondy, who as early as 1950 had outgrown youthful surrealist imitations and developed his own artistic program of so-called total realism.[1]

From the perspective of Czech cultural history, literature, art, and politics, the Czech underground, in the narrow sense of that term, involved only one of the unofficial communities that were gathering in Czechoslovakia toward the end of the 1960s: the one that, at the beginning of the 1970s, still consisted mostly of fans of the Plastic People of the Universe, the band that had formed in 1968, inspired by the aesthetics of Andy Warhol's pop art and by the sound and performances of Lou Reed and John Cale, founders of the the Velvet Underground, in New York. This group of fans notably incorporated the word and label "underground" for self-identification, reflecting a type of influence that was quite extraordinary in the Czechoslovakia of those years.

The Plastic People were also one of the very few groups in the Czechoslovak Socialist Republic of the early 1970s that refused to submit to the state's supervision of all kinds of cultural and political activity. From that point on, then, the group was inevitably pulled into a literal underground, in the sense of *illegal activity:* in the 1970s and 1980s, the term "underground" gradually became a label for a number of unofficial, illegal groups. Thus, in the broadest sense, the term "underground," in its Czech translations *(podzemí* or *podzemní),* can be seen as applying to every kind of illegal, unofficial, banned cultural activity that took place during the four totalitarian decades (1948–1989), and especially during the 1950s, the 1970s, and the 1980s. Hence the term applies as well to samizdat activity, which was also quite characteristic of political dissent in the 1970s and 1980s.

The difference in substance between the cultural role played by underground activities in the narrow sense, as embodied in the Plastic People and their circle, and the role played by most other underground activities in the Czechoslovakia of the 1970s and 1980s, as embodied in unofficial, illegal, dissident, *podzemní* movements, can be found in their different cultural backgrounds, which in turn came from different historical trends, as suggested by the seven approximate phases in the history of Czechoslovakian social life: (1) the period between 1945 and 1948, years in which plurality of opinion was guaranteed and there was a democratic society, with no need for illegal activities; (2) 1948–1956, the period of terror, Stalinist dictatorship, and totalitarianism; (3) 1956–1968, a time of gradual liberalization in social life; (4) 1968–1969, the time of the Prague Spring, a short period that saw complete liberalization in social and cultural life, as well as the collapse of the dictatorship; (5) 1969–1977, the period when terror and totalitarianism were reintroduced along with the so-called normalization of social life; (6) 1977, the year of Charter 77 (a declaration of human rights, the first oppositional platform to appear since 1968), and the year when terror reached its climax; and (7) 1977–1989, the period when totalitarian terror and the dictatorship gradually disintegrated.

In phase 2 (1948–1956), only a very few artists were committed to continuing their work on an illegal basis, and of those who were, even fewer attempted to reflect the new social situation with the help of new, more adequate artistic means. In phase 3 (1956–1968), most artists were able to work legally, but only with a certain degree of self-censorship, since all cultural activities were still under state supervision; those who worked in publishing also had to take the tastes of readers into account. Many artists during this phase tried not only to pursue the variety of artistic currents and literary trends that had existed in Czechoslovakia before the coup of 1948 but also to keep abreast of contemporary Western trends. In phase 4 (1968–1969), near-complete liberalization permitted all types of orientations and confrontations, but of course this period was very short; the impulses assimilated during this time formed the foundation of most illegal cultural activity during the subsequent two decades.[2] In phase 5 (1969–1977), the best-known authors who had managed to publish their work within the few liberal years became dissidents (if they decided not to leave the country). With the help of samizdat editions and Czech publishing houses in exile, they tried to maintain the continuity of their liberal views and ideals. By contrast, the Plastic People and their underground circle kept their distance from the formerly prominent dissidents, followed their own radical Western patterns, and soon discovered and took inspiration from several Czech protounderground authors of the 1950s, beginning with Egon Bondy. By phase 6 (1977) and the first year of phase 7 (1977–1989), the separate, individual *podzemní* currents, including the underground community of the Plastic People, had to some degree found their way to one another through Charter 77.

On the basis of the preceding overview, I offer two propositions. First, the illegal, underground dissent of the 1970s tried both to preserve and to generate a rich variety of democratic cultural forms (in literature and in art, for example) as they had existed before 1948 and, in part, in the 1960s. Second, the writers and artists of the Plastic People community, in the face of the totalitarian regime, experienced a helplessness that formed their basic, primary attitude toward life. Feeling isolated, almost without predecessors, and uprooted, they were drawn to establishing a community of a new kind, and to creating autonomous, completely independent expressions in art and literature, no matter how inferior or unworthy of attention their fellow artists of dissent might judge such expressions. This situation, of a "ghetto within the ghetto," certainly contributed to the type of underground samizdat texts that were actually produced.

The underground literature I am considering here—the literature concerned with the Plastic People circle of the 1970s and the 1980s, which looked to literary texts by Bondy that had been written in the 1950s—is usually connected if not identified with several Czech literary currents that reflected the social situation and position in which underground artists found themselves. These artists were outlaws, as it were, engaged in illegal activity, and very often Bondy's early program of so-called total realism is quoted as a *pars pro toto* of the whole underground literary scene of the Plastic People circle. Nevertheless, the designation "total realism," as Gertraude Zand has convincingly argued,[3] actually involves only a single aspect of the broad concept that had to do with depoeticizing, primitivizing, or barbarizing literary texts (and other art phenomena), as this concept was applied and first used by Bondy and his friends Hrabal, Krejcarová, and Vodseďálek. Zand argues that this concept was an adequate reaction to the terror of Bondy's and his contemporaries' era, a period that misused art and wanted it wholly subordinated to the state and ruled by only one ideology (in this case, the ideology of Stalinist Communism) but parallel to similar concepts—for example, the concepts of Jiří Kolář (1914–2002), Jan Hanč (1916–1963), and Karel Maryčko (1915–1988), who used "eyewitness poetics" or "diary poetics" in some of their samizdat works from the 1950s. This type of poetics was also approached—with heightened emphasis on the factual, and a weakening of most traditional poetic devices—by some older poets, such as Jakub Deml (1878–1961) and Vladimír Holan (1905–1980) in the collections *Rudoarmějci* (1947) and *Tobě* (1947), and by a number of other authors, including Jan Zahradníček (1905–1960), whose literary works of the 1950s offered evidence of life in the prisons and labor camps. Václav Havel (1936–), too, used eyewitness poetics in some early poems of the mid-1950s. Ideological, dogmatic pressure was also resisted in prose, with eyewitness poetics partially applied in a number of Hrabal's short stories and in the novel *Zbabělci (The Cowards)*, by Josef Škvorecký (1924–), the latter work written in the late 1940s but published officially only in 1958, at which point it aroused indignation and scandal—Škvorecký was accused of being "too explicit." Jan Zábrana (1931–1984) also wrote several short stories of a similar kind in the 1950s, these published only after 1989.

It is surely also possible to understand such concepts as depoeticization and emphasis on the factual as direct reactions to the rigidity of official socialist realism, which was all that was permitted in the Soviet bloc in the 1950s. These concepts, akin to 1950s ideals of French existentialism, were also, in a way, reactions to the exclusiveness and sophistication of "vanguard" (Czech or French) surrealism. Simplification of the means of expression can also be understood as an unconscious parallel to American action painting and to French tachism, but many of the illegal Czech literary works of that period are rich in neodadaist poetic principles (remarkable especially in Ivo Vodseďálek's concept of the poetry of "embarrassment"), anticipating the iconography and poetics of so-called new figuration, pop art, and hyperrealism. Frequent renunciation of rhyme, metaphor, and most other traditional poetic devices (or their ironic or parodic use), along with explicit politics and a disregard for taboos, reflected the feeling of having discovered a new way of seeing and of having established a system of new, nontraditional values. It has only recently become possible, thanks to preservation of these 1950s Czech poets' texts, to find in their work parallels to the work of some American poets of the Beat Generation, especially in explicit expressions of their hopeless position in society, of their disregard for taboos, and of their effort to establish a new autonomy of values.

In the 1950s, the reality of a world divided into two poles seemed definitive, final—"total"—and provided the ground for the very existence of such literary texts. Feelings of helplessness and powerlessness were an appropriate, almost inevitable reaction to such a reality; adequate reflection of such feelings needed and, in fact, demanded new artistic forms. In these conditions, literary production was anything but ordinary, normal, or routine; for just that reason, the texts and their preservation and dissemination are all the more important.

The history of the Plastic People of the Universe, and of the band's underground community of fans during the 1970s and the 1980s, is now well known.[4] The members of the band, by comparison with their forerunners of the 1950s, enjoyed much more access to information about what was happening on the other side of the Iron Curtain. Czechoslovakia in the 1970s and 1980s was strongly influenced by the Anglo-American rock scene and by the "flower power" and nonviolence of the 1960s hippies. Czech translations of a number of Beat Generation writers were also available by then. Milan Knížák (1940–), who founded the experimental, proto-underground rock group Aktual in 1966, supplied young Czech artists with much valuable information about the original New York underground scene; about Fluxus, the avant-garde artists' group of which he was a member; about Andy Warhol; and about such musicians as the Fugs, the Velvet Underground, David Peel, the Jefferson Airplane, the Grateful Dead, the Mothers of Invention,[5] and Captain Beefheart, who all later had a strong influence on the Czech underground scene. At the same time, young artists were looking for information about the suppressed local artistic traditions of the 1950s, the prewar Czech vanguard, and the generation of turn-of-the-century symbolist and decadent artists and poets. Some of them also turned an interest in Christianity, which had been pushed aside during the 1950s and even the 1960s by the official atheistic propaganda, almost into a kind of underground resistance, whereas others became interested in various Oriental teachings and exotic religions. But this effort to absorb cultural values coming from the West was soon violently interrupted and crushed by the state and its dogmatic ideology. Artists who refused to conform to the new rules were terrorized at every turn and deprived of possibilities to realize their works.

It is important here to emphasize the role of the art historian Ivan Martin "Magor" Jirous (1944–). Thanks to his outstanding organizational skills, a number of illegal concerts and even festivals were held in addition to exhibitions and poetry readings. It was also Jirous who organized several samizdat anthologies of underground poetry and provided the impetus for the founding, in 1979, of *Vokno*, the first underground journal of the circle of the Plastic People. As a result, he was jailed several times in the 1970s and the 1980s and spent almost nine years in prison. It was also Jirous, as early as 1972, who had made young musicians and artists aware of Bondy's literary work. The Plastic People of the Universe read it with great enthusiasm and began setting it to music. Later, they called their first illegal record *Egon Bondy's Happy Hearts Club Banned*. It can be said, without much exaggeration, that had it not been for the music written by the Plastic People, Bondy's poems probably would have vegetated at the fringes of samizdat readers' attention until 1989. Thus it was the underground circle of the Plastic People that rehabilitated the work of Bondy's group of 1950s poets: a few manuscripts, preserved purely by chance over two decades, had helped set in motion a whole series of activities of all kinds. Since the early 1970s Bondy himself, inspired by the interest of his new friends, has been at work on new artistic projects. In 1974 he published (in samizdat) a chef d'oeuvre for the underground community: a philosophical, anti-Utopian science-fiction novel, *Invalidní sourozenci* (The Disabled Siblings).

A number of other poets and writers also gathered around the Plastic People. Of these, the most outstanding were Milan Koch (1948–1974), who during his short life created a specific Czech variant of Allen Ginsberg's litanic poetry, and Vratislav Brabenec (1943–), in whose poems the tradition of Czech Hussite protestantism and the biblical ideals of the Bohemian Brethen[6] mingle with a sort of biophile, egalitarian pantheism. It was also Brabenec who supplied the Plastic People with texts by a little-known but quite remarkable Czech Nietzschean philosopher and writer, Ladislav Klíma (1878–1928) and created arrangements for several New Testament texts, which the Plastic People used as the basis of two of their most important records, 1978's *Pašije* (Passion Play), and 1979's *Jak bude po smrti / Slavná Nemesis* (Afterlife / Glorious Nemesis). Yet another was Pavel Zajíček (1951–), founder of the well-known underground band DG 307,[7] whose early texts were appeals bordering on reproaches to Old Testament prophets. Gospel songs and parables written and sung by the priest Svatopluk Karásek (1942–) also aroused keen interest in the underground public. Also popular were the poetic experiments using déclassé language of Andrej Stankovič (1940–2001) and Fanda Pánek (1949–) and, of course, the unskilled, "primitive" rock lyrics of Josef Vondruška, Miroslav Skalický, František "Jim Čert" Horáček, and many others. This community enjoyed, at the fringes of Czechoslovak society, a rich, autonomous cultural life reminiscent of life in a "merry ghetto,"[8] in sharp contrast to the overwhelming gloom, depression, and hypocrisy of the times.

It should be mentioned at this point that the underground writers' samizdat activities, always fruitful and varied, mostly took the form of so-called wild, unestablished samizdat texts—that is, samizdat texts not organized into volumes or editions, and mostly unauthorized. Sometimes mysterious imaginary editions were even produced, expressly to baffle the police. Moreover, the underground community of the 1970s and 1980s subscribed to communal ideals, and the thought of a work of literature as individual property, not to mention the notion of a copyright, was mostly alien to this group. Texts and books were often retyped for the purpose of further distribution, and, unfortunately, their self-appointed editors often worked rather willfully. As the number of unauthorized editions grew, unplanned textual variations occurred, along with more and more borrowings and quotations that made no mention of the originators (but unattributed quotations can also be seen as deliberate attempts to protect authors from the police). Authors often changed their pseudonyms or remained anonymous, a fact that multiplied the number of errors and misprints. Moreover, not all samizdat texts made by authors themselves survived to 1989 and the end of the dictatorship, since the police regularly destroyed confiscated materials after a given period had elapsed.

This complicated situation has greatly contributed to the difficulties involved in textual studies, literary historical studies, and the work of editors after 1989. The existence of "wild" underground samizdat texts also tells us something about the type of literature they contained. It is obvious that in such texts the message was a very vital component, and that even the most manifestly literary text often had an extraliterary purpose or aim.

But this kind of cultural ferment could not be sustained for long in the Czechoslovakia of the 1970s. In 1976, soon after one of the illegal festivals, most of the leading figures of the underground community were arrested, and about ten of them were eventually jailed for allegedly fomenting a "disturbance." Their trial caught the attention of prominent Czech dissidents who had not previously been interested in underground activity, and it also aroused the interest of some Czech journalists as well as foreign writers abroad such as Ivan Hartel, Heinrich Böll, Kurt Vonnegut Jr., Ed Sanders, and Allen Ginsberg. Police terror became more intense, peaking in 1977, when most of the underground artists and their friends and fans united around Charter 77. Thus it was a combination of police repression and the solidarity of the underground people with the Charter 77 political dissidents that brought about the considerable disintegration of the underground ghetto, with the accompanying destruction of its spirit of coherence. Moreover, many leading figures of the underground were forced to leave the country under pressure from the police, and permanent police repression made any kind of major underground action almost impossible.

It is remarkable that the more impossible it became to organize underground gatherings, such as concerts, poetry readings, and exhibitions, the more active underground authors became in writing texts and publishing them in samizdat form. When the underground writers later established connections with prominent dissidents and exiles, their works were published in established samizdat form for the first time, as well as in such exile periodicals as Václav Havel's review *Expedice*, Pavel Tigrid's Paris-based journal *Svědectví*, and Zbyněk Benýšek's Vienna-based *Paternoster*. Respectable publishing houses, such as Josef Škvorecký's Sixty-Eight Publishers, in Toronto, also expressed interest. Thanks again to Czech exiles and foreign friends, the first Plastic People of the Universe record was released in Britain, in 1978. In this way, the Western public finally came to learn something about the Czech underground.

The 1980s saw considerable dispersion of underground activity, on the one hand, and, on the other, its nearly desperate efforts to survive, especially in the area of "publishing" (i.e., dissemination of samizdat texts). Even though police surveillance made even private concerts before small audiences impossible, new illegal records by the Plastic People and DG 307 were distributed and subsequently released—but only abroad, of course. Also in the 1980s, Ivan Jirous wrote his seminal text on the history of the underground culture, *Pravdivý příběh Plastic People* (The True Story of the Plastic People),[9] which he conceived as something of a chronicle of the vanished era, a legacy for future generations. Egon Bondy concentrated on writing his voluminous history of philosophy, dedicated to the underground community and conceived both as a challenge of sorts to academicians and state-supported scholars and as a manifestation of the still-living underground.

The early 1980s also saw the founding of a number of new underground journals; and new rock bands and other musical groups, inspired by the old underground, came into being. Several remarkable younger poets, most born about 1960, made their debuts as well, again inspired by the resistance of the older underground generation. (The evidence of that resistance was now often found only in texts, since many of the earlier underground writers were in prison in the 1980s or had been forced into exile.) Among the new writers it is necessary to mention, first, Jáchym Topol, author of harsh naturalistic poetry and prose, and then J. H. Krchovský and Luděk Marks, who together brought about an ironic revival of late-nineteenth-century decadent poetry, and, finally, Petr Placák, who wrote visionary, Beat-like poems and diary-style verse in addition to one of the most characteristic works of the Czech literary underground: an ironic, experimental autobiographical novel, *Medorek* (1985). Also notable is Jan Pelc, who in 1983, in a provincial town in the north of Bohemia, wrote a harsh, largely factual documentary novel, *Děti ráje* (Children of Paradise).

The year 1989 brought the end of the Czechoslovak cultural underground movement. Hundreds of samizdat publications are now gathered and filed in archives, primarily in Prague's Libri Prohibiti, the Library of Samizdat and Exile Literature. Since the end of 1989, underground literature, along with all the other types of samizdat, dissident, exile, or banned literature, has been prepared for printing presses. As these texts appear, the challenge for textual studies is once again evident, not just on technical grounds but on ideological grounds as well: a text that emerges from such a history carries a substantial part of its meaning in that history itself, and so the fact that the text appears in the form of an aesthetic object—that is, in the normalizing context of a printed book—tends to enhance the text's importance at the cost of obscuring its historical origins, and therefore a good part of its meaning.

If we count the writers of the underground, between 1990 and 2001 about 150 volumes of original poetry, fiction, essays, and memoirs were published in Czechoslovakia, later the Czech Republic. Official Czech literary history has recorded these volumes, but it must be said that today's prominent literary historians and critics give them scant attention. With only a few exceptions—Bondy's *Invalidní sourozenci*, Placák's *Medorek*, the poetry of Jirous, Krchovský, and Topol—this literary heritage has been as seriously neglected, even denied, by the professional literary class as it surely would have been by the Communist *kulturträgers* of the ancien régime.

There are certainly a number of reasons for this neglect. To begin with, these texts are a departure from both official and unofficial mainstream literature. They were often written for too narrow a circle of readers, most of whom found themselves in the same existential situation as the authors, and they reflect that ghettolike condition. Moreover, they are too focused on their own times, on a concrete sociopolitical situation; as such, these texts, even those that seem purely literary, often took the place of political journalism or political action. Further, they often require concrete interpretation or framing (for example, as lyrics set to music), and they usually have to be read within the special atmosphere of a conspiracy. In addition, because there were very few attempts to review samizdat writings—any reviews that did appear, mostly in the second half of the 1980s, were found in the pages of various samizdat periodicals—it is obvious that most of these texts were never influenced by the feedback of a wide readership or book reviewers. Regardless of their vaunted "antiliterary" character, then, these texts are actually rather exclusive, and a number of underground texts whose literary value cannot be denied are clearly out of step with the aesthetics and tastes of the average mass-market reader, who is himself often the object of the underground writers' irony, derision, and disrespect. Thus the underground texts necessarily, if inadvertently, constitute an indictment against the average reader; their mere existence accuses him of passivity and silent collaboration with the totalitarian regime.

Even this brief survey of underground Czech literature shows the troubled nature of textual study in such circumstances. It is evident that literary historians may be severely challenged in retrieving the relevant details of this literary history, just as it is clear that, if this work is to be preserved, it will be crucial for literary historians to decide precisely which details *are* relevant, and to link these texts to the flow of seemingly chaotic events. Moreover, textual editors will be confronted with publishing patterns and practices that radically complicate the idea of editing. How does one even determine what will count as a text, when artistic work emerges from so dense a matrix of cooperation and resistance? Nevertheless, and regardless of the difficulties, this challenging work must be undertaken because of its importance for our understanding of the rich dynamic— and the stress—of cultural life in such conditions.

The value of Czech underground literary works written in the 1970s and 1980s is especially visible in these works' anarchic enthusiasm. They delighted in shared resistance and defiance, but they also created a community in which writers, poets, philosophers, musicians, and artists of the most varied provenance were able to confront one another's works freely and exercise mutual influence. The underground movement thus occasioned several artistic conjunctions that probably never would have occurred under so-called normal conditions. In some of the samizdat poetry anthologies, for instance, politically explicit and provocatively anti-Soviet (though leftist) "Maoist" lyrics by Bondy found their place next to the tender, refined, formalist poetry of Věra Jirousová and alongside revivals of Czech Catholic tradition by Ivan Jirous, which in turn appeared in the same neighbourhood as the perverse, quasi-satanic, primitive texts of Josef Vondruška and Dino Vopálka—all of it a paradoxically harmonious whole.

Such mutual tolerance, such mingling and mixing of texts derived from very different poetics (but from similar ideals), such "interdisciplinary" unity of purely literary texts with "antiartifacts" and "documents," undoubtedly contributed to this writing's relative lack of popularity with most Czech readers of the time, and with most reviewers and literary historians, who tended to comply with the tastes of the broad reading public. And the writings of the underground remain half forgotten in today's Czech Republic, perhaps mostly because they are too adequate, too radical, in mirroring the true face of the late totalitarian regime. This fact, as much as the inherent fascination of undertaking what is difficult, makes the textual preservation of this literature essential.

NOTES

1. Between 1990 and 1993, Bondy's poetic work, which now consists of about forty collections of poems and lyric epopeés, was published in Prague as *Básnické dílo Egona Bondyho*, in nine volumes. Between 1991 and 2001 most of his novels and other prose writings were also published in Prague, as were his numerous philosophical works, such as *Poznámky k dějinám filosofie* (Remarks on the History of Philosophy). Of his early samizdat texts, the most typical and remarkable ones are the collection *Totální realismus* (1950); *Für Bondy's unbekannte Geliebte* (For Bondy's Unknown Love, 1951), parts of which were written in German; and *Ožralá Praha* (Hammered Prague, 1952), with its pseudoprimitive verses and dominating "antipoetic" sound. Other Bondy masterpieces of the period are his lyric epopees *Pražský život* (Prague Life, 1951), *Zbytky eposu* (Remnants of an Epic, 1955), and *Nesmrtelná dívka* (Immortal Girl, 1958). For additional information, see the translator's introduction and the note on the author and the translator in *Egon Bondy: The Consolation of Ontology*, trans. Benjamin B. Page (New York: Lexington Books, 2001).

2. It is also interesting that a number of authors who took little if any advantage of the Prague Spring liberalization, perhaps striving for an even higher degree of freedom, were later on associated if not identified with the underground circle of the Plastic People.

3. Gertraude Zand, *Totaler Realismus und Peinliche Poesie: Tschechische Untergrund-Literatur, 1948–1953* (Frankfurt: Peter Lang, 1998).

4. The richest source of commentary is Jaroslav Riedel, ed., *The Plastic People of the Universe: Texty* (Prague: Maťa, 1997), available in English as Jaroslav Riedel, ed., *The Plastic People of the Universe*, trans. Olga Záhorbenská, Paul Wilson, Jan Jonák, Marek Tomin, and Yosef Yanda (Prague: Matta, 1999). The essays of the art historian Ivan Jirous, artistic director of the Plastic People of the Universe, have recently been published in one volume; see Michael Špirit, ed., *Ivan M. Jirous: Magorův zápisník* (Prague: Torst, 1997). One of Jirous's essays, of essential relevance to the history of the Plastic People underground, was published in English; see Ivan Jirous, "Report on the Third Czech Musical Revival," in *The Merry Ghetto*, catalog enclosed with the album *Egon Bondy's Happy Hearts Club Banned* (London: LTM and Boží Miýn Productions / The Plastic People Defense Fund / SCOPA Invisible Productions, 1976, 1978). Of great importance as well are the memoirs of Milan Hlavsa, *Bez ohňů je underground* (Prague: BFS, 1992). Some problems of underground literature, involving both the Plastic People underground and several of its 1950s predecessors, are discussed in Martin Pilař, *Underground: Kapitoly o českém literarním undergroundu* (Brno: Host, 1999). See also Wolfgang Eichwede, ed., *Samizdat: Alternativí kultur in Zentral- und Osteuropa: Die 60er bis 80er Jahre*, vol. 8 (Bremen: Edition Temmen, 2000) and Josef Alan, ed., *Alternativní kultura. Příběh české společnosti 1948–1989* (Prague: NLN, 2001).

5. Frank Zappa of the Mothers of Invention wrote the song "Plastic People" (1966), and it was from this song that the Plastic People of the Universe took their name.

6. The Bohemian (or Moravian) Brethren formed a fifteenth-century religious community that attempted to renew the faith of the first Christians. Radical Hussites, the Bohemian Brethren split off from the Roman Catholic Church in 1467. Many of the group's adherents, heavily persecuted during the period of re-Catholicization, fled to Poland and Silesia. In 1575 they joined the Lutherans to create the *Confessio Bohemica* and were granted religious freedom by Rudolf II in 1609.

7. The band reportedly got its name from the members' mistaken belief that DG 307 was the diagnostic code for schizophrenia.

8. *The Merry Ghetto* was the title of the catalog that accompanied *Egon Bondy's Happy Hearts Club Banned*, the first album by the Plastic People of the Universe; see n. 4 above.

9. In Špirit, ed., *Ivan M. Jirous: Magorův zápisník*.

PART V

Electronic Text

The Reality of Electronic Editions

SUSAN HOCKEY

Much hype currently surrounds discussions on hypertext, electronic textuality, theory of electronic text, and related topics, especially in relation to the preparation of electronic editions and archives. Leading textual scholars have embraced the idea of electronic texts and textuality and have speculated at length about this new medium, both in print and on the Internet.[1] In practical terms, however, we are very much farther behind. Few implementations exist, and most of these are, in my view, poorly designed and weak in functionality. They tend to have too much dependence on the HyperText Markup Language (HTML) and native Web technology and to incorporate too many multimedia gimmicks. They also fail to provide the user with adequate tools to manipulate and analyze the material, and thus they do not fully exploit the real power of the technology.[2]

It is all too easy to be seduced by the medium and lose sight of the scholarly objectives of a project. I want to argue here that we should take a back-to-basics approach, and a more scientific approach to defining a workable model for electronic editions.[3] We need to reach consensus on a model that will serve current and future scholarly needs and not be overtaken by rapid changes in technology. That model must be flexible enough to address the needs of a variety of users and must also be amenable to many kinds of computer processing. We need to prove that the concept of electronic editions is viable for the long term and formulate a path for arriving at that proof. A scientific approach calls for building on existing expertise, developing models, evaluating those models, and documenting what we have learned. In this, as in much computer-based work, methodological issues are in the forefront. It is impossible to avoid the question of "how" in starting an electronic project. Given the expense of creating electronic information, it makes sense to consider a generalizable framework for the "how" and to aim to build a framework and tool set that will satisfy many purposes.

It also makes sense to start from what we know. In this case, we have a reasonably well defined model for printed editions, one that has evolved over a period of time and that works as well as it can, given the limitations of the medium in which it is published (it was of course these limitations that led scholars to begin experimenting with electronic editions in the first place). Working in electronic form, we are no longer limited by what can be made to fit on rectangular pieces of paper that are bound together into a book. A publication can be, theoretically, any size, even of unlimited size; but, in more practical terms, its size is perhaps limited by what the reader can conceptualize as still being part of the publication. Material in an electronic publication does not have to appear in a single, linear stream; it can be organized in many different ways. In reality, however, readers very soon get lost unless they can perceive some kind of structure within the framework. The print model, with its linear stream of text and footnotes, offers a well-understood and very simple framework, one that works reasonably well when there is only one version of the text, and when the information in the footnotes applies only once and is not repeated anywhere. It works less well with more complex texts where it is very difficult to present multiple versions, or for annotations that need to be repeated and thus can be signaled only by cross-references, perhaps even to earlier volumes. For an electronic edition, we need to build on these structures, not by attempting to replicate the printed page but by organizing the information into its component parts, which can then be manipulated as necessary.

We also now know a fair amount about electronic texts, particularly about how to create electronic texts and about the kinds of processing that can be successfully carried out on them. Humanities computing began in 1949 with Father Busa's *Index Thomisticus*, a concordance to ten million words of St. Thomas Aquinas and related authors.[4] Until recently, much work in literary and humanities computing has focused on the detailed analysis of scholarly electronic texts.[5] The computer is extraordinarily good at finding patterns and at counting and sorting them, provided that those patterns are clearly defined. Concordances can be excellent tools for philological, linguistic, and stylistic applications. Many of the scholars using concordance tools have worked on very complex texts that they needed to represent in fine detail in electronic form. This work has led to research into methods of representing or encoding electronic text, an area where I do think that significant progress has been made, and where, as is shown by developments with the Extensible Markup Language (XML, discussed below), the humanities computing community has been leading the field.

Electronic texts are much more useful when markup or encoding is inserted within them. Markup makes explicit for computer processing things that are implicit for the human reader. Markup thus puts intelligence into texts, providing information to help computer programs perform more meaningful operations on them.[6] It was soon realized, for example, that markup is needed to identify titles or names of manuscripts, or to distinguish notes from the main text, but early projects then faced the question of what that markup should look like. In print format, typographic markup, in the form of font changes or location on the page, distinguishes such features as headings, titles, authors' names, and page numbers. This form of markup is intended to aid the reader by reinforcing what the text says, but it is designed for print and does not translate well to the electronic medium, where other operations, such as indexing or the insertion of hypertext links, will also be performed on the text. For example, italics may be used to represent both titles and emphasized words in the same text, thus making it impossible for a computer program to search only within titles. As another example, font changes are used extensively within dictionary entries to distinguish headwords, definitions, etymology, quotations, etc., from the body of an entry, but an examination of an entry in the *Oxford English Dictionary* will show that italics are also used for etymologies and titles within quotations. As yet a third example, a critical text may be in a recognized format that the reader expects, but that format may be difficult for a computer program to analyze in order to extract names of manuscripts or variant readings.

Research on the creation and use of markup schemes has illuminated the problems in using so-called prescriptive markup, which indicates the functions that are to be carried out on the text. Prescriptive markup restricts the functionality of the electronic text because the text, once marked up in this fashion, can really be used only for the functions prescribed in the markup. By far the most widely used form of prescriptive markup is that created by word-processing programs. Many directors of editorial projects have gone to extreme lengths to get their material word-processed into carefully designed pages, with page numbers, footnotes, and other annotations, only to find that they cannot use their electronic texts for anything else, even something as simple as a word index.

Descriptive markup is much more powerful and flexible.[7] The concept behind descriptive markup is very simple: instead of indicating what the computer is to do with a given component of the text, descriptive markup merely says what that component *is*. This approach has the obvious and extremely useful side effect of allowing different functions to be performed by different computer programs on the same component, without making any changes to the text itself. Well-designed descriptive markup has another advantage, particularly for scholarly work: it enables the construction of a model that corresponds exactly to the text but that also can be extended if the need should arise for new features to be encoded. By contrast, many older markup schemes require the fitting of the text into a predefined model that, more often than not, fails to reflect the actual characteristics of the text; the graphic representation of the text has to be simplified to make it fit the model, and all subsequent processing is carried out on this simplified model, to the detriment of the scholarship being carried out on the text. It makes more sense all around to design a model that corresponds to the existing text rather than fit the text to an existing model.

Those who have begun to use HTML as an encoding model for electronic editions justify their choice not by the virtues of the encoding scheme itself but by the fact that HTML is directly interpreted by Web browsers. Thus an "edition" can be disseminated very quickly, and it can easily incorporate links to images, notes, and other apparatus. The World Wide Web has now become so ubiquitous that people who are relatively new to computing tend to assume that computing *is* the Web, and that HTML is an accepted format in much the same way that the layout of printed pages is the accepted format for books. In fact, however, the Web has been in existence for only a few years, and it is developing all the time, with various enhancements to HTML and more possibilities for multimedia. For this reason alone, HTML does not seem to be an appropriate encoding scheme for scholarly editions.

A more detailed examination of HTML can also help to illustrate the points made earlier while suggesting future directions. HTML consists of markup tags embedded in text in such a way as to surround the textual features to which the tags are applied. These tags contain information that a Web browser will display in a particular way. Thus, for example, the tags <h2> and </h2> are placed, respectively, at the beginning and the end of a phrase that is intended to be viewed as a second-level heading:

<h2>Second-Level Heading</h2>

These tags and this placement cause the text "Second-Level Heading" to be interpreted and displayed (at least by Netscape and Internet Explorer) as text that is flush left in large bold type.

The *concept* of using tags to surround textual components works well on the World Wide Web and, as implemented in HTML, does allow tags to be nested within other tags. But the real problem with HTML is in the *actual* tags, and in what they indicate. HTML uses a rather curious mixture of simple structural tags (for example, <p> to indicate a paragraph, <ul> to indicate an unordered list, and <h*n*> to indicate heading level *n*) and some typographical tags (for example, <i> to indicate italic, <u> to indicate underlining, and even, in some versions of HTML, <blink>, to indicate that the text should blink on and off in the user's browser window). Very few of these tags are of much use for any intelligent searching of the text. The current generation of Web browsers does incorporate a Find command on the Edit menu, but this command causes the entire document to be searched; it would be much more useful to be able to search only within titles, or only within quotations from the Bible, or only within a list of variants, but these types of searches cannot be conducted unless the document's encoding corresponds precisely to the actual components of the text.

Standard Generalized Markup Language (SGML) and the Extensible Markup Language (XML) make it possible to create a set of encoding tags that directly correspond to the components of the text.[8] An SGML / XML–based data model can avoid many of the simplification problems associated with HTML and can easily be extended if additional features have to be encoded. The principles of SGML can be summarized briefly as follows:

1. An SGML / XML–encoded text is a plain *ASCII file*,[9] which can be read independently of any specific word-processing program. XML supports Unicode as well. Thus the same text can be used for many different purposes and will outlast the computer on which it was created.

2. SGML / XML itself is a *syntax* or *framework* for *defining* markup languages, and the set of specific markup tags for one particular project is called an *SGML/XML application.*

3. These markup tags, and the relationships among them, must be defined in a *document type definition* (DTD) in SGML and XML (and possibly in a *schema* in XML), which gives a formal specification of the document's structure.

4. Almost anything, from a complete text down to the detailed interpretation of one part of a word (for example, the *"ur"* portion of the term *"ur*-text), can be encoded in SGML / XML. It is up to the designer of a DTD to determine what is important and what should be encoded— a process known as *document analysis.*

HTML is in fact a simplified version or subset of SGML, and looking at an HTML document can be a useful way of beginning to understand SGML concepts.

SGML / XML has a very useful mechanism for handling nonstandard characters—*é, à, ü*, and the like—which otherwise are not easily transferred from one computing platform to another. It handles such characters by means of what it calls *entities*. An entity (simply the term used to denote any piece of a text, long or short) begins, in SGML, with an ampersand and ends with a semicolon, and it consists of only those characters that can safely be transmitted across networks. Standard sets of entities exist for commonly occurring nonstandard characters; thus, for example, the entity *é* is used to represent é (*e* with an acute accent). But the entity mechanism is in fact even more general: it can be used to set off boilerplate text, thus ensuring that the same phrasing is used throughout for identical boilerplate elements, and it can even be used to denote whole chapters or works that are still in an incomplete state, functioning as a placeholder until they are complete.

Because of the DTD mechanism, an SGML-aware computer program—that is, a software application used for processing SGML-encoded material—can read the DTD first, using the information derived from it to validate the markup tags and, more generally, to know what to expect in working through the text. The processing ability of the SGML-aware program, by contrast with that of an HTML-dependent Web browser, is not restricted to or limited by what is contained in a small number of generic, predefined markup tags. After the document has been analyzed and the DTD has been created, an *SGML / XML editor* helps the user insert markup tags by offering a "pick" list of only those tags that are valid at a given point in the text. An *SGML / XML retrieval program* is aware, via the DTD, of the structure of the text. It can thus search for a word only in the context of a footnote, or find all the Biblical quotations within those sections of the text that are in Latin. The precision offered by an SGML / XML retrieval program, in conjunction with the Boolean search operators AND, OR, and NOT, enables the editor of an SGML / XML–based edition to offer a whole range of tools to the user of that edition. Other SGML / XML programs allow hypertext links to be associated with certain SGML / XML elements, perhaps also only when certain conditions apply.

When the time comes to print an SGML / XML–encoded document or format it for the user's screen, style sheets—that is, sets of formatting specifications—come into play. Several style sheets may be associated with a single document, according to the display views or print-based presentation that the editor wants to provide. In each style sheet, there is a style associated with every one of the document's components. For example, a quotation within a footnote may have a different format from a quotation in the main body of the text. A style may also be "inherited" from components that are farther up in the document tree structure. For example, the style applied to scenes within a play may form the basis of the style applied to speeches within the scene, or the style applied to sections may be applied to paragraphs within the section.

Software that performs most of these functions already exists, although some of these applications may be expensive for humanities scholars. SoftQuad's Xmetal[10] is perhaps the most widely used XML editor, and versions of the TEI Lite DTDs (see the discussion, below, of the TEI, the Text Encoding Initiative) for use with Xmetal are available on the Internet. A shareware Windows version of the emacs editor with SGML is now also on the Internet.[11] A list of SGML tools and vendors is maintained on the Internet by Steve Pepper.[12]

Fortunately for editors of electronic editions in our field, a good deal of SGML (and, more recently, XML) work has already been done in the humanities. The Text Encoding Initiative (TEI), a major international project sponsored by the three text-analysis computing associations, has developed a modular, extensible SGML application suitable for the humanities and for what the European Union calls the "language industries." The TEI involved more than one hundred volunteers in some twenty countries, who worked together over a period of six years to define some four hundred features that might be of interest in electronic texts and to specify SGML / XML tags for them. The TEI published its *Guidelines for Electronic Text Encoding and Interchange* in 1994, in two very large volumes.[13] The TEI guidelines are just that: guidelines that may be applicable as they stand for some projects, but that can also act as a base on which individual encoding schemes can be built for particular projects. The TEI addresses a number of specific application areas, including critical apparatus, specialized forms of names and dates, simple linguistic analysis, and dictionaries, but it has been criticized for its apparent inability to encode the physical attributes of a text.[14] The problem is not that the TEI's SGML application cannot be used at all for this kind of encoding, but that when the TEI was doing its work, no volunteers could be found to address this topic. In fact, it would be quite possible, by using the TEI's modular and extensible system, to add a tag set that would allow the TEI application to encode the text's physical appearance.

SGML / XML does present one problem for the representation of humanities material: it assumes that the text consists of a single hierarchic structure. To put this problem in the simplest terms, a play might consist of the title, the name of the author, and a list of the characters, and then one or more acts, each act containing one or more scenes, and each scene containing speeches and stage directions. A speech would consist of the speaker's name and the text of the speech. Within the text of the play, various other items of interest, such as quotations from other sources, or names of persons and places, might also be encoded. But a problem can arise in lineation and line numbering, especially when a speech is a half-line or less, so that two or more speeches are on the same line and have the same line number. This is one example of an overlapping structure, a phenomenon that occurs frequently in humanities material. Page breaks are another instance of the same problem. The designers of SGML assumed that it would be used for encoding new material that was not yet paginated, but most humanities projects are encoding existing material, often printed versions of texts that also exist in manuscript form. It is useful to record the page breaks and page numbers of the printed edition, but normally these have no defined relationship to the manuscript folios; a new folio will not start on a new page. SGML does not handle this kind of structure well.[15] It can only be handled in SGML through the insertion of what is called an "empty" tag (a tag that marks a point in the text but does not surround any part of the text), but because empty tags have no scope, they cannot be validated in the same way as other tags.

Some other markup schemes are capable of handling overlapping structures. Perhaps the best-known of these is the COCOA (word COunt and COncordance on Atlas)[16] scheme used by the Oxford Concordance Program (OCP) and, in an extended version, by the text-analysis computing tools (or TACT) suite. The COCOA markup is really intended for canonical referencing schemes rather than for such textual features as quotations and abbreviations. Because it has no end-tag syntax, it can identify the end of a component (for example, a poem within an anthology) only by the start of a new instance of that component (that is, by the start of the next poem in the anthology), or by a null instance. This feature offers some flexibility for handling overlapping structures that involve pages and folios, as described above, but it also means that the markup cannot be validated (since the structure of the text is not predictable). The COCOA scheme also becomes very clumsy when encoding is needed for textual features; attempts to use it for any kind of critical apparatus have failed because its structures are not powerful enough.

The Wittgenstein Archives Project at the University of Bergen has defined an encoding scheme called MECS (Multi-Element Code System) that can handle overlapping structures. It contains some of the properties of SGML, but it also contains additional, simpler mechanisms for representing structures that are cumbersome in SGML. Unlike SGML, MECS allows overlapping elements and does not require a DTD, although it allows (but does not require) the specification of a similar (though simpler) code-definition table.[17] MECS incorporates some interesting ideas, but it can be processed only by way of software written at Bergen, which, as far as I can ascertain, is specific to the requirements of the Wittgenstein Archives Project.

The processing functions provided by OCP and TACT can be extremely valuable for editorial work. Both programs are able to carry out searches for words and phrases. TACT is designed primarily for interactive retrieval.[18] OCP creates concordances, word indexes, and frequency lists.[19] Word processors, Web browsers, and other commonly used programs tend to assume a very simple definition of a word—namely something delimited by spaces. With OCP and TACT, the user specifies the letters and other symbols that make up words as well as the alphabetical order in which they are to be sorted. This means that hyphens, apostrophes, and other symbols that are not in the normal twenty-six-letter alphabet can be treated as parts of words. The user can specify whether they are to be taken into account when the words are being indexed for retrieval or sorting, or whether they are merely carried along with the words and displayed in the search results. Thus OCP and TACT can also be used to search for punctuation, if that is of interest. OCP and TACT have two disadvantages, however. They are both DOS-based programs that have not been updated recently, and neither is SGML-aware. Recently, more Web-based programs have appeared, but they too are not generally SGML / XML–aware. There is a real need now for a good Windows-based concordance program for the humanities; Rob Watt's Concordance is among the first.[20]

Of course OCP, TACT, and every other text-retrieval program in widespread use can only search for sequences of characters, not for "words" in the normal sense, or for concepts. These programs are unable to separate homographs (words that are spelled the same with different meanings, such as "record" and "record") or to lemmatize words (that is, put them under their dictionary headings). More sophisticated processing of electronic text can be carried out only if programs are given more information to help them. This information is best provided by an electronic dictionary or lexical database from which a retrieval program can derive possible dictionary headwords for a word as well as morphological and, possibly, syntactic forms, and synonyms and synonym relationships (such as the relationships represented by hypernyms and hyponyms).[21] Research in this area is still very experimental as far as the humanities are concerned, but it is a very important area for the development of natural-language understanding systems and thus has potential applications that are much wider. Most current effort is focused on modern prose texts, such as technical and scientific material, that has commercial value or is of interest for defense-related activities.

To summarize so far, the editor who is interested in making an electronic transcription of material and manipulating that transcription does have some useful tools at his or her disposal. The Text Encoding Initiative's application of SGML contains many if not all of the encoding elements that might be needed, but getting started with the TEI is not particularly easy for the individual scholar. Fortunately, some institutions are now offering summer schools or short courses on the TEI and SGML / XML in the humanities. Concordance tools can be a valuable aid to detailed study of transcriptions, but many tools in current use are not particularly easy for beginners. The editor who is embarking on a long-term project would be well advised, in my view, to invest time in learning SGML / XML and to plan for the availability of better tools in the future. For more immediate needs, a simple style sheet or computer program can convert an SGML / XML application to HTML for delivery over the Web. Starting with HTML is perhaps a useful way to learn more about markup, but continued use of HTML will severely limit the possibilities for the future, in terms of both representing the scholarly objectives of the project and delivering and manipulating the edition.

Much interest at the moment is focusing on digital imaging—what I can perhaps call the other hype.[22] Some projects, as an alternative to microfilm, are using imaging, a new form of preservation, even though it is not at all clear how long any form of digital technology will last. But the main attraction of imaging is access. Imaging enables scholars and students to see material that otherwise could be examined only through a visit to the library or repository in which it is held. Imaging technology is a much more recent development than the technology for working with text, and so there is a smaller body of knowledge on how best to work with images, on the material that should accompany images, and on how they should be described.

Most discussion about imaging has been concerned with the optimum resolution for scanning and storing images. Humanities material, particularly manuscripts, really needs to be at a high resolution before it can be studied effectively. Even with file compression, however, high-resolution images can generate very large files requiring large amounts of disk space. Moreover, images scanned a few years ago now look very poor because their resolution was constrained by the space available for storing them. Hardware costs continue to fall, and hard drives get bigger, but it seems that the proportion of disk space taken up by images does not fall, because image resolution gets higher and more storage is needed for each image. When all the costs are taken into account, it seems that much of the cost of imaging goes to taking the object to the scanner or camera, setting it up, and then returning it to its place. It makes sense, therefore, to make the master image at as high a resolution as possible, since redoing it will be costly. Note that the situation discussed here is rather different from that involving an electronic text, to which new encoding can easily be added incrementally.

There seems to be a tendency to forget that a digital image is a surrogate, not the real thing. Nor does the surrogate need to be an exact copy, since it is so easy to manipulate or enhance images. Imaging projects often touch up images, using such programs as Photoshop, with the intention of making the images better, but participants in these projects only rarely record what they have done to an image or what effect their manipulations and enhancements may have on its use. The viewing of images is also affected by the properties of a computer screen's display and by the type and quality of the computer's video card. Modern file-compression programs are reasonably good, but very few people understand the algorithms used to reduce an image's size.

Image manipulation and enhancement are now beginning to be used as research tools in the humanities. Perhaps the best-known and most influential example of these activities is the work done on the *Beowulf* manuscript in the British Library, where the use of ultraviolet light in scanning has made it possible to read a portion of the manuscript that was previously illegible.[23]

Images on their own are not very helpful. They need contextual material in order to be retrieved and used sensibly: users need to know what the images are and why they are being made available. Some image database projects use relational database technology for this descriptive material but then often find themselves at the limit of what their databases can do, particularly in terms of flexibility. Images, like other kinds of material, are not good candidates for work involving proprietary databases, since such databases restrict the use of the images to certain functions and do not migrate well to new systems.

Because an image's contextual information is normally text, it is sensible to make that text subject to the same concerns as other electronic text. Text associated with images falls into three broad categories:

1. *Descriptive material* is essential to helping users find an image and then learn exactly what it is and what its electronic properties are.

2. *Annotations* are often needed, to provide further explanatory material, perhaps for only one area of an image.

3. Some type of *explanation* is needed when an image is linked to something else in hypertext, to tell the user why the link is being made.

These categories overlap, to some extent; for example, an explanation of a link is really an annotation of the link. In any case, it makes sense for the same encoding format and syntax to be used for all three kinds of text, and for that format and syntax to be the same as for any other textual material in the project.

The use of hypertext has also become very popular in humanities scholarship.[24] It provides a way of making connections between pieces of information, thus modeling what many humanities scholars actually do. Hypertext has been popularized by the World Wide Web more than anything else, but the Web's linking mechanisms are fairly weak.[25] They allow only one-to-one links, not one-to-many, and a link is made, in effect, to the start of a Web document or to a point within the document, not to a span of information. Nor does the Web offer any easy way of placing annotations on a link; if an explanation is needed, it must be provided in the document from which the link is being made rather than on the link itself.

Research on how people use hypertextual publications is still at a fairly early stage, but getting "lost in hyperspace" is recognized as a common problem. It is all too easy to keep following links and lose track of where one has got to. The users of a hypertext feel they would like to have some idea of its overall structure, of where they are in it, and of how they got there.[26] The linking structures in the hypertext environment model the real world in being more like a web than a tree, but the web model is more difficult to conceptualize from the human point of view, as well as more difficult for computer programs to work with.

SGML / XML, in addition to offering the possibilities already discussed, can help with some of these linking questions. SGML-encoded information can be "chunked" in many different ways, with SGML tags identifying what the various chunks are. SGML can also be used to encode the links between chunks in a more sophisticated way than is possible with HTML. Moreover, annotations explaining why the links are there can also be encoded in SGML. Thus SGML can be used to put some "intellectual frameworks"[27] around the material, and these frameworks can help to give human users some points of reference as they navigate through a hypertextual publication. Such frameworks also provide the markup that helps computer programs operate on the information that the material contains. (Perhaps a better term than "intellectual frameworks" is "underground tunnels,"[28] since such frameworks are mostly hidden from the user but are essential to the workings of hypertext.) It seems to me that one role of the editor of an electronic edition is to decide on the frameworks that will be used for the edition and use them to privilege the navigation routes that determine the user's view of the material. Just to present a mass of material is less helpful. The material must be organized to support and strengthen the interpretations that the editor wants to make. SGML provides the best tool I know of for organizing the material in this way.

Thus research on electronic editions should concentrate more on the design and testing of these intellectual frameworks. In this way, we will be able to work toward a commonly accepted model that will last into the future. Few projects have such a methodological orientation, however; most are geared to preparation of specific editions, with less interest in the long-term implications of how these editions are being prepared. Nevertheless, the Model Editions Partnership (MEP) is one that is methodological.[29]

The MEP, a consortium of seven documentary editing projects and three coordinators, received substantial funding from the National Historical Publications and Records Commission for a project that would explore what an electronic documentary edition should look like, and that would build some models to test various hypotheses about electronic editions. Two of the MEP's editing projects are preparing image editions. The other five are creating traditional print publications. In the first stage of the MEP, the three coordinators visited all seven projects, to learn more about the projects and investigate their current methods of working. The projects were then shown some tiny mockups of what can be done electronically and were invited to "dream" about what they would do if they were not restricted to the format of paper or microfilm. The "dreams" were then put together into a prospectus for electronic documentary editions. The prospectus stresses five principles: that electronic editions should

(1) maintain current standards of scholarly editorial excellence;

(2) facilitate changes in scholarly editorial practice;

(3) allow postpublication enhancements of editions;

(4) allow multiple forms of publication; and

(5) conform to relevant standards for electronic text, images, and other material.

The MEP has built samples from each of the seven projects, and its work is firmly grounded in the use of SGML / XML to represent the projects' intellectual frameworks. The MEP has developed a specialized version of the TEI DTDs that includes an SGML envelope for images as well as textual tags, and it plans to produce a detailed analysis of how well the project has been able to meet its objectives.

Attention must now turn to the development of better document-delivery tools. The MEP and some other SGML-based projects are using INSO Corporation's DynaText suite of tools. These offer good searching of the SGML structures, but they also provide a model that is very much that of a book rather than pieces of information that can be chunked and organized in different ways. DynaText products that appear to organize material in different ways do so by precomputing all of them rather than generating them on the fly.[30] This approach may be feasible for a project that has an obvious set of structures to present. It is less obviously feasible for one in which the range of possibilities is greater.

Another development has turned out to be even more important: Extensible Markup Language (XML), which was adopted by the World Wide Web Consortium in February 1998 as a new markup language for the Web.[31] XML was developed in response to growing recognition of HTML's limitations, in both the commercial and academic sectors. To explain this markup language very briefly, XML is a cut-down version of SGML that enables the user to create documents marked up with his or her own tag sets, not HTML's. XML is intended to run on the World Wide Web and on intranets, and XML documents will be accompanied by style sheets that the next generation of Web browsers will use to determine how to display the documents. XML also incorporates more sophisticated interdocument linking mechanisms, which are modeled on those defined by the TEI.

At present, XML offers a way forward, enabling more complex document models to be delivered over the Web. In the meantime, I would like to reiterate my plea for more basic research and development on what an electronic edition should look like and on how it can best maintain and enhance current standards of editorial scholarship.

NOTES

Every effort has been made to ensure that addresses on the World Wide Web are correct and current, but some may have changed or expired while this volume was in production. The reader is urged to use online search engines to locate current URLs.

1. Jerome McGann, "The Rationale of Hypertext," *Text: An Interdisciplinary Annual of Textual Studies* 9 (1996), 11–32, which is also found at http://www.iath.virginia.edu/public/jjm2f/rationale.html.

See also Kathryn Sutherland, "Waiting for Connections: Hypertexts, Multiplots, and the Engaged Reader," in Don Ross and Dan Brink, eds., *Research in Humanities Computing,* vol. 2, series eds. Susan Hockey and Nancy Ide (Oxford: Clarendon Press, 1994), 46–58; Richard J. Finneran, ed., *The Literary Text in the Digital Age* (Ann Arbor: University of Michigan Press, 1996), especially Simon Gatrell's contribution, "Electronic Hardy", 185–92.

2. Peter Robinson's Canterbury Tales Project, of which the first CD-ROM, *The Wife of Bath's Prologue,* was published in 1996 by Cambridge University Press, is one of the very few projects that does provide a range of analytical tools for the user.

3. The *Guidelines for Electronic Scholarly Editions* compiled by the Modern Language Association Committee on Scholarly Editions at http://sunsite.berkeley.edu/MLA/guidelines.html provide what is, in my view, an excellent description of the various possibilities for scholarly electronic editions, but they do not, nor is it their role to, discuss how these editions might be created.

4. Roberto Busa, ed., *Index Thomisticus* (Stuttgart–Bad Cannstatt: Frommann-Holzboog, 1974–80). The same author reflects on his work and "progress" in literary and linguistic computing in Roberto Busa, "Half a Century of Literary Computing: Towards a 'New' Philology: Reports of Colloquia at Tübingen," *Literary and Linguistic Computing* 7 (1992), 69–73.

5. For an overview and analysis of the uses of electronic texts in the humanities, see Susan Hockey, *Electronic Texts in the Humanities: Principles and Practice* (Oxford: Oxford University Press, 2000).

6. James H. Coombs, Allen H. Renear, and Steven J. DeRose, "Markup Systems and the Future of Scholarly Text Processing," *Communications of the ACM,* 30 (1987), 933–47, is generally considered the seminal article in the development of markup systems.

7. Allen H. Renear, "Representing Text on the Computer: Lessons for and from Philosophy," *Bulletin of the John Rylands University Library of Manchester* 74 (1992), 221–44, emphasizes the arguments in favor of descriptive or content-based markup.

8. Charles Goldfarb, *The SGML Handbook* (Oxford: Clarendon Press, 1990), gives a detailed specification of SGML. A good but rather technical overview can be found in Eric van Herwijnen, *Practical SGML,* 2nd ed. (Dordrecht: Kluwer, 1994). For an introduction to SGML, see Lou Burnard, "What is SGML and How Does It Help?," *Computers and the Humanities* 29 (1995), 41–50, which is also found at http://www.uic.edu/orgs/tei/sgml/teiedw25. See also C. M. Sperberg-McQueen and Lou Burnard, eds., "A Gentle Introduction to SGML": http://www.tei-c.org/Guidelines/SG.htm. A very comprehensive Web site on XML/SGML is maintained by Robin Cover: http://www.oasis-open.org/cover.

9. ASCII stands for American Standard Code for Information Interchange. An ASCII text file, also called a "text-only file" or a "plain-text file," contains characters, spaces, punctuation, end-of-line markers, and sometimes tabs and an end-of-file marker, but it contains no other machine-control codes or formatting information (that is, no encoding that would give text a specific appearance, such as 12–point bold centered, or 9–point italic justified).

10. See http://www.sq.com/top_frame.sq for descriptions of all of SoftQuad's products.

11. See http://users.ox.ac.uk/~tess/TESSswar.htm and http://www.umanitoba.ca/faculties/arts/linguistics/russell/ebenezer.htm.

12. See "The XML Cover Pages": http://www.oasis-open.org/cover/publicSW.html.

13. C. M. Sperberg-McQueen and Lou Burnard, eds., *Guidelines for the Encoding and Interchange of Electronic Texts* (Chicago and Oxford: ACH [Association for Computers and the

Humanities] / ACL [Association for Computational Linguistics] / ALLC [Association for Literary and Linguistic Computing], 1994). Further information about the TEI and information about how to obtain the TEI guidelines is on the TEI Web site: http://www.tei-c.org.

14. Ian Lancashire, "Early Books, RET Encoding Guidelines, and the Trouble with SGML" (Nov. 11, 1995), for the Electric Scriptorium Research Network, Calgary Institute for the Humanities, University of Calgary, at http://www.chass.utoronto.ca/~ian/calgary.html (see also the discussion in the postings by Ian Lancashire); C. M. Sperberg-McQueen, Patrick Durusau, Robin Cover, Martin Mueller, and Steven DeRose, *Humanist Discussion Group* 9, nos. 343 (Dec. 2, 1995), 349 (Dec. 3, 1995), 358 (Dec. 5, 1995), 362 (Dec. 6, 1995), 365 (Dec. 9, 1995), 395 (Dec. 18, 1995), and 429 (Jan. 4, 1996), accessible via http://www.kcl.ac.uk/humanities/cch/humanist.

15. Some solutions for handling multiple hierarchies are proposed in David Barnard, Lou Burnard, Jean-Pierre Gaspart, Lynne A. Price, C. M. Sperberg-McQueen, and Giovanni Battista Varile, "Hierarchical Encoding of Text: Technical Problems and SGML Solutions," *Computers and the Humanities* 29 (1995), 211–31. Earlier work by Barnard and his team at Queen's University is reported in David T. Barnard, Ron Hayter, Maria Karababa, George M. Logan, and John McFadden, "SGML Based Markup for Literary Texts: Two Problems and Some Solutions," *Computers and the Humanities* 22 (1988), 265–76. See also Allen Renear, Elli Mylonas, and David Durand, "Refining our Notion of What Text Really Is: The Problem of Overlapping Hierarchies," in Hockey and Ide, eds., *Research in Humanities Computing*, vol. 4, 263–80.

16. Chap. 2 of the *Micro–OCP Manual* (Oxford: Oxford Electronic Publishing, 1988) describes the COCOA / OCP scheme, and further examples of its use can be found in the *Oxford Concordance Program Users' Manual* (Oxford: Oxford University Computing Services, 1988). The TACT version of COCOA is described in Ian Lancashire, in collaboration with John Bradley, Willard McCarty, Michael Stairs, and T. R. Wooldridge, *Using TACT with Electronic Texts* (New York: Modern Language Association, 1996) 12–22.

17. See Claus Huitfeldt, "Multi-Dimensional Texts in a One-Dimensional Medium," *Computers and the Humanities* 28 (1996), 235–41.

18. Among the many publications discussing applications of TACT are T. Russon Wooldridge, ed., *A TACT Exemplar,* Working Paper no. 1 (Toronto: Centre for Computing in the Humanities, 1991); Ian Lancashire, "Phrasal Repetends in Literary Stylistics: Shakespeare's *Hamlet* III.1," in Hockey and Ide, eds., *Research in Humanities Computing*, vol. 4, 34–68; Edward A. Heinemann, "Mapping Echoes with TACT in the Old French Epic the *Charroi de Nimes,*" *Literary and Linguistic Computing* 8 (1993), 191–202; and Willard McCarty, "Peering Through the Skylight: Towards an Electronic Edition of Ovid's *Metamorphoses,*" in Hockey and Ide, eds., *Research in Humanities Computing,* vol. 4, 240–62.

19. See Susan Hockey, "Textual Databases," in John Lawler and Helen Aristar-Dry, eds., *Using Computers in Linguistics: A Practical Guide* (London: Routledge, 1998), 101–37, for examples of the functions performed by OCP.

20. See http://www.mjcw.freeserve.co.uk/wics.htm. For other tools, see http://info.ox.ac.uk/ctitext/mesguide2000/contents.shtml.

21. One of the best-known tools for concept-based searching is WordNet: http://www.cogsci.princeton.edu/~wn. WordNet is an online lexical reference system developed by George Miller and his team at Princeton, initially for research in cognitive science and psycholinguistics.

22. One good starting point for imaging in the humanities is Howard Besser and Jennifer Trant, *Introduction to Imaging* (Santa Monica, Calif.: The Getty Art History Information Program, 1995), also found at http://www.getty.edu/research/institute/standards/introdimages/index/html. Another is Peter Robinson, *The Digitization of Primary Textual Sources* (Oxford: Office for Humanities Communication, 1993).

23. See http://www.uky.edu/~kiernan/BL/kportico.html for examples. See also Kevin S. Kiernan, "Digital Preservation, Restoration, and Dissemination of Medieval Manuscripts," in Ann Okerson and Dru Mogge, eds., *Scholarly Publishing on the Electronic Networks: Gateways, Gatekeepers, and Roles in the Information Omniverse,* proceedings of the Third Symposium, Nov.

13–15, 1993 (Washington, D.C.: Association of Research Libraries, 1994), also found at http://www.uky.edu/~kiernan/welcome.html. In addition, see Kevin S. Kiernan, "Digital Image Processing and the Beowulf Manuscript," *Literary and Linguistic Computing* 6 (1991), 20–21; Espen Ore, "Project Litera: Computer Aids in Restoring Partly Preserved Letters in Papyri," in Susan Hockey and Nancy Ide, eds., *Research in Humanities Computing*, vol. 2, 226–31; and the collection of papers on computers and ancient documents edited by Alan Bowman and Marilyn Deegan in *Literary and Linguistic Computing* 12:3 (1997).

24. The concept of hypertext, but not the name, was first proposed by Vannevar Bush, "As We May Think," *Atlantic Monthly*, July 1945, 101–8, also found at http://www.isg.sfu .ca/~duchier/misc/vbush. The term *hypertext* was coined by Ted Nelson in 1965; see http://www.cinemedia.net/xanadu/bibliography.html. This term did not become popular, however, until the advent of the Macintosh computer, with its HyperCard system, in the late 1980s. The literature on hypertext in the humanities is now enormous. A good starting point is a search for the term *hypertext* on the Voice of the Shuttle: http://vos/ucsb/edu.

25. For a discussion of the linking facilities required for a hypertextual approach to biblical material, and thus by analogy to other complex textual material in the humanities, see Steven J. DeRose, "Biblical Studies and Hypertext," in Paul Delaney and George P. Landow, eds., *Hypermedia and Literary Studies* (Cambridge, Mass.: MIT Press, 1991), 185–204. DeRose's ideas are analyzed further by Patrick W. Conner, "Hypertext in the Last Days of the Book," *Bulletin of the John Rylands University Library of Manchester* 74 (1992), 7–24.

26. Early hypertext systems—such as Intermedia, developed at Brown University— provided better mechanisms for users to keep track of where they were. See George P. Landow, "The Rhetoric of Hypermedia: Some Rules for Authors," in Delany and Landow, eds., *Hypermedia and Literary Studies*, 81–103.

27. The phrase "intellectual frameworks" is used by David Chesnutt, director of the Model Editions Partnership. See section 1 of the partnership's prospectus: http://adh.sc.edu/mepinfo/ MEP-Docs/proptoc.htm.

28. The term "tunnels" for the role of SGML is emphasized in Yuri Rubinsky, "Electronic Texts The Day After Tomorrow," in Ann Okerson, ed., *Scholarly Publishing on the Electronic Networks: The New Generation: Visions and Opportunities in Not-for-Profit Publishing*, proceedings of the Second Symposium, Dec. 5–8, 1992 (Washington, D.C.: Association of Research Libraries, 1993), 5–13, also found at http://www.arl.org/scomm/symp2/Rubinsky.html.

29. See http://adh.sc.edu for a description of the MEP.

30. This appears to be the approach taken by Peter Robinson for *The Wife of Bath's Prologue*.

31. A full specification of XML and associated activities under the auspices of World Wide Web Consortium is at http://www.w3c.org/XML.

Imagining What You Don't Know
The Theoretical Goals of the Rossetti Archive

JEROME MCGANN

I

In a trenchant metatheoretical essay, Lee Patterson has investigated what he calls "The Kane-Donaldson *Piers Plowman*," that is to say, the 1975 Athlone Press edition of the B Text.[1] I say "metatheoretical" because the edition itself constitutes the primary theoretical event. Patterson's essay elucidates the theory of that extraordinary work of scholarship.

According to the editors themselves, their edition is "a theoretical structure, a complex hypothesis designed to account for a body of phenomena in the light of knowledge about the circumstances which generated them."[2] Needless to say, this "body of phenomena" is problematic to a degree. Patterson studies the evolution of Kane and Donaldson's "complex hypothesis" about these phenomena as the hypothesis gets systematically defined in the edition itself. These are his conclusions:

> As a system, this edition validates each individual reading in terms of every other reading, which means that if some of these readings are correct, then—unless the editorial principles have been in an individual instance misapplied—they must all be correct. This is not to say that the edition is invulnerable, only that criticism at the level of counterexample . . . is inconsequential. . . . Indeed, the only way [criticism] could be effective would be if [it] were part of a sustained effort to provide a contrary hypothesis by which to explain the phenomena— to provide, in other words, another edition.[3]

Patterson's startling last judgment—deliberately outrageous—is not simply a rhetorical flourish. He is aware of the intractable character of the *Piers Plowman* materials. But he admires, justifiably, the comprehensiveness and the rigor of the Kane-Donaldson work. Even more, he admires its visionary boldness. In thinking about Kane and Donaldson's project, was Patterson also thinking of Blake?

> I must Create a System, or be enslav'd by another Man's
> I will not Reason and Compare, my business is to Create.[4]

If he wasn't, he might have been; perhaps he should have been. For Patterson's essay is acute to see what is so special about the Kane-Donaldson edition: not merely that it is based upon a clearly imagined theory of itself but that the theory has been given full realization. "Counterexample" will not dislodge the "truth" of the Kane-Donaldson edition. Indeed—Patterson himself does not say this, though it is implicit in his argument—even a different "theory" of the *Piers Plowman* materials will necessarily lack critical force against the *theoretical* achievement represented in the Kane-Donaldson edition. Only another theory of the work *that instantiates itself as a comprehensive edition* could supplant the authoritative truth of the Kane-Donaldson text.

Why this requirement should be the case is one part of my subject in this essay. The other part, which is related, concerns procedures of theoretical undertaking as such. In this last respect, my focus will be on electronic textuality.

Let me address the first issue, then: the theoretical status of what William Carlos Williams called "embodied knowledge"[5] (which may be rendered in the Goethean proverb "In the beginning was the deed"). There is an important sense in which we should see the Kane-Donaldson project as a gage laid down, a challenge to scholars to imagine what they know or think they know. The edition begs to be differed with, but only at the highest level—only at an equivalent theoretical level, in another edition. In this respect, it differs from other editions that have seen themselves as theoretical pursuits. Here I would instance Fredson Bowers's *The Dramatic Works of Thomas Dekker* or almost any of the editions of American authors that were engaged under the aegis of the Greg-Bowers theory of editing. These works do not go looking for trouble, as the Kane-Donaldson project did (so successfully). They imagine themselves quite differently, as is readily apparent from the scholarly term they aspired to merit: *definitive*. In this line of work, the scholar proceeding with rigor and comprehensiveness may imagine a de facto achievement of critical completeness. Not that other editions might not be executed, for different reasons and purposes; but the "theoretical structure" of the so-called critical edition, in this line of thought, implicitly (and sometimes explicitly) argues that such undertakings would be carried out within the horizon of the definitive critical edition.

In the past fifteen years or so, scholars have all but abandoned the theory of the "definitive edition," although the term still appears from time to time. The Kane-Donaldson theoretical view—that a critical edition is a hypothesis "designed to account for a body of phenomena in the light of our given historical knowledge," must be judged to have gained considerable authority during this period. As Patterson's essay suggests, theirs is fundamentally a dialectical and dynamic theory of critical editing. Not, of course, that a Greg-Bowers approach need fail to appreciate the indeterminacy of particular editing tasks and problems—on the contrary; but the general theoretical approach is different. Bowers, for example, inclines to technical rather than rational solutions to problematic issues, as his famous insistence on collating multiple copies of a printed work clearly demonstrates. This is a procedure that flows from a disciplined theoretical position. But it differs from the theoretical posture adopted by Kane and Donaldson, who take a much more skeptical view of the authority of positive data.

Over against these two theoretical approaches to editing stands that great tradition of what Randall McLeod would call (I think) "unediting": that is, the scholarly reproduction of text in documentary forms that reproduce more or less adequate replicas of the originary materials. Until recently, this approach has scarcely been seen as "theoretical" at all. But McLeod and others have been able to show the great advantages to be gained by using theoretically sophisticated forms of documentary procedures. Many doors of perception have been cleansed by R. W. Franklin's work on Emily Dickinson's manuscripts, by Michael Warren's work on Shakespeare, and by the astonishing genetic texts that have come to us from Europe, such as D. E. Sattler's work on Friedrich Hölderlin.[6]

Let us remind ourselves about what is at stake in these kinds of work. In another day—say, in the late nineteenth century—an edition like Warren's would have emerged from the influence of institutions such as the Early English Text Society. To that extent, it would be seen as an archival work meant primarily to preserve and make accessible certain rare documents. But of course Warren's edition is very different: it is an investigation into the character and status of documents and their relationships (intra- as well as extratextual). Like Sattler's great edition, it instantiates a self-conscious and theoretical argument. Moreover, Warren's immediate subject, *King Lear*, is implicitly offered as a strong argument for rethinking the textuality of the Shakespeare corpus as a whole. The play isn't seen precisely as *representative* because the case—which is to say, the documentary material—is too idiosyncratic. This unusual documentary survival, however, is used to encourage and license new acts of attention toward the whole of the Shakespeare canon, as well as to analogous texts beyond.

More speculative theoretical undertakings operate very differently

from works like Warren's and Sattler's. Having emerged from the genre
of the scholarly essay and monograph, speculative theory tends to move
an argument through processes of (as it were) natural selection. Paul De
Man was a careful builder of the absences he presented, sieving his materials with great discrimination.[7] In textual and editorial works, by contrast, the whole of each phyla as they have ever been known—every
individual instance of all the known lines—lays claim to preservation
and display. All come to judgment: strong and weak, hale and halt, the
ideal and the monstrous.

They come, moreover, *in propria persona,* and to that extent they come
on their own terms. Franklin's edition of Dickinson points up the theoretical advantage that flows from this method of proceeding. His fidelity to the original manuscripts was so resolute that the documents would
eventually be called to witness against him—or rather, against certain
of Franklin's less significant ideas about Dickinson's texts. Franklin's
work exploded our understanding of Dickinson's use of the physical
page as an expressive vehicle. We now see very clearly that she often
designed her textual works in the manner of a visual or graphic artist.
These unmistakable cases have come to be something like the case of
King Lear—strange survivals helping to elucidate surfaces that might
otherwise seem commonplace and unremarkable. Franklin himself has
resisted and even deplored many of the critical moves that his own work
made possible. His edition did not set out to demonstrate some of its
most important ideas: that Dickinson used her manuscript venue as a
device for rethinking the status of the poetic line in relation to conventions of print display, for example; or that the execution of the (private)
fascicles and the (public) letters together comprise a "theory" of verse
freedom every bit as innovative as Whitman's; or that fragmentary
scripts might possess an integrity that develops through a dynamic
engagement between a text and its vehicular (material) form.[8] These
ways of thinking about texts are real if unintended consequences of
Franklin's work. The edition itself, however, was clearly undertaken
through a different set of ideas. Most apparent, it was a kind of preliminary move toward producing a new print edition of the poems, this
time organized by fascicle rather than by hypothetical chronology or top-
ical areas (the two previously dominant ordering systems). Franklin has
now completed that print edition. And while it may have considerable
success—Dickinson is one of our central American myths—it is unlikely
to match the theoretical achievement of his edition of the manuscript
books. That achievement is being pursued elsewhere, in the textual

works being organized through the so-called Dickinson Archive, a scholarly venue sponsoring a variety of approaches to editing Dickinson materials.[9]

Projects of this kind have a strong documentary orientation. They are also electronic. Why? Because digital technology has created a field of significant new possibilities for facsimile and documentary editing projects. In this respect, remarkable genetic editions like Sattler's, although they come to us in codex form, prophesy an electronic existence. They are our age's incunabula, books in winding sheets rather than swaddling clothes. At once very beautiful and very ugly, fascinating and tedious, these books drive the resources of the codex form to its limits and beyond. Think of the Cornell Wordsworth, a splendid example of postmodern incunabula.[10] Grotesque systems of diexis and abbreviation are developed in order to facilitate navigation through labyrinthine textual scenes. To say that such editions are difficult to use is to speak in vast understatement. But their intellectual intensity is so apparent and so great that they bring new levels of attention to their scholarly objects. Deliberate randomness attends every feature of these works, equally well read as postmodern imaginative constructions and as scholarly tools because their enginery of scholarship is often as obdurate and nontransparent as the material being analyzed.

The works I have been talking about suggest how editions may constitute a theoretical presentation. Their totalized factive commitments give them a privilege unavailable to the speculative or interpretive essay or monograph. Because the three documentary editions just discussed—Franklin's, Warren's, and Sattler's—call special attention to the theoretical status of textual materials, including their own mediating qualities and procedures, these works represent a vanguard for new levels of critical reflexiveness.

Their greatest significance, however, only appeared after they were drawn into the orbit of another, more encompassing textual innovation: electronic hypertextuality. It gradually became clear that had each of these editions been conceived and executed in digital forms, their documentary and critical imperatives would have discovered a more adequate vehicle. That understanding encouraged an imagination of a different editorial approach. Lee Patterson might have called it a "true" theory of documentary editing; Randall McCloud, an (un)serious effort at Unediting. Or call it a hypermedia archive with a relational and object-oriented database. Its truth as theory is twofold: as a fully searchable set of hyperrelated archival materials, and as a reflexive system capable of self-study at various scales of attention. In 1993, the Rossetti

Archive was begun as an effort to realize this double theoretical goal. In describing it then (in my introduction to the demonstration model of the archive's Web site), I said that its aim was to integrate for the first time the procedures of documentary and critical editing.[11]

But this initial purpose was governed by received understandings of these two approaches. Formed through a long history of scholarship grounded and organized in codex forms, these understandings would have their imaginative limits searched and exposed in the practical work of designing and executing the Rossetti Archive. This result was inevitable. Although the Rossetti Archive was not conceived as a tool for studying the theoretical structure of paper-based textual forms, it has proved very useful in that respect. Translating paper-based texts into electronic forms entirely alters one's view of the original materials. Thus, in the first two years of the archive's development, we were forced to study a fundamental limit of the scholarly edition in codex form of which we had not been aware: using books to study books constrains the analysis to the same conceptual level as the materials to be studied; electronic tools raise the level of critical abstraction in the same way that a mathematical approach to the study of natural phenomena shifts the theoretical view to a higher (or at any rate to a different) level.

II

That last idea, which still seems an important one, led me to write "The Rationale of HyperText" in 1995.[12] The further development of the Rossetti Archive since that time has brought new alterations to the work's original conception and purposes. Or perhaps they are not so much alterations as supplements. For the project "to integrate the procedures of documentary and critical editing" (as I said in my introduction to the archive's demonstration model) keeps turning to worlds unrealized. The Rossetti Archive seemed to me, and still seems to me, a tool for imagining what we don't know. The event of its construction, for example, gradually exposed the consequences of a crucial fact we did not at first adequately understand: that the tool had included itself in its own first imagining. We began our work of building the archive under an illusion or misconception—in any case, a transparent contradiction: that we could know what was involved in trying to imagine what we didn't know. Four years of work brought a series of chastening interdictions, stops, revisions, compromises.

In the end, despite these events, I see more clearly how one can indeed imagine what one doesn't know. One can build something like the Rossetti Archive, which is just such an imagining, and it can be fashioned to reveal its various (and reciprocal) processes of knowing and unknowing. These can be either intramural or extramural. The Rossetti Archive's self-exposures, for example, emerge from two of the project's basic understandings (they are reciprocals): first, the archive can build into itself the history of its own construction (the ongoing histories of its productions and its receptions); and, second, it can expose those historicalities to each other at various scales and levels.

These self-exposures might be of many kinds. To provide a good general sense of what we have done, let me focus on one aspect of the archive's work: the decision to make digital images the center of the project's computational and hypertextual goals. This decision followed our aspiration to marry critical and facsimile editing, and our belief that electronic textuality had arrived at a point where the desire might be realized. Thus, in 1992, we began trying to bring about the convergence of these ancient twain.

Let me recapitulate a bit of the recent history of humanities computing initiatives. Current work in electronic text and data management falls into two broad categories that correspond to a pair of imaginative protocols. On one hand, we have hypertext and hypermedia projects—information databases organized for browsing via a network of complex linkages. These databases characteristically deploy a mix of textual and image materials that can be accessed and traversed by means of a presentational markup language like HTML. On the other hand, we have databases of textual materials organized not so much for browsing and linking / navigational moves as for in-depth and structured search and analysis of the data. These projects, by contrast, require more rigorous markup in full SGML. If they deploy digital images, the images are not incorporated into the analytic structure. They will be simple illustrations, to be accessed—perhaps even browsed in a hypertext—for reference purposes.

One kind of project is presentational, designed for the mind's eye (or the eyes' mind); the other is analytic, using a logical structure that can free the conceptual imagination of its inevitable codex-based limits. The former kind of project tends to be image-oriented; the latter is inclined to be text-based.

To date, almost all of the most impressive electronic text projects have been text-based: Peter Robinson's Chaucer project, Willard McCarty's Ovid, Hoyt Duggan's *Piers Plowman*, the University of Bergen's Wittgenstein project. Set beside these kinds of works, even the most complex hypertext—the Perseus project, for instance, or the literary "webs" developed by George Landow at Brown University—will seem relatively

primitive scholarly instruments. (The great exception to this general-
ization would be those nonproprietary and wholly decentered projects
that grow and proliferate randomly, like the network of early gopher
servers or—the spectacular instance—the World Wide Web's network
of hypermedia servers.)

So far as localized hypermedia projects are concerned, works like those
developed in Storyspace have a distinct attraction, as the amazing success of the Web demonstrates. Crucially, they operate at the macro level
of our human interface. Elaborated front-end arrangements reinforce an
important message: that however strange or vast the materials may
sometimes appear to be, the user can maintain reasonable control of what
happens and what moves are made. The buzzwords that iconify such
a message are "user-friendly" and, most widespread of all, "interactive."

Not without reason do hypertext theorists regularly imagine their
world in terms of spatial and mapping metaphors. Not without reason
did the greatest current hypertext project (the World Wide Web) decide
to code its data in HTML (it could have supported a more rigorous document type definition, or DTD, for its materials), or make the accessing
of images (rather than the analysis of their information) a key feature
of its work. The Web's success derives from its humane—indeed, its
humanistic—interface. Of course, the World Wide Web, like all hypermedia engines, is grotesquely pinned down by the limits of the color
monitor. Still, though limited by the monitor (whether in two or three
dimensions), hypertexts like the Web can simulate fairly well the eye-
organized environment we are so used to.

By contrast, SGML-type projects need take little notice of the eyes'
authority. They are splendid conceptual machines, as we see when we
reflect on the relative unimportance of sophisticated monitor equipment
to text-based SGML projects. The appearance of text and data is less crucial than their logical organization and functional flexibility.

The computerized imagination is riven by this elementary split. It
replicates the gulf separating a Unix from a Mac world. It also represents the division upon which the Rossetti Archive was consciously built.
That is to say, from the outset we held the project responsible to the
demands of hypermedia networks, on one hand, and to text-oriented
logical structures, on the other. This double allegiance is fraught with
difficulties, even with contradictions, as would be regularly shown during the first period of the archive's development (1992–95). Nevertheless,
I determined to preserve both commitments because each addressed a
textual ideal that seemed basic and impossible to forgo. We knew that
we did not have the practical means for reconciling the two demands—

perhaps they can never be reconciled—but even products like DynaText, imperfect as they were (and are), held out a promise of greater adequacy that spurred us forward. Besides, the tension fostered and exacerbated by this double allegiance might prove a kind *felix culpa* for the project, a helpful necessity to mother greater invention. This was my initial belief, and events have only strengthened that faith.

So our idea was to build the archive along a kind of double helix. On one hand, we would develop a markup of the text data in SGML for structured search and analysis of the archive's materials. On the other, we would design a hypertext environment for the presentation of the primary documents—the books, manuscripts, proofs, paintings, drawings, and other designs of Dante Gabriel Rossetti—in their facsimile (i.e., digital) forms. A key problem from the outset, then, was how to integrate these different organizational forms. We arrived at two schemes for achieving what we wanted. One involved a piece of original software that we would develop, now called the Image Annotation Tool, or Image Tool (see below). The other plan was to develop an SGML markup design that would extend beyond the conceptual framework of the Text Encoding Initiative (TEI), the widely accepted text-markup scheme spun out of SGML that has become the standard protocol for organizing the markup of electronic textual projects in humanities.

This is not the place to enter into a full critique of the limitations of the TEI approach to text encoding.[13] Suffice it to say that the linguistic orientation of TEI did not suit our documentary demands. Bibliographical codes and the graphic design of texts are not easily addressed by TEI markup, but those features of texts are among our primary concerns; after all, we had chosen Rossetti as our model exactly because his work forced us to design an approach to text markup that took into account the visibilities of his expressive media. What we wanted was a text-markup scheme that could deal analytically with the whole of the textual field, not simply a TEI subset of its linguistic elements. Therefore, in 1992, we began the effort to design an SGML-based documentary markup for structured search and analysis of all Rossetti's work.

Those initial design sessions immediately involved us with the problem of textual concurrencies. SGML markup of text organizes text fields as a *series* of discrete textual units. Each unit can comprise embedded subseries, and further subseries can be developed indefinitely. But SGML processors have no aptitude for marking up *concurrent* textual features. A classic instance of concurrency would involve the effort to permit simultaneous markup of a book of poems both by page unit and by poem;

in SGML, the user is led to choose either one or the other approach as the logical basis of markup design.[14]

At that point, we had two options: to abandon SGML and look for a markup language that could process concurrent structures, or to try to modify SGML to accommodate the needs of the Rossetti Archive. In choosing the latter option, we consciously committed ourselves to an inevitable set of unforeseeable problems. These problems turned out far more critical than we initially expected them to be, for the truth is that all textualizations—but, preeminently, imaginative textualities—are organized through concurrent structures. Texts have bibliographical and linguistic structures, and those are riven by other concurrencies: rhetorical, grammatical, metrical, sonic, and referential structures. The more complex the structure, the more concurrencies are set in play.[15]

We made our choice for SGML largely because we could find no other system that possessed the analytic depth or rigor that SGML offered for dealing with concurrencies, and because our project was not the designing of a new markup language for imaginative discourse. True, building a general model for computerized scholarly editing depends on an adequate logical conception of the primary materials, and it does not bode well to begin with a logic one knows to be inadequate. But what were the choices? If natural languages defeat the prospect of complete logical description, an artistic deployment of language is even more intractable. In such cases, adequacy is out of the question. Besides, SGML is a standard system. We are aware of its limitations because the system is broadly used and discussed. As Hamlet suggested, we seemed better off bearing the ills we had than flying to others we knew nothing of. And there was one other important consideration: the basic concurrency of physical unit versus conceptual unit might be addressed and perhaps even accommodated through other parts of the archive's design structure—through the markup of images, through software for analyzing image information, and through the hypermedia design.

Thus, in 1992, we began building the Rossetti Archive with what we knew were less than perfect tools, and under clearly volatile conditions. Our plan was to use the construction process as a mechanism for imagining what we didn't know about the project. In one respect, we were engaged in a classic form of model building whereby a theoretical structure is designed, built, tested, and then scaled up in size and tested again at each succeeding juncture. The testing exposes design flaws and leads to modifications of the original design. That process of development can be illustrated with excerpts from one of our SGML markup protocols:

the DTD (again, the document type definition) for marking up every Rossetti Archive document, or RAD. This DTD is used for textual (as opposed to pictorial) documents of Rossetti's work, as well as for important related primary materials (like the pre-Raphaelite periodical *The Germ*). It defines the terms within which structured searches and analyses of the documents will be carried out. My immediate interest is not the SGML design as such but the record of modifications to the design. That record appears as a list of dated entries at the top of the DTD.

Before discussing some of these entries, however, let me point out several matters of importance. First, the date of the initial entry is given as "6 Oct 94"—just about one year after we completed the first design iterations for the Rossetti Archive DTDs. Although a great many modifications to the initial design were made during that year, and before October 6, we did not at first think to keep a systematic record of the changes. Thus there is a prehistory of changes, held now only in volatile memory—that is, in the personal recollections of the individuals involved, and in paper files that contain incomplete records of what happened in that period.

Second, the record does not indicate certain decisive moments when the archive was discovering features of itself of which it was unaware. In these cases, no actual changes were made to the DTDs. For example, we regularly discovered that different persons implementing the markup schemes were liable to interpret the intent of the system in different ways. We tried to obviate this situation by supplying clear definitions for all the terms in use, as well as a handbook and a guide for markup procedures. But it turned out—surprise, surprise—that these tools were themselves sometimes ambiguous. The archive is regularly reshaped, usually in minor ways, when we discover such indeterminacies.

Third, external factors have also had a significant impact on the form and content of the archive, and we found ourselves driven in unimagined directions. One of the most interesting shifts came about because of our problems with permissions and copyrights. The cost of these exploded as the archive was being developed, and in certain cases we were simply refused access to materials. This problem grew so acute— the date is 1994—that I decided on a completely new approach to the issue of facsimile reproduction of pictures and paintings. Rather than construct the first installment of the archive around digital facsimiles made from fresh full-color images (slides, transparencies, photographs), I determined to exploit a vast contemporary resource: the photographs made of Rossetti's works during and shortly after his lifetime, many done by friends and other early pioneers in photography. Rossetti is one of the first modern artists to have taken a serious interest in photography; the photographs he made of Jane Morris and Fanny Cornforth with J. R. Parsons are themselves masterpieces of the art.[16]

Whether extramural or intramural, however, these changes to the Rossetti Archive are, first, the realized imaginings of what we didn't know; and, second, clear instances of a theoretical power beyond the range of strictly speculative activities. Let's consider for a moment some examples of intramural changes, as coded in the historical log of the RAD DTD. The recorded alterations in that DTD design were made as we scaled the project up from its initial development model (which involved only a small subset of Rossetti documents). This is a record of a process of imagining what we didn't know. The imagining came through a series of performative moves that created a double imaginative result: the discovery of a design inadequacy, and a clarification of what we had wanted but were at first unable to conceive.

Some modifications are relatively trivial—for example, this one:

```
<!--div1 ornLb added to titlePage 11-20-96 A.S.-->
```

The change permits the markup of an ornamental line break (*ornLb*) on title pages. Small as it is, the change reflects one of the most important general demands laid down by our initial conceptions: to treat the physical aspects of the documents as expressive features.

A more obviously significant change is the following:

```
<!--revised: 9 Mar 95 to add r attr to l, lg and lv (seg)-->
```

It calls for the introduction of the attribute *r* (for "reference line") to all line (*l*), line group (*lg*), and variant line (*lv*) values in the archive. This small change defines the moment when we were able to work out a line-referencing system for the archive that would permit automatic identification of equivalent units of text in different documents. We had known, of course, that we wanted such a system from the outset, but we were unable to feel confident about how the system should be organized until we had three years of experience with many different types of textual material.

Working out this scheme for collating Rossetti's texts revealed an interesting general fact about electronic collating tools: that we do not yet have any good program for collating units of prose texts. The poetic line is a useful reference unit; in prose, the textual situation is far more fluid and does not lend itself to convenient division into discrete units smaller than a paragraph. The problem is especially apparent when one tries to mark up working manuscripts for collation with printed texts. The person who discovers a reasonably simple solution to this problem will have made a signal contribution not just to electronic scholarship but to the theoretical understanding of prose textuality in general.

But, returning to the history of RAD revisions, let us look at the notation for June 14, 1995:

<!--revised: 14 Jun 95 to add group option to rad for serials-->

A large-scale change in our conception of the archive's documentary structure is concealed in this small entry. The line calls for the use of the "group" tag in the markup structure for serials (like *The Germ*) that are to be included in the archive. Behind that call, however, lies a difficult process that extended over several years. The problem involved documents (like periodicals) containing multiple kinds of materials. The most problematic of these documents were not the periodicals, however, but a series of primary Rossettian documents, the most important of which were composite manuscripts and composite sets of proofs. In these materials the problems of concurrency became so extreme that we began to consider the possibility of abandoning SGML altogether—which would have meant beginning the whole project again from scratch.

As it turned out, we found a way to manipulate the SGML structure so as to permit a reasonably full presentation of the structure of these complex documents. That practical result, however, was not nearly so interesting as the insights we gained into general problems of concurrency and into the limitations of SGML software.

Consider the following situation. Rossetti typically wrote his verse and prose in notebooks of a distinctive kind. Two of these survive intact to this day, but the fragments of many others are scattered everywhere. Many are loose sheets or groups of sheets; many others come down to us as parts of second-order confederations of material that Rossetti put together, or that were put together by others (during his lifetime or after his death) as other second- or even third-order arrangements. Problem: devise a markup scheme that will reconstruct, on the fly, the initial but later deconstructed orderings; or—since, in many cases, we can't identify for certain which pages go with which notebook phylum—devise a markup scheme that constructs, on the fly, the various possibilities; or devise a system that lays out an analytic history of the reorderings, including a description of the possible or likely lines by which the distributed documents arrived at their current archival states.

An instrument that could perform any or all of these operations would have wide applicability for textual scholars of all kinds and periods. I am sure it could be developed, perhaps even within SGML. It is an instrument that was imagined into thought by our building of the Rossetti Archive. We saw it as we were trying to devise markup systems that would accommodate the composite proofs and manuscripts that are so characteristic of Rossetti's extant textual materials. It is an instrument that we would like to develop ourselves—but we're far too busy with so many other basic problems and demands.

III

The examples I have been discussing illustrate what I would call the "pragmatics of theory," as well as the sharp difference between theory, on one hand, and hypothesis or speculation, on the other. In humanities discourse this distinction is rarely maintained, and the term "theory" is characteristically applied to speculative projects—conceptual undertakings (gnosis) rather than specific constructions (poiesis). Scientists work within the former distinction, and in this sense the Rossetti Archive seems a "scientific" project. Patterson's discussion of the Kane-Donaldson edition of *Piers Plowman* implicitly affirms the same kind of distinction, where "theory" operates through concrete acts of imagining.[17]

The virtue of this last kind of theorizing is that it makes possible the imagination of what you don't know. Theory in the other sense—for instance, Heideggerian dialectic—is a procedure for revealing what you *do* know but are unaware of. Both are intellectual imperatives, but in humanities disciplines the appreciation for theory-as-poiesis has grown attenuated. The need to accommodate electronic textualities to humanities disciplines, which are fundamentally document- and text-based, is bringing a radical change in perspective on these matters.

The force of these circumstances has registered on nearly every aspect of the Rossetti Archive, as I've already indicated. Up to this point, however, I've used examples that illustrate the praxis of theory, since it is an example of a methodological process we are familiar with, though perhaps not so much in a humanities context: the process of imagining what you know, testing it, scaling it up, modifying it, and then reimagining it; and then the process of repeating that process in an indefinite series of iterations.

At this point, I want to give one more example of that process. It is the history of the development of the Image Annotation Tool, a piece of software I mentioned earlier. More than an exemplum of theory-as-poiesis, the story indicates, I believe, the "strange days" that lie ahead for humanities scholars as we register the authority of these new electronic textualities.

The Image Tool was originally an idea for computing via images rather than with text or with the data represented in text. Because information in bitmapped images cannot be coded for analysis, our technical people were asked if it would be possible to lay an electronic transparency (as it were) over the digital image, and then use that overlay as the vehicle for carrying computable marked-up data and hypertext links. The idea was to treat the overlay as a kind of see-through page on which one would write text that elucidated or annotated the imaged material seen "through" the overlay. (The idea originates in scholarly editions that utilize onionskin or other transparent pages to create an editorial palimpsest for complex textual situations.)

As with virtually all work undertaken at the Institute for Advanced Technology in the Humanities, this tool's design was influenced by many people who came to have an interest in it. Consequently, because I was initially most preoccupied with designing the Rossetti Archive's markup structure, my interest in the development of the Image Tool hung fire. My own early thought had been that such a tool might enable the Rossetti Archive to incorporate images into its analytic text structure and thus establish a basis for direct searches across the whole of the archive at the image level. As I worked more and more closely with SGML markup, however, I began to suspect that the same result might be achieved through the design of a DTD for images. That idea, plus the technical difficulties in building the Image Tool, drew my attention away from the tool's development.

The Image Tool thus began to evolve in ways that I (at any rate) had not anticipated. As others looked for features that would answer their interests, the tool emerged as a device for editing an image with multiple-style overlays that, if clicked, would generate a text file carrying various annotations to the image. These annotations would be saved as part of the total archive structure and hence could be embedded with hypertext links to other images or archival documents.

At that point—the date is early 1995—my practical interest in the tool was revived. This happened because my work on the DTDs for the archive, nearing completion, began to expose certain limitations in the overall design structure. It was growing very clear that the archive's two parallel universes continued discontinuous in fundamental and (in this case, I thought) unhelpful ways. The Image Tool had become a device with two primary functions: (1) it allowed one to build a random set of

image points or areas to which one could attach text materials of varying kinds; and (2) it allowed one to embed hypertext links to those materials. Therefore, while the tool created navigational paths from text to
image and vice versa, thus connecting the two basic (and different) kinds
of objects in the archive, and while it drew these image-related texts (and
hence the images as well) into the full computational structure, it did
not organize these materials *within a logical structure readable in the
archive.* Any searches of the materials would have to be, in effect, string
searches. (The Image Tool in its first iteration, for example, could not
function in close cooperation with the indexable fields of information
as established through the archive's DTDs.)

This limitation in the tool recalled my attention to the archive's basic
contradiction and double allegiance. The full evolution of the markup
structure—the building of the DTDs for all text and image documents—
had not been matched by a corresponding development in the Image
Tool, at least not for those who would want, as I did, a tool that could
function within the SGML-marked database (texts as well as pictures).
This discrepancy arose because the first version of the tool, unlike the
DTDs, was not mapped to the logical (DTD) structure of the files in the
archive. It would be formally integrated with the SGML-marked database only when it could summon its materials within pre-established
indexable categories. Furthermore, an adequate integration would
require some kind of mappable relation between those indexable forms
and the SGML-marked database.

To address these problems, I suggested that we limit our consideration, at least initially, to textual images—that is, images of manuscripts,
proofs, and printed documents—since these are far simpler than pictorial images. We began by posing the question "What is the formal structure of a text page?"

This initial query arose through a pair of presuppositions implicit in
the Rossetti Archive. The first reflected the archive's practical delivery
of its images, which the archive manipulates as units of either single
pages or single sets of two facing pages. That procedure flowed from a
second assumption about texts in general. We assumed that a "text" is
a rhetorical sequence organized by page units, with each page centered
within a structure created by a sequence of lines commonly running from
top to bottom, from left to right, and inside some set of margins, which
themselves may be reduced to nil (practically) on one or more sides.

In marking up the formal structure of the text image, these general
conventions defined the shape of the page and governed the markup.
Consequently, I proposed that the page be formally conceived as a struc-

ture consisting of different spatial areas. I initially proposed four marginal areas (left and right margins, plus header and footer) and a central text area stacked into four equal horizontal sections. This design was found to be more complex than necessary, however, and so we eventually settled on a page design of three stacked horizontal areas that eliminated the four marginal areas from the page structure.

The essential point of this structure was and is to permit SGML-marked textual materials to be mapped directly to digitized images. An indexable key or code is supplied to the digitized images so that a formal relation can be established between the two conceptual states of any text (i.e., any text conceived as simultaneously a linguistic field and a bibliographical field, the latter being the totality of a given text's typographical and page-design features). SGML markup has little to say about the *physical* status of the materials so marked, since SGML markup is not conceived in terms of spatial relations. For example, even if a set of SGML fields were to be defined for the bibliographical features of a text, no formal structure would exist to connect the digitized images of the text to the SGML-marked texts, since the SGML-marked texts would not have been defined conceptually in relation to the digitized images.[18] In the case of textual materials, formalized representation of a bibliographical field would serve primarily to facilitate the study of documents with "irregular" textual conditions (e.g., documents with many additions, corrections, and erasures, or documents, such as Blake's illuminated texts, with nonlinguistic elements). At least that was the initial imagination for the scheme.

The Image Tool has now been developed along these lines, and its functions have been applied and adapted by the editors of the Blake Archive. The results can be seen in the Blake Archive's release of its first installment: an edition and study tool for *The Book of Thel* created by Morris Eaves, Robert N. Essick, and Joseph Viscomi.[19]

But not all the results are immediately apparent. The practice of the theory of the Image Tool has revealed some interesting ideas about computerizing textual materials in relation to a database of images. For instance, it is apparent that in such cases one should define the basic textual unit as the *page* (as is done in the Blake Archive) rather than as the individual *work* (as is done in SGML and—alas—in the Rossetti Archive). Only if the basic unit is the page (or the page opening) can the lineation in the digital image be logically mapped to the SGML markup structure. Of course, if SGML software were able to handle concurrent structures, this consequence would not necessarily follow.

The Blake Archive's work conforms to the original thought about the

Image Tool: that it be shaped to integrate any editorial (SGML) meta-data directly to the digital images that constitute the metadata. As the tool was being adapted by the Blake Archive editors, however, their work exposed more severely than ever the problem of analyzing the data of digital images. Blake's work lent itself to the idea of the Image Tool because that idea was fundamentally a textual one; and while Blake's works are profoundly iconological, they are also, at bottom, texts, not pictures.

We still do not have any means of carrying out on-the-fly analyses of the iconological information in pictures (let alone pictures that are aes-thetically organized). Our work with the Image Tool shows how far one might go—and it is pretty far, after all—to integrate an SGML approach to picture markup and analysis. But the limitations of such an approach are also painfully clear.

I have no idea how or when this nexus of problems will be overcome, though I do have some thoughts on experimental avenues that might be explored. Nevertheless, electronic textuality is so intimately bound up with the manipulation of images that the issues must remain at the fore-front of attention. Logical markup through schemes derived from lin-guistic models, powerful though they are, cannot even serve the full needs of textual scholars, much less those of musicologists, art historians, film scholars, and artists in general. The Pentagon and the infotainment indus-try have committed large resources to research into these problems, whose importance is clear to them. While scholars and archivists lack those kinds of financial resources, we would be wrong to stand aside while the issues are being engaged and theorized. Indeed, scholars like ourselves typi-cally possess a phenomenological understanding of such materials that is obscure to technoscientific researchers. Therefore, it is extremely important that traditional scholars and critics experiment with the study of digital images, and—what is perhaps even more useful—set their stu-dents to play and experiment with these materials. If ever there were a situation calling us to imagine what we don't know, this is one.

Notes

Every effort has been made to ensure that references to the World Wide Web are correct and current, but some addresses may have changed or expired while this volume was in pro-duction. The reader is urged to use online search engines to locate current URLs.

  1. See Lee Patterson, "The Logic of Textual Criticism and the Way of Genius: The Kane-Donaldson *Piers Plowman* in Historical Perspective," in Jerome J. McGann, ed., *Textual Criticism and Literary Interpretation* (Chicago: University of Chicago Press, 1985), 55–91; William Lang-land, *Piers Plowman: The B Version*, ed. George Kane and E. Talbot Donaldson (London: Athlone Press, 1975).

2. Langland, *Piers Plowman,* 212.

3. Patterson, "The Logic of Textual Criticism and the Way of Genius," 69.

4. William Blake, *Jerusalem,* pl. 109, 11.20–21.

5. William Carlos Williams, *The Embodiment of Knowledge,* ed. Ron Loewinsohn (New York: New Directions, 1974).

6. See Emily Dickinson, *The Manuscript Books of Emily Dickinson,* ed. R. W. Franklin (Cambridge, Mass.: Belknap Press of Harvard University Press, 1981); William Shakespeare, *The Parallel King Lear: 1608–1623,* ed. Michael Warren (Berkeley: University of California Press, 1989); Friedrich Hölderlin, *Sämmtliche Werke: Frankfurter Ausgabe,* ed. D. E. Sattler (Frankfurt am Main: Verlag Rater Stern, 1975).

7. See, for example, Paul De Man, *Blindness and Insight* (Oxford: Oxford University Press, 1971).

8. [See, in this context, Marta Werner's essay in this volume.—Eds.]

9. See Martha Nell Smith, Ellen Louise Hart, and Marta Werner, eds., The Dickinson Archive: http://www.iath.virginia.edu/dickinson

10. That is to say, the ongoing set of print editions of Wordsworth's poetry being issued by the Cornell University Press; for one example, see W. J. B. Owen, ed., *The Fourteen-Book Prelude by William Wordsworth* (Ithaca, N.Y.: Cornell University Press, 1985).

11. See http://jefferson.village.virginia.edu/rossetti/index.html.

12. See Jerome McGann, "The Rationale of HyperText": http://jefferson.village.virginia .edu/public/jjm2f/rationale.html.

13. The creators of the TEI instance of SGML have initiated this critique themselves in several papers; see, for example, Steven DeRose, David Durand, Elli Mylonas, and Allen H. Renear, "What Is Text, Really?," *Journal of Computing in Higher Education* 1:2 (1990), 3–26, and Allen Renear, David Durand, and Elli Mylonas, "Refining Our Notion of What Text Really Is," in Susan Hockey and Nancy Ide, eds., *Research in Humanities Computing,* vol. 4 (Oxford: Clarendon Press, 1996), 263–80. Most recently, this critical investigation has been extended by Daniel Pitti and John Unsworth in "After the Fall: Structured Data at IATH," a paper presented at the conference of the Association for Literary and Linguistic Computing / Association for Computers held in Debrecen, Hungary, in 1998. See also Jerome McGann, *Comp[u/e]ting Editorial F[u/ea]tures,*" in Neil Fraistat, ed., *Re-Imagining Textuality* (Milwaukee: University of Wisconsin Press, 2002), 17–27.

14. It is true that the CONCUR feature is part of the ISO markup standard (ISO is the anomalous acronym for the International Organization for Standardization), but we had no way to implement that feature or to test its operation. This problem is more complex than appears from the simple example of overlapping page and work structures, for the fact is that imaginative texts—unlike expository texts—do not merely *exhibit* some concurrent features, they *are* organized systems of multiple concurrencies. This radical character of imaginative texts suggests that no SGML processor would ever be able to implement the CONCUR feature except in the most minimal ways.

15. One classic paper seems to espouse a different view of "text": that the expository text is "real" text, or the model of the textual condition; see DeRose, Durand, Mylonas, and Renear, "What Is Text, Really?" Makers of imaginative texts see the matter very differently. But whether the form of exposition or the form of poiesis is thought of as the normal state of textuality, it is clear that the two forms are very different, that SGML/TEI is a design built for expository text, and that the SGML/TEI design consequently has fundamental limitations when laid upon poetical texts.

16. This shift to early photographic resources—the materials date from the mid-1860s to about 1920—has two great advantages, one both scholarly and practical, the other scholarly. First, the move allows us to temporize on the extremely vexed issue of copyright; we use whatever fresh full-color digital images we can afford, and we work toward developing standards for the scholarly use of all such materials. Second, we now comprehensively represent Rossetti's visual work in the medium that was probably its major early disseminating vehicle,

and we simultaneously create a digital archive of great general significance for studying both the history of photography and the history of painting.

17. See Patterson, "The Logic of Textual Criticism and the Way of Genius."

18. The problem here essentially replicates the problem of textual concurrency. In the Rossetti Archive, we have marked up the presence of various bibliographical features of our texts. Nevertheless, because these features fall within the horizon of "the page" and "the book" rather than within the horizon of the linguistic and semantic text, they stand outside the logical envelope that organizes the SGML/TEI "text." They are locatable in the textual field, but they are not integrated into the textual field's logical form.

19. See http://www.blakearchive.org.

PART VI

Textual Maintenance

Old and New
in Italian Textual Criticism

CONOR FAHY

In preparing this essay, it has been almost impossible for me not to take as my starting point the volume *Contemporary German Editorial Theory*,[1] which sets out to do in detail what I can only begin to do here: present to scholars of one particular language tradition the state of textual criticism in another. In his introduction to that volume, the distinguished critic Hans Walter Gabler writes, "If it is just to say that in the Anglo-American debate encounters with the German school of textual criticism have not been sought, . . . the reverse is equally true: German textual scholarship, beyond taking marginal note of analytical bibliography, has remained oblivious of Anglo-American developments."[2] This national isolationism is a general feature of modern-language textual scholarship. How many English-language textual critics, for example, have read the works, or even know the name, of the leading Italian exponent of the theory and practice of textual criticism in this half-century, Gianfranco Contini (1912–1990)? For their part, Italian textual critics would be astonished to read that "Anglo-American editing may be described as the most influential and successful undertaking in the history of modern language scholarly editing."[3] It is true that for the last ten years Italian textual critics have had at their disposal a volume similar to the German one, containing the translation into Italian of key articles by W. W. Greg, Fredson Bowers, and others.[4] This publication has been quite effective in helping to alert the younger generation of Italian textual scholars to their lack of technical expertise in the field of analytical bibliography, but it has had no impact whatever on the discussion of theoretical issues.[5] Italian textual critics are quite satisfied with the substantial indigenous theoretical and practical activity that has taken place in their discipline during the last half-century, and they would certainly regard it as highly successful if not, perhaps, particularly influential outside the national boundaries.

A self-satisfied account of this activity can be found in a 1991 article published (in Italian, unfortunately) in a special number of the American journal *Romance Philology*.[6] Its title can be translated as "Textual Criticism and Italian Medieval Literature." And here we have, in this title, the beginnings of an explanation of the major distinctive feature of modern Italian thinking about textual criticism. Dante, Petrarch, and Boccaccio, arguably the three greatest Italian writers, whose influence permeates every period of Italian culture, lived and died a century or more before the invention of printing. The transmission of all of their major works, and almost all of their minor ones, is by way of the written, not the printed, word. Even today, despite the European importance of many later Italian writers from the age of print, Italian textual criticism remains preoccupied with the manuscript. In fact, I do not know a single Italian theoretical discussion of textual criticism that does not explicitly or implicitly confine itself to manuscript transmission. As a consequence, Italian textual criticism still shows strong links with nineteenth-century classical and Biblical textual criticism. Karl Lachmann lives, in fact! But slimmed down, and in modern dress.

A good place to start is a book by the classical scholar Giorgio Pasquali, first published in Florence in 1934 under the title *Storia della tradizione e critica del testo* (which can be freely translated as "Textual Criticism and the History of Textual Transmission").[7] This book started as a review of Paul Maas's *Textkritik,* a handbook of classical textual criticism published in 1927,[8] which contained a rigorous and mechanistic codification of Lachmannian stemmatics. Pasquali did not openly criticize Lachmann's method, but his main point was that, even among classical texts, many were unsuited to pure Lachmannian treatment, either because there was no split in the tradition or because some of the transmission had been horizontal, not vertical. In other words, the tradition was contaminated; it was what Pasquali called "open," as opposed to the "closed," vertical transmission envisaged by Lachmann. Pasquali even claimed it was possible, in the tradition of a few classical works, to identify authorial variants. In all these cases, the study of the history of the transmission of the text was vital.

The relevance of these views to the textual criticism of medieval vernacular literature is obvious and was explicitly indicated by Pasquali. With the chain of surviving witnesses usually going back at least to something fairly close to the author's holograph, authorial variants are relatively commonplace, while the prevalence, in the transmission of most vernacular texts, not of professional scribes, but of amateurs who copied for personal pleasure and use, makes conflation and contamination widespread.[9] In other words, the typical medieval vernacular work has an "open" tradition, in which, too, there is a high probability of finding authorial variants.

Pasquali's views served to clarify and give theoretical coherence to a practice that was already established among Italian textual critics in the first half of the century. Following the lead of the French medievalist Gaston Paris, they had attempted to apply Lachmannian principles to the editing of medieval Romance texts. These principles were particularly attractive to them because of the help they seemed to offer in bringing some sort of order into traditions with large numbers of surviving witnesses, which are numerous in medieval Italian literature. One need look no further than to its greatest work, Dante's *Divine Comedy,* of which there are more than six hundred surviving manuscripts. The earliest of these postdates the author's death by several years, as does the earliest witness whose text can be reconstructed, though the manuscript itself is now lost. The task of providing a critical text of the *Comedy* has dominated the development of Italian textual criticism in much the same way as the problem of the Shakespearean text shaped the history of the discipline in the English-speaking world. By the middle of the present century, Italian textual critics had identified some of the requirements and the new possibilities of vernacular textual criticism but had not come to terms with the radical challenge mounted to Lachmann-based vernacular philology in the 1920s by the French scholar Joseph Bédier. According to Bédier, the biggest weakness of the Lachmann method as applied to medieval texts was that it almost always produced a bipartite stemma; thus, in the end, after the elimination of obvious errors, often few in number, the scholar was left, where the readings of the two families differed, with a subjective choice between two competing readings. Bédier mischievously suggested that medieval textual critics had a tendency subconsciously to manufacture these bipartite stemmata, so as to leave themselves a margin of autonomy when it came to constituting the text; better by far, Bédier suggested, to follow the reading of a single, authoritative manuscript. In that way, at least, one would produce a text with some historical basis, not one manufactured eclectically by a modern scholar.[10] A lot of modern French textual criticism is still based on Bédier's principle of the "good manuscript"; I remember taking part in a discussion with some French scholars in Italy in the 1980s, from which it was clear that *éclectique* was still a dirty word in French textual criticism.

It was principally Gianfranco Contini who met the challenge of Bédier's arguments. Contini's views on textual criticism were expressed in articles and introductory material to editions; some of the most important have now been collected in a small volume whose title can be translated as "Breviary of Textual Criticism."[11] How do Bédier and his followers decide, Contini asked, which of the surviving witnesses of a work is the one on which to base their text? Unless their choice is wholly aleatory, or directed by convenience, they must make an assessment that is based on some sort of comparison of the readings of possible candidates. In other words, they must carry out an operation similar to the collations required by Lachmannian stemmatics, after which they must make a critical (i.e., subjective) choice. And, when constituting the text, they do not just slavishly copy their source, obvious errors included; their editions always contain an element of interpretation. Every critical edition, Contini reminds us, however compiled, is, like any other historical reconstruction, just a hypothesis. What counts in textual criticism, Contini believes, is precisely what Bédier seems to regard as its weakness: the use the critic makes of his critical faculties.

Modern Italian textual criticism continues to be what Contini calls neo-Lachmannian.[12] Lachmannian stemmatics can be useful, and are used, where the witnesses are numerous or their relationships are not immediately clear. For example, Lachmannian stemmatics formed the basis of the biggest event so far this half-century in Italian textual criticism: a new critical edition of the *Divine Comedy*,[13] published in 1966–67 and based on the twenty-seven manuscripts that predate the editorial exertions of the first serious Dante scholar, Giovanni Boccaccio, whose activities in the 1350s greatly influenced the subsequent transmission of the text of Dante's work. Lachmannian stemmatics still form the backbone of the training and practice of students and scholars operating out of the many departments of Italian and of Romance philology in the Italian university system. But the fact is that, in many cases, and particularly in those where the transmission is solely printed (of which more later), Lachmannian stemmatics are of little relevance because for many vernacular texts, even those transmitted by manuscript—for example, Petrarch's *Canzoniere,* or Boccaccio's *Decameron*—it is not a question of trying to recover a lost original. We have the originals.[14] What textual criticism must do (and has been doing for centuries in the two cases just mentioned, with varying degrees of awareness) is examine and document the stages of the author's compositional journey. Much of the attention of Italian textual critics in this half-century has been devoted to the two elements indicated in 1934 by Pasquali—the history of the transmission of the text, and authorial variants—thus bringing recent developments in Italian textual criticism into line with those apparent elsewhere.

Interest in the history of textual transmission, already present in the Italian cultural humus through the work of literary historians of the positivist school at the turn of the century, was much stimulated in the 1940s and 1950s by the publications of the medievalist Giuseppe Billanovich and his pupils. They have devoted much of their research to studying the history of those classical or medieval manuscripts that passed through the hands of, or were created by, the scholars responsible for the intellectual movement known as Italian humanism. Billanovich's brilliant reconstruction of the stages by which Petrarch succeeded in recovering for posterity what had survived of the text of Livy can serve as an example of this trend.[15] This is not textual criticism, of course, but Billanovich's influential activities reminded textual critics that manuscripts are never just letters in a Lachmannian stemma; they always have a cultural importance relative to the time and place of their production and fruition.

In this context, it is worth mentioning that Italian textual critics have always approached the concept of final authorial intention with more circumspection than have traditional Anglo-American textual critics. This is partly because Italian literature contains a blatant and famous instance, dating from the age of print, of the nonfunctionality of this concept as an editorial criterion: Torquato Tasso's great epic poem *Gerusalemme liberata*. While still engaged in an agonized revision of the text, Tasso, who was a paranoiac and also probably a schizophrenic, drew a dagger in the presence of the Duke of Ferrara and was understandably incarcerated for several years. While he was in prison, the *Liberata* was published without his consent, as it stood, to immediate and lasting acclaim. On his release, Tasso disowned the poem as published, rewrote it in conformity with Counter-Reformation ethics and poetics, and published the heavily revised version in 1593 with a new title, *Gerusalemme conquistata*. There is no doubt what Tasso's final intention was, yet Italian textual critics have never faltered in regarding their task as that of trying to produce a critical edition, not of the *Conquistata*, but of that earlier, unrevised, and subsequently disowned version of the poem, which profoundly influenced Italian and European culture for two centuries and has ceaselessly delighted readers from its first publication to the present day.[16]

For various reasons, then, modern Italian textual criticism has been open to the idea that each separate witness of a literary work may constitute an independent version and has, at the very least, its own cultural validity, which textual criticism should not ignore. But what Italians themselves indicate as the distinguishing mark of their textual criticism in this half-century is its interest in authorial variants and, in general, in the evidence that enables the textual critic to document the genesis of a work. The presence of these features in the tradition of vernacular works has attracted the attention of Italian scholars for a long time (I think, for example, of Federico Ubaldini's 1642 edition of an early, autograph version of Petrarch's *Canzoniere*).[17] Over the centuries many studies of Italian authors, and editions of their works, have contained information about authorial variants and about earlier, or later, versions of all or parts of these works, and I expect that the same is true of other modern languages. What distinguishes the modern Italian interest in these phenomena from earlier efforts is its intensity and self-awareness. This modern interest is usually dated from the work of a brilliant but isolated scholar, Santorre Debenedetti, teacher of Contini, who proposed in the 1920s to publish a critical edition of Ariosto's *Orlando furioso* that would include in the apparatus not only the authorial press variants of the definitive edition of 1532 but also the variants of two earlier authorized editions of the poem. This project was vetoed by the general editor of the series, the philosopher Benedetto Croce, who did not want the purity of the text sullied by a messy apparatus, and so Debenedetti's edition appeared in 1928, with just the 1532 authorial variants, and these were relegated to an appendix.[18] A few years later, however, he published the surviving autograph fragments of the new material that Ariosto had added to the 1532 edition.[19] This publication provoked a brilliant essay by the young Contini, entitled "How Ariosto Worked." This essay also signaled the emergence of one of the most characteristic features of modern Italian textual criticism, personified in the career of Contini himself: the close link between textual and literary criticism.[20]

If textual criticism is to concern itself with the history of a work and of its dissemination and fruition as well as with the constitution of the text, the presentation of its results, in the form of a critical edition, becomes a crucial issue. Contini has spoken of the desirability of constructing an apparatus that enables the user to reconstruct the physiognomy of the text in its passage through time, or at least at certain selected moments of this passage. He was thinking of a work like the *Divine Comedy,* disseminated in manuscript after the author's death, though the practicalities of following his advice are formidable. But Contini and others have also considered the case of works where preliminary versions survive. Clearly, the skeletal apparatus normally given in Lachmannian editions of classical texts is quite inadequate, though such material needs to be included, where relevant. It belongs to the part of the apparatus that Italians call "synchronic," or "critical," the purpose of which is to justify the critical text. But there is another function of the apparatus, which is to document the changes introduced by the author in surviving texts of the work. This part of the apparatus is variously called by Italian critics "diachronic" or "genetic"; another term, "evolutionary," has recently been introduced to describe the variants of partial textual re-elaborations subsequent to that on which the edition is based. Many editions illustrating these approaches to the constitution of the apparatus have been published in the last forty years.[21]

It is interesting that many of the editions that show these concerns are of texts transmitted through the medium of print. The practice of Italian textual critics, unlike their thinking, has never restricted its focus to manuscript transmission. But, until recently, printed texts were edited as though they were manuscripts. Only a few scholars—like Ariosto's editor Debenedetti, or like Michele Barbi, another great figure of the first half of the century—arrived at an understanding of the phenomenon of press variants, but they did not try to incorporate their experiences into a general view of textual transmission, and this aspect of their work, though much admired, was dismissed as dealing with exceptional cases. Only in the 1980s did knowledge of textual bibliography begin to reach the Mediterranean. After twenty years, more or less, of mild indoctrination, I think it can be said that Italian textual criticism has begun to assimilate the part of the message of textual bibliography that it considers relevant. This is, in effect, the technical side—that is, the study of printed witnesses by means of the techniques of analytical bibliography. On the theoretical side, younger textual critics have paid some attention to Greg's ideas.[22] They were already familiar with the distinction between substantives and accidentals; that distinction had been made in identical terms by an Italian textual critic in the sixteenth century,[23] while in our own day Contini had drawn attention to the presence of these two types of variants in manuscript transmission, calling them variants of "substance" and of "form," and pointing out that Lachmannian stemmatics should properly take account only of the former.[24] As regards printed transmission, there was already an interesting example of Italian thinking on these matters in an edition of two dialogues, by the notorious Renaissance author Pietro Aretino, *Ragionamento della Nanna e della Antonia* (1534), and *Dialogo nel quale la Nanna insegna a la Pippa* (1536), edited in 1969 by Giovanni Aquilecchia, an Italian scholar working in Britain.[25] For the *Ragionamento,* Aquilecchia had to choose between two editions, the earlier one likely to be closer to the author's holograph, and the later with substantive variants, probably authorial, but also with linguistic changes that ran counter to the author's known position in the age-old Italian debate on the Italian literary language.

The editor opted for the earlier edition, because of its more authentic accidentals, but declined to incorporate into his text the substantive variants of the later one.

What interests Italians in Greg's article is precisely the idea of divided authority for these two elements. Nevertheless, a difficulty with transferring Greg's suggestions to the Italian scene lies in the substantial and enduring linguistic divisions of the peninsula. To take one example, Castiglione, author of the Renaissance classic *The Book of the Courtier*, was a Mantuan who wrote in Italian with a strong North Italian patina. This patina is present in the final manuscript version of the work, written mainly by a secretary of Castiglione, with some autograph additions, which served as printers' copy for the first edition of 1528. But, at the request of the printers, and with the approval of the author, the text was subjected to linguistic revision in a "normalizing" sense, an operation that removed many of its North Italian features. The fact is, most Italian authors from the Renaissance to the present day, like Castiglione but unlike Aretino, have humbly acquiesced in the bringing of their regional Italian into line with the Tuscan-based norm approved by publishers and followed by printers. Occasionally, however, particularly in the sixteenth century, the normalizing edition, intended for interregional consumption, was preceded by a local edition, in which regional features were still present. Obviously, each case has to be treated on its merits, but it is clear that the historical circumstances of the Italian language are very different from those of English, and it is the latter circumstances that underlie Greg's "rationale"; therefore, eclectic editions in the Gregian sense are less likely to provide satisfactory answers to the editorial problems of Italian texts.

The age of the compact disc has some obvious attractions for Italian textual critics, and the potential of CDs naturally occupies the attention of the youngest generation. A group of research students and young lecturers in the arts faculty of Naples University has recently initiated an immense, long-term project aimed at finally bringing under control the hundreds of manuscripts of the *Divine Comedy*.[26] The scheme envisages both the reproduction and the transcription of each manuscript, and then the preparation of a complete list of variants, organized in such a way as to permit the user to generate, for any part of the work, the sort of apparatus he wants. It sounds like the promised land, but I doubt that I am the only skeptic who believes the organizers have underestimated the enormousness of the task. But surely the computer will contribute in some way or another to resolving outstanding textual problems in Dante studies.[27] The possibility of using the computer to record and reproduce the texts of all the surviving witnesses, so that the reader can put himself into the position of a critical editor and construct his own critical text, has naturally occurred to Italian textual critics, but no one yet seems to have the answer to the problem of commercial support. There is also a certain built-in resistance to such ideas: at a recent conference, a proposal put forward by a young scholar to do something along these lines for the text of Castiglione's *Book of the Courtier* provoked heated discussion and some opposition.

Such hostility to change, however, is not typical of Italian textual criticism, which has developed in markedly original ways since the trauma of the Fascist era and the Second World War and has shown a real ability to incorporate insights from other countries and other fields into a still largely traditional concept of the task of textual criticism and so continually to renew itself.

Notes

1. Hans Walter Gabler, George Bornstein, and Gillian Borland Pierce, eds., *Contemporary German Editorial Theory* (Ann Arbor: University of Michigan Press, 1995).
2. Ibid., 15n23.
3. Hans Zeller, "Structure and Genesis in Editing," ibid., 95.
4. See Pasquale Stoppelli, ed., *Filologia dei testi a stampa* (Bologna: Mulino, 1987), which contains Italian translations of W. W. Greg, "The Rationale of Copy-Text," *Studies in Bibliography* 3 (1950–51), 19–36; Philip Gaskell, "The Transmission of the Text," in *A New Introduction to Bibliography* (Oxford: Oxford University Press, 1972), 343–57; G. Thomas Tanselle, "The Concept of Ideal Copy," *Studies in Bibliography* 33 (1980), 18–53; Fredson Bowers, "Multiple Authority: New Problems and Concepts of Copy-Text," *The Library* 27 (1972), 81–115; G. Thomas Tanselle, "The Editorial Problem of Final Authorial Intention," *Studies in Bibliography* 29 (1976), 167–211; and Conor Fahy, "The View from Another Planet: Textual Bibliography and the Editing of Sixteenth-Century Italian Texts," *Italian Studies* 34 (1979), 71–92.
5. This is not to say that the points of view of English-language textual critics have never been put before Italian scholars. In addition to Stoppelli's anthology, summaries of the views of Greg, Bowers, Tanselle, and Jerome McGann on final authorial intention can be found in Alfredo Stussi, *Introduzione agli studi di filologia italiana* (Bologna: Mulino, 1994), 192–94, and there are frequent references to the work and views of English-language textual critics in the essay by the British-trained scholar Neil Harris, "Filologia dei testi a stampa," in Alfredo Stussi, ed., *Fondamenti di critica testuale* (Bologna, Mulino, 1998), 301–26.
6. Cesare Segre and Gian Battista Speroni, "Filologia testuale e letteratura italiana del Medioevo," *Romance Philology* 45 (1991–92), 44–72.
7. Giorgio Pasquali, *Storia della tradizione e critica del testo* (Florence: Le Monnier, 1934). A second, enlarged edition was published in 1952 and reissued in 1962. The latest edition, with an introduction by Dino Pieraccioni, was published in 1988.
8. Later published in Leipzig by Teubner (1957).
9. The classic description of this situation in the transmission of Italian medieval literature can be found in Vittore Branca, "Copisti per passione, tradizione caratterizzante, tradizione di memoria," in *Studi e problemi di critica testuale: Convegno di Studi di Filologia italiana nel Centenario della Commissione per i Testi di Lingua (7–9 Aprile 1960)* (Bologna: Commissione per i Testi di Lingua, 1961), 69–83, a volume of conference proceedings. The contents of this volume give a panoramic view of the interests and achievements of modern Italian textual criticism, as is also

true of a more recent volume of conference proceedings; see *La critica del testo: Problemi di metodo ed esperienze di lavoro: Atti del Convegno di Lecce 22–26 ottobre 1984* (Rome: Salerno, 1985).

10. Joseph Bédier, "La tradition manuscrite du *Lai de l'Ombre*: Réflexions sur l'art d'éditer les anciens textes," *Romania* 54 (1928), 161–96, 321–56.

11. Gianfranco Contini, *Breviario di ecdotica* (Milan and Naples: Ricciardi, 1986).

12. The continued interest of Italian culture in the figure of Karl Lachmann, an interest tempered by a healthy and well-informed critical attitude, is well illustrated in Sebastiano Timpanaro, *La genesi del metodo del Lachmann* (Florence: Le Monnier, 1963); see also the new and enlarged edition of this work published in Padua by Liviana in 1981.

13. Dante Alighieri, *La commedia secondo l'antica vulgata*, 4 vols., ed. Giorgio Petrocchi (Milan: Mondadori, 1966–67). The neo-Lachmannian apple-cart has recently been upset by the publication of a resolutely Bédierian edition of the *Divine Comedy*, based on the oldest surviving Florentine manuscript; see Dante Alighieri, *La commedia: testo critico secondo i più antichi manoscritti fiorentini: Nuova editione*, ed. Antonio Lanza (Anzio: De Rubeis, 1996).

14. For Petrarch, codice Vaticano latino 3195, largely autograph; for Boccaccio, codice Hamilton 90, Staatsbibliothek, Berlin, entirely autograph.

15. See Giuseppe Billanovich, *La tradizione del testo di Livio e le origini dell'Umanesimo* (Padua: Antenore, 1981).

16. Also influential in inserting doubts into the minds of Italian textual critics over the validity of the principle of final authorial intention was Luigi Firpo, "Correzioni d'autore coatte," in *Studi e problemi di critica testuale*, 143–57. Firpo's contribution to that volume deals with the changes imposed on authors by religious or political censorship. It is in the context of a discussion of final authorial intention, and of cases in which Italian textual critics have opted not to follow this criterion, that the views of Anglo-American critics are introduced in Stussi, *Introduzione agli studi di filologia italiana*.

17. Federico Ubaldini, ed., *Le rime di M. Francesco Petrarca estratte da un suo originale* (Rome: Grignani, 1642). The manuscript is cod. Vat. lat. 3196. Ubaldini's faithfulness to the manuscript included respect for Petrarch's writing two successive verses of a sonnet on the same line. This was itself a reflection of the thirteenth-century habit of writing the whole of the tercet or quatrain of a sonnet on a single line, the textual significance of which has recently been stressed in an important study; see H. Wayne Storey, *Transcription and Visual Poetics in the Early Italian Lyric* (New York: Garland, 1993).

18. See Ludovico Ariosto, *Orlando furioso*, 3 vols., ed. Santorre Debenedetti (Bari: Laterza, 1928). The projected edition with the earlier variants was published by his nephew, Cesare Segre, after Debenedetti's death; see Ludovico Ariosto, *Orlando furioso secondo l'edizione del 1532 con le varianti delle edizioni del 1516 e del 1521*, ed. Santorre Debenedetti and Cesare Segre (Bologna: Commissione per i Testi di Lingua, 1960).

19. Santorre Debenedetti, *I frammenti autografi dell'"Orlando Furioso"* (Turin: Loescher, 1937).

20. See Gianfranco Contini, "Come lavorava l'Ariosto," in *Esercizi di lettura* (Florence: Parenti, 1939); see also the editions published in Florence by Le Monnier (1947) and in Turin by Einaudi (1982). Contini was a close friend of the poet Eugenio Montale and a perceptive critic of Montale's work. He also championed the work of other avant-garde writers, such as the novelist Carlo Emilio Gadda. The link between textual and literary criticism is equally clear in the work of Cesare Segre, the other major figure in Italian textual criticism in this half-century. Segre's main importance outside the field of textual criticism has been as mediator of structuralist and semiotic theories; see, for example, Cesare Segre, *I segni e la critica* (Turin: Einaudi, 1969), and Cesare Segre, *Semiotica filologica: Testo e modelli culturali* (Turin: Einaudi, 1979). It is largely thanks to Segre that modern Italian literary criticism, while fully up to date, has a human face.

21. See, for example Debenedetti and Segre's 1960 edition of Ariosto, *Orlando Furioso*; Giuseppe Parini, *Il giorno*, ed. Dante Isella (Milan and Naples: Ricciardi, 1969); Giovanni Verga, *Mastro-Don Gesualdo*, ed. Carla Riccardi (Milan: Mondadori, 1979); Gabriele D'Annunzio, *Alcyone*, ed. Pietro Gibellini (Milan: Mondadori, 1980); Eugenio Montale, *L'opera in versi*, ed. Rosanna

Bettarini and Gianfranco Contini (Turin: Einaudi, 1980); Giacomo Leopardi, *Canti,* ed. Emilio Peruzzi (Milan: Rizzoli, 1981); Giacomo Leopardi, *Canti,* ed. Domenico De Robertis (Milan: Polifilo, 1984).

22. W. W. Greg, "The Rationale of Copy-Text."

23. Vincenzio Borghini (1515–1580); see Brian Richardson, *Print Culture in Renaissance Italy: The Editor and the Vernacular Text, 1470–1600* (Cambridge: Cambridge University Press, 1994), 161.

24. Contini, *Breviario di ecdotica,* 38. For a recent contribution to this subject, see Guglielmo Gorni, "Restituzione formale dei testi volgari a tradizione plurima: il caso della 'Vita Nova,'" *Studi di filologia italiana* 56 (1998), 5–30.

25. Pietro Aretino, *Sei giornate: Ragionamento della Nanna e della Antonia (1534); Dialogo nel quale la Nanna insegna a la Pippa (1536),* ed. Giovanni Aquilecchia (Bari: Laterza, 1969).

26. See Vittorio Russo and Alfredo Iannone, "La tradizione manoscritta della *Commedia:* Progetto per un'edizione elettronica 'in progress,'" *Filologia e critica* 20 (1995), 200–16.

27. Since this essay was written, a much more promising collaboration has developed between the Società Dantesca Italiana of Florence and an international group of scholars headed by Peter Robinson. On the society's Web site (www.danteonline.it) there is already a complete list of all the manuscripts of the *Comedy,* together with the text of seventeen of the most important. The same partnership is also preparing for publication on CD-ROM a version of the seven manuscripts used as the basis of a new critical edition of the poem (forthcoming).

Hagiolatry, Cultural Engineering, Monument Building, and Other Functions of Scholarly Editing

PETER SHILLINGSBURG

Because scholarly editing takes a great deal of time, is often tedious, requires meticulous care over masses of minute detail, involves decisions that can easily go wrong, and is seldom rewarded by wealth or early promotions; because every fifty years or less some new hotshot editor comes along, demanding that the work scholarly editors have been doing needs complete overhaul and replacement; because so little reward seems to come from so much investment of time and intelligence, I am led to ask: Why do we create scholarly editions? Why do we spend our time and our lives in this way?

This essay has three main parts. The first, "The Everlasting Nay," rehearses a variety of motives for scholarly editing that have been or should be discarded. They include hagiolatry, monument building, cultural preservation, and cultural engineering. The second part, "The Center of Indifference," addresses what we lose and what we gain by discarding the high-sounding but weak, false, and decayed motives rehearsed in "The Everlasting Nay." The third part, called, ironically enough, "The Everlasting Yea," presents some conclusions about what scholarly editing, stripped of its pretensions, actually can and should strive to achieve.

The Everlasting Nay

I present as a confessional the following meditation on motives for scholarly editing: reasons for editing I have held and discarded. The first is that scholarly editing might be pursued out of some sense of self-importance or some delusion about the importance of editing. One could start with references to A. E. Housman, who famously chose what he considered to be a third-rate writer to edit, in order to create a more perfect work and lasting monument. We could ask how many people know Housman as the editor of the works of Manilius, or in what way Housman's significance as a thinker and writer and scholar is memorialized in that edition. While pondering that question, one might ask how few people purchased and cited in their subsequent scholarship my

Garland edition of William Thackeray's *Vanity Fair,* of which about three hundred copies were printed, or my edition of Thackeray's *Pendennis,* of which one hundred eighty copies were printed.[1] Of course, one then needs to sort out whether the value of an edition, or of any work, is to be gauged by the number of people who respond positively to it, or by some less subjective standard—remembering that we live on a planet with approximately six billion people, and in an age when the phrase "objective standard" is considered an oxymoron.

In a whimsical chapter of *Resisting Texts,*[2] of which I imagine about ninety copies will ever be sold, I survey a range of possible meanings of scholarly editions: the meanings of their binding and weight and type. I thought perhaps the acid-free paper chosen for these editions, and guaranteed to last for three hundred fifty years, was an attempt to preserve the editor's work as much if not more than the author's. And if we ask how much money we make as scholarly editors, or how many people are out there clamoring for our new editions, it might be tempting to think that we do what we do because, at least within certain small circles, we gain reputations and feel virtuous. Those are well-deserved rewards for scholarly editing when it is done well, but is that the extent of it? Would we be satisfied if we did what we did solely for the personal rewards found in doing it? I have invested too much of my life in scholarly editing to be able to stand the idea that the Thackeray edition now in progress will fulfill its function in the world by making my name known as Thackeray's editor, or by legitimizing my invitations to take part in academic conferences.

So perhaps we should spurn the cynical view of scholarly editing as a self-serving activity and adopt a more noble view—one in which the editor serves the author and the author's public by worshipful actions that protect the work from the author's own neglectful or ill-considered actions regarding revisions, or that protect it from the predations of fools and quacks (other quacks, plague take them) who have undertaken to edit it, or actions that resurrect and perpetuate the memory of authors whose reputations have dropped below the horizon of modern consciousness. In pursuing such goals, editors have adopted strategies that minimize readers' awareness of the editorial presence in the text; for, of course, it is the *author's* work that is important. But that is no reason why, in professional communication with each other, we should continue to pretend that we are objective, scientific, principled scholars whose pursuit of truth produces the foundational rocks for significant criticism. The solid rocks of textual scholarship we have hung around our necks weigh about the same as millstones, not just from the weight of paper but also from the weight of cultural significance with which they have been freighted. I don't think the extreme tediousness or length of scholarly commitment to editorial projects is fully justified by these notions of noble actions on behalf of authors, because in the end these action don't withstand close scrutiny.

To take up and dismiss two more items in my title can be quickly compassed. Hagiolatry, the sanctification of literature or authorship, has been battered sufficiently in other critical circles to keep us from justifying our work publicly the way we did years ago, when phrases like "preserving and restoring our cultural heritage" were spoken without a blush. In recent years it has become far more common for editors to provide access to historical texts than for editors to provide established texts that render textual problems and complexities transparent. It is more likely that an editor will speak of placing a text in its context than that the editor will claim to have established the definitive edition of a literary work. It is common now for editors to refer to their work as acts of criticism or as choices among several viable editorial acts. And yet paper editions continue to be issued in formats developed to preserve, once and for all, the definitive editions of the 1960s. I'm not complaining about that, just suggesting that there is a disjunction between what we are now saying about the paper editions and the formats in which we package them.

The phrase "cultural engineering" in my title refers to the way in which collective efforts to produce scholarly editions can be seen as driven by the cultural preconceptions of the class of people from which scholarly editors derive—it has been said often enough, for example, that the majority of editions approved by the Center for Editions of American Authors were of the works of dead white males. Indeed, most of the editors are, or soon enough will be, dead white males also. But the phrase "cultural engineering" could refer to the possibility that collective editorial efforts shape or change cultural preconceptions. I do not, however, think of scholarly editing as one of the leading-edge professions in social and cultural revolutions. An increase in the number of scholarly editions of women and minority authors, postcolonial texts, or folk writing is more likely to be the result of cultural forces driving editing than the other way around. An increase in the number of electronic editions is also more likely to be the result of cultural forces dragging us into cyberspace than of forward-thinking scholarly editors pushing the envelope of electronic innovation. Or perhaps there has been in the breasts of some editors the notion that their editions would help cement a cherished author's place in history or would even spark a resurgence of critical interest. Scholarly editions of William Gilmore Simms, Charles

Brockden Brown, and William Makepeace Thackeray have had such effects—on a scale so small that no one has noticed. I am hard pressed to name a major twentieth-century edition that has revolutionized an author's reputation and critical standing. I recall Gary Taylor arguing at a Society for Textual Scholarship conference that perhaps a new edition of Thomas Middleton—or, better yet, several editions—might restore Middleton to the critical stature and popular reputation relative to Shakespeare that he once enjoyed. (I can't remember just now: was it Middleton or some other author?) But I am not convinced that these motives for editing—that we might rehabilitate authors' reputations or alter cultural awareness—rise above wishful thinking or even self-deception.

The sea changes in editing, made possible and even necessary by electronic media for editions, also reveal motives that ring false. When the first serious attacks on the notion of "definitive" texts were mounted, editors first defended their work by declaring that it was the *edition*, not the *text*, that was definitive. What the scholarly edition made possible, they said, was the serious study of texts and their variants, because the list of emendations made possible the reconstruction of the copy-text, and the historical collation made possible the essential reconstruction of other authoritative texts. Thus the text and apparatus combined to present a definitive source for study of the author's text and for checking on the editor's work. One hesitates to ask how many people have used a scholarly edition to reconstruct a copy-text, or how many, bent on reconstructing other authoritative texts, have found everything essential to such work in a historical collation. In fact, the scholarly print edition could not sustain the burden of being called a definitive edition, either: too much had to be left out because it was too expensive to print, or because the available technologies of printed editions made such goals impractical. Students interested in the bibliographical matrixes and cultural contexts of works demand more than print editions can supply. The editions are not definitive.

Some of the current arguments for electronic editions sound ominously like renewed attempts by editors to be definitive. One claim for electronic editions is that they are archives of texts; the editor's meddling hand has been curbed one stage earlier than was possible in any printed work. The computer makes possible, we are told, the juxtaposition of all the relevant texts in their linguistic variants, and in their bibliographic variant forms, as digitized images. Thus a library of electronic texts, linked to explanations and parallels and histories, becomes accessible to a richly endowed posterity. To the extent that such archives

contain accurate transcriptions, high-resolution reproductions, precise
and reliable guides to the provenance and significance of their contents,
and to the extent that they are comprehensive, to that extent they are
"definitive"—until the next generation of critics and scholars, with new
interests, notices some other aspect of texts that scholarly editors of the
past (by then, that will be us) took for granted and ignored. But already
information overload has set in. The comprehensiveness of the electronic
archive threatens to create a salt, estranging sea of information, separating the archive user from insights into the critical significance of textual histories.

The Center of Indifference

I should pause to say that I don't think this line of argument leads to
the conclusion that electronic archives should not be undertaken. The
same cogent arguments for the accumulation of major libraries apply
to the accumulation and preparation of major electronic archives. The
arguments for the creation of library catalogs and other reference works,
to explore the significance of libraries and archives, remain cogent as
reasons to accumulate and explain textual histories of individual works.
But there is something imposed upon editorial work by the drive for
objectivity and comprehensiveness and endurance that leaves the results
in some important way unsatisfactory. My task in this essay is to try to
track down the source of that dissatisfaction and to gauge its importance.

One approach to this problem is to ask what textual critics and scholarly editors lose when they give up the words "definitive," "objective,"
"established," "standard," "authoritative," "exhaustive," "comprehensive," and "complete." What do we lose if we acknowledge some pretty
well-known but shushed facts about scholarly editions: that they are
infrequently cited in critical articles, infrequently used as classroom texts,
infrequently cited in term papers; that copy-texts and alter-texts are more
easily and satisfactorily reconstructed through obtaining a photocopy
(or an authentic exemplar) than through examining emendations tables;
that nobody can or will read an electronic text of a long prose work, let
alone an electronic archive of them; that in order to use an "unedited"
text or archive to discover how a work was written and what difference
that makes to a reading of the work, one must collate and compare and
analyze the relevant texts. What do we lose if we acknowledge that our
best editorial efforts and the best efforts of our publicists will soon cause
our work to join the largely silent chorus of has-been editions, discredited in the light of new ways of conceiving texts, textuality, and textual
scholarship? What do we lose if we grasp firmly the contradictory truths,

first, that the reader must do the textual work for herself in order to fully appreciate and understand the significance of variations in texts, not only linguistic and bibliographic but contextual, and, second, that if the scholarly editor does not do it for the reader, it probably will not get done?

First, let me say what I think we do not lose. We do not lose a reason to edit texts, or to preserve them, or to archive them, or to annotate them, or to examine them for their linguistic and bibliographic histories or their cultural, economic, and generic contexts. We do not lose a reason for trying to discover as much as can be known about how texts have become and how they have worked. And, perhaps the most important thing that is *not* lost, even when we give up this list of noble-sounding terms, is the desire or necessity to be accurate in our work.

But we do lose a lot of excess baggage, inflated rhetoric, electronic hype, a false sense of importance and accomplishment, and the narrow grounds from which to bash the work of other editors. I assert that we lose these unnecessary things, though I do not intend to prove that it is so. But I speak from experience. And with these happy losses, I say, we gain a great deal of freedom. What a relief it is to an editor to be able to express an opinion without having to claim it as the standard opinion, to be able to assume that the user of an edition can and should know that an edition is a work of literary criticism, anchored in evidence, but to be used skeptically. How refreshing it is to be able to create an edition that represents no more than our best ability to respond to the textual evidence we have found. How light the burden becomes, and how interesting the chase, when we cease to pretend objectivity in building monuments to the literary heroes of yore. How many times have scholarly editors failed to follow an enlightened instinct because the rules of definitive editing prescribed some other action?

I recall, as an example, Gordon Haight's Clarendon edition of George Eliot's *The Mill on the Floss*.[3] Haight did a superb job of locating and identifying primary materials and articulating the compositional and publication history of the *Mill*. The introduction to the Clarendon edition provides a convincing and well-written account of how Eliot read the proof for one edition but not another, how she prepared copy for a third edition by marking up a copy of the second, and how the printers had in each printing incrementally toned down and conventionalized the dialect spelling in the speech of her countrified characters. Faced with a textual situation in which the author had taken an active role, and believing that Eliot might have deliberately passed up the chance to reimpose dialect spellings, the editor prepared a text representing a fusion of Eliot's and the printers' work on the text. Although the surviving documents include a manuscript, the first edition, the second edition (for which Eliot read proofs but did not supply copy), and a copy of the second edition with Eliot's manuscript corrections and revisions for the third edition, the editor nevertheless chose as copy-text the third edition, which Eliot had not proofread. Why did the editor pick the first nonauthoritative text as the copy-text? Because, he said, much as he personally preferred the dialect spellings of the manuscript, or even the slightly toned-down versions in the first edition, the third edition represented a more corrected version and might incorporate Eliot's surrender to the publisher's and perhaps the public's need for more conventional spellings. Haight actually sounds sorrowful as he expresses his regret at the loss of authorial forms, and he sounds nearly apologetic about the typos introduced in the third edition, which he now had to emend, thus calling special attention to the most trivial variants in the whole textual history. But he was impelled, by some notion of the rules of editing and of definitiveness, to make an editorial decision that few other people would have made or, if they had, would not have made for his reasons. Quite frankly, had Haight followed his critical inclinations, his edition would have conformed accidentally to the editorial norms of his day even more than they did as a result of his effort to do the normative thing. But that is a separate problem. That is to say, I am not now focusing on editorial acts taken by editors who do not fully understand their business, or who do not articulate well either what they have done or why they have done it. I am instead focusing on the effects upon texts worked by a "desire to do right" or a desire to "be definitive" or to eliminate individual critical judgment from editions. Those desires too frequently lead editors to reject their own best thinking in favor of what they believe to be the prevailing rules of editing, which are designed to inhibit the exercise of individual judgment—and gain longevity for the edition. Forlorn hope.

And, of course, there are reasons to behave in that way. Elsewhere I have told the story of how my edition of Thackeray's *Vanity Fair* was rejected by the Modern Language Association's Committee on Scholarly Editions (CSE) in the year I retired as chairman of that organization. In matters such as these it is good to remember that there is an inside view and an outside view, so that my assessment of that debacle is not likely to be the only one; but from my point of view, the CSE that year wanted a conventional edition more than it wanted one that was sensibly edited. I remember that the inspector wanted me to reject the manuscript as copy-text because it had survived for only a part of the book. The underlying reason, I suspect, was that in any case the inspector preferred

editorial policies that regularly chose printed copy-texts over manuscript ones. There are, I know, outspoken advocates of that position in
the profession, but the rationale proposed by the CSE inspector was
not one of those frequently heard today. It was merely that the mixture
of manuscript and printed copy-texts produced an inconsistent texture
for the work—a fact I had explicitly brought to his attention in my introduction and had dismissed as not compelling. A few years later, another
CSE inspector and committee approved what was essentially the same
edition.[4]

As I see it now, the desire for consistency, like the desire for definitiveness, is a force driving toward an edition with a reading text that can
stand for the work itself—one in which the editor has fulfilled the perfection that author and publisher must have wanted and would have
achieved had they had time and a grant from the National Endowment
for the Humanities. Most scholarly editors have now abandoned such
hopes, but there are two radically different ways in which to do so. Some
editors retreat to the archive, increasing their insistence that the editor's
personal judgment be curbed—believing that the exercise of individual
judgment is what caused the problem with those misguided attempts
to achieve textual perfection. The other way to abandon such misguided
hopes is to recognize that editing *inevitably* involves the exercise of individual judgment, that texts have *always* been in some sense unsatisfactory, and that the *best* work of any editor, like the best work of any critic,
will appear dated before long and be in want of replacement. What a relief
to be able to produce an edition that represents the editor's best thinking rather than his or her most conventional thinking. What a relief to
acknowledge that the purpose for the new edition is to arrange the evidence in a way that lends coherence to the editor's best insights into the
author, the text, and the cultural milieu of text creation—or of some other
combination of forces the editor has identified as relevant. What a relief
to cast off the burden of trying, in the scholarly edition, to establish the
text as the standard for all time.

My sense of relief is based on the acknowledgment that editions incorporate distinct components. The first is evidence. The second is editorial insight. Evidence is found, not created. It is what it is. We cannot do
anything *about* evidence. But we can do things *to* evidence. We can represent it. But every act of (re)presentation is an act of criticism, an act of
interpretation. Every new edition, every digitized image, every hyper-
link establishing a relationship between bits of evidence is interpretational. Editorial insight can be narrow or comprehensive, convincing or
unconvincing, well or ill articulated, but it remains insight and is not to

be confused with evidence. The important things to remember are that the evidence cannot be presented without interpretation and that editorial insight is a necessary component of editions. I suspect that this will be anathema to some editors. If it is not, then perhaps the editor is in denial, charitably thinking that I do not believe what I am writing.

I could list any number of writers on editorial practice who pay lip service to the notion that editorial insight and interpretation are necessary components of editions, but who immediately bring to bear rules of editing designed to prevent editors from exercising individual judgment. The recently published *Contemporary German Editorial Theory* is occupied primarily with explanations of how German editorial practice acknowledges the difference between "the artifact" (which is hard evidence) and the "aesthetic object" (which is an editorial construct) and then imposes rules that will prevent the exercise of individual judgment.[5] Hans Zeller, for example, proposes the imposition of blanket rules designed to avoid the worst excesses of intentionalist, idealist editing—but at the terrible cost of adopting uncritically the introduction of textual faults by so-called authorized (re)transmitters of the text. Zeller was unhappy with the result of his own recommendations—as well he should have been:

> A new problem presents itself here which I regard as fundamentally unsolvable. It is best known through M. Bernays's (1866) discovery of the fatal effect of Himburg's corrupt pirated editions (1779) on Goethe's revision of his *Schriften,* specifically on the *Werther* of 1787. In the textual comparison with the initial edition of 1774 the corruptions are so blatant and scandalous that one would hesitate to allow the principles developed here to apply to this text.[6]

"Fundamentally unsolvable" Zeller says, because the only way to solve such problems is to abandon the principles developed to prevent editors from doing what they think is best. That is pure sophistry, combined with cowardice and perhaps a modicum of pomposity about the objectivity of scholarly editions. The barriers to solving Zeller's problem were erected by Zeller himself and by other editorial theorists who pursue definitiveness (by whatever name they prefer) and oppose individual judgment in the false belief that objectivity is the goal of scholarly editing. If it is, woe be to us all.[7]

My point is that the fundamental dissatisfaction one feels with scholarly editions is not that they don't get the recognition they merit, but that they have pretensions they cannot actually fulfill. We do not feel comfortable pretending to accomplishments that are false. We know they are false—whether the public does or not.

The Everlasting Yea

When Thomas Carlyle got to his everlasting yea, he found that doing work was better than being purposeless in life. But I cannot bring myself to say that editing is better than being purposeless. I live too close to the land that produced the song "I Ain't Doing Nothing But I'm Not Quite Done" to believe that editing is a cure for purposelessness. Carlyle's everlasting yea did not entail a belief that any thing made by man would last for very long; but, like Carlyle, I think we can develop a positive attitude toward editorial work that can withstand scrutiny. As usual, my proposed view of our enterprise comes with names and distinctions that, for me at least, remove the confusions and dissatisfaction involved in mistaking one thing for another, or in using one name to refer to two unlike activities.

When we look at the textual condition, its materials, its events, its players, and its mental states, we see many things that need to be done, many things that are the scholarly editor's responsibility, many things that have been called editing. But some of them are not editing, though editors frequently do them. If we separate out these activities, we can see why one person's view of the editing task might fail to satisfy another person's needs.

The first activity is the collection of evidence—making libraries and archives of artifacts, material documents, and mechanically reproduced images of them. Without this foundation of collection and archiving, editors could not claim to be historical. This archiving activity is not, however, editing. It is collecting, describing, cataloging, and indexing.

Second (though there is nothing particularly sequential in this list), there are the acts of introducing and annotating texts. These activities have been called editing for as long as any other activity has gone by that name. They are important activities, and in recent years they have come into their own as vehicles for insight into the cultural, social, economic, and political contexts of texts. But no one gives the writing of introductions or of annotations the label "textual editing." It can easily be argued that a textual editor who has not annotated the text for its cultural and other contexts is not in a position to conduct textual editing with much sophistication, but annotating is not editing.

The third activity is representing the evidence of texts in reproducible form, such as in editions, both print and electronic. Since every act of representing evidence is critical and interpretive, we must strive for clarity about what we did and about why we did it, erring on the side of excess when presenting supporting materials and explanations, and when pointing out relationships between documents, or between the text and historical events and places. We strive for accuracy and clarity not because they will ensure the longevity of our editions but because accuracy and clarity are the foundations of good scholarship and good criticism. We can never forget that the compilation of a scholarly edition is the interpretive best thinking of an editor and is *not* the establishment of a text for all time. Representing texts, delineating their textual and formal histories, and sorting out the agents of change in those histories is editing. No two editors would produce the same results. It is not science.

As for the fourth activity, I am particularly concerned that the critical, interpretive consequences of archiving, annotating, and editing not be lost as needles in a haystack of apparatuses, and so we should emphasize forums for presenting the best insights of textual criticism. I have said many times that editors, having spent enormous energy exploring the textual richness of the works they investigate, then hide the best things they have discovered—in clear reading texts, or in piles of evidence in apparatuses. What we have discovered is richness and the relevance of textual criticism, yet we do not write enough critical essays explaining the ways in which our work affects our understanding of the texts we edit. We do not write enough reviews of scholarly editions, showing how textual criticism changes our reading of texts. We do not bring textual and editorial insight often enough into conference sessions, other than to those sessions devoted to textual criticism. We spend too much time talking and writing to "the choir" and not enough to critics and students generally. This fourth matter is not editing, but it is something I think more editors should undertake. In their very different ways, Hershel Parker and Jerry McGann have done as much as any of us to focus attention on the interpretive significance of textual histories.[8] They have accomplished this primarily through critical analyses of texts, rather than through the production of the works they have edited. It is the essays and books they have written that have brought the consequences of textual insights to the wider attention of literate people. My view is that Parker has been less influential than his basic insight deserves because his method of presenting it demands assent more than it exercises persuasion. McGann's far more influential position is marred, in my view, by a tendency, which he shares with European editors, to let blanket decisions override the exercise of better judgment in specific instances. But both writers have written passionately, entertainingly, intelligently, and knowledgeably about the effects that variant forms of texts have on understanding and interpretation. If the people who do the real work of examining texts closely will also write about the interpretive consequences of their hard-won knowledge, the difference between understanding texts and dancing around them—or taking airy flights from them, as most critics do—may become more evident in our profession.

NOTES

1. William Makepeace Thackeray, *Vanity Fair: A Novel without a Hero*, ed. Peter L. Shillingsburg, with commentary by Nicholas Pickwood and Robert Colby (New York: Garland, 1989); William Makepeace Thackeray, *The History of Pendennis*, ed. Peter L. Shillingsburg, with commentary by Nicholas Pickwoad (New York: Garland, 1991).

2. Peter L. Shillingsburg, *Resisting Texts: Authority and Submission in Constructions of Meaning* (Ann Arbor: University of Michigan Press, 1997).

3. George Eliot, *The Mill on the Floss*, ed. Gordon Haight (Oxford: Clarendon Press, 1980).

4. An extended account of the Thackeray edition is in Peter Shillingsburg, "Editing Thackeray: A History," *Studies in the Novel* 27 (1995), 363–74.

5. Hans Walter Gabler, George Bornstein, and Gillian Borland Pierce, eds., *Contemporary German Editorial Theory* (Ann Arbor: University of Michigan Press, 1995).

6. Hans Zeller, "Structure and Genesis in Editing: On German and Anglo-American Textual Criticism," in Gabler, Bornstein, and Pierce, eds., *Contemporary German Editorial Theory*, 116.

7. I repeated this charge in Peter Shillingsburg, "A Resistance to Contemporary German Editorial Theory," *editio* 12 (1998), 138–49. Its publication prompted a response that puts Zeller's argument in a better light; see Bodo Plachta, "In Between the 'Royal Way' of Philology and 'Occult Science': Some Remarks About German Discussion on Text Constitution in the Last Ten Years," *TEXT* 12 (1999), 31–47.

8. See Hershel Parker, *Flawed Texts and Verbal Icons* (Evansville, Ill.: Northwestern University Press, 1984); Jerome McGann, *The Textual Condition* (Princeton, N.J.: Princeton University Press, 1991).

THE CONTRIBUTORS

WINAND M. CALLEWAERT is professor of Sanskrit and Hinduism at the Catholic University Leuven in Belgium. Professor Callewaert has studied and worked in India since 1965 and holds degrees in Hindi, Sanskrit, and philosophy. He is the author or co-author of thirteen books on India in Dutch and of nineteen others in English. His publications include *Shri Guru Granth Sahib* (1996), *The Hagiographies of Anantadas: The Bhakti Poets of North India* (2000), *The Millennium Kabir—Vani, 1. Pad-s* (with Swapna Sharma and Dieter Taillieu, 2000), and *Devotional Literature in South-Asia: Current Research, 1997–2000* (with Dieter Taillieu, 2000).

ROGER CHARTIER is *Directeur d'Études* at the École des Hautes Études en Sciences Sociales in Paris and Annenberg Visiting Professor at the University of Pennsylvania. He is one of the world's leading historians of postmedieval book culture. His numerous books include *The Order of Books: Readers, Authors, and Libraries in Europe between the Fourteenth and Eighteenth Centuries* (1994), *Forms and Meanings: Texts, Performances, and Audiences from Codex to Computer* (1995), *On the Edge of the Cliff: History, Language, and Practices* (1997), and *Publishing Drama in Early Modern Europe* (The Panizzi Lectures, 1999).

PHYLLIS CULHAM is professor of history at the U.S. Naval Academy. She is co-editor of *Classics: A Discipline and Profession in Crisis?* (1989) and editor and translator of *Seneca: On Favors* (1995). Professor Culham has published widely on both Greek and Roman history and epigraphy and is currently working on a book on literacy, records, construction of memory, and perceptions of time from the Sumerians through the first Christian millennium. Her essay in this volume and her other published articles are related to this project.

PAUL EGGERT is professor of English, director of the Australian Scholarly Editions Centre, and head of the School of Language, Literature and Communication at the University of New South Wales, Australian Defence Force Academy, Canberra. He has edited titles in the Cambridge

University Press *Works of D. H. Lawrence* and in the Academy Editions of Australian Literature series, of which he is general editor. He also co-edited the collection *The Editorial Gaze* (1998) and is currently working on a book *(The Golden Stain of Time)* about the restoration of historic houses and monuments. Professor Eggert is a fellow of the Australian Academy of the Humanities.

CONOR FAHY is professor emeritus of Italian at the University of London. A specialist in Italian sixteenth-century printing history and in the application of bibliographical method to problems of Italian textual transmission, Professor Fahy is the editor of Z. Campanini's 1789 manual *Istruzioni pratiche ad un novello capo-stampa* (1998), the only Italian manual for printers to survive from the hand-printing period. His many publications include *Saggi di bibliographia testuale* (1988), *L'"Orlando furioso" del 1532: profilo di una edizione* (1989), and *Printing a Book in Verona in 1622: The Account Book of Francesco Calzolari Junior* (1993). He is currently working on the 1528 Aldine first edition of Castiglione's *Book of the Courtier* and other contemporary Aldine editions. Professor Fahy gave the Sandars Lectures in Bibliography at the University of Cambridge in 2002.

JOHN MILES FOLEY is Curators' Professor of Classical Studies and English and W. H. Byler Endowed Chair in the Humanities at the University of Missouri–Columbia. Recognized for his groundbreaking studies of oral traditions in ancient Greek, South Slavic, and medieval English cultures, Professor Foley is the author of numerous books, including *Immanent Art: From Structure to Meaning in Traditional Oral Epic* (1991), *Teaching Oral Traditions* (1998), *Homer's Traditional Art* (1999), and *How to Read an Oral Poem* (2002). He is the founder and director of the Center for Studies in Oral Tradition and the founding editor of the journal *Oral Tradition*.

DAVID GREETHAM is Distinguished Professor of English, Medieval Studies, and Interactive Technology at the City University of New York Graduate Center. He was the founder, the first executive director, and then the president of the interdisciplinary Society for Textual Scholarship and for many years was co-editor (with W. Speed Hill) of the society's journal *Text*. His books include *Textual Scholarship: An Introduction* (1992, 1994), the standard survey of the field; *Textual Transgressions* (1998), a partly autobiographical account of the development of textual speculation over the last two decades; and *Theories of the Text* (1999), a major reassessment of the conceptual grounds for textual study. He is now working on several electronic projects involving digital morphing, electronic identity, and digital copyright.

SUSAN HOCKEY is professor of library and information studies and director of the School of Library, Archive, and Information Studies at University College, London. She was the first director of the Center for Electronic Texts in the Humanities (CETH) at Rutgers and Princeton Universities and the Canadian Institute for Research Computing in Arts (CIRCA) at the University of Alberta. Professor Hockey is the author of *Snobol Programming for the Humanities* (1986) and of *Electronic Texts in the Humanities: Principles and Practice* (2000). She is also the editor (with Nancy Ide) of the series *Research in Humanities Computing,* published by Oxford University Press.

H. J. JACKSON is professor of English at the University of Toronto and a founding member of the university's collaborative Book History and Print Culture program. She is the author of numerous articles on eighteenth-century and Romantic literature and editor of selected poetry, selected letters, and selected works by Samuel Taylor Coleridge. She also edited volumes 3 through 6 of Coleridge's *Marginalia* (with George Whalley) and *Shorter Works and Fragments* (with J. R. de J. Jackson) in the Bollingen edition of Coleridge's *Collected Works.* Professor Jackson's most recent book is *Marginalia: Readers Writing in Books* (2001). She is currently working on a book about reading practices during the Romantic period.

MARTIN S. JAFFEE is professor of international studies at the University of Washington, where he teaches in the Comparative Religion and Jewish Studies programs. Formerly the Stroum Chair of Jewish Studies and the Golub Chair of International Studies, Professor Jaffee is the author or editor of dozens of essays and many books on the history of classic Rabbinic literature and ancient Judaism. His most recent book, *Torah in the Mouth: Writing and Oral Tradition in Palestinian Judaism, 200 BCE–400 CE* (2001), studies the history of oral tradition in early Rabbinic Judaism. Professor Jaffee also serves on the editorial boards of the *Journal of the American Academy of Religion* and *Oral Tradition.*

MARTIN MACHOVEC is a writer, editor, and publisher in Prague, with major interests in the twentieth-century Czech literary scene, especially the underground literature of the 1950s, 1960s, and 1970s. He has formed close contacts, dating from 1970, with independent, legally banned artists, writers, editors, and publishers and has taken part in publishing samizdat books and periodicals. He has published many studies and essays and translated the work of Allen Ginsberg, John Fowles, Anne Waldman, and the Beat poets. He has also edited a number of literary texts, among them nineteen volumes of Egon Bondy's works, and, more recently, *Milan Knížák: Zpěvník Aktualu* (2002) and *Pavel Zajíček: Zápisky z podzemí* (2002).

JEROME MCGANN is John Stewart Bryan University Professor at the University of Virginia and Thomas Holloway Professor of Victorian Media and Culture, Royal Holloway, University of London. His extensive scholarship and criticism have altered radically the direction of both Romantic and textual studies and have formed the basis for Marxist and New Historicist perspectives on literary works. His numerous influential books include *A Critique of Modern Textual Criticism* (1983, 1991), *The Textual Condition* (1992), *The Poetics of Sensibility: A Revolution in Literary Style* (1996), and, more recently, *Dante Gabriel Rosetti and the Game that Must Be Lost* (2000) and *Radiant Textuality: Literature after the World Wide Web* (2001). Professor McGann is the editor of the seven-volume Oxford edition of *Lord Byron: The Complete Poetical Works* (1980–93) and is currently editing the online *Complete Writings and Pictures of Dante Gabriel Rossetti: A Hypermedia Research Archive.*

RANDALL MCLEOD is associate professor of English at the University of Toronto. He is the editor of *Crisis in Editing* (1994) and the author of seminal essays on "unediting" canonical Renaissance writers. His essays, which have appeared in a variety of journals and books, include "FIAT *f*LUX" and "Enter Reader" (on Herbert) and "UN *Editing* Shak-speare" and "*Gon.* No more, the text is foolish" (on Shakespeare). Professor McLeod is currently completing three books: *Material Shakespeare;* a photo-facsimile edition of all extant seventeenth-century manuscripts of Donne's poem "To His Mistress Going to Bed"; and the Rosenbach Lectures delivered at the University of Pennsylvania in 1999, on works of two continental printers, Castiglione's *Il libro del Cortegiano* (printed at the Aldine Press in 1528) and the first Hebrew Bible printed in France (at the press of Robertus Stephanus, from 1539 to 1544).

RAIMONDA MODIANO is professor of English and comparative literature and director (with Míčéal Vaughan) of the program in textual studies at the University of Washington. A scholar of S. T. Coleridge, Modiano is the author of *Coleridge & the Concept of Nature* (1985) and co-editor of Coleridge's marginalia to German works for volumes 2 through 6 in the

Bollingen edition of his *Collected Works* (1984–2001). In addition to publishing articles and book chapters on British Romanticism, Professor Modiano has edited (with Nicholas Halmi and Paul Magnuson) *Coleridge's Poetry and Prose* (2003), the Norton critical edition. Her numerous honors include the University of Washington's Distinguished Teaching Award. She is currently completing a book titled *Contracts of the Heart: Sacrifice, Gift Economy, and Literary Exchange in Coleridge and Wordsworth.*

SCOTT B. NOEGEL is associate professor of Near Eastern languages and civilization at the University of Washington. A specialist in Egyptian, Mesopotamian, and biblical languages, Professor Noegel is the author of numerous articles and book chapters, coauthor of *Historical Dictionary of Prophets in Islam and Judaism* (2001), and co-editor of the volume *Prayer, Magic, and the Stars in the Ancient and Later Antique World* (2001). In the monograph *Janus Parallelism in the in the Book of Job* (1996) and the edition *Puns and Pundits: Word Play in the Hebrew Bible and Ancient Near Eastern Literature* (2000), he explores word play in ancient texts. He recently completed a monograph, *Nocturnal Ciphers: The Allusive Language of Dreams in the Ancient Near East,* on ancient dream interpretation. His "Okeanos" Web site: http://faculty.washington.edu/snoegel/okeanos.html is a premiere resource for the study of the ancient world.

LUDO ROCHER is professor of Sanskrit and W. Norman Brown Professor of South Asian Studies at the University of Pennsylvania. His extensive publications in various fields of Indology include *Paulinus A. S. Bartholomaeo: Dissertation on the Sanskrit Language* (1977), *Ezourvedam: A French Veda of the Eighteenth Century* (1984), and *The Purāṇas* (1986), a volume in the new *History of Indian Literature*. Professor Rocher's primary research focuses on the history of Hindu law from ancient to modern times, covering such subjects as Hindu legal procedure, Hindu law in general, and Hindu law of inheritance. He is currently preparing a first edition of a Sanskrit text on legal procedure and a study of the law applied to Hindus by the British in the eighteenth and nineteenth centuries.

LEROY F. SEARLE is associate professor of English and comparative literature at the University of Washington and formerly taught at the University of Rochester. He is co-editor (with Hazard Adams) of *Critical Theory Since 1965* and has published widely in literary criticism and theory, photographic criticism, and computer applications in the humanities. Professor Searle has also created several pieces of original software. He is currently at work on a book, *Democratic Literacy and the Politics of*

Reading, and (with Hazard Adams) a new edition of *Critical Theory Since Plato.* He is also one of the founders of the Society for Critical Exchange.

PETER SHILLINGSBURG, formerly at the University of North Texas, is professor of English at DeMontfort University, Leicester, England. A former chair of the Modern Language Association's Committee on Scholarly Editions, he is the author of essays and books that include the influential *Scholarly Editing in the Computer Age* (1984), now in its third edition; *Resisting Texts: Authority and Submission in Constructions of Meaning* (1997); and *Pegasus in Harness: Victorian Publishing and W. M. Thackeray* (1992). Professor Shillingsburg is general editor of *The Works of W. M. Thackeray* and editor of the Norton critical edition of Thackeray's *Vanity Fair.* His latest book is *A Literary Life of Thackeray* (2001).

MARTA WERNER is assistant professor of English at D'Youville College, Buffalo. A specialist in American literature and textual studies, Werner is the author of *Emily Dickinson's Open Folios: Scenes of Reading, Surfaces of Writing* (1995) and the editor of *Radical Scatters: An Electronic Archive of Emily Dickinson's Late Fragments and Related Texts* (1999). She is also co-editor (with Paul Voss) of a special issue ("The Poetics of the Archive") of *Studies in the Literary Imagination* (1999). Professor Werner's recent work on cancellation in Dickinson's manuscripts appeared in *La littérature à ses limites: genèse, censure, autocensure* (2002). She is currently preparing an edition of Nathaniel and Sophia Hawthorne's *Common Notebooks.*

INDEX

Adi Granth, earliest manuscripts of, 121

Agency, 26, 29, 172. *See also* Literature and literary works; Shillingsburg, Peter

Aktual (rock group). *See* Knížák, Milan

Alija, Djerdjelez, 116

Allographic-autographic distinction, 168–69

Amory, Hugh, 162

Anacreon, 61

Antinomies of Reason. *See* Kant, Immanuel

Anxiety: insufficient, 42; Matthew Arnold and, 23; and the monstrous, 45; of print, 42

Aporia, 5

Arché, 17

Aretino, Pietro, 407

Ariosto, Ludovico, 406

Aristotle, 59, 40

Arnold, Matthew, 22–33 *passim;* and Aristotle, 34; and cultural pessimism, 31; and disinterestedness, 32; and high moral seriousness, 33

Authenticity, and hierarchical relations with corruption and descent, 27

Author: and personal agency, 174; and pseudonyms, 352

Authorial function, 3, 12

Authority: readerly, 172; textual, 11–13, 164

Autographic-allographic distinction, 168–69

Baccylides, 59

Barbi, Michele, 407

Bartók, Béla, 112

Beat Generation, 350

Beattie, Brad, 29

Bédier, Joseph, 32, 403

Benjamin, Walter, 170

Benýšek, Zbyněk, 353

Beowulf, 101, 115; manuscript of in British Library, 371

Bhabha, Homi K., 32

Bhakti literature. *See* Literature and literary works

Bible, 31; and Old Testament prophets, 352. *See also* Klíma, Ladislav

Bibliography: and decay of bibliographic perceptions, 24; shrinking of, 162

Billanovich, Giuseppe, 404

Blake Archive, 394

Blake, William, 6, 73, 394

Boccaccio, 402

Böll, Heinrich, 353

Bolter, J. David, 36; and writing space, 40

Bombay High Court, 339

Bondy, Egon, 346; and "total realism," 349

Bonjour, Adrien, 115

The Book of Thel (William Blake). *See* Blake, William

4288328

hill

boundary of BVC